*The Tuba Family*

# THE
# TUBA FAMILY

by

Clifford Bevan

*2nd edition*
*revised, enlarged and updated*

*Piccolo Press*
10 Clifton Terrace
Winchester

First published in 1978 as
THE TUBA FAMILY
by Faber & Faber Limited
second edition, revised, enlarged and updated
published 2000 by
Piccolo Press
10 Clifton Terrace, Winchester
Hampshire, SO22 5BJ
England


Text computer typeset at Piccolo Press
in 10½ pt on 13½ pt Bembo.
Printed in Great Britain by
Itchen Printers, Southampton
ISBN 1 872203 30 2

British Library Cataloguing in Publication Data
available on request from The British Library

FOR
JEANNETTE
WHO, HAVING LIVED
THROUGH IT ALL ONCE, HAD
TO LIVE THROUGH IT ALL AGAIN

# Contents

## Contents

# Illustrations

## TABLES

## MUSIC EXAMPLES

# Preface to the Second Edition

THERE are two main reasons for producing a second edition of *The Tuba Family*. One is that the first edition has long sold out and, while flattered, I was growing tired of being bombarded with requests for a reprint. Recently the Internet has carried a second-hand book dealer's advertisement for a copy of the first edition at a price of $500.00, and no impoverished author could be pleased by that development. The other reason is that we now know so much more about the predecessors of the tuba and their music, as well as low brass performance in the mid-nineteenth-century, than we did twenty years ago when the first edition of this book appeared.

Perhaps surprisingly, the tuba itself is now one of the best-documented instruments in existence. The enormous *Tuba Source Book* that appeared in 1996 is a remarkable testimony to the various skills of numerous tuba experts in compiling this everything-within. One review included the comment '. . . it is hard to avoid asking why the book was written'. On investigation, this particular criticism turned out to have been written by a retired trombonist. I use my copy every week, and I suspect that if I were American I should use it every day. In addition, the quarterly *TUBA Journal* updates the low brass community on developments, products and an increasing number of activities.

There are no music lists in the revised edition of *The Tuba Family* since *The Tuba Source Book* has provided annotated lists for tuba (pages 11-314) which are regularly expanded in *Tuba Journal*, while up-to-date catalogues, including music for other brass instruments, are regularly issued by June Emerson Wind Music, Windmill Farm, Ampleforth, York YO6 4HF, U.K. and Robert King Music Sales, 140 Main Street, North Easton, Massachusetts 02356, U.S.A.

I must admit that when I was preparing the first edition of this book I did not have tubists in mind. It seemed far more important to try to inform composers, conductors, teachers and others who often control a tubist's destiny in either the long or short term. But in preparing the second edition I have constantly thought of the low brass players I have met, have taught or have corresponded with. As the Acknowledgements indicate, I have also often asked their advice . . .

Perhaps at this point I should apologize for having concentrated to some extent on activities in the United Kingdom. There is a vast amount of continuing tuba research in the United States, Germany and France, and all three have a considerable tuba family literature. However, as a resident I have the advantages of easier access to and an innate understanding of what happens (and has happened) in these small islands, so I hope that my geographical bias is therefore justified.

Owing to the ambiguous way in which the tuba family has been named composers can find it difficult to discover essential information about matters like compass and timbre. In some cases an instrument specified in a score published in one country means something completely different in another, and it is to be hoped that composers, conductors and players will all find clarification here.

This is a discursive book, with time and space taken to explore the delightful byways and discover unexpected curiosities. There are few footnotes, but there are many cross-references and a detailed index. Acoustics are dealt with from an essentially practical point of view—how the instruments work, why the player finds certain things difficult. There are plenty of other books dealing with acoustics in depth, and a number by highly-qualified instructors explaining the technique of the instruments.

It is pleasing that the word 'tubist' has now been generally accepted as meaning 'tuba-player'. The famous instruction: 'Im 14 Takt schlägt der Tubist Triangel' (translated on page 341) on the part of Berlioz's 'Marche Hongroise' in the Breitkopf edition is proof that the term has been around for many years.

The word 'Flügel horn' (with an umlaut) has generally been adopted. The etymology is given in Chapter VI and it will be seen that this version adapts the original German to English, retaining a word with meaning (Flügel) as opposed to the English (flugel) which has none and the American (Fluegel) which apparently seeks to relate the instrument to part of a chimney at least. 'French horn' is also used since it seems the only non-ambiguous word for that particular instrument.

Many years ago, shivering in a rehearsal room with the cold brass of my Eb tenor horn chilling my bare blue legs, I was puzzled by its name as it so clearly played the alto parts. I have thus used the American 'Eb Alto Horn', thereby also solving a problem for all those vociferous pundits who for almost a century have been trying to drive the tenor horn from the British brass band.

I have followed tradition in making the named pitch of a valved instrument refer to the second harmonic of the open fundamental (e.g. 'Euphonium in Bb'). Although it is possible to play several pedal notes on all the valved bugle-horns it is normal practice to give the pitch of brass instruments by reference to the first playing mode—the instrument's second harmonic with no valve tubing in use. The named pitch of serpents and ophicleides refers to the fundamental of the instrument with all side-holes closed.

As far as possible I have adopted the usual terms for the lower instruments:

F tuba:—Tuba pitched in F.

Eb Tuba:—Medium-narrow-bore tuba with three valves in Eb.

EEb Tuba:—Full-bore tuba with four or more valves in Eb—a term used by both manufacturers and players.

CC tuba:—Tuba in C (as opposed to the Small French Tuba in c).

BBb Tuba:—Tuba in Bb. Sometimes the three-valve medium-narrow-bore type is said by makers to be 'in Bb' but this can cause confusion as to the player and organologist the Bb Tuba is the Euphonium in Bb.

The inconsistency is apparent: Eb and EEb refer to differences in bore and construction; C and CC to differences in pitch. Following this slight foretaste of the nomenclature problems to come I should like to commend the reader to a careful perusal of the helpful people and organizations named in the Acknowledgements and finally request that any information, differences of opinion or abuse be sent to me c/o the publisher.

*Winchester,*
*Hants.*

*Note*

The following system of pitch notation is used in the text:

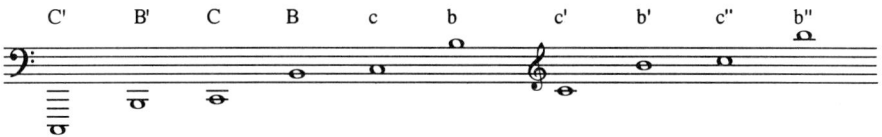

# *Acknowledgements*

I AM immensely grateful to the large number of people and institutions who have been so generous with their time and assistance.

First of all to my daughter Vicky, who typed the whole of the first edition of *The Tuba Family* on to disc so that it could be appropriately amended. Using technology that was not available when the initial edition was prepared through typewriter, glue and sticky tape, she saved me an unquantifiable amount of time. The impetus for this revised version came from David Murphy of the Irish Low Brass Association who deluged me with e-mails sent to him from all directions, each full of the anguish of those born too late to buy a copy of the first edition. I am grateful also to Winifred Genin (Aunty Winnie) for her very practical encouragement. The contributions of the following have been invaluable:

Gebrüder Alexander; Tom Prem of Červený; Donald E. Getzen of DEG Music Products; Charles Ford of the Getzen Co.; Gregory Schoeneck, Getzen International Corporation; Glassl of Nauheim; Ted Kexel of Frank Holton & Co.; Mike Zucek of the Mirafone Corporation; Kellie Edwards of UMI; Yamaha-Kemble Music UK Ltd; and John Myatt of John Myatt Woodwind & Brass who eventually opened the doors of Boosey & Hawkes where lesser mortals failed.

Many of the above generously provided photographs. Others were provided by John Carmichael (back cover); Carolino Augusteum, Salzburg (Fig. 4.10); the late Rex Conner (original of Fig. 1.9(c)); David Rendell and staff conductor Nic Wilks of the Hampshire County Youth Orchestra (Fig. 4.5); Ursula Jones and the late Philip Jones (Fig. 12.6); The Horniman Museum and Gardens (Figs. 2.7, 3.1, 13.3(d), 15.4, 15.10); the Local History Department of the London Borough of Hammersmith & Fulham (Fig. 15.2); Donald C. Little, University of North Texas (Fig. 11.5); Philippa Lunn (Figs. 2.5 and 2.10); John Taylor (Fig. 11.6); Martin Thacker, Librarian, Henry Watson Library and the author Michael Kennedy, for assistance with Fig. 12.2 and, along with Stuart Robinson, for documents relating to the Hallé Orchestra.

Jack Allison provided information on Tug Wilson, the Sander tuba, Barlow Tubas and more besides. My long-standing friend, instrument-maker Derek Farnell, helped me with many technical problems, gave me the opportunity to play the Farnell cimbasso (now the property of Kevin Morgan, to whom I am indebted), provided the exploded valve-cluster from which Fig. 4.1 was drawn and also information on the Manchester serpent. Craig Kridel has offered continuing and invaluable assistance over the years. His contributions have covered the areas of bass horn and serpent, Mendelssohn, the location of obscure journals and reference books, tracing sources, guiding me around United States collections and the provision of Fig. 2.8. Arnold Myers, also, has made available his expertise in acoustics, opportunities to play instruments from the Edinburgh University Collection and the generous provision of the photographs for Figs. 3.3, 5.2, 62, 10.1, 12.3 and 14.1 along with willing responses to a host of queries.

Information on aspects of repertoire and instrumentation were kindly provided by Bridget Carr, archivist of the Boston Symphony Orchestra, who drew my attention to its valved bass trombonist; Stewart Carter (nineteenth-century American low brass); Tony George (ophicleide solos); Beryl Kenyon de Pascual (details of Spanish practices and collections in connexion with a wide range of instruments); and Robin Norman (British tuba repertoire).

Details of serpents, their use and repertoire were provided by Bernard Fourtet (to whom I am particularly grateful for the copy of Sacem CD 300 002.2); Michel Godard; my colleague Phil Humphries, who provided much information on the Melstock Band, serpent parts in various film and television scores and the unique serpent shown in Fig. 2.2; Paul Schmidt; Major Roger Swift, Royal Military School of Music, Kneller Hall, who gave valued information on the serpents and bass horns in its collection; and Doug Yeo, who provided recordings of contemporary works. Alan Lumsden was uniquely helpful in preparing the serpent section of the first edition; I am grateful to him, his colleagues in the original London Serpent Trio and photographer Michael Fear for the original photograph of Fig. 2.10. I have also been able to utilize much of the material amassed by the late Christopher Monk. Margaret Gregory generously gave material collected by the late Robin Gregory; Lisbet Torp, Musikhistorisk Museum, Copenhagen and Veronika Gutmann, Historisches Museum, Basel responded willingly to queries about keyed and valved ophicleides; Ralph Dudgeon and Robert E. Eliason with information on keyed bugles. Corp.-Major Frearson, curator of the Life Guards Museum at Windsor, Band Sergeant-Major Peter Wise of the Blues and Royals and A. E. Woodbridge of the Household Cavalry Museum provided information requested with true military efficiency.

The bulk of the printed material consulted was housed in the British Library (which also gave permission for the reproduction of Fig. 9.1) and University of London Library, Senate House. In addition, Westminster Music Library, Greater London Archives, the Henry Watson Library and Local History Library at Manchester, the Public Libraries of Bristol, Fulham, Guildford and Winchester all gave much help. Peter Linnett and Patrick Johns of the BBC Sheet Music Library provided invaluable assistance in locating obscure Verdi scores. Michael Ball of the National Army Museum and Juliet Jewell of the Natural History Museum gave freely of their expertise. The Family Records Centre and Maggie Gibb of the Royal Society of Musicians provided access to documents relating to British musicians, while the Norfolk Record Office allowed material relating to the Norwich Festival to be consulted.

Activities in specific areas and events were explained by Chris Aspin (memorial to Adam Westall); Liverpool Record Office (programme for the first English performance of *St Paul*, 1836); Mike Lomas (the serpent in southern England); Harry Woodhouse (church bands in Cornwall); John Shepard, New York Library for the Performing Arts (copies of Mendelssohn correspondence); Peter Ward Jones, Bodleian Library, Oxford and leading Mendelssohn scholar, for much information on that composer; William Waterhouse for a range of information on instruments (particularly the Viennese Concert Tuba); Carl Willetts for demonstrating that Sterndale Bennett's *May Queen* included ophicleide, not serpent; Philip Atkin, National Railway Museum, York and Jean-Marc Combe, Musée français du Chemin de Fer for information on the use of the bugle by nineteenth-century railways; David Aird provided weights and dimensions of his tuba and case and Peter Shearer allowed me to abstract information from his copy of Kappey's Tutor.

Many foreign embassies in London gave invaluable assistance. Ladislav Müller of the Embassy of the Czech Republic was particularly enthusiastic; the Military Attaché to the Italian Embassy, Lt.-Col. Luigi Caligaris was of great help in the area of the bersag horn. In cimbasso research, the librarian of the Conservatorio Statale di Musica, Firenze; Licisco Magnagnato of the Musei e Gallerie d'Arte, Verona; Pierluigi Petrobelli, visiting lecturer at King's College, London; Marcello Conati of the Istituto di Studi Verdiani, Parma; Giampiero Tintori of the Museo Teatrale alla Scala, Milan, and Tom Wrigley, late of the RLPO and now of the Costa del Sol, all provided clues to help in solving the Great Cimbasso Mystery. Renato Meucci generously provided me with a copy of his original article in *Studi Verdiani*; Sean O'Neil enthusiastically arranged for me to hear the cimbasso in performance and also provided the photograph for Fig. 13.1. Nick Perry provided details of his early cimbasso, opportunities to play it and also the photograph for Fig. 13.3(c).

Further photographs and technical details were provided by Laurence Libin, Metropolitan Museum of Art, New York (Saxtuba); Harold Nash (Mahillon Wagner Tuben); Gerhard Zechmeister (Viennese Concert Tuba and Contrabass Trombone). Robert Tucci not only contributed to the English F Tuba hunt but also provided details of the Perantucci mouthpiece range. Ron Davis provided the photograph for Fig. 11.3 and the opportunity to meet his tuba and euphonium students at USC.

Dieter Krickeberg of the Staatliches Institut für Musikforschung, Berlin went to immense trouble to provide me with the fullest details of the Moritz Baß-Tuba in the museum's collection (including the photograph for Fig. 4.8) and to him I am truly grateful. He also helped me to trace the original patent, and I should like to express my gratitude to the Zentrales Staatsarchiv for their permission to reproduce this in translation. To Heidi Herbert, who made enlargements of the none-too-good microfilm, and Veronica Lawson, who undertook the task of translation from archaic German script, go my sincerest gratitude.

In one way or another all my tubist colleagues have contributed to this book, but I should particularly like to thank George Wall, who contributed in many ways, including Figs. 7.1(c), 8.2 and 12.4(a). Jim Anderson, Andrew Botter, John Elliott (with Figs. 11.2 and 15.6), Martin Fry, Horst Görgen, Carlo Ingrati, Gerard Middendorp, Kevin Morgan, Paul Lawrence, Stephen Wick (with Fig. 8.4) and trombonist/ophicleidist Tom Winthorpe (Fig. 3.4) were all of great help, while Rys Gilbert, Fernand Lelong and Roger Vaillant explained the unknown world of the French orchestra. Raymond Young of Louisiana Tech University helped unravel the U.S. baritone/euphonium situation.

The English F Tuba hunt was greatly assisted by Nicholas Alford, Jack Allison, Jim Anderson, Mark Carter, Marcus Cutts, Steve Freeman, Mike Johnson, Paul Lawrence, Arnold Myers, Harold Nash, Norman Shaw, Bob Tucci, George Wall and Stephen Wick.

Composers Michael Gibbs and Darrel Runswick kindly provided me with Exx. 14.6 and 14.5, and Alan Cohen with Ex. 5.6 plus help in locating certain jazz references. Carey Blyton was most informative on the contemporary use of old instruments and kindly provided Exx. 2.4 and 3.4.

Hilary Forshaw and Yvonne Milliet came to my assistance when Italian and French became too idiomatic for me to understand. Otherwise, all translations are my own.

I am grateful to the Beacon Press, Boston, Mass., for permission to reprint the excerpt from Harry E. Dickson's *Gentlemen, More Dolce Please!*; to Victor Gollancz Ltd for permission to use extracts from David Cairns's edition of the *Memoirs of Hector Berlioz*; to the editor of *Melody Maker* for permission to quote from the account of a concert written by Martha Sanders Gilmore; and to Denis Dobson, publishers, for permission to reproduce the drawing from *The Hoffnung Symphony Orchestra*. I am also grateful to those publishers who have given me permission to quote a number of the music extracts in this book. They are listed and duly acknowledged in the List of Music Examples.

Finally, if I have overlooked any copyright holders I should like to apologize. With the volatile nature of publishing companies, their mergers, take-overs and disappearance, it has sometimes proved impossible to trace them, as a number of returned letters demonstrates. In apologizing I should also like to make it clear that I do understand: when I walked into a southern European museum and was faced with life-size enlargements of photographs from the first edition of *The Tuba Family* on the walls my faith in intellectual property rights suffered a blow from which it has still to recover.

# CHAPTER I

# The Valved Bugle-horn and its Acoustics

One blast upon his bugle-horn
Was as a thousand men!
—*The Lady of the Lake,*
Sir Walter Scott (1810)

THE TUBA and its relatives make up a family called by organologists 'the valved bugle-horns'. Their common and unique characteristic is a markedly conical profile resulting from the bore's more or less regular expansion from mouthpipe to bell. This is in clear contrast to the comparatively cylindrical profile of the trumpets and trombones and the french horn's less gradual rate of expansion. In fact both the french horn and the valved bugle-horns are descended from the medieval bugle-horn, but whereas the former was modified during its early stages of development, the latter retain the distinctive profile of the original.

*Bugle* can be traced back to the Latin *buculus* or *boculus*, a young bullock. By the fourteenth century 'bugle-horn' was a term in common use for a drinking vessel or musical instrument made from the horn of one of these animals. Similar words were found in Ireland: *corn buabhall* (buffalo horn) or simply *buabhall*, derived from the Latin *bubalus*, meaning a wild ox or buffalo; and in Wales: *bual, buelin, bualgorn* and *corn buelin* (D[17], 136)*. In *The Canterbury Tales* ('The Franklin's Tale') Chaucer presents a vivid picture of a medieval new year:

> Ianus sit by the fyr with double berd
> And drynketh of his bugle-horn the wyn,
> Biforn hym stant brawers of the tusked swyn;
> And Nowel crieth euery lusty man (C[19], 359).

(Ianus = January; brawers = flesh; swyn = bear.)

More than 500 years later, Tennyson's Lady of Shalott notes on first catching sight of Sir Launcelot:

> And from his blazon'd baldric slung
> A mighty silver bugle hung (T[7], stanza 10).

*see Bibliography.

Its important role in pleasurable pursuits like drinking and hunting, together with its distinctive shape, quickly established a unique mythology for the bugle-horn. An illustration dated 1639 shows Puck, liberally surrounded by phallic symbols including a bugle-horn (reproduced by Maureen Duffy (D[22], pl. 10)). Even today, there are parts of the world where the aphrodisiac qualities of powdered animal horn contribute to the comfortable living of the unscrupulous trading on the credulous.

The practical problems of piercing a hole in the point of the horn are considerable, as a significant length of this end consists of solid material. It seems likely, therefore, that initially the idea of the bugle-horn as musical instrument arose from the discovery of a horn which had been damaged in some way. Producing more than one note on a bugle-horn is extremely difficult, and it is probable that the sound made by the bugle-horn over the centuries has dropped in pitch. Juliet Jewell of the Natural History Museum, London has pointed out to the author that during the high middle ages (twelfth and thirteenth centuries) cattle were very small with correspondingly small or even tiny horns, while in the later middle ages (fourteenth and fifteenth centuries) there was in many places great improvement in cattle, and some beasts were very large with massive horns. The equivalent horn in a present-day breed might be that of a Hereford or Welsh Black cow (Fig. 1.1).

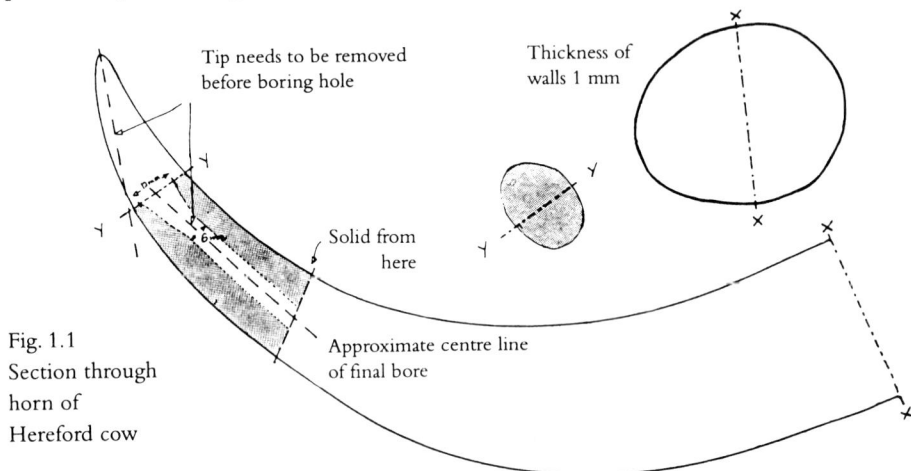

Tip needs to be removed before boring hole

Thickness of walls 1 mm

Solid from here

Fig. 1.1
Section through horn of Hereford cow

Approximate centre line of final bore

The larger and less bucolic *oliphant* was originally made from an elephant's tusk. Probably introduced into Europe some time before the tenth century, oliphants were later made of ivory, bone, wood or copper, often with considerable ornamentation. A number of these instruments may be found in collections, the prestigious instruments of the nobility, bringing a Byzantine exoticism to war and hunting. The Horn of Ulph at York Minster was given by King Canute to Ulph Thoroldsson as an indication of good faith on the transfer of lands to him, and Ulph in turn passed it on to the Minster authorities when the lands were transferred into their ownership (Fig. 1.2).

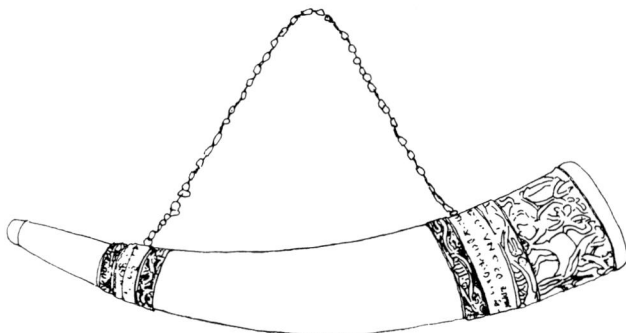

Fig. 1.2
The Horn of Ulph,
York Minster. A
decorated elephant's
tusk given as a
perpetual token
of the gift of lands
by Ulph, son of
Thorold in the
eleventh century.

The oliphant's function of charter horn was found throughout medieval and renaissance times. A twelfth-century bronze horn cast in oliphant shape is to be found in the Winchester City Museum. It is 500 mm long, weighs 6 kg and the mouth is decorated with four lions and two bishops, indicating the balance between royal and ecclesiastical interests in the medieval town. This *moot horn*, producing four notes, was originally used to summon citizens to town meetings, though by the late thirteenth century it was being played by the watch. It is now appropriately celebrated as the logo of the city's museum service (Fig. 1.3).

Fig. 1.3
The twelfth-
century
Winchester
moot horn
as logo of
the city's
Museum
Service.

WINCHESTER
MUSEUMS
SERVICE

The idea of the oliphant as musical instrument was held in parallel to its symbolic functions. The *Chanson de Roland*, probably written shortly after the First Crusade in 1099, tells how the eponymous hero, at the mercy of the Saracens, blew on his oliphant and the sound reached Charlemagne, thirty leagues distant. Alphonse Sax made a version of this instrument called the *cornet-trompe*, a copper oliphant with an extended tube wound round it externally. Théodore Grégoire of Nancy made a more complicated variety—really a type of *cor de chasse*—under the name *Trompe de Lorraine*, French Patent 76072, 7 July 1867. The spiral tubing, 4700 mm long, is contained *within* the horn.

Fig. 1.4
Bugle-horn as
part of the
insignia of
the Light
Division.

The military valued the bugle-horn's ability to convey signals over the field and in the mid-eighteenth century a metal bugle, still following the semicircular shape of the original, was adopted by the British army. This was reflected in two operas by William Shield, *The Noble Peasant* (Little Theatre in the Haymarket, 1784) and *The Woodman* (Covent Garden, 1791) where bugle-horns appear in military-style numbers. They were also sometimes introduced into bands—for example the Royal Artillery had a 'Bugal horn' in 1789, and on its establishment in 1800 The Rifle Brigade (part of the Light Division which in 1814 was given permission to incorporate a bugle-horn in its insignia (Fig. 1.4)), boasted a band of '30 bugle-horns' (T[15], 210). The tone was found attractive, but its musical potential was limited. The familiar shape, in which the tubing is looped back on itself twice, was not finally adopted until 1858. By this time the duty bugle's present status had been confirmed since keys and later valves had been added elsewhere to bring into existence the family of valved bugle-horns.

Bugles without valves are found in the modern orchestra in just one composition: eight, pitched in bb—but written at concert pitch—in four parts, occasionally muted, specified in Britten's *Noye's Fludde*. The instrument's martial function continues to this day, while its ability to draw attention to itself has been exploited by such makers as Čeverný of Hradek Králové whose 1866 *Sokolovka* or *Turnerhorn* was intended for sports club use and the *Jägerhorn* of 1867 for general use; and Anborg of Como who made a cyclist's bugle. M. B. Martin's British Patent 27,746 of 16 December 1907 was for a bugle or other instrument made from flexible tubing of coiled metal or of tube sections connected by india-rubber joints. The drawing in the specification shows an instrument looking like a cross between a duty bugle and a vacuum cleaner.

Any reference work able to devote more than one sentence to the valved bugle-horns mentions the incredible confusion of nomenclature relating to the family. Some manage to complicate the matter even further, like Forsyth who developed an intricate system using a code of numerals along with upper- and lower-case letters to differentiate between instruments. Table 1.1 gives the names in four languages of the various valved bugle-horns, excluding only those which are markedly the product of interbreeding with another brass family (like the Wagner Tuben). The names in the table have been compiled from scores, orchestral parts, references in the literature and word-of-mouth. Trade names are followed by the name of the maker. Further references may be found in Appendix B and the Index.

Table 1.1 THE VALVED BUGLE-HORNS

Instruments pitched in b'b (superseded by Piccolo Bb Trumpet)

| *English* | *German* | *French* | *Italian* |
|---|---|---|---|
| **Saxhorn** | **Sax-horn in B** | **Petite Saxhorn** | **Flicorno** |
| **Suraigu** | **alto** | **suraigu** | **sopracuto** |
| *Narrow-bore* | | | |
| Super-acute | | | |
| Soprano | | | |
| Saxotromba | | | |

Instruments pitched in e'♭

| English | German | French | Italian |
|---|---|---|---|
| **E flat Soprano** | **Flügelhorn** | **Petit bugle** | **Flicorno** |
| **Flugel Horn** | **Pikkolo in Es** | | **Sopranino** |
| Sopranino | Altflügelhorn | Bugle mi bémol | |
| Saxhorn | Diskanttuba | Petit saxhorn | |
| | Hochflügelhorn | | |
| *Narrow-bore* | | | |
| Sopranino | Kleine | Saxotromba | |
| Saxotromba | Saxotromba | soprano | |

Instruments pitched in b♭

| English | German | French | Italian |
|---|---|---|---|
| **Flugel Horn** | **Flügelhorn** | **Bugle si bémol** | **Flicorno** |
| **[U.K.]** | **in B** | | **Soprano** |
| **Fluegel Horn** | | | |
| **[U.S.A.]** | | | |
| Alto Flugelhorn | Hochflügelhorn | Bugle à cylindres | Clavicorno |
| Alto Saxhorn | Kornett | Bugle à pistons | Flicorno |
| Soprano Saxhorn | Sopransaxhorn | Contralto | Sax. [coll.] |
| Valve Bugle | Tuba Soprano in B | Saxhorn contralto | Biucolo [Neap.] |
| Ebor Corno | | Saxhorn soprano | |
| [Dodworth] | | Bugle ténor [Belg.] | |
| *Narrow-bore* | | | |
| Soprano | | Saxotromba | |
| Saxotromba | | contralto | |
| *French horn-shape* | | | |
| Koenig Horn | Könighorn | | |
| *Tuba-shape* | | | |
| Contralto | | | |
| Saxhorn | | | |

Instruments pitched in eb

| English | German | French | Italian |
|---|---|---|---|
| **Tenor Horn** [U.K.] **Alto Horn** [U.S.A.] | **Althorn** | **Alto** | **Genis** |
| Alto Saxhorn | Altkornett | Althorn | Clavicorno |
| Tenor Flugel Horn | Alto | Bugle alto | Flicorno |
| Tenor Saxhorn | Flügelhorn | Bugle contralto | Contralto |
| Dog Horn [coll.] | Alto Tuba | Bugle ténor | |
| Peck Horn | Altsaxhorn | Saxhorn alto | |
| [U.S.A. coll.] | Alt-tuba | Saxhorn ténor | |
| Althorn [arch.] | Alt-trompete [arch.] | Ophicléide-alto | |
| Valve Ophicleide | | à pistons [arch.] | |
| [arch.] | | Baryton aigu | |
| | | [Besson] | |
| Contrahorn | Contrahorn | Contrehorn | |
| [Lamperhoff] | Kontrahorn | Néo-alto [Rivet] | |
| Ebor Corno | | | |
| [Dodworth] | | | |
| Tenor-valve | | | |
| Ophicleide | | | |
| [Jordan] | | | |
| *Sweet-toned(!)* Obbligato Alto Horn [Červený] | Althorn Obbligat Obligat-Althorn | Alto obligé | |
| *Narrow-bore* Clavicor Alto Saxotromba | | Clavicor alto Saxotromba alto-ténor | Clavicorno |
| *Wide-bore* Herculesophone [Sediva] | Herkulesofon | Herkulesofon | |

Instruments pitched in e♭ *(continued)*

| *French horn-shape* | | | |
|---|---|---|---|
| Primhorn<br>[Červený] | Cor Alto<br>Corhorn<br>Oktavwaldhorn<br>Primwaldhorn<br>Primhorn<br>[Aust.] | Alto cor<br>Cor alto<br>Cor ténor | |
| *Trumpet-shape* | Baßtrompete<br>[Stölzel] | | |

Instruments pitched in B♭ ('normal bore')

| *English* | *German* | *French* | *Italian* |
|---|---|---|---|
| **Baritone**<br>**Baritone Horn**<br>[U.S.A.]<br>Alto Horn<br>Baritone Saxhorn<br>Althorn [arch.]<br>Barytone [arch.]<br>Tenor Euphonium<br>[arch.]<br>Tenor Horn [arch.]<br>Glycleide (with<br>    rotary-change to<br>    A) [Červený] | **Tenorhorn**<br>Baritonsaxhorn<br>Barytonsaxhorn<br>Tenorflügelhorn<br>Tenorsaxhorn<br>Bassflügelhorn<br>[Aust. & Ger. arch.] | **Baryton**<br>Alto<br>Barytone<br>Bugle baryton<br>Bugle ténor<br>Grand bugle<br>Saxhorn baryton<br>Saxhorn ténor | **Flicorno Tenore**<br>Basso Flicorno<br>Tenore |
| *Sweet-toned*<br>Obbligato Alto<br>    Horn [Červený] | Obligat-Althorn | | |

*(continued)*

Instruments pitched in B♭ ('normal bore') *(continued)*

| | | | |
|---|---|---|---|
| *Narrow-bore*<br>Baritone<br>  Saxotromba<br>Clavicor | | | Clavicorno |
| *Wide-bore*<br>Herculesophone<br>  [Červený]<br>Imperial Baritone<br>  [Červený] | Herkulesofon<br><br>Kaisertenor | Herkulesofon<br><br>Ténor impériale | |
| *French horn-shape*<br>Amateur Voice<br>  Horn (in C)<br>  [Distin]<br>Ballad Horn (in C)<br>  [Distin]<br>Ballad Horn (in B<br>  flat) [U.S.A.] | | | |
| *Trumpet-shape* | Tenortrompete<br>  [Stölzel] | Bugle ténor (in C) | |
| *Helicon-shape* | Tenorkornett<br>  (narrow-bore)<br>  [Červený] | | |

Instruments pitched in B♭ (wider bore)

| English | German | French | Italian |
|---|---|---|---|
| **Euphonium** | **Baryton** | **Basse** | **Eufonio** |
| Tenor Tuba | Tenor Tuba | Basse-à-cylindres | Tuba Tenore |
| Alto Horn | Bariton | Basse-à-pistons | Basso Flicorno |
| Bass Flugel Horn | Barytonhorn | Bugle baryton | Basso Tuba |
| Bass Saxhorn | Barytonsaxhorn | Bugle basse | Bombarda a 4 |
| Bass Tuba | Barytontuba | Clairon-basse | pistoni (with four |
| B flat Tuba | Baßflügelhorn | Clairon-contrebasse | valves) |
| Bass Horn [U.K. | Baßtuba | Cor-basse ténor | Bombardino |
| arch. & U.S.A.] | Baßtube | Saxhorn baryton | Flicorno (with three |
| Bombardin [arch.] | Kleine Baß | Saxhorn basse | valves) |
| Euphonic Horn | Tenorbaß | Tuba | Flicorno Basso |
| [arch.] | Tenorbaßhorn | Tuba basse | Pelittone |
| Euphonion [arch.] | Tuba Baryton | Tube | |
| Sommerophone | Euphonikon [arch.] | Baryton-à-bocal | |
| [arch.] | Euphonium [arch.] | [arch.] | |
| Valve Ophicleide | Primbass [arch.] | Ophicléide-à- | |
| [arch.] | | cylindres [arch.] | |
| Baroxyton | | Ophicléide-à- | |
| [Červený] | | pistons [arch.] | |
| Hell's Horn [Hell] | Hellhorn | | |
| Phonikon (with | | Phoneion | |
| bulbous bell) | | Emboliclave | |
| [Červený] | | [Coëffet] | |
| | | Néo-alto [Rivet] | |
| | | Piston-basse | |
| | | [Périnet] | |

*(continued)*

Instruments pitched in B♭ (wider bore) *(continued)*

| | | | |
|---|---|---|---|
| Herkulesofon<br><br>Kaiserbariton | Herkulesofon<br><br>Baryton impériale<br>Basse impériale | | |
| Barytonkornett<br>(narrow-bore)<br>[Červený] | | | Pelittone |

Instruments pitched in F

| *English* | *German* | *French* | *Italian* |
|---|---|---|---|
| **F Tuba**<br>Bass Tuba<br>Bombardon<br>Tuba<br>Bass Horn [U.K.<br>  arch. & U.S.A.]<br>Bombardin [arch.]<br>Valve-ophicleide<br>  [arch.]<br>Barlow Tuba<br>  [Besson] | **Baßtuba**<br>Baßtube<br>Bombardon<br><br>Baßhorn [Stölzel] | **Tuba basse**<br>Bombardon-à-<br>  cylindres<br>Clairon contrebasse<br>Saxhorn basse<br>Tube<br>Ophicléide-à-<br>  cylindres [arch.]<br>Ophicléide-à-<br>  pistons [arch.]<br>Ophicléide monstre<br>  [arch.]<br>Piston-basse<br>  [Périnet] | **Tuba Bassa**<br>Basso Tuba<br>Bombardone<br>Flicorno Basso-<br>  grave<br>Pelittone |
| *Wide-bore*<br>Imperial Bass<br>  [Červený] | Kaisertuba<br>Kaiserbaß | | |

*(continued)*

Instruments pitched in F *(continued)*

| | | | |
|---|---|---|---|
| *Wide-bore*<br>Imperial Bass<br>[C̄ervený] | Kaisertuba<br>Kaiserbaß | | |
| *Helicon-shape*<br>Helicon | Helikon<br>Baßkornett<br>(narrow-bore)<br>[C̄ervený] | | Elicon |

Instruments pitched in E♭

| *English* | *German* | *French* | *Italian* |
|---|---|---|---|
| **EE flat Tuba** | **Baßtuba** | **Tuba basse** | **Tuba bassa** |
| Bass | Baß | Bombardon-à- | Basso Tuba |
| Bass Tuba | Baßtube | cylindres | |
| Bombardon | Bombardon | Bombardon | Bombardone |
| Contrabass Saxhorn | Bordunsaxhorn | contrebasse | Flicorno Basso- |
| Deep Bass Saxhorn | Großer Baß | Clairon contrebasse | grave |
| EE flat Bass | Kontrabaß-saxhorn | Contrebasse | Pelittone |
| E flat Bass (three | Tiefes Baß-saxhorn | Flugelhorn | Gabusifono |
| valves, medium- | Baßhorn [Stölzel] | contrebasse | [Gabusi] |
| narrow bore) | | (three valves) | |
| E flat Tuba (three | | Sax-contrebasse | |
| valves, medium- | | Saxhorn basse | |
| narrow bore) | | Tube | |
| Tuba | | Tube de contrebasse | |
| Double E [coll.] | | Piston-basse | |
| Bass Horn [U.K. | | (Périnet) | |
| arch. & U.S.A.] | | | |
| Bombardin [arch.] | | | |

*(continued)*

Instruments pitched in Eb *(continued)*

| | | | |
|---|---|---|---|
| Valve Ophicleide [arch.] | | Ophicléide-à-cylindres [arch.] Ophicléide-à-pistons [arch.] Ophicléide monstre [arch.] Sax-tubar [arch.] | |
| *Narrow-bore* Bass Saxotromba | | Saxotromba basse | |
| *Wide-bore* Herculesophone [Sediva] Imperial Bass [Červený] | Herkulesofon Kaiserbaß | Herkulesofon Basse impériale | |
| *Helicon-shape* Helicon Sousaphone Circular Bass Holtonphone [Holton] Sonorophone [Metzler] | Helikon Susaphon Baßkornett (narrow-bore) [Červený] | Soubassophone [Couesnon] | Elicon Pelittone |
| *Snail-shape* | | Antoniophone [Courtois] | |

Instruments pitched in C

| English | German | French | Italian |
|---|---|---|---|
| **CC Tuba** | **Kontraß-tube** | **Saxhorn** | **Tuba Bassa** |
| Contrabass Tuba | Baßtuba | **Contrebasse** | Basso Tuba |
| Bass Tuba | Baßtube | Tuba basse | Flicorno |
| Tuba | Bombardon in tief C | Saxhorn bourdon |   Contrabbasso |
| Double C [coll.] | | Tube | |
| Bass Horn [U.S.A.] | | Tube de contrebasse | |
| *Wide-bore* | | | |
| Imperial Bass | Kaiserbaß | | |
|   [Červený] | Kaisertuba | | |
| *Helicon-shape* | | | |
| Helicon | Helikon | | Elicon |
| Imperial Helicon | Kaiser-Helikon | | Pelittone |
|   (wide-bore) | | | |
|   [Červený] | | | |

Instruments pitched in B'♭

| English | German | French | Italian |
|---|---|---|---|
| **BB flat Tuba** | **Kontrabaßtuba** | **Saxhorn** | **Tuba Bassa** |
| Contrabass Tuba | Baßtuba | **contrebasse** | Basso Tuba |
| Bass | Baß | | Flicorno |
| Bass Tuba | Baßtube | Tuba basse |   Contrabbasso |
| BB flat Bass | Bombardon in tief B | Bombardon | Pelittone |
| B flat Bass (three | Bordunsaxhorn |   contrebasse | |
|   valves, medium- | Kontrabaß-saxhorn | Clairon contrebasse | |
|   narrow bore) | Tiefes Baß-saxhorn | Contrebasse | |
| Contrabass Saxhorn | | Flugelhorn | |
| Contrebass Saxhorn | |   contrebasse (three | |
| Double-bass | |   valves) | |
|   Saxhorn | | Saxhorn bourdon | |
| Tuba | | Sax-contrebasse | |

*(continued)*

Instruments pitched in B♭ *(continued)*

| | | | |
|---|---|---|---|
| Bass Horn [U.K. arch. & U.S.A.] Double B [coll.] Double Bass [coll.] | | Tube Tube de contrebasse Sax-tubar | |
| *Narrow-bore* Contrabass  Saxotromba Double-bass  Saxotromba | | Saxotromba  contrebasse | |
| *Wide-bore* Imperial Bass  [Červený] | Kaiserbaß Kaisertuba | | |
| *Helicon-shape* Helicon Sousaphone Circular Bass Holtonphone  [Holton] Imperial Helicon  (wide-bore)  [Červený] | Helikon Susaphon Kontrabaß-kornett  (narrow-bore)  [Červený] Kaiserhelikon | Soubassophone  [Couesnon] | Elicon Pelittone |

Instruments pitched in E♭

| *English* | *German* | *French* | *Italian* |
|---|---|---|---|
| **Subbass Tuba** [Sax] | | **Sax-bourdon  mi bémol** Saxhorn bourdon  [Sax] | |

*(continued)*

Instruments pitched in B''♭

| English | German | French | Italian |
|---|---|---|---|
| **Contrabass Tuba** Subcontrabass Tuba [Sax] Subcontrabass Tuba (in C' and F') [Červený] | | | |

TABLE 1.2    DIMENSIONS OF VALVED BUGLE-HORNS IN CURRENT USE

| | | BORE | | BELL DIAMETER | | OVERALL HEIGHT | | WEIGHT | |
|---|---|---|---|---|---|---|---|---|---|
| Instrument | Approx. open tube length [1] | Min. mm | Max. mm | Min. mm | Max. mm | Min. mm | Max. mm | Min. kg | Max. kg |
| Flügel Horn Bb | 1320 mm | 10.5 | 16.00 | 134.62 | 177.8 | — | — | — | — |
| Mellophone Bb | 1320 mm | 11.7 | 11.89 | 254.00 | 279.4 | — | — | 1.7 | 2.72 |
| Alto Horn Eb | 1945 mm | 11.7 | 17.00 | 197.00 | 311.00 | 381.00 | 520.7 | 1.587 | 1.757 |
| Baritone Bb | 2640 mm | 12.00 | 14.5 | 210.00 | 300.00 | — | 800.00 | 2.2 | 3.3 |
| Euphonium Bb | 2640 mm | 13.00 | 16.8 | 250.00 | 340.00 | 660.00 | 860.00 | 3.2 | 4.8 |
| French c Tuba | — | 10.00 | 15.00 | 266.00 | 300.00 | 612.00 | — | — | — |
| F Tuba | 3550 mm | 17.5 | 21.2 | 350.00 | 480.00 | 790.00 | 1020.0 | 5.7 | 7.8 |
| Eb Tuba [2] | 3955 mm | 14.2 | 21.00 | 310.00 | 483.00 | 780.00 | 1080.0 | 5.6 | 9.3 |
| C' Tuba | 4800 mm | 16.89 | 23.00 | 360.00 | 508.00 | 830.00 | 1050.0 | 8.0 | 10.00 |
| B'b Tuba [2] | 5355 mm | 15.49 | 22.00 | 355.6 | 508.00 | 800.00 | 1120.0 | 5.4 | 11.4 |
| Sousaphone Eb | 3955 mm | — | 14.20 | — | 600.00 | — | — | — | — |
| Sousaphone B'b | 5355 mm | 14.2 | 18.64 | 610.00 | 665.00 | — | — | — | — |
| Helicon B'b | 5355 mm | 18.20 | 22.20 | 500.00 | 500.00 | 1030.0 | 1100.0 | 7.00 | 7.80 |

1. The precise length of tubing is affected by the bore.
2. Includes both three-valve and four-valve instruments of this pitch.

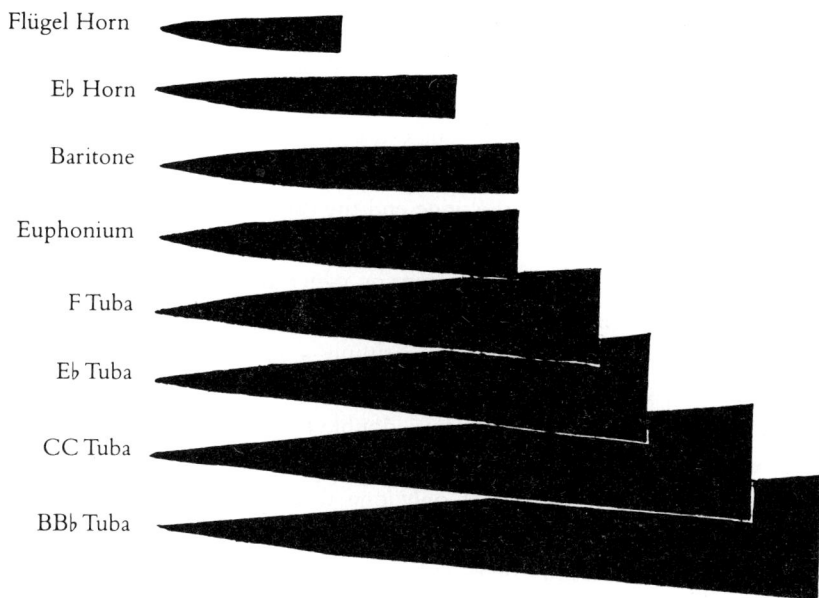

The basis of these diagrams is the mean profile of each type of instrument calculated from dimensions drawn from Table 1.2 as follows (in mm):

|              | Tube length | Bore  | Bell   |
|--------------|-------------|-------|--------|
| Flügel Horn  | 1320        | 10.9  | 149.2  |
| Eb Horn      | 1945        | 11.85 | 184.15 |
| Baritone     | 2640        | 13.15 | 249.25 |
| Euphonium    | 2640        | 15.45 | 277.7  |
| F Tuba       | 3550        | 18.15 | 387.35 |
| Eb Tuba      | 3955        | 16.85 | 441.00 |
| CC Tuba      | 4800        | 19.00 | 482.6  |
| BBb Tuba     | 5355        | 19.6  | 482.6  |

For purposes of comparison, the bore at the second valve has been assumed to be reached at a point one-third of the tube-length from the mouthpiece. The orifice of the receiver has been taken as zero. The scale of width is double the scale of length.

Fig. 1.5. Comparative Profiles of the Valved Bugle-horns.

# THE ACOUSTICS

The acoustics of any brass intrument are extremely complex, and still not fully understood. The following generalized account is intended for non-scientific readers, though every attempt has been made to ensure that it is accurate.

The modern tuba and other valved bugle-horns consist of a tube with a widely-expanding bore. At the narrow end is a *mouthpiece* forming the junction between the player and the instrument; at the wide end the tube expands into a flare or *bell*. The *valves* (Figs. 4.1, 4.2) provide the player with a wider choice of notes than is obtainable from the simple horn. The means by which this is achieved are explained later in this chapter.

Without a player any brass instrument is simply a tube containing air. When an air-column vibrates regularly a musical sound is heard. The player places his (or her) lips on the mouthpiece where they form a double heterophonic reed. (*Heterophonic* means that the reed is capable of a wide range of vibrations, as opposed to an *idiophonic* reed which can vibrate at only one frequency.) By using the tongue behind the upper teeth as a valve the player can control the passage of air from his lungs through the lips causing these, and consequently the air-column, to vibrate. The air-column vibrates not only as a whole but simultaneously in fractions of its length. The longer the vibrating air-column the lower the note. Thus the parts produce higher notes than the whole. The note given by the vibrations of the entire column is called the *fundamental*, those given by the vibrating parts are *harmonics*. Only one series of harmonics can be obtained from an air-column of given length, using conventional playing techniques, and this is called the *harmonic series*. Ex. 1.1 shows the harmonic series for the open tube (i.e. with no valves in operation) of the euphonium pitched in B♭. Harmonics 2-6 are familiar as the notes played by a bugle (albeit in this case a bass bugle); harmonic 8 is the highest normally demanded of the valved bugle-horns.

Although it is customary to describe the player's action as 'buzzing the lips' this is not an accurate description of the process. Very often brass players can control their lips to the extent that they are able to demonstrate their function whilst playing by producing notes consisting of tuned versions of the sound known in the nursery as 'blowing a raspberry'. This is a much coarser action of the lips than actually takes place when playing the instrument. The mode of vibration has been shown to be extremely complex, similar in fact to the action of the larynx. It was thought at one time that the vibrations of the air-column were produced by frequent and recurrent

Fig.1.6
Baritone with forward-
facing bell and three front-
valves.

1. Bell wire
2. Bell flare
3. Bell
4. Mouthpipe ferrule
5. Mouthpipe (leadpipe)
*6. Mouthpiece
  (for details see Fig. 1.8)
7. Bell/bottom bow
  ferrule
8. Stay flange
9. Stay barrel
10. Bottom bow
11. Bottom bow cap
12. Large branch
13. S-bend
14. Slide ferrule
15. Slide bow
16. Reinforcing ring
17. Inner slide
18. Water-key
19. Water well
20. Water-key carriage
21. Outer slide
22. Valve casing
23. Right-hand finger-ring
24. Casing stay
*25. Valves
  (for details see Fig. 4.2)
26. Third valve-slide
  finger-ring
27. Second valve-slide
28. First valve-slide
29. Main-slide

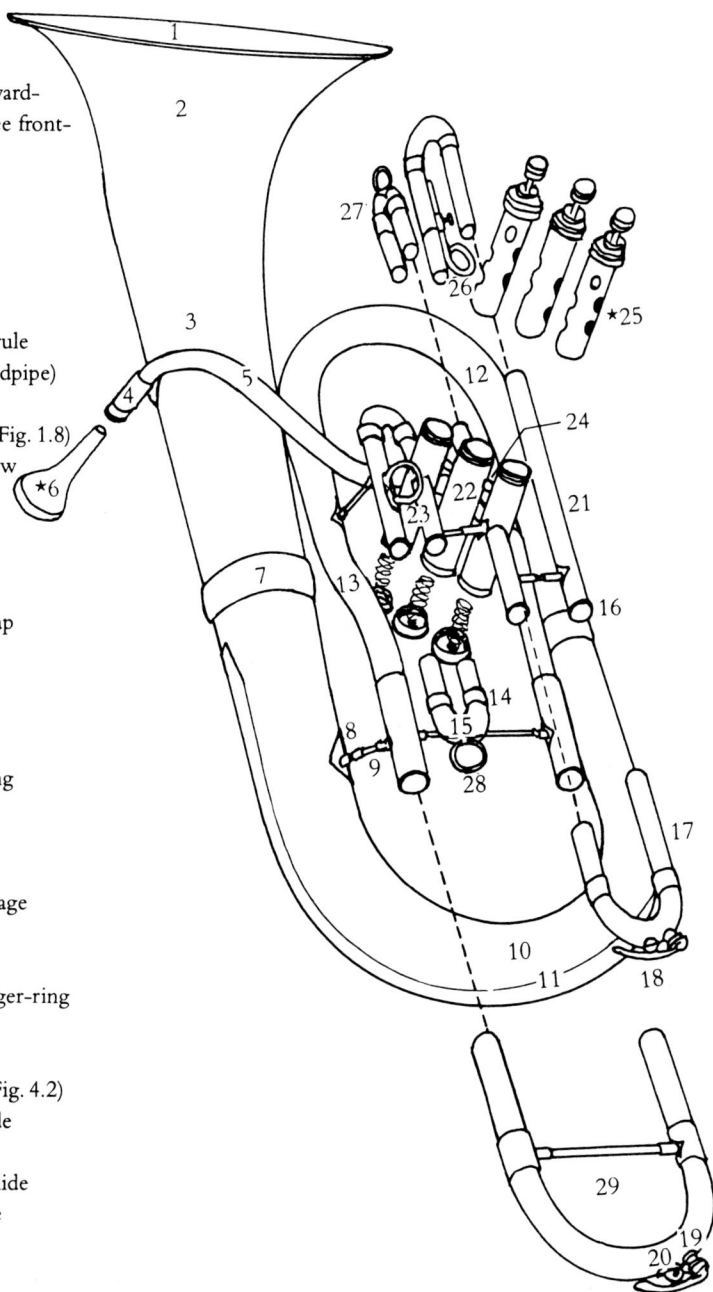

UMI makers of Conn Musical Instruments

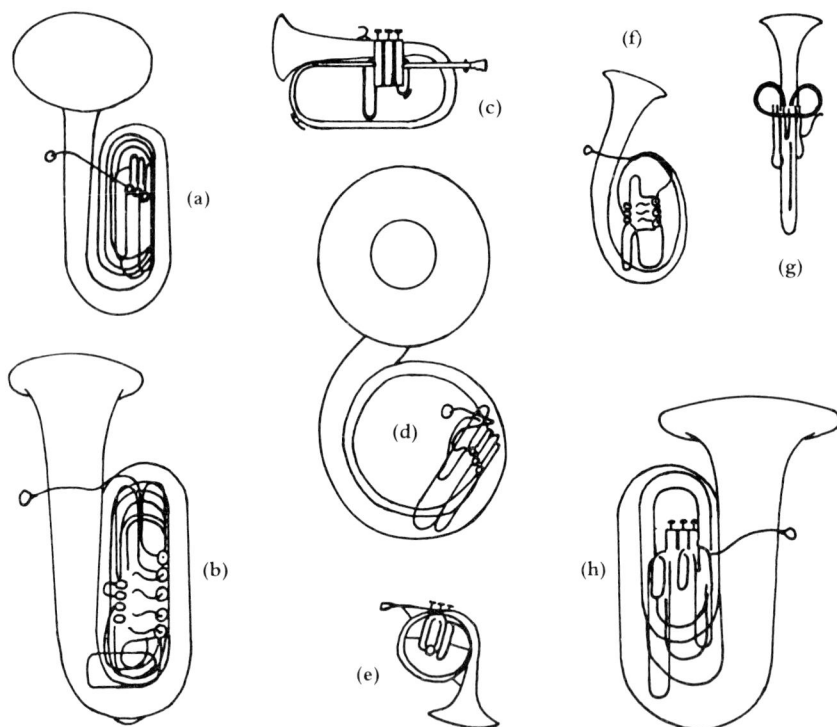

*Not to scale*

Fig. 1.7. Valved bugle-horn shapes. (a) Forward-facing bell tuba with front-valves (York); (b) Left-facing tuba with rotary valves (Červený); (c) Trumpet-shape flügel horn with top valves (Couesnon); (d) Helicon-shape sousaphone (Reynolds); (e) French horn-shape mellophone (Olds); (f) Oval-shape alto horn with rotary-valves (Alexander); (g) Bassoon/ophicleide-shape valved ophicleide with *Wiener-ventile* (Uhlmann); (h) Right-facing tuba with top-valves (Holton).

puffs of air from the lips. Filming at high speed through a transparent mouthpiece has shown that this is not the case and it is now thought that the harmonics are caused by the production of a sound pressure so high as to distort the sound–wave as it travels down the air-column.

A note is initiated by the vibrating lips building up oscillations of the air-column resonance nearest to that of the lips themselves. As the oscillations increase in amplitude the pressure they create in the air-column reacts on the lips. This is the reason for the deeper instruments speaking more slowly than those of higher pitch: owing to the greater mass of the air-column the time required for this system to come into operation is longer than in a smaller instrument. For this reason tubists, who often have the additional disadvantage of being placed at the rear of the concert platform some distance from the conductor and audience, often have to anticipate the conductor's beat and 'tongue' the note early. (*Tonguing* is the action of releasing the air built up under pressure between the tongue and the roof of the mouth so as to initiate vibration of the lips: the whole action takes only a fraction of a second and is preferably assisted by raising the diaphragm either simultaneously or as part of a longer controlled act of exhalation in which the glottis may also be involved as a further controlling factor. Current practice is sometimes to avoid use of the tongue altogether, relying totally on the use of the diaphragm to initiate the note.)

Ex. 1.1                         HARMONIC SERIES OF Bb EUPHONIUM

| Open tube | 2nd valve | 1st valve | 3rd or 1st & 2nd valve(s) | 2nd & 3rd valves | 1st & 3rd (or 4th) valve(s) | 1st & 2nd & 3rd (or 4th & 2nd) valve(s) |
|---|---|---|---|---|---|---|

NB. Seventh harmonics are too flat to be used in performance.

Another difficulty which often results from the tubist's seating position is caused by the proximity of drapes and other absorbent surfaces. The oscillation necessary for the production of tone will not occur until the energy input through the lips is balanced by the minor losses into the walls of the instrument and the frequently considerable losses into the tabs and flies. Hence the necessity for increased blowing pressure in these surroundings and in the open air. It is not unusual for the tubist to be seated by the timpani, which may link up tidily with the score but gives the tuba-player an almost impossible work-load since he feels that the harmonics he produces are absorbed to a considerable extent by the complex harmonics produced by the drums.

The profile of the tubing is of major importance in determining an instrument's tone-quality. Lower harmonics are produced more readily in an instrument with a wide bore, and higher notes are more difficult to obtain—both consequently characteristics of the bugle-horns. The outstanding difficulty caused by wide

Ex. 1.2          PRACTICAL FINGERING-CHART FOR B♭ EUPHONIUMS

**First staff**

| | | | | | | | | | |
|---|---|---|---|---|---|---|---|---|---|
| 3-valve | 1 / 3 | 2 / 3 | 1 3 / 2 | 1 | 2 | 0 | | | |
| 4-valve | 4 1 / 3 | 2 / 3 | 1 3 / 2 | 1 | 2 | 0 | | 1 / 2 / 3 / 4 | 1 / 3 / 4 | 3 2 / 4 3 / 4 |
| 4-valve compensated | 4 1 / 3 | 2 / 3 | 1 3 / 2 | 1 | 2 | 0 | 1 / 2 / 3 / 4 | 1 / 3 / 4 | 2 / 3 / 4 | 1 / 2 / 4 |

**Second staff**

| | | | | | | | | | |
|---|---|---|---|---|---|---|---|---|---|
| 3-valve | | 1 / 2 / 3 | 1 / 3 | 2 / 3 | 1 3 / 2 | 1 | 2 | 0 | 1 / 2 / 3 | 1 / 3 |
| 4-valve | 1 1 / 4 2 / 4 | 2 1 / 4 2 / 3 | 4 1 / 3 | 2 / 3 | 1 3 / 2 | 1 | 2 | 0 | 2 1 / 4 2 / 3 | 4 1 / 3 |
| 4-valve compensated | 1 / 4 | 2 1 / 4 2 / 3 | 4 1 / 3 | 2 / 3 | 1 3 / 2 | 1 | 2 | 0 | 2 1 / 4 2 / 3 | 4 1 / 3 |

**Third staff**

| | | | | | | |
|---|---|---|---|---|---|---|
| All types | 2 / 3 | 1 3 / 2 | 1 | 2 | 0 | 2 / 3 |

**Fourth staff**

| | | | | | | |
|---|---|---|---|---|---|---|
| All types | 1 3 / 2 | 1 | 2 | 0 | 1 / 2 | 1 |

**Fifth staff**

| | | | | | | |
|---|---|---|---|---|---|---|
| All types | 2 2 / 3 | 0 1 / 2 | 1 | 2 | 0 | 2 / 3 |

**Sixth staff**

| | | | | | | |
|---|---|---|---|---|---|---|
| All types | 1 3 / 2 | 1 | 2 | 0 | 1 3 / 2 | 1 |

conicity is the relative lack of control exercised by the air-column. This creates extra demands on the player's lips which have to vibrate the note more accurately than in the trumpet or trombone where the more cylindrical profile of the air-column gives more control.

The mouthpiece can help or hinder to a great extent. Instruments of the bugle-horn family use a more or less cup-shaped mouthpiece, as opposed to the shallow trumpet and more funnel-shaped french horn mouthpiece. The rim of the mouthpiece (Fig. 1.8(a)) supports the lips and defines how much of their area is free to vibrate and contribute to the functioning of the system. The greater the area able to vibrate the greater the flexibility with which the lips may be changed from one frequency of vibration to another, but the less control they have over the stability of each note. Increasing the diameter of the mouthpiece has the added result of making the entire instrument flatter in pitch, reducing resonance in the higher register and making the tone fuller but more sombre. These characteristics are not primarily caused by the enlarged diameter but by the increased volume thus created.

The same results follow from making the cup deeper, though they may to some extent be mitigated by enlarging the backbore. This increases the fulness of tone while sharpening all but the lowest notes, giving more resonance in the higher register and less in the middle. In practice, enlarging the throat gives much the same results as increasing the volume, except that the decreased resonance is noticeable over much more of the compass while the upper register becomes both sharper and more difficult to 'fill' owing to the diminished resistance to the air-stream. Lengthening the throat flattens the upper register and gives more resistance in this part of the compass. It also increases resonance in the middle and low registers but overall may give a smaller, brighter sound.

It will be apparent that the player has many decisions to make when choosing a mouthpiece and manufacturers have been generous in the alternatives they offer. A contemporary manufacturer's list is printed in Table 1.3. There are also craftsmen who will make mouthpieces to players' requirements. Furthermore, from time to time models with unexpected applications appear on the market, such as 'THE CURVED RIM MOUTHPIECE (a boon to the player with artificial teeth)' introduced by Boosey & Hawkes in 1932. In this, the section *along* the rim (as opposed to through the rim) was concave in two parallel planes. British Patent 3662, taken out on 20 February 1901 by H. Herring and G. E. Case, was for a rim depressed at each side to fit the lips more accurately than the normal straight rim.

Instrument-makers insist, with few exceptions, that the pattern of mouthpiece should be dictated by the instrument, not the player. Anton Helleberg, the distinguished American tubist, agreed with this theory. He designed a basic shape which was rather more inclined to the funnel than the cup and adapted it to individual instruments as required (Fig. 1.8(B)). Mouthpieces of this type are still made by several manufacturers and are popular with players, although the tubist tends to have a favourite mouthpiece regardless of the particular model of

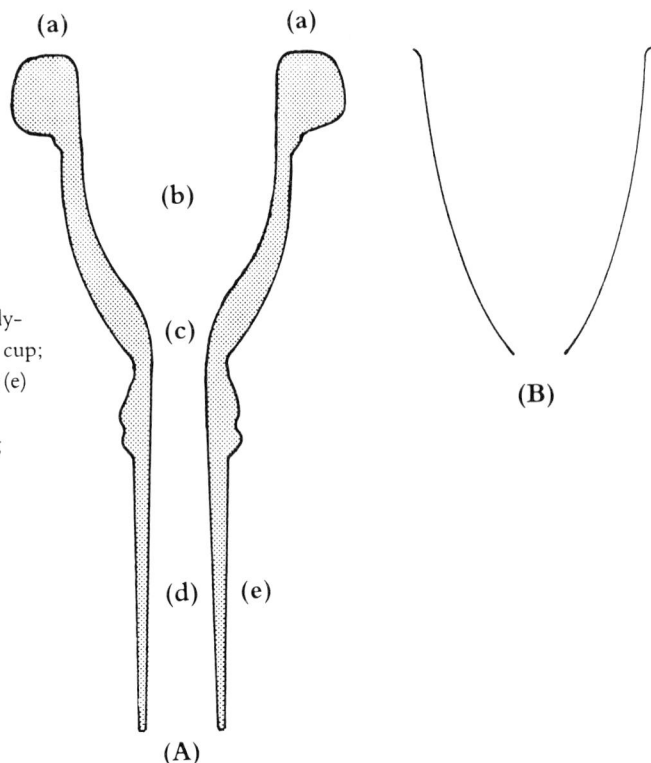

Fig. 1.8
Tuba mouthpieces.
(A) Bach 24AW, a widely-used model: (a) rim; (b) cup;
(c) throat; (d) backbore; (e) shank.
(B) Profile of Helleberg mouthpiece cup.

instrument that he plays. In fact the greater change in timbre is brought about by the alteration of cup volume not cup shape, and it has been demonstrated that the player's oral cavities (probably even throat and chest cavities) exercise some influence on the final tone. Certainly different players produce different timbres when playing the same instrument with identical mouthpieces. An attempt to provide players with the opportunity to adjust mouthpiece dimensions at will was made by A. J. Burr, whose British Patent 24,526 of 5 November 1907 was for a

Table 1.2                     PERANTUCCI MOUTHPIECES

American-style
(Funnel-cupped)

| MODEL | CUP DIA. mm | CUP DEPTH | RIM WIDTH mm | RIM EDGES | THROAT BORE mm | NOTES |
|---|---|---|---|---|---|---|
| PT-30 | 32 | medium | 8.0 | v. round | 8.3 | versatile: all tubas |
| PT-32 | 32.5 | med-large funnel | 8.0 | rounded | 8.3 | versatile: all tubas |
| PT-34 | 32.5 | med/round | 7.5 | sharp inner, round outer | 8.4 | versatile |
| PT-36 | 33 | deep-funnel | 7.5 | sharp inner, round outer | 8.3 | symphony orchestra |
| PT-38 | 34 | deep-funnel | 7.5 | rounded | 8.3 | symph; large lips |
| PT-42 | 33 | deep-funnel | 7.5 | rounded | 8.3 | contrabass tubas |
| PT-44 | 33 | medium- large- funnel | 7.5 7.5 | round inner sharp outer | 8.4 | CC tubas |
| PT-48 | 33.5 | deep-funnel | 8.0 | rounded | 8.5 | large-bore CC & BBb |
| PT-49 | 33.5 | deep-funnel | 8.0 | rounded | 8.5 | versatile large mouthpiece |
| PT-50 | 33 | deep-funnel | 7.5 | flat rim, sharp inner | 8.3 | advanced players |

German-style
(Round-cupped)

| MODEL | CUP DIA. mm | CUP DEPTH | RIM WIDTH mm | RIM EDGES | THROAT BORE mm | NOTES |
|-------|-------------|-----------|--------------|-----------|----------------|-------|
| PT-60 | 32.0 | small-round | 9.0 | mod r'd inner, v. r'd outer | 7.00 | versatile: for F tubas |
| PT-62 | 32.0 | small-round | 9.00 | round inner, v. r'd outer | 7.00 | cushion-rim PT-60 |
| PT-64 | 32 | mod. shallow bowl-shaped | 9.00 | very round | 7.8 | F, Eb or CC tubas |
| PT-66 | 32.5 | med-bowl | 8.00 | rounded | 8.0 | quick response, clarity |
| PT-68 | 32.5 | med, very round at bottom | 8.00 | rounded | 8.0 | F tuba, powerful |
| PT-70 | 32.5 | deep, very round at bottom | 8.00 | small, sharp inner | 8.00 | quick response, broad |
| PT-72 | 32.5 | deep, mod. round at bottom | 8.00 | small, sharp inner | 8.1 | F, Eb; student CC, BBb |
| PT-80 | 32.5 | deep, very round at bottom | 8.5 | cushion | 8.0 | F, Eb tubas |

*(continued)*

German-style *(continued)*

| PT-82 | 32.5 | mod, shallow, round cup | 8.0 | round, slightly sharp inner | 8.2 | large, mellow |
|---|---|---|---|---|---|---|
| PT-83 | 33.0 | med. deep | 7.5 | mod r'd, fairly sharp in. | 8.4 | CC, BBb all-purpose |
| PT-84 | 32.0 | deep, bowl | 8.0 | rounded | 8.0 | Eb, powerful |
| PT-86 | 33.7 | wide dia., mod. depth | 7.5 | slightly r'd inner | 8.3 | round & weighty |
| PT-88 | 33.5 | wide, deep bowl, r'd at bottom | 7.0 | very r'd inner, very r'd outer | 8.2 | CC, BBb advanced players |

mouthpiece with an oval rim and the ability to change the depth of cup and size of throat by means which could include springs acting in notches.

Many new instruments are still supplied with ludicrously small mouthpieces. Lower notes and  larger tones are obtainable only with  the greatest diameter acceptable to the player, a factor the manufacturer often seems to ignore. On using a larger mouthpiece the player will find the instrument below pitch, sometimes to a considerable extent, unless the maker has had the wit to build the instrument sharp to allow adjustment of the *main-slide*, a U-shaped slide working inside two legs of the main tubing. This may be pulled out to adjust the pitch, which in consequence can only be flattened. Since the major British manufacturer uses very small mouthpieces during the tuning process, the problems are literally built into the product, despite continuing representations from players over many years.

At low frequencies the drop in pitch is equivalent to the addition to the instrument of a length of tubing containing the same volume as that of the mouthpiece cup. After shortening the mouthpipe to compensate for the mouthpiece intended by the maker for use with the instrument the pitch of the fundamental remains unchanged but the higher harmonics are flattened. Players who have adopted a larger mouthpiece will find the phenomenon familiar.

The challenges and opportunities offered to mouthpiece designers by the various requirements of tubists and their instruments are graphically illustrated by the range designed by Daniel Perantoni of Indiana University and Robert Tucci of Munich, manufactured under the name of Perantucci. These two players and teachers began their work in 1970 as the result of the limited choice of mouthpieces for players of tuba and euphonium and have since assembled a comprehensive range. The suggested functions of each model are given in Table 1.3 above.

Intonation is affected by other aspects of the instrument's form. The interval between the fundamental and second harmonic in a completely conical instrument is an octave, but in practice part of the narrow end has to be cut off to provide an orifice large enough to allow the lips to function. This has the effect of increasing the interval. There is actually considerable variation in intonation between the notes. The designer has to calibrate the bore so as to ensure that the points of maximum and minimum air-column vibration (*antinodes* and *nodes*) coincide as far as possible with the harmonic series of the tube. For generations this has been done empirically and, except in the cheapest instruments, generally satisfactorily. Increasingly, however, computers are being used in the design process.

A bad bruise at a crucial place may cause changes in pitch affecting certain notes but not others. This happened in the case of one tubist of my acquaintance who fell downstairs with a rather deficient instrument. The result was a badly-dented tuba on which some notes which had previously been of very doubtful intonation were now as good as the others. Reflections of the sound-waves caused by sharp bends in the tubing, small holes. a poorly-adjusted water-key cork or irregularities in the tubing (for example badly-butted sections) can also affect the intonation of certain notes. It was possibly to help overcome this problem that H. H. Lake (on behalf of H. F. Keyes, M. Smith and F. T. Smith) took out British Patent 6166 of 9 March 1897 for helical ribs inside the mouthpiece shank to give the air-column a helical movement. Whether this would be practical either in theory or in practice is yet to be proven. The temperature of the air-column is important for overall pitch: although in practice modified by the heat of the breath, an increase in temperature from 2.7 °C to 32.2°C will raise the pitch a semitone. In any case an air-column is more easily excited when warm than when cold.

A great deal of influence is exerted by the bell, which is far from being a mere ornamental flourish. Both the size and shape have a strong effect on intonation. The acoustic length of an instrument is rather more than the actual length of the tubing, though the precise difference is affected by the bore. The distance between the acoustic length and the end of the actual tube is called the *end correction*. This can be reduced to some extent by increasing the diameter of the bell, highly desirable since the smaller the end correction the more intense the higher *overtones* (parts of the complex tone, but not necessarily harmonics). If the bell diameter is increased excessively the effect is reversed, which is particularly to be avoided in the valved bugle-horns as their wide conicity will have already weakened any high partials created earlier in the system.

The bell also acts as a radiator for the sound. As its diameter is increased so its efficiency improves, particularly in relation to the lower frequencies. This is the reason for larger instruments having wider bells and a relative lack of brilliance. The large bell also is more directional, sometimes a disadvantage to a player with an upright-belled instrument. Directional properties are more pronounced at lower frequencies, which is why a BBb tuba player may find more discomfort in these situations than a performer on the Eb alto horn. Some of Adolphe Sax's six-valve instruments had bells which could be rotated to direct the sound. Other attempts to introduce this useful feature are discussed in Chapter XV.

The presence or absence of the higher overtones is affected by several factors. The characteristic *timbre,* or tone-colour, of a brass instrument is at its strongest when the dynamic is a healthy *mezzo-forte* or thereabouts. When played extremely quietly or loudly the tone quality tends to approach that of other instruments (for example, a quiet tuba may sound like a bassoon, an overblown euphonium like a trombone) owing to the distortion of the individual instrument's wave form. The *wave-form* is the most important arbiter of an instrument's timbre and consists of a diagram of the sound pressures in simultaneous existence at points along the sound wave. The single frequency of a pure tone gives a sinusoidal wave but the considerable number of overtones present in the sound of the bugle-horn gives an extremely complex wave-form.

The wave-form itself is the result of the profile of the tubing. At the ultimate *pianissimo* (with a relatively uncharacteristic tone) resonance occurs mainly at the frequency of the note being vibrated by the lips but as the volume increases due to the increase in pressure of the breath extra harmonics contribute to the tone, coming into action in the order of second, third, etc. By the time a good *fortissimo* is reached all the harmonics within the tone are fully involved. At the entry of the third harmonic the pitch will begin to rise as a sharpened fundamental is more favourable to oscillation at this stage. Players of brass instruments sometimes utilize this phenomenon as part of their technique, reducing breath pressure if a note sounds slightly sharp and vice-versa. If, on the other hand, breath-pressure is increased beyond fully-developed oscillation the lips may suddenly cease to function, a phenomenon not unknown in practice.

The high notes of any brass instrument are difficult to obtain because of an additional reason to those possibly inherent in the chosen mouthpiece: they are not so strongly assisted by other harmonics as notes in the middle and lower registers. At the other extreme of the compass, the pedal notes (which are normally obtainable on the valved bugle-horns) are not easy to play in a well-defined manner at the lowest dynamic levels. Although stronger than in some other classes of brass instruments, the fundamentals in practice scarcely exist, the notes of those pitches being supplied by the interaction of the second and third harmonics of the notes vibrated by the player's lips. The production of notes an octave below the fundamentals (which is often feasible) is the result of a similar interaction. These *factitious notes* can also include others between the highest fundamental and the lowest second harmonic. On some tubas (for example the Holton Mammoth BBb) they may be sounded with some power by an experienced player.

Sousa's euphonium virtuoso, Joseph De Luca, and his tuba soloist Anton Helleberg featured chords in their performances.Up to four notes may be heard at the same time, the technique being to hum one note while playing another. If they have the appropriate relationship the result will be a difference tone (a note with the frequency of the difference between the two notes sounding) and summation tone (a note with the frequency of their combined frequencies). There is no particular merit in the trick, as the eccentric nineteenth-century horn-player Eugène Vivier—a prolific chord-sounder—discovered when an inn-keeper insisted on charging him for the three guests in his room.

So far the acoustic system has been considered mainly in terms of a simple tube giving what a player understands as one harmonic series and an acoustician more precisely as *modes of vibration*. Apart from the duty bugle this is in practice far too restrictive for musical purposes. A system of valves allowing the instantaneous addition of extra tubing is necessary. A length of tubing lowering the fundamental by a semitone, for example, will also give a harmonic series half a tone lower than the original tube-length (Ex. 1.2). At least three extra lengths are necessary to give a full chromatic range over the compass with alternative fingerings allowing more convenient playing of faster passages and slightly flatter or sharper versions of some notes to improve intonation without making excessive demands on the lip. (Tone can suffer when the embouchure is required to exercise control over intonation.)

Overriding the vibrating air-column can become tiring to the *embouchure* (in this sense the lips and muscles controlling them). Eugene Anderson has calculated that over a four octave range—forty-nine notes—a five-valve tuba gives almost 500 possible fingerings, each of which may have particular advantages in any given situation (A[12], 2). The valves are often used in combination, but this leads to problems, particularly in the lower instruments. These difficulties and attempts to overcome them are outlined on pages 191-202 below.

It will become evident that the tuba in particular has a large compass. Including harmonics its frequency range is considered to extend from 60 c.p.s. (cycles per second) to 7,000+ c.p.s., the main output lying in the area between 100-300 c.p.s. This wide range makes mute construction difficult. A normal tuba mute fits in the bell as shown in Fig. 1.9(a). Brass instrument mutes work roughly on the principle of the Helmholtz Resonator, the tuba mute absorbing strongly in the 200-300 c.p.s. frequency region. High harmonics are thus accentuated in relation to low, changing the timbre. It has to be said that theoretically-correct calculations do not always lead to successful mute design and some of the most effective have been built along empirical lines. The sheer size of the tuba mute is daunting to the potential builder and it is rare to find anything other than straight and practice mutes, as opposed to the many varieties used by the trumpet and trombone. Owing to the enormous variation in sizes of tuba bells mutes are often custom-made. It is doubtful, for example, that Robert Schopper of Leipzig had the tuba in mind when he took out German Patent 14258 of 1893 for a brass instrument mute made of glass. The use of aluminium for the body and wooden ends (as advocated by Ron Apperson of Boise, Idaho and the N. P. Griffith Co. of Ralston, Nebraska) has the advantage of reducing the potentially considerable weight of this relatively large object with beneficial results in both carrying the mute and inserting it into the bell during performance. R&S tuba and euphonium mutes, made by Jet-Tone of Elkhart, Indiana have neoprene-tipped adjustable spacers mounted through their polymer walls which enable them to be used in a range of instruments. The distinctive design, and the resonant nature of the material of which the mute is made, provide an alternative timbre to that produced by the more conventional aluminium or fibre mutes.

In the 1970s a radical form of mute resulted from the collaboration of Ben Gossick and tubist Rex Conner of the University of Kentucky. By appropriate design of the outlet duct of the mute in relation to the volumes of both the mute and the bell of the instrument the tone quality was made more uniform over the

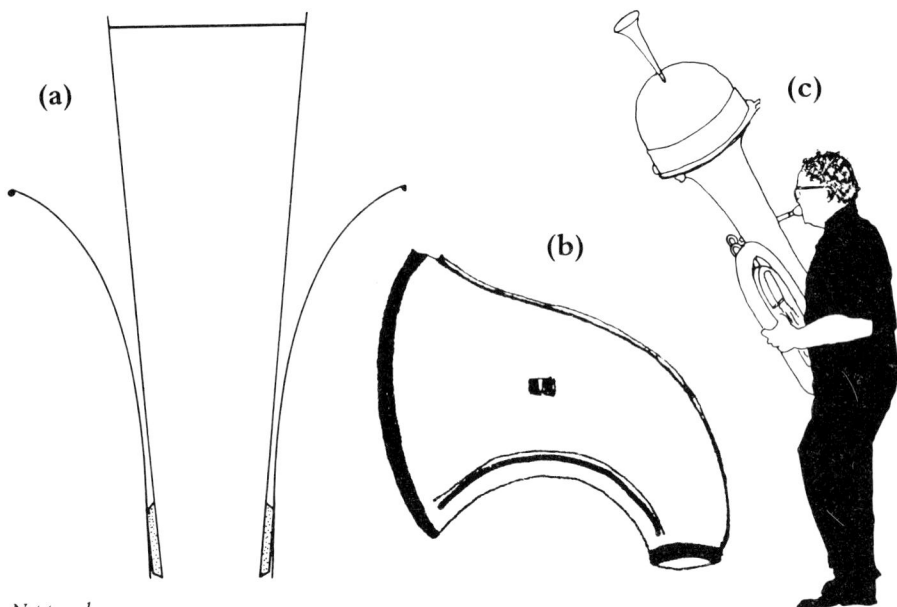

Not to scale

Fig. 1.9. Tuba mutes: (a) Typical mute showing position in tuba bell. Three pieces of cork are fixed to the mute, bearing against the walls of the instrument to hold it in the correct position; (b) sousaphone mute (Humes & Berg); (c) improved tuba mute (Conner & Gossick).

entire range and—a particularly attractive point since traditional mutes are deficient in this area—the low notes were made easier to articulate. It was claimed that in practice they were actually easier than on an unmuted instrument. Since the outlet duct is detachable other ducts providing different timbres may be substituted. Practical considerations have prevented its being widely adopted (Fig. 1.9(c)).

An even more radical form of mute was introduced by Yamaha under the name Silent Brass in 1994. Tubists had had to wait for some years for a version designed for this largest of all brass instruments, but the principle of a mute containing a microphone to pick up the sound which can then be transmitted to a headphone worn by the player has enabled a range of possibilities to be realized. The prime function is, of course, that of a practice mute, allowing instruments to be played without annoying the neighbours. But the electronic element also facilitates the addition of reverberation to the basic sound, enables it to be recorded (either alone or mixed with other instruments using similar mutes) and also offers the possibility of playing to a pre-recorded accompaniment. Mutes of this type are now available for all brass instruments.

The principle had actually been demonstrated some forty years earlier, in J. W. T. Roope's British Patent 679,158 of 19 March 1951. The abstract is worth quoting in full:

A mute comprises a cylinder of metal or plastic closed at one end and clipped at the other end to the bell of the intrument. Inside this cylinder and secured to a flange at its open end is a second cylinder of spongy rubber, closed at its other end and enclosing a volume of air equal to that enclosed by the instrument. Sound-absorbing material is packed betwen the two cylinders. In the open end of the mute is suspended a microphone supplying, through a volume control and an amplifier, headphones worn by the player.

It is doubtful that the mute was actually made as a number of practical problems had to be overcome, not least, in the case of the tuba, the difficulties caused by the need for the mute to contain a volume of air equal to that of the instrument.

There remains one factor which has only been touched upon so far: the material of which the instrument is made. Normally this is brass, often epoxy-lacquered, silver- or nickel-plated. Acousticians are quite clear that the actual material is of little importance in the acoustic system of a wind instrument. Coltman, for example, states that 'It has been shown that, all other factors being equal, the materials of which a flute is made have no effect on its tone quality' (C[28], 212). In 1890 Blaikley confused an audience of musicians by playing metal and paper bugles out of sight; six years later, F. Coeuille of Philadelphia constructed a trombone in which the final 480 mm of the bell was made from lead, a state of affairs not perceived by any of the audience of musicians before whom he played it; more recently Backus covered a cornet in putty to demonstrate that the sound quality remained the same; Mahillon actually made an instrument from cheese to prove that not the material but the proportions were crucial. It is impossible to gauge the likely effect of T. G. Ghislin's proposal that 'a marine plant, *eiklonia buccinalis*, is treated by chemical and other processes, and used for covering and ornamenting horns and other musical instruments' (British Patent 2661 of 31 October 1860). Similarly, Martin's French Patent 12,823 of 14 September 1855 for instruments in aluminium claimed incontrovertably that the instruments would be lighter in weight, but his contention that they would also be sonorous is debatable.

Currently numerous makers make great claims for gold brass bells, while UMI state that nickel-silver causes sound to become brighter. As can often be felt, wall vibrations *are* present in brass instruments but they are limited and do not affect the vibrating air-column; neither do they radiate enough sound to affect the quality of tone perceived by the listener.

The effect of modifying the interior of the tubing is something that has from time to time occupied the minds of inventors but so far seems not to have been tested practically. Adolphe Sax's British Patent 112 of 13 January 1865 was one such:

Brass and like wind instruments are provided with an inner double jacket for the reception of tar or other antiseptic liquid. Or the sides of the the instrument may be coated, so that the air inhaled by the performer is impregnated with the vapours of these substances.

His French Patent 60,296 of 30 September 1863 concerned glazing the inside surface of the tubing of woodwind instruments. So far as is known, the idea was not put into practice, although in theory (only) it could be advantageous for brass players also.

Bowsher and Watkinson, researching the behaviour of brass instruments at the University of Surrey, made a collection of the claims made by manufacturers about the musical qualities of their instruments in relation to the material of construction. Their six-page article (B[49], 25-30) should be read by anyone with an interest in this topic, or techniques of persuasion in general. As an example, yellow brass bells were claimed by Bach to produce a 'brilliant, lively tone'; by Miraphone, to produce 'that big, yet centred tone'; Yamaha, 'high resonance and superb sonority'; Schilke, 'with a yellow brass, it is necessary to anneal it at two different points . . . if this temper were left in the bell, we would find the quality of sound had become very dark'; Paxman stated that 'yellow brass makes for warm sonority'.

But why do players react in one way to instruments with thin walls, another to thick-walled instruments? What is the indefinable 'feel' of an instrument—not only the 'feel' when blown but when felt with the fingers? Does 'blowing in' a new instrument really consist of the player him- or herself adjusting to its particular characteristics? Scientifically there is an absolute and discouraging answer to all these questions, but fortunately music and the instruments used to create it transcend science. Therein lies their magic.

# CHAPTER II

## Serpents and Bass Horns

... the true bass of the cornett is performed with the serpent ...
—Marin Mersenne *Harmonie universelle*, 1635

... a canon of Auxerre, Edme Guillaume, invented the disastrous machine
called the serpent ...
—organist L.-S. Fanart during a seminar on reforms to French church
music reported by Morelet *Revue de la musique religieuse*, 1845

*ab antiquo serpent libera nos, domine* [God save us from the ancient serpent]
—musicologist Charles Bordes (1863-1909) quoted in J. Viret
*Le chant grègorien*

THERE are illustrations from as far back as the eleventh century of players using
bugle-horns with finger-holes to give additional notes. These instruments were the
immediate ancestors of the *cornett*, a gently curved or straight wooden instrument
with side-holes and a cup-mouthpiece. The date of its introduction is unknown,
but it was undoubtedly of great antiquity—and longevity, since it remained in use
until the middle of the nineteenth century. (For a masterly account of the cornett,
its history, development and repertoire by a leading player and scholar, the reader
should consult Bruce Dickey's contribution on the subject to *The Cambridge
Companion to Brass Instruments* (D[12], 51-67).) The cornett had six finger-holes, one
thumb-hole and a virtuoso potential exploited magnificently by composers like
Giovanni Gabrieli in the sixteenth and seventeenth centuries. Benvenuto Cellini
was an exponent: 'My dear son,' said his father, '. . . will you not promise sometimes
to take in hand your flute and that seductive cornett, and play upon them to your
heart's content, inviting the delight of music?' (C[16], 14).

In the sixteenth and early seventeenth centuries there was a tenor cornett pitched
a fifth below the normal treble. Presumably it was the 'most unlovely and bullocky'
sound described by Praetorius (P[22], 36) which accounted for its relative
unpopularity. Players would have found the instrument's length of a metre or more
unwieldy, despite its being built in the form of a somewhat flattened S. Bass
cornetts were also made. Used particularly in France (D[12], 56), they were
sometimes called *lysarden* in England. Some terminated in snake's heads, an excess
which was later to be found in the *basson russe* (Fig. 2.6).

Contrary to the opinions expressed by some authorities, the serpent is not a member of the cornett family, owing to its more conical bore, thinner walls, and the absence of a thumb hole. Its serpentine shape should not cause too much surprise as there had been other examples of wind instruments with relatively long tubes bent to facilitate playing or carrying, apart from the deeper cornetts. Duffin points to depictions of S-shaped trumpets dating from as early as the end of the fourteenth century, some 200 hundred years before the invention of the serpent (D[21], 114). However he does not include in his very thorough account the painting in St Peter's Church, Wenhaston, Suffolk. Dating from c. 1480, this dramatic depiction of the Last Judgement, probably the work of a monk from nearby Blythburgh Priory and known as 'The Wenhaston Doom', shows heaven and hell in some detail, the latter place including the serpentine instrument shown in Fig. 2.1.

Fig. 2.1
Serpentine instrument
depicted in 'The
Wenhasten Doom',
Suffolk, c. 1480.

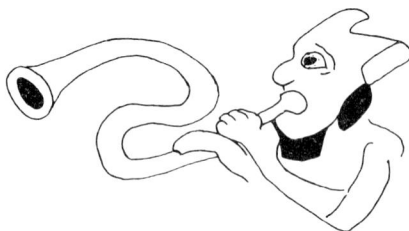

# THE SERPENT

Following the Council of Trent (1542-63), *Concilium Tridentinum* 6:754 included the following (here in translation):

The provincial Council will prescribe, according to the custom of the country, the normative usage for other things that concern the Divine Office. It will determine the right manner of chanting and singing that must be observed . . . The Bishop, with the help of at least two canons, one chosen by himself, and another named by the Chapter, may organize and effect whatever he may judge useful and necessary (H[16], 28).

Thus, the good Bishop of Auxerre, Jacques Amyot encouraged the comptroller of his household, Canon Edmé Guillaume, in his experiments aimed at adapting the tenor cornett to the function of supporting the choir singing plainchant.

The only account so far discovered of the instrument's invention is given by the historian Abbé Lebœuf (or Lebeuf) in his *Mémoire Concernant l'Histoire Ecclésiastique et Civile d'Auxerre* (L[10], I, 643). Lebœuf was himself born in Auxerre, but it is unlikely that his claim resulted from chauvinistic motives: quite the reverse if the comments below (pages 74 and 93) are typical of those who heard the instrument. For the present, his claim has to be accepted as being based on fact: although it has not been confirmed from any other source, no serious counter-claim has been discovered (but see below, page 70). The arrival of the serpent was well-timed, given the growing need for strength in the cantus firmus sung by the bass voices essential in both *chant figuré* (chant with ornamentation and figuration) associated with the new 'neo-Gallician' breviary issued in Paris in 1680, and *l'art de fleuretis en chant sur le livre*, with its improvised counterpoint. Here the serpent reinforced the requisite strictness of measure to the cantus firmus (itself a radical approach) above which the higher voices improvised their florid melodies, although it is to be noted that the female religious were expressly forbidden to sing 'the so-called "figured" chant' (H[16], 29).

The range of this music rarely exceeded an octave, and the cantus firmus, which might be conveniently transcribed into modern notation using mainly minims and semibreves, gave time for the serpent-player to stabilize each note before proceeding to the next pitch. Mersenne had pointed out in 1637 that: 'It seems that the irregular distance of the holes of the serpent makes its diapason more difficult than that of the other instruments . . .' (M[28], 29). Abbé Beaugeois remarks: '. . . the student needs a good ear, because many of the notes are only given by the lips'(B[18], 106). But the serpent was designed specifically to play a simple, slow-moving, sustained part, a function it exercised in France into the nineteenth century (in some cases, the twentieth: see page 119 below). Mersenne refers to its capability of 'supporting twenty very strong voices . . . And the tone can be softened so that it will be suitable to join with the soft voices of chamber music . . .(M[28], 29). Bazin's painting *Procession à Saint-Sulpice* (in the Parisian church of that name, and reproduced on the cover of *Le livre d'orgue de Montréal*, Sacem CD 300 002.2) gives a vivid impression of the appearance of the serpent in its ecclesiastical setting. It is also a timely reminder that far from playing an obscure and sympathetic role, the serpent was prominent in the Church's intimidating pomp and ceremony, carefully-calculated techniques exercised with a success all too evident in the postures of the women in the congregation pictured here. Bernard Fourtet is the serpentist who appears on several of the tracks on the disc, while Hiley (H[26], 620) gives useful sources for further research, including contemporary treatises and compositions.

As originally made, the serpent consisted of a conical tube, about 2150 mm long, with six finger-holes. It was normally wooden, preferred species including walnut, maple and such trees as plum, pear, sycamore and sorb (other trees related to apple and pear), though softwoods (poplar or linden) are sometimes found (S[36], 49). The two halves were carved out separately and glued together lengthwise (a traditional cornett-building technique), then bound in leather. The operation needed great skill. From a bore of some 12 mm the tube expanded regularly to about 100 mm at the bell and the walls were a mere 6-7 mm thick. The main reinforcing elements in this method of construction were simply the glue and the leather binding, although Mersenne refers to binding with beef sinews to strengthen the first curve (M[29], III, 278). Philip Bate, dissecting an old and decrepit serpent, was surprised to find that the wood's butt-joints had been covered with old strips of document vellum to add support (B[14], 49).

Fig. 2.2 shows an interesting exception to conventional methods of construction. While appearing to be a traditional church serpent, and in fact modelled on a specimen in Shaftesbury Museum, Dorset, it was made from a series of softwood cross-sections by retired nuclear engineer and amateur euphoniumist Burchell Gladwyn. Phil Humphries, its owner, finds it playable, though a later smaller model in F is more satisfactory. The main disadvantage is its weight, which is considerably more than the 11 kg of a comparable Christopher Monk instrument.

The typical serpent mouthpiece was of cup shape, with a small throat and very narrow rim, about 30 mm inside diameter. It was made of ivory, sometimes of horn, and fitted into the narrower end of a bent brass crook (today called by Americans a *bocal*, the original French term) some 235 mm long which in turn entered the tube of the serpent proper where the bore was roughly 20 mm. The six holes, each about 13 mm in diameter, were arranged in two groups of three, one for each hand, 350 mm or so apart. The distance between holes (centre to centre) was approximately 45 mm.

By the end of the seventeenth century the serpent had crossed the Channel and a rather different method of construction became normal in England. Here it was built up from overlapping half-sections joined by iron staples and glue. The leather

Fig. 2.2. Phil Humphries with serpent by Burchell Gladwyn. Similar in appearance to a traditional instrument, it is in fact constructed from a series of softwood sections glued together.

exterior (sometimes parchment, or even brown wrapping paper) (S³⁶, 49) was then applied over a layer of canvas, either of which may also have been treated with a lead-pigmented and probably oil-based black paint (S³⁶, 22). (There are useful drawings and photographs showing this method of construction in Philip Bate's article 'Some further notes on serpent technology' (B¹⁵, 124-9).) The introduction of iron staples and a secondary binding clearly strengthened the instrument considerably. Finally, the interior of the bell was often painted a shade of red.

The description of the serpent given by James Talbot in Christ Church Library, Oxford, MS. 1187, c. 1685-1701 (B⁶, 18-19) shows that the familiar form of the instrument had already been established by that time. Talbot seems to have based his information on serpents belonging to Le Riche, one of the most renowned of contemporary players, and Lewis. Where they performed is unfortunately not stated, although about this time there was some work available in the theatre. They may have been associated with the private chapels of embassies, the only places in London where the Mass was officially allowed to be celebrated. Le Riche was presumably of French origin. Perhaps one or other played the brief serpent part in John Eccles's music for *Macbeth,* produced some time after 1695 (Ex. 2.3). These instruments were made from 'wallnut' with a brass crook, an ivory mouthpiece, and 'a brass loop to whch a Ring for a ribband is fastened'. Talbot provides a wealth of dimensions, and states that 'half-notes are made by stopping half a hole'.

The most thorough treatment of the serpent is probably that in BL Add MS. 27681, ff. 3-15 (17), dating from c. 1801 and catalogued as: *MATERIALS for a dictionary of music, derived from the works of Grassineau, Burney, Chambers, Walther, Overend, and others, with essays, notes, copies of letters, etc., by John Wall Callcott; 1797-1802. Thirty-six volumes. Paper. Small Quarto.* The compilation begins with a brief definition:

Hawkins. I. 354 . .

### Serpent

This is a wind instrument similar to the Horn & Trumpet in respect of blowing and yet played with the fingers like the Hautboy & Baſsoon.

Its Compaſs extends from double Gamut, of which the four first notes GABC without the intermediate semitones are formed by the breath alone without any alteration of the fingering all the six holes being stopt. [This is a reference to the four notes formed by fingering the instrument as for the lowest note, C, and then lipping down: factitious notes (see page 58 above). The reference is interesting in confirming that this technique was known to players of the time.]

The manuscript then continues with fingering charts for various scales, fingering for similarly-named notes in all octaves, and arguments of every sort presented at great length and with extraordinary thoroughness. It ends with *God Save the King* and *March* in notation with the fingering indicated below each note. It would be an interesting exercise for a serpentist with enough years remaining to test all of Callcott's theses.

Between 1779 and 1781 Johann Zoffany painted the members of the Sharp family on their sailing barge at Fulham. The painting is now in the National Portrait Gallery. This musical family gave regular fortnightly performances from the 1750s onwards, including water concerts, and most of the subjects are shown with their instruments (W[6], 69). James Sharp, son of William (surgeon to George III), holds a serpent. Zoffany is renowned for his accurate representations of musical instruments, and here he paints in great detail a church serpent, dangling vertically from its ribbon, and conveniently resting between the knees while not being played. Church serpents are rarely seen in English iconography, and its presence could well indicate that its owner, a member of a wealthy family, purchased it when abroad. Just below the bell a chain is fastened, possibly to use in hanging up the serpent when it is not in use. This device may have been designed by James himself, an engineer by profession. (An inventory of instruments owned by Samuel Hellier, who died in 1784, also includes 'One Serpent [Silver ornaments] made at Paris in a Red leather Case' (H[17], 6).)

At about this time, in his serenata *Ascanio in Alba*, first performed in 1771 in Milan, Mozart included parts for two 'Serpenti (in Fa)' which contribute an attractive *Andante grazioso* duet to Aria No. 25. These are two *cors anglais* (English horns) built in serpentine shape. In his Introduction to the Neue Ausgabe edition of the work (S[13], IV, 1095), Ernst Fritz Schmid points to the use of the term *biscione inglese* (from *biscia*, 'snake' with the affix *one* implying a larger variety) in the Milan area to describe this instrument. Problems raised by the reference to an H. Liconi who made a 'serpentone' in Florence in the fifteenth century (V[2], 40) are resolved if this particular instrument is accepted as a contrabass cornett. There are extant examples of Italian tenor, bass and contrabass cornetti in serpentine form probably made in the sixteenth or seventeenth centuries, and Liconi's instrument is likely to have been one of these.

Confusion was caused when Chouquet described a contrabass cornett in the Paris Conservatoire collection as a *serpent italien* in the 1875 catalogue. This gave rise to the misconception that the serpent first appeared in Italy. In 1884 Valdrighi compounded Chouquet's anti-chauvinistic stand, conjuring up some bizarre 'facts': 'Sometimes its coating of skin is decorated with arabesques in gold or silver; and it is also made from boiled leather, and in copper, in brass and also in iron' (V², 39). There are in all three pages of this type of misinformation. (For further discussion of this matter see M⁴⁰, 53-56.)

Schmid, incidentally, indicates a solution to the problems raised by the presence of the word *biscione* in the records of San Petronio, Bologna, also in northern Italy. Schnoebelen (S¹⁵, 48) cites a reference to 'bissone' in lists of the church's musical establishment around 1700 and suggests that the word may be a corruption of 'buisine', and thus a trombone. However this is unlikely, as players of the trombone are listed under the name of the instrument in the church records. The bissone's inclusion in specific works may indicate that it was a cor anglais, used for much the same purpose as the oboes introduced about the same time: to strengthen the parts played by the cornetti which were regular members of the church's musical establishment. A *serpentone* player is listed in the expenses for the first Sunday in Lent, 1696 and the placing of the 'bissone' near the trombones in a 1700 seating plan is further evidence that this instrument could have been associated with the cornetti, which were customarily allied to the trombones.

*Serpent technique*

Until well into the nineteenth century even orchestral players usually stood while performing. At first the serpent was played vertically, a method still used in French churches in the nineteenth century, but Abbé Lunel, serpentist at Notre-Dame de Paris 1772-80, is said to have devised the method of holding it diagonally. The playing position assumed greater importance with the introduction of the serpent into the military band round about the end of the eighteenth century. There is a tradition that George III (1738-1820) suggested it should be held sideways to prevent its entanglement with the marching bandsmen's legs and that the bell should be turned outwards to increase the volume of tone (though most of the sound comes from the tone-holes). An engraving in the British Museum (Crace Coll. Pf. XI, Sh. 11, No. 11) of *The Band of a Regiment of Guards entering the Colour Court, St. James's Palace*, dating from about 1790, shows the serpent-player using the standard English diagonal or horizontal hold. It has been suggested that this may be a representation of the band of German musicians imported into the Coldstream Guards some time after 1783, so this playing position may already have been used in Germany, or alternatively Lunel and George III's practical suggestions may have been generally adopted by this date (C[35], 153).

In all serpents, the group of holes closer to the crook is fingered by the left hand, the other by the right. The first octave is produced by opening up the finger-holes from the bell end. In the vertically-held church serpent this results in the fingering system's essentially following that of any other wind instrument. In the course of time the right hand sometimes adopted a palm upwards position giving better support but causing the fingering to be reversed to the disadvantage of those who came to the serpent from other wind instruments. The right-hand fingering must also be reversed when the serpent is held horizontally (as is the case with English military serpents). Some of the holes therefore need to be relocated to allow for the variation in the lengths of the fingers.

In his *Méthode*, published in Paris c. 1817, Hermenge illustrates alternative ways of holding the serpent. He demonstrates the necessity of placing some holes in different positions according to whether or not keys are to be used. He also shows two different hand positions, both for use when the serpent is held horizontally despite the tutor's French origins. This may have been because the work was dedicated to Fréderic Berr, bandmaster of the 8th Regiment of the Royal Guard and Director of the Gymnase Musical Militaire, and Hermenge consequently wished to emphasize ways in which marching with serpents could be facilitated. He recommends the position shown in Fig. 2.3 (a) as this allows the arms more freedom, the head to be held erect and breathing to be easier as a result of the good posture required. The position shown in Fig. 2.3 (b) allows more rational fingering, but most of the advantages of position (a) are then lost.

With all holes closed it is possible to obtain harmonics as high as the eighth, but the fingering for other notes in the various octaves clings only tenuously to basic principles. While semitones were originally played by half-stopping, subsequently cross-fingerings were adopted (Ex. 2.1). Paradoxically, both tone and intonation generally become firmer as higher harmonics are played, providing a strong argument for using a contrabass serpent so that the playing compass begins with C, its second harmonic. In practical terms, this course of action is available to only a limited number of players as few contrabass serpents have been built (see pages 77-9 below).

Fig. 2.3 (a) Method of holding the serpent recommended by Hermenge, c. 1817.

Fig. 2.3 (b) Alternative method which allows rational fingering to be used. Hermenge comments that this approach requires 'Key No. 12' (the C♯ key) to be repositioned.

Ex. 2.1

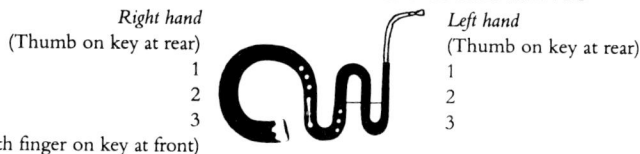

PRACTICAL FINGERING-CHART FOR SERPENTS

Where there is only one fingering this is based on Hermenge, c. 1817. Note that the fingering for the right hand is reversed (see diagram). Alternative fingering, in a column to the right, may be found advantageous in certain circumstances; the player should experiment on the instrument concerned. Fingering to the right of the vertical line is that for three-keyed serpent. Some notes below C can be obtained by using the fingering for C and lipping down to the desired pitch.

One of the daunting aspects of serpent fingering-charts is their tendency to give identical fingerings for adjacent notes, the most familiar example probably being the all-holes-covered position for both Bs and Cs. The charts themselves differ considerably, and not surprisingly when the rate of expansion of the tube is examined. The abrupt conicity makes it obvious that the player is by far the most important element in this system, and the player will in turn wish to modify his fingering-system to the particular instrument he is playing at any given time. He may, in particular, wish to 'vent' some notes, a technique in which certain holes within the group of consecutive covered holes for a particular note are left open. Some notes can be lipped up or down a fourth or more, and for this reason the player needs a very keen sense of intonation.

It is difficult to imagine an abundance of musicians able or willing to make each note so carefully at the embouchure, and this doubtless accounts for the many unfavourable opinions expressed on the serpent. Viret describes the serpent in its liturgical context as 'a type of clumsy and unsightly cornett——*ab antiquo serpente libera nos, Domine [God save us from the ancient serpent]*, Charles Bordes [1863-1909; French early music authority] said ironically not long ago . . .' (V[7], 19).

There are also problems caused by the variation in tone and volume between different notes. Berlioz mentions three notes, d, a and d', as being more powerful than the others (B[25], 230). The instrument in fact gives C with all holes closed, but French church pitch (*ton de chapelle*) had been a tone lower than *ton de chambre* up to the end of the eighteenth century and it was conventional amongst French musicians to consider the instrument as being pitched in B♭, sounding a tone below the written notes. (In his *Traité* he states that 'it must be written a whole tone above the real sound, like the ophicleide in B♭'.) Berlioz thus meant that the c, g and c' were the prominent notes—the second, third and fourth harmonics of the complete tube-length's fundamental. The note D is, like D♭, poor on the serpent in the first and second octaves, and often the player has to decide whether to try to match to it the quality of better notes in order to avoid the kind of contrast noticed by Berlioz. Forsyth  stated firmly and erroneously that 'the serpent was a B♭-serpent' (F[19], 287). Since he described the instrument in the 'Obsolete Wood-Wind' section of his *Orchestration*, his statements do not merit being taken too seriously. Froelich (F[22], 37) makes a puzzling reference to the 'serpent in E♭, the most common in wind music today. The older ones and those used in orchestral music are in D, as it is easier transposed to other keys from there'. The twentieth-century makers Christopher Monk and Rainer Weber have offered serpents in D (the latter also made serpents in F), and the museum of the Royal Military School of Music, Kneller Hall contains serpents in D♭ and B♭, but as a result of the numerous changes in pitch and temperament during the serpent's long lifetime it is not possible to be totally specific about pitch.

The matter of what might be termed 'prevailing pitch' at any given time is particularly complex in relation to the serpent as it has often been closely connected with singers—much more so than most other wind instruments, including cornetts and sackbuts. The significant difference between the way in which these were used and the way in which the serpent was used is that while the former were found in accompanying ensembles the latter was very often the only instrument involved with the choristers, a situation acknowledged in some French church records where serpentists were included on the strength of the choir.

The combination of rapidly-expanding profile, a cup-mouthpiece for generating the sound and side-holes for changing the pitch, along with the need to lip many notes one way or the other, creates a unique timbre, certainly not caused by the materials used in construction. Writing in 1635, Mersenne stated that already serpents of brass and other metals had been manufactured (M[29], III, 278). Carl Fleming (b. 1764) made one of brass, and in the early nineteenth century the Glasgow instrument-maker Joseph Taylor made one of copper with four keys (left-handed), now in the Edinburgh University Collection of Historic Musical Instruments. Some French metal serpents terminated in putative bell flares. A twentieth-century copper serpent by Rob Stewart of Arcadia, California, is illustrated in Fig. 2.4 with owner, Claude Engli. Several nineteenth-century papier-mâché serpents exist, and others are known to be in the course of construction. Lander, of Mere in Wiltshire, is said to have made a metal serpent around the middle of the nineteenth century, while Carl Grenser of Dresden and Herr Feidhart of Leipzig were others who used metal rather than wood. Feidhart's contribution is significant in that he was by trade a tinsmith and his instruments of pewter are the only musical instruments he is known to have made. This is an interesting example of a technological development made by an inventor not professionally involved in the area of its application. (Although not so extreme a case perhaps as Herr Weinrich, the Thuringian shoemaker who in 1828 designed—and built—his *Psalmelodicon*, a type of serpent with twenty-five keys and a name indicating its liturgical function. Ernst Schmidt of Heiligenstadt made a similar instrument some three years later. This was the *Appollo-Lyra* with forty-two keys, six finger-holes, a four-octave range, and the claimed capacity to imitate both horn and clarinet.)

Fig. 2.4. Left to right: Claude Engli, with a copper serpent by Rob Stewart, Arcadia, California, 1988; Alan Lumsden, serpent by Forveille, Paris, 1821; Clifford Bevan, serpent by Christopher Monk, Churt, Surrey, 1987 photographed at the South Carolina Serpent Festival 1989.

Feidhart's serpent, dating from about 1822, is reported to have carried a key below the third hole. In an attempt to improve the tone by increasing the size of the holes, and intonation by rationalizing their position, keys had been introduced towards the end of the eighteenth century. This is later than one might have expected since in 1619 Praetorius had illustrated a tenor cornett with one key at the hole nearest the bell. The three-keyed serpent—one each for B, C♯ and F♯—soon became standard, possibly owing to the attention being paid to military band reorganization. In his *Méthode elémentaire de serpent ordinaire et à clé*, Hermenge actually uses the term *serpent d'harmonie* ('band serpent') for the type with three keys. However, in 1839 D'Almaine of London offered for sale serpents with three, four or five keys (P[21], 25).

An attempt to overcome the serpent's inconvenient width is exemplified by an instrument by Embach of Amsterdam from about 1825 (illustrated in B[5], No. 683) in which the curves are closer than usual and the first bend turns back on itself. A more spectacular compact design is that of an instrument by B. Coldwell, probably of Sheffield, made around 1831 and described and illustrated by Robert Pacey (P[1],132). Here the tube turns back on itself at an angle of 45 degrees after the second curve from the bell, bringing the mouthpiece into the middle of the instrument. This serpent is also unusual in not being covered by leather but simply presenting a stained wooden tube.

The *Gazette musicale* for 1839 reported an attempt four years earlier to make a *serpent contre-basse*, but concluded that it was not successful owing to its conical profile and the large *ouverture* (bell-opening) (W[30], 155). However, about 1840 the hand-loom weavers Joseph and Richard Wood from Upper Heaton, Yorkshire, succeeding in making a contrabass serpent, twice normal size, which was played in Almondbury church, near Huddersfield, possibly York Minster, and elsewhere (Fig. 2.5). They may have been inspired to build their giant instrument by the presence of the double-sized ophicleide at the 1835 Yorkshire Grand Musical Festival, particularly as the preview in *The Yorkshireman* referred to this as a 'keyed serpent'. The instrument made by the Woods, which inevitably came to be called the 'Anaconda', is essentially a military serpent scaled up 100 per cent, with a bell diameter of 200 mm, a tube length of 4600 mm and a vertical height of 1370 mm. As six of its eleven keys cover normally open finger-holes the fingering-system is relatively rational. The mouthpiece is of a unique pattern, made of copper with a profile showing parallel walls terminating in a shallow hemispherical cup. Despite experiments with modern tuba mouthpieces, this unpromising original has proved

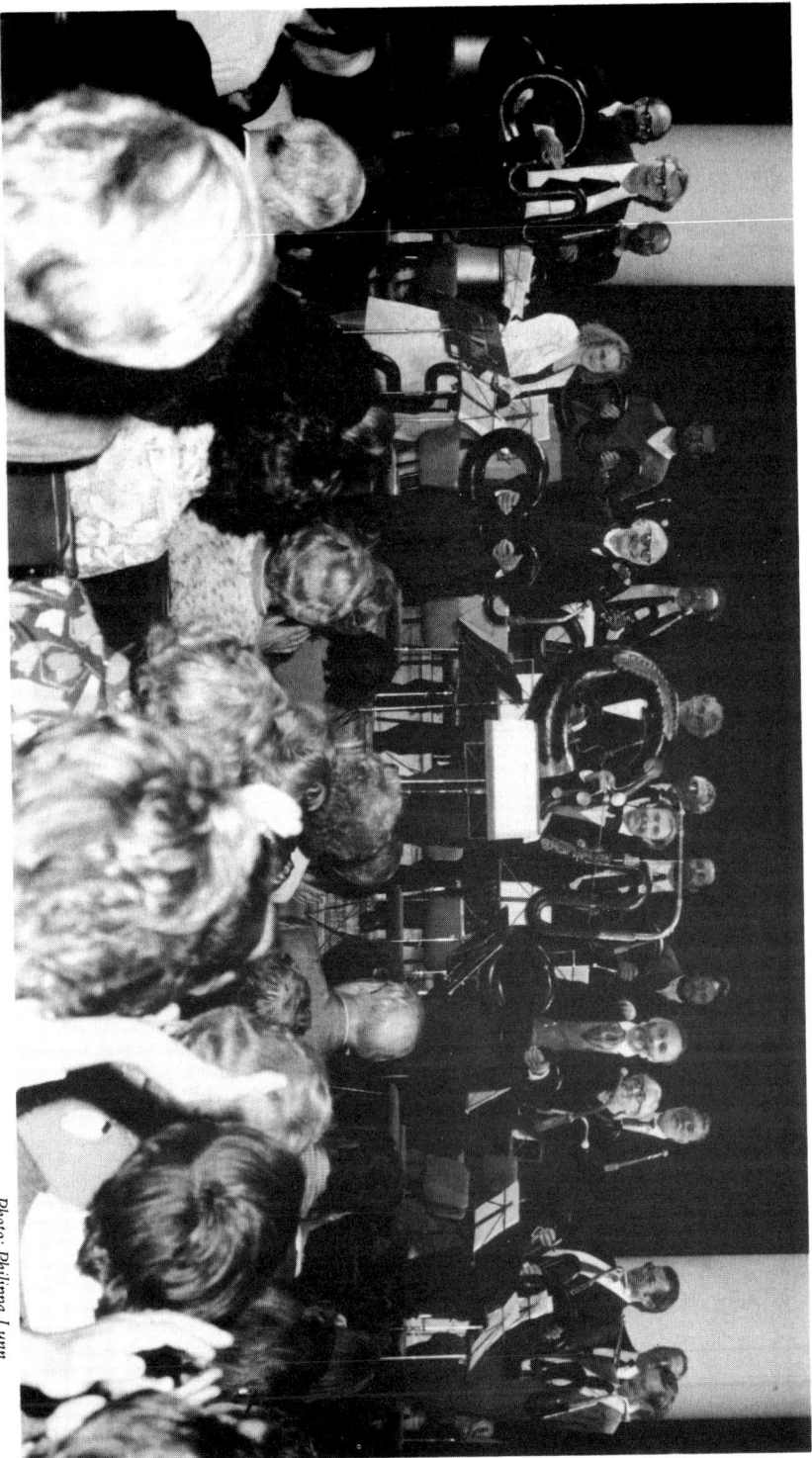

*Photo: Philippa Lunn*

Fig. 2.5. The finale of the 1990 Serpent Celebration at St John's Smith Square, London. Andrew van der Beek displays the Anaconda. Christopher Monk, who was later to make the first twentieth-century contrabass serpent, is on his right.

to be the most effective over the entire three-octave range of the instrument. The 'Anaconda' is now in the Edinburgh University Collection of Historic Musical Instruments.

In 1989–90 Christopher Monk built a contrabass serpent, known as George I. He adopted a vertical shape, with all holes covered by keys. George II, completed in 1997 by the Christopher Monk Workshops, included some modifications to the key-work. Monk also constructed miniature serpents ('worms').

The English military serpent (widely used in church bands) was distinguished from the church serpent through its more robust construction, a squatter shape, curves of a smaller radius and the use of brasswork (including stays) to strengthen and support the tubing. Often ivory chimneys inserted in the finger-holes could be adjusted in order to improve intonation. The differences between the French *serpent d'église* (*serpent ordinaire*) and *serpent militaire* were more pronounced.

## UPRIGHT SERPENTS

The first upright serpent appears to have been conceived by J. J. Régibo, a musician at the College of Saint-Pierre at Lille, who made a serpent in the shape of a bassoon which he advertised in Framéry's *Calendrier Universel Musical* for 1789. Little more is known about this instrument, but it seems to have been built in three detachable sections and played like a normal serpent, although it had a stronger tone. Perhaps it was this characteristic that led to its adoption by Belgian and Prussian army bands. It would in any case have been better for use on the march, better balanced for carrying and more robustly constructed.

The advertisement in the Paris Conservatoire *Méthode* for a new form of serpent invented by Piffault of Paris in 1806 states, with an unusual degree of candour:

This serpent is much easier to use in military service than the original serpent; the lower part is held to the right, like the bassoon. In view of this advantage, the inventor has named it SERPENT MILITAIRE. This serpent has all the characteristics of the other, the same fingering; the same problems with C♯, whether high or low; but the sound is brighter, the tube is not covered with leather as in the original serpent.

Baines (B[5], 681) illustrates an example in the Royal College of Music Museum of Instruments, showing its anticipation of saxophone form (Fig. 2.6).

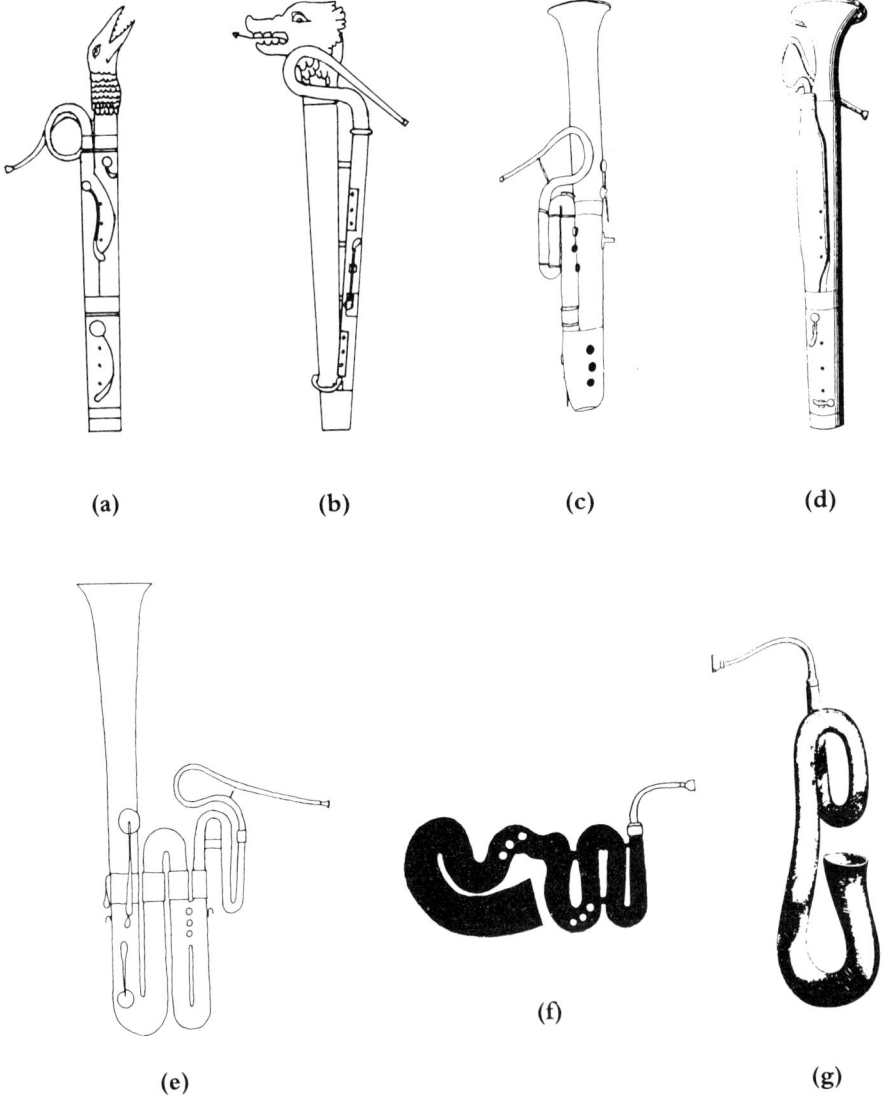

Fig. 2.6. (a) Russian bassoon; (b) Russian Bassoon; (c) Serpent Forveille; (d) upright serpent erroneously identified by Kastner as 'Contre-basson autrichien'; (e) Contra-bass-horn (Coëffet); (f) serpent by anonymous Spanish maker (Barcelona Museo de la Música, 802); (g) French military serpent (Serpent Piffault).

There followed a spate of upright serpents. The common Continental variety (also made elsewhere: there is an extant model by Francis Pretty of London (W[3], 33)), although originally *serpent basson*, came to be called *basson russe,* for no clear reason, though Nagy's suggestion that this may have been a corruption of *basson prusse* (a logical name in view of the early adoption of the instrument by Prussian army bands) deserves serious consideration (N[1], 55). Its close relationship to the serpent is confirmed by Berlioz who follows French serpent practice in his *Traité*, notating its scale a tone higher than it sounds. The instrument consisted of two parallel tubes, often bored in the same piece of wood and always close together. It was made in four sections, like a bassoon, and at the base was a bassoon-type butt with three holes for the right hand. The three left-hand holes were in the wing joint, which terminated in the mouthpiece crook; the bell joint was normally surmounted by either a flared brass bell or a painted snake's head, often complete with red tongue. The holes in the butt could be bored through the relatively thick wood at an angle that ensured their being placed both conveniently for the fingers and in roughly the correct acoustic positions. Usually three or four keys were provided. The crook of the Russian bassoon was somewhat longer than that of the serpent so the less abrupt expansion of the bore would have given slightly more resonance and control (Fig. 2.6(a) and (b)).

Berlioz recounts an amusing experience when working with the orchestra at Brunswick during a conducting tour of Germany in 1843. 'Then a Russian bassoon, called by the performer a double-bassoon. I had much trouble in undeceiving him as to the nature and name of this instrument, which emits the sound just as it is written and is played with a mouthpiece like the ophicleide . . .' (B[27], 298). (The contrabassoon is, of course, a double-reed instrument. Like the double bass, its music is written an octave higher than it sounds.) This German player was not alone in confusing his instrument with the double-bassoon. No less an authority than Kastner describes a Russian bassoon as a *contrebasson autrichien* in his *Manuel de musique militaire* (Fig. 2.6(d)).

There was an immmense variety of upright serpents. The type found in Italian opera houses, the only orchestral environment in which it made a regular place for itself, had a relatively narrow bore. This was the prototype *cimbasso* (Fig. 13.3(c)). There is an example in the Yale University Collection with three keys, made by Garignani Brothers, Milan about 1820. It is likely that the 'bass horn' seen by Spohr at La Scala, Milan in 1816 was also a Russian bassoon (S[32], i, 258). The August 1825 issue of *The Harmonicon* shows a plan of the orchestra there which includes 'serpent'. The scores of many early nineteenth-century Italian operas include a stave for *serpentone*. Lichtenthal's musical dictionary, published in Milan in 1826, devoted one and a half pages to the *serpentone*, an indication of its importance in Italy at that time. The cimbasso is considered in more detail in Chapter XIII.

The *Serpent Forveille*, made partly of wood and partly of metal, appeared at the 1823 Paris Exposition de l'industrie. The invention of the instrument-maker Forveille, its conformation was clearly influenced by the ophicleide's vertical bell section (Fig. 2.6(c)). This instrument possibly presented the first example of what was to become another nineteenth-century custom—that of inventors naming their new instruments after themselves.

Five years later the *Ophimonocléide* appeared, invented by Jean–Baptiste Coëffet of Chaumont-en-Vexin (French Patent 2338 of 2 May 1828). This upright serpent had a metal bell below which an open-standing key (as on an ophicleide) was provided with the intention of facilitating the playing of sharps and flats. It was to be closed only for all Cs and C♯s, the E♭ and F of the fourth octave, and the B and F of the third octave. The instrument was built at *diapason de l'opéra*, but if the entire lower part of the butt was pulled out about two inches ('deux pouces') it dropped to *diapason de la cathédrale*, the pitch of *serpents ordinaires*. At its lowest point, the crook had a reservoir where any water collected. It was, in effect, a wooden ophicleide. An example by Coëffet is in the Royal College of Music Museum of Instruments, while another, by Darche of Paris, is in the Stearns Collection, University of Michigan, Ann Arbor. There is an example of Coëffet's *Contra-bass-horn*, dating from about 1840, in the Leipzig Museum (B⁵, No. 687). The crook contains a considerable proportion of straight tubing, although it travels through three curves before reaching the wooden portion, emerging into a soaring vertical bell section. The overall impression is that of an instrument combining elements of English bass horn, serpent and tugboat. Gebrüder J. & A. Lamperhoff of Essen patented their similarly-named *Contrahorn* (a keyed bass horn) in 1844. Other upright serpents included the *Serpent droite* and the *Ophibaterion*, known only as a name. Was the *Ophy-baryton* designed by Forveille in 1823 and built by Turlot identical to the *Ophibariton* by George Bachman of Brussels patented in 1840? Both were probably types of Russian bassoon.

A four-keyed *Fagottserpent* was made by Hess of Munich (there is an example in the Leipzig Museum), part of a general tendency to increase the number of keys. Johann Streitwolf of Göttingen built his elegant *Chromatische Basshorn* in 1820, the upright serpent that probably most accurately followed the form of the bassoon. There were twelve holes and ten keys. Even the *serpent ordinaire*, which was still alive and writhing, became the subject of additional key-work. By 1840 there were specimens with up to thirteen keys. At the Royal Military Exhibition in 1890 a model with fourteen keys was shown, made not inappropriately by Thomas Key of London. In 1841 Key had made improvements to the serpent which, claimed one of the instrument's devotees in the *Musical World* (3 June 1841), would enable 'the fine quality of the tone of the serpent . . . to be available in the orchestra and the hog-song of the ophicleide speedily tacitted . . .'

Others were also fighting rearguard actions. Heinrich Haseneier of Coblenz produced his ten- or eleven-keyed *Bass Euphonium* as late as 1850, mischievously giving it the name of the successful valved instrument invented by Sommer of Weimar some seven years earlier. An upright serpent made of wood with a brass bell and crook, it had ten or eleven keys, two of them open-standing. Writing in 1903 of the eleven-keyed version in the Leipzig Museum (one of only two extant examples), Paul de Wit commented that the large size of the keys of this type of bass horn gave it unfavourable blowing characteristics (W[24, 144]).

The extent to which makers were committed to updating the serpent to combat the encroachment of valved instruments is best demonstrated by a bass horn thought to be French built in the shape of a tuba and at present in the Horniman Museum, London (Fig. 2.7). This is described as a *serpent de cavalrie* in the caption to its photograph in *Grove V* (M[43], VII, pl. 59, 5). There is another example in the Vleeshuis Museum, Antwerp (No. 245). While the form is rational, it is not known what effect the extra bends in the tubing necessary to bring the serpent into a more modern configuration had on the production of the sound.

On the basis of form, there appear to have been five main types of upright serpent, references to any of which might be found under the name of bass horn:

1. Russian bassoon (wooden body, normally with a dragon's head bell).
2. (French) military serpent (wood, saxophone—later sometimes tuba—form).
3. (Italian) cimbasso (long crook, wooden body, metal bell).
4. (French) Serpent Forveille (section terminating in bell wooden, remainder metal).
5. English bass horn (metal, V-shape).

Care has to be taken with later references to the bass horn. An advertisement placed by Thomas Croyer of 17 Devonshire Street, Queen Square, London in *The*

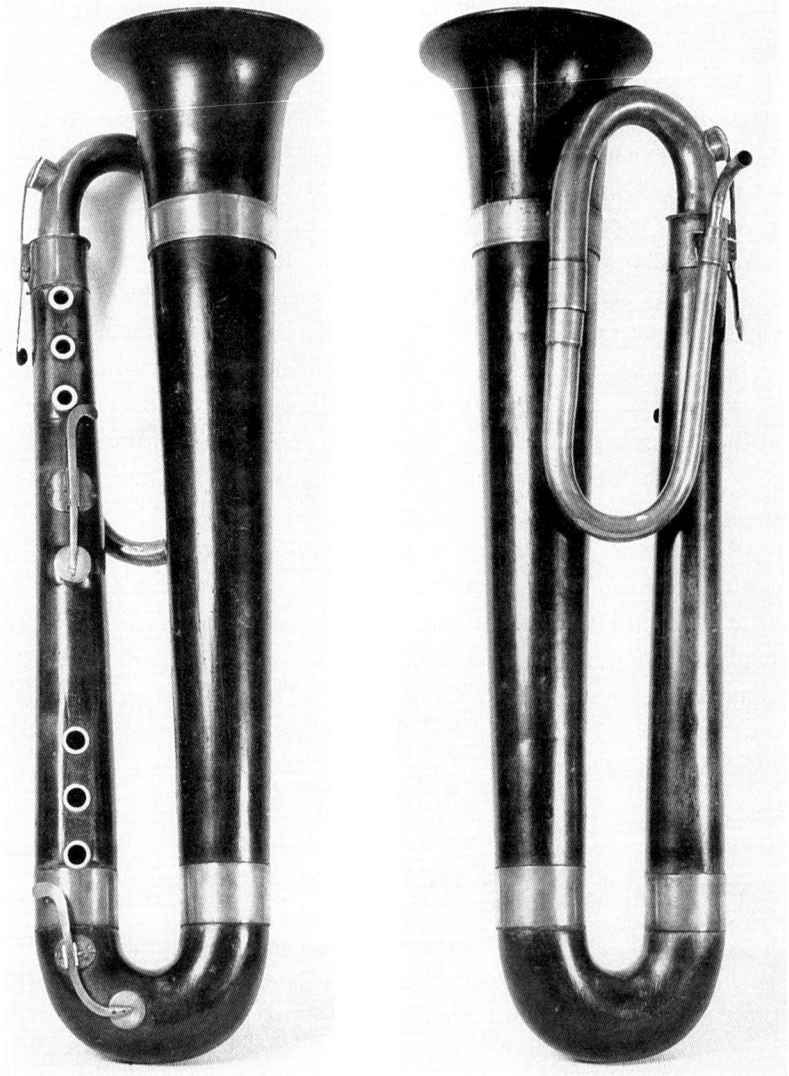

*Horniman Museum & Gardens, London*

Fig. 2.7. Bass horn in tuba shape thought to be by a nineteenth-century French maker.

*Musical Times* of 1 February 1860 includes details of brass instruments on offer. His obsessive use of the term 'horn' could have caused problems were any older players looking for new instruments (M[52], 1.2.60, 216).

| | | | |
|---|---|---|---|
| Cornet, in Bb | 4. 0. 0 | Baritone Horn, in C and Bb | 6. 6. 0 |
| Soprano Horn, in Eb | 3.10. 0 | Bass Horn, in C and Bb, 3 valves | 7. 7. 0 |
| Alto Horn, in Bb | 4. 4. 0 | Bass Horn, in C and Bb, 4 valves | 8. 8. 0 |
| Tenor Horn, in F and Eb | 5. 5. 0 | Contre-Basse Horn in Eb, 3 valves | 10. 0. 0 |

Yet there is evidence that conventional serpents were still being commercially produced after the middle of the nineteenth century. An example by Wood & Ivy, 50 New Compton Street, Soho, London bears the date 1854 (a date by which the firm had previously been considered to have gone out of business—see W[3], 435). It also carries the name of the retailer, Frederick Wroe, 13 King Street, Manchester. (P[16] shows him at 8 Back King Street in 1841, while S[27] gives his address as 5 & 7 John Dalton Street in 1851.) This instrument, now in private ownership, is thought to have been played in church bands in the Blackburn and Clitheroe area.

Demonstrating his unparalleled ability to present misinformation as established fact, Algernon Rose, writing in 1894, stated: '. . . the last maker of this weird instrument [the serpent] was Huggett, who lived in Kensington. Through no fault of his, his trade died out, and he was last seen 12 months ago touting for advertisements' (R[8], 187). In fact the Huggett family lived and worked in *Kennington*. To confuse the grand Royal Borough with a lower-middle class area then in decline is a social solecism that it might have been though even beyond the ability of Rose to commit.

# THE ENGLISH BASS HORN

The English bass horn is well documented although the number of surviving specimens is not large. There is a strong case for considering it to be an instrument in its own right, though clearly related to the serpent. Unlike other upright serpents, characterised by their bassoon configuration and the use of mainly wooden tubing, this instrument is distinguished by the use of metal in construction (usually copper, with some parts made of brass) and a relatively long crook, beginning with a straight section which expands rapidly into the wing joint.

There are many indications that it was widely used, and in his Baß-Tuba

Patent of 1835 (see Appendix A) Wieprecht uses it several times as a familiar basis for purposes of comparison with his new instrument, but a thorough assessment of its performance characteristics still remains to be carried out. The serpent authority Christopher Monk maintained that the English bass horn was a type of serpent only in the broadest sense since its fingering, its blowing characteristics and its timbre were all significantly different from those of the traditional church or military serpent. Although at present the only serious player of the English bass horn is the American Craig Kridel, the reasons for the instrument's popularity in the early nineteenth century are becoming increasingly clear.

The origins of the English bass horn lie in a period of increasing revolutionary activity, when some were straightening the serpent and others were fighting for the Rights of Man. One of the refugees from the French Revolution was Alexandre Frichot (1760-1825), who came to England in 1793. Here he designed his *bass horn*, which was manufactured by the London instrument-maker George Astor (not John Astor as erroneously stated elsewhere). The instrument was a copper serpent built in V-shape, the crook going into one end and a widely-flared bell terminating the other. (A rarer wooden version finished in a cor anglais-type bell.) It had the serpent's usual six holes and three or four brass keys (Fig. 2.8). The relatively narrow bore, along with a crook that accounted for almost one-third of the total length, also contributed to the clarity of sound as well as conferring more control over the pitch of individual notes, but only when appropriate fingering was evolved: there is less scope for the player to exercise persuasion through the embouchure than with the normal serpent. Frichot himself published the first complete scale for his invention in 1800.

By 1804, following the Treaty of Amiens, Frichot was back in Lisieux. In 1806 he presented a brass serpent which he called *Base-cor* to the Conservatoire. In 1810 he patented the somewhat altered intrument under the name *Basse-trompette* (French Patent 404 of 31 December 1810). Later it become known as *Tromba*. It had a potential chromatic range of over four octaves, using either a serpent, trombone or trumpet mouthpiece. Frichot suggested that it might function as a substitute trombone (more fluency and greater compass); or a substitute trumpet (it was entirely chromatic whereas the trumpet of the time could play only one harmonic series). It could also, if called upon, deputize for the horn. But like many upright serpents it life-span was brief, albeit full of variety.

The English bass horn, however, quickly became popular, especially in bands, and versions were made in many Continental centres: extant specimens include the products of makers in Dresden, Dublin, Leipzig and Lyons. Bass horn nomenclature is an indication of type, not place of origin or of use. Waterhouse refers to both an extant bass horn and Russian bassoon by Dubois & Couturier, active in Lyons c. 1834-54 ($W^3$, 97). The English bass horn was widely used on the Continent. As shown in Fig. 2.8, the construction of the tube and chimneys anticipates that of the later ophicleide. Other types of bass horn were made mainly from wood with two parallel tubes like the bassoon on which their designs were based.

Correspondence from the Royal Artillery Band archives printed by Farmer indicates that the Deputy-Adjutant General considered the bass horn superior to the serpent for military band use:

PURCHASE OF BASS HORN

Woolwich, 10th Oct. 1803

To Brigade Major Macbean,

Dear Major,
I saw with the Duke of Kent's Band the other day, what is called a Base Horn, for which James & William Power, 36 Tighe Street, Dublin have a patent. I have received the Master General's directions to write to Colonel Manley to order one to be made for the Artillery Band. The Instrument is made of copper, and the vents, mouldings, ornaments, &c., of brass.

I am . . .
J. Macleod ($F^3$, 25).

Ireland, which was to produce the keyed bugle itself, seemed a hot-bed of bass horn inventors. In 1802 the Royal Irish Artillery already had a two-keyed bass horn of the type patented by James and William Power played by Gunner Patrick Carty. The instrument delivered to the Royal Artillery at Woolwich also proved a success as some two years later Captain C. A. Quist, Commanding Officer R.A. Band, wrote a letter reading in part:

. . . The band of Music has 26 musicians, counting the drummers etc., 3 Tromboners, 2 Trumpetts, 2 French Horns, 2 Bassoons, 1 Serpent & 1 Bass Horn . . . The Small Flute and the Bass Horn are quite new and Mr. Eisenherdt [Master of the Band] would like another Bass Horn instead of the Serpent . . . ($F^3$, 4).

Fig. 2.8 Craig Kridel with English Bass Horn by Rob Stewart, Arcadia, California.

Bass horns were not only made in Dublin, but music for them was published there. In 1810, for example, 'Three Grand Overtures entitled *The Conversation of Five Nations* compoſed for Military Bands and dedicated to the Hon^ble Col^l Foster, Louth Reg^t by Signor Domenico Briscoli, Profeſsor of Muſich of the Royal College of the Pieta de Torckini of Naples and Composer & Director of Music to the Louth Regt' included a part for 'Corno Basso'.

A list of the bandsmen of the 24th (2nd Warwickshire) Foot dated 1812 includes 'Thomas Hinton Bass Horn (likely to be a good one)', followed immediately by 'Samuel Miller learning the 2nd horn—not likely to play' (T[16], 113). A bass horn also appeared in a York Subscription Concert in 1817. Unfortunately no details of the programme are available—particularly regrettable as the bass horn was unusual in an orchestral context. In 1825 Henry Bishop composed music for *The Coronation of Charles the 10th* (British Library Add. MS. 33570), probably a Drury Lane production although it is not listed in *The New Grove Dictionary of Opera*. This involved both an onstage military band and an orchestra in the pit. The lowest stave in the band score is for 'Serpano & Baſs Horn', in unison throughout its joyous repetitions of *For He's a Jolly Good Fellow*.

A continuing connexion between the English bass horn and bands is confirmed by the presence on 'Baſs Horn' of a Mr Maccheow in the military band formed especially for the Royal Entertainment on Lord Mayor's Day at the City of London Guildhall on 9 November 1830. The conductor, Sir George Smart, assembled a band of twenty-seven for this function, and Maccheow was one of those paid £1.1.0 for the concert and a rehearsal five days earlier. (Principal payers received £2.2.0.) The event was actually postponed 'In consequence of the Duke of Wellington fearing there would be rioting' [as this notoriously unpopular prime minister passed through the streets on his way to the Guildhall]. However, Smart intervened on behalf of the performers and they were paid five months later, though the total received was one pound short of that due.

The English bass horn remained in use for only a few years, ousted by the valved instruments which solved so many problems in the bass range. Even so, in their 1839 catalogue D'Almaine of London included brass and copper bass horns, both models with '4 Elastic Plug Keys' (the improved type of stuffed kid pads) (P[21], 24). The French composer Adolphe Adam, writing from Berlin in 1840, referred to 'the *corno basso*, an instrument that is completely unknown to us, and which has a powerful effect' (see page 305 below). However it was certainly well-known to the Berlin military bandmaster Wieprecht (see Appendix A).

There seems to have been just one contrabass English bass horn, made by Thomas Key in 1823 in a shape which clearly reflected the influence of the ophicleide. This was the *Hibernicon* patented by Rev. Joseph Cotter, Vicar of Castlemagner, Co. Cork (British Patent 4849 of 9 October 1823). The instrument has a tube-length of some 5000 mm expanding from 13 mm at the mouthpiece to 240 mm at the bell. (A tenor version was also included in the patent.) The six holes are covered by keys, and two additional key-covered holes extend the compass downwards. Pitched in D', the contrabass has a range of over two chromatic octaves. The only example known, in the Bate Collection, Oxford, is illustrated in M[42], II, 216.

*Methods for Serpents*

Pedagogic material for serpent is surprisingly scarce, bearing in mind the instrument's immensely long lifetime, but most instruction during its first two centuries was given in association with choir schools where learning was done by rote. The responsibilities for the teaching of plainsong were laid down as early as 1411 at Notre-Dame de Paris in a *doctrina* which stated:

> 5. Moreover, the master of music shall teach the boys at the statutory hours primarily plainsong and counterpoint, and some honest discants, but no dissolute or ribald songs . . . (W[28], 166-67)

Much of the material in the following list either forms part of works concerned with plainchant or is connected with teaching in nineteenth-century French music schools. An interesting link—made explicit in the title of his *méthode*—is provided by Abbé Nicolas Roze (1745-1819) who was cleric, composer, serpentist and the first librarian of the Paris Conservatoire. The establishment of the Conservatoire in 1795 was largely the result of post-Revolutionary educational philosophy. The training of musicians for bands which were to take the compositions of sympathetic composers to the public was a prime aim. *Méthodes du Conservatoire* were compiled. One hopeful was Métoyen, on the title-page of whose *Méthode* in the library is a manuscript note stating that it had not been approved by the authorities, who had ordered another to be compiled by Gossec, composer and one of the Conservatoire's inspectors, in conjunction with Roze, Ozi and Étienne Rogat (bassoonist and manager of the Conservatoire's music shop). This was approved by Sarrette on 25 August 1812 for use in Conservatoire classes.

The author Hardy is probably Alexandre Hardy, a bassoonist who taught there. It was normal to double on the two instruments as either might be called upon to support the singing of plainchant. (Joseph Rogat, who taught bassoon and *solfège* at the Institut National, had also played serpent and bassoon at Notre-Dame in 1789.) Imbert was serpentist at Saint-Benoît. Two of the works below deal with newly-invented instruments, the English bass horn and Serpent Forveille, while only one has its origins in Germany. Two other works, both from Italy, are fingering-charts for the cimbasso. Three of the authors—possibly four, if there is an error in Signor Feraboschi's initial—also compiled methods for ophicleide (see page 160 below).

Anon., *Scale for the Serpent* [No. 4], London, c. 1835.

Anon., *Tavola della Scala Cromatica Digitata pel Cimbasso* [see M$^{28}$, Table 2], ?, [1830].

Asioli, B., *Trasunto dei principj elementari di musica compilati dal celebre M°. B. Asioli & breve metodo per ophicleide e cimbasso* [includes 'scala cromatica del cimbasso'] [see M$^{28}$, Fig. 1], Bertuzzi, Milan [1825].

Beaugeois, Abbé, N$^{elle}$ *méthode de plain-chant, de musique et de serpent*, Amiens. 1827; 3rd edn, 1854.

Bertini, A., *New system for learning, and Acquiring Extraordinary Facility on, All Musical Instruments* [includes fingering-charts for various instruments], Longman, London, 1830, 1837; 1849 as *Phonological System . . .*

Conservatoire Impériale de Musique, *Méthode pour l'étude du serpent,* Paris, 1812.

Foraboschi, S. (M.P.S.R.), *New and Complete Tutor for the Serpent* ['with Scales, Exercises, &c.'], D'Almaine, London, by 1839.

Frichot, A. & J. Astor, *A Complete Scale & Gamut of the Bass Horn, A New Instrument Invented by Mr. Frichot & Manufactured by J. Astor,* London, 1800.

Froelich, J., *[Serpent-]Schule,* Bonn, c. 1811.

Gossec, F. J., l'abbé N. Roze, Ozi & Rogat, *Méthode de serpent pour le service de culte et le service militaire,* Paris, 1814 (repr. Geneva, 1974).

Goulding & D'Almaine [publ.], *Scale for the Serpent,* London, c. 1823-34.

Hardy, A., *Méthode de serpent contenant les Gammes naturelles, Dézées et Bémolisées, et une explication raisonée de la manière de se servir de cet instrument* [Zanetzfotell], Paris, c. 1815.

Héral, A., *Méthode de serpent droit contenant les principes de la musique et du Plain-chant, Tablature et les principes de l'instrument, les gammes, exercices, Leçons élémentaires, douze petits aires et douze duos,* Lyons, n.d.

Hermenge, C., *Méthode elémentaire de serpent ordinaire et à clé,* Paris, c. 1817.

——, *Méthode elémentaire pour le Serpent-Forveille,* Paris, 1835.
Imbault [publ.], *Gamme du serpent,* Paris, n.d.
Imbert, M. [Imbert de Sens], *Nouvelle Méthode de Plein-Chant* ['contenant auffi une Méthode de Serpent'], Paris, 1770.
Lucan, M., *Méthode de Plain-Chant* [with 'trois figures représentant l'instrument appelé SERPENT, avec ses différentes gammes chromatiques, etc.'], Dijon, 1826.
Métoyen, *Méthode de serpent* [Premier ouvrage fait pour cet instrument], Paris, c. 1792-5.
Schiltz, *Méthode complete et raisonne de serpent,* Paris, post-1836.

# THE MUSIC

*The serpent in church*

The serpent's prime function was to support the choir in plainsong. It was adopted by churches throughout France, although later Berlioz was to claim (incorrectly) that it blended poorly with voices and Lavoix, writing in 1878, remarked that the ophicleide was preferred for supporting choristers, the serpent—unlamentably—no longer being made (L[6], 144). In England, however, it was reported that Sir Michael Costa strengthened the male voices in his Sacred Harmonic Society oratorio performances as late as 1880 by placing two serpents amongst them.

Some informed observers thought the serpent particularly apt for its purpose. In 1771 Dr Burney made a notably shrewd assessment of the instrument, pointing out the advantages of its lack of attachment to the equal-tempered scale which it shared with those favourite supporters of voices in parts, the trombones.

In the French churches, there is an instrument on each side the choir, called the *serpent,* from its shape, I suppose, for it undulates like one. This gives the tone in chanting, and plays the base when they sing in parts . . . it mixes with them better than the organ . . . is less likely to overpower or destroy by a bad temperament, that perfect one, of which the voice only is capable . . . The *serpent* keeps the voices up their pitch, and so is a kind of crutch for them to lean on (B[64], 11-12).

The experienced Abbé Beaugeois expressed concern about the practical problems of two widely-separated serpentists playing in tune with each other (B[18], 128).

The serpent's claims to improve the performance of plainsong in French churches seem to have lost legitimacy by the nineteenth century. Fétis contrasts the practice of plainsong sung by the choir alone both in Paris and French provincial churches 'in a stiff and repulsive manner, the disagreeable effect of which is augmented by the serpent' with the more sensitive approach adopted elsewhere in Europe (F[13], 407-8). As late as the middle of the nineteenth century the composer Adolphe Adam complained: '. . . in Paris, at the hub of the arts, one cannot enter a church without being followed by one or sometimes two serpents' (A[4], 63). When Léon Battu and Jules Moinaux, the librettists of Offenbach's *Pépito* in 1853, included serpent playing as one of the Figaro-like hero's many skills they knew that audiences at the Théâtre des Variétés would understand.

It seems that serpentists quite often introduced their own ornaments into the plainsong and sometimes extemporized cadenzas between lines. Hillsman prints versions of the *Pange Lingua* as sung and (according to Imbert de Sens, serpentist of Saint-Benoît) as it might be played (H[27], 11). Hermenge expressed strong disapproval of the practice in his *Méthode*.

The serpent seems to have carried out its prime function routinely only in France and the Low Countries. In Spain, where similar practices might have been expected, the instrument commonly used for suporting the choir was the *bajón* (curtal or dulcian), replaced during the nineteenth century by bassoon, ophicleide or even euphonium (see pages 153-4 below). Beryl Kenyon de Pascual notes the presence of serpent in a number of 'draft' scores in the archives of the Sanctuary of Aránzazu, but since it is known that there was no serpent in the monastery and since there is also a bass drum part it is to be assumed that these were played by extra-numerary musicians in processions on special feast days (K[12], 142).

Hugh Keyte has pointed out that in English parish churches few hymns were sung from the Reformation until the last decade of the seventeenth century, and then they were usually metrical psalms (K[13], 669-71). The developing style of singing these in country churches was characterised by increasingly slower tempi and a nominal unison which in practice meant varying speeds, held notes and individual embellishments. In some churches this approach was utilized as late as the nineteenth century, but elsewhere by the 1740s single bass instruments (usually bassoon or bass viol) were used for accompaniment. By the 1770s higher instruments were also often present, though at St Feock, Cornwall there were seven bassoons (M[1], 25) and at Brightling, East Sussex no fewer than nine (M[2], 127). MacDermott found that the most frequently used bass instrument in Sussex was the bassoon (eighty-nine instances), next bass viol (twenty-eight) and finally serpent (twelve). Weston found evidence of only two serpents in Northamptonshire, at Milton Malser and Warmington (W[10], 311-12). Individual cases sometimes demonstrated bizarre practices: at Heathfield, Sussex the total band consisted of two bassoons, a bass horn and a 'brass serpent' (possibly an ophicleide) (M[1], 30). The serpent in the band at the Wesleyan Methodist Church at Poole, Dorset was seperseded by organ between 1865 and 1870 (M[52], 1.6.17, 264). From the 1830s Anglican clergy, influenced by the so-called Oxford Movement, began to introduce barrel-organs and harmoniums, mainly, it seems, in order to achieve some control in situations where the instrumentalists and singers in the west gallery had grown increasingly powerful, their behaviour in many cases verging on the anarchistic.

The context in which village musicians performed will stand more thorough investigation. Hardy gives many clues, there are more in county archives and the members of the West Gallery Music Association are committed to breathing new life into the old materials thrown up by their researches. Even the smallest piece in the jigsaw can be valuable, though often raising as many questions as it answers. Woodhouse, for example, refers to a Thomas Reed who played in the Trenoweth Chapel, Mabe (W[26], 73). He emigrated from Cornwall to America in 1851, taking with him his serpent and his manuscript book, both of which still exist. The copperplate handwriting in the book is accounted for by a descendant as the result of his grandmother's ambitions for him to become a lawyer's clerk, paying for him to stay at school until fifteen or sixteen. His father, however, had other plans, and Thomas spent his days working on family farms in Mabe parish, playing the serpent with the church band on Sundays. One wonders who taught him to play and read music, and what was the standard of the band's performances.

This may be an appropriate place to clarify the function of the serpent in English churches, which was always the provision of the bass line in an ensemble where singers and instrumentalists read from shared parts. At the time of the serpent's introduction the Reformation in England was well under way, and with it the development of a distinctive style of Protestant cathedral music. Church bands or quires first appeared shortly after the Restoration (1660) to fulfil the function of the organs which had been largely destroyed during the Commonwealth, immediately preceding. Foreign commentators have sometimes overlooked the fact that from 1563 until 1829 the rights of Catholics in the United Kingdom were severely restricted. A Statute of 1699 actually offered a reward of £100 for information leading to the arrest of a priest who said Mass. Burney's pleasure when seventy years later he came upon the serpent fulfilling its original liturgical function is thus all the more understandable. When plainsong was finally reintroduced into England the day of the liturgical serpent had drawn to a close in most places. Thomas Helmore of the London Gregorian Choral Association, writing in 1877, suggested that the voices might be supported by 'some solemn instrument, such as the euphonium or ophicleide' (H[26], 9).

## The serpent in the community

English village musicians were accustomed to providing their services for a wide range of occasions requiring music. The close relationship of liturgical and military performance is confirmed by the extract from Q's 'The Looe Die-Hards' (see page 133 below), which also introduces the name 'scorpion' for the instrument, as was occasionally the practice in Cornwall (W[26], 7, 21). While Hardy's *Under the Greenwood Tree* places the village musicians centrally throughout the action, four of his short stories are also of value in assisting us to picture them in his native Dorset (the page references are to H[7]). Of particular interest is the ascription of a date, 'March 28, 182-', to *The Three Strangers*. Here the serpent becomes a metaphor for the entire musical activity in Shepherd Fennel's cottage:

At seven the shrill tweedle-dee of this younger had begun, accompanied by a booming ground-bass from Elijah New, the parish clerk, who had thoughtfully brought with him his favourite musical instrument, the serpent. Dancing was instantaneous . . . (12)

Mrs Fennel, seeing the steam begin to generate on the countenances of her guests, crossed over and touched the fiddler's elbow and put her hand on the serpent's mouth . . . (12)

While he stood, the boom of the serpent within the adjacent house . . . reached the spot as an accompaniment to the surging hiss of the flying rain on the sod . . . (13)

And just as the dancing was ushered in by the serpent, so its cessation was made audible through the the serpent's silence:

At last the notes of the serpent ceased, and the house was silent . . . (14)


In *The Fiddler of the Reels* Hardy, whose own father had played fiddle in a Dorset village band, gives an interesting indication of the familiarity of the serpent to the local population:


'He could no more play the Wold Hundredth to his true time than he could play the brazen serpent', the tranter would say. (The brazen serpent was supposed in Mellstock to be a musical instrument particularly hard to blow.) (403)


The instrumentation of a complete band is listed in *The Grave by the Handpost*:


On this night [Christmas eve] there were two or three violins, two 'cellos, a tenor viol, double bass, hautboy, clarionets, serpent and seven singers. (827)


Christmas eve was one of the most important nights of the year for the performance of Christian music, so the band would doubtless be at its fullest. In the uproarious (and apparently factually-based) story *Absent-Mindedness in a Parish Choir*, the Longpuddle band is described in great detail:


There was Nicholas Puddingcome, the leader, with the first fiddle; there was Timothy Thomas, the bass-viol man; John Biles, the tenor fiddler; Dan'l Hornhead, with the serpent; Robert Dowdle, with the clarionet; and Mr Nicks, with the oboe . . . (463)


Following the band's unacceptable behaviour, and their public dressing-down from the pulpit by the parson


. . . 'twas a sight to see Nicholas Puddingcome and Timothy Thomas and John Biles creep down the gallery stairs with their fiddles under their arms, and poor Dan'l Hornhead with his serpent . . . (465)


Guy de Maupassant's attitude to peasants and their environment was diametrically opposed to Hardy's. His purpose in introducing a serpent as part of a description of the christening of a new boat in a seaside village in the 1820s was more akin to Berlioz's using it to disparage the Catholic church (see page 110 below).

Then came three old cantors, one of them limping, then the serpent, then the priest . . . Every time they paused for breath the serpent continued its mooing, the player's little grey eyes disappearing into his swelling cheeks as he blew. The skin of his forehead and neck seemed to have become loosened from the bone with his blowing . . . The priest, having ended his prayers, trotted along behind and the cantors and the serpent disappeared down an alley to take off their vestments more quickly . . . (M[22], 53-56).

## The serpent in the wind band

The passage of the serpent through a French municipal band is described in Georges Durand's factual *Notice historique sur la Musique Municipale du Mans*. The local authority formed a Garde Nationale as ordered by the decree of 10 October 1791. By 1808 the original six musicians had grown into a band of thirty-seven, including two serpents, M. Fourniols and M. Vinchon. Fourniols took on the additional post of treasurer from 1815. He demonstrated his loyalty on 27 December 1827 when the band disgraced itself in connexion with a procession to the cathedral. Of the twenty-three members then on the role, thirteen went absent. The mayor, M. de Chateaufort, summoned the director of music, M. Bizeray, to the town hall and demanded to know the reasons why. Present-day members of bands may wish to make a note of these reasons:

Brichet (1st Clarinet): Illness of wife. Had to mind the shop.
Hélix (Oboe): Travelling for two months.
Comtois (2nd Clarinet): Ill with a swelling.
Dureau (2nd Clarinet): Sick in the nose, causing breathing difficulties.
Duval (1st Horn): Ill with a very heavy cold.
Farin (1st Horn): Water on the knee.
Jarossay (Trumpet): Instrument not yet arrived from Paris.
Lemercier (Trumpet): Recovering from an illness.
Pons (1st Bassoon): Sick.
Didier (2nd Bassoon): His daughter was sick and he had to stay at home.
Ménard (Cymbals): Travelling.
Pattier (Jingling Johnny): Told that he could not come.
Housseau (Bass Drum): After going into the countryside had to rest because of the severe headache to which he is subject.

However, serpentist Fourniols was present, alongside him M. Demause playing 'Ophycléïde' (a mere six years after the instrument was patented). This gives some indication of the speed with which the ophicleide established itself in French bands.

In 1830 the band consisted of thirty-three players, including Fourniols and his nephew. The young man did not stay for many years, and in 1840 his uncle retired from his posts of serpentist and treasurer, possibly as a result of the new instrumentation, with *bugle* (flügel horn), valve trumpet, alto ophicleide, two bass ophicleides and bass trumpet shown in the band list that year.

The introduction of the serpent into British military bands is often dated 1783, the year when a band was recruited in Hanover for the Coldstream Guards. One of its twenty-four members played serpent, and within a decade most British staff bands had adopted the instrument. It is likely that some other regiments already had serpents as there is a part in William Abington's *Royal East India Slow March* composed in 1777. As a lieutenant in the 1st Regiment of Royal East India Volunteers he presumably scored his march for the band as it existed at the time. The eleven year-old Samuel Wesley's *March in D* dates from the same year. This also includes serpent and is thought to have been written for a Guards band. It is clear from Appendix C 1 that the last thirty years of the eighteenth century and the first twenty of the nineteenth saw the serpent at its peak of military use. An interesting Situations Vacant notice in *Caeciliá*, 3 July 1824, referring to a serpentist and a bassoonist required by a Dutch regiment, shows that some modern practices had already been established (C[1], 58). Preference was to be given to players able to double on a stringed instrument, particularly cello.

The serpent first appeared in French Revolutionary music during the 1770s, around the same time that it was found in both England and in some German states. Here it formed part of the gradual augmentation of the standard *Harmonie* (wind band) which by the middle of the century had become established as pairs of oboes, clarinets, horns and bassoons. Nagy (N[1], 55) refers to the presence of a serpent in a Grenadier Regiment's band in Pirmasens (Hesse-Darmstadt) in 1772. *Wiener Zeitung* for 25 February 1789 carried the announcement of the local wind instrument-maker Friedrich Lempp's 'Newly invented bass serpent, never before made in this area, 14, 16 and 18 duc.' Lempp generously credited his twenty-three year-old son 'who has discovered how to play and make the instrument known as a serpent (a bass instrument); he has already made his third serpent' (W[21], 464). In 1790 a serpent was included in the stage band of a Russian opera, Sarti, Canobbio and Pashkevich's *Natshalnoie oupravlinie Olega*. The Italian composer Giuseppe Sarti, at the time director of the Russian Imperial Chapel, was renowned both for his use of unusual wind instruments and the introduction of marches into his operas (M[25], 184).

In 1790 also was established the predecessor of the Conservatoire Nationale Supérieur de Musique, the École de Musique de la Garde Nationale Parisienne. Shortly after it opened Jean Mathieu was appointed *Professeur de 1$^{re}$ classe* at a salary of 850 l. to teach serpent. (P[12], 37). He was joined on 1 October 1793 by Gaspar Veillard, a member of the *musique des gardes françaises* since 1771. Veillard was discharged from the École in year X (1801) but returned three years later to teach *solfège*, and played in the orchestra of the Opéra until 1813. Another serpent-teaching appointment, in 1793, was *Professeur de 1$^{er}$ classe* Jacques Cornu who in 1789 had played serpent and bassoon at Notre-Dame, in 1794 became bassoonist at the Théâtre Feydeau, played trombone at the Opéra 1805-26, and was also assistant director of music at Notre-Dame.

A concert given by students at the Théâtre Feydeau on 29 May 1793 included a *Symphonie* by Devienne for strings, two oboes, two horns, bassoon and two serpents. Another, on 20 November, included Gossec's *Symphonie concertante* for eleven wind instruments. The *concertante* group consisted of 'petite flûte, grande flûte, clarinette, hautbois, cors, bassons, serpent et contreclairon'. This last mysterious instrument was described in the report of the concert in the *Journal de Paris* the following day as an invention of the performer (actually clarinettist and composer) Hostié 'to nourish the part of the bass . . . he still has need to perfect it.' The *contreclairon* had first appeared in 1791, as an experimental reconstruction of 'the ancient deep bugle'. Its subsequent fate is unknown.

The list of sixty classes held at the Institute (P[12], 97) which succeeded the École de Musique does not include any for serpent, but at the annual concert on 6 November 1794 Catel's *Ouverture* for wind instruments was played by an ensemble including four serpents. The *Chœur patriotique* sang music by Lesueur accompanied by a wind band in which three serpents and a *tuba-corva* [sic.] were present. The Conservatoire announced in 1795 to supersede the Institute was to provide six serpent teachers for twenty-four students (compared with one teacher for four trombone students, eighteen for seventy-two bassoonists and twenty-six for 104 clarinettists). A student wind orchestra of one hundred was to include '6 serpens'. Four serpents were also listed under *Enseignement* (teaching) and '8 serpens' under *Exécution* (performing) (P[12],181).

By 1836 there appeared to be neither serpent nor ophicleide professor at the Conservatoire, although Boileau *fils* of quai de la Mégisserie 16 and Forveille, rue de la Cerisiaie 16, were still offering serpents for sale in Paris and in Saint-Omer Cuviller made *serpent-bassons*. Tuition was still available elsewhere, however. In Basoche (Landes) Biedau described himself as 'professeur de serpent'. In Dampierre (Seine-et-Oise) there were no fewer than three such professors, Ballard, Lefèvre and Tousez. For a village with a population of under 800, the provision of serpent tutition was uniquely generous. In nearby Rochefort Lefèvre and Martin offered tuition, but in Paris the ophicleide seemed largely to have overtaken the serpent by this date. An amateur, M. Dunand, of quai des Ormes, played both serpent and ophicleide, but outside the church the serpent seemed to be restricted to military bands: three players (Bonvoust, Peters—who sometimes partnered Caussinus on ophicleide (see page 169 below)—and Faivre) in the V$^e$. Légion, Garde Nationale (with one ophicleide); another three (Barrard, Cheron, Jonghmans) in the VII$^e$. Légion (one ophicleide); one, Brindel, IX$^e$. Légion (three ophicleides); Peters and Holtzem (later a tubist) in the X$^e$. Légion (six ophicleides) (P[19], 88, 91-3).

Compared with this profusion, the Austro-Hungarian Empire seemed ill-served, for there substance was added to the bass not by serpent but through the double bassoon. It was rare therefore for serpent parts to be provided by Austrian, Hungarian and Moravian composers or arrangers, although occasionally an indication that a part might be played by either contrabassoon or by serpent is found.

Percussion instruments began to appear in bands from the early eighteenth century, when the rulers of Poland and of Russia were presented with complete Turkish or 'Janissary' bands. In 1725 the latter consisted of three or four treble shawms, one or two tenor shawms, fife, kettledrums, bass drum, three pairs of cymbals and triangle (F[3], 41). By 1770 'Turkish percussion' was common in many European military bands, and was shortly afterwards introduced into the opera orchestra by Mozart in *Die Entführung aus dem Serail* (1782). It is curious therefore to find that in certain publications (for example, *Musique Turque*, which appeared in Hesse-Darmstadt between 1812 and 1818) a part was provided for serpent, an instrument with neither Turkish nor any other eastern European connexions (not least because it played no part in the Orthodox liturgy). A serpent was also included with piccolo, two flutes, clarinet, bass trombone and percussion in the 'Turkish group' of Paul Mašek's *Harmonie mit Türkischen Musick* of 1815. Beethoven specified serpent in his *Military March* (1816), commissioned by a Viennese officer who requested a 'march for Turkish music'. About 1825 Crusell made an arrangement of Beethoven's Septet for a somewhat larger ensemble of ten instruments, including serpent (S[40], 131, 134]. Another Viennese work, Hummel's *Parthia in Eb* is in eight parts, 'con Serpente ad libitum'.

The geographically widespread use of various types of serpent in wind bands in the late eighteenth and early nineteenth centuries is not surprising. Provision of a strong bass part has always presented a problem in ensembles without cellos and double basses. Castil-Blaze states that four bassoons were used in Paris as early as 1763, the number sometimes being increased to six or eight (C[13], II, 354). The need to address the problem become more urgent as the band of the *gardes françaises* grew from sixteen players in 1762 and 1770 to twenty-four in 1788 and thirty-two in 1789. Large-scale free open-air concerts began in Versailles (1777) and Paris (1782) (B[52], 60-61) After the Revolution works by citizen composers were heard. Méhul's *Le Chant de départ* was first performed on 4 July 1794 by a standard *Harmonie* group of two clarinets, two bassoons, trumpet, serpent and timpani; ten days later its second performance was given by a band of sixty-three including ten serpents, the greatest number of any single instrument on that occasion.

In 1817 Rossini's opera *Armida* was first produced, at the Teatro San Carlo, Naples, and his *serpentone* (which would have been called a cimbasso, see Chapter XIII) is very much in evidence at the opening of the *Sinfonia*, or overture. This begins with a *pianissimo sotto voce* slow march scored for two horns, two bassoons, timpani and a *serpentone* which contributes a nicely-calculated bass part. As shown in Ex. 2.2 (a) the general tessitura is relatively high: in the second bar, for example, the serpent plays in unison with the second bassoon and second horn. Later there is a passage where the three trombones and serpent play chords. Although the serpent often has the lowest note, sometimes it is actually written higher than the lowest trombone (Ex. 2.2 (b)). This is not unique to this passage, but suspicions that there may have been a convention of writing for the serpent an octave higher than it sounds are allayed when contemporary fingering-charts are scrutinized. The serpent line in this particular case is written identically to the double bass part so the situation was no doubt simply the result of a composer's oversight as he worked frantically to meet a deadline. Similar oversights have been found in scores by several composers, including Paganini and Verdi.

A belt-and-braces approach was taken by Sir George Smart who for the 1837 Royal Entertainment provided an 'Instrumental Band' which included Jepp on serpent and Ponder on ophicleide. Their fees were £1.1.0, generous in comparison

Ex. 2.2

(a)

Andante maestoso
Bassoons
pp sottovoce
Horns
pp sottovoce
Serpentone
pp sottovoce
Timpani
pp sottovoce

Ex. 2.2
(b)

Rossini: *Armida*

with the side-drummer who had to be recruited as a last-minute deputy from the Artillery Company and was paid a mere 2s. 6d. When, some time before 1859, Sir Michael Costa orchestrated Prince Albert's *Invocazione all'Armonia* for soloists and chorus, below the alto, tenor and bass trombones in the score he also placed 'Ophicleide & Serpent'. While the inclusion of a serpent in a composition by a member of the royal family is worthy of comment, it is merely in unison with the ophicleide throughout, confirming Costa's conservative approach to orchestration.

The method of producing octaves by writing in unison for serpent and double bassoon subsequently adopted by Mendelssohn and others, based on the convention of cello and double bass parts where a written unison becomes a sounding octave, seems to have been overlooked by band arrangers as the two instruments tended to be available only in different countries. Both instruments are capable of producing effective staccato notes to mark the beats. The practice of considering the serpent as a substitute double bassoon is less understandable. The two instruments had more or less identical *written* compasses, and yet A.B. of Paddington, in the *Musical World* of 24 February 1837, was far from unique in considering that 'being a *wooden* instrument, its tones must necessarily, in many instances, be *softer* and *more mellow* than those of the ophicleide, and more in accordance with those of the bassoon, to which it forms a suitable double bass' (M[52], 151). However, the most striking aspect of the serpent's presence in the classical period is not how often it is included in scores but how rarely. Stoneham, Gillaspie and Clark refer to vast numbers of compositions for wind ensemble in their encyclopedic sourcebook, yet the name of the serpent appears only twenty times in a total of 432 pages.

Brass music was important for the Moravian community in eighteenth- and nineteenth-century America, providing a direct link with the *Stadpfeifer* tradition (K[19], 136), but the serpent was as rare amongst emigrants as it was in the country they had left. It appears only once in American Moravian Collections: Louis von Esch's Military divertimentos, composed around 1800, for 2 Flutes, 2 Clarinets, 2 Bassoons, 2 Horns, Trumpet, Serpent and Drum (K[19,] 141): a *Harmonie* ensemble of the type already well-established in America. The U.S. Marine Band had a serpent before 1812, although it had disappeared by 1842 (K[14], 41), and in 1819 a serpent was included in the 'Kennebec March' forming part of *The Instrumental Director.* (The other brass instruments were two horns, trumpet and trombone.) William Webb's *Second Sett of Grand Military Divertimentos,* dating probably from the 1820s, includes a brass section of trumpets, bugle and serpent or trombone (S[25],V, 204).

Fig. 2.9
The memorial to
serpentist Thomas
Maynard (1780-1807)
at Minstead, Hampshire.

Michael Lomas's considerable researches into the bands of southern England (see Bibliography) have unearthed few serpent references. Amongst these are the instruments belonging to the Loyal Stroud Volunteers c. 1798; the serpent in the Horsham band, 'about 1835 or 1845'; and the delivery of a serpent to David Tiddy of the Modbury band on 18 July 1838. The latest reference to the use of a serpent by auxiliary forces is the pen and ink drawing of *The Band of the North Gloucestershire Militia*, c. 1869 in the Gloucester Regimental Museum.

Woodhouse has found references to thirteen serpents in Cornwall between 1799 and 1860. Illustrations of church bands there depict military serpents, making it likely that the instruments were used in (and provided by) the militia when not in church. A military serpent is depicted on the tombstone erected

To the Memory of
THOMAS MAYNARD who departed
this life July 19th 1807 aged 27 Years

--------

*The Band of Musicians of*
*the South Hants Yeomanry*
*(of which He was a Member)*
*Caused this Stone to be Erected.*

The grave is beside the tiny church of All Saints, Minstead, in the New Forest, Hampshire (Fig. 2.9). Tom would doubtless also have played in the band in the west gallery, built in the late 1700s. In 1818 an upper gallery was erected to house the poor, the young and others best kept out of sight. Church musicians were also almost certainly amongst the three serpent-players in the Patrington Band at the Burton Constable Contest, Yorkshire, in 1845 (J[1], 101). Other bands present included ophicleides and valved basses in their instrumentation. Alas, Patrington's performance of a 'pot pourri of country airs' did not secure them a prize.

As a native of Saxony Handel had something of a shock when, visiting England, he heard his first serpent. 'Aye, but not the serpent that seduced Eve', he is said to have rumbled. Nonetheless, the 'authentic' recording of *Music for the Royal Fireworks* directed by Charles Mackerras in 1972 has been followed by many other performances including a serpent. At least one discography has praised the recording directed by Johannes Somary for its authenticity although there are two serpents present. There appears to be no historic basis for having even one serpent in the band. Furthermore, Eric Halfpenny referred to this in a note to an article about the serpent in the *Galpin Society Journal* in 1969 (F[6], 95), so Handel's deliberate act of omission has been known for a long time. The list of instruments in the manuscript score (BM Handel MSS. RM.20.g.7) is specific in its requirements, as follows:

Tromba 1/[3] per parte
Tromba 2 /[3] per parte
Principal/[3] per parte
Tymp./ [ ] per parte
Corn. 1/3 per parte
Corn. 2/3 per parte
Corn. 3/3 per parte
Hautb. 1/12 per parte e Violino 1.
Hautb. 2/8 per parte e Violino 2.
Hautb. 3/4 per parte e Viola.
Baffon 1/8 per parte e tutti li[ ] Violoncelli e Contra Baffi.
Baffon 2/4 per parte/
Contra Baffone e Serpente.

(Figures in [ ] are bound into the spine and therefore reprinted from H[5], IV, 13, 61).

The word 'Serpente' has been very strongly deleted, and it is not reinstated elsewhere in the score. The style of the deletion—hasty, clumsy and unambiguous—matches Handel's other corrections. There are many eye-witness accounts of the Royal Fireworks and the reports of some of those present at the performance find space to refer to the numbers of instruments involved, but none referring to the presence of a serpent has so far been found. A possible reason for the deletion may be Handel's awareness of the convention in some of the German States of writing the serpent and double bassoon part as one on the same stave. When he realized that it did not play at the same pitch as the double bassoon but merely doubled the second bassoon he found it redundant, an interloper in a bass line provided by multiple bassoons with a double bassoon at the lower octave. Alternatively, he may not have liked what he heard during the public rehearsal the previous week.

A further mystery is posed by the question of where the serpentist might normally have worked. The date of 1749 was apparently prior to the introduction of the serpent into Guards' bands. Did Handel import a German player, or was the serpentist attached to an embassy chapel? English Catholics had worshipped only covertly since 1640. In 1689 an Act was passed requiring known or suspected Papists to reside at least ten miles from Westminster, the centre of political power. Perhaps Handel had only *hoped* to include a serpent-player, but in the event none was available. Whatever the reason, it is pleasing to note that both Trevor Pinnock and Robert King have recorded authoritative performances using precisely the numbers of instruments specified—and not subsequently deleted—by Handel.

'New' musical instruments have often appeared in the theatre before being heard in concert performances. Mozart, for example, used trombones and Turkish percussion in operas but not symphonies, and Beethoven restricted his demands for harp to the pit. A hundred years earlier the English composer John Eccles (c. 1668-1735) showed a gift for dramatic music that was considered by some at the time to put his contemporary Purcell in the shade. When a playhouse was established at Lincoln's Inn Fields in 1695 he was responsible for overseeing the music for something like ten years. The music for the semi-opera *Rinaldo and Armida* (1698) no longer exists, but the libretto (British Library Add. MS. 29378) includes a reference to 'The Serpent and Basses softly under the Stage'. Fiske refers to Eccles's flair for this type of ghost music (F[16], 10). There is another example in Eccles's opening 'Symphony' to *Macbeth* (British Library Add. MS. 12219; another copy 29378). Neither the dates of performance nor the names of the players are known. These twenty bars, written below the (figured) bass stave represent the only place in the entire score where a specific instrument is named (Ex. 2.3). Possibly the performer doubled on a different instrument during the remainder of the work. Eccles's background is obscure and there are no clues as to how he knew of the serpent's existence. His coming from a Quaker family intensifies the mystery.

When Haydn visited England he was commissioned to compose several military marches. As the most professional of composers he will have scored them for the instruments available. These are minor works, often sharing common material, so they are not of any great significance other than in demonstrating the presence of the serpent in a number of English military bands of the time.

*Two Marches composed by J. Haydn, M.D. for Sir Henry Harpur, Bart. and presented by him, to the Volunteer Cavalry of Derbyshire; Embodied in the Year, 1794. London, Printed for Sir Henry Harpur, Bar.* by *Will^m. Simpkins, Clements Inn* are scored for Trombe in E, Corni in E, Clarinetto ^1mo., Clarinetto ^2do., Fagotto ^1mo., Fagotto ^2do. and Serpent. *March for the Prince of Wales* (?1792) and *Grand March composed expressly for*

Ex. 2.3

Eccles: 'Symphony' *(Macbeth)*

*and presented to the Royal Society of Musicians, London, by Joseph Haydn, Mus. Doc.
Oxon. 1792* (a reworking of this material) also include a serpent. Works ascribed to
Haydn but considered doubtful or spurious in Feder's *New Grove* article (F[8], 378)
include two Divertimenti in F (2 oboes, 2 horns, 2 bassoons and serpent) and a
Divertimento in Bb with identical instrumentation including the *St Antony corale*.

### The serpent in the orchestra

A performance of Haydn's *Creation* given in Paris on 23 May 1804 used a serpent
to play the part written for double bassoon, an instrument in short supply in
nineteenth-century France (P[18],108). The reporter, in *La Correspondance des amateurs
musiciens* of 23 May 1804, maintained that 'the serpent produced in a wind section a
better effect than the double bass in a string section'.

In general, however, the serpent attracted rude comment to an extent only too
familiar to players of large instruments. There seems to be something about low-
pitched notes that brings out the most puerile excesses in usually moderate
commentators. Berlioz, of course, was moderate only in moderation. He made the
serpent an excuse for a characteristic attack on the Church. 'The truly barbaric
tone of this instrument would be much better suited for the bloody cult of the
Druids than for that of the Catholic Church, where it is still in use—as a monstrous
symbol for the lack of understanding and coarseness of taste and feeling which have
governed the application of music in our churches since times immemorial' (B[25],
230). Even the superior Russian bassoon he thought 'might be dropped from the
family of wind instruments without the least injury to art'. As a result of these
particular feelings Berlioz utilized one ophicleide and one serpent in the original
version of the weirdly satirical 'Dies Irae' of his *Symphonie fantastique* (begun in
1830). It should not be overlooked that both of these instruments would have been
familiar to his audience in an ecclesiastical setting, so their sounds were also
intended to recall an everyday (or at least weekly) experience.

Mendelssohn made wide use of various types of serpent (considered in detail in
Chapter XVI). Balfe included 'serpentone' in his 'grand serious opera' *The Maid of
Artois* (Drury Lane, 1836) and when, on 2 June 1843, Sir George Smart provided a
small orchestra of eighteen, along with eleven singers, for the royal christening of
the Princess Alice at Buckingham Palace he included a serpent, presumably to give
sympathetic support to the voices as no instrumental work specifying serpent in its
scoring was performed. The full range of the serpent's duties is vividly illustrated by

comparing Smart's use of the instrument with the functions that it would have fulfilled in Fuller Brothers' Olympic Circus of 1835. This American organisation featured the Lafayette Band, directed by Mr Tallis and consisting of flute, two clarinets, trumpet, keyed bugle, french horn, trombone, bass horn and bass drum. In the following year the band of the American Arena Co. had three clarinets, bugle or trumpet, two horns, two trombones, serpent, cymbals and drum (D[20, ]60).

In 1843 Wagner asked for serpent in *Das Liebesmahl der Apostel*. Here it is positioned below four bassoons in the score while a tuba is placed below the three trombones. In his 'Norma, il predesse'(1839) the serpent is below the trombones. The instrument's capabilities are shown particularly well in *Rienzi*, composed in 1840 but subsequently much revised by the composer and others. The orchestra includes both serpent and ophicleide, the latter because Wagner hoped for a première at the Paris Opéra. The ophicleide appears in the score as 'Ophicleide [Bass tuba]' at the foot of the brass; the serpent is 'Serpent [Kontrafagott]' below the woodwind. The serpent part ranges from d' down to G'. It is possible to lip down the official lowest note of C for a few semitones, but a good strong G' is available only to a skilled player. These extremely low notes  appear regularly, particularly in Act 2, and it is possible that Wagner (who gave an *ossia* for a B'♭ and A'♭ appearing earlier) also fell into the trap of constructing the serpent part by uncritically copying bass parts elsewhere in the score.

The serpent in *Rienzi* fulfils the following functions:

(1) doubling the double basses at the higher octave (i.e. written in unison) when they are playing a melody or are otherwise separate from the cellos;
(2) unison with cellos;
(3) unison with double basses;
(4) unison with cellos and double basses alone below voices;
(5) unison with double basses and bass trombone;
(6) octave below bassoons;
(7) bass part in staccato quavers with ophicleide and timpani;
(8) solo passage in unison with second horn.

The dynamics are consistent with the woodwind, and there is no emphasis on the instrument's clearer or stronger notes; the writing is chromatic and includes semiquavers and acciaccaturas which sometimes make considerable demands on fingering technique. The part may be summarized as a true bass part, often playing with the double basses (the ophicleide being associated with trombones and other brass), and quite frequently including passages of crotchet bass notes on each beat of the bar, an idiom with which the serpent can cope well.

Whether Wagner had actually heard a serpent before he wrote the part, or whether he would have preferred a double bassoon but chose to avoid specifying an instrument virtually unknown in France at the time, are debatable points. It seems unlikely that before the twentieth century a serpent was ever chosen by a composer solely, or even partially, for its specific tone colour. It was usual for it to be included simply to strengthen the bass part, an effect called by Christopher Monk 'thickening the gravy'.

If serpents and bass horns were scarcely found in the symphony orchestra, they came into their own during the English music festivals, those orgies of oratorio that have offended sensitive ears for the last 200 years. The orchestra lists year after year include a serpent or two. The apotheosis was at York in 1825 and 1828 with eight serpents and bass horns; in 1835 there were two bass ophicleides and one *monstre ophicleide* (see pages 149-53 below), four serpents (played by André of London, Ainsworth of Huddersfield, Costello of York and Stead of Halifax) and a Hibernicon played by Mr. Hull who travelled all the way from Brighton. They liked bass instruments in Yorkshire. A member of George III's band named Hurworth came from nearby Richmond. He was famous for playing flute variations on the serpent. The contrabass serpent made by the Wood brothers of Upper Heaton, near Huddersfield, is described above, pages 77-9.

The German composer Ludwig Spohr (1784-1859) was something of a bass horn addict. While his inclusion of 'Basshorn' in the *Notturno für Harmonie- und Janitscharenmusik,* opus 34, is not surprising, given that it was composed in 1815 for the Hautboisten-Corps in Sonderhausen, the part for it in his Symphonie 9 'Die Jahreszeite', opus 143 was unusual. This was composed in Kassel between December 1849 and April 1850. When he came to compose his next symphony, in Kassel seven years later, he used a Baß-Tuba as the lowest of the brass. Of greater significance is that in two earlier works, *Vater Unser,* one of two pieces for male voice chorus and orchestra composed in 1838, and the opera *Die Kreuzfahrer,* composed in 1843-44, he specified ophicleide. The nature of this particular instrument is discussed below, pages 213-20.

Though symphonic composers were not often drawn to the serpent, Italian composers, for both opera house and band, used it regularly. The reasons for believing that the upright serpent was the protoype *cimbasso* are summarized in Chapter XIII with details of its use by Rossini, Verdi and others in Chapter XVI. Although seated beside the trombones, this instrument did not totally fulfil the function of the bass tuba: the latter is a contrabass instrument while the range of the former extends no lower than that of the F bass trombone. Elsewhere, Zaslaw notes the presence of two serpents at the Paris Opéra in 1793 (Z[1], III, 727) and Carse lists one at a Hanover Square Rooms Subscription Concert in 1842 (C[10], 53). It seemed that the serpent's final employment was to be in Klose's *Das Leben ein Traum* composed in 1899—the same year as Elgar's *Enigma Variations* and Schoenberg's *Verklärte Nacht.*

In 1900 Breitkopf published a version of Berlioz's *Symphonie fantastique* edited by the Paris Opéra archivist Charles Malherbe and the conductor Felix Weingartner. In their note on the 'Witches' Sabbath' they state that 'in the autograph [is] a Bb instrument which was formerly used in churches but is now entirely neglected, namely the *Serpent* . . .' (B[31], xxxvii).

# THE PLAYERS

The early role of the serpent and its players in French churches and cathedrals is a subject that has attracted relatively little research since Westrup delved into the archives of Avignon and Carpentras (Provence) and reported his findings in 1927 (W[13], 635-7). These need to be read with care, since he made the erroneous assumption that references to the bassoon at the time could include references to the serpent. Nonetheless, they throw an interesting light on the situation in French churches in the seventeenth century.

At Notre-Dame des Doms, Avignon, the serpentist in 1602-03 was Michel Tornatoris. He was also *maître de chapelle* and organist as well as sometimes playing bassoon. In 1630 the Chapter of Saint-Agricol at Avignon recommended that 'A esté conclud de recepvoir un serpent au pris et gage de quatre escus et le maistre aura la charge de le chercher, et qui joue bien' ('Agreed that a serpent should be obtained, and engaged at the rate of four écus, and the master [of music] to be responsible for finding him, and that he should play well'). The serpentist at Carpentras in 1611 was M. Labeau, and in 1641, M. Roux. In 1639 Mons. Pelissier was paid ff.5.0.0 (5 florins=1 écu=60 sous) 'pour avoir ioué de serpent despuis la veille de la noël iusques aux rois . . .' ('for having played serpent from Christmas Eve until Epiphany'), deputizing for M[r]. Barbier who was sick.

Meanwhile, at San Petronio, Bologna, Pietro Chaboud (his surname indicating that he was possibly of French nationality or descent) appears amongst the numerous trombonists from 1679 until 1685 as 'Musico di Serpente o Fagotto'. He seems to have provided an alternative possibility as one of a number of basso continuo instrumentalists rather than being an individual serpentist, or perhaps one of a pair, whose function was the support of plainsong. There is just one reference in the church records to the presence of a player of the *serpentone* itself, on the first Sunday in Lent, 1696 (S[15], 49).

From the mid-sixteenth century until the beginning of the eighteenth, there was no shortage of wind instruments to support voices in sacred music. These generally took the form of cornetts and trombones—usually, though not always, together—found from Naples to Durham, South America to Bohemia. It is tempting, and logical, to imagine ensembles of cornetts and serpents. Mersenne himself wrote that he considered the serpent to be the true bass of the cornett (M[28], III, 278). Yet the only reference to an ensemble of this type is made by Palmer (P[3], 6) who in turn refers to Marcelle Benoit's monumental *Versailles et les Musiciens du Roi* (B[21], 36). Sadly, neither on this page nor on any other can a reference to the serpent be found. However, in another of Benoit's invaluable investigations into seventeenth- and early eighteenth-century music in France, *Musiques de Cour, 1661-1733* (B[20]), there is ample evidence of the part played by serpentists in the royal establishment, although there are no indications of the serpent's ever forming part of ensembles of wind or brass instruments. The players often doubled on other instruments, most frequently bassoon or cornett, and it was likely that in concerted performances these were the instruments that they played.

*Officiers de la Musique* are listed under the *chapelle* (the royal chapel) or *écurie* (stables). In the former case, serpentists are in the division headed 'Chantres, Chapelains, Serpents' (Cantors, Chaplains, Serpentists). It is interesting to note that serpent-players sometimes had responsibilities in both chapel and stables. Two of the three serpent-playing sons of serpentist Claude Ferrier, Pierre (who also played bassoon and cornett) and Antoine François, were associated with the Hautbois et Musettes de Poitou de l'Écurie, while Charles François Grégoire de la Ferté was affiliated to the Vingt-Quatre Violons de la Chambre, and may also have played cornett. Pierre Dubois, meanwhile, was classed as a chapel *symphoniste*, which may imply that he also composed.

A detailed account of serpent-players in la Saint-Chapelle de Paris from 1651 to 1785 is to be found in Michel Brenet's *Les Musiciens de la Saint-Chapelle du Paris* (B[51]). Saint-Chapelle, the royal collegiate church situated on the Isle de la Cité at the opposite end to Notre-Dame, may be more typical of the environment in which the majority of sixteenth- and seventeenth-century French serpentists worked. Here there is no doubt of the players' ecclesiastical status. The tenor clerk Pousson was reimbursed for his purchase of 'an instrument of serpent or bassoon' on 24 June 1651, while on 3 June 1793, two livres were given to Pierre Monnet, a choirboy who wished to learn serpent, to buy an instrument. (The worth of the livre (l.) changed over time, from the value of one pound's (500 grammes) weight of silver c. 1100 to less than the value of 5 grammes on the adoption of the metric system in 1799.) Chein, described as a priest who played the serpent in the church, was allocated a room on 30 May 1674. He was made assistant churchwarden on 11 April 1682, continuing to play serpent. There is more evidence of the Chapter's generosity towards its serpent-players in the account of an interview with François Belé on 11 May 1686.

The source of apprentice serpentists is explained by regular references to the admission of novices wishing to learn the instrument. One such was Jean-Baptiste Marchand, admitted on 2 May 1697, who was reimbursed nine francs on the following 29 January for repairs to a part of his serpent which had broken off. On 23 January 1726 two serpent-playing clergy were upgraded. Étienne André, a priest from the village of Sedan, was received as an ordinary chaplain and Melon Joly was received as cleric. Joly had first appeared at Saint-Chapelle with Goubert on 24 December 1723 when both were received as novices, clerics, 'to play the serpent'. Elevation of a different nature occurred on 22 October 1785 when serpentist Decombes became an alto. Others progressed musically. François Capelle, who played bassoon and serpent, was received as a novice on 18 January 1727. He subsequently played bassoon at the Opéra and *Concerts spirituels*, performing a concerto in 1750. Others stayed in the service of the Church for long periods. During the night of 5 December 1723 Jean Du Quesne, a clerk who played serpent, died of smallpox 'which is very dangerous this year'. He had served since 8 October 1701, over twenty-one years. There is an enlightening reference for 3 July 1725 to a 'payment of 20 l. for five ecclesiastics who were engaged to strengthen the music of the Saint-Chappelle performed during the procession to Sainte-Genevieve, "namely two basses, a serpent, a tenor and a contralto".'

As western European countries sought to expand their influence over increasingly wider areas, there is evidence of a fortuitous spread of serpentists. Gallat-Morin (G[1], 12-13) recounts the adventures of Jean Girard, a cleric who in 1724, at the age of twenty-eight, left Saint-Privé-les-Bourges to take up the posts of organist and choirmaster at Notre-Dame in Montreal and teacher at the local school. Girard learned to play serpent at the age of sixteen as a choirboy at the Saint-Chapelle of Bourges, progressing to his clerical status along the route followed by many serpentists. He took to *la Nouvelle France* two books of organ music, some of which has been recorded on *Le livre d'orgue de Montréal*. Gallat-Morin explains that French organ music of the seventeenth and eighteenth centuries had a liturgical function, consisting mainly of short verses alternating with sung verses. The serpent, sensitively played on this recording by Bernard Fourtet, supported the choir in these latter sections. This *alternatim* style was instigated at Notre-Dame de Paris in the middle ages, organ and one of the physically-separated halves of the choir performing odd-numbered verses and the full choir in unison the even verses, those which later were to be supported by the serpent (W[28], 157).

Events in France towards the end of the eighteenth century upset the status quo at both court and cathedral, ending the possibility of serpentists transferring between royal and ecclesiastical employment. The authorities of the Conservatoire saw the provision of *méthodes* for each instrument as a priority. Métoyen compiled one for serpent. On the title-page of the copy in the library of the Conservatoire is a hand-written note to the effect that it had not been approved and the Conservatoire had ordered Gossec and Roze to compile another. As the list on pages 91–2 above confirms, many existing methods for serpent had merely formed part of instruction books on the performance of plainchant.

The situations in which serpentists performed around the beginning of the nineteenth century brought them more prominently before the public and gave rise to the appearance of players who, in some instances, became widely known. The first was Frichot, the inventor of the English bass horn. He was serpentist at the London Antient Concerts in 1793, shortly after arriving from France, but would play solos only on his own invention. J. Doane's *Musical Directory* for 1794 lists him along with four other serpentists who were all members of military bands: Hurst and Joseph Wilmshurst, Guards First Regiment (later The Grenadier Guards); Sickel, Guards Second Regiment (later The Coldstream Guards); and Tingy, Guards Third Regiment (later The Scots Guards). Later, Richard Bentinck played with the 23rd Regiment of Foot at the Battle of Waterloo (1815) (S[22], 1.4.1995).

The most illustrious serpentist in England was André, who sometimes played an arrangement by Christian Kramer of a Corelli concerto. This was noted in a report in the *Musical World* of a City [of London] Amateur Concert on 16 December 1819, which included a 'Sonata, arranged by Kramer, with orchestral accompaniment and Serpano obligato, Mr. Andra, of his Royal Highness the Prince Regent's Band . . . Corelli' (C[10], 153). On another occasion the virtuoso double-bass player Dragonetti was in the audience. He knew the Corelli concerto well—it was one of his own show-pieces—and he congratulated André on the serpent version.

The Prince Regent's Band, subsequently George IV's Household Band, included one serpent *obbligato* and three serpents *ripieno*. André had been a member of the band from being a boy. When it disbanded in 1830 he joined the Montpellier Band at Cheltenham, but his presence amongst royalty was noted again in 1837 when he appeared at Windsor as a member of Queen Victoria's Private Band (M[53], 22.12. 37, 552). By 1840 the serpentist at Cheltenham, Mr. Collins, doubled on ophicleide and André had retired to keep a public house in Gloucester, where he died.

Then there was Mr. Jepp who played serpent in the band which accompanied Queen Victoria's visit to the City of London Guildhall on 9 November 1837, alongside Ponder on ophicleide. In October that year he took part in a performance promoted by Richmond (Surrey) Harmonic Society. According to a report in the *Musical World* of 3 November 1837 (M[53], 137) the 'gem of the evening was Neukomm's *Septetto* for flute, clarinet, oboe, horn, trumpet, bassoon and serpent. It was charmingly played by Messrs. Beale, Lazarus, Keating, Horne, Handley, Godfrey and Jepp.' A copy of this work has yet to be discovered. It is possible that Jepp was the bass horn player in the first English performance of Mendelssohn's overture to *A Midsummer Night's Dream* (see page 484-5 below).

A reference to another lost work for serpent has been discovered by David Guion. An article in the first issue of the *American Musical Journal*, dated March 1835, mentions a Mr Young who 'on the 24th ultimo . . . was announced at the Park Theatre to perform a concerto for the first time in America, on the keyed serpent . . .The instrument which Mr. Young professes is, in reference to a military band, exactly what the double bass is to that of an orchestra. The serpent is the last instrument in the world we wish to hear figuring in a concerto within doors. Mr Young really plays beautifully' (S[22], 1.4.99, 6).

William Ponder played serpent in the 1830 series of Oratorio Concerts at Covent Garden and Drury Lane. He was on bass horn for the Philharmonic Society performance of *A Midsummer Night's Dream Overture* on 18 June 1832, and serpent in *Meerestille und Gluckliche Fahrt* on 22 February 1836. Foreseeing the futures of both of these instruments, he subsequently changed his allegiance and became a distinguished ophicleidist.

These serpent-players, highly regarded in their own time, were remarkable musicians. Although there is ample evidence that in comparison with those of today orchestral performing standards in the nineteenth century were appallingly low (some of us can remember embarrassing moments even in the mid-twentieth century), there is no question that the serpent is the most difficult of all cup-mouthpiece instruments to play to an acceptable standard. In the circumstances it is amazing that by the end of the ninetenth century it had maintained a continuous presence for some 300 years, particularly bearing in mind the constant attacks made upon it (especially by those who had probably not heard it). 'Authorities' on orchestration had very firm views. Mandel, in 1859, claimed that the serpent produced a 'howl rather than an intelligible scale, and, therefore, is inferior to the bass horn and ophicleide' (M[11], 22). In his book on orchestration Evans opined that 'the serpent was such an odious affair that nothing short of compulsion could explain its employment' (E[13], II, 84). Even Burney, consciously or unconsciously adapting and Anglicizing Praetorious's remarks of 200 years before, wrote of 'a great hungry, or rather angry, Essex calf', although in fairness it must be noted that he generally showed a certain enthusiasm for a well-played serpent and these comments were made after an unfortunate experience in Antwerp where the serpent was 'over-blown and detestably out of tune' (B[65], 36). Those who had not heard the serpent derided its appearance. Forsyth wrote with schoolboy glee of this instrument which 'presented the appearance of a dishevelled drainpipe which was suffering internally' (F[19], 287).

In line for an Oxford professorship, Jack Westrup was not unduly reticent about his wide-ranging musical expertise, writing:

Stalwarts who make it their practice to deplore the fading of the past are sometimes heard to say that the tone of the serpent was 'rich'. But they remain an heroic minority, and I am more inclined to trust the result of my own experiments than a tradition which is probably due to professional pride (W[13], 635-6).

No doubt he would have derided the natural trumpet in the same way after trying a little clarino playing.

There is an early nineteenth-century serpent at Amherst College, Massachusetts, one of the first universities to be established in the United States. The instrument is particularly significant because the written records of the college society to which it belonged, and at whose functions it was played, are still held in the archives. However, despite the generally-held view that universities are in the business of discovering and disseminating the truth (in the words of Brian Fender, 'to guard our cultural inheritance' (F[9], 22)), the authorities of Amherst College find the presence of a serpent on their campus so embarrassing that they have flatly refused the offer of a benefactor to have it suitably restored and displayed.

Maybe certain types of academic mind and appreciation of the serpent are incompatible. It doubtless requires the simple wisdom and unaffected candour of someone like like Mr. Penny in Hardy's *Under the Greenwood Tree*, to appreciate that 'Old things pass away 'tis true; but a serpent was a good old note: a deep rich note was the serpent'. Hillsman quotes four references to the use of the serpent in French churches during the twentieth century: Curt Sachs thought that the serpent and ophicleide were still to be found in 1920 (S[1], 263, 267); MacDermott stated that the serpent was in use in 1922 (M[2,] 41); Maguy Andral stated that it was heard in the first quarter of the century (A[13], III, 1013); and Monsieur l'abbé Jean Bihan, of the Institut Catholic in Paris, remembers a player of either serpent or an ophicleide at his parish church in Normandy about 1932 spitting on the sawdust covering the floor after every line or two of music (H[27], 8).

This reluctance to give up the 'good old note' was also evident in the Belgian town of Kortrijk where the serpent was used to play the *Miserere* during funeral processions until 1925, having appeared regularly in churches in the area until about 1830 and various bands until the end of the century. With increasing age, the player changed to baritone, on which he performed until his own death in 1932. In 1973 the serpent still formed part of the fantasy carnival group Moncrabeau in nearby Namur (H[18], 120).

# THE SERPENT REVIVAL

Although the serpent is generally considered to be an 'historic' instrument, invented in the late sixteenth century and thought obsolete by authorities writing in the late nineteenth century, in actual fact it has now been in continuous use during some four centuries. At the court of Louis XIV serpent-players were outnumbered by those performing on crumhorn and trumpet marine. In such a sound-world the serpent was obviously at home, and quite possibly at an advantage: the other instruments were to become defunct, while it remained. However, although Klose included it in his composition of 1899, it is true to say that in most parts of Europe and North America it was not in common use at the time.

Harvey Grace, in his article 'A Note on the Serpent' ($M^{52}$, 1.11.1916, 500-1) begins his account like a Victorian explorer explaining his reason for venturing into an African desert or South American jungle: 'Hearing that a specimen of that obsolete instrument, the serpent, had been unearthed in Devonshire . . . I went to see it.' There then follows a description of a five-keyed serpent by D'Almaine (and therefore no older than a century) along with an account of his enthusiastic, well-meaning amateur attempts to produce a note. It seems that this particular instrument had been played in Ashburton Church by a Thomas Bastow in the 1830s.

In 1897 Ebenezer Prout recounted how several years earlier he had emerged from between his dull brown covers to arrange a performance of Mendelssohn's *St. Paul*. There was no serpent player available 'in the whole of London' and the part had to be played on the tuba ($P^{23}$, I, 242). However, if Prout had looked farther afield he would have been able to engage the enterprising Richard Marsden who, in addition to playing tuba and (probably) ophicleide in the Hallé Orchestra between 1873 and 1886, took up serpent specifically for performances of *St Paul* in Manchester and Liverpool in 1882 ($M^{15}$, 156). With less regard for authenticity, at the first English performance of *St Paul*, which also took place in Liverpool (on 7 October 1836), the serpent part was played by William Ponder who travelled from London . . . especially to play it on ophicleide. This part was regularly heard on the 'modern' ophicleide during the nineteenth century. At the 1874 Leeds Festival Samuel Hughes followed the practice in a performance conducted by Costa. During the 1886 Festival a bass tuba appeared for the first time, played by Felix A. Lee and used in both *St Paul* and *Elijah* (which has an ophicleide part).

There were sporadic revivals of the serpent around the turn of the century. W. W. Starmer, another pioneer, described in *The Musical Times* a performance of Mendelssohn's *St Paul* by Tunbridge Wells Vocal Association on 29 March 1897 in which Mr Callingham, having practised for six months, played the serpent part on the correct instrument. The enlightened Starmer adds: 'At subsequent performances . . . the serpent part has been played by the bass tuba. However, if I am privileged to conduct the work again after the war, I shall use my best endeavours to find a player so that the serpent can be used' ($M^{52}$, 1.12.1916, 549-50).

A serpent played the title-role in the short film *The Case of the Mukkinese Battlehorn* (Spike Milligan, 1956). Possibly Prince Charles's enthusiasm for Goon humour was initiated through an interest in serpents inherited from George III (see page 70 above). It is to be hoped that this is the only one of his ancestor's characteristics that the present heir to the throne will exhibit. In 1958 the Anaconda was taken from Yorkshire to London for an appearance in the Hoffnung Music Festival. Here it featured in Gordon Jacobs's *Variations on Annie Laurie* alongside two piccolos, heckelphone, two bass clarinets, two double bassoons, serpent, subcontrabass tuba, hurdy-gurdy and harmonium. A new, post-war, interest in the serpent seemed to be in the course of becoming established.

A worldwide survey of makers of historical musical instruments published in 1960 (G[4], 70-87) included only one making serpents, Rainer Weber, of Bayerbach/ü. Ergoldsbach b. Landshut. Otto Steinkopf of Berlin-Steglitz was preparing to begin production. In fact the later twentieth-century revival of the serpent was due principally to one man: Christopher Monk. Monk's credentials as a participant in the authentic performance movement were impeccable. He had read History at Oxford but also studied trumpet with George Eskdale of the London Symphony Orchestra. In 1955 he made his first cornett and in that same year became the first to broadcast on the instrument in the UK. With missionary zeal, in 1968 he and a colleague devised a way of making inexpensive cornetts from resin, thus allowing anyone who was interested to purchase, and become familiar with, the instrument and its music.

Having spent nine months carving his first serpent from the plank he realised that if he was to offer reasonably-priced instruments to those attracted to deeper notes he would have to devise methods of making traditional instruments by modern means. He succeeded in doing this through adapting machinery originally designed for precision metal working. Monk's historian's ability to look simultaneously forwards and backwards led him in 1988 to persuade Philip Drinker and John Bowsher of the University of Surrey at Guildford to asssist in identifying the reasons for poor intonation in some of the notes of his serpents. Later the same team measured the bore profile of the Anaconda. Their account of this work, along with some interesting illustrations, is to be found in an article in *Historic Brass Society Journal* (D[19], 119, 123-8).

Another English maker, David Harding of Appleton, uses a synthetic material with similar properties to hardwood for his serpents. They look remarkably traditional and weigh about the same as conventional serpents: their playing characteristics have improved over the years. With the prices of wooden serpents rising steadily, these instruments now offer a viable alternative for the increasing number of enthusiasts.

In 1976 Christopher Monk, with Andrew van der Beek and Alan Lumsden, formed the London Serpent Trio, which first appeared in public on 1 April that year. The ensemble was built on paradox—inevitably, given Monk's whimsical sense of humour: the exercise could scarcely be considered authentic, for this was the first serpent trio in history. It was also a paradox uniquely suited to the instrument, for it is still not completely accepted as part of the authentic performance movement. One reason may be that historically it prowled on its own, and has a closer relationship with choirs singing plainsong than any of the instrumental early music ensembles now in existence. It is called upon to perform in wind ensemble or orchestra relatively infrequently. However, in such groups as The Mellstock Band the serpent can make a valid contribution to a particular genre. In this case it is a repertoire built around early nineteenth-century Dorset as celebrated by Thomas Hardy. In addition to performing in Britain and America, the group has been heard and sometimes seen in films like *The Woodlanders* and *Tess of the D'Urbevilles*. The serpentist concerned, Phil Humphries, was prominent in the band playing for a country ball in the BBC's televison adaptation of Jane Austen's *Pride and Prejudice* (1994). There is no doubt that one sequence, during which an important exchange of ideas took place between the leading protagonists, featured the longest unbroken serpent passage so far recorded on film.

The serpent has characteristically established its own distinctive place in contemporary performance. In September 1986 Christopher Monk held a serpent class as part of the Amherst Early Music Festival. The First International Serpent Festival, arranged by Craig Kridel in South Carolina in 1989, was followed by the 1990 Serpent Celebration in London, where a capacity audience in St John's Smith Square went into rapturous applause as fifty-nine serpentists from all over the world gave a performance of Tchaikovsky's *Overture solenelle '1812'*. Recent high-profile serpent appearances have been in works like Simon Proctor's concerto for serpent and orchestra, first performed in Columbus, South Carolina, by Alan Lumsden in 1989 and then in 1997 by Doug Yeo with the Boston Pops Orchestra conducted by John Williams in Symphony Hall. This work skilfully parodies styles of twentieth-century middlebrow music in a way appropriate to a solo instrument with a history of several centuries of populist performance.

It also exploits the serpent's ability to facilitate wide leaps in pitch. These are difficult to achieve on valved brass instruments, but presumably because its acoustic system partakes of some of the characteristics of woodwind instruments the same problems are not evident in serpent technique. The greater problem found by

*Photo: Michael H. Fear*
Fig. 2.10. The original London Serpent Trio. Left to right: Alan Lumsden with a possibly unique iron-keyed church serpent by Forveille, Paris, Paris, 1821; Christopher Monk with a church serpent by Baudouin, c. 1810; Andrew van der Beek with a military serpent by Pretty, London, c. 1840.

players with traditional brass instrument training who come to the serpent is that of overblowing, for the serpent's vocal characteristics are more readily achieved by a low breath pressure like that utilized historically by sackbut players. The staccato rhythmic effects which undoubtedly led to the serpent's being adopted in bands are readily produced by a clean attack and, particularly, use of the diaphragm, although this is unlikely to have been a technique used before the late twentieth century. The question of authenticity is thus raised once again: should the techniques of earlier periods be adopted in performances to audiences accustomed to contemporary standards of performance? It is certainly a fact that players of modern instruments who should know better are quite willing to perform on the serpent in a way that does justice neither to their own standards, the potential of the instrument, or the trust of their audiences. The reverse side of this coin is presented by players who are

Ex. 2.4

Blyton: *The Revenge of the Cybermen* [see also Ex. 3.4]

understandably jealous of their reputations as brass performers. Although not so much the case in Britain, there are serpent players elsewhere who do not attempt to use mouthpieces which are in any way 'authentic'.

These problems do not, of course, appear when the serpent is deliberately used as a unique voice by contemporary composers. Since the 1970s it has been investigated not only by those interested in old music but by those keen on 'new sounds'. Carey Blyton was commissioned to compose the music for a BBC television serial featuring Dr Who, a science-fiction character of high repute amongst those addicted to Saturday tea-time television. Blyton's problem was to conceive music which would add to the frightening qualites of the Cybermen, last seen seven years previously and possibly no longer scary. For some time he had specialized in the use of instruments like crumhorn, cornett and sackbut and in this case he solved the problem by scoring for serpent and ophicleide in addition to cornett, with modern percussion and electronic organ (Ex. 2.4).

The titles of some of the films in which the serpent has been used give an idea of its function: *The Devils* (Peter Maxwell Davies, in the section composed by David Munrow, 1970), *White Witch Doctor* (Bernard Herrmann, 1953) and *The Golden Voyage of Sinbad* (Miklos Rosza, 1973). Maxwell Davies also used the serpent in the stage-band of his opera *Taverner* (1970). Music by Jerry Goldsmith for the films *Tora! Tora! Tora!* (1970) and *Alien* (1979) was put on to CD by the Royal Scottish National Orchestra in 1997. The serpent parts were played by Phil Humphries in supra-authentic performances: when the original sound-tracks were originally recorded the parts had to be played on bassoon as no serpentist could be found in the Hollywood area.

Two French serpentists illustrate the extremes of serpent style. Bernard Fourtet, who plays trombone, sackbut and serpent in a number of distinguished early music ensembles, is Professor of Serpent in the Early Music Department of the CNR de Toulouse where he has maintained more consistently than anyone else the traditions of original serpent-playing. A totally different direction has been taken by the jazz tubist and serpent-player Michel Godard with *Le Chant du Serpent* and several other serpent/tuba CDs.

During the last two decades of the twentieth century advances in serpent technique, led by players like Alan Lumsden, Phil Humphries and Douglas Yeo, have been remarkable. The fact that the serpent is now often used in non-historic ways helps explain why it has had such a long continous performing life. Despite the technical problems it poses it is to be found in situations ranging from re-created church bands to the London Serpent Trio's *James Bond* and *West Side Story* selections; from folk music to Michel Godard's ethnically-influenced improvisations; from historically-informed recordings of Mendelssohn to enjoyable massed serpent orgies. When, in 1975, Gary Stewart remarked that a serpent's tonal flexibility conferred 'the capacity to be played in "C", "Db", or even "D" ' (S[36], 26), he was being realistic for that time. However, players now accept that, as with all brass instruments, a strong sounding regime will come into operation when all the elements are favourable, and it is the player's responsibility to provide the majority of these. There are, in fact, no more than two or three notes in the serpent's chromatic range of more than three octaves where it is not possible to achieve this.

# CHAPTER III

# *Keyed Bugles and Ophicleides*

If you do succeed in lifting off your hat in time, it is very
little better off than on, for you are obliged to hold it up in
the air, whilst all the solos are being played, with
innumerable variations, on the cornet, bassoon, ophicleide,
and piccolo . . .
> —from an article on the problems caused by hats
> during promenade concerts
> *Punch*, 1850

In Mozart's masterpiece, while Don Juan's private band is
playing the naive music of the *Cosa Rara,* an incredible solo
on the ophicleide has been introduced . . .
> —from a report by Berlioz on the opera in London, 1851
> quoted in A. Ganz, *Berlioz in London*

## THE KEYED BUGLE

ON 5 May 1810 Joseph Haliday, bandmaster of the Cavan Militia, took out British
Patent 3334 for 'Certain Improvements in the Musical Instrument called the Bugle
Horn'. He bored five holes in the instrument, each covered by a key, which enabled
two chromatic octaves to be played. Soon afterwards he added an open-standing
key to increase the range and improve the intonation. This became the standard
keyed bugle, pitched in c' but provided with a crook to lower it a tone.

It seems likely that Haliday (mispelled with two 'l's in the patent document) did
not benefit from his patent, but sold the rights to the Dublin instrument-maker
Matthew Pace for £50 and that John Bernard Logier, whose *A Complete Introduction
to the Art of Playing the Keyed Bugle* was published in 1813, may have renamed
Haliday's intrument *Royal Kent Bugle* (presumably in homage to the Duke of Kent,
Queen Victoria's father, sometime G.O.C. in Ireland until cashiered for excessive
brutality in his disciplinary methods). Logier also fraudulently claimed the right to a
patent.

Ralph Dudgeon, the American virtuoso keyed bugle player and leading authority
on the instrument, has published the results of his dedicated research, which
included tracing present-day descendants of Haliday, in his fascinating book *The
Keyed Bugle* (D[20]). The reader is strongly urged to refer to this for detailed

information on the many varieties of keyed bugle, their players, and those who made and sold the instruments.

The instrument was remarkably successful, in contrast to previous attempts to apply side-holes to brass lip-reed instruments. This was probably because the profile of the bugle was more amenable to the system than the more cylindrical keyed trumpet of the Viennese Weidinger (1801) and the moderately conical *Amorschall* invented by Kölbel of St. Petersburg in 1760. The latter was a french horn with possibly two keys mounted on a hemispherical bell with two perforated covers, one lying over the other—hence *amor* as in *oboe d'amore* plus *schall*—used in this case not as German for 'sound' but as an abbreviated form of *Schall-stück* or bell.

The keyed bugle was almost always made of copper (occasionally brass, or copper with brass fittings), although U.S. Patent 4132 of 4 August 1845 in favour of G. W. Shaw of Thompson, Connecticut, was for keyed bugles made of tortoise-shell. These instruments were constructed by welding together five separate parts and it was claimed that the tone was unimpaired but the instrument was lighter in weight and safe from bruising as the material possessed a certain elasticity. There is an example in the Smithsonian Institution (USNM 251,393). Exquisite American presentation keyed bugles in silver and gold dating from the mid-nineteenth century are described and illustrated by Eliason (E[5], 32-40).

From a bore of some 12 mm the keyed bugle expanded conically, reaching 25 mm in three-quarters of its 1250-1350 mm tube-length. There was then an aprupt expansion to the 150 mm bell. Models with more than six keys were made—up to twelve, in fact, although it is difficult to ascertain the precise function of many of the extra keys. There were also sopranino instruments pitched in e'♭ and f', and possibly also d'♭ (D[20], 27). The first became particularly popular in the United States as a solo instrument and may well have been the major single influence on the prevailing pitch of American bands in the mid-nineteenth century (see page 427 below). A model by Henry Sibley of Boston with nine keys is also exhibited at the Smithsonian Institution (USNM 237,775). Like his European colleagues a man of many parts, Sibley appeared in Boston directories from time to time as a musician, machinist, instrument-maker and wooden leg-maker.

Although principally a band instrument, the keyed bugle was used in the orchestra to a limited extent. George MacFarlane played it at Drury Lane Theatre and Thomas Wallis, first trumpet at Covent Garden in 1818-20, was paid an extra 5s. 0d. for doubling on it. His musical director, Sir Henry Bishop, gave the keyed bugle a solo in *The Miller and his Men* (1813), and also included it in *Guy Mannering*

(1816). It appeared in opera scores by Meyerbeer (*Robert le diable*, 1831) and Rossini (*Semiramide,* 1825). Its use in Spain is attested by a manuscript fingering-chart with French and Spanish titles for seven-keyed bugle *(clarín de siete llaves*—an unusual term for an instrument normally called *corneta de llaves)* (K[12], 147). José de Juan Martinez was appointed teacher of trumpet and *clarín de llaves* on the foundation of the Real Conservatorio in Madrid in 1830. There is seven-keyed *corneta de claus* by Bernareggi of Barcelona in the city's Museu de la Música, No. 808 (illustrated in M[46], 371).

The keyed bugle was particularly welcome in bands, as here at last was a full-toned soprano brass instrument to carry the melodic line. The first West Point bandmaster, Richard Willis (who had studied with Logier) is said to have introduced the keyed bugle to the United States as early as c. 1815 (G[6], 99). Dudgeon reprints a reference to a performance in New York in 1816 and presents evidence confirming Willis's important role in teaching the instrument throughout New England (D[20], 48). Subsequently a number of American circus bands were also to include keyed bugle (D[20], 59-60). With so much active interest in the instrument

Ex. 3.1 FINGERING-CHART FOR KEYED BUGLE (BASED ON HALIDAY'S CHART FOR A FIVE-KEYED INSTRUMENT)

improvements were inevitable. Clementi of London, for example, sold 'T. Harper's Improved Royal Kent Bugle', although it is possible that the appropriation of the name of the the country's leading slide-trumpet player may have done more for sales than any improvement to the basic design. Thomas Harper's *Instructions for The Trumpet* also dealt with the keyed bugle as well as the 'Russian Valved Trumpet' (see page 186 below). The high-powered publicity put out by the Distin family led some to believe that the keyed bugle was invented by John Distin, including M. B. Foster, author of *The History of the Philharmonic Society of London 1813-1912* (F[20], 188).

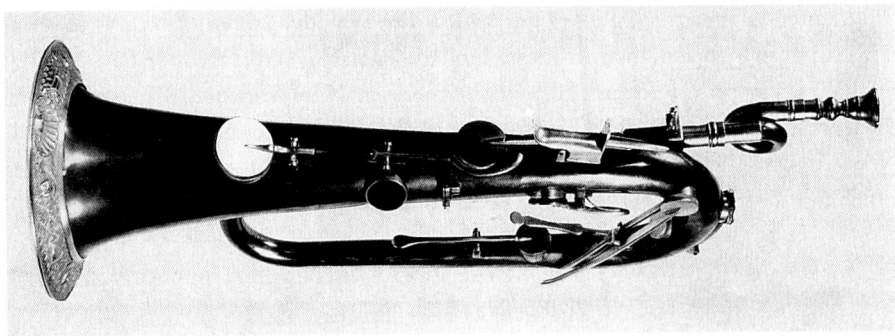

*Horniman Museum & Gardens, London*
Fig. 3.1. Keyed bugle by Jonathan Fentum, London c. 1820-40. It has a b♭ crook, ratchet tuning-slide and eight keys. Note the bell garland with a design in relief.

The keyed bugle was, without doubt, one of the most familiar instruments in the first half of the nineteenth century. *Professeurs* like Villequin (Calais), Bergeret (Louviers) and Guillen (Paris) taught it in France (P[19], 15, 20, 262), and at the first known brass band contest in England, held in Burton Constable near Hull in 1845, the Patrington Band included two keyed bugles alongside its three cornopeans (early cornets) (J[1], 101). It had entered the world of banding much earlier: Baines points out that John Clegg played one in Besses o' th' Barn band as early as 1818 (B[3], 197). It was also found in the itinerant street bands of that socially divisive and noisy age. The artist George Scharf I (1788-1860), who recorded so much London musical activity, includes keyed bugle players in two of his black lead drawings in the British Museum. One is drawn on two slips, each including a bugle (1862-6-14-1976 . . . 977). Another, also dating from the 1830s, shows a band of five with another musician passing round the hat (1900-7-25-51 (vol. II, 11, 13). Keyed bugles (and ophicleides) are also shown in *Studies of Wind and Brass Instruments* (1862-6-14-929 . . .930 (vol. I, 47)); *Band of the Royal Marines in the Officers' Mess, Woolwich, 1826* (1900-7-25-101 (vol. I, 45)); *The 'Fancy Fair', in aid of the Charing Cross Hospital, at Spring Gardens, Charing Cross . . . 1830* (Grace Coll. Pf. XII. Sh.A5, No. 82) and *Street Musicians with a Juvenile Audience, 1839* (1862-6-14-975). These illustrations are reproduced in $C^{35}$, pl. 115, 116, 121, 123, 125, 128, 129.

There are references to the keyed bugle in English church bands. The most detailed deserves to be taken seriously as its author, George Eliot (Mary Anne Evans) was musically knowledgeable. We know which reference books she consulted prior to writing musical episodes in her novels and, on a practical level, the grand piano on which she participated in performances of Beethoven's violin sonatas is exhibited in Nuneaton Museum. 'The sad misfortunes of the Reverend Amos Barton', the first of the three stories in *Scenes of Clerical Life* published in 1858, deals with the incumbent of the parish church of Shepperton, based on Chilvers Coton in Warwickshire where Eliot was herself born and baptised. The period is 'five-and-twenty years ago' (about 1833) and the story begins with a description of the church when 'the innovation of hymn books was as yet undreamed of . . .'

And the singing was no mechanical affair of official routine; it had a drama. As the moment of psalmody approached . . . a slate appeared in front of the gallery, advertising in bold characters the psalm about to be sung . . . Then followed the migration of the clerk to the gallery, where, in company with a bassoon, two key-bugles, a carpenter understood to have an amazing power of singing 'counter', and two lesser musical stars, he formed the complement of a choir regarded in Shepperton as one of distinguished attraction, occasionally known to draw hearers from the next parish . . . But the greatest triumphs of the Shepperton choir were reserved for the Sundays when the slate announced an ANTHEM . . . in which the key-bugles always ran away at a great pace, while the bassoon every now and then boomed a flying shot after them ($E^7$, 6).

Stephen Weston has found references to keyed bugles in two churches in the adjacent county of Northamptonshire, at Milton Malsor and Silverstone (where there were two) ($W^{10}$, 311) An illustration in J. & M. Lindsay's *The Music Quotation Book*, reproduced here as Fig. 3.2, shows a church band which includes two players of sopranino or pocket keyed bugles. It has not been possible to discover the provenance of the illustration, nor to decipher the artist's name. In the mid-nineteenth century Mr. Haskell played keyed bugle in the chapel at Verwood, Dorset, alongside tenor saxhorn, trombone, piccolo, flute, clarinet, violin and cello. Saffron Walden Museum, in northern Essex, contains a keyed bugle known to have been used in the local church (B[35], 94), and records at Feock, Cornwall, refer to one being bought for the church in 1836 (W[26], 377). Another reference to its presence in Cornwall is found in 'The Looe Die-Hards', a short story by

Fig. 3.2. A church band with two sopranino or pocket keyed bugles.

'Q' (Arthur Quiller-Couch). Set in the early years of the nineteenth century, it tells of a French cornet-player's being found in a store-hut used by the Looe Volunteer Artillery. His appearance is fortuitous as there is an urgent need to form a band to play the 'Dead Marching Soul' [i.e., Handel's 'Dead March' in *Saul*] at the anticipated funeral of a sick volunteer.

> 'But what about this key-bugle, monsieur? And the other instruments?—not to mention the players'.
>
> 'I've been thinking about that,' said Captain Pond. 'There's Butcher Tregaskis has a key-bugle. He plays "Rule Britannia" upon it when he goes round with the suet . . . then we have the church musicians—Peter Tweedy, first fiddle; Matthew John Eade, second ditto; Thomas Tripconey, scorpion——'
>
> 'Serpent,' the Doctor corrected.
>
> 'Well, it's a filthy thing to look at, anyway . . .' (Q[1], 66)

Lomas (L[17], 82) refers to a painting by J. Archer, *The Arrival of William IV and Queen Adelaide at 'The Friars', Lewes* which shows two keyed bugles in a welcoming band of fifteen. It is thought there were two keyed bugles in the band at Horsham, in the same county of Sussex, during the late 1830s.

These sightings are sparse, but they are widely separated geographically, implying that the keyed bugle was played in an area covering at least the southern half of England. In fact the instrument was known throughout the length and breadth of the United Kingdom as it was a favourite with coach guards. Their merry improvisations heralded the arrival of the mail until the railways were appointed to take over their function in 1838. Even so, as late as the 1850s the traveller W. E. Adams found himself sharing a bed with a drunken keyed bugler at the Black Bull in Kendal (A[5], I, 294-96).

Much as Hardy was given to using the serpent as an indication of time and place, so Dickens referred to the keyed bugle—valuable descriptions in view of his ability to reproduce detail of speech and action so accurately. In *Martin Chuzzlewit* (1844), William Simmons, working for a 'large stage-coaching establishment at Hounslow' hoped to become a regular driver:

> He was musical besides, and had a little key-bugle in his pocket, on which, whenever conversation flagged, he played the first part of a great many tunes, and regularly broke down in the second. [There is a pocket keyed bugle, in b♭, in the

Royal College of Music Museum of Instruments.]
'Ah!' said Bill, with a sigh, as he drew the back of his hand across his lips, and put his instrument in his pocket after screwing off the mouthpiece to drain it; 'Lummy Ned of the Light Salisbury, *he* was the one for musical talents. He *was* a guard. What you may call a Guard'an Angel, was Ned' (D[9], 82). [The amazing complexity of this pun is revealed on page 135 below.]

In *The Posthumous Papers of the Pickwick Club* (1837) the keyed bugle becomes a device on which to hang a vivid picture of travel by road in early Victorian times:

The lively notes of the guard's key bugle vibrate in the clear cold air, and wake up the old gentleman inside, who carefully letting down the window-sash half way, and standing sentry over the air, takes a short peep out, and then carefully pulling it up again, informs the other inside that they're going to change directly; on which the other inside wakes himself up, and determines to postpone his next nap until after the stoppage. Again the bugle sounds hastily forth, and rouses the cottager's wife and children, who creep out at the house-door, and watch the coach till it turns the corner . . .
And now the bugle plays a lively air as the coach rattles through the ill-paved streets of a country town . . . (D[10], 223)

Here the most accurate chronicler of early nineteenth-century England seems to be presenting vivid pictures of contemporary life. But did these fondly-remembered events actually occur? A series of letters published in 'The Country House' column of *The Field* ('The Country Gentleman's Newspaper') in 1873 presented conflicting evidence (F[14], 264). This was summarized by H. E. Malet in his *Annals of the Road*. Here he refers to events and players recollected by the correspondents, one of whom remembered

How Prettyman, guard of one of the Manchester coaches, used to wake the echoes in some of the sleepy agricultural villages we passed through in those days! Brandt, also, on the Leicester 'Union', was an accomplished player, and could bring many to the windows and doors of their houses by the sweet music of his bugle . . . I know one guard who had a bugle snugly stowed away, and brought out to the delight of the people who lived clear away from the smoke [outside London] (M[8], 43-48).

L.R.P., at one time a guard on the Holyhead mail, remembered playing the keyed bugle when passing his father's house on the outskirts of Chester. However, 'Ex-Mail-Coachman' contended that

the bugle was no part of the mail. The tin horn [known as 'the angel'] was there, whether for the purpose of raising up an old pikeman in the dead of night to have his gate open, to warn the next change, or to let the market gardener who was fast asleep on the shafts of his cart know that the whole of the road was not his perquisite, and also to inform him that Her Majesty's mail, half an hour late and going at twelve miles an hour, was close behind him.

The writer of the original letter than wrote again to explain that he spoke of the use of the keyed bugle on one special occasion only: the procession of mail coaches from Millbank, Westminster to the General Post Office annually [from 1791 to 1838] on the king's birthday. He remembered seeing as boy the keyed bugles laid out in the shop of a musical instrument-maker in Westminster, ready for the use of the mail guards in the annual procession. The regulations limited the guards to the post-horn only, but he doubted that the rule was enforced. (The instrument-maker concerned would have been none other than Pace, established in Dublin by Matthew Pace in 1798. From 1814 until 1913 members of the family operated from a number of addresses in Westminster as well as Soho, Bloomsbury, Pentonville, Bristol and Sheffield. Charles & Frederick Pace, at Lower Crown Street, Westminster 1819-27, described themselves as 'Martial musical instrument makers, and original makers of the Royal Kent Bugle') (W[3, 289]).
'Deadfall' added:

I fancy I hear Goodwin playing 'Or che in cielo' from the opera of *Marino Faliero* [Donizetti, 1835] while I am writing this letter! . . . What a pity that so fine an instrument should be supplanted! It's [sic.] 'round' tone has never yet been rivalled, and if ever I become a millionaire I will have a band of my own with the lead on six bugles. The appearance of a well-kept bugle was always so good. What could be handsomer than the black shining copper of the instrument itself, and the inch of polished brass round the bell, and its seven bright keys? . . .

The impression gained from both this correspondence and from information provided by Macintyre, sometime guard of the London-Brighton coach who had been asked by the Inspector-General of Mails to play on the keyed bugle during the procession of 24 May 1834, is that its use was permitted. The angel and 'three feet of tin' [straight post-horn] were provided by the guard, and were his property. Paragraph 6 of the *Official Instructions for Mail Guards* reads:

> He is to sound his horn as a signal for carriages to turn out of the way upon the approach of the mail-coach [which had priority over all other vehicles on the road], also to warn turnpike men of its coming, that no unnecessary delay may be occasioned, and likewise to prepare postmasters against its arrival, and horse-keepers to bring out their horses at each of the changing-places; and he is to sound it always as a signal to passengers when the time is expired that is allowed in the time bill for their stopping to refresh, and use his utmost exertions to prevent delay in all cases whatever ($M^8$, I, 397-98).

There is no shortage of mail coach illustrations, and so long as Christmas remains commercialized the number can only increase. However, none seems to include a keyed bugle, although the angel and the yard of tin are often prominently displayed. But there is evidence that it was also played on coaches not carrying mails.

Harper refers to the annual gathering of one hundred *stage* coachmen and guards in September 1834 at the Green Man, Dunchurch (on the present A5 trunk road) ($H^9$, I, 275-77). As they made their approach there were 'in some cases two, or even three, being perched on one coach and making the welkin ring with the notes of their bugles, in solos, duets or trios . . . ' At the dinner 'Bob Hadley was put in the chair . . . and on mounting his perch he returned thanks on his bugle in the favourite hunting air of "Old Towler".' Harper also discusses the part played by musical performance in the final days of coaching, an interesting topic in view of its presenting an aspect of proletarian music-making hitherto overlooked:

> The last twenty years of the coaching era were remarkable for the development of musical ability on the part of the guards, both of the mail- and stage-coaches, who, relieved from their old-time anxieties and fears of highwaymen, kept their blunderbusses safely stowed away, and, turning their attention, like so many scarlet-coated Strephons, to the ballad-music of the moment, became expert practitioners on the key-bugle. That instrument came over from Germany in 1818 [sic.], and for a time pretty thoroughly displaced the old 'yard of tin' the earlier guards had blown so lustily . . . the roads became excruciatingly lively

when every gay young blood of a guard learned to play 'Cherry Ripe', the 'Huntsman's Chorus', 'Oh! Nanny, wilt Thou gang wi' Me?' and half a hundred others (H[9], I, 279-80).

Harper confirms that the Post Office forbade mail-guards to play keyed bugle, so they bought their own and played them when clear of London 'to the great admiration of the country joskins'. The Gilbertian nature of the whole arrangement was confirmed annually during the parade from Westminster to the City when the guards were encouraged to perform on the keyed bugles that their superiors did not know they were able to play. Furthermore, there were indications of early stirrings in the field of authentic performance when on 1 June 1887 the Post Office began to send parcels from London to Brighton by road again rather than by rail. James Nobbs, the oldest guard in its service, was appointed guard for the day:

An even more enthusiastic admirer of the bygone days produced a key-bugle so that Nobbs might play 'Auld Lang Syne'. He tried, but the attempt was not a success. The results were feeble, in consequence, as he explained, of his having lost his front teeth. (H[9], I, 256).

The Post Office's decision may have been misread by the London instrument-makers Henry Keat & Sons when they exhibited their telescopic coach horn in 1885. Algernon Rose claimed in 1894 that the company was making 1,000 coach horns annually (R[9], 352), but for what market it is difficult to discover. (By 1924 Keats had ceased to manufacture and were only carrying out repairs.)

The extent to which coach passengers themselves may have played keyed bugle is worth considering. An illustration entitled 'The Road' in an *Illustrated London News* feature about Derby Day 1844 (I[1], 25.5.44, 336) shows crowds riding and driving to Epsom. An outside passenger on a coach in the foreground appears to be performing on the instrument. ('Derby Day', a highly satirical illustration by Leech in the same journal a year later (I[1], 31.5.45, 349), includes a patient nag drawing a cart containing a man playing tailgate trombone.)

The part played by the bugle in railway transport was minimal. There is an unattributed illustration in Brooks's *Railway Ghosts* (B[56], 5) showing a train hauled by a locomotive identified as a Robert Stephenson 'Patentee' 2-2-2 dating from the 1830s. The artist shows a bugle, along with several passengers—all apparently seated in the tender. There are further references to a railway bugle in Dickens's description of a rapid journey from London to Paris by train and boat, 'A Flight' (*Reprinted Pieces*). A bell is used to signal the departure at English stations, but there is a change of tone in France. Here the traveller is sleeping, experiencing a vivid dream of escape. 'We are up the chimney, we are on the guard-house roof, we are swimming in the murky ditch, when "Qui v'là?" A bugle, the alarm, a crash! what is it? Death? No, Amiens.' After a further halt: 'Bugle, shriek, flight resumed' (D[11], 133).

The instrument Dickens heard appears to have been a straight horn, about fifty centimetres in length, used by the formidable French lady crossing-keepers. (Dollfus & de Geoffrey illustrate two such in about 1845 and 1891) (D[15], 71, 177).

The French did not use the duty bugle (*clairon*) itself until 1823, when it was introduced by Courtois at the request of the War Minister. The keyed bugle was therefore called *trompette à clef, trompette à clés* or *trompette chromatique* before adopting the more correct names of *clairon chromatique* or *bugle à clefs*. A related case of inappropriate nomenclature (though reversed) is that of the *Regent's Bugle*, which has been shown to be a slide-trumpet and as such outside the scope of this book (W[14], 65). Berlioz, having thoroughly demolished any musical pretension the simple bugle may have had, turned to the keyed bugle which he assessed characteristically: 'It does not lack agility, and some artists play it excellently; but its tone is exactly that of the plain bugle' (B[25], 226).

Agility the keyed bugle certainly does not lack. This was undoubtedly one of the reasons why on both sides of the Atlantic it was so frequently played by leaders of bands. These tended to be civilian bands in America, like that at Woburn, Massachusetts, which included two keyed bugles and two ophicleides after reorganisation in 1841 (K[18], 6), but more often military bands in England. In 1834 John E. Jones, Assistant A.D.G. of the Royal Artillery, wrote to Bandmaster McKenzie expressing his joy on hearing the 93rd Regiment at Canterbury: 'The Master of the Band played the Kent Bugle very well' (F[3], 100). The first bandmaster of the 1st Battalion, The Rifle Brigade, was also a keyed bugler. William Miller occupied the post for an astonishing thirty-eight years, during most of which he was known as 'Billy the Bugler'. Turner prints a photograph of the silver Kent Bugle presented to him on his retirement by the officers of the regiment 'in token of their regard and appreciation of the zeal and energy which he has always displayed' (T[16], 210-213).

Elsewhere whole sections of keyed bugles were found, as in the private Cyfarthfa Band at Merthyr Tydfil in South Wales. Morgans refers to two E♭ buglers, T. Chirm and Ned Richardson, who sat alongside William Jones, a Bb bugle player and original band member (M[38], 1839).

Schwartz gives an exciting account of a contest in 1856 between cornet virtuoso Patrick Gilmore and Ned Kendall 'celebrated all over New England as the greatest keyed bugle virtuoso of his day' (S[21], 31-6). Kendall played an Eb sopranino and the outcome of the contest was very close indeed, but inevitably in Gilmore's favour. The keyed bugle retained its popularity longer in the United States than in Europe, although there were plenty on display at the 1851 Great Exhibition in London. During the Crimean War (1854-56) Andrew Henry, principal keyed bugle of the Royal Artillery, was the first musician in the British Army to be awarded the highest honour for special individual acts of bravery, the Victoria Cross.

A fondness for the warm tone of the Royal Artillery's keyed bugle was to remain for many years, sometimes coupled with regret at the passing of the bass horn. Amongst the correspondents who contributed to the debate on the mail-coach guards issue referred to above was E.L.L. On 21 June 1873 he remarked:

Allow me to re-echo the regret of 'Deadfall' at the gradual supplanting of the fine old key bugle by the cornopean . . .

I for some years hoped that the example of Mr. Distin, who, with I believe his sons also, used to lead their fine horn band on the key bugle, would induce many still to give the preference to this beautiful instrument . . . Certainly for richness of tone the copper key bugle far surpasses anything that could be produced from the cornet-à-piston, whether of brass or silver; but I suppose the much greater facility of learning and blowing the latter instrument gave it an immense recommendation in the eyes of the modern horn blowers.

Still the superiority of the copper over brass musical instruments is not wholly unrecognised. The Royal Artillery have, or had some four or five years since, a band of considerable numbers, consisting entirely of copper instruments, and a very rich-toned, splendid band it was; it used to play regularly on parades on Woolwich Common.

I only wish the C.O.'s of regiments would take a hint from this example and endeavour to introduce a couple of key bugles and a couple of bass horns of copper into their bands; the general richness of tone in our regimental bands would be immensely enhanced thereby (F[14], 21.6.73, 597).

A letter from the renowned Jack Goodwin on 12 July 1873 confirmed this:

In comparing the tone of the cornet with the bugle, the latter most decidedly. The highest authority I had was Kœnig. He told me the bugle most certainly (F[14], 12.7.73, 43). [Kœnig was a celebrated cornet soloist who appeared regularly in Jullien's concerts. He was also a composer, and his *Post Horn Galop* is still regularly performed.]

The keyed bugle was familiar, and popular in every sense of the word, on both sides of the Atlantic, and there was an awareness of the instrument at least as far east as Hungary, where the Hungarian for horn *(kürt)* formed part of its name, *billentyüskürt*. Part of its appeal undoubtedly lay in its being the first brass instrument to allow its players to reach the levels of solo virtuosity attained by flute and clarinet soloists. John Distin's keyed bugle artistry, in fact, appears to have been the direct cause of the invention of the ophicleide. Following the Battle of Waterloo there was review in Paris of the victorious allied troops. The Russian Grand Duke Konstantin was greatly impressed by the playing of Distin, then solo keyed bugle player in the Grenadier Guards, and asked for a similar instrument. By the time this could have been obtained from London the Grand Duke would have returned to Russia, so Distin's keyed bugle was copied by the Parisian intrument-maker known as Halary.

Two years later, in 1817, a series of 'new instruments' was submitted to the Académie royale des Beaux-Arts by Jean Hilaire Asté, otherwise called Halary.

# THE OPHICLEIDE

The name *ophicleide* is formed from two Greek words, *ophis* (serpent) and *kleid* (that which serves for closing). Halary's French Patent, No. 1849 of 24 March 1821, was for:

*Clavitube* or *trompette à clef*, a keyed bugle made in f', eb', c' and bb;
*Quinticlave*, *trompette-quint* or *quinte à clef*, an alto keyed bugle in f or eb built in bassoon shape;
*Ophicléide*, *serpent à clef*, *basse* in c or Bb; and *contrebasse* in F, all in bassoon shape;
*Clairon métallique*, a metal clarinet.

The latter was included as the patent specification was 'for keyed musical wind instruments', but as a reed instrument it is outside our terms of reference. The specification reprints the report of the Académie which gives full details of the instruments. It states that the ophicleide was designed to replace the serpent (which it subsequently often did), offering superior tone and intonation. The original ophicleide had nine keys, and a mouthpiece like that of the serpent or trombone.

In the specification is also a reference to a M. Dumas who had submitted similar instruments to the Académie in 1811 as *Basse* and *Contrebasse guerrières*. This scarcely prejudiced Halary's application as these were in fact bass and contrabass clarinets. Similar confusion is shown by Lavoix, who describes the *Bass-orgue*, a bass clarinet invented by Sautermeister in 1812, as analogous with Frichot's *Basse-trompette* (see above, page 86) (L[6], 131). They actually *looked* very much like each other.

The Académie declared that Halary had rendered a genuine service to the art of music, particularly through the *contre-basse d'harmonie,* which went down to a tone and a half below orchestral double basses. (The three-stringed variety, with G' as the lowest note, was common in orchestras up to the twentieth century.) It then awarded him a medal for the first three instruments. The quinticlave subsequently became known as the alto ophicleide, accepted in military bands but not orchestras owing to its unreliable intonation. Its tone is distinctive, with a mischievous clarity reminiscent in some ways of the Eb clarinet. It is, however, even more difficult to avoid bending the note when attacking it or releasing it than when playing the bass ophicleide (Fig. 3.3). In his youth the conductor Rivière played alto ophicleide in a French band which also had eight bass ophicleides (C[7], 38). It was generally replaced by the clavicor after 1838, and shortly afterwards by the alto saxhorn.

Fig. 3.3
Alto ophicleide
(quinticlave) in Eb by Gautrot
*aîné,* Paris, c. 1844. It has nine keys.
*Edinburgh University Collection of*
*Historic Musical Instruments.*
*Photo: Antonia Reeve*
*Photography, Edinburgh.*

The fingering-chart in the patent specification confirms that the lowest note available to the F contrabass ophicleide (all keys depressed) was E', a semitone below the first pedal of the bass tuba in F. (The lowest note of any ophicleide is always a semitone below its basic pitch, obtained by closing the open-standing key on the bell.) Halary even suggested that the lowest notes might be written an octave higher, as is the convention with the double bassoon and double bass. Berlioz considered that the instrument's lack of use resulted from the huge amount of breath it required (see page 149 below). In fact breath control is a major factor in playing any ophicleide as once the breath has passed through the crook the instrument's widely conical bore provides virtually no more resistance. The instrument itself thus confers less control over pitch than the tuba, and if constant attention is not payed to diaphragmatic support there can be some very undesirable results. The profile of the crook itself is also a major factor in controlling intonation. Had French players possessed greater lung capacity the contrabass ophicleide could have had a lasting effect on the attitude of French composers towards the lowest of the brass, but time was not to allow this as the Baß-Tuba appeared in Germany in 1835, a mere fourteen years after the ophicleide was patented.

Ophicleides were normally made of brass, sometimes silver-plated. They were conical in profile, bassoon-shape in form and all the side-holes were covered by keys. The affinity in the construction of the ophicleide and the English bass horn can be clearly seen in Figs. 2.10 and 3.4. The exclusive use of metal in both instruments and similarity of key-heads and seatings leads to suspicions that Halary may have been influenced in his invention by both the English bass horn and the keyed bugle, producing an improved English bass horn in which the V-conformation was changed to a U. (The Hibernicon showed other similarities.) The eventual number of keys varied between nine and twelve, eleven becoming normal. In view of the desirability of certain notes being vented in serpent-playing (see above, page 74) it is noteworthy that all ophicleides required venting when their tenth and eleventh keys (if present) were depressed. This was usually, though not always, arranged to take place automatically, through the keywork. There was a circular or elliptical crook (in the latter case normally incorporating a tuning-slide) into which the mouthpiece fitted. Further tuning adjustment was possible through a screw on the open-standing key; the smaller the gap between key-pad and orifice the lower the instrument's pitch. The mouthpiece was either cup-shaped or funnel-shaped, like French trombone mouthpieces of the time. Caussinus, in his *Méthode*, gives the following ideal dimensions for a mouthpiece, recommending that it should be made of metal rather than of ivory or horn:

| | |
|---|---|
| Overall length | 72 mm |
| Depth of cup | 34 mm |
| Diameter of cup | 27 mm |
| Width of rim | 5 mm |
| Diameter of throat | 7 mm |
| Diameter of shank where it enters the mouthpipe | 10 mm |

These should be compared with details of the mouthpiece used by Samuel Hughes, one of the last nineteenth-century players of the ophicleide.

HUGHES (BY COURTOIS)
(details from W[12], 10)

| | |
|---|---|
| Diameter of rim | 39 mm |
| Diameter of cup | 26 mm |
| Depth of cup | 20 mm |

The following are comparative dimensions of ophicleides in Bb by Charles Sax (c. 1830) and Henri et Martin (c. 1855: illustrated on the back cover of this book).

Table 3.1.    COMPARATIVE DIMENSIONS OF OPHICLEIDES BY C. SAX
AND HENRI ET MARTIN
[Dimensions in millimetres]

| | SAX | HENRI ET MARTIN |
|---|---|---|
| Overall length of tubing | 2745 | 2598 |
| Length of main tube | 1829 | 1628 |
| Length of crook | 916 | 970 |
| Bore where mouthpiece is inserted | 12.5 | 12 |
| Bore where crook is inserted | 35.5 | 34 |
| Diameter of bell | 213 | 236 |

(The later instrument is compared with a Moritz Baß-Tuba on page 471 below.)

The compass of the ophicleide was three octaves or more, depending upon the player. Since all the holes were covered by keys they could be placed in more acoustically-correct positions and intonation was thus more secure than on the serpent, although the existence of conflicting fingering-charts indicates that it was

Ex. 3.2.  FINGERING-CHART FOR OPHICLEIDE IN C (BASED ON HÉRAL)

The keys are numbered along the tubing from 1, closest to the bell. 10 is an
additional key above 7; 11 additional between 6 and 7

not totally secure. Interestingly, the ophicleide repertoire in general required far more use of the left hand than the right. As with the serpent, each player needed to become familiar with his individual instrument since fingering in each octave did not follow a totally logical progression.

In 1822 Jacques Labbaye *fils* introduced a ten-key ophicleide, giving B♭b, described in a ten-year French Patent, 1327 of 9 February 1822 for 'Changements faits à une basse d'harmonie, appelée *ophicleïde*'. To assist portability his instrument was made in four sections and weighed a mere four pounds ('quatre lives'). Lavoix claimed that Labbaye was responsible for the ophicleide's 'unique timbre of horn-cum-bassoon-cum-serpent', although the Académie's report on Halary's quinticlave had already referred to its tone being midway between the human voice and the bassoon, and louder than that of the bassoon.

In 1827 François Sautermeister of Lyons patented his *Basse d'harmonie ou nouvelle ophicléide* with eleven keys (French Patent 2158 of 22 June 1827). He described the tone as being an amalgam of serpent and buccin (dragon-headed trombone), 'a bass producing majestic sounds; it copes with all sorts of modulations in every key, in the medium register as well as in the bass, and without any change to the tone-quality'. Its eleven keys were placed under the fingers as in playing the serpent, thus providing an attractive and practical method of luring serpentists to the new instrument. Four or ten[!] of the holes were closed 'according to the wish of the *artiste-musicien* . . .' Keys 3, 5, 6, 8, 10 and 11, which represented the holes of the serpent, could be either open-standing or closed; keys 2, 4, 7 and 9, for semitones, were closed. A double tuning-slide to lower the basic pitch of the instrument a semitone was provided, and a potential range of three octaves was promised. The mouthpiece could have either a round or conical cup, while the body of the instrument could be made of wood and metal or totally of metal, and substitute bells were available: a serpent's head, a bowl or 'tout autre'. There is evidence that the term *basse d'harmonie* had a fairly general application at one period, not surprisingly as the name translates not as 'bass of the harmony' but as 'band bass'. Pontécoulant defined Cotter's Hibernicon as 'a rationalized and carefully calculated *basse d'harmonie*' (P[20], I, 132).

By 1836 there were at least four ophicleide-makers in Paris: Antoine Halary, making 'les ophicléides altos, basses et contre-basses' at rue Mazarine, 37; Labbaye at rue de Caire, 17; Gambaro at rue des Vieux-Augustins, 18; and Raoux at rue Serpente [sic], 11 (P[19], 85-6). At some time prior to 1843 the distinguished ophicleidist Joseph Caussinus, author of a renowned *méthode*, added a key improving the note F♯. 'Formerly', wrote Berlioz, '[it] could be produced only very imperfectly with the lips and left much to be desired as regards intonation and steadiness . . . It now sounds as well as the other notes' (B[25], 316). (In the Richard Strauss edition of Berlioz's *Treatise* 'key' is translated confusingly as 'valve'.) Halary himself was awarded a silver medal in 1849 for his *Omniton*, another type of improved ophicleide. An ophicleide invented by Couturier of Lyons had six keys and one valve. In 1854-5 Gautrot *aîné* produced an ophicleide with a rotary change from C to B♭ on the crook and another with twelve keys and a similar change of pitch controlled by a tuning-slide in the butt. (As early as 1822 Halary had introduced a twelfth key, but with apparently little success.)

The eminent English player Samuel Hughes may have been involved in a number of improvements to his instrument, itemised by Stephen Weston who has diligently researched both instruments and player (see Bibliography). One of these consists of a roller mechanism on the right-hand thumb key facilitating movement from E or D♯ to G♯. A number of instruments exists with this useful modification, no doubt dating from late in Hughes's career (during his period at Covent Garden, see page 180 below) (W[11], 113). Weston concludes that Hughes's system approaches near perfection, the only defect remaining consisting of problems caused by the F to F♯ fourth finger slide (for which Weston himself has suggested a solution). Four of the ophicleides owned by Hughes are still in existence, three of them made by Courtois of Paris which incorporate a venting hole with a diameter of some 70 mm in the bell. The purpose of this appears to be to enhance the tone-quality (as in some types of organ pipe). It is not easy to decide by practical demonstration whether in fact the theory has been proven. All notes except the B' obtained by closing the open-standing key closest to the bell are produced by opening tone holes and the bulk of the sound therefore emanates from the open holes rather than through the bell. However, the function of the venting hole could be seen as helping to ensure that all notes, including B', sound through vents, thus resulting in a more even tone over the range (see Fig. 3.4).

British makers were widespread, including Birmingham-based George Smith and George & John Cottrell; Henry Smith of Wolverhampton; Roger Ward and James Jordan, both of Liverpool; George Wigglesworth of Otley; Thomas Macbean of Edinburgh; and John Pask of London. Others imported ophicleides from France, stamping them with their own names, sometimes preceded by the word 'maker'. D'Almaine's 1839 catalogue offered keyed ophicleides in the price-range £7.10s. – £16.16s. (P[21], 25). At the time an ophicleidist engaged by the Philharmonic Society could expect £3.13.6d for four rehearsals and three concerts: 10s.6d (half a guinea) per session. The 16 gn. price of the best eleven-key ophicleide would thus be covered by working thirty-two sessions. At 1999 rates similar sessions would generate about £1,440, roughly one-third of the list price of a Besson EE♭ tuba. The 1999 player would therefore need to work for three times as long in order to buy his instrument.

Fig. 3.4
Tom Winthorpe, Royal Opera House, Covent Garden, with ophicleide in C by Courtois played by Samuel Hughes with the Royal Italian Opera in the same theatre, c. 1870s. The distinctive vent in the bell should be noted.

The *Serpentcleide*, one of the few wooden ophicleides, was an intriguing British variant, invented either by a Mr. Beacham, T. M. Glen or Charles Huggett, depending upon which source is deemed correct. What is certain is that Huggett made the serpentcleide played by Prospère in Jullien's *Concerts d'hiver* at Covent Garden in 1846. *The Musical World* (1 August 1846) considered that this instrument combined 'in a superior degree the excellence of the serpent and the ophicleide, possessing the power of the one and the softness of the other', a description which subsequently appeared in *The Musical Times* of 1 September 1846 . . . reprinted from the *Worcester Journal!* (M53, 1.9.46, 26). The wooden ophicleide in the Brussels Musée Instrumental (Mahillon 2454) may be an example. It is marked 'Approved by Prospère, manufactured by Huggett, warranted and sold by Jullien at his Royal Conservatory of Military Music, 214 Regent Street, London, Patent No. 84'. (A patent document with this number has yet to be traced.)

Thomas Key registered a 'Design for the new improved Regimental Cased Serpentcleide' (BT45/12/2379) on 16 July 1850. To prevent the wooden bell (fitted in order 'to preserve the fine, sonorous tone') from splitting when the instrument was used in the tropics, it was cased in copper in order to (as John Webb has neatly pointed out) 'preserve the wooden bell' (W[4], 52). Thomas Key, really to confuse matters, included a metal serpentcleide in his 1855 price-list, describing it as 'made of pure copper . . . and better fitted for extreme climates than the serpentcleide'. Problems likely to beset  players of the wooden ophicleide who were intent on expanding the Empire were clearly being seriously addressed. At the Great Exhibition James Jordan of Liverpool exhibited his 'Newly-invented Euphonic Serpentcleide' which was apparently pitched a complete octave lower than the normal bass ophicleide. Previous monster ophicleides had been only a fifth lower.

A six-key wooden ophicleide made by Pierre-Paul-Ghislain-Dupré of Tournai in 1824 was called, inevitably, the *Tuba-Dupré*. His aim was to make out of wood instruments normally made in metal. There is an example in the Brussels Musée Instrumental. British Patent 13601 of 24 April 1851 was taken out by Joseph Robertson for a similar instrument. (He also developed methods of making everything from artifical marble to railway carriages and wooden ships.) The Paris Musée de la Musique contains a wooden ophicleide in F by the French maker Lefebvre. Another, of unknown make, with a square section looking like part of a nineteenth-century Methodist chapel, was for some years in London but is now thought to be in Japan. Morgans (M[37],138) refers to a Welsh player named Coleman who made an ophicleide out of paper (see page 171 below).

# MONSTER OPHICLEIDES

The contrabass or monster ophicleide in F or E♭ was a full 1500 mm tall. They 'are very little known,' said Berlioz. 'Up to the present nobody in Paris has been willing to play them because of the volume of breath required' (B$^{25}$, 228). A valid reason for the instrument's lack of use, but, even so, the monster ophicleide appeared every now and again throughout the century. In 1834 William Ponder played one at the Birmingham Festival, sitting alongside the local ophicleidist Mr Thurston (H$^6$, 99). Robert Merrick, later translator of Shiltz's ophicleide tutor, published in 1853, reported that Ponder's was a new instrument, specially made for the festival. 'The volume of sound it emits is immense, but the tone is richly rounded and blends well with the voices'.

*The Yorkshireman* considered Ponder and the Birmingham instrument worth mentioning in an article giving a foretaste of the forthcoming 'Yorkshire Grand Musical Festival'.

. . . The Birmingham Festival committee have kindly lent their *monstre ophicleide* (or keyed serpent) for the approaching grand occasion. This is the largest wind instrument ever invented; it was made at Lyons, France [in this case the most likely builder was Couturier], and is the only one in the kingdom. It is called the *monstre ophicleide*, in distinction to the *contra bass ophicleide*, from its size and the depth and power of its notes. It has been already received in this city by Dr. Camidge [organist of York Minster], and will form a splendid addition to the powerful and effective band engaged for the Festival, and a peculiar and attractive feature in the orchestra. Mr. Ponder is the gentleman engaged to perform upon this *ponderous* instrument (Y$^2$, 22.8.1835, 1).

*The Yorkshireman*'s review of the performance of Handel's *Messiah* in the Minster in its issue of 12 September 1835 noted that 'In the chorus "Let all the Angels", we particularly observed the great aid afforded by that powerful and deep-toned instrument, the monster ophicleide, which was well played by Mr. Ponder.' The orchestra list also shows the presence of two bass ophicleides, played by Thurmston of London and Tuckwell of Blackburn, as well as four serpents (see page 112 above). Significantly the leaders of the orchestra, the principal viola and Ponder were accorded the privilege of having 'Mr.' placed before their names in the programme book. Later in the year Prospère performed on a monster ophicleide at the Hanover Square Rooms, London, where the account implies that it was the original instrument used by Ponder since it was described as having been specially made for the Birmingham Music Hall.

Fig. 3.5. Prospère and his giant ophicleide, as shown in the *Illustrated London News,* 24 June 1843.

Fig. 3.5 shows the depiction of Prospère and his instrument that stood above a lengthy article on the man and his music in the *Illustrated London News* of 24 June 1843. This was headed:

THE "GIANT" OPHICLEIDE, WITH A NOTICE OF MONS. PROSPERE.

. . . let not our readers imagine that the instrument our artist has placed in the hands of M. Prospere is exaggerated in size, such being in truth about the relative proportions of himself and the gigantic ophicleide manufactured expressly for the purposes of the Birmingham Music Hall. When seen the other day by the audience at the Hanover Square Rooms slowly ascending, as it were from out of the floor, among the gentlemen of the orchestra, considerable consternation arose, some imagining that, as steam is now made to do everything, they were about to witness a novel application of its powers to the manufacture of "sweet sounds" by means of some machine of which the funnel was the first part introduced to their notice. But when Prospere stepped forward, and, boldly grasping the brazen pillar, proved that one small mouth could bring out its mighty tones, merriment and delight took the place of surprise, and perhaps dismay.

The powers of the ophicleide have been so fully illustrated in the metropolis and the principal cities of our country by the subject of this notice that we will now quit the instrument and address ourselves to the man . . .

. . . he has now been about two years and a half in England, and those who have the pleasure of knowing him would be loath that he should quit us. Few would imagine, on seeing that grave face in the full blow of its seriousness, when just about to commence a solo, what a man of mirth, and "quips and cranks", and all sorts of bedevilment lies beneath. As composers shall hereafter enable him to unfold the powers of the ophicleide, so greater popularity will be in store for him as an artist; as a man, his popularity is only bounded by the limit of his acquaintance ($I^1$, 24.6.43, 442).

In 1833 an account in the Parisian *Revue musicale,* which had originally appeared in *Courier de Lyon,* referred to the use of an ophicleide in place of the organ at Saint-Nizier, Lyons, commenting: 'It is a strange thing and truly fantastic, the sounds offered by this *monster* instrument, which is no more than seven feet in height and is armed with nine enormous keys, nonetheless easily operated by the player's fingers. It provides the band with new possibilities, and the modern school could draw on the unforeseen effects of this double-bass of wind instruments' (R[5], VII, 46, 372). Morelot, who disapproved of the ophicleide in church, was particularly critical of the policy at Saint-Nizier, '. . . where, not content with the normal dimensions of this instrument, they have intentionally constructed an edifice . . .' (M[39], 133).

The French *pied* (foot) of the time measured 324 mm, so the height of this instrument was some 2268 mm: the size of a true monster ophicleide (see Fig. 3.5)—and indeed it is described as being both a 'monstre' and a double bass instrument. The first reference to the monster ophicleide in England, just two years after the French account, was to an instrument said to have been made in Lyons for the Birmingham Festival. Were two monster ophicleides made in Lyons, one for local playing (where the effect was so exceptional as to merit a report in a journal published in the capital itself) and the other for Birmingham? Or was the instrument one and the same, built and used in Lyons, perhaps proved there in liturgical performance, and then sold to the Birmingham Festival? Sadly, it—or they—seems no longer to exist.

At Drury Lane in 1850 M. Lerey played the contrabass ophicleide in the first performance of Jullien's *Great Exhibition Quadrille*. When Jullien went to the United States in 1853 he held his own great exhibition—of the 'World's Largest Ophicleide' in  a shop-window on Broadway as publicity for his concerts. One wonders if it was the instrument made by Boston manufacturer E. G. Wright. He was in business from 1842 to 1871 and  his contrabass ophicleide was mentioned in the catalogue of the Chickering Exhibition in 1902, although by that time its whereabouts were unknown.  The last recorded contrabass seems to have been designed by Julien Tollot with ten keys and one valve and made by Halary around 1858. Morley-Pegge (M[41], 5.40, 172) illustrates an *ophicléide monstre* in F in the Paris Musée de la Musique with eight keys, a piston-valve giving a drop of a semitone in place of the usual B key and a mass of additional tubing leading from the mouthpiece. Alongside it he shows one of Couturier's instruments, patented in 1853, a bass ophicleide with six keys and one rotary-valve which is a useful indicator of scale. Giampiero (G[13], II, 811) refers to a 'contra-ophicleide' in F made by Červený in 1840, which was probably valved. For details of this and other valved ophicleides see pages 213-20 below.

The presence of the monster ophicleide in a performance of Handel's *Messiah* emphasises the lack of adherence to the score which prevailed not only at the great British music festivals but even in the capital and in European countries where a more enlightened approach might have been expected. Reporting on a performance of Beethoven's *Missa Solemnis* by the Philharmonic Society directed by Costa, the *Illustrated London News* of 9 May 1846 boasted: 'Our band was far superior [to that at Bonn] . . . The brass at Bonn was quite a failure . . . But our ophecleide [sic.] and trombones were magnificent . . .' ($I^1$, 306). On 1 August 1846 the same periodical previewed performances of the *Missa Solemnis* and the premiere of Mendelssohn's *Elijah* at the Birmingham Festival, stating that there would be three ophicleides in the orchestra on these occasions ($I^1$, 78). Later in the year (12 December 1846) a review of Mendelssohn's *St Paul* at the Vienna Music Festival referred to the presence of 'trombones, ophicleides, & c., 12' ($I^1$, 378).

*The ophicleide in Europe and America*

The ophicleide was widely used in France, England, Italy, Spain and the United States. There was an awareness of its existence throughout most of Europe, as the Romanian *oficleid* and Russian *ofikleíd* testify (in both cases probably through Italian influence). Kenyon de Pascual points out that the name of the instrument caused problems for Spanish speakers ($K^{12}$, 142). From the early variant *ofixlier* it progressed through *ofigle* to the final version *figle*. She cites iconographic evidence of the instrument's being used in a procession in Barcelona in 1828, and there is an official record of the appointment of a player to the Royal Chapel in 1830 specifically for the funeral service of the King of Naples. Two *ofigles* were present at the memorial service for Fernando VII in 1834. There are also extant a manuscript copy of a partial translation into Spanish of Gobert's tutor (published by Halary c. 1823) and also manuscript band music. The first trombone teacher at the Madrid Conservatory, Domingo Broca, was also an ophicleidist, but the Barcelona Conservatory had an ophicleide class as late as 1882. An 1842 guide to Barcelona lists two professional ophicleidists, and there were two players in the orchestra of the Teatro Real in Madrid in 1850. However, in his *Escuela de Composición* (1870) Hilarió states that by that time the ophicleide was rarely used in bands.

Kenyon de Pascual also refers to the numerous cathedral chapter records from the 1830s and later which contain ophicleide references. There is evidence that some players had been army musicians, such as Mariano Tafall, appointed to Burgos cathedral in 1836, and the first ophicleide player from the garrison in Tuy who was appointed to the cathedral in 1843. Here a *bombardino* (euphonium) had been acquired by 1876. At Valladolid cathedral the musical establishment was reorganised in 1843, the second organist's post going to the first dulcian, who also played ophicleide and violin. A funeral march composed for the cathedral by Joaquín Piña includes an ophicleide alongside buccins. The ophicleide replaced the dulcian at Segovia cathedral in 1854, where on some special occasions voices were accompanied by organ and ophicleides. When Alfonso XII ascended the throne in 1875 the *Te Deum* was sung there accompanied by ophicleides only.

The ophicleide lingered into the twentieth century in Spain, with a part in the Mass composed for the Royal Chapel in 1900 by Pablo Hernández, another in Celestino Vila's *Veni Creator* composed for Segovia cathedral in 1907, and a decision by the chapter of Palencia cathedral the following year that if no bassoonist could be found an ophicleide should be acquired. Gonzalo Castrillo Hernández, the choirmaster in 1920, composed Easter music including ophicleide, while a *Vidi acquam* for three voices composed by B. Aguilera Gil for Burgo de Osma cathedral also included the instrument. In response to Kenyon de Pascual's incredulous enquiry, Juan José de Mur, composer of a *Salve Regina* for Huesca cathedral in 1986 explained that the *figle* part it contained simply implied any bass brass instrument!

The majority of ophicleides used in the country seem to have been imported from France, although José Ramis of Madrid was listed as the maker of a range of brass instruments of which this was one. In her researches, Kenyon de Pascual has found only eight extant ophicleides in Spain.

The instrument was rarely found in Germany. In 1827 the composer Maurice Hauptmann, then a member of the orchestra in Kassel, was totally unaware of the nature of the ophicleide specified by Rossini in his *Siege of Corinth*: the part was played on trombone. Sixteen years later there was still no ophicleide in the important orchestral centres of Berlin, Brunswick, Hanover and Mannheim. They existed, however, in Hamburg and Darmstadt—well played, too. Leipzig possessed an 'abject brass instrument masquerading under that name'. In addition to being pitched in the unfortunate key of B it had 'practically no tone . . . so was declared null and void' ($B^{28}$, 47 et seq).

The lack of keyed ophicleides in Gemany was certainly not the result of a lack of awareness of the instrument's existence. The influential firm of Schott, long-established in Mainz, regularly referred to the instrument in the columns of its journal *Caeciliá*. In 1827 this included a French language fingering-chart for nine-keyed ophicleide (see page 161 below), in 1828 a description of the instrument was printed ($C^1$, 34, 1828, 130) and in 1829 Schott's nine-key 'Pariser Modell' in brass or copper was advertised ($C^1$, 39, 1829, 12).

The ophicleide was also found in the United States, where the first maker is thought to have been Edward Torrins of New York, about 1835 (G$^{24}$, 158). George Warren, of Weston, Massachusetts, paid thirty-two dollars for an ophicleide in 1842, playing it in the town band and Unitarian church until about 1850, one of many exponents in New England. Raphael R. Triay, leader, bought the U.S. Marine Band an 'Oficlayde' on 13 June 1849 for thirty dollars (K$^{14}$, 57). The ophicleide may have travelled there via Ireland as there exists a specimen made in Dublin in 1829, the year William Ponder was still described in the London Oratorio Concerts orchestra as 'serpent'. The keyed bugle was sent across the Atlantic by Dublin makers prior to its being made in the U.S.A. about 1825 and Morley-Pegge suggests that the ophicleide may also have reached England by way of Ireland.

It was soon found in army bands, but remained with the British military for a shorter time than it stayed in the orchestra. The instrument was fragile, with delicate key-work and extremely thin walls. Farmer gives the instrumentation of 'an ordinary cavalry regiment' band (citing the 4th Light Dragoons c. 1842) as two horns, five trumpets, three cornets, keyed bugle, three trombones, ophicleide and timpani (F$^5$, 114-155). In 1848 the Grenadier Guards stores list mentions two ophicleides and a 'bombardono'. The 1850 lists remarks that a former ophicleidist had transferred to bass tuba. However, Turner prints a striking coloured plate of a 'Bandsman, 93rd Foot with ophicleide 1850' in Highland dress (T$^{15}$, pl. II).

French infantry bands retained two ophicleides alongside their four valved *saxhorns contrebasses*, even after the reforms of 1845. Details of the bands of the Garde Nationale given in an 1836 directory (P$^{19}$, 84-96) indicate the contribution the instrument made to French military music of the time:

*I$^{ere.}$ Légion:* six ophicleides (Buttry, Galême, Lebeau, Maurage with amateurs Dunand and Lance).

*II$^{e.}$ Légion:* three ophicleides (Becherias, Divoire, Guillon (amateur) with the great Dieppo on trombone).

*III$^{e.}$ Légion:* four ophicleides (Garré, Pavart, Sault (amateur), Aussondon (*quinte*).

*IV$^{e.}$ Légion:* five ophicleides (Caussinus, Leudet, Marchand, Mutel, Obez).

*V$^{e.}$ Légion:* one ophicleide (Mongin, the first ophicleidist (see page 161 below)).

*VI$^{e.}$ Légion:* four ophicleides (Guillon, Lebrun and two amateurs, Mutel, Cognet).

*VII$^{e.}$ Légion:* four ophicleides (Charramond, Garré, Marsaux, Dunand).

*VIII$^{e.}$ Légion:* one ophicleide (Dayet).

*IX$^{e.}$ Légion:* three ophicleides (Arnault, Dunand, Marche).

*X[e.] Légion:* six ophicleides (Bernard (amateur), Butry, Cacheleux, Dayet, Henricet, Leclus).

*XI[e.] Légion:* six ophicleides (Crozier, Caussinus, Duzart and three amateurs: France, Husson and Moreaux).

*XII[e.] Légion:* five ophicleides (Bossus (amateur), Bruyas, L. Maurage, Seyder, Vallod).

*Légion à cheval:* (two bass ophicleides, Larsillière and Limberger; one *quinte*, Reinard).

Appearing on the scene at the time of a decline in the number of European wind ensembles, for social and political reasons, the ophicleide signally failed to fulfil any sort of role in the civilian wind band. While Stoneham, Gillaspie & Clark (S[40]) can muster twenty references to the serpent, the ophicleide scores a risible total of four, one of which probably does not refer to the keyed instrument. An ophicleide was included in the French composer Antoine-Edouard Batiste's *Symphonie militaire* of 1845 (along with flute, two oboes, two clarinets, two horns, two bassoons, trumpet and trombone); there are solos for horn, cornet and clarinet with accompaniment for two clarinets, bassoon and ophicleide by Prince Michele Enrico Francesco Vincenzo Paolo Carafa di Colobrano (born Naples 1787, died Paris in 1872); and a part in the Parisian Louis François Dauprat's *Solo de Cor* (solo horn, two clarinets, bassoon, ophicleide). In *Cycle Symphonique Nr. 6* 'Elégie' by Hippolyte Chelard (1789-1861) it joins a flute, three horns, three trombones, two harps, percussion, two cellos and a double bass.

In 1989 the horn-player and musicologist Chris Larkin discovered in the Bibliothèque Nationale the *Nonetto en ut mineur* by Félicien-César David (1810-1876) which is scored for two cornets, four valved horns, two trombones and ophicleide. This significant work, composed in 1839, is in four movements and lasts twenty minutes in performance. Larkin deals with it in some detail, including music examples, in his article in *Historic Brass Society Journal*, V (L[3], 192-202). He has also edited a number of quartets by Joseph Forestier (1815-1881) which are scored for two cornets, Eb saxotromba and ophicleide. Johann Wenzel Kalliwoda's *Six Pièces d'Harmonie pour Musique militaire* (c. 1845) is for large wind band, including both ophicleide and bombardon. Born in Prague and dying in Karlsruhe, it is probable that his understanding of the ophicleide was as a valved rather than as a keyed bass.

There were ophicleides in English brass bands, shown by the Burton Constable Contest (see page 130 above), the two present in the Bramley Band in Yorkshire by

1830 (L[17], 96), and the famous 1860 photograph of Besses o' th' Barn Band reproduced by Baines (B[3], pl. XIV, 1) and elsewhere. Lomas points out that he has found no evidence of ophicleides in brass bands in the south of England. It must have been a rare treat for locals, then, when in 1860 the Crystal Palace Brass Band Contest massed band concert included 133 ophicleides in addition to 155 Eb basses and two BBb basses. In that same year British Patent 2967 of 3 December 1860 for brass wind instruments was taken out by G. Macfarlane, W. E. Newton and R. Carte. This included an ophicleide, keyed bugle and serpent in ophicleide shape with all keys open-standing; movable bells, to throw the sound in any direction; a mute 'to effect echoes and swells': a disc or two perforated plates 'which may be changed in position for the production of diminuendos or crescendos'. The normal method of achieving these effects through changing breath velocity seems to have been overlooked by the inventors in their commitment to technological wizardry.

Berlioz realized that the ophicleide did not blend well enough with trombone tone to be used regularly as an independent lowest part, but should preferably double the lowest at the octave (but cf. Ex. 8.2). He considered it 'excellent for sustaining the lowest part of massed harmonies'. In the higher range it was agile, but less so in the lower, and staccato passages were 'scarcely practicable in fast tempos . . . the sound of [the] low notes is rough', he added, 'but in certain cases, under a mass of brass instruments, it works miracles. The highest notes are of a ferocious character which has not yet been utilized appropriately. The medium range, especially if the player is not skilled, recalls too closely the tone of the serpent and cornett; I believe that it should rarely be used without the cover of other instruments' (B[25], 227). When revising the *Symphonie fantastique* he ameliorated the quality of the poorer notes by specifiying one ophicleide in C and another in Bb.

In practice, Berlioz obviously considered that the most useful contribution the ophicleide could make was to strengthen the bass in louder passages. A dynamics count of all the works in which he used the instrument gives the following results:

TABLE 3.2. OPHICLEIDE DYNAMICS IN BERLIOZ'S WORKS

| *ppp* | 4 | *mf* | 53 |
|-------|-----|------|------|
| *pp*  | 41  | *f*  | 196 |
| *p*   | 110 | *ff* | 427 |
| *mp*  | 0   | *fff*| 1 |

Listeners were in general more complimentary about the tone of the ophicleide than that of the serpent. Some delighted comments were expressed on Prospère's playing which put into perspective silly remarks like 'Mr. Balfe has added an enormous ophicleide to the band [Drury Lane] which absolutely blows one out of the house' (S[7], 46). The instrument seems mainly to have upset writers on orchestration like our sensitive Evans who resorts to the inevitable pastoral analogy and calls it a 'chromatic bullock'; and Kling, who in 1902 wrote '. . . it has gradually and justly been put aside, as its croaking, unmusical and false tones are, to say the least, quite disagreeable . . . as a solo instrument it would be quite disgusting' (K[16], 158). Forsyth linked the ophicleide (which he called 'a sort of musical hobgoblin') with the keyed bugle as being 'shockingly defective in intonation' (F[19], 174). Adolphe Sax is another on record as having a low opinion of the ophicleide. His statement that 'The Ophicleide, for example, which reinforces the trombones, produces such an unpleasant sound that it cannot be used indoors because one cannot modify the tone' appears perverse, until put into its context: French Patent 3226 of 21 March 1846 for the saxophone.

The ophicleide invariably pleasantly surprises those who hear it for the first time. It is not easy to be objective about timbre, but perhaps a baritone with a modicum of alto saxophone to round off the edges and add to the fulness of tone might be an appropriate description. It responds well to being played with a low breath pressure, which makes it easy to understand why it superseded the serpent in accompanying plainsong. With an increased breath velocity the bulk of its notes can be very positively produced, although owing to the presence of some pitches with dubious intonation (particularly at the top of the lowest octave) the player needs to be able to devise alternative fingerings where necessary to avoid a dull tone. There is no doubt that some adverse comments resulted from those who heard ophicleides being overblown, resulting in a particularly unpleasant hard, bloated sound. However, the ophicleide became one of the most familiar instruments to those living in western Europe and the United States in the mid- to late nineteenth century. About 1852 Henry Mayhew was informed that 'opheicleides' were introduced into the English street bands 'about ten years ago . . . and saxhorns about two years since' (M[23], 521). There were also mechanical ophicleidists like that in a 'London Street Organ', where it is pictured as one of six automata wearing Chinese hats (I[1], 19.12.46, 397). And right up to the middle of the twentieth century the cover of *Punch* showed an angelic ophicleidist, puzzling those who came to the journal long after the instrument had disappeared from the musical scene (Fig. 3.8).

*Methods for ophicleide*

Although the period during which the ophicleide was in normal use was short—like canals and railways, a good idea was overtaken by a better idea soon after it appeared—there is striking testimony to its widespread adoption in the number of published methods. The impression is given that there may sometimes have been an urgent need for pedagogical material for the ophicleide as more than a few of the following methods are substantially copies of each other. The instrument (called by Christopher Monk 'a high-tech serpent') appeared at a time of increasing general wealth, active attempts to promote literacy, and a spectacular spread in the availability and performance of musical material resulting from a number of technological and sociological stimuli. The technical skills needed to build an ophicleide were to be matched by increasing musical skills that would contribute towards the gradual improvement in performance standards still taking place today.

Of the authors, only Cornette and Joseph Caussinus (an acknowledged virtuoso) are known to have played ophicleide. They both also compiled methods for other instruments and were obviously well-informed musicians, Cornette also organist of St Sulpice and l'hôtel des Invalides, Caussinus teaching instruments other than brass. Frédéric Berr (a clarinettist) was the first director of the Gymnase Musical Militaire, where Caussinus taught. Clodomir, whose real name was Pierre-François Mathieu de Borrit, was a cornet-player who also compiled several other instrumental methods. Cam and Kastner produced numerous others. Cam played in the orchestras of the Théâtre Italien and Opèra Comique, but his instrument is not known. Schiltz was another cornet-player who also compiled a serpent method. Boscher and Guichard's ophicleide works form part of their band methods. Th. Garnier's work deals only with valved ophicleides and was compiled with both Périnet valves and Berliner-Pumpen in mind. Kastner's includes a section on 'ophicléide à très pistons ou bombardon'. There is a copy of an Italian version of Kastner's work in the Biblioteca Musical de la Diputació de Barcelona (P[8,] I, 204). The French language fingering-chart published by B. Schott's Söhnen of Mainz as part of *Caeciliá* for 1827 is an interesting curiosity. Like many publications of its kind, this journal carried a great deal of advertising for its owners, who were not only also publishers of music but instrument makers and retailers with branches in Paris, London and Antwerp. There are indications that it may have been copied from the plates forming part of Halary's original French patent of 1821.

Ashdown & Parry [pub.], *Chromatic Scale for Ophicleide*, London, c.1860.

Asiolo, B., *Transunto dei pricnipj elementari di musica compilati dal celebre m°. B. Asioli & breve metodo per ophicleide e cimbasso*, [see M[28], Figs. 5 & 6], Bertussi, Milan, [1825].

Berr, F. & J. L. V. Caussinus, *Méthode complète d'ophicléide*, [Maissonnier, cat. 842], Paris, n.d.

Bertini, A., *New system for Learning, and Acquiring Extraordinary Facility on, All Musical Instruments* [includes fingering-charts for various instruments], Longman, London, 1830, 1837; 1849 as *Phonological System* . . .

Bonini, G., *Nuovo metodo per ofichleide* [sic.] *o bombardone* [deals only with the valved ophicleide], [MS.], 1888.

Boscher, A., *Méthode de ophicléide en sib, à 9, 10 et 11 clefs (extrait de la méthode générale d'ensemble)*, Paris, 1875.

Cam, E., *Méthode pour l'ophicléide basse et pour l'ophicléide alto*, Paris, 1868.

Capelli, G., *Metodo elementare per oficleide o bombardone*, Paoletti, Florence, n.d.

Caussinus, J. L.V., *Solfège-méthode pour l'ophicléide basse, en 2 parties*, Paris, 1843.

Clodomir, P., *Méthode élémentaire pour Ophicléide*, Paris, 1836.

Cornette,V., *Méthode d'ophycléide alto et basse*, Paris, 1835.

Dodworth, A., *Dodworth's Brass Band School* [includes fingering-charts for 'C Ophecleide' and 'Bb Ophecleide', reproduced in G[6], 2], New York 1853.

Foraboschi, G. (M.P.S.R.), *New and Complete Tutor for the Ophicleide* ['with Scales, Exercises, &c.'], D'Almaine, London, by 1839.

Frosali, G. B., *Oficleide in fa* [Metodi popolari per strumenti a fiato], Braccialini, Florence, n.d.

Garnier, Th., *Méthode élémentaire et facile d'ophicléide à pistons ou à cylindres* [deals only with the valved ophicleide], Paris, 1844.

Gobert, A., *Méthode pour l'ophicleide basse* [6[ème] partie of his method for various instruments, published by Halary], Paris, c. 1823.

Guichard, M., *École de fanfare* [a brass band method with a separate volume for each instrument], Paris, c. 1865.

Hartmann, *Méthode pour l'ophicléide basse et alto* [Aulagnier, cat. A.A.476], Paris, c.1845.

Héral, A., *Méthode d'ophicléide, contentant les principes de musique, ceux de l'instrument, les gammes, 24 leçons, 12 duos* [Cartroux], Lyons, n.d.

——*Méthode pour ophicléide à neuf, dix & onze clés*, [Kelmer] Paris, n.d.

Kastner, J. G., *Méthode élémentaire pour l'ophicléide*, Paris, 1845.

——*Metodo elementare per Officleide, seguito d'esercizi e varj pezzi aggradevoli*, Lucca,

Milan, [1849].

Palazzi, E., *Metodo per bombardone servibile anche per l'officleide, pelittone, contrabbasso e basso-d'armonia in do,* Lucca, Milan [1853].

Paoli, F., *Metodo progressivo per oficleide o bombardone,* Lucca, Milan [1866].

Ricordi [pub.], *Scala cromatica e sue posizioni per Basso d'armonia, ossia Opikleide,* Ricordi, Milan [1832].

Schiltz, *Grande méthode d'ophicléïde basse et d'ophycléïde quinte à l'usage des musiciens de la garde nationale* [Gambaro, cat. 125], Paris, n.d.

——trs. Merrick, *Tutor for the Ophicleide (Bass and Alto)* [No. 12 of Cock's & Co's Modern tutors for Wind instruments], London, 1853.

Schott's, B. [pub.], 'Ophiclëide ou basse d'harmonie' [fingering-chart for nine-key ophicleide with French text] in *Caeciliá,* 34, Mainz, 1827.

Steiger, *Méthode élémentaire et graduée d'ophicléïde* [Schoenberger], Paris, n.d.

——*Metodo elementare e graduato di officleide contenente i principj di musica, l'intavolatura, le scale, esercizj, studj, arie e duetti d'opere favorite,* Ricordi, Milan [1844].

# THE MUSIC

The ophicleide's first appearance (which few can actually have seen) was at the Paris Opéra amongst the stage band in Spontini's short-lived opera *Olimpie,* in the company of four horns, eight trumpets and three trombones. It was played by M. Mongin (presumably he who was to take out French Patent 4636 of 19 October 1849 'to make instruments chromatic or non-chromatic at will') on 22 December 1819—two years before it was patented. It took some years to become totally accepted by French composers and some sections of the press reacted in a markedly negative way. 'The invasion of brass instruments of all sorts and sizes has begun to upset the balance and tone of the basses even at the Opéra, where they are smothered by the ophicleides and trombones', fulminated the *Revue musicale* in 1827 (W[30], 469). Nine years later, the only Parisian theatre orchestra to admit to including ophicleide was the Opèra Comique, where it was played by M. Mutel, although the orchestra of the Gymnase Musical had three trombones and ophicleide (M. Dayet) (P[19], 76). The low brass of the (symphony) orchestras of the Académie royale de Musique and Concerts Musard apparently comprised four trombones, though it is possible that one or more of the players may have doubled on ophicleide, or the management may simply have listed all the low brass as trombonists. Mutel would not have found the 'Ophycléïde' part in Hérold's *Zampa* (produced at the Opéra Comique in 1831) demanding. Apart from the overture (largely in unison with 'Trombonne 3') it plays only seventy-nine bars. Even here the lowest part tends to be given to the third trombone. French opera scores during the 1830s frequently include a note like that in Meyerbeer's *Robert le diable*: "L'Ophyclé ïde (dans toute l'opera) toujours avec le 3ᵉ Trombone, toutes les fois, qu'il n'y aura pas le mot *solo*' [the ophicleide (throughout the opera) always in unison with the third trombone except where marked *solo*]. Waldteufel's *España* includes a bb in unison with the first trombone above the third trombone.

The ophicleide generally took over the functions of the serpent in French churches during the nineteenth century, sometimes maintaining the objectional habits developed by serpentists. Stéphen Morelot, in his article 'Du vandalism musical dans les églises' (M³⁹, 133), complains about ophicleidists in Troyes accompanying the chant with 'roulades of all sorts, diatonic and chromatic scales, finally following-up with the most foreign sounds to the key of the piece which overlap, echo, fighting against verve ['luttent de verve'] and daring to make the singing unintelligible and the listener suffer'. In 1849 William Kelly wrote of 'the eternal boo-boo of a wretchedly-played ophicleide' in French churches (H²⁷, 12)).

In 1850 no less an authority than Fétis considered the relationship of the various ophicleides to the *cor à clefs* (keyed bugle). Having recommended the bugle as an instrument better able to cope with the weaker notes of the clarinet, he suggested that the various keyed bugles along with alto and bass ophicleides formed a 'complete system of instruments of the same genre with matching sonorities'. For this reason he also recommended the introduction of a tenor ophicleide, since: 'As for the use of the bass ophicleide to play tenor parts, this is barbarous; for the big tone of the instrument is not suitable for this intermediate part; the volume of the tube must be proportionate to the character of the voice'. Fétis also correctly considered it wrong to give the same part in bands to ophicleide, serpent and Russian bassoon, or (as was apparently often the practice in military bands) alto ophicleide and alto trombone, again because of their divergent timbres (F¹², 345-6).

By and large, the Spanish shared French conceptions of the ophicleide. The instrument assumed the function previously carried out by the bassoon in Spanish churches, where the serpent had rarely, if ever, been used to support plainsong (see references in the Bibliography to articles by Kenyon de Pascual). Sacheverall Sitwell, clearly knowing of the serpent's historic role in France, found himself in great organological difficulties when he tried to identify the instrument that he witnessed participating in the liturgy at the cathedral of La Seo, Zaragoza. It was  probably an ophicleide, but if the reference to piston valves is accurate it might equally have been a tall, thin euphonium on the French model familiar in Spain; the euphonium is known to have been used in Spanish churches (see pages 93, 153 above). The date of Sitwell's exciting experience is not given, but as he first visited Spain in 1919 he is presumably describing practices some time after World War I.

> . . . you heard the procession advancing towards you, looming larger and louder at every step . . . while, immediately behind them, came a man in a frock coat holding a brass instrument, a trombone or bass clarionet [sic.], upon which, every now and then, he blew a low, rumbling note. The visual image was that of a man in a frock coat blowing a conch or a seashell, until you caught the brass glitter of the instrument and the telescope movement of the piston valves . . . At a moment when the whole procession was hidden behind the *coro* it blew again . . . It is an effect made by Berlioz in certain moments of his *Grand Messe des Morts* . . . I cannot think otherwise than that Berlioz must have heard this very effect in his childhood in some village church in his native Dauphiné where the sexton and the gravedigger, both posts in one, blew, as well, the 'serpent' . . . A note blown by a devil, not an angel . . . and at the mock day of Judgement staged by an anti-Christ before he is interrupted by the real One . . . Again and again it sounded. The procession came past in front of us on its last turn of the cathedral. The man in the frock coat lifted the 'serpent' to his lips; the shuddering, forlorn note died back against the ceiling . . . the man in the frock coat blew the last note on the 'serpent' and the chanting ended . . . (S[26], 132-33)

Although unclear about the instrument he had stumbled across, Sitwell points with startling clarity to the chilling paradox of a *serpent*—once evicted from the Garden of Eden—flagrantly performing in church.

The ophicleide also appeared in English church bands. Woodhouse found references to five ophicleides in Cornwall and prints a photograph of Tregajorran choir and band about 1860 in which both the incoming ophicleide and the outgoing serpent are present (W[26], 47). An ophicleide was also on duty with the Hellesveor choir when in 1874 it sang Christmas carols throughout the night (W[26], 92). Macdermott refers to ophicleides being played in Penshurst church, Kent (by James Payne, early nineteenth century); Seend, Wiltshire, c. 1830; and Winkburn, Nottinghamshire, c. 1850. An 1850 entry in the diary of the incumbent at Rockhampton, Gloucestershire, reads: 'Spoke to Woodward about not playing the ophicleide which obliged Farmer Pinnell to go out of church' (M$^1$, 30-31). Ophicleide and serpent were found side-by-side in church at Winchester, Massachusetts, in the first half of the nineteenth century. After the American Civil War changes to musical practice were introduced along the lines of those which had driven the serpent from English churches. Organs replaced church bands and choirs as congregational and gospel singing were encouraged by ministers (K$^{18}$, 5).

Sometimes the pivotal ophicleide and incoming tuba were found side by side, as Berlioz remarked in 1843: 'Most modern scores include a part for either ophicleide or bass tuba, sometimes for both'. (Berlioz himself scored for both in several works, see Chapter X.) Jullien included both instruments in his 1850 *Concerts d'hiver* at Drury Lane.

The ophicleide was a valuable soloist. *Punch* wrote of Jullien in 1852:

> With ophicleides, cymbals and gongs
> At first thou didst wisely begin,
> And bang the dull ears of the popular throngs,
> As though 'twer to beat music in (P$^{24}$, xxiii, 260).

Jullien was not above adding four ophicleides to Beethoven's fifth symphony (1849) but it was all in the good cause of bringing the symphonic repertoire to a new public. He also performed 'Locke's celebrated music to Macbeth, with *Hecate* by Mons. Prospère on the ophicleide, *1st Witch* by Herr Koenig on the cornet, *2nd Witch* by Mons. Barret on the oboe, *3rd Witch* by Mons. Jancourt on the bassoon'. (The order of the soloists should be noted.) Prospère was one of Jullien's most valued players, although some correspondents of the *Musical World* did not approve of the ophicleide as a solo instrument.

Canny publishers quite often hedged their bets when issuing ophicleide solos. While Kummer's op. 62, *Variations for Ophicleide,* was clearly intended for solo ophicleide with piano accompaniment, Labitzky's *Scène et Bolero* (op. 288) is 'pour Euphonium ou Ophicleïde', and Demersseman's *Introduction et Polonaise,* 'pour Basson ou Ophicléïde en Ut'. Opportunities for players to spend happy evenings together were provided through the publication of works like the *Dix Duos pour deux Ophicleïdes* extracted from the *Méthode* compiled by Hartmann, 'Professeur au Conservatoire de Cracowie et membre de la Société Lyricale'. These works, and others of their ilk are largely unremarkable, their composers showing no particular awareness of the instrument's strong or weak points.

Despite his German nationality, Wagner's requests for ophicleide often imply the familiar French keyed version since most of them anticipated production in Paris. The lowest brass part in *Der Fliegende Holländer* (1841) may be played either on tuba or ophicleide for this reason. In September or October 1839 his aria for Bellini's *Norma* ('Norma il predesse'), also including ophicleide, was premiered at his benefit concert in Riga. This, too, was composed in the hope of interesting the Parisian musical establishment, but it was equally unsuccessful. There is another very demanding ophicleide part in *Rule, Britannia!*, composed in Königsberg and first performed in Riga during the winter of 1836-37. He sent the score to the London Philharmonic Society in 1837 but failed to make a favourable impression. The part in *Nikolay*, a *Volkshymn* composed to celebrate the birthday of Tsar Nicholas and first performed in Riga on 21 November 1837, may well have been for valve ophicleide. More details are given in Chapter XVI about Wagner and Verdi's use of ophicleide. Rossini's *Petite Messe Sollenelle*, which he rescored with orchestral accompaniment in 1869, and the *Messa da Gloria* of the student Puccini (1880) include parts for keyed ophicleide. The instrument stayed for a long time in Italian orchestras, although Verdi's feelings about its presence were unequivocal (see page 413 below).

In England Michael Balfe's opera *The Bohemian Girl* (Drury Lane, 1843) included ophicleide and eight years later it appeared more anonymously, playing the double bassoon part in the grave-digging scene in a production of Beethoven's *Fidelio* at Her Majesty's Theatre ($C^{10}$, 489). The English musical establishment certainly did not overlook this useful instrument. Sterndale Bennett included one in his 'pastoral' *The May Queen* (not serpent as has been stated elsewhere). This received its premiere under the composer's direction at the first Leeds Festival in 1858. Originally published by Kistner of Leipzig as *Die Mai-Königin*, opus 39, in 1860, a superior version was engraved by Novello in 1882. The ophicleide fulfils a number of useful roles in the work, functioning at times as strengthening for the bass trombone (which part could be played on tenor), sometimes as a contrabassoon, and at other times providing more general support by playing along with the double basses.

There was an ophicleide present in the Crystal Palace Orchestra until 1880 when Costa, whom we have seen to be somewhat conservative, still employed Alfred Phasey as the player. Offenbach's orchestra of 100 for his 1876 season at Gilmore's Gardens, New York, included a brass section of two cornets, three trombones and ophicleide.

On the evidence of the part for 'Ophicleide or Bass Tuba' in his *Overture di Ballo* (1888) Arthur Sullivan was more finely attuned to the instrument's capabilities than many of his contemporaries. It is scored between the trombones and 'Extra Bass Tuba (ad lib.)', covering a wide compass from B'♭ to e♭ with an unusually great expressive range. Here the monolithic approach typical of much of Berlioz's writing gives way to some delightful pianissimo quaver bass parts, quiet staccato rhythms reminiscent of Mendelssohn's woodwind writing in *A Midsummer Night's Dream Overture*, and yet includes a fortissimo low register rumbustious waltz accompaniment shared with the less-important 'Extra Bass Tuba'. Sullivan was not satisfied, however, and felt the need to move with the times. Writing to the Leeds Festival chorus master on 18 January 1888, prior to an anticipated performance, he states: 'The *contra fagotto* can play for the *serpent*, and the *tuba* (most important) for the *ophicleide*' (J[3], 264). He presumably had in mind the 1874 Festival when, under Costa, Samuel Hughes played ophicleide in the orchestra—and it is doubtful that any other player would have handled the part in *Di Ballo* with more skill. At the same event, however, Mendelssohn's *St Paul* was performed, and Hughes played the serpent part on ophicleide. Sullivan's anxiety to have this serpent part played on double bassoon is understandable, but it would have been more appropriate for an ophicleide rather than a tuba to contribute the lowest line of the brass section in *St Paul*, as at the premiere (see page 120 above). When the Royal Liverpool Philharmonic Orchestra recorded *Di Ballo* in 1968 I enjoyed the experience of playing the ophicleide part on euphonium, aiming to achieve the light tuba tone that Sullivan required.

Writing in 1885, Gevaert believed (correctly) that the ophicleide still remained in use in France (G[12], 265), although it was replaced in 1874 at the Paris Opéra, which it had entered in 1819. Parts like that given to it by Delibes in his ballet *Coppélia*, premiered there in 1870, are delightful, but totally unsuited to a large modern tuba (see Ex. 3.3). (A medium-size F tuba might be appropriate in modern performances.) In its 1878 catalogue the firm of Jérome Thibouville-Lamy still offered two distinctive types of ophicleide. The ten-keyed version cost forty-eight francs (the price also asked for an F tenor saxhorn), with the *nouveau modèle* at sixty-four francs; the eleven-keyed was seventy francs (*modèle du Conservatoire*, eighty francs; *nickelé* [nickel-plated] ninety-six francs). A three-valve F or E♭ contrabass saxhorn is shown in the catalogue for about the same price.

It comes as something of a shock to read the following in Banister's *Music* (1892); 'Several other brass instruments . . . are occasionally used in ordinary orchestras, as

Act I, No. 1, Valse.

*ff*

*en elargissant*

**Tempo I**

*ff*

**1.**   **2.**

Act II, No. 13

**Lento**

Tbns.

Oph. *p*

*pp*

*dim.*

Act II, No. 10   **Moderato**

Hns, Bsn

Oph.   [Soli]

*pp*

Delibes: *Coppélia*

the BASS-TUBA, the EUPHONIUM, &c. But the above specified [serpent and ophicleide] are those in most common use' (B[10], 229). Yet there are indications that Harry Barlow, the first distinguished British orchestral tubist, may have been appointed to his position in the Hallé Orchestra, Manchester in 1894 to play both ophicleide and tuba as he is shown as playing the former on 7 March 1895, possibly in two pieces from Massenet's *Scènes Pittoresques*. Only the death of Sir Charles Halle the following year, an interregnum when the orchestra was conducted by Sullivan among others, and the appointment of Hans Richter, who had banished the ophicleide from his London orchestra seven years earlier, firmly established the tuba there as the lowest of the brass.

Even in darkest Warrington, H. P. Hughes wrote in 1905 of 'the now almost extinct ophicleide . . .' (H[34], 14). It is interesting to note that while it was considered almost extinct in Warrington, in Dresden there may have been attempts in 1900 to revive it, according to a letter from Balakirev to Charles Malherbe published in *Revista musicale italiana* (January 1930). But this also may have been a different type of ophicleide . . .

Morley-Pegge, an extremely reliable source, refers to its final disappearance from the Couesnon catalogue in 1916. Couesnon themselves claim they made their last ophicleide in 1850. Some of their stock seems to have sat on the shelf for a long time. It is possible that elsewhere remaining devotees of the ophicleide were happily tootling away their declining years. Garofalo & Elrod print a wonderful photograph of George J. Wolfer, a George Bernard Shaw lookalike, with his ophicleide in 1917 (G[6], 66). A member of the Aurora Colony, Oregon, he may have been the oldest surviving player in the United States at the time.

## THE PLAYERS

Although in 1829 William Ponder was playing the serpent, five years later he played ophicleide in Westminster Abbey, along with Mr. Hubbard. In the same year he appeared at the Birmingham Music Festival. Ponder's name crops up regularly during the 1830s—as soloist in *The Death of Nelson*, for example. He was a familiar sight and sound at the great English music festivals, although the hardships of his chosen profession should not be underestimated. On the return journey to London from the Manchester Grand Musical Festival in 1836, for example, he was involved in a coach accident when the *Pevril of the Peak* overturned near Bedford, suffering arm injuries which prevented him from performing for a time. (M[53], 16.9.36, 12).

The account published in the *Gloucester Journal* of his death five years later while in the city for the Three Choirs Festival presents a vivid contrast to the spectacular funeral of the locally-famous Adam Westwell in 1859 (pages 175-6 below).

SUDDEN DEATH OF ONE OF THE PERFORMERS AT GLOUCESTER MUSIC MEETING.—On Sunday night [5 September 1841], Mr. Wm. Ponder, a performer on the ophicleide, died suddenly at the Marquis of Granby inn, Barton-street, at which inn he was lodging, having arrived in Gloucester from London, under engagement to perform at our Music Meeting. He had been ill, it seems, some time previously, but his disease, which was internal, had not assumed an immediately dangerous aspect, though it was of that nature which certainly rendered it necessary that he should abstain from the violent exertion of the lungs caused by performing on the above named instrument. He went to bed about half-past ten o'clock on Sunday night, but rose again in consequence of his cough being troublesome. On its becoming more easy he again went to bed in about an hour afterwards, when his cough returned with so much violence that Mr. Band, the landlord of the inn, went to his room and proposed to fetch a medical man to his assistance, to which Mr. Ponder assented, saying he thought he should be choked. Mr. Clutterbuck, surgeon, was accordingly called in, but death took place in a few minutes from the bursting of one of the blood vessels of the lungs, which produced suffocation. An inquest was held next day, before Thos. Bailey, Esq., coroner for this city, when the jury returned a verdict of died by the visitation of God (G[16], 11.9.1841, [3]).

A certain amount of Ponder's work was taken over by Prospère, the brightest light on the English ophicleide scene—as the distinguished critic Davison remarked, 'one of the stars of Jullien's orchestra'. Born Jean Prospère Guivier in 1814 at Vilna in Lithuania (his father had been taken prisoner by the Russians during the retreat from Moscow), he joined a French military band and later became a horn student at the Paris Conservatoire. Having taken up the ophicleide in the 1830s he appeared as soloist in Musard's Paris concerts. (Joseph Caussinus, born in 1806, and his colleague Peters, who was also a serpentist in the bands of the V[e]. and X[e]. Légion, Garde Nationale, formed the ophicleide section in 1837.) Prospère joined Jullien's first orchestra at the Jardin Turc and presumably came over to London with him and several of his musicians about 1840, although if that were so it did not prevent him from playing the part of Hecate on the ophicleide in

Musard's Drury Lane concerts version of Locke's *Macbeth* in the same year, a part he was to play for Jullien the following year (see page 164 above). Caussinus also appeared with both Jullien and Musard during their English tours, although unlike Prospère he preferred not to stay. Prospère was to be a featured soloist of Jullien's orchestras for many years, performing such items as *Rule, Britannia!* 'set forth from his leviathan instrument with a majesty and grace that no single one ever before equalled' (C[7], 46). And he could play quietly: he had, it was reported, 'subdued his giant instrument . . . to every shade of softness . . . Truly this gentleman's execution and power of subduing this normally obstreperous instrument passes all understanding' (I[1],10.12.42, 49). *The Illustrated London News* (6 December 1845), writing of Jullien, stated: 'He is supreme in brass . . . Prospère and Chipp [timpanist] are his attendant demons—they are his familiars' (I[1], 366).

By the mid-1830s the enormous number of ophicleide players in Paris demonstrated a significant demand for the instrument. Planque lists over twenty *professeurs* in 1836 (P[19], 258-67). Some of them doubled on trombone (for instance Marchal, Seyder, Davise and Pavart, who was first trombone at the Opéra), and Reinhart played both alto ophicleide and valved horn. Caussinus, who directed the ophicleide class at the Gymnase Musical Militaire in 1837, played at the Théâtre Italien and in two Garde Nationale bands. In a directory of 'Artistes pour bals et soirées' (P[19], 190-205) ten more ophicleidists are named, some doubling on cello and others on double bass. Drobert also played double bass and violin, Labalte double bass, bassoon and trumpet, Marchand violin. Amongst the five amateurs, Bossus doubled on serpent and trombone while Dunand and Bernard also played serpent. On the basis of the lists in Planque's directory, Paris in 1836 supported over sixty professional ophicleidists, and there were, of course, others elsewhere in France. In Colombes Poisson taught ophicleide, horn and trombone (amongst other instruments); Moreau, a Dijon piano-tuner, taught stringed instruments and ophicleide; in Orléans Vinceaux was the *professeur d'ophicléide*.

In 1846 Prospère appeared as soloist on a new instrument, the serpentcleide. When Jullien went on his American tour in 1853 he chose to stay in town (not a particularly wise decision as it turned out: M. Moirato's promenade concerts, at which he was one of the soloists, were a failure). Jullien took with him Samuel Hughes, once a member of the Cyfarthfa Brass Band, who was partnered in the U.S.A. by the American player Freising. Jullien's decision to present Hughes as one of the leading soloists in his orchestra were much appreciated by transatlantic audiences, particularly in the mammoth *American Quadrille* (L[7], 365). The Boston critic John Sullivan Dwight praised Hughes's contribution to Jullien's selection from *Don Giovanni* (which he thought overall to be a form of blasphemy), particularly when in 'the sublime and freezing harmonies of the ghost scene . . . those ponderous marble tones of Hughes's ophicleide spoke gravedly for the statue' (L[7], 373). Hughes also contributed spectactularly to *Les Huguénots* (L[7], 453, fn.). Although Prospère rejoined Jullien on his return, he still retained the connexion with the master showman and in *The Siege of Sebastopol* played the recitative representing a dying Zouave.

Morgans boasts that the Cyfarthfa Band had the three best ophicleide players in the country: Hughes, Coleman and Walker (M[37], 136). Coleman, who later emigrated to the United States, was solo ophicleide in the early 1850s, before Hughes. He reputedly made a 'paper ophicleide' notable for its soft tone (M[38], 138). This was probably made from papier-mâché rather than rolled-up copies of the *Merthyr Tydfil Advertiser*. When Hughes left, he recommended that John Walker be appointed to the solo chair. Walker was awarded the prize of a euphonium as performer of the best ophicleide solo at the Crystal Palace Contest in 1860, and died in 1890, in his sixty-ninth year, from 'affection of the throat' (B[55], 4.90, 167).

There can be no doubt that Hughes's playing was of a superior quality to that of most other English ophicleidists and his earnings far exceeded those of other known ophicleide players who, on the available evidence, mainly lived in modest circumstances, often close to barracks as army musicians. Alfred Phasey was living at 137 Cambridge Street, Pimlico, London in 1862 when his son Handel was born. Although he himself had been born in Pimlico on 19 February 1834, Cambridge Street was developed from 1842 until around 1860, so it is likely that Phasey was the original tenant. The area was initially considered 'an abode of gentility' where the houses had bathrooms, w.c.s and most families maintained one or two servants. However, by 1852 it was described as being 'prolific in loose women'. Phasey may have chosen to live near barracks as he was still in the Coldstream Guards in 1859 (M[16, 114]). (In 1887 the tubist and ophicleidist Guilmartin, an ex-Scots Guards euphonium-player, lived nearby at 118 Alderney Street (see page 377 below).)

In 1880, when the Hallé Orchestra performed Berlioz's *Symphonie fantastique* at St James's Hall in London to general acclaim, two local ophicleide players were engaged. C. Dannby lived at 44 Vincent Square, Westminster. This is close to Pimlico, and there is little doubt that Dannby also was a military bandsman living near barracks with the advantage of easy access to the West End. I. W. Horrocks lived at 3 Prospect Place, Trafalgar Road, Greenwich, the main road linking the

Royal Naval Schools on the west to Woolwich Road on the east. It traversed an area of tremendous contrasts, from the 180-acre park with its Wren buildings to a typical south London shopping street which in 1900 was the site of one of London County Council's first slum-clearance schemes. Its proximity to Woolwich Arsenal and the Royal Artillery barracks is likely to have been the reason for Horrocks's living there. Richard Hopkinson, who played ophicleide with the Hallé in the 1868-69 season, lived at 77 Clowes Street in the Manchester suburb of West Gorton. This area of mixed industry and terraced housing was close to Belle Vue Gardens, so he possibly succeeded Medina in its brass band. Medina himself lived at 38 Bedford Street in the working-class district of Hulme.

In contrast, Samuel Hughes's move in 1870 to Trentham House, 34 Avenue Road on the Mill Hill Estate, Acton's first select suburban development, was an indication of his comfortable circumstances. (The property cost £800, and he took out a £400 mortgage.) The road followed the line of Mill Hill Park Avenue which had been a prominent feature of the grounds of a previous house and was known locally as 'The Avenue'. This familiar reference in an account of Hughes in the local newspaper has led to his address's being given slightly inaccurately in some biographical accounts. Hughes was born the son of a bricklayer at Trentham, Staffordshire on 9 December 1823 and by 1844 was working as a china painter. By April 1852 he was a rail agent at Williams Town, Merthyr, playing for the Cyfarthfa Band, although his second son was baptised at Trentham parish church in 1855. Six years later he was established at 124 Camden Villas, Camden Road, London as 'professor of the Ophicleide'.

Weston refers to his commanding a fee of thirteen pounds a week for a three-month engagement with Jullien on the American tour of 1853 and being re-engaged at double that figure on his return (W[12], 4). At this time school teachers, clerks and lower-level managers earning between £150 and £300 a year were buying pianos and culture for their children (E[1], 71), while in 1865 Sterndale Bennett told a government committee that a suitable new director for the ailing Royal Academy of Music would need to be paid £1,000 per annum (E[1], 92). A classical concert fee of up to one guinea (£1.1s.) was paid to orchestral players almost to the end of the century, when it dropped to 15s, although principals were paid more (E[1], 142). By December 1885 Hughes was 'incapacitated from following his profession from the loss of teeth'. He supported his request for financial assistance from the Royal Society of Musicians with a letter from A. P. Robertson, L.D.S., a Glasgow dental surgeon who had regularly treated him 'during his stay in the North'. 'I am quite of the opinion that the difficulties in the way of his continuing to play any instrument which may necessitate pressure against the lips, or teeth, are altogether insuperable,' he wrote. By October 1886 Hughes was living at 1 Lansdowne Villas, Harlington, Middlesex and on 1 April 1898 he died at Three Mile Cross, near Reading of 'old age' (or, as the doctor told Hughes's son—still living in Acton at 5 Mill Hill Grove—of 'general decay'). His widow Martha was 'left totally unprovided for', with only 'a few shillings' and household furniture.

Remembered with affection by George Bernard Shaw in 1889 ('It seems only the other day that Mr. Hughes was playing "Oh, Ruddier than the Cherry". . . at Covent Garden') (S[24], 58), he and J. H. Guilmartin were the last eminent ophicleide-players in London. Guilmartin also often performed 'O, Ruddier than the Cherry', and is said to have 'played on the tuba mouthpiece to which he is accustomed'. He played for Sullivan in the Royal Aquarium Concerts in 1876 and was still shown as 'Professor of the Ophicleide' in the 1901 *Musical Directory*. Seven years earlier Hughes was ophicleide professor at the Guildhall School of Music, a post he is known to have held as early as 1881, a year after the school was founded. He occupied an identical position at the Royal Military School of Music, Kneller Hall and a photograph of him with Alfred Phasey (professor of euphonium) and Thomas Sullivan (father of Sir Arthur Sullivan, chief professor of clarinet, known also to have taught bombardon) is reproduced by Binns (B[40], pl. opp. 60).

The programmes of the Leeds Musical Festivals between 1858 and 1886 indicate the pattern of work for these distinguished players, with rehearsals on Monday and Tuesday and performances from Wednesday to Saturday. In 1858 Prospère played ophicleide in the premiere of Sterndale Bennett's *The May Queen* and also in Mendelssohn's *Elijah*. Samuel Hughes was ophicleidist at the 1874 Festival, playing the ophicleide part in Sullivan's *Di Ballo* and presumably the serpent part in Mendelssohn's *St Paul* (on ophicleide). He appeared again in 1877 for *Elijah*, in 1880 for *Elijah* and *The May Queen,* and in 1883 again for *Elijah*. (How many bars' rest he counted over the years is impossible to compute.) That year there was a ten per cent increase in fees. 'An excellent spirit was thus infused into the orchestral players' (S[31], 244). In 1886 a bass tuba was used for the first time, played by Felix A. Lee in *Elijah*, *St Paul* and (more appropriately) the overture to Wagner's *Die Fliegende Holländer* and the premiere of Sullivan's *The Golden Legend*. J. H. Guilmartin played bass tuba in 1889, in Mendelssohn's music to *A Midsummer Night's Dream*, and also Berlioz's *Damnation of Faust*, Brahms's *German Requiem*, the third act of Wagner's *Tannhäuser* and *The Golden Legend*.

Fig. 3.6. Part of a depiction of Jullien's orchestra performing the *National Quadrille* published in *Harper's Monthly Magazine*, New York, December 1853. Hughes and his ophicleide are shown in the background, with Winterbottom (trombone), Lütgen (cello), Bottesini (double bass) and Kœnig (cornet).

The original ophicleide player in the Hallé Orchestra, England's first permanent symphony orchestra, was Signor Angelo Medina, who was appointed in 1858 and stayed until his untimely demise on 13 January 1869 at the age of forty-seven. This occurred at Belle Vue Gardens, known to brass players mainly as the venue for the brass band contests held annually from 1853 until the closure of the Gardens (a zoo and amusement park) in 1982. It is likely that Medina was working there as a member of the professional brass band established in 1851. The death certificate shows the cause of his death as 'Disease of Liver', a condition not unknown amongst brass players. Medina played in Rossini's overture *Le Siège de Corinth* in the initial Hallé concert on 30 January 1858. During that first season, on 13 February, Mendelssohn's overture *A Midsumer Night's Dream* was performed. On 6 March 'The music to Shakspere's "Midsummer Night's Dream"', with Solo and Chorus' appeared again, this time presumably in the complete version. Samuel Hughes probably took part, as he performed an ophicleide solo in the same programme 'On Airs from "La Sonnambula" Arranged by Bottesini'. He returned on 24 April to delight Mancunians with his celebrated solo, 'O, Ruddier than the Cherry'.

The next season, on 22 September 1858, Medina himself appeared as a soloist, along with other orchestra members. The occasion was the performance of a 'Grand Selection: Robert le Diable—Meyerbeer (With Solos for Flute, Oboe, Clarinet, Bassoon, Violoncello, Cornet and Ophicleide, by Messrs. De Jong, Jennings, Grosse, Raspi, Vieuxtemps, Richardson and Medina)'.

Distinguished ophicleide players were not restricted to orchestras. Twenty miles north of Manchester, in Accrington, Adam Westwell died the following year. *The Accrington Free Press* (15 October 1859) stated that on the day of the funeral 'Abbey-street, Blackburn-road, and Church-street, were lined by a vast assemblage of persons, and a dull funeral haze overhung the town.' *The Blackburn Weekly Times* (8 October 1859) printed an account in which, in characteristic style, the name of the deceased (confirmed from his death certificate) was consistently mispelled:

FUNERAL OF THE LATE MR. ADAM WESTALL, MUSICIAN.—Mr. A. Westall, the well-known instrumentalist, expired on Tuesday, the 4th inst., in the thirty-sixth year of his age, after a lingering illness of several months. The disease from which the lamented gentleman has so long suffered, was a derangement of the nervous sytem, which had the effect of gradually impairing his mental faculties. The remains were interred at St. James' church, Accrington, on Saturday last. The funeral was one of the most solemn, but magnificent scenes, ever witnessed in this town. Not less than ten thousand persons [5-6,000 persons according to the *Free Press*] assembled around the church and lined the streets through which the mournful *cortége* had to pass. The far-famed Accrington band, accompanied by many whose names rank high in the musical profession, preceded the hearse from his residence to the church, playing the "Dead March in Saul" conducted by Mr. Geo. Ellis, of Blackburn. The sad ceremony was rendered the more affecting by the united choirs of St. James's, Christ Church, and Church Kirk performing that requiem-like anthem from the book of Job. But the most touching part of the proceedings was at the conclusion of the burial rites, when the band drew around the grave, and with tears trickling down their manly cheeks, paid their last musical tribute to the memory of their departed brother in harmony by playing the Hundredth Psalm. The effect may possibly be imagined, but language cannot describe it. The sobs of the multitude were heard between the trembling notes of the band. It may be truly said that the Accrington brass band will never look upon his like again. He was acknowledged to be the best ophecleidist in the country. He travelled fourteen years [*Free Press*: eight years] with Wombwell. May he rest in peace (B[41], 2).

The (professional) band of Wombwell's Menagerie had a high reputation, but it is not clear what took Westwell back to Accrington. In 1855 and 1858 Accrington Band won the national contest at Belle Vue, Manchester, and it was placed third in 1854 and 1856. *The Free Press* mentions that Westwell was a member of the band for nine years up to his death, and Aspin (A[19], 18) refers to his playing a greatly-applauded duet with George Ellis (cornet) after the 1855 contest. Westwell's tombstone in St. James's churchyard, Accrington, is the only one known to depict an ophicleide (Fig. 3.7).

Fig. 3.7
Adam Westwell's
memorial at St. James's
church, Accrington,
which shows an
ophicleide.

While Adam Westwell's fame was restricted to the Rossendale cotton towns, his contemporary, the Neapolitan ophicleidist Colosanti, built an international reputation, playing in concerts directed by Jullien and others. He also composed for his instrument, and a performance he gave of one of his compositions in Florence in 1853 caused some amazement. 'A piece for ophicleide in a concert could appear a marvel, and truly seemed like that to us, especially when listening to this instrument, which resembles the trunk of an elephant, producing smooth and melancholic sounds like a flute' ($I^3$, 13.4.53, 121). In 1855 Colosanti took part in the final concert of the Bordeaux Philharmonic Society's season, and was once again 'found marvellous on his instrument', playing with precision and passion ($I^3$, 28.4.55, 136). In 1858, shortly after a successful appearance in Leipzig, he died in Aix-la-Chapelle ($I^3$, 17.3.58, 88).

By the beginning of the twentieth century the ophicleide was considered defunct even in the city of its birth. Referring to the 'March to the Scaffold' in the 1900 Breitkopf version of Berlioz's *Symphonie fantastique* the editors, Malherbe and Weingartner, commented: 'As ophicleides are no longer met with in symphonic orchestras they have been replaced by tubas in C [Small French Tubas in c]. In the few passages where the notes lie too high for the tubas an exchange of notes had to be made between these and the trombones' ($M^9$, xxxvii).

In London, *The Descriptive Catalogue . . . of the Royal Military Exhibition* (1891) remarked that tuba and euphonium had replaced the ophicleide. It seemed the end of a thousand years of instruments with cup-mouthpieces and side-holes.

# THE OPHICLEIDE REVIVAL

However, ophicleides continued to make sporadic appearances, sometimes in unlikely contexts like Royal Military School of Music concerts and the 1950 National Brass Band Championships, where a quartet of eminent bandsmen performed on early instruments. The ophicleide was played on this occasion by Alex Mortimer, conductor, euphoniumist, and tubist of the Liverpool Philharmonic Orchestra 1939-49.

In 1962 a Berlioz Centenary Committee was established to co-ordinate the British celebrations of the centenary of the composer's death. During 1969 a new edition of his *Memoirs* was published, a plaque was unveiled on the London house where he stayed in 1851, there was a commemorative exhibition at the French Institute, the recently-initiated complete edition of his works continued publication and numerous performances of his compositions were given.

The only thing missing was an ophicleide, for in those carefree days the lowest brass part was simply played by the same tubist who played the lowest brass part in everything else. There were however always those who voiced concerns over the appropriate instrument to use for ophicleide parts following its apparent demise. Tom Wotton, for example, referred to the German conductor and composer Fritz Volbach (1861-1942), who used two euphoniums in Berlioz's *La Damnation de Faust*, and the French conductor Édouard Colonne (1838-1910), who directed some 150 performances of the same work and who preferred two tubas (W[27], 179). In fact the two conductors reached virtually identical solutions, as the Small French C Tuba (a tone higher than the euphonium) was then standard in France.

A number of enthusiasts, including Alan Lumsden and David Rycroft, occasionally played ophicleide from the mid-1960s. Carey Blyton, whose use of serpent in television music was considered on pages 124-5 above, also scored for ophicleide (Ex. 3.4). Probably the first complete ophicleide recital ever was given by the author of this book accompanied by Alison Pink at the Horniman Museum, London on 11 November 1990. A much wider awareness of the instrument was achieved with the release of the seminal recording of Berlioz's *Symphonie fantastique* on period instruments under the direction of Roger Norrington made in 1989. The players concerned were Stephen Saunders and Stephen Wick, who later admitted: 'We just had to work away together, teaching ourselves how to do it. The whole exploit was like an experiment, and we felt like pioneers' (B[38], 4). Later Stephen Wick played serpent in John Eliot Gardiner's recording of the earlier version of the work.

Subsequent performances (and particularly recordings) with two tubas do now sound less appropriate than they would have done before the 1989 watershed, the full tone of the tubas lacking the eeriness of the ophicleides. However, any expected ophicleidists' bonanza has failed to materialise, perhaps because the frequency of Berlioz performances is now far lower than it was during the celebrations of his centenary. This is less a reaction against his style than a situation resulting from his mammoth orchestral requirements. They could be satisfied in the 1960s, but not during a period of financial recession.

When no extra expenditure is involved the ophicleide continues to make inroads into mainstream performance. During the 1996-97 London opera season, trombonist Tom Winthorpe of the Royal Opera played the 'Ophicleide 1' part in the single number where it appears in Saint-Saëns's *Samson et Dalila* of 1877, using

Ex. 3.4

[DOVE VOGANS *seen in distance* (L.S.). *They approach* DOCTOR *and*

Blyton: *The Revenge of the Cybermen*

Ex. 3.5

Berlioz: 'Dies irae' *(Symphonie fantastique)*                          *f*

Samuel Hughes's own ophicleide (see Fig. 3.4). (The composer gives permission for the second part to be played on tuba.) This instrument, marked with the initials 'R.I.O.' (Royal Italian Opera), had been discovered by Winthorpe in store at Covent Garden when preparations were being made for the theatre's renovation. Sadly Hughes himself had not played this particular part as he ceased performing in 1885 and the first Covent Garden performance (not staged) took place eight years later. Also during 1996-97 John Elliott played ophicleide in the English National Opera production of Berlioz's *The Damnation of Faust* at the Coliseum. Elsewhere the ophicleide is being more frequently used in performances of Rossini's *Petite messe*, Puccini's *Missa da Gloria*, Mendelssohn's *Elijah* and (incorrectly, as it turns out) *A Midsummer Night's Dream*.

Fig. 3.8. *Punch*'s angelic ophicleidist.

# CHAPTER IV

## Valves, Valve-Systems and the First Tubas

I have learned a lot about who I am and who I
want to be through playing tuba.
—Joseph Skillen, Professional-in Residence
Louisiana State University in
*Tuba Journal*, Winter 1999.

Everybody does silly things to help them think.
Well, I play the tuba.
—Longfellow Deeds in the film *Mr. Deeds
Goes to Town* (Frank Capra, 1936)

THE VALVE to nineteenth-century instrument-makers was like the philosophers'
stone of the middle ages: they applied themselves with all the fanaticism of the
alchemists to the task of discovering a means of turning acoustically-imperfect side-
holes and restricted harmonic series into golden chromaticism.

All there was to discover had been found by mid-century, a mere thirty-five years
after the prototype valve appeared, although earlier attempts to provide chromatic
facilities on brass instruments other than by side-holes or a slide should be
mentioned. The first seems to have been in 1777 when Johann Maresch of St
Petersburg bound together two horns pitched a minor third apart. Shortly
afterwards Charles Clagget, an Irishman resident in Long Acre, London, patented a
*Chromatic Trumpet and French Horn* (British Patent 1664, 15 August 1788, illustrated
in his *Musical Phenomena*, No. 1, 1793).This consisted in 'uniting together two
French horns or trumpets in such a manner that the same mouthpiece may be
applied to either of them instantaneously during the time of performance, as the
music may require'. The mouthpipes of the instruments, one pitched in eb and one
in d, were brought together in a box. The mouthpiece entered the opposite side of
the box and could be directed towards either instrument, the other being switched
off by means of 'a piece of elastic, gum, or leather or otherwise'. The whole idea
seems highly theoretical and far from air-tight, but Fétis mentions a soloist on the
instrument named M. Mortella and Galpin prints an illustration of it (G³, 229).

In 1813 or shortly afterwards the first valve appeared. Gottlob Bierey, conductor
at the Breslau Theatre, wrote an article in the 3 May 1815 issue of the *Allgemeine*

*Musikalische Zeitung* about a 'New Discovery'. A horn player named Heinrich Stölzel (sometimes spelled Stoelzel or Stöelzel), recently a member of the Breslau Theatre orchestra but currently in the private band of the Prince of Pless, had devised a method of obtaining a chromatic scale without hand-stopping. Two years later an article in the same periodical by Friedrich Schneider, at the time director of the Leipzig Municipal Theatre, confirmed Stölzel as the inventor of the *Ventil*, described as an air-tight piston depressed by the player's finger and returned to its normal position by means of a spring (A[7], 26.11.1817, cols. 814-16).

There is a good deal of conflicting evidence about the actual circumstances of its invention, but it seems probable that Stölzel had applied his valve to a horn as early as July 1814, and the following year he approached the Berlin firm of Griessling & Schlott who agreed to manufacture instruments incorporating it; so far as we can tell it was a tubular valve. In 1816 or 1817 Stölzel went to live in Berlin, where he played horn in the Royal Opera orchestra and was also chamber musician and instrument repairer to the King of Prussia. In December 1817 he played a solo on a two-valve horn in a concert at Leipzig. Pless (the present-day Pszczyna) was situated in Silesia, so it is likely that it was here that he met Friedrich Bluhmel, a member of a Silesian mining company's band, who in 1817-18 was working to perfect a box valve *(Kastenventil)* inspired by a type of air-pipe valve used in Upper Silesian blast furnaces. The Berlin maker J. C. Gabler is known to have been working on two instruments using the box valve in February 1818. Together, on 12 April 1818, Stölzel and Bluhmel took out a ten-year Prussian Patent for the tubular and box valves. Kunitz (K[25], 827) and Day (D[4], 182) state that Bluhmel sold the valve, which he had invented in 1813, to Stölzel in Breslau. Subsequent detailed research by Herbert Heyde has substantially confirmed the above narrative.

For the next ten years and longer there were constant claims and counter-claims as to who was the actual inventor of the valve. On the expiry of the patent Bluhmel personally attempted to take out another, for the *conisches Drehbuchsenventil*, without success despite having produced evidence allegedly showing that he had sold the original valve to Stölzel. It appears that the latter's tubular valve had certain limitations, probably because—assuming it to be like that subsequently known as the Stölzel Valve—the air-column had to make an abrupt turn on entering the piston in order to leave it at the base. In addition the makers had to develop a whole new technology to construct this delicate piece of mechanism, involving precision brazing and close tolerances. On the other hand the square valve, sometimes called the *Schuster Box Valve* after the Karlsruhe firm that made it, was clumsy but the windways were not restricted, allowing easier blowing. Wieprecht, who later was to design a valve called the *Stecherbüchsenventil* or *Berliner-Pumpe*, combining the lightness of one with the free windways of the other, relates that the Berlin players were not attracted to the valve in any form at first, but after certain improvements the tubular valve was accepted and used for many years.

The virtuoso Prussian trombonist Friedrich Belcke was possibly the first soloist on Stölzel's new *Tenorhorn* (baritone); the band of the Jäger Guards had valve horns in 1825 and valve trumpets three years later. Prussian Infantry bands had their first valve instruments in 1830. Spontini, the Italian conductor at the Berlin Royal Opera, sent some Prussian valved instruments to Paris in October 1826. French manufacturers copied them (the International Patents Convention was not signed until 1883) and in 1827 the Parisian horn-player Meifred in conjunction with the manufacturer J. C. Labbaye *père* was awarded a medal at the Paris Exposition de l'industrie for a two-valve horn. In the same year Labbaye patented a trumpet with three valves, evidence conflicting with the statement by some authorities that the third valve was introduced by Müller of Mainz in 1830. Spontini quite clearly mentions two- and three-valve instruments being sent to Paris, and Wieprecht states that Stölzel arrived in Berlin with a three-valve horn as early as 1816 or 1817.

It has been suggested that valved instruments arrived in England by way of Russia (see pages 186-7 below), but be that as it may they were certainly being imported direct from Germany or France by 1830. The *Harmonicon* for July 1830 includes an account of a visit to Thomas Percival's in St. James's Street, London, where the writer saw a *Chromatic Bass*, folded like a bugle-horn. It had 'three moveable stops'. Valves were being added in Vienna by makers like Leopold Uhlmann and Joseph Riedl before 1830. In that very year the former patented his *Wiener-Ventil* (Austrian Patent 2053) or Vienna Valves, a twin-piston system like the Glossop farmer John Shaw's invention of 1824 (British Patent 5013, 7 October 1824). There the resemblance ends, for whereas Shaw's *Transverse Spring Slides* had limited success the Vienna Valve was to become one of the three main types of valve, still offered by Meinl-Weston as an option for two models of F tuba. Fig. 4.10 shows a valved ophicleide by Uhlmann with valves of this type.

Another valve of major significance was patented by the horn-player Josef Kail with Joseph Riedl of Vienna in 1835 as the *Rad-Maschine* or *Drehventil* (Austrian Patent of 11 September 1835) (D[23], 154). Although Bluhmel may have experimented with rotary-valves as early as 1811, Kail and Riedl's version was the first practical European valve of this type, and a tribute to its inventors in that it

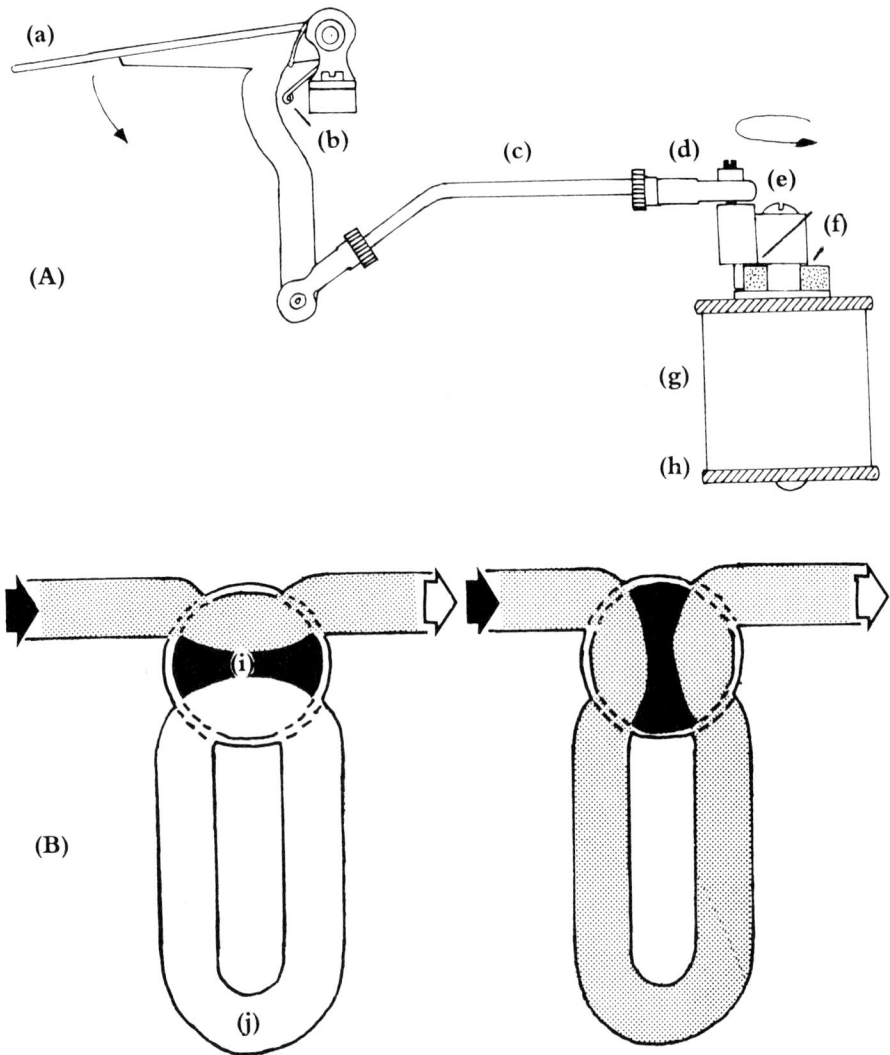

*Not to scale.*

Fig. 4.1. Rotary-valve. (A) Side view of typical mechanism, with arrows showing the direction of spatula movement and motion imparted to rotor; (B) position of rotor and passage of air with valve 'open' (left) and after depression of spatula (right). (a) spatula or touch-piece; (b) spring; (c) arm; (d) stop arm head; (e) stop arm head screw; (f) cork buffers; (g) casing; (h) valve cap; (i) rotor; (j) valve slide.

remains virtually the same to this day. Its operation is shown in Fig. 4.1 along with the two alternative methods of turning the rotor, by cranks or cord. (Various claims have been made for the distinction of having been the inventor of string action, but Thomas Paine of Woonsocket, Rhode Island, was certainly using it before 1855) (E[3], 93).) Cranks are mechanically more reliable, but string action is quieter although in practice it has normally been used only for valves with a relatively small diameter. The action, of either type, is returned to its normal position by a clock spring enclosed in a drum or by a plain spring. Virtually all rotary-valve tubas now in production utilize the latter method. In 1994 the makers Willson perfected their Rotax valve, a beautifully-made rotary-valve with no fewer than 113 precision elements. In this the volume of the entire airway remains constant no matter what position the rotor is in at any particular moment. It is perhaps significant that Willson are based in Flums, Switzerland so may have approached their task along lines informed by the precision watch-making techniques developed in the country (K[26, 26-30]).

Not long after the appearance of the piston-valve in Europe American inventors were experimenting with rotating valves. On the U. S. Frigate *Constitution*, in the Navy Yard at Charlestown, Massachusetts, is a trumpet inscribed 'Permutation Trumpet/Invented & Made by N. Adams, Lowell, Mass/Paul Heald/Carlisle/Mass. 1825'. It is made in brass with three keys which, when depressed, operate valves containing vanes which rotate and deflect the air into the appropriate windway. The connexion between the key and the rotor is by two wires. (This instrument is illustrated in B[5], fig. 770.) Nathan Adams (1783-1864) was bandmaster on the ship during the War of 1812 and later a musician and instrument-maker at Lowell and repairer of ship's chronometers at Nantasket, Masachusetts.

Two widely-used valves in nineteenth-century America offered certain advantages over the Riedl rotary-valve. Thomas Paine's version, invented in 1848, had three windways through the rotor rather than the usual two, enabling it to function by making only one-eighth of a turn rather than a quarter. Paine played tuba, and Eliason presents evidence suggesting that his valve may initially have been used on one of these instruments (E[3], 92). In 1850 J. Lathrop Allen devised a long thin rotary-valve, broadening and flattening the tubing as it approached the valves in order to enable them to turn more quickly. As confirmed by many of the illustrations in G[6], it was widely used during the Civil War, when it vied for supremacy with the more robust Berliner-Pumpe. From about 1870 onwards it was gradually ousted in the face of the increasing popularity of the Périnet piston-valve.

As in more recent technological history, American mechanical ingenuity may have been matched by events in Russia. The *United Service Journal* for 1831 included an item headed 'Presentation of Silver Kettle Drums to the 2nd Life Guards' which took place on 6 May 1831. It records that 'the drums were then put on the horse and "God Save the King" was immediately played by the famous Russian chromatic trumpet-band of the 2nd Life Guards, (the only one in England), in which the drums performed their part with brilliant effect'. The report of the jury at the 1851 Great Exhibition mentions that the introduction of valves was 'due to the munificence of the Emperor of Russia, who about 24 years ago presented a complete set of brass instruments with valves to the band of the Second Life Guards' (G[20, 330]).

We know the circumstances under which the gift was made: Earl Cathcart, the British ambassador to the Court of Russia in 1805-6 and 1812-20 and colonel of the regiment, had expressed his appreciation of the St Petersburg Band of the Imperial Guards which was equipped with similar instruments. There is another reference in the *Musical World* of 29 December 1837: '. . . for the origin of the system of valves we are indebted to the Russians, who first invented and applied them to their trumpets and horns' (M[53], 29.12.1837, 254). Thomas Harper's *Instructions for the trumpet, with the use of the chromatic slide, also the Russian valve trumpet, the Cornet à pistons, or small stop trumpet, and keyed bugle, & c, & c* had been announced by Cramer, the publisher, in 1836. What was the nature of these valves? The casual observer would have found it difficult to discover anything as the bandsmen were instructed to cover them in performance (a touch of mystery present also in the story of the Hibernicon). Perhaps Algernon Rose had a hazy recollection of the truth when in 1895 he claimed of Thomas Key that 'In 1809 [sic.] he made the first circular bass tuba with rotary action used in this country . . . for the Second Life Guards' (R[9],103-4).

The mythology of the Life Guards' valved instruments is strongly established. Reporting on musical instruments shown at the 1862 International Exhibition, *The Musical Standard* for 15 December 1862 referred to the first 'rude cornet-à-piston' produced some forty years earlier by Miggenhofen [a maker who has so far remained elusive] of Frankfort and Miller [C. A. Müller] of Mainz.

A few years after the appearance of the Mainz cornets, the Emperor of Russia possessed bands of valved brass instruments; and Lord Cathcart brought to England a set of them as a present to the 2nd Life Guards, who vainly attempted to keep the peculiarities of these instruments a secret by partially covering them in bags when playing in public (M$^{51}$, 15.12.1862, 132).

There is also a reference to this ploy in an article on 'The Life Guards Band' by Lieut. W. J. Gibson (G$^{14}$, 6), at the time the regiment's director of music. A commonsense view rejects the ominous official secrets act implied here as it is still the practice of bandsmen to keep the lower parts of larger instruments covered by canvas bags which can be easily blancoed, thus avoiding the need for frequent polishing of the intricate tubing of the valve-slides and lower branches (see Fig. 14.2). Mr A. E. Woodbridge of the Household Cavalry Museum, Combermere Barracks, Windsor has kindly drawn my attention to a footnote appended to the *United Service Journal* account as reprinted in J$^{10}$ (1-3) in which R. G. Harris agrees with this suggestion. He prints two illustrations of oil paintings by John Frederick Taylor, one dated c. 1831 entitled *2nd Life Guards Changing Quarters*, and the other painted later in the same decade. The detail of the instruments is not sufficient to enable the mechanism to be established, and Harris points out several inaccuracies which lead to the conclusion that this iconographic evidence is of little real value.

The missing link in this saga has been discovered by the trumpeter and musicologist Edward Tarr, who points out in a footnote to the first part of his article on 'The romantic trumpet' (T$^3$, 238-9, 261) that there is in Moscow an instrument with two valves of the Stölzel type resembling that illustrated in Harper's method, marked 'I. F. Anderst, St. Petersburg' with the date 1825. He gives further references to sightings by others and quotes Heyde who notes that the Tsar made his presentation to the Life Guards by 1827 (H$^{24}$, 11). The instruments could have been taken to Russia before then by the German director of the St Petersburg Guards Regiment, Dörffel: there are other early Russian brass instruments with similar valves.

In 1833 Wilhelm Wieprecht, with the maker Johann Moritz, devised the *Berliner-Pumpe*, a piston valve with a large diameter allowing the windways in the piston to be curved, thus overcoming the Stölzel valve's great disadvantage. Dullat reproduces Patentrag 12.8.1833 for *Berliner Pumpenventil* (D$^{23}$, 151). Heyde (H$^{23}$, 54-58) presents evidence for earlier, more free-blowing valves on principles which Wieprecht could utilize in working to achieve his ultimate aim:

1. 1827. A rejected patent application by Stölzel for an improvement on Bluhmel's box valve, the *Schiebekastenventile*.

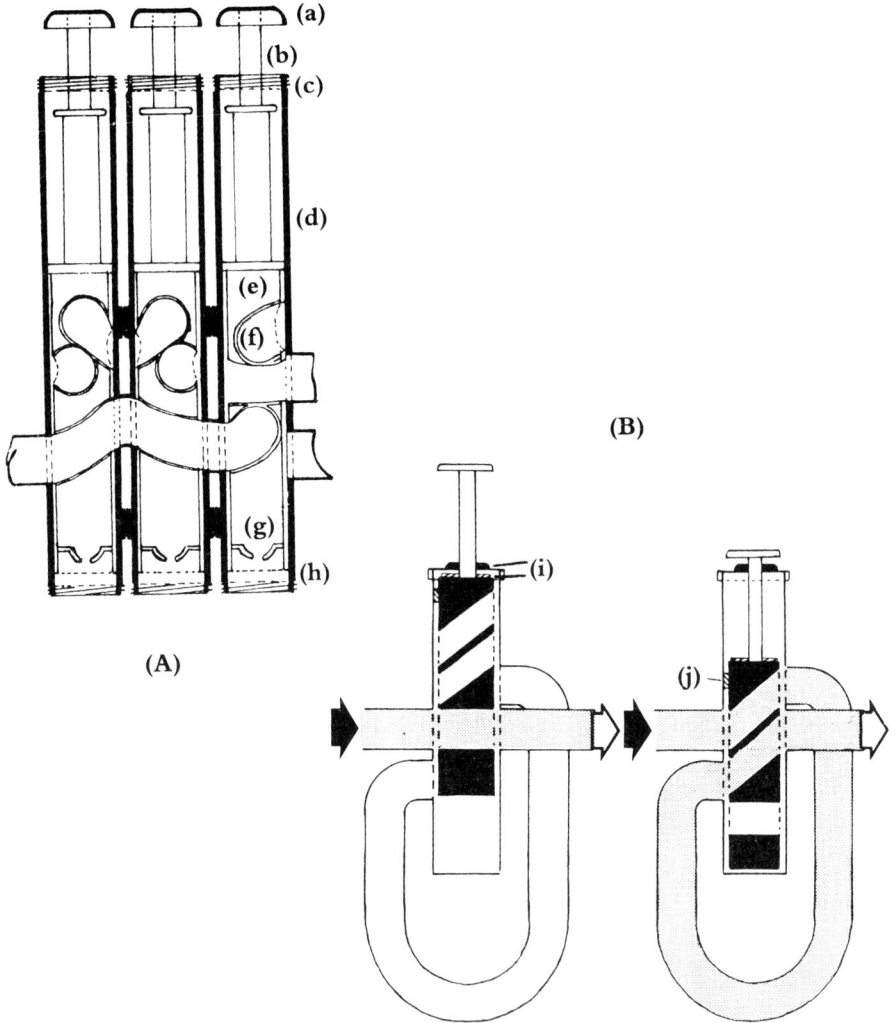

*Not to scale.*

Fig. 4.2. Piston-valves. (A) Cluster of three Périnet valves; (B) diagrammatic representation of valve in 'open' position (left) and when depressed (right). The valve spring in (A) is positioned around the wider section of the valve pillar above the piston; in (B) it is placed between the valve bottom and the valve bottom cap. (a) finger-top; (b) valve pillar; (c) valve top cap; (d) valve casing; (e) piston; (f) port leading to valve passage or *coquille*; (g) valve bottom; (h) valve bottom cap; (i) cork or felt washer; (j) guide-pin running in slot in casing.

2. 1828. Bluhmel's three-airway rotary-valve.

3. 1829. Large-bore tubular versions of Stölzel's improvement, noted in (1) above.

4. 1832. Kail's rotary-valve, half the size of Bluhmel's.

The latter vied for popularity in Germany with Stölzel's later cylindrical valve. It may be that Wieprecht and Moritz's work on developing the Baß-Tuba necessitated their evolving a method of continuing a relatively large bore through the valve windways. Or it may equally have been that having contrived a piston-valve which could accommodate a wider tube than previously they were ready to create the Baß-Tuba two years later, in 1835.

In 1843 Adolphe Sax achieved a smoother windway still through pistons of the Berliner-Pumpe type by arranging for the windways to cross at angles of 105° and 75° rather than the previous 90° (H²³, 58). Instruments using these valves are illustrated in Fig. 6.1.

In 1839 the French maker Étienne François Périnet designed the valve known by his name, an improved version of Stölzel's tubular valve which is substantially the piston-valve used today (Fig. 4.2). It may be returned to its normal position by means of a spring positioned below the piston, or by means of a spring positioned between the top of the piston and the top of the casing. (The first example of this 'top-spring' seems to have been J. Bossi's British Patent 13,865 of 13 October 1887.) Three years after the introduction of his valve, Périnet applied it to his *piston basse*, invented specifically to replace the ophicleide. The piston-valve found general application in France, Belgium and Britain, the rotary-valve in German-speaking countries. There is no clear reason for their individual preferences, but it is interesting to note that attempts by French and English makers to develop rotary-valves have generally met with little success. When in 1841 Berlioz recorded that the piston had virtually been abandoned in Germany, claiming that Sax had 'demonstrated the superiority of the cylinder system over the piston method', he was not differentiating between piston- and rotary-valves but rather instruments *à pistons* (with Stölzel valves) and *à cylindres* (with Sax's wide-diameter valves of the Berliner-Pumpe type) (B²⁸, 277).

Later in the century manufacturers attempted to decrease the distance piston-valves had to travel. With the introduction of automatic compensation systems necessitating more windways and larger bores this became a major problem, particularly in the case of tubas. Tradition has it that when Theodore Distin dropped his trumpet in 1864 the new elliptical bore gave a brighter sound. The idea of making elliptical windways through valves (with no decrease in area, but allowing a shorter stroke) followed on from this. Rudall, Carte in England, Conn and Holton in the United States have all made 'short-action' valves.

In 1855 Gustave Besson devised a system in which the bore remained constant whether the instrument was open or any valve or combination of valves was in use. He had achieved something which many other inventors, notably John Shaw with his *Swivel Valves*, Köhler with his *Patent Lever Valves*, Halary with his *Placques Tournants* (all more or less impracticable types of disc-valve as opposed to piston- or rotary-valves) and the Lichfield winner of a Great Exhibition award, Dr. John Oates with more conventional piston-valves, had been attempting for twenty years.

The problem of the considerable lengths of cylindrical tubing introduced into the conical profile of bugle-horns with the addition of valves still remained to be solved. Although this difficulty was eventually overcome, most nineteenth-century manufacturers do not seem to have considered it of particular importance. It is easy to provide a short mouthpipe on instruments with upright piston-valves, resulting in the valves being close to the narrower end of the tubing and thus creating less interference to the profile which can then expand regularly to the bell. Curiously, many French manufacturers seem to have gone out of their way to position the valves much further along the main tubing.

Alphonse Sax took out Belgian Patent 4363 of 3 May 1848 for double valve loops with expanding bore applicable to both positions of a valve. Myers & Tomes point out that this was rarely used in practice, although a Thibouville-Lamy euphonium exists in which the fourth valve utilizes the principle (M[57], 111). They do go into some detail, however, in considering the attempt by Rudall, Carte to devise a method of ensuring that the bore of an instrument gradually increased from mouthpiece to bell regardless of how many or how few valves were depressed. This was marketed from 1905 as the 'Patent Conical Bore' (PCB) (British Patent 21,295 of 31 December 1903 in favour of Henry Klussman, Montagu George and Julius Zambra, the partners in the company). The bulk of the instruments made using this principle were cornets and trumpets, but the authors list a number of others, including tenor cors, flügel horns, Eb horns, baritones, euphoniums (in C, Bb and A), bombardons in F, Eb, Bb, BBb and a BBb 'circular' (helicon) model. There is also a euphonium with Samson finger-slide valves featuring bore increments between valves in the Edinburgh University Collection of Historic Musical Instruments (No. 198). Present-day rotary-valve instruments usually vary the bore of the valve-tubing (and diameter of the valve) more or less appropriately, but a more urgent problem had to be tackled before time and effort could be spent on such niceties as maintaining a constant profile: overcoming the poor intonation resulting from the use of valves in combination, particularly the third valve.

The conventional three-valve system in which the first lowers the pitch by a tone, the second by a semitone and the third by a tone-and-a-half was soon well established. There were to be variants—there still are, in fact—but players were already becoming accustomed to this arrangement. However, there was one great acoustic disadvantage in using three valves: the cumulative errors of pitch resulting from the use of more than one valve at a time. If a tube of length $a$ sounds a tone lower with the addition of length $b$ (first valve) or a semitone lower with the additional length $c$ (second valve), then $(a+b)$ will need a proportionately greater additional length than $c$ to lower the combined length by a semitone (Fig. 4.3).

For example, the fundamental of a euphonium, B'♭, is produced by an effective acoustic length of 2929 mm. To achieve A', a semitone lower, an extra 174.5 mm of tubing is added by the second valve. If A'♭ is required the first valve is depressed and an extra 360 mm of tubing is joined to the open instrument. The third valve adds 554 mm, lowering the instrument one and a half tones to G'. The first and third valves together thus give an additional length of 914 mm.

For the production of the note F' a tube-length of 3910.5 mm is required. To play this note the first and third valves are depressed, but this gives only 3843 mm (the open instrument's 2929 mm + combined first and third valves' 914 mm). There are 67.5 mm too little—in musical terms the note is .295 semitone sharp. The combination of all three valves gives an even more marked error, the notes they give being .522 semitone sharp.

Owing to the shorter tube-lengths the differences are not so pronounced in the higher instruments, but they quite obvious in the lower brass, as any bass tuba player will enthusiastically confirm.

In order to ameliorate the intonation problems it became the practice to lengthen the third valve-slide. Notes playable on the third valve alone can alternatively be played on a combination of first and second valves where they are reasonably well in tune (actually .1 semitone sharp, small enough to be lipped down). If the third valve-slide is lengthened so that it becomes .187 semitone flat the error given by the combination of all three valves is reduced to .191 semitone sharp. At the same time the total number of notes over the entire range with inherent intonation defects is actually increased, although the errors themselves are not so pronounced. There are many thousands of such instruments currently in use.

Ex. 4.1                    PRACTICAL FINGERING-CHART FOR TUBAS

*(First system — bass clef, ascending chromatic notes)*

| Tuba | 1 | 2 | 3 | 4 | 5 | 6 | 7 | 8 | 9 | 10 | 11 | 12 | 13 | 14 | 15 |
|---|---|---|---|---|---|---|---|---|---|---|---|---|---|---|---|
| F TUBA 5 valves (3 = 1½ tones, 5 = 2 tones) | 41/3 | 2/3 | 1/2 | 1 | 2 | 0 | 1/3/4/5 | 31/42/54/5 | 12/34/45 | 41/53/5 | 2/3/5 | 21/42/5 | 4 | 2/3 | 1/2 |
| F TUBA 5 valves (3 = 2 tones, 5 = ¼ tone) | 4 | 3 | 1/2 | 1 | 2 | 0 | 1/3/4/5 | 1/2/3/4 | 2/3/4 | 1/4/5 | 1/3/5 | 2/4 | 42/3 | 3 | 1/2 |
| EE♭ TUBA 4 valves (3 = 1½ tones, compensated) | 1/2 | 1 | 2 | 0 | 1/2/3/4 | 1/3/4 | 2/3/4 | 1/2/4 | 1/4 | 2/4 | 4 | 2/3 | 1/2 | 1 | 2 |
| CC TUBA 5 valves (3 = 1½ tones, 5 = 2 tones) | 0 | 1/3/4/5 | 31/42/54/5 | 12/34/45 | 14/35/5 | 2/3/5 | 21/42/5 | 4 | 2/3 | 1/2 | 1 | 2 | 0 | 21/42/3 | 41/2/3/4 |
| BB♭ TUBA 3 valves (3 = 1½ tones) | | | | | 1/2/3 | 1/3 | 2/3 | 1/2 | 1 | 2 | 0 | 1/2/3 | 1/3 | 2/3 | 1/2 |

*(Second system — bass clef, ascending chromatic notes)*

| Tuba | 1 | 2 | 3 | 4 | 5 | 6 | 7 | 8 | 9 | 10 | 11 | 12 | 13 | 14 | 15 |
|---|---|---|---|---|---|---|---|---|---|---|---|---|---|---|---|
| F TUBA 5 valves (3 = 1½ tones, 5 = 2 tones) | 1 | 2 | 0 | 21/42/5 | 4 | 2/3 | 1/2 | 1 | 2 | 0 | 2/3 | 1/2 | 1 | 2 | 0 |
| F TUBA 5 valves (3 = 2 tones, 5 = ¼ tone) | 1 | 2 | 0 | 2/4 | 42/3 | 3 | 1/2 | 1 | 2 | 0 | 3 | 1/2 | 1 | 2 | 0 |
| EE♭ TUBA 4 valves (3 = 1½ tones, compensated) | 0 | 21/42/3 | 41/2/3/4 | 2/3 | 1/2 | 1 | 2 | 0 | 2/3 | 1/2 | 1 | 2 | 0 | 1/2 | 1 |
| CC TUBA 5 valves (3 = 1½ tones, 5 = 2 tones) | 2/3 | 1/4 | 1 | 2 | 0 | 2/3 | 1/2 | 1 | 2 | 0 | 1/2 | 1 | 22/3 | 01/2 | 1 |
| BB♭ TUBA 3 valves (3 = 1½ tones) | 1 | 2 | 0 | 2/3 | 1/2 | 1 | 2 | 0 | 1/2 | 1 | 22/3 | 01/2 | 1 | 2 | 0 |

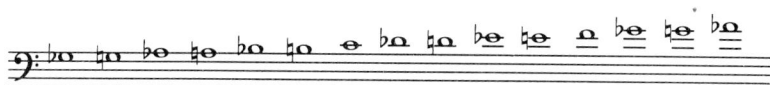

| | | | | | | | | | | | | | | | |
|---|---|---|---|---|---|---|---|---|---|---|---|---|---|---|---|
| **F TUBA 5 valves** (3 = 1½ tones, 5 = 2 tones) | 1 / 2 | 1 | 2 2 / 3 | 0 1 / 2 | 1 | 2 | 0 | 2 / 3 | 1 / 2 | 1 | 2 | 0 | 1 / 2 | 1 | 2 2 / 3 |
| **F TUBA 5 valves** (3 = 2 tones, 5 = ¾ tone) | 1 / 2 | 1 | 2 3 | 0 1 / 2 | 1 | 2 | 0 | 3 | 1 / 2 | 1 | 2 | 0 | 1 / 2 | 1 | 2 3 |
| **EE♭ TUBA 4 valves** (3 = 1½ tones compensated) | 2 2 / 3 | 0 1 / 2 | 1 | 2 | 0 | 2 / 3 | 1 / 2 | 1 | 2 | 0 | 1 2 / 2 | 1 | 2 2 / 3 | 0 1 / 2 | 1 |
| **CC TUBA 5 valves** (3 = 1½ tones, 5 = 2 tones) | 2 | 0 | 2 / 3 | 1 / 2 | 1 | 2 | 0 | 1 2 / 2 | 1 | 2 2 / 3 | 0 1 / 2 | 1 | 2 | 0 | 2 / 3 |
| **BB♭ TUBA 3 valves** (3 = 1½ tones) | 2 / 3 | 1 / 2 | 1 | 2 | 0 | 1 / 2 | 1 | 2 2 / 3 | 0 1 / 2 | 1 | 2 | 0 | 2 / 3 | 1 / 2 | 1 |

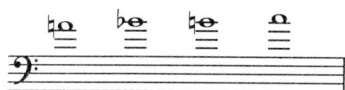

| | | | | | |
|---|---|---|---|---|---|
| **F TUBA 5 valves** (3 = 1½ tones, 5 = 2 tones) | 0 1 / 2 | 1 | 2 | 0 | |
| **F TUBA 5 valves** (3 = 2 tones, 5 = ¾ tone) | 0 1 / 2 | 1 | 2 | 0 | |
| **EE♭ TUBA 4 valves** (3 = 1½ tones compensated) | 2 | 0 | 2 / 3 | 1 / 2 | |
| **CC TUBA 5 valves** (3 = 1½ tones, 5 = 2 tones) | 1 / 2 | 1 | 2 | 0 | |
| **BB♭ TUBA 3 valves** (3 = 1½ tones) | 2 | 0 | | | |

There is a fingering-chart for Small French C Tuba on page 360.

Charts for other instruments are listed under 'Fingering-charts' in the Index (page 616).

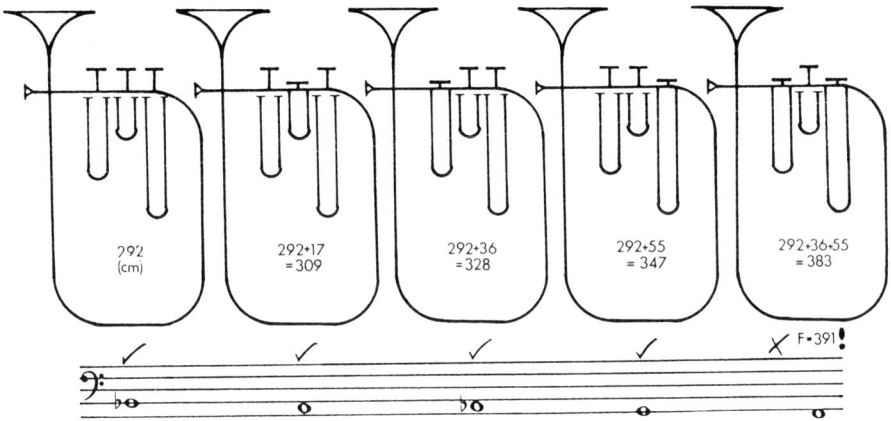

Fig. 4.3. Problems caused by additions to an instrument's open tubing. With no valves depressed 292 cm (approximately) gives B♭. The addition of the second valve-slide gives a total of 309 cm, sounding A. The first valve added to the open tubing gives A♭, with 328 cm. The third gives G, with 347 cm. The addition of first and third (total 383 cm) is too little for F, which requires 391 cm (see above).

It was almost exclusively the French and British who seemed anxious to devise methods of overcoming these problems either automatically or semi-automatically. Manufacturers in German-speaking countries seemed to ignore the whole question and there is no record of players being particularly dissatisfied with their instruments. This may well have been because of the general use of the rotary-valve in these areas, resulting in the bell of the instrument's facing left (as the player sees it) and bringing the valve-slides into a position convenient for the player to manipulate during performance if necessary (Fig. 11.6). (The provision of valve-slides was the brainwave of horn-player Meifred, and although they now seem to us absolutely essential there was at least one instance where they were not used in the design of an instrument on the grounds that they were acoustically a liability—see Fig. 6.1.) Until a method of positioning piston-valves at right-angles to the plane of the instrument was evolved their use inevitably caused the bell to face to the right, making it impossible for the player to have sufficient access to the slides for them to be adjusted with accuracy whilst playing. The Berliner-Pumpen on Wieprecht's original Baß-Tuba gave this facility since they were built into the instrument at the same angle as modern front-valves, if not precisely in the same positions, but the possibilities were not appreciated at the time. Had they been, much subsequent work on overcoming intonation problems could have been avoided.

# COMPENSATING DEVICES

There were three general directions taken by inventors in their attempts to improve the existing valve system. One was to rethink the whole principle and provide a separate valve for each additional harmonic series. The second was to provide additional valves and tubing which could be brought into operation when required to temper the most noticeable errors. The third involved the provision of valve-tubing in lengths different from the norm.

Adolphe Sax was attracted to the first method and in 1852 conceived a system involving six piston-valves. Each, when operated, cut off a length of tubing and was therefore classed as an ascending valve in contrast to the more normal descending valve which adds tubing (Fig. 6.2). Robert Kerrison of New York is said to have invented a similar valve between 1835-41 (G$^{24}$, 88). (The ubiquitous John Shaw's 1824 Transverse Spring Slides provided the first known example of ascending valves.) G. Metzler and J. Waddell's British Patent 1836 of 12 August 1858 included a third valve which raised the pitch one and a half tones. The first valve lowered the pitch conventionally by a tone and the second by a semitone. Used together in combination with the third valve the open tube's harmonic series was produced.

The second method of *compensation* (i.e. compensating for the errors in intonation) had several adherents. One of the more industrious was Gustave Besson who introduced the *barillet* in 1853. Each valve-slide carried a barillet, a rotary-valve operated by a trigger adjacent to the valve casing. So far as the player was concerned the method of operation was similar to that of the triggers on present-day trumpets, but the slides themselves did not move—an extra length of tubing was brought into use through the valve. In 1856-57 the same maker substituted a fourth valve, acting in a horizontal plane, through which all the valve-tubes passed. In conjuction with M. Girardin he produced an improved version two years later known as the *transpositeur*.

Systems involving the use of additional valves bringing in extra lengths of tubing as required were developed in Paris by de Retter and Courtois (1856), in Lyons by Léon Cousin (1873) and as late as 1916 by Thibouville-Lamy who made a five-valved trumpet designed by Merri Franquin of the Paris Conservatoire.

There were also some one-off ideas, like Besson's 1855 two-way rotary-valves. They could be turned either clockwise or anti-clockwise depending upon which of two touch-pieces the player chose. Alternative tubing of different lengths was thus available through each valve, giving numerous combinations plus the lack of constriction associated with rotary-valves. Presumably its lack of success was due to a factor which was not always taken into consideration by these undoubtedly ingenious inventors: the players' unwillingness to learn a new fingering system.

In 1874 Thibouville-Lamy added two keys which, placed near the bell, made it possible to adjust the air-column to the theoretically correct length when using valves in combination. Combining keys and valves was not, however, a new idea: Garofalo & Elrod illustrate an over-the-shoulder soprano saxhorn by Wright of Boston, dating from about 1853, with three rotary-valves and five keys (G[6,7]). Adolphe Sax took out French Patent 22148 of 3 January 1859 for the addition of keys to the bell in order to facilitate high notes, but they adversely affected intonation (Fig. 6.1). There is an example in the Brussels Musée Instrumental, No. 1269. François Sudre, in 1881, introduced a mechanical device which automatically extended the valve-slides. Although too fragile to be practicable, it obviously provided the inspiration for Arban's system which appeared two years later. In addition to providing a fourth valve giving an extra tone and a half he added a lever mechanically extending the third valve-slide to give an extra semitone. The touch-piece of the fourth valve was also linked to the first and second valve-slides. Complicated to describe, it must have been even more complicated to use.

By the 1870s it was obvious that the most satisfactory method of compensation would be completely automatic (possibly the players' lack of enthusiasm for extra valves, levers and keys was striking home). With this in mind, in his company's catalogue, *Manufacture d'instruments de musique*, published in 1878, Jérôme Thibouville-Lamy wrote an article headed '*Conseil aux chefs de musique sur l'accord des instruments de cuivre*' ('Advice to musical directors on the tuning of brass instruments'). In it he argues that the ability to produce the most frequently-used notes through using only one valve for each would improve intonation and overcome variations in tone-quality (T[8], 114-15). Ex. 4.2 shows how he demonstrated this in musical notation.

He then compared the existing system (*perce droite:* straight bore) with his own *perce pleine compensée:* compensated full bore, and announced that all valve instruments produced by his company would henceforward be made on the new principle (T[8], 117). Although it meant that players needed to learn a new fingering-system, this was not markedly different from the conventional system. The drop in pitch of three semitones given by using the third valve alone is an alternative available on the majority of instruments, although it is often not well in tune.

# Ex. 4.2 THIBOUVILLE-LAMY: ADVICE TO MUSIC DIRECTORS ON THE TUNING OF BRASS INSTRUMENTS

## ACCORD GÉNÉRAL
### [OVERALL HARMONY]
Particulier à tous les Instruments de cuivre

ACCORD COMPARATIF & SIMULTANÉ DES INTRUMENTS ENTRE EUX

Petit Bugle, Mi♭, Alto & Cor Mi♭
C. Basse, Mi♭

Cornet à Pistons, Bugles,
Baritons, Si♭

Thibouville-Lamy was not to know that the first completely automatic compensation system, using conventional fingering, had appeared three years earlier. Although not absolutely perfect it was to serve generations of players satisfactorily and is used to this day on the most popular British tubas and euphoniums in professional use as well as on others made elsewhere. It was the brainchild of the acoustician David Blaikley who in 1874 introduced his *compensating valves*, basically a three- or four-valve system which in the former case brings into operation the required extra lengths of tubing when the third valve is used in combination, and in the latter is operated by the fourth valve (Fig. 4.4). In his British Patent 4618 of 14 November 1878 he described the system succinctly:

The tubing connected with the third valve is passed through the first and second, in such a way that, when the third piston is depressed, air passes through passages in the first and second valves, besides the two passages ordinarily arranged in the third. Additional tubing D, E is connected with the first and second pistons respectively, to add two air passages to each of their valves. When the first or second piston is depressed with the third, the length of the passage is increased by D or E. When all three are simultaneously depressed, the whole of the additional tubing is employed, compensating for the lowering of the pitch of the instrument which is caused by depressing the valve 3.

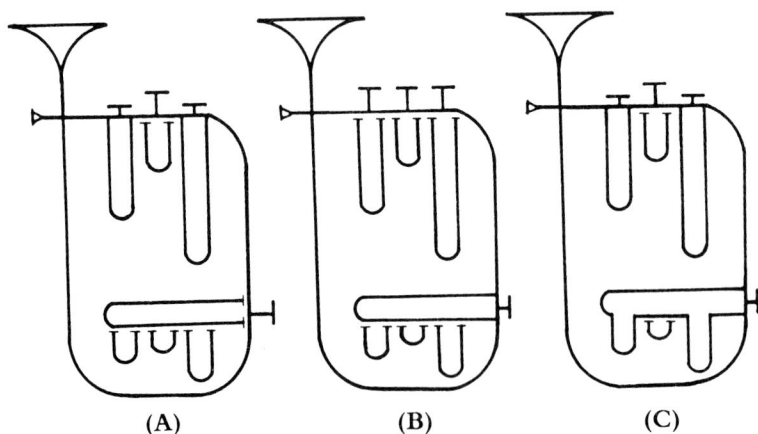

(A)                    (B)                    (C)

Fig. 4.4. The Blaikley Compensating System. (A) First and third valves are depressed giving, in the case of a B♭ instrument, a sharp c. (B) The fourth valve only adds the correct amount of tubing for an in-tune c. (C) With the first, third and fourth valves depressed extra tubing is brought into operation giving an in-tune C.

*Hampshire County Youth Orchestra*                                    *Photo: David Rendell*
Fig. 4.5. Euphoniumist Charis Snell rehearsing for the first performance of the orchestral arrangement of Hartmann's *Rule Britannia* with the Hampshire County Youth Orchestra. The photograph shows the compensating slides, on the side of the instrument closest to·the player.

Similar systems were developed by Daniel and Sudre (1884), Arban and Bouvet (1858–88), Mahillon (1886) and O. Hawkes and P. F. Maurice (British Patent 29,613 of 20 December 1910). Fontaine-Besson's British Patent 6649 of 30 April 1890 was scarcely innovative, being for brass wind instruments 'employing one of the valves for two purposes: first, the ordinary purpose of lowering the pitch; second, opening a new wind passage, the object being to enable the instrument to be played more exactly in tune'. As Boosey's works manager, Blaikley made a significant contribution to the company's reputation for quality euphoniums and tubas. Its two leading British rivals in the field, Besson and Hawkes, found it necessary to introduce similar systems, named respectively the 'Enharmonic Patent' and 'Dictor'.

One compensating system which seems not to have been put into production was that designed by C. Moore and J. W. Clay (British Patent 21,026 of 6 October 1908). They proposed that a chain should pass through slotted extensions to the valve pistons. 'When two or more are operated simultaneously, pulleys attached to the valve extensions tighten the cord or chain, so that the U-shaped [tuning-]slide is shifted by an amount varying according to which valves are operated . . . A spring is provided to return the slide to its normal position.'

Until the 1970s the firm of Adolf Egger, of Basle, made a five-valve F/C tuba employing a method of compensation very much like that found in compensating horns. The right hand operated four valves—1, ½, 1½ and 2½ tones—while the fifth valve switched the instrument's pitch from F to C as required. Gronitz of Hamburg made similar double-tubas in BBb/F which have a high reputation. The final batch of five was produced in 1998. In 1997 Kalison of Milan introduced a range of tubas incorporating an ascending valve system (AVS) conferring two parallel pitches on each instrument. The concept was of a four-valve tuba which can become a tuba in a different pitch by activating a fifth valve. Thus, the Bb tuba can be put into C, the C into D, the Eb into F and the F into G. This allows the smallest number of valves to be used for any given note.

The third method of attempting to improve the traditional valve system by substituting unconventional lengths of valve-tubing has had considerable success. The provision of a drop of two tones instead of a tone and a half when the third valve is depressed is common on Continental tubas, French and Belgian euphoniums and around 1880, according to Kappey, on English tubas also (K[2], 2). The system completely avoids the combination of second and third valves, the coupling with the poorest intonation. The only disadvantage is that fewer alternatives are available for other notes, but this may be a small price to pay.

Other methods involve the addition of valves. The most common is the use of the fourth valve, primarily intended to fill the gap between the fundamental and lowest second harmonic. This valve's tubing, lowering the instrument by two and a half tones, may be used instead of combined first and third valves which theoretically lower by the same amount but owing to the involvement of the third valve result in poor intonation. Blaikley himself provided for the addition of a fourth valve shortly after introducing his compensating system.

Wieprecht's Baß-Tuba was fitted with an unconventional five-valve system in an attempt to improve intonation (see page 203 below). The English Barlow F tuba, described in Chapter XII, also had five valves arranged in an unorthodox way.

Fig. 4.6
(a) Meinl-Weston Dual-Purpose
Fifth Valve, showing pre-set slides.

(b) The slides arranged as
for BBb Tuba (with fifth
valve depressed).

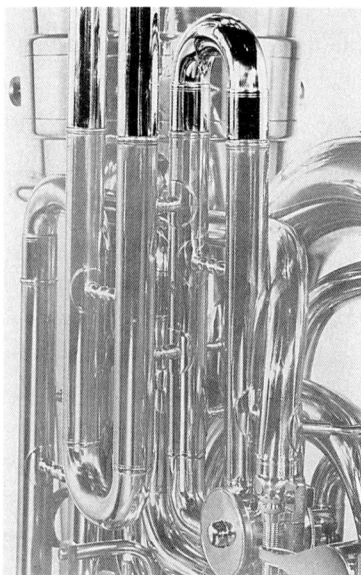

*Getzen Co. Inc.*

Very often a fifth valve—which is always provided to improve intonation rather than to extend the compass—can be arranged to give an interval decided by the player. Its most usual function is as a ¾-tone valve used in place of the second (½-tone) valve in the lower register where intonation problems are most pronounced. An unusual CC tuba built by Rudolf Sander of Wolfstein has five rotary valves, the first three acting in the normal way, the fourth lowering the pitch by two tones and the fifth by two and a half tones. (The instrument also has some other unusual features. It was built from copper, rather than the usual brass, and white metal; the fifth valve (for left hand operation) is a piston-valve acting on a rotary-valve; and by coiling the tubing once more than in the conventional CC tuba a more compact form was achieved (Fig. 8.1).)

At one time Meinl-Weston five-valve CC tubas had a dual-purpose fifth valve. The suggestion of Arnold Jacobs, it gave a tone when arranged as in Fig. 4.6(a), two tones (Fig. 4.6(b)), or as at Fig. 4.6(c) converting the instrument into a BB♭ for as long as the fifth valve is held down. The company's current Walter Hilgers 45 H-L Large 6/4 F tuba has five rotary-valves with optional quint valve and second valve trigger. (The quint, giving a drop of five semitones, is a version of the sixth valve fitted to some of the company's Klemens Pröpper models.) B&S offer whole-tone fifth valves with two-tone extensions. The two available fifth-valve slides for their 4098 GI Mel Culbertson model give a choice of either a seven-eighth or nine-eighths of a tone drop. Currently most serious tuba-makers offer a basic instrument which can be tailored to the player's specific requirements. B&S, Rudolph Meinl, Meinl-Weston and Miraphone for example, give the option of four- or five-valve versions of several of their instruments; Hirsbrunner, five or six valves; Kalison *(Flicorno Basso Grave in Fa Daryl Smith)*, a fifth valve arranged either for right- or left-hand operation.

Details of the Small French C Tuba are given in Chapter X; contemporary attempts to improve the intonation of low notes are surveyed in Chapter VII.

# THE FIRST TUBAS

There is only one instrument in the modern orchestra of which we know the precise date of birth: Prussian Patent 19 was taken out on 12 September 1835 by Wilhelm Wieprecht and Johann Moritz of Berlin for the *Baß-Tuba*. The event was announced in a small paragraph on the front page of the *Allgemeine Preussische Staats-Zeitung* for Wednesday, 16 September 1835, in the following words:

Dem kammer-Musikus W. Wieprecht und dem Hof-Instrummenten-macher J. G Moritz zu Berlin ist unterm 12. September 1835 ein Patent auf das von ihnen durch Zeichnung und Beschreibung nachgewiesene Blase-Instrument-Baß-Tuba—so weit daßelbe für new und eigent-humlich erachtet worden, auf Zehn Jahre, von jenem Termine an gerechnet, und für den Umfang der Monarchie ertheilt worden (A⁸, 1).

This was certainly not the first valved instrument, nor was it the first valved bass instrument, but it was the first valved bass instrument to be called the *Baß-Tuba*. There is an example dating from 1838-40 in the Musikinstrumenten-Museum, Berlin (No. 4456) and I am deeply indebted to Dieter Krickeberg who provided the following details and the profile shown in Fig. 4.7. The instrument itself is illustrated in Fig. 4.8.

Overall height: 841 mm
Overall length of tubing: 3540 mm
Distance from mouthpipe entry through valves: 910 mm
Valve-tubing: whole tone: 452 mm
        semitone: 230 mm
        one and a half tones: 605 mm
        compensating valve: 285 mm
        two and a half tones: 1277 mm
Overall length of bell: 1266 mm
    (this includes the flare, 447 mm)
Bore, from entry to mouthpiece to end of valves: 14.8 mm
    increasing to 33.4 mm at beginning of bell.
    157 mm is reached by the point where the flare begins.
Diameter of bell: 193 mm
Thickness of walls: 0.5 mm

The instrument is pitched in F with five Berliner-Pumpen. The three valves for the right hand are arranged to give 1, ½ and 1½ tones; the pair for the left give ¾ and 2½ tones. Significantly an attempt was made to overcome the defects in intonation; the instrument was designed to play down to the fundamental, although owing to the relatively narrow bore the lower notes—as Berlioz was to remark—were not strong; and it was made mainly in brass with German Silver fittings, the normal materials of Continental tubas today. Wieprecht's new instrument thus established several of the characteristics of later tubas.

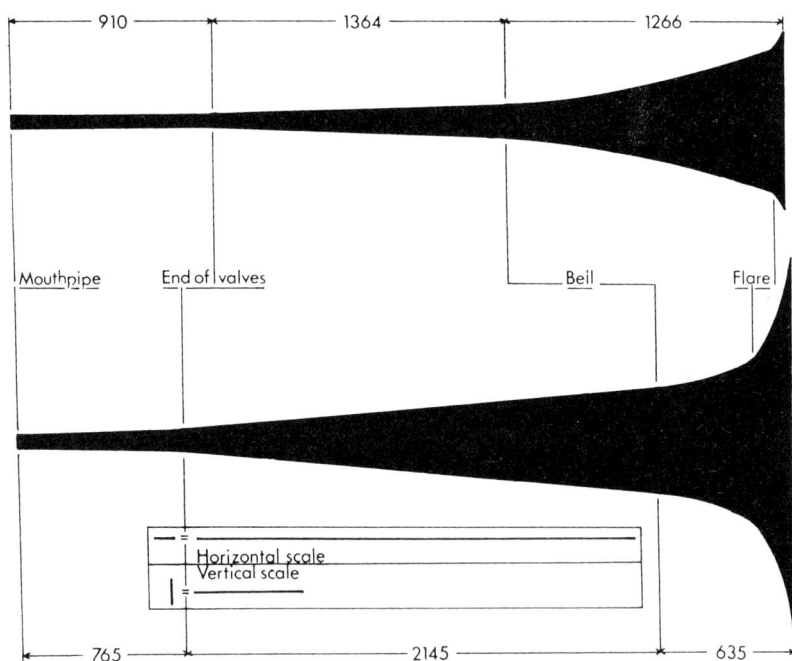

Fig. 4.7. Comparative profiles of the Wieprecht and Moritz Baß-Tuba and a tuba of the same pitch by an unknown East German maker, c. 1960 (Fig. 8.3). Dimensions are given in mm.

The Baß-Tuba (a term used throughout this book to indicate an instrument built to Wieprecht and Moritz's original design) also represented a link between the bassoon/upright serpent/bass horn/ophicleide shape, in which the instrument is held more or less vertically, the player's left hand positioned above the right, and the bugle/keyed-bugle/flügel horn form, in which the extra tubing forms one or more large loops parallel to the bell section, while valves are grouped together for playing by the fingers of a single hand. The Baß-Tuba's five valves followed keyed ophicleide convention, with the two valves for the left hand positioned above the three for the right (in his patent Wieprecht relates this to the bassoon and English bass horn), but its overall form was that of a vertical keyed bugle. The Baß-Tuba was thus a synthesis of the ophicleide and the Austrian *Ventilbugelhorner* of the 1820s derived from the conical *Signalhorn.* These latter instruments seem to have been

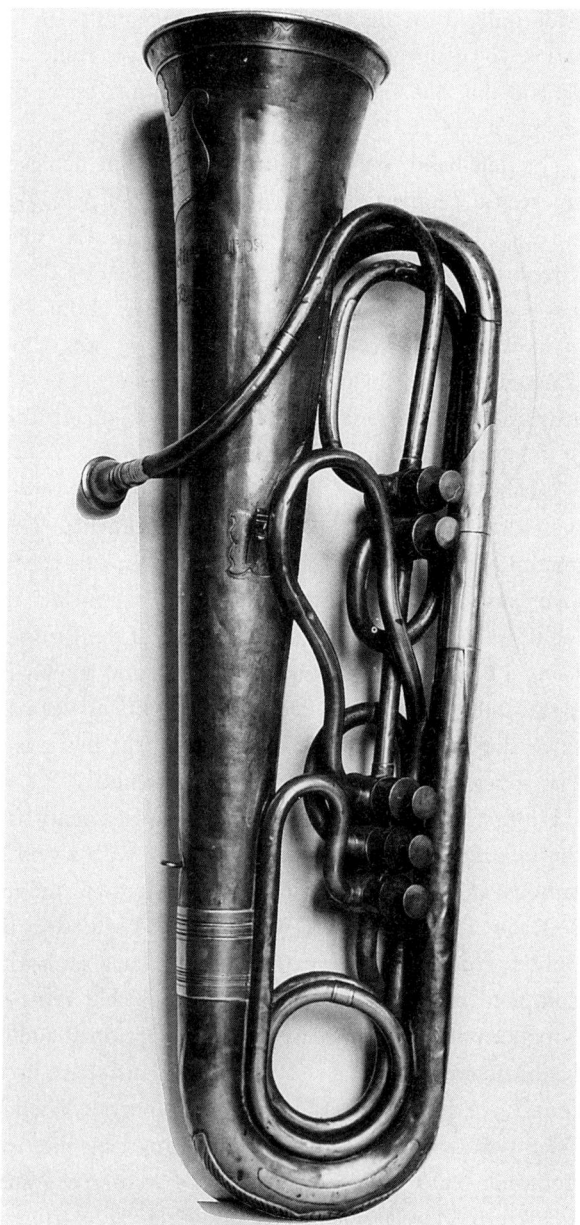

Fig. 4.8
Baß-Tuba by
J. G. Moritz, 1838-40.
Moritz and Wieprecht
patented the instrument
in 1835. (See also Fig. A1.1.)

made only in the higher pitches, the *Altkornett*—not to be confused with the later cornet (*à-pistons*): the earlier instrument was really a flügel horn—pitched in f' or e'b, and the *Althorn*, an octave lower. Kunitz terms the Baß-Tuba a *Ventilkornett* in bass pitch (K$^{25}$, 832).

The left-hand above right-hand position achieved some popularity in mid-nineteenth-century America prior to a brief period during which the French-style top-valved intrument was more popular. A striking photograph of Joseph Kingsbury dating from c. 1861 is reproduced by Garofalo & Elrod (G$^6$, 71). His Eb bass was possibly made by Samuel Graves about 1855 and has five string-action rotary-valves. Graves's Trombacello (in F) was also built along the lines of the Wieprecht and Moritz Baß-Tuba between about 1840 and 1850 (Fig. 11.1). Of instruments in current use, the Viennese Concert Tuba gives the clearest impression of the relative position of the hands (Fig. 8.5).

Valves were initially conceived as a quick way to change crooks and were therefore first applied to existing instruments. The possibility of making brass instruments capable of taking the top line in the band was of interest to both inventors and bandmasters, and it is significant that by 1828 Wieprecht had included in his revised instrumentation of the Prussian Dragoon Guards *Trompeten-Corps* a high *B-Trompete* with two valves and an *Alt-Trompete in Es* along with some of Stölzel's instruments. Deeper bugle-horns were more of a technical challenge since they would require larger valves, but this was exactly the type of challenge that appealed to the extraordinary Wieprecht.

He first came on the scene at the age of twenty as a violinist in the orchestra of the Leipzig Stadttheater, not an orchestra with a very high reputation, although the famous trombone virtuoso and beer-garden proprietor Carl Queisser was his colleague. Two years later Wieprecht had settled in Berlin, where by means known only to himself he persuaded the military authorities to entrust him with the complete reorganization of their bands. He remained a civilian (which in the Kingdom of Prussia was itself quite exceptional) and his success must have relied on his having the sort of personality found attractive by the military. One clue may be found in a letter of Berlioz's which describes Wieprecht after a successful concert: 'The worthy man positively cracked my ribs, interspersing his interpolations with Teutonic oaths beside which Guhr's were Ave Marias' (B$^{28}$, 340). (Guhr was the Frankfurt *Kapellmeister* with a wide reputation not only as an orchestral disciplinarian but also as the man most likely to curse for Prussia in any international competition.) It was fortunate for the progress of the tuba that

Wieprecht had influence and successfully advocated the inclusion of two Baß-Tubas in each band.

The instrument made its first appearance on 27 February 1835 in the 2nd Infantry Guard Regiment, Berlin and ten years later Wieprecht claimed that he had sold a total of eighty-four to various customers. Later in 1835 Wieprecht made a *Bombardon*, which was also pitched in F, wider-bored and three- or four-valved. Berlioz considered its tone less noble that that of the Baß-Tuba, but the bombardon he discusses in his *Treatise on Instrumentation* ($B^{25}$, 229) may be an earlier instrument than the Wieprecht type as in his memoirs he describes the Baß-Tuba as 'a huge brass instrument, derived from the bombardon' ($B^{27}$, 326).

In the 1820s Johann Riedl of Vienna had used the name bombardon for a bass ophicleide (as late as 1864 F. L. Schubert defined bombardon as 'a bass instrument with keys or valves'), and Kalkbrenner claims that the bombardon was introduced into Jäger Bands in 1831, four years before Wieprecht's invention. Wenzl Riedl of Vienna also used the name, this time in an Austrian Patent for three- and four-valved instruments dated 4 September 1833 ($H^{23}$, 223). The description of the bombardon by Fétis, published in *Gazette Musicale* of 15 February 1834, is translated by Morley-Pegge and contains some intriguing inconsistencies.

'. . . a kind of large trombone with three tubes that can be opened or closed at will by piston valves. Its tone, though less round is far more powerful than that of the ophicleide and, in fact, equals that of several trombones in unison. The bombardon is no more diffciult to play than the bass slide trombone, while its gamut is the same. It is built in B♭, and its compass extends from low E♭ to D of the double octave. Herr Riedl intends to add an extra tube and a fourth piston to extend the compass upwards to E, so that the bombardon will then be not only the most powerful of brass instruments but also that with the largest compass.

The bombardon is destined to become an integral part of the military band as its indispensable bass. It has already been adopted by the band of the Prince of Hesse-Hamburg's 10th Regiment, commanded by Count Franz Gyulay, the bandmaster of which is a musician of merit, by name Nemet ($M^{40}$, 6.40, 199).

In 1828 Stölzel had advertised a *Basshorn oder Basstrompete in F oder Es* along with other valved instruments. Baines reasonably suggests that the affix *-horn* indicated ophicleide shape and *-trompete* trumpet shape ($B^{8,}$ 579). It is possible, therefore, that the valved *Basshorn* was popularly known by the name of a more familiar instrument of similar appearance, the *Bombardon* (rather as in the case of the valved ophicleide). Berlioz even states that the bombardon's '. . . timbre differs only little from that of the ophicleide', yet if it was wider in bore than the Baß-Tuba its tone would have been a further stage removed from the ophicleide's. In describing Wieprecht's Baß-Tuba as 'a kind of Bombardon, whose mechanism has been improved by Herr Wieprecht . . . its tube, like that of the Bombardon, produces the tones of the F-major chord' Berlioz was not putting the cart before the horse. Whereas Wieprecht invented *the* Baß-Tuba he subsequently made *a* bombardon, the distinctive features of the Baß-Tuba being not only its bore and valve-system but his new Berliner-Pumpen, the improvement to the mechanism mentioned above. Berlioz also implies, by using it as a term of reference, that the bombardon was the more familiar instrument to his readers—in other words, that it had been around longer. This argument both explains the otherwise puzzling passage in *Instrumentation* and reveals an error in the assertion by Marcuse that because the Baß-Tuba was patented as a five-valve instrument other makers were able to circumvent the patent by making similar instruments with three, four or six valves which they called bombardons. Since the makers were not in Prussia there was no need for them to circumvent the patent as they were outside the area of its protection. Sachs's assertion that the difference between a Baß-Tuba and a bombardon is that the former had five valves and the latter had four (S³, 54) is logical and probably correct when applied to the period in which Wieprecht worked.

The name 'bombardon' has always had band connotations as opposed to the orchestral 'tuba' (see page 386 below for a twentieth-century anecdote illustrating this). Verdi and other Italian composers reserved the name *Bombardone* (*Flicorno basso-grave in fa o mi♭*) for stage bands, although models of Baß-Tuba in E♭ were soon manufactured as well as those in the original F.

Fortunately, just about the time the Baß-Tuba was becoming known in the German States Berlioz was there on an extended conducting tour and his excitement on discovering the instrument is as clear in his letters to friends in France as is the initial frustration caused by the virtual non-existence of the ophicleide there. His correspondents must have been intrigued. Writing from Dresden he remarks: 'The military band is very good . . . There are no ophicleides, the bottom line is taken by Russian bassoons, serpents and tubas'. Then from Brunswick: '. . . as to the ophicleide, there was none of any kind . . . I was offered as a substitute a bass tuba (a magnificent instrument of which I shall be speaking in connexion with the military bands of Berlin)—but the young man who played it did not seem to have thoroughly grasped its mechanism, being uncertain of the true range'. At the Opera in Berlin itself, where one might have expected a tuba, there was neither tuba nor ophicleide but two bass trombones. Berlioz found the effect 'disastrous', but this may not necessarily have been the case (see pages 494-5 below). Two valved F bass trombones were used in stage bands at the Vienna Opera as late as 1883 (Z⁴, 24).

Following a performance of the overture *Les Francs Juges* by the 600 players of Wieprecht's massed bands, including twelve Baß-Tubas, Berlioz at last throws light on this mysterious new instrument:

The bass tuba, which I have mentioned several times in previous letters, has completely dislodged the ophicleide in Prussia, if indeed the latter was ever prevalent there, which I doubt. The bass tuba is a large brass instrument derived from the bombardon [sic] and fitted with a mechanism of five rotary valves [*an error in translation:* Berlioz actually writes 'cylindres' (Berliner-pumpen)] which gives it an enormous range in the lower registers.

The lowest notes of all are a little blurred, it is true, but *when doubled an octave higher by another bass tuba* [my italics], they take on an amazing richness and resonance, and in the middle and upper registers the tone is impressively noble, not at all flat like the ophicleide's but full and vibrant and well matched with the timbre of trombones and trumpets, to which it serves as a true bass, blending perfectly with them. Wieprecht is the man who popularized the instrument in Prussia. Adolphe Sax now makes admirable tubas in Paris (B²⁸, 335).

Lavoix mentions that the collection of autograph scores at the Bibliothèque Nationale shows Berlioz's replacement of ophicleides by tubas in almost every case. Where Berlioz did not make the alteration his publishers did. Other orchestral composers, however, were generally slow to take up the tuba. Adolphe Sax's 'admirable tubas' were made in Paris not for orchestras but for bands. Manufacturers were similarly engaged in Paris and in Königgrätz, Prague, Vienna, Stockholm and elsewhere. 'The effect of a great number of bass tubas in a large military band is beyond imagination', wrote Berlioz. 'They sound like a combination of trombones and the organ'. In 1869 at the National Peace Jubilee, Boston, Massachusetts, the band of the Garde Républicaine was to impress its audience by just this quality. Including eight saxophones and 'large, conically tapered tubas' it 'was so round, full and soft that all musicians were captivated with the deep diapason of sound' ($S^{21}$, 71).

The tuba had certainly solved the problem of a satisfactory bass for the band. As Ridley points out, historically there had often been difficulties in the provision of related bass instruments, problems not by any means restricted to ensembles including brass ($R^8$, 29). By the time the tuba appeared, therefore, orchestral composers had long accepted substitute bass instruments. In the score of Haydn's oratorio *The Creation* of 1798 a double-bassoon is placed immediately below the three trombones. The *Reglamento per la Musica, e Cappella di Corte,* issued on 27 April 1827 on the reoganisation of the musical establishment at the court of Modena, Italy, placed the first and second bassoons below the trombone ($V^1$, 43).

In bands, also, there seemed to be no attempt at any homogeneity of sound. There are strong indications that any and all instruments capable of playing the deepest notes were included in the hopes of producing sufficient volume and fulness of tone. Kastner gives details: *l'Infantrie impériale,* two serpents and one *buccin* (*buccine,* a trombone with a dragon's head); 'une grande musique d'infantrie', two contrabassoons; Prussian, Saxon, Austrian and Hanoverian regiments generally, a *quartfagott* (a fourth below the normal bassoon) or serpent ($K^5$, 171-188). A correspondent of the *American Musical Journal* in 1835 gave his recommendation for a 'full band', including one serpent and one bass horn. The low brass section in the monster concert presented in New York on 16 April 1842 under the title of the Heinrich Musical Festival included 'one Bombardo, one Ophicliede, one Serpent, one Bass Horn' ($B^{58}$, 16.4.42, 75). During the transitional period after the tuba's introduction but before the other instruments were dropped there were sections like the Prussian Infantry's serpent and tuba, bombardon or bass horn and the Russian bassoon, three ophicleides and bombardon of the *Guides de Bruxelles.*

Little by little, inevitably, the Baß-Tuba appeared in an increasing number of German orchestras. By 1844 there was one at both the Berlin Court Opera and the Dresden Court Opera (in the previous year the Hanover Court Opera borrowed a player as required from the local military band), and by 1850 Brunswick and Darmstadt also had bass tubas (or valved ophicleides), while a valved ophicleide was present at the Vienna Music Festival in 1843. From these known facts it would be safe to assume that the instrument was by mid-century widespread in the German States. And, as we shall see, there were also other varieties of bass tuba, members for the most part of large simultaneously-conceived families as opposed to the solitary Baß-Tuba.

The deep valved brasses were also being made in the United States by the middle of the nineteenth century. Writing in 1850, A.D. describes American brass bands of the period:

The lowest and largest Brass instruments in general use at the present time, are the C and B *flat* Opheclides, F Trombacella, Bass Tuba in F, and the Contra Bass Saxhorn in E *flat*. Very rarely that Instruments of larger size are ever used, although many have been made, but found too heavy for practical purposes.

The Saxhorn is the most general favorite, and very justly so, as it stands in E *flat*; most of the notes used are open tones, and the quality of the tone is more sonorous than any of the others. The Opheclide, some few years back, was universally used; its tone is too short, and does not amalgamate with the other Instruments of the band. . . . The next in quality is the Trombacella, which is simply a Bass post-horn, and, like that Instrument, deficient in power, arising from the smallness of the tubing. The next are the Bass Tubas, they are certainly fine Instruments, and are Bass Trompets, the tubing being a little larger than the Trombacella, and consequently, as much improved as the tube is enlarged. The last I shall speak of are the Saxhorns; these, like all the Instruments of the name, have the most decided preference given them by all, as they are in better proportion than any other (A[2], 361).

Although A.D.'s motives are sometimes suspect (the passage quoted is only the initial section of an article which culminates in a plea for recognition of the unsurpassable quality of American-made instruments), he had correctly identified the source of an instrument's tone quality. The saxhorns are covered in the next chapter. The Trombacello (Fig. 11.1) was the deepest instrument made by Graves of Winchester, New Hampshire by 1844. The company may have begun making brass instruments as the result of being joined by James Keat, third son of the London instrument-maker Samuel Keat, about 1837 (E[4], II, 74). The general characteristics of what is quite probably the first American-designed bass brass instrument, closely follow those of the Baß-Tuba, thus strongly differentiating its maker's approach from that of his contemporaries in Britain and France where the more open saxhorn conformation was already being more generally adopted.

All of these instruments occupied an ambivalent position in their earlier days. Berlioz's *Instrumentation* heads the appropriate article 'THE BASS TUBA (The double bass of the wood wind)' (in the original, '*d'harmonie*': 'of the band' (B[24], 229)).

Mandel wrote in 1859: 'It must be observed that those brass instruments such as bass-bombardons, and sometimes, also, euphonium, which play the principal bass part, are, practically, to be considered wood instruments' ($M^{11}$, 5). Writers on bands like Kastner (1848) tend to list the tubas or their equivalent with the bass instruments of the wood-wind rather than after the trombones. Musically there was neither a reason for nor a result of this in either band or orchestral scoring, but it does indicate the uncertain attitude of even the best-informed commentators of the time.

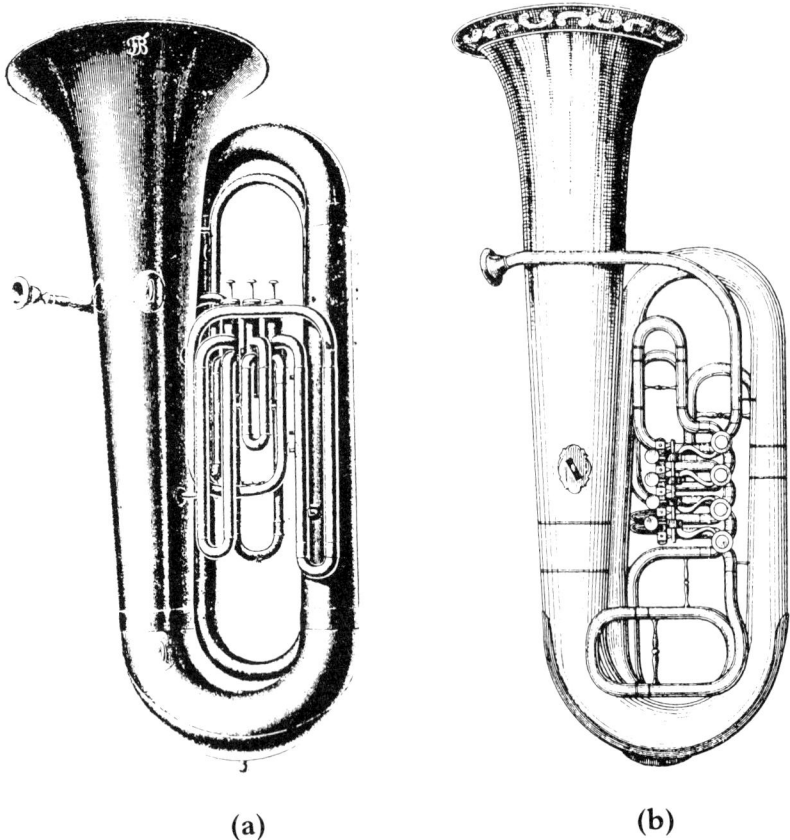

(a)                                    (b)

Fig. 4.9. (a) *Contre-basse sib* (illustrated by Fontaine-Besson, 1910); (b) *Kontrabasstuba* (illustrated by Niloff, 1908): two instruments of identical pitch showing the distinctive French and German conformations which still prevail in the twenty-first century. Note that the bells actually face in opposite directions: (a) is shown from the player's side, (b) from the audience's side.

References to natural bass tubas in European musical instrument collections are explained by pitch relationship rather than mechanism. One was made by G. Ottensteiner of Munich in 1865. Its shape is that of a typical German tuba, but its notes consist only of the harmonic series in G. Another exists made in F in 1860, while an instrument built in Paris in 1845, in which Adolphe Sax is thought to have had a hand, appears to be a natural baritone, in French tuba-shape.

## VALVED OPHICLEIDES

In the letter quoted above (page 209), Berlioz stated that the tuba had 'completely dislodged the ophicleide in Prussia, if indeed the latter was ever prevalent there, which I doubt'. Almost twenty-five years had elapsed between the ophicleide's first public appearance at the Paris Opéra and Berlioz's German tour. In Paris the ophicleide had become familiar in situations ranging from Musard's popular concerts, where it was in use by 1833, to performances of major works by Berlioz himself. It was used in a performance of Haydn's *Creation* at the Opéra in place of the double bassoon (a rare instrument in France), and was also to be heard in town bands throughout the land.

Yet the ophicleide was not unknown in Germany. Breitkopf & Härtel had included a part in the first published edition of Mendelssohn's *Midsummer Night's Dream Overture* (parts published 1832, score 1835); there was an ophicleide at the Frankfurt Festival in 1838, the year in which Spohr, living in Kassel, included ophicleide in the first of his *Zwei Männenchöre* (G[7], 11). An 'Oplick.' was shown alongside the Baß-Tuba in a plan of the orchestra at the Berlin Opera and an 'Orphikleide' at the Darmstadt Hoftheater by 1844 (G[7], Plans 9, 11). In his book of advice for conductors published in that year, Gassner does not refer anywhere in the text to the Baß-Tuba (reserving his references for the Plans), but he does list 'Ophycleyde' (G[7], 77), leading to the inference that this, as the more familiar instrument, had been around longer. He groups it with bassoon, bass trombone 'and similar new bass instruments' in a list of those providing the lowest parts (G[7], 94).

In 1838 Johann Strauss, the elder, brought his orchestra to London's Hanover Square Rooms. 'The trumpet and ophicleide performers distinguished themselves by the power and beauty of the tone they brought from their respective instruments,' reported *The Musical World*. 'M. Strauss has taught the public the real power of the ophicleide' (M[53], 19.8.38, 264). The ophicleide in Strauss's orchestra was possibly not the ophicleide to which London concert-goers were accustomed:

it was more likely to have been valved (*Ventil-Ofikleide*) than keyed (*Klappen-Ofikleide*), although in general it was considered that the latter produced the better sound. The reviewer should not be blamed for confusing the two. The reader is invited to inspect the photograph of Besses o' th' Barn Band in 1860 (B[3], pl. XIV, 1) and try his luck at differentiating between valved and keyed low brass of the time.

   Further challenges are presented in the numerous photographs of over-the-shoulder (OTS) and upright saxhorns in Garofalo & Elrod's book on American Civil War instruments (G[6]). By their very nature, OTS basses retained the long, straight, relatively narrow bore associated with valved ophicleides (Fig. 14.1). It is interesting to note that the tubing profiles and tallness of bell characteristic of upright instruments of the time in America are largely indistinguishable from OTS. There seems to have been a general desire for the relatively thin, incisive tone produced by these instruments, despite associated intonation problems. Contemporary wider-bore instruments also followed the traditional French tall upright form with top-valves—a surprising development in view of the earlier Trombacello's marked Baß–Tuba characteristics.

   The German ophicleide repertoire amounts to no more than a handful of parts. Berlioz's suggestion that the ophicleide may have been rarely used in Prussia is supported by the small number of these instruments to be found in museums in German-speaking countries, the area in which brass instrument-making has been cultivated more actively than anywhere else in Europe. The paucity of surviving examples indicates that keyed ophicleides were made there extremely infrequently. One of the few examples known to have been produced in the German States is the ophicleide with eight keys by August Heiser of Potsdam in the Frankfurt Museum.

   The weight of evidence suggests that most Teutonic ophicleides did not have key-covered side-holes but were examples of a variety of narrow-bore valved tuba made in ophicleide shape, i.e. the valves and associated tubing were not enclosed within loops of the main tubing but were arranged across, or alongside, the vertical bell section. One such by A. Barth (Munich) & A. L. Stegmann (Magdeburg) is in the Historisches Museum Basel. More are to be found in the catalogue of the Leipzig Musikinstrumenten-Museum (H[22], 62-71). No. 1767, by Michael Saurle of Munich, c.1835-40 is described as *Bombardon (Ventilophicleide)*. This has three Sattler valves '*Spätform*' (backwards) for left-hand operation. (The Sattler valve is a type of double, or Vienna, valve, which is activated by being lifted, hence the need to provide a 'backwards' touch-piece for the player to depress.) Leipzig No. 3600, an anonymous *Bombardon* with four Vienna valves, also has a narrow bore. Heyde points to the inferior tone-quality of both of these instruments, confirming the views of Caussinus who ascribed the dull quality of tone to the valve mechanism itself, while also deprecating its poor intonation (page 219 below) (C$^{14}$, 5).

The widespread presence of German orchestral players in the nineteenth century, perhaps most clearly shown in the symphony orchestras formed then in England and the United States, makes it essential to be cautious when references to ophicleides are found. Lévachkine, or example, cites William Schönekerl, one of a number of German and Austrian members of the orchestra of Moscow's Bolshoi Theatre (L$^{11}$, I, 24). He is listed as playing ophicleide in 1861, but tuba in 1865. It is likely that both instruments had valves. (The paucity of Teutonic names in Appendix C 2 presents a remarkable contrast to most lists of nineteenth-century orchestral musicians.)

The *Bombardon Ophocleide* [sic.] for which Michael Pfaff of Kaiserlautern, Bavaria was awarded Honourable Mention at the 1851 Great Exhibition, was also more bombardon than ophicleide, with 'four valves and mouthpiece'. This helps explain why the number of F ophicleides made in Germany seems disproportionately large in comparison with the number known to have been made in France and Britain. The latter were, of course, keyed instruments, but the German models were valved. While the ophicleide in F by Charles Kretzschmann of Strasbourg in the Copenhagen Musikhistorisk Museum has twelve keys, and the eleven-keyed ophicleide in F in the Germanisches National Museum, Nürnberg has been identified by Baines with the *Contradon*, *Kontrastbombardon* or *Kontrabombardon* built by the Munich maker Andreas Barth in 1840, in terms of a *valved* instrument to play the lowest part, the pitch of F was ideal, as Wieprecht demonstrated in 1835. Červený made his *Serpentbombardon* on this pattern in 1842. Leopold Uhlmann made a valved ophicleide in 1835, fitted with a set of his *Wiener Ventil* (Austrian Patent 2053 of 1830 (Fig. 4.10). It is to be supposed that the ophicleide by Joseph Meinlschmidt of Vienna (1866-93) was also valved, unless he was living in a time-warp. Stegmann's ophicleide (see page 214 above) was made in the third quarter of the nineteenth century.

The most detailed information on this type of instrument is to be found in French Patent 4936 of 14 June 1836, taken out by Jean-Auguste Guichard of Paris 'pour un instrument perfectionné à pistons'. The description begins significantly with the phrase 'Cet ophicléide à pistons . . .', showing that Guichard was prepared to acknowledge the source of his instrument's shape. It was pitched in Eb, and could

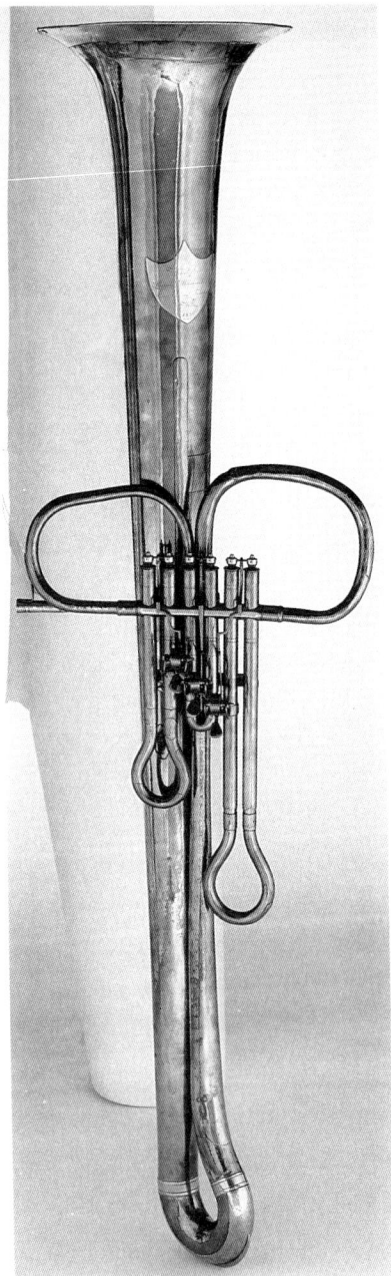

Fig. 4.10
*Ventil-Ophikleide*
by Uhlmann, 1835.
The touch-pieces
of the three Vienna
Valves (invented by
him in 1830) are
positioned conveniently
in front of the second
valve-slide.

be lowered to C by means of an alternative slide, or to B using an alternative double slide. The patent document states that the three valves are operated by keys, but precise details of the mechanism are not given. The drawing shows an ophicleide-shaped instrument, about 110 cm in height overall, with three Stölzel valves mounted horizontally across the body, while the keys are situated on the opposite side, between the bottom bow and the valves (Fig. 4.11).

The *Bass-Bombardone* 'with twelve keys or machine' (*maschine:* valve mechanism) advertised by the Viennese maker Wenzl Riedl seven years earlier, in 1829, may have been similar, since the description implies that the valve mechanism could be operated either through keys acting on valves, or directly by the valves themselves. In 1833 Riedl took out Austrian Patent 1558 for a *Bass-Pumpathon* 'mit einer Maschine', a valved bass bombardon likely to have been in ophicleide form. In the Brussels Musée Instrumental is yet another variation on the valved ophicleide, (No. 2021) a *basse en ut* by J. Finck of Strasbourg. Between the two parallel branches are mounted three rotary valves. The crook enters one branch, the other is terminated by the bell, and the two are joined at the foot in a pleasing curve.

Another spectacular *basse en ut*, by Raoux ('seul fournisseur du Roi, rue Serpente [bis.], à Paris') was exhibited at the Paris Exposition of 1844 and is now No. 1275 in the Brussels collection. The three valves work on the system invented by Coëffet and called by him *emboliclave* ('piston-key'). Each involves two connected parallel tubes, with the all the disadvantages conferred on an air-column forcing its way through complex passages. In this instrument the mechanism is disposed to one side at the foot of the long bell branch, giving it a marked ophicleide profile (M7, 423-24, 439-441).

The valved ophicleide was not restricted to Germany and France. An Italian *Ventilophikleide,* or *Ophicléide monstre,* from c. 1850-55 (Leipzig Museum No. 1765) is pitched in F, with three rotary valves. Heyde mentions that a previous cataloguer, Kraus, had in 1878 referred to this instrument as an *ophicléide à rotation*, and states that in Italy this model was also known as a *cimbasso*. In 1845 Giuseppe Pelitti of Milan built his *Pellitone* or *Controficleide,* probably the instrument described as a valved ophicleide pitched an octave lower than usual for which he was awarded a silver medal by the Istituto Lombardo that year. The Istituto withheld the gold medal as it considered that the instrument did not reach the level of perfection attained   by Wieprecht's Baß-Tuba (M33, 305), confirmation of Berlioz's initial assessment of Wieprecht's invention as having exceptional attributes. In 1844 Pelitti made a *Pelittifono* or *Pelittifero in do a cilindro,* an ophicleide made from leather-

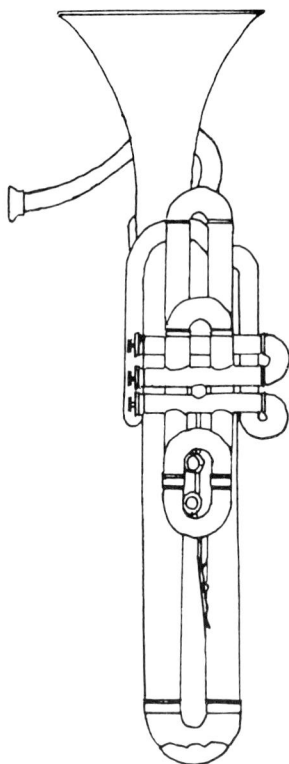

Fig. 4.11
Guichard's
*Ophycléide à pistons*
of 1836.
*(After the patent drawing.)*

covered wood which had three Vienna valves and was played with a french horn mouthpiece (M[33], 307). It can only be assumed that its lack of general adoption was caused by this unique combination of obstacles to the easy production of a good sound. Giovacchino Bimboni's *Contrabbasso a Fiato* ('wind contrabass') invented in Florence in 1842 was also probably valved, in view of Bimboni's interest in building unusual valved instruments. The 'vertical bombardino' designed by Giuseppe Gabusi and built by Spada which was exhibited at the 1881 Bologna Exhibition is likely to have been a euphonium of the ophicleide type. Similar instruments were made in Britain, where at the 1851 Great Exhibition James Jordan, in addition to exhibiting his euphonic serpentcleide, showed a tenor-valve ophicleide (perhaps anticipating Spada's instrument), both products of his Liverpool workshop.

   The word 'ophicleide' seems rarely to have been applied to valved instruments in Britain, where the Halary keyed ophicleide was firmly established, and so far no references to indigenous performers have been located. D'Almaine's 1839 catalogue includes ophicleides with nine or eleven keys and also 'With Patent Valve Stops' at a considerably higher price. This term is also applied to their trombones ('Alto . . . Tenor . . . Bass . . . Do. with Valve Stops') so implies a valved variety. (See also above, page 183, for 'three moveable stops'.) In view of the existence of numbers of the superior French saxhorns in England by this date, it is not surprising that the valved ophicleide failed to establish a place here. It is significant, however, that all three references to 'ophicleide' amongst the twenty-nine specifications for improvements to brass instruments identified by John Webb in the Public Record Office imply the valved variety. These consist of:

BT45/3/433 of 7 April 1845 for 'The Albert Valve for . . . Ophicleides, etc.' (Robert Bradshaw, Dublin.)
BT45/3/594 of 1 December 1845 for 'Design for . . . Ophicleide'. (George Macfarlane, London.)
BT45/4/700 of 16 April 1846 for 'Design for a Four-valve . . . Ophicleide'. (Thomas Key, London.) (W[4], 48-50)

*Ophicléides-à-pistons* (sometimes known as *ophicléides monstres*) appeared in French makers' catalogues for some years in the nineteenth century. In his ophicleide tutor Caussinus writes: 'L'Ophicléïde à piston est généralement moins juste que l'autre' ('The valved ophicleide is generally less well in tune than the other') (C[14], 5). Kastner's *Méthode pour l'ophicléide* also deals with the 'ophicléide à trois pistons ou bombardon', while in 1845 Garnier's *Méthode élémentaire et facile d'ophicléide à pistons* appeared, a work which does not even mention the keyed instrument.

Berlioz is sure to have known about Guichard's invention as he kept a wide-open ear on Parisian musical activity, and he is likely to have come across valved ophicleides during his conducting tour. He refers to the situation in Hamburg, where 'I also found a vigorous ophicleide . . .' (B[27], 303) and, more intriguingly in Brunswick, where he writes 'There was no ophicleide *of any sort* at Brunswick' (B[27], 297) (my italics). That he seemed to ignore the valved ophicleide in both his letters and his *Grand traité* may well have been because he thought it unworthy of consideration. We have already noted that Guichard's *ophicléide-à-pistons* was considered by Caussinus as being inferior to the traditional ophicleide owing to its intonation problems. These would be inevitable in a three-valve uncompensated deep brass instrument with a relatively narrow bore. However, in view of a tradition of valved instruments that began in 1813 the German States are unlikely to have looked favourably upon the keyed ophicleide, based on an acoustic principle that had never merited serious consideration by Teutonic makers of low brass. The valved ophicleide provided an alternative timbre to Wieprecht's Baß-Tuba, and as it happened, given the profile of the tubing, one that was probably not too far removed from that of Halary's original keyed ophicleide.

The use made of the instrument by composers was limited. About 1845 Johann Kalliwoda, in Donaueschingen, composed his *Six Pièces*, for large wind band including bombardon alongside an ophicleide; Spohr, in addition to the work of 1838 mentioned above (page 213), specified an ophicleide in his opera *Die Kreuzfahrer* of 1843-44 intended for Kassel. One of the most intriguing examples of a German request for ophicleide occurs in Schumann's *Das Paradies und die Peri*, composed for solo voices, chorus and orchestra and performed in Leipzig in 1843. This is considered, along with Schumann's sole request for tuba, on pages 312-15 below.

The publishers Breitkopf & Härtel were clearly moved by commercial considerations in changing Mendelssohn's requirement for a bass horn to the printed 'Ophicleide' in both the *Midsummer Night's Dream Overture* (published in 1832-35) and the later incidental music (1848). Both German and British first performances of the *Overture* correctly utilized the English bass horn. However, this instrument was becoming increasingly scarce by the 1830s, and had always been restricted to bands rather than finding a place in the orchestra, so the decision to print 'Ophicleide' in the published version made the works more viable for German performance (in, for example, Frankfurt, Kassel and Darmstadt, where orchestras included the valved type). As in England, performances involving large choral forces used augmented orchestras. In Vienna, a performance of Handel's *Alexander's Feast* in 1841 involved three ophicleides and two double-bassoons. Haydn's *Creation* in 1844 had three ophicleides and four double-bassoons, and an ophicleide was also present at the 1846 Vienna Music Festival.

The valved ophicleide remains a somewhat isolated experiment, restricted in the numbers made, in the period of its use and in the area in which it was used. Wieprecht's Baß-Tuba itself was to be superseded during the 1840s as increasing numbers of inventors set to work on making improvements. By the middle of the century the valved ophicleide was effectively extinct, although as a final tribute François Sudre's family of Sudrephones, invented in 1892, was built in this form (Fig. 15.7). Inevitably, it was a failure.

# CHAPTER V

## *Tenor Tuba and Euphonium*

As early as high school, she had dreamed of being a musician at Walt Disney World. She even chose the University of Central Florida (UCF) for her undergraduate work because of its proximity to the theme park.

—on euphoniumist Gail Robertson, from an article by Tom Mackim on Walt Disney World's The Tubafours in *TUBA Journal*, Spring 1998

West Riding Asylum, Menston, near Leeds. WANTED, Euphonium player, who will be required to Act as Attendant. Must be a Good Player, and able to Read Music at sight. Salary to commence at £30, increasing £2 10s. annually up to £55, with Board, Lodging, Uniform and Washing. Apply personally, or by letter, to the SUPERINTENDENT, at the Asylum.

—*The Era*, 14 June 1893

IN 1838 Carl W. Moritz of Berlin built a tenor tuba pitched in B♭. The instrument had a relatively wide bore and four valves, two for each hand. There is an example in the Städtliches Musikinstrumentensammlung, Munich (No. 40/206). The tenor tuba was superseded about 1843 by the *Euphonion* (Greek *euphonos*, 'sweet-voiced'), invented by *Konzertmeister* Sommer of Weimar, apparently a tenor tuba with an even wider bore. (Later in the century the publishers Boosey & Co. differentiated between parts for the instrument in bass clef and parts in transposed treble clef by naming the former 'Euphonion' and the latter 'Euphonium', but this did not become standard practice.)

The name 'tenor tuba' in translation is still used for the euphonium by players in Italy and Holland: the Haags Gemeentemuseum has five of these instruments in tuba, helicon and oval shapes mainly by Dutch makers. The bell and mouthpipe dimensions (the bore is not available) are closer to the average baritone than the average euphonium but it should not be supposed that this implies a precise use of the term 'tenor tuba' since the Besson euphonium is also known by this name in the Netherlands. Additionally 'tenor tuba' is sometimes used in English-speaking countries when referring to a group of tubas in various pitches. It is then generally applied to both euphoniums and baritones as opposed to the lower bass tubas.

Kunitz claims that the Sommer instrument was a tenor tuba of *narrower* bore than its predecessor, later becoming known as *Baritonhorn, Bariton* or *Baryton*, sometimes *Tenorbasshorn* or *Tenorbass* (K[25], 880). However as early as 1829 Wieprecht's new instrumentation for the *Trompeten-Corps* had included a three-valve *Tenorbasshorn in B*. Baines has suggested that this may have been a wider-bore version of the *Tenorhorn* and thus the prototype euphonium, which seems logical. It is supported by the subsequent occasional German use of *Tenorbasshorn* for euphonium and *Tenorhorn* for baritone. If it is impossible at this distance of time to be definitive about the use of these terms it seems sensible to compromise by accepting German *Baryton* as meaning euphonium and German *Tenorhorn* as meaning baritone. It is likely that the North American practice of calling the euphonium by the name 'baritone' (which has now all but died out) resulted from the large number of nineteenth-century German immigrants.

The application of the appparently self-contradictory term *Tenorbasshorn* is based on a keen awareness of the compass and function of the instrument. A comparison of the euphonium's compass with that of the ophicleide shows that if we accept the older instrument as a bass we should do likewise with the newer. The euphonium is, after all, precisely the same pitch as the French *saxhorn-basse* and approximately the same pitch as the orchestral cello. When it is used in the orchestra it frequently doubles the bass tuba at the octave, and the bass tuba is really a contrabass instrument (cf. *violoncello* and *contrabasso*: Berlioz said of the bass tuba, 'Its position in the trumpet family [is] exactly equivalent to that of the double bass in the violin family') (B[25], 229).

On the other hand, in bands the euphonium plays a predominantly tenor role and, as will be obvious from some of the music examples below, usually fulfils a similar function when required to appear in the symphony orchestra. We must therefore conclude that it fulfils both tenor and bass functions. Military band arrangements, particularly those following conventions established towards the end of the nineteenth century, often juxtapose phrases demonstrating the two contrasting roles, and in a typical concert programme the euphonium can be called upon to cover a compass of A' to b'. The appellation 'cello of the band' is thus applied to the euphonium with accuracy as well as feeling

Fig. 5.1. An ensemble playing King 625-SB 'baritones' with the satin silver-plated finish popular in the early twentieth century reintroduced by United Musical Instruments in the late 1990s.

*United Musical Instruments U.S.A. Inc., makers of C. G. Conn brass instruments*

# THE INSTRUMENT

The euphonium is pitched in B♭ (occasionally in c and even more rarely in A), and its music is normally written in bass clef at concert pitch or, in brass bands, treble clef a ninth above the sounding note. (The few exceptional cases are dealt with later in this chapter.) There are from three to five valves, the placing of the valves and positioning of the bell normally following bass tuba practice.

Except for cheaper models, euphoniums made in England are always compensated on the Blaikley system, with the advantage that $B^1$ can be obtained (Ex. 1.2). The bore of the average euphonium is about 15 mm. Possibly this is ideal for a bass pitch conical instrument as there is no doubt that it speaks more readily, is played in tune with more ease and found more responsive generally than the larger tubas. It is also, as Kunitz puts it (K[25], 882), 'a decided *Gesanginstrument*' while at the same time its agility allows the euphonium to occupy the undisputed position of most important lower instrument in the band—once again, an analogy with the orchestral cello.

In brass band scoring cello and bassoon passages are automatically allocated to it, and often horn solos as it is much more distinctive in tone than any of the higher saxhorns. If the instrument has a disadvantage it is this lack of anonymity. While it can provide a good octave reinforcement to the bass, the bass itself in relatively lightly-scored passages, and be a superb tenor melodist or counter-melodist (its constant and continuous function in older arrangements), it is folly to put the euphonium on a unimportant note in a chord or give it a disjointed harmonic line. Its tone is so compelling that the arranger's error becomes compulsive listening.

Comparison with the ophicleide as a solo instrument is to the advantage of the euphonium since, precisely as in the case of the cornet and the keyed bugle, the valved instrument's agility is sometimes frankly incredible and it is much more easily managed by the player (see Ex. 5.1). Sousa employed some renowned euphoniumists in his band (almost all with Italian names) and during his 1904 world tour the brass players in the Leipzig Gewandhaus Orchestra were only convinced that Simone Mantia's triple-tonguing was not produced by three little balls in each valve when they were allowed to unscrew the valve-caps and inspect the interiors. Mantia specialized in playing cornet solos on a five-valve euphonium with two bells which could be used for echo effects. (See pages 476-9 below for details of this type of instrument.)

Ex. 5.1

Hartmann: *Variations on Rule Britannia*

*Double-*and *triple-tonguing* are fast articulation methods achieved by utilizing the normal tonguing technique *T* and the consonant *K* in the patterns *T-K* or *T-T-K* respectively. They are extremely effective on the euphonium or higher brass instrument but difficult on the deeper tubas owing to the longer time it takes to make the note 'speak'.

Jullien featured the euphonium, of course. In his *British Army Quadrilles* there is a 'recit, by euphonium, descriptive of issuing the orders'. The player of the bombardon solo in the same work was Herr Sommer, a member of Jullien's orchestra who also played the euphonium and Sommerophone. (His name sometimes appears as Sommers.) The Sommerophone was exhibited at the 1851 Great Exhibition, where F. Sommer (Prussia) received Honourable Mention and a comment in the *Reports by Juries* on the 'euphonic horn . . . an instrument of great power, as well as sweetness of tone' (G[20], 331). Not only this, but the report (written by an anonymous member of the jury, which included Hector Berlioz) digresses at some length in a discussion of the diminished power of the organ removed from its cathedral and put into the Crystal Palace (G[20], 330). 'So . . . deprived of a building to whose column of air it acts as the sounding-body to bring

it into resonance . . . it is eclipsed by an insignificant-looking "Sax" or euphonic
horn . . . and to induce even the multitude to listen to the organ . . . it has
been found necessary to get one of these small wind-instruments to mingle its
more expressive and exciting sounds. I allude to the combined performance of the
euphonic horn and organ, which has been so often heard in the Crystal Palace . . . '
Sir Henry Bishop strongly denies in a footnote that it was necessary to draw the
crowds by this stratagem (only one example of the highly amusing battle of words
between the anonymous juror and Bishop, the official Reporter) but our interest
lies in the presence of Herr Sommer in Jullien's band playing Sommerophone solos
concurrently with a *Kapellmeister* named Sommer from Prussia playing solos on his
instrument at the Crystal Palace.

Herr Sommer first appears in Jullien's programmes as the Sommerophone soloist
in 1849. Fétis, having explained that Sommer invented the euphonium in 1844,
goes on to describe recitals he gave in Frankfurt-am-Main, Breslau and Prague
during 1844-5, but this otherwise invaluable reference lets us down badly by giving
Sommer no forename. One is almost driven to conclude that he had only a
surname, as in none of the several references to Sommer is there any more positive
identification, save for the initial in the Great Exhibition *Reports.*

Lavoix states that Sommer invented the Sommerophone (or *baryton-à-bocal*), 'a
sort of ophicleide with valves or pistons', in 1844 (L[6],145). Pontécoulant relates
how Sommer, having invented his instrument in Silesia (what a fertile area for brass
that was), took it to Vienna where further improvements were made by Franz Bock
and after two concerts it was perfected by Ferdinand Hell who patented the
instrument under the name *Hellhorn* (P[20], I, 425). It seems more likely that
Sommer's instrument was actually *built* by Bock, who then took out an Austrian
Patent for *Euphonion* on 1 April 1844. Heyde prints an illustration of the prototype
(H[24], 298). The Hellhorn was in fact patented on 5 April 1844, and Heyde's
illustration of this instrument clearly shows its four rotary-valves, but there is no
confirmation of any of the other events in Pontécoulant's saga. Hell's 'new
invention called "Hell's-horn"' was also exhibited at the Great Exhibition, which
might have proved embarrassing to one inventor or the other.

Is it safe to assume that the Sommerophone was the euphonium, an unsuccessful
attempt to preserve its inventor's name for posterity? Sachs (S[3], 350) defines
*Sommerophone* as 'baryton' (i.e. euphonium), and I am inclined to agree that they
were one and the same. But of the Sommerophone, or Sommer, no more was heard
after 1851.

As a footnote to this investigation into the origins of the euphonium, Pelitti's *bombardino* should be mentioned. 'Bombardino' is a term in common use by both Italians and Spaniards for the euphonium, widely familiar as the name on the front of the part for that instrument in Verdi's stage bands. Giuseppe Pelitti of Milan claims to have invented it in 1835, the year Wieprecht invented the Baß-Tuba. In a detailed account of its early history Meucci refers to a dispute in 1847 between Pelitti and Adolphe Sax over the identity of the true inventor (M[32], 305). Why this disagreement did not occur until twelve years after it was claimed that Pelitti's instrument had appeared in Milan, and why either of the two inventors bothered when the euphonium itself had been patented in 1844, is difficult to understand.

In 1848 the prolific Červený brought out his *Baroxyton*, which shares its name with a 'four-valved bombardon' invented by Ferdinand Stegmaier of Ingolstadt about the same time (W[3], 384). Červený's version was a four-valve euphonium with a range of three octaves and a third from B♭ to d″. The Russians adopted it as first bass in their infantry bands. Made in tuba, ophicleide and helicon shapes, there were other models in F and E♭. Červený also made the *Phonikon* or *Zunkoroh*, a euphonium with a cor-anglais type of bulbous bell. (This is one of the instruments illustrated in Červený's 1859 catalogue, reproduced by Lévachkine (L[11], I, 23).) In 1861 Rott of Prague invented the *Glagol*, a *baryton* (euphonium) with adjustable bell, while around 1887 Fratelli Rossano of Bari built their *Clavicorno Fagotto*, apparently yet another variety of euphonium.

It is possible (though unlikely) that alterations were made to the euphonium by the London player Alfred Phasey, already encountered as an ophicleidist. He was the featured euphonium soloist in Luigi Arditi's concert season at Her Majesty's Theatre in 1865, where the assistant conductor was Dan Godfrey, snr. The orchestra included two bombardons and two euphoniums. Writing in 1912 Clappé describes the euphonium as a modification of the B♭ bass saxhorn 'that is, when retaining the proportions introduced some forty years ago by Mr. Phasey of London' (C[26], 127). Phasey's obituary in the *British Bandsman* states that 'he bought a Courtois saxhorn baritone at the Paris Exhibition in 1857 and made many improvements. M. W. Balfe [the composer of *The Bohemian Girl* who conducted at Her Majesty's Theatre from 1845-52] and others suggested that he should call it 'Phaseyphone' but he named it euphonium' (B[55], 11.1888). *The Musical Times* (M[52], 1.9.1888, 552) refers to his having played ophicleide in the Coldstream Guards Band at the early age of fifteen [in 1849], 'and it was while there that he took up the Saxhorn baritone of Courtois, remodelled and renamed it the Euphonium, an instrument now so

Fig. 5.2. *Kaiserbaryton* (euphonium) with four rotary-valves by Červený, c. 1900.

popular in our military bands'. Farmer states that the Continental euphonium used in Britain was of medium bore and Phasey's improvement consisted of enlarging the bore thus enabling it to replace the ophicleide in British orchestras (F$^5$, 12). However, this raises the question as to why Phasey bought a *saxhorn baritone* rather than a *saxhorn basse*, an instrument of the same pitch but with a real euphonium bore plus the four valves necessary in an instrument to be used for orchestral playing. As early as 1845 Sax's patent drawing showed expansive profiles in the lower instruments.

Alfred Phasey began his career as an ophicleidist and finished it, according to the *British Bandsman*, 'without rival on the euphonium' (B$^{55}$, 11.1888, 33-4). He joined the Crystal Palace Orchestra in 1862 and was still there playing ophicleide and bass trombone in 1880. From 1879-82 he directed his own band at the Palace, and was bandmaster of St George's Rifles/Earl of Chester's Yeomanry for fifteen years. In the midst of all this, he found time to play with Queen Victoria's Private Band and the Musical Amateurs' Society as well as touring with the Courtois Union. He was involved with brass bands and published a number of arrangements including a *Fantasia on Verdi's opera Attila* 'for Euphonium or Ophicleide and Pianoforte', published about 1860. In 1868, Chappell published as No. 63 of its Army Journal his arrangement for cornet and euphonium duet with military band accompaniment of 'D'un tenero amore' from Rossini's *Semiramide*. Phasey also compiled instruction books for euphonium and trombone. He died in Chester on 17 August 1888, possibly having gone there to play ophicleide in *Elijah* during the Chester Music Festival on 25 July. He was fifty-four years of age, just three years older than his son, Handel Victor Phasey, when the latter died on 18 September 1913. Alfred's occupation was given as 'Professor of Music', while Handel's was simply 'Bandmaster'. In 1893 Handel was Dan Godfrey jnr's euphonium soloist in the inaugural season of his Bournemouth summer season band. He appears in the band photograph, displaying both his euphonium and a fine walrus moustache (M$^{35}$, opp. 118). The Orchestral Band which succeeded it (and became the Bournemouth Symphony Orchestra) included Handel on euphonium and bass trombone. He also published at least one composition, a piano solo *Shamrock the third*, issued by Witmark of New York.

In the United Kingdom virtuoso euphoniumists tend to be restricted to the brass band. While the idea of even a euphonium and tuba event is relatively new, the National Euphonium and Baritone Festival arrived in Manchester in 1998. With the band movement's strong emphasis on family involvement, it is not surprising that there is at least one present-day brass band euphonium dynasty, that of John Childs, his two sons Bob and Nick and third generation David (see page 242 below). All three have brought an enhanced awareness of the euphonium's solo and duet potential. Stephen Mead took a conscious decision to attempt what had previously been thought impossible: a career based on being a freelance euphonium soloist. In fact he has had remarkable success on both sides of the Atlantic, actively involved in giving master-classes and arranging low brass events. He is also leader of the British Tuba Quartet, a brass band-based ensemble of two euphoniums and two E♭ tubas. This particular group, and these virtuoso players, emphasize the differences in approach between the band euphoniumist and the orchestral tenor tubist. There still exists an apparently unbridgeable gap in stylistic terms in contrast to the increasingly orchestral approach of brass band trombone sections.

# THE MUSIC

In the wind or brass band the euphonium is prime bass soloist, after the solo clarinet or solo cornet the most strongly featured instrument. There was a distinctive attitude towards the euphonium in orchestras, particularly in England and France, up to the beginning of the twentieth century. A part for the instrument was often included in light orchestral sets whereas the thought of including a tuba would never have crossed publishers' minds. Its entry into Parisian theatres as the *saxhorn basse* is recounted on pages 253 and 341 below. In 1895 the orchestra at the Alhambra, London's most extravagant variety theatre, consisted of forty-one players including a euphonium but no tuba. It is possible to appreciate R. Farban when he states: 'For dance music I prefer the euphonium to the 'cello; it emphasizes the bass more distinctly' (V³, 244). But in 1901 A. C. Venables made a more questionable suggestion: 'The euphonium may be occasionally employed as a substitute for the bass trombone. It is easier to learn (having the same fingering as the cornet), and is therefore safer in the hands of amateurs than the trombone' (V², 98). Kappey remarks in his bombardon tutor (c. 1874): 'Euphoniums in B♭ and C are replacing the ophicleide and serpent which are now out of date' (K², [1]) .

The inclusion of a euphonium in the orchestra was neither restricted to England and France nor to light music. In the programme of a concert on 17 April 1905 under the auspices of the Cercle des Étrangers de Monaco Asé is shown as playing *bombardino* (euphonium) alongside Rose and Maquarre on trombones, representing a transition between the ophicleide and Small French Tuba in c.

The euphonium would appear to have been one of the most familiar instruments in the late nineteenth-century, with a place in bands and orchestras of many types, but then, as now, there were pockets of ignorance in all classes of society, as shown by this extract from *The Musical Times* of 1 February 1891:

The *Daily Telegraph* is responsible for the following:
'During the dense fog on Saturday night a young German musician, who was very drunk and disorderly at the time, annoyed the inhabitants of Aldgate by persistently blowing some fearsome instrument which neither the bystanders nor the policeman could describe. One said it was a sort of cross between a beer-barrel and a coffee-pot—whatever the product of such a union might be—and the only elucidation another could offer was that the noise it gave forth was "enough to make a Quaker kick his mother-in-law"—a fearful aberation into the land of metaphor which can only be excused by the fact that the strains were so hideous as to drive the listeners into incoherent anger. Alderman Sir Andrew Lusk, before whom the offender was brought at the Mansion House, inquired whether it might not be a bassoon, or a serpent, but all the constable, careful of his oath, could venture to affirm was that it was "a great big hollow thing". Was there no one to suggest that after all it was only a fog-horn? The Alderman was in a lenient mood, and, after most properly insisting that all persons in this realm, whether English or foreign, must obey the law, let the foolish young Deutscher off with a caution.' One would think that a half-century of German bands had familiarised London policemen with the appearance, sound, and name of that instrument—we admit that it is one of torture—called an [sic.] Euphonium. But this ignorance is by no means uncommon. There are comparatively few amateurs of music who know even the names of all the instruments commonly used in the orchestra (M[52], 1.2.1891, 83-4).

A reminder of this golden age sometimes appears in orchestral programmes—Bax's *Overture to a Picaresque Comedy*. Written as late as 1930, this lively work includes a part for 'Tuba in Bb' notated in the bass clef a tone higher than it sounds (like a *saxhorn basse* part). Its demands for agility and lightness make it likely that the composer anticipated its being played on euphonium (Ex. 5.2).

Orchestral tenor tuba parts are also played on the euphonium. No permanent orchestra has a euphoniumist on the pay-roll and if a bandsman is engaged there is a danger that the instrument may sound like a euphonium rather than a tenor tuba.

Ex. 5.2

Bax: *Overture to a Picaresque Comedy*


(Succinctly, the former is usually played with vibrato and the latter without.) Often a trombonist plays the instrument, sometimes the fourth player who specializes in bass trumpet and tenor tuba. Often a tubist plays it, and in this case has the advantage of being accustomed to a conical instrument and normally adjusting intonation with his lip. The trombonist's cylindrical instrument has a very different feel and he automatically adjusts intonation with his slide. On the other hand the tubist, even if he has previously been a euphoniumist, will not have an embouchure accustomed to playing high notes so the lip may tire before a trombonist's.

In the 'Bydlo' movement of Mussorgsky's *Pictures from an Exhibition* orchestrated by Ravel there is a solo written for tuba (originally the Small French Tuba in c) which may be played by the tubist on his normal instrument or a euphonium; by one of the trombonists on the euphonium (the trombones are tacet in the movement) or by a specialist player brought in to play only 'Bydlo' (Ex. 5.3). (This applies to ordinary mortals. In the recording made by Raphael Kubelik and the Chicago Symphony Orchestra in the early 1950s Arnold Jacobs plays 'Bydlo' on a Penzel BBb/F double tuba, and it is claimed that an F tuba is regularly used in Russia. There have also been performances in the U.K. on EEb and F tuba.)

There are occasions when a true euphonium is required in an orchestral setting. These occur not in the symphonic repertoire but when a specific additional character is needed. There is an unmistakable band feeling about the tone of the euphonium, and in consequence Verdi and others included a *eufonio* in their stage bands. It has been used in films from time to time, and sometimes on the stage. The Alun Owen play *Progress to the Park* begins with a small Salvation Army band on stage and the line adapted from Shaw: 'God's euphoniums!'. The instrument was used in the orchestra pit during the John Barry musical *Billy* (Drury Lane, 1974–6)

Ex. 5.3

Mussorgsky/Ravel: 'Bydlo' *(Pictures at an Exhibition)*

where the addition of euphonium countermelody to the 'big band' sound reminded the audience that the action was taking place in a small Yorkshire industrial town and not in the sophisticated world in which the hero imagined himself. It has also been used in radio and television programmes, where a single phrase used as a link between scenes or a more extended signature tune places the proletarian scene with tongue-in-cheek precision.

The tenor tuba's first appearance in the symphony orchestra came about accidentally. Richard Strauss's *Don Quixote* had its first performance in 1898 and *Ein Heldenleben* was premiered the following year. They both contained a part for tenor tuba and so far as is known the first performances—in Cologne and Frankfurt-am-Main respectively—were satisfactory. Strauss's tenor tuba was the higher Wagner Tuba (see page 461 below), surprisingly, regarding his own stated views on these instruments. He wrote in 1904:

> . . . one modern composer . . . showed me the score of a comedy overture, in which the four 'Nibelung' tubas carried on a most lively dance with the rest of the brass . . . Had not Wagner really 'invented' them with such wisdom and sure imagination to depict the sombre world of the Nibelungs? (B[25], 99)

It is difficult to reconcile this statement, in Strauss's revision of Berlioz's *Orchestration* where he gives ample evidence of being the prime Wagnerophile, with the character of Sancho Panza that the instrument is required to portray in *Don Quixote* (Ex. 5.4).

In December 1899 the noted Strauss conductor Ernst von Schuch was preparing a performance of the work in Dresden. 'My tenor tuba player cannot play the part well', he wrote to Strauss, 'and I have therefore arranged for a *Baryton* [euphonium] tomorrow'. Strauss subsequently claimed the credit, writing in the same book: 'I myself have frequently written a single tenor tuba in Bb as the higher octave of the bass tuba; but performances have shown that, as a melodic instrument, the euphonium (frequently used in military bands) is much better suited for this than the rough and clumsy Wagner tubas with their demonic tone' (B[25], 361). He had had ample opportunity of hearing the capabilities of the euphonium as during the Sousa band visit to Berlin in 1900 he went not only to all the concerts but, according to the players, to all the rehearsals as well.

Bernard Shaw once stated: 'I believe that a taste for brass instruments is hereditary' (S[24], 76) and Strauss may have offered confirmation of this as his father, Franz, was first horn of the Munich Hofoper. When Richard wanted to include baritones in his early opera *Guntram* he had to write to his father to discover their pitch and range (which may be thought a strange method of orchestration). It has been suggested that Franz was concerned in the origination of the Wagner Tuben: he certainly played in the first performances of *Tristan*, *Meistersinger* and *Parsifal*. Wagner thought highly of his horn-playing although there was an intense hatred between the two men, well-documented in stories of arguments at rehearsals. (In an article on Strauss's operas David Murray includes the telling phrase: 'Though his father sought to protect him from Wagner's music as long as possible . . .' (M[45], iv, 565).) Strauss snr had the last laugh: when Wagner's death was announced the orchestra stood in silent tribute –all except the first horn.

Richard Strauss used an accepted Wagner Tuba notation for *Don Quixote* and *Heldenleben*: bass clef, a tone higher than the sounding note. Coincidentally this was the identical notation to that used in French bands for the *saxhorn basse*, the euphonium being in both cases effectively the instrument concerned. Players of the orchestral low brass are accustomed to reading at concert pitch but a number of composers later adopted Strauss's notation for tenor tuba (euphonium) parts. Strauss also asks for a mute to be used in both tenor and bass tubas in *Don Quixote*, probably the first time for both.

Bartók includes '2 Tube Tenori in sib' in his symphonic poem *Kossuth*, composed in 1903. The parts are allied to the bass tuba and trombones, obviously not written

Ex. 5.4

(a)

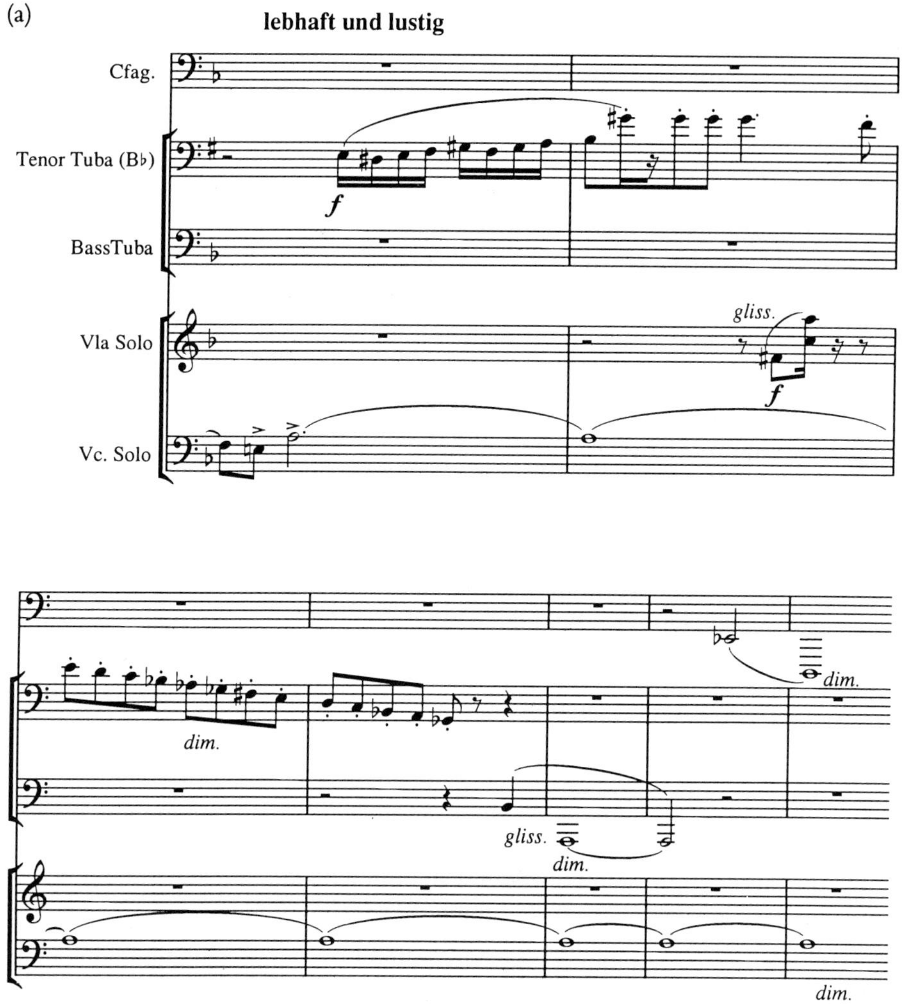


(b)

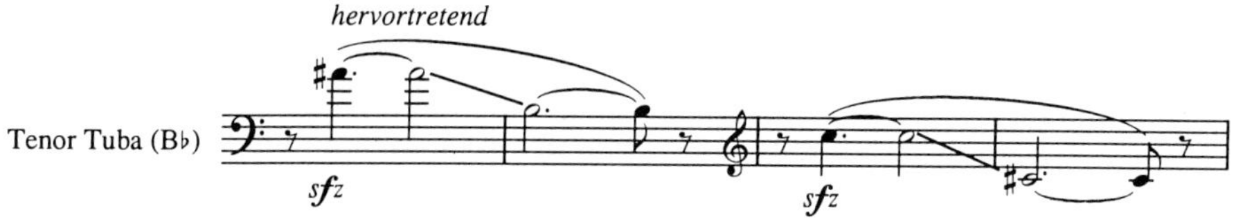


Strauss: *Don Quixote*

with the Wagner Tuba in mind. The compass of the 'Tuba Tenore I' ranges from concert C to concert b♭ and in its higher reaches utilizes the tenor clef, but is still written a tone above the sounding note—surely a unique use of the tenor clef?

The Czechoslovakian composer Janáček wrote two consecutive works including tenor tuba. The first was the *Sinfonietta* (1926) which includes two amongst the numerous brass instruments. This was followed by the *Capriccio* for piano (left hand), for flute doubling piccolo, two trumpets, three trombones and a virtuoso but sympathetic tenor tuba. The preface to the score points out that the two works are linked by common military inspiration: the *Capriccio* (written for pianist Otakar Hollmann whose right arm was paralysed in World War I) is 'a protest against the senselessness and horrors of war' in contrast to the brilliant and colourful *Sinfonietta*. Both parts are notated in treble clef for a B♭ instrument (sounding a ninth below written pitch). Janáček's opera *From the House of the Dead* includes a part for bass trumpet in B♭ doubling tenor tuba. The latter instrument is used only for a section of the 'Pochod' (March) in Act 2 and is notated in treble clef at sounding pitch. Janáček's distinctive approach to orchestration results in the tenor tuba's adopting an unusually ominous presence in these works.

Gustav Holst, who had been a professional trombonist, included a tenor tuba in his suite *The Planets*, first performed in 1918. There is no mistaking the instrument he required—like Janáček he notates the part in brass band treble clef. There are

Ex. 5.5

(a)

Holst: 'Mars' *(The Planets)*

passages requiring the greatest dexterity, but the instrument's appearance in 'Mars', where it issues a war-god's challenge above the insistent five chords to the bar of the triple-*forte* strings, is possibly the tenor tuba's moment of supreme triumph (Ex. 5.5(a)). The reappearance of the motif later in the same movement played in canon with unison trumpets is the supreme affirmation of the claim that the instrument's timbre is sufficiently individual to be heard through the *fortissimo* of the largest orchestra (Ex. 5.5(b)).

Slightly eccentric composers from Anglo-Saxon cultures have sometimes been attracted to the euphonium. The Australian Percy Grainger, who often scored for flexible ensembles, used one alongside tuba in his *English Dance* of 1899-1909, but when rescored in 1924-25 substituted two tubas; there is also a euphonium in *To a Nordic Princess, Marching Song of Democracy, Hill Song No. 1* (where there are no trombones or tuba) and *Lincolnshire Posy*, for military band. The music is always notated in bass clef at sounding pitch. Havergal Brian required two euphoniums alongside the two tubas in his Symphony 1, 'Gothic'. He also scored for euphonium (as well as tuba) in Symphonies 8, 10, 11, 12, 13, 14, 15, 16, 17, 19 and 20 (under the name 'tenor tuba'). Euphonium and tuba begin the eighth symphony with a muted duet over three muffled snare-drums. Brian's notation varies from work to work between sounding pitch bass clef, bass clef written a tone higher than sounding, and treble clef written a ninth higher than sounding (as in the brass band).

Karlheinz Stockhausen scored for euphonium in *Lucifers Tanz*, a version of No. 53 from his opera *Samstag* of 1984. At the premiere, in Berlin in 1988, the extended euphonium solo was played by a member of his own ensemble, Michael Svoboda.

Mention should also be made of its regular inclusion alongside the saxhorns and flicorni. It appears as *eufonio* in Verdi's stage bands, as has already been noted; as *sax-horn-basse à 4 cylindres en sib* in Meyerbeer's *Le Prophète* (Ex. 6.2); and as a pair of *Flicorni bassi* contributing the lowest part of the '6 Buccine' required in the last few pages of Respighi's *Pini di Roma*.

Possibly owing to the undesirable connotations of its timbre the euphonium took a long time to find its way back into jazz, once having given up its place in New Orleans brass bands. It can however provide a useful addition to a full rich unison, as Ex. 5.6 by Alan Cohen shows. (This composer has occasionally used a pair of euphoniums in his jazz scores.) A euphonium also sat by the four french horns in the orchestra assembled in London in 1964 for Benny Golson. The euphonium has now been adopted by a significant number of jazzmen. Foremost amongst these, not least for his pioneering role, was the American Rich Matteson (1929-1993) who 1992 was *Down Beat* magazine's Lifetime Achievement Award winner (see Fig. 11.5). In 1976 he had formed the Matteson-Phillips Tubajazz Consort, consisting of three euphoniums, three tubas and three rhythm, in co-operation with tubist Harvey Phillips. Four years later Matteson was responsible for the introduction of jazz improvisation competitions for both euphonium and tuba. (Jazz tuba is dealt with at greater length on pages 440-6 below.) Kiane Zawadi (Bernard McKinney) has doubled euphonium and trombone with numerous bands where his distinctive euphonium bop solos have established a new role for the instrument. There has also been a certain demand for euphonium in commercial music, not as an individual distinctive voice but as a part of a group of instruments to provide an alternative and 'different' sound. It is not unknown for as many as four to be used in a backing, but inevitably they are unrecognizable in the final mix.

Ex. 5.6

Cohen: *It is*

Following in the steps of the ophicleide, the euphonium was favoured by buskers, possibly because of the favourable effect on the potential donor of an instrument played cradled in the arms. In the late 1960s Geoffrey Fletcher sketched and interviewed a player in London's Oxford Street—a man whose sense of humour seemed to have been strongly influenced by the music hall, as the following extract demonstrates:

You needs good breath for one o' these. It's called a euphonium. Write it down, same as when a man makes a euphemism at dinner . . . I can't play the cornet, as it is, but that's because I have only one tooth, as I'll show you . . . central eating, as you say, Guv . . . I'm 73, too old for a job. But I don't want a job, I have this—the euphonium. Life is an adventure . . . My mother-in-law is staying with us so we have plenty to eat. She gives me the cold shoulder . . . (F[17], 50).

Table 5.1.    SOME ORCHESTRAL SCORES INCLUDING EUPHONIUM

| COMPOSER | TITLE | NOMENCLATURE | NOTATION | DATE |
|---|---|---|---|---|
| Bartók | Kossuth | [2] Tuba tenori Sib | 𝄢 and 𝄡 tone above | 1903 |
| Bax | Overture to a Picaresque Comedy | Tuba in Bb | 𝄢 tone above | 1930 |
|  | Symphony 4 | Tenor tuba in Bb | 𝄢 tone above | 1932 |
| Brian | Symphony 2 | [2] Euphoniums | 𝄢 concert and 𝄞 9th above | 1930-31 |
|  | Symphony 8 | Euphonium in Bb | 𝄢 tone above | 1949 |
|  | Symphony 10 | Euphonium in Bb | 𝄢 tone above | 1953-54 |
| Gounod | Faust (stage band) | Saxhorn [basse] Sib | 𝄢 tone above | 1859 |
| Grainger | Works with 'elastic scoring' | Euphonium | 𝄢 concert |  |
| Harris | Symphony 5 | Baritone tuba (opt.) | 𝄢 concert | 1943 |
| Holst | The Planets | Tenor tuba | 𝄢 concert | 1914-16 |
| Hovhaness | several works | Baritone | 𝄢 concert |  |
| Janáček | Capriccio | Tenor tuba | 𝄞 9th above | 1926 |
|  | From the House of the Dead: 'Pochod' | Tenor tuba (doubling Bb bass trumpet) | 𝄢 concert | 1927-28 |
|  | Sinfonietta | [2] Tenor tubas | 𝄞 9th above | 1926 |

| Composer | Work | Instrument | Clef/Transposition | Date |
|---|---|---|---|---|
| Meyerbeer | Le prophète | Saxhorn-basse à 4 cylindres en si♭ | 𝄢 tone above | 1836-49 |
| Mussorgsky-Ravel | Pictures at an Exhibition: 'Bydlo' | Tuba (small French in c] | 𝄢 concert | 1922 |
| Ponchielli | La Gioconda (stage band) | Bombardino | 𝄢 concert | 1876 |
| Respighi | Pini di Roma | [2] Flicorni bassi | 𝄢 concert | 1923-24 |
| Shostakovich | The Bolt | [2] Baritono treble) | 𝄞 9th above | |
| | The Golden Age | Baritono treble | 𝄞 9th above | 1927-30 |
| | The Tale of the Priest and his Blockhead Servant | Baritono treble) | 𝄞 9th above | |
| Strauss (R.) | Don Quixote | Tenor tuba | 𝄢 tone above | 1896-97 |
| | Ein Heldenleben | Tenor tuba | 𝄢 tone above | 1897-98 |
| Turnage | Three Screaming Popes | Euphonium | 𝄢 concert | 1989 |
| Verdi | Stage bands | Eufonio | 𝄢 concert | |
| Wood | Fantasia on British Sea Songs | Euphonium | 𝄢 concert | 1905 |

The euphonium soon established a place in the standard brass band contesting quartet of two cornets, E♭ horn and euphonium. And its chamber music role was not restricted to the United Kingdom. Isidoro Rossi (1813-1884) composed his *Gran sonata in Do minore* for a Milan exhibition. Unpublished, and probably no longer extant, it was scored for E♭ cornet, E♭ trumpet, trombone and euphonium *(bombardino)* (V[1], 25-6). Reference to the pages shown under 'Stage bands' in the Index will demonstrate the importance of the euphonium in this field in many countries.

Ex. 5.7

Bouillon: air varié *Souvenir d'Ostende*

There are now several concertos for euphonium and brass band, serious compositions presenting the instrument in a serious light. The first, and arguably still the best, is that composed by Joseph Horovitz for Trevor Groom in 1972. Surprisingly, no version for euphonium with orchestral accompaniment is yet available. When David Childs won his way to the final of the BBC Young Musicians 2000 competition the concerto by Philip Wilby had to be arranged for orchestra especially for the occasion.

The combination of solo euphonium and orchestra, rarely heard since the nineteenth century, was shown to work extremely effectively when Charis Snell played the author's arrangement of John Hartmann's *Rule Britannia* (Ex. 5.1) with the Hampshire County Youth Orchestra conducted by Nicholas Wilks in 1999 (Fig. 4.5).Otherwise, television viewers who can bear to watch the jingoistic proceedings of the annual 'Last Night' of the BBC Henry Wood Promenade Concerts may hear a euphonium play 'The Saucy Arethusa' in Wood's *Fantasia on British Sea Songs*. Few of them will realise that the chosen key is possibly the most awkward that could have been found for the player, and yet this was not the arranger's intention. The common use of euphoniums built in pitches other than B♭ is shown by two classified advertisements in a 1908 edition of *Wright & Round's Brass Band News*:

FOR SALE—Euphonium, Besson's Prototype (Class B) with A natural shank for Concert . . .

FOR SALE—Euphonium (Orchestral). Short model in C with B flat attachment, 4 valves . . .(W[32], 21.3.08, 423).

Either one of these instruments would have considerably simplified the fingering of the *Sea Songs* solo.

Amilcare Ponchielli's *Concerto per flicorno basso* (for euphonium and wind band) was composed in 1872 for the Banda Cittidina in Cremona of which he was director. The work was rediscovered by the American Henry Howey, who produced modern performing editions with the accompaniment of wind band, brass band or piano, playing it himself for the first time in 1992 (H[33], 49). Like the Hartmann work, it is both technically demanding and delightfully typical of the time and place of its composition.

# CHAPTER VI

## Saxhorns and Other Families

*Tenor Horn & Baritone*
These two sections of a band include the
highest proportion of girls. You can see . . .
why the boys make jokes about the girls
'cuddling their baby tubas' .
—A. Ben-Tovim & D. Boyd
*The Right Instrument for Your Child*
(London, 1985)

ANTOINE JOSEPH SAX, known as Adolphe, was born in the Belgian town of Dinant on 6 November 1814. His father, Charles, was a musical instrument-maker who numbered amongst his inventions an omnitonic horn, patented in 1824. After studying flute and clarinet at the Brussels Conservatoire the younger Sax set up a workshop in Paris in 1842. He found no welcome from manufacturers already established there, but he did secure the support of Berlioz amongst others. In a newspaper article Berlioz extolled the virtues of

this man of keen, lucid and stubborn spirit, well-proven perseverance and humility, always willing to use his skill to assist workmen incapable of understanding and executing his plans; simultaneously mathematician, acoustician and, if necessary, builder, turner or carver. A man of thought and a man of action; an inventor and a craftsman . . . (J⁹, 3).

Sax was a prolific inventor, and his activities were not limited to brass instruments or even to the field of music. This may be one of the reasons why over the years numerous errors have crept into written accounts of his patents. Even the most reliable authorities have fallen at the patent fence, and sources with a reputation for unimpeachable accuracy like Bate, Kunitz, Lavignac & Laurencie, Scholes, Waterhouse and the first edition of this present work must all share the blame. In an attempt to clarify the situation once and for all, the following list of Sax's French patents for brass instruments is given, with a brief description of their claims.

It should be remembered that patents in France were often granted for short periods so it was necessary to renew then periodically, and also that Sax took out patents in Britain and other countries. Some of these are cited elsewhere in the present work.

The following are examples of the abbreviations used in giving the locations of the specification extracts listed below: II = Series II; 86 = Volume 86; C.17 = Class 17; 4 = Sub-class 4; p. 11 = page 11; pl. X: = plate X.

17 August 1843. 9434. [I, 68, pp. 256-57, pl. XX.] *Système d'instruments chromatiques.* A 'nouveau système d'instruments chromatiques,' including the 'adaptation de coulisses aux cylindres'. This is a compensation system incorporating a slide which can be adjusted to rectify problems in intonation caused by increases in the length of tubing brought about by the use of more than one valve simultaneously, while avoiding the need for new fingering to be learned. The illustrations show the invention applied to existing instruments: *bugle, trompette-ténor, trompette-chromatique and contre-basse d'harmonie.* The latter (Fig. 6) is in the form of a Wieprecht Baß-Tuba, pitched in F, with 3 + 3 valves. Fig. 5 shows a model in E♭, its three valves placed low down on the instrument's large branch (0 + 3). Fig. 4 (a B♭ tenor trumpet) is also in upright form, narrow bore, its three valves placed horizontally about the centre of the large branch. All valves are of the Berliner-Pumpe type, no doubt in Sax's improved version.

13 October 1845. 1592. [II,6, p. 163, pl. XXXI.] For 15 years. *Pour des instruments en cuivre.*
Saxo-tromba forms suitable for military bands and particularly for playing on horse-back. Fig. 9 shows an instrument with three Berliner-Pumpe valves looking like an E♭ horn but called by Sax *saxo-tromba.* The larger instruments have a fourth valve 'to complete the lower octave.' The third valve lowers the pitch by two whole tones. It is claimed that the rounder conformation of tubing facilitates production of the sound. Sax writes:

Un des grands avantages du système que j'ai adopté pour le saxo-tromba, c'est qu'il peut s'appliquer aux sax-horns, trompettes, cornets et trombones; que tous ces instruments ont alors le même doigté et se jouent de la même manière.

This sentence apparently contains the first reference to the saxhorn under that name by Sax himself, and also highlights one of the aspects of the saxhorns that from the beginning made them attractive to amateur bands: the fact that the fingering is the same for all pitches of instrument.

5 May 1849. 4361. [II, 15, p. 186, pl. XIII.] For 15 years. *Pour des instruments a vent.* [With *certificat d'addition* 20 August 1849; and 23 April 1852.]
This is the Saxtuba patent, the intention being that sonority is improved by

making all the instruments in the orchestra face in the same direction.

9 October 1856. 16752. ['Au sieur SAX, à Bruxelles' [bis.].] [II, 57, pp. 397-404.]
For 15 years. *Instruments en cuivre.* [With *certificat d'addition* 30 April 1859.]

Sax states that the proportions of an instrument's tubing confer its distinctive
tone. His 'pistons ascendants et descendants' conserve the instrument's overall
conicity regardless of their position. The homogeneity of sound is thus retained as
the nodes of vibration are formed regularly through a tube of regular conicity from
mouthpiece to bell. He refers to a 'new system of ascending piston-valves with six
ports and a conical column of air devised by a French maker in 1848'. This patent
includes six piston-valves, three ascending, three descending, with twelve tubes in
all.

3 January 1859. 22148. [II, 70, pp. 131-137.] For 15 years. *Pour des nouvelles
dispositions applicables aux instruments de musique en cuivre.* [With *certificat d'addition* 30
April 1859.]

Eight improvements are listed, including instruments with both valves and keys,
and movable bells. He refers to a patent of 1845 and also to the saxotromba and
saxtuba, possibly meaning trumpet and tuba conformations. In addition he refers to
the ascending valve system made in 1852, i.e. four years before the patent of 1856
but four years later than the reference he makes in that same patent to their having
been made in 1848. The fingering system is given as follows:

C and its harmonics are obtained by using valve No. 1

| B  | ,, | ,, | 2 |
|----|----|----|---|
| Bb | ,, | ,, | 3 |
| A  | ,, | ,, | 4 |
| Ab | ,, | ,, | 5 |
| G  | ,, | ,, | 6 |
| Gb | ,, | ,, | 7 |

F with no valves depressed.

19 May 1862. 54212. [II, 83, c.17, 4, pp. 7 & 9, pl. 1 & 2.] *Pour des modifications
apportées aux instruments de musique à pistons.*

This is concerned with retaining the tone quality of the instrument by avoiding
the use of conventional valves. He suggests pistons consisting of two small parallel
tubes moved by a kind of *spatule à ressort* (spring-loaded spatula). This is illustrated
in the plates, along with all contemporary patterns of valve including his own
version(s) of the Berliner-Pumpe.

8 March 1881. 141575. [(III), 39(3), 4, pp. 8-15, pl. V-VII.] *Pour des perfectionnements aux instruments de musique.*

This massive specification includes instruments with six dependent descending valves; six dependent and independent valves, along with modifications of form (as in the Saxtuba); independent ascending valves and associated tubing; instruments with a single tube and proportional subdivisions; instruments with up to twelve valves; instruments based on seven and eight independent valves; instruments with seven independent valves; transposition; methods of modifying timbre. Cleaning, dismantling and repairing instruments without the need to unsolder them. Octave and two-octave keys for mouthpiece instruments and for flutes. New layout for instruments with six valves and independent tubing, and for the six-valved contralto. Trumpets with six independent valves. *Trompe militaire* or *trompe Sax*. *Cornet-à-pistons*. Echo cornet. *Trompe-olifant* (an elongated *trompe de chasse* in the form of an oliphant). Parabolic vocal reflector for theatres.

The saxhorn was not an original idea in itself, in fact little more than the name was new. It was essentially the same instrument Wieprecht had introduced into the Prussian army in 1828—a type of valved bugle-horn, or flügel horn. The first saxhorns even had Berliner-Pumpen, copied from two instruments purchased from Moritz of Berlin. But everything was new about the *saxhorns* as a matching family. Here was a range of instruments pitched from b'♭ down to B"♭ alternately in E♭ and B♭. Their relative proportions were fairly constant (with minor exceptions which we shall note) and consequently their timbres matched. This has been singled out as Sax's really important discovery—that the profile of the instrument confers its timbre.

Saxhorns were made in these pitches:

*Petit Saxhorn Suraigu en si bémol.* This instrument, specified by Berlioz in the 'Bénédiction des drapeaux' of his *Te Deum*, sounds a seventh above the written note. It was played by no less a virtuoso than Arban in the first performance. A model in c", one tone higher, may also have been made (see Sachs ($S^3$) 'Kleines Saxhorn').
*Petit Saxhorn en mi bémol.* The equivalent of the English brass band E♭ soprano cornet.
*Saxhorn Soprano en si bémol.* This instrument was the same pitch as the B♭ cornet, but its tone was considered less vulgar.
*Saxhorn Alto en mi bémol.* Although this is the instrument which tends to be thought of as *the* saxhorn, until recently it has never been considered totally satisfactory.

There are still sporadic attempts to find substitutes for the three normally used in the English brass band, and it has virtually been replaced in the American concert band. Widor in 1904 thought it 'rather inferior . . . not a soloist . . . a kind of orchestral padding' (W[20], 93). It replaced the alto ophicleide, another unsatisfactory instrument.

All the saxhorns are written as transposing instruments, those above in treble clef, those below in bass clef. (Orchestral tuba parts are, of course, always written in concert pitch bass clef).

*Saxhorn Baryton/Saxhorn Ténor en si bémol.* The equivalent of   the present-day baritone, considered by Widor to be the perfect saxhorn. Sax also made a version in A, a semitone lower, especially for cavalry use.
*Saxhorn Basse en si bémol.* The same pitch as the *Saxhorn Baryton*, this was a wider-bore instrument, similar to the euphonium. It was normally made with four valves, sometimes five. This instrument and those of lower pitch are all of proportionately wider bore than those from *baryton* upwards. Widor wrote: 'Such is, till some better instrument has been invented, the usual bass of the brass instruments; so far it is the most currently employed and most practical. Doubtless the future has something better in store for us' (W[20], 95).
*Saxhorn Contrebasse en mi bémol.* This was the equivalent of the Eb tuba, although at the time it was first constructed the bore of the saxhorn was wider than that of the tuba. Later the two became indistinguishable, just as did the *saxhorn basse* and euphonium, the tuba and bombardon.
*Saxhorn Contrebasse en si bémol.* Identical in pitch to the BBb tuba.
*Saxhorn Bourdon en mi bémol.* This subbass was pitched in Eb.'For such an enormous bass a peculiarly built man is wanted to use it', wrote Kappey, accurately if not grammatically. Built in 1851, it was 1650 mm high, the bell diameter 800 mm.
*Saxhorn Bourdon en si bémol.* This subcontrabass was 2750 mm high with a bell diameter of 1500 mm. It was constructed in 1855 specifically for that year's Paris Exposition Universelle.

While the key relationships of these instruments show a clear and logical progression, manufacturers were free to build saxhorns and similar instruments in other pitches. In 1858, for example, the Cyfarthfa Band library included parts for 'Bugle Primo' (in Db, sometimes Bb), 'Third Bugle' (in Ab), 'Repiano Bugle' (in Db), 'Sax Horn Primo' and 'Sax Horn Second' (in Db, sometimes Eb) (H[19], 5-7).
Donizetti was anxious to use saxhorns in *Don Sebastian*, produced at the Paris Opéra in November 1843. He was prevented  by industrial action taken by some of

Ex. 6.1.          COMPASS OF THE SAXHORNS

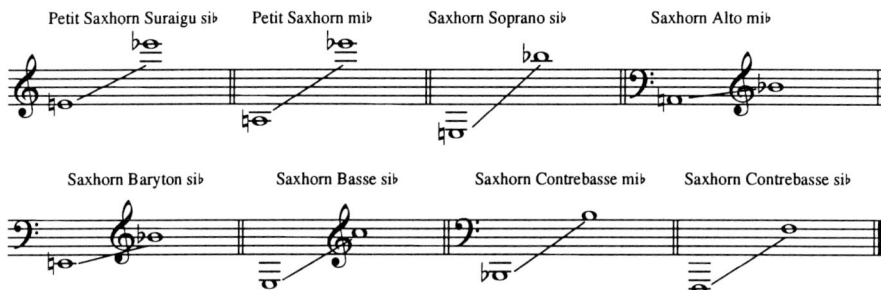

the orchestra members who were also instrument-makers. In the spring of the following year the Distin family met Adolphe Sax. John Distin, last noted as solo keyed bugle player with the Grenadier Guards, had since become a distinguished performer on the slide-trumpet, regarded as second only to Thomas Harper. By 1837 he had begun touring with his four sons playing on miscellaneous brass instruments—including 'that rare instrument the Tenor Horn'—his wife at the piano and his daughter singing.

The Distins went to the Continent as a family for the first time in 1844, playing in Belgium and later in Paris. Berlioz had organized a concert at the Salle Herz primarily to publicize Sax's instruments, and composed a work expressly for this purpose (more correctly, arranged—circumstantial evidence points to a version of his *Chant Sacré*). Sax himself played the saxophone and Arban performed upon the 'improved bugle' or saxhorn. The Distins, appearing in the same programme, were immensely impressed by the tone of this instrument.

At that time Sax had in his possession an E♭ *petit saxhorn*, B♭ *soprano* and E♭ *alto* which they borrowed, played and coveted. Having suggested some improvements they stayed in Paris until a set of five instruments had been made for them. Berlioz arranged another concert, this time at the Opéra Comique, and the Distins played a selection from Meyerbeer's *Robert le Diable*. That evening they performed at the Conservatoire, and the committee gave each a silver medal. Subsequently Louis Philippe, to whom they played on a number of occasions, gave them a complete set of engraved solid silver saxhorns (or so the story goes).

The Distins' first concert in London with saxhorns took place only seven weeks after Sax himself had introduced the instruments at the Royal Adelaide Gallery in the Strand, during October 1844. Even though his 'Sax horn band' once again included the great Arban, Sax's concerts were not a success and the ensemble left London before the scheduled end of the season. The Distins, who were at an advantage in not only being good players but accustomed to performing as a regularly-constituted ensemble, were more successful, and also appeared as soloists at Jullien's Covent Garden concert on 7 December.

But the great attraction of the evening was the Distin family, who have been for the last six months in Paris and Germany, during which time they have lost no opportunity of improving themselves or their instruments. The latter, now used by them, are of silver, and were presented to them by Louis Philippe, in consequence of the pleasure he received from their performance during the late *Exposition*. Their instruments, termed 'Sax Horns' were originally invented by M. Sax, of Paris, but have been greatly improved by the Distins who performed on Tuesday, the magnificent, 'Robert, toi que j'aune [j'aime]' and Donizetti's touching 'Fra Poco'—the finale to 'Lucia di Lammermoor,' in both of which they were most enthusiastically received. We really advise all who have not heard them to take an early opportunity of so doing (I[1], 7.12.44, 365).

Reluctant to let well alone, the next issue of the same journal continued the Distin saga, demonstrating that the family's PR was at least as good as its performing abilities.

THE DISTIN FAMILY

The first appearance of these highly-gifted gentlemen at M. Jullien's concerts, was noticed in our journal of last week. They have repeated their performances, with increased effect, during the past week.

Mr. Distin and his four sons have been for several years before the public. Mr. Distin, sen., for more than nine years was principal trumpet in the private band of King George IV. The Distin Family have visited various parts of Scotland, Ireland, and England, and have given upwards of seven hundred concerts. In December, 1843, they proceeded to the continent, and were invited to make a trial of some newly-invented instruments, manufactured by M. Adolphe Sax, in Paris. Upon the introduction of the Distin's [sic.] improved Sax Horns in Paris, they at once ensured success.

Invariably receiving the most enthusiastic applause, Mr. Distin was requested by M. Habeneck, the Director of the 'Conservatoire Royale de Musique,' to perform some of Sebastian Bach's and Handel's compositions—(the former, in particular, having very difficult passages for the trumpet)—which he did, and also the obligato [sic.] to Handel's 'Let the Bright Seraphim.'—This composition had not been played in Paris for many years, as no French trumpet-player would attempt it.

Mr. Distin's reception was a most brilliant one, the audience and orchestra manifesting their delight by presenting him with a handsome silver medal, accompanied with a very flattering letter and address (an honour unprecendented for an English artist in Paris). Mr. Distin and his four sons were also presented with a splendid silver medal by the Committee of the 'Societé libre des Beaux Arts,' with a very complimentary address for their performance at their great concert at the Hotel de Ville.

The Distins are at present the only performers on the Sax Horn, which unites the powers of the French horn and those of the cornet-à-piston, but is infinitely superior to both, for it combines the mellowness and sweetness of the former, with all the brilliancy and power of the latter. The pieces which the Distins perform are of their own arrangement, and do credit to their musical skill (I[1], 14.12.1844, 384).

Depending upon the source, Henry Distin's account written in 1896 or a number of French references (which tend to show Sax in the same light as American writers show George Washington—though if Sax had chopped down the cherry tree he would have patented his axe), it is clear that the Distins made the Saxhorn's reputation . . . or vice-versa. John Distin stated that Sax had originally intended to call the instruments *Bugles à cylindres* (a name already used in France for existing instruments along with *Bugles à pistons*) but the Distins suggested the name 'Saxhorn'. In view of the chronology of appearances of the term (see pages 249-50 above), this may well be true.

More importantly, during the quintet's tours the instruments became known all over the United Kingdom, where they gave impetus to the early development of the brass band movement. In 1853 the Mossley Temperance Saxhorn Band won a resounding success at the Belle Vue Contest. Hawick Saxhorn Band appears to have been formed about the same time. But eight years earlier, in 1845, a band at the Burton Constable Contest had included three Sax instruments and two years later the Cyfarthfa Band included four Sax instruments. 1845 was the year in which Henry Distin became Sax's London agent, no doubt benefiting from the appearance of 'WIZARD'S MONSTER BAND of Sax Horns and Cornopeans' which performed at Covent Garden in April 1846. He also supplied the set of instruments (all in tuba shape) with which the Mossley Band won at Belle Vue. In this same year, 1853, Distin himself became a manufacturer, and Sax transferred the agency to Rudall, Rose & Co. Yet the Distins had lost no time in exploiting their early introduction to Sax's instruments. John Webb refers to a document in the Public Record Office, BT45/2/345 of 1 January 1845: 'Design for a Sax-horn (a musical wind instrument)' that was registered by Messrs. Distin of London a mere thirteen months after the family had first played the original instruments in Paris. 1844 had been a busy year! (The design, which incidentally shows four Berliner-Pumpen, claimed 'a free passage through the instrument without the obstruction of sudden angles as in other wind instruments' (W⁴, 4).)

The Distins continued to tour until the early 1850s, travelling extensively in Europe and visiting the U.S.A. in 1849, a year after the Bethlehem Concert Band was formed in Pennsylvania. This already included three E♭ alto saxhorns, two B♭ baritone saxhorns and three E♭ contrabass saxhorns. Indigenous makers were also active. Valved alto horns and tenor horns called *ebor corno* were developed by Allen and Harvey Dodworth of the Dodworth Band in New York around the middle of the century. The music supplement to *The Message Bird* of 1 October 1851 consisted of an arrangement by Allen Dodworth of 'Then You'll Remember Me' for 'E♭ Bugle or a Saxhorn, B♭, 2 Ebor Cornos and Bass Tuba or Opheclide'. Their use was restricted, however, in the face of the saxhorns' rapid advance. We have already read A.D.'s opinion that '. . . the Saxhorns . . . have the most decided preference given them by all . . .' In 1869 the University Band of Notre Dame, near South Bend, Indiana consisted of twenty-four saxhorns, all in tuba-shape. This pattern, in a range of pitches, was advertised in the *Musical Times* for 1 March 1860 by Croyer of London (M⁵², 1.3.1860, 237). A flügel horn in tuba-shape made by J. H. Ebblewhite, who worked in London from 1883 to 1901, is in the Royal College of Music Museum of Instruments.

In the meantime Spontini was asked to reorganize French army bands. A commission met on 25 February 1845 to consider three instruments submitted for approval. One, a *flügel-horn à pistons* similar to an Austrian flügel horn recently examined, was rejected as mechanically unsound. The next was an *Emboliclave*, recently invented by Coëffet, of Ophimonocleide fame, a type of rotary-valve which the commission adjudged too fragile for military use (see page 217 above for description). The third was a valved E♭ *contrebasse*, 'a variety of the Austrian bombardon', as Kastner called it, considered inferior to both the Emboliclave and ophicleide. A fortnight later Sax gave the commission his views on the suggested reorganization and this was followed by a play-off, a band of Sax's instruments against existing bands conducted by Carafa, director of the Gymnase Musical.

As a result it was recommended on 19 August 1845 that infantry bands should each include twelve saxhorns (four being E♭ contrebasses) while still retaining two ophicleides; cavalry bands should each include twenty-two saxhorns and two saxotrombas; the bands of the light infantry would each comprise thirty-six players, thirty of whom would use saxhorns; each company would have an additional six men, including five saxhorn players. Later in the year army bands were deprived of their french horns, oboes and bassoons, instruments of Sax's development and manufacture being substituted, leading to his having a complete monopoly.

It is universally agreed that his instruments were well made, and having the active support not only of eminent composers like Berlioz, Halévy, Donizetti and Meyerbeer but also the theorist Kastner and Général de Rumigny, aide-de-camp to Louis Philippe, he could scarcely have failed to succeed in France just as Wieprecht had in Prussia.

Except for the deeper instruments, which infiltrated the orchestra more slowly than the bass tuba in most other countries ('Ambroise Thomas, in *Hamlet* [1868], has given the lead in the replacement of the ophicleide by the Saxhorn basse', wrote Lavoix in 1878), the saxhorns made little impression on the orchestral score. Meyerbeer succeeded where Donizetti had failed and in the 'Coronation March' of *Le Prophète,* produced at the Opéra on 16 April 1849, introduced a large stage band consisting almost exclusively of Sax's instruments. Since the parts were all transposed he thought it necessary to show the actual pitch of the instruments in the conductor's score by means of a phrase from the march (Ex. 6.2).

Gounod's *Faust* (Théâtre Lyrique, 1859) also involved a stage band including Sax instruments. Lavoix mentions a Rossini pastiche entitled *Robert the Bruce* in which they featured (L[6], 425). Produced in 1846 this must have been their first appearance in an orchestral score. In Berlioz's *Les Troyens* (1856-58), Act I, No. 11 (Final. 'Marche Troyenne'); Act IV, No. 29 (1er Tableau. 'Chasse Royale et Orage'); and Act V, No. 52 ('Imprécation') the saxhorn requirements are as follows, although the composer had to modify his demands for the premiere on 4 November 1863 at the Théâtre Lyrique for reasons of economy:

Petite Saxhorn Suraigu en Si♭
2 Saxhorns Soprani en Mi♭ (ou Trompettes à cylindres en Mi♭)
2 Saxhorns Contralti en Si♭ (ou Trompettes à cylindres en Si♭)
2 Saxhorns Ténors en Mi♭ (ou Cors à cylindres en Mi♭)
2 Saxhorns Contre-Basses en Mi♭ (ou Tubas en Mi♭) (B[29]).

In a BBC Radio 3 *Music Now* broadcast (24 June 1981), the authority John Warrack emphasised that the composer really did want the 'rougher sounds of the saxhorns'. These will already have been heard in the stage band in Verdi's *Jérusalem* (1847) which comprised a little E♭ saxhorn, two B♭ valved trumpets, two B♭ saxhorns, two E♭ saxhorns, two B♭ valved trumpets or sax-trombas, B♭ baritone saxhorn, B♭ bass saxhorn, contrabass saxhorn and two side drums. (B[63], I, 353; III, 114). The instruments were to become familiar in a theatrical setting, not least because of Sax's position as director of stage bands at the Paris Opéra. (In this respect, the testimonial from M. Holtzem on page 258 below is significant, coming as it does from a player who relied on Sax for engagements there.) The scale of

Ex. 6.2

2 Petits Saxhorns en Mi♭ aigu

2 1ers. Saxhorns en Si♭ Contralto

2 2mes. Saxhorns en Si♭ Contralto

1er. et 2me. Cornets à *Cylindres* en Si♭

1er. et 2me. Trompettes à *Cylindres* en Mi♭

2 1ers. Saxhorns Altos en Mi♭

2 2mes. Saxhorns Altos en Mi♭

1er. et 2me. Saxhorns Barytons en Si♭

4 Saxhorns Basses à 4 *Cylindres* en Si♭

2 Saxhorns Contrebasses en Mi♭

2 Tambours militaires

(1) L'effet réel de tous les instruments de Sax est indiqué par la demi-mésure qui suit le nom des Instruments.

Meyerbeer: 'Coronation March' *(Le Prophète)*

Sax's involvement in productions could be considerable, as details of the 1860 *Tannhäuser* show. Amongst the 'special costs' for each performance listed by the general administrator are:

| | |
|---|---|
| Brass band *(fanfare)*, 24 persons hired from M. Sax | 240 francs |
| Orchestra under stage in Act III, 29 musicians | 290 francs |

These items account for 530 francs of extra costs totalling 860 francs. In addition, there is note that 'M. Sax has to be paid an indemnity which varies from 500 to 1,000 francs according to the quantity of work for each instrument, which he will decide himself, and which might add up to 2 or 3,000 francs or more' (N[8], 34).

Thirty years later Saint-Saëns came closer than anyone to integrating the instruments into the orchestra. The second act of his oratorio *Le Déluge* tells the story of the building of the ark and the coming of the flood. The movement begins *ppp* and works up by way of a long orchestrated crescendo to the moment when the choir sings ' . . . se heurtèrent les flots et les vents furieux . . .' At that instant six Sax chromatic trumpets, five trombones and three contrabass saxhorns suddenly play a *fortissimo* phrase in octaves over tremolando strings. *Vents furieux* indeed!

Although the French repertoire probably contains more works involving multiple tubas than that of any other country this work is a rare instance of three being required, two *contrebasses en mib* and one *en sib*. Later they have contrapuntal entries, and the two Eb Saxhorns play right up to the *pianissimo* end of the act. But even Saint-Saëns had not gone so far as Widor would have wished: 'It would be well to admit the Saxhorn group into our orchestra. This perfectly homogeneous mass, with a total compass of five octaves, would serve as a firm and mellow background for the brilliant flourishes of the Trumpets and Trombones' (W[20], 91). Is this perhaps Widor the organist rather than Widor the composer writing? Lavoix thought that the instruments owed their lack of employment in the orchestra to the impairment of tone given by the complex tubing. This idea was widespread in France for some time, affecting attitudes to all valved instruments, and although there are indications that it originated amongst the more conservative players it resulted in attempts by makers to meet performers halfway, evidenced by instruments with circular valve-slides or no movable slides at all apart from the main-slide (Fig. 6.1(d)).

Many Parisian instrument-makers had already marketed similar brass instruments to the saxhorns. They were furious when Sax had the temerity to patent his own versions. Halary and Besson went into print, questioning his right to the name 'Saxhorn'. Others, including Gautrot, demanded that the patent be annulled. Rivet, of Lyons, took Sax to court but lost the case, having to pay not only the costs but also damages to Sax. We have details of Rivet's instruments, which were described

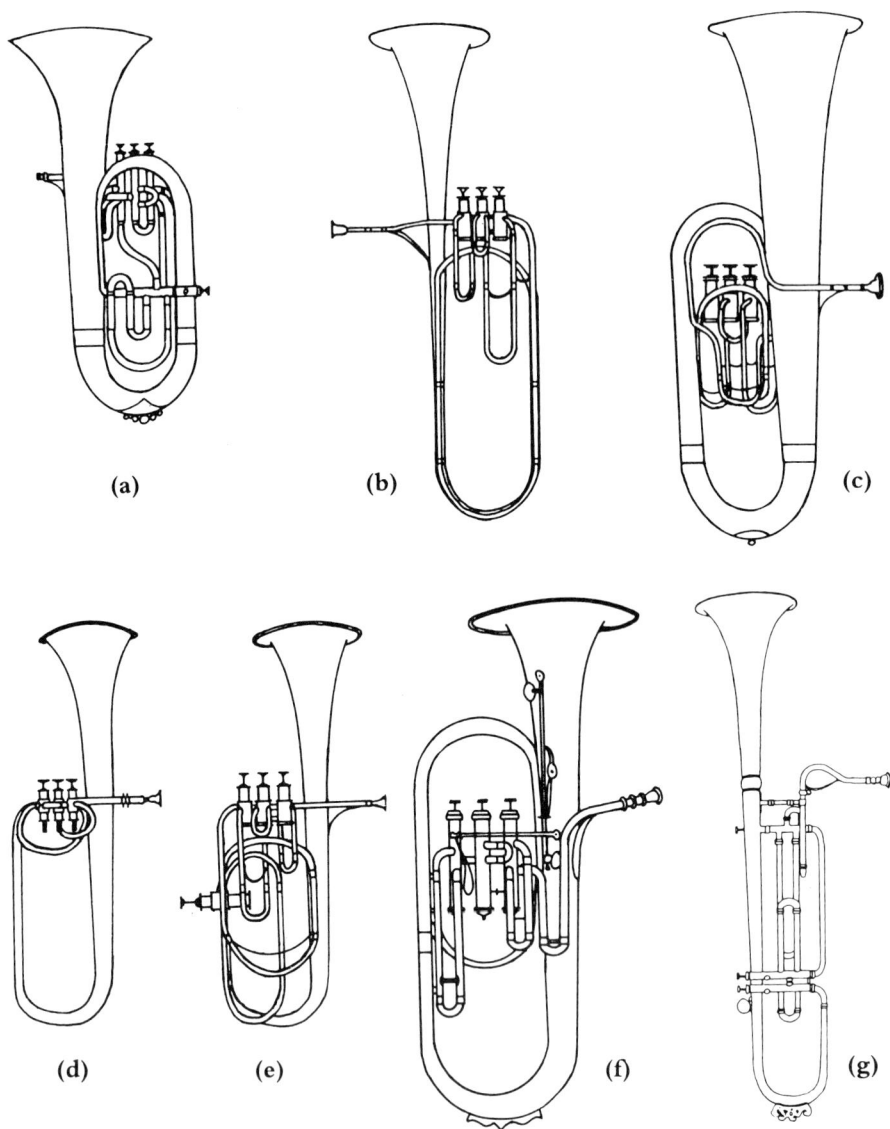

*Not to scale*

Fig. 6.1. (a) Four-valve *Bombardon* si♭ *Bas* [sic.] with Stölzel valves (Rivet); (b) B♭ Baritone Saxotromba with three Berliner-Pumpen (Sax); (c) three-valve F saxhorn with Berliner-Pumpen (Sax); (d) saxhorn in b♭ with three Berliner-Pumpen and no valve-slides (Sax); (e) E♭ alto horn with four Berliner-Pumpen (Sax); (f) saxhorn with three Perinét valves and two keys; (g) clavicor in C with two Stölzel valves for the right hand and one for the left (Guichard).

and illustrated in support of his claims. One of his groups was the *Famille de Néo-Alto et Bombardon*, ranging from f tenor to Eb contrabass with three or four valves. The f, eb and c instruments were called *Néo-alto* and the Bb and Eb instruments *Bombardon*. The three-valve *Bombardon* he named alternatively *Flugelhorn contrebasse*. At first glance they look very much like upright Saxhorns, not distinguishable by eccentric figuration of tubing or other peculiarities. Rivet even makes a note: 'Notice that all these instruments have the same attitude and shape as those patented by M. Sax on 13 August 1845, after these had been on sale for a long time'. However, the illustrations show Stölzel valves, which were far less efficient than those on Sax's instruments, whether Berliner-Pumpen or Périnet (Fig. 6.1(a)).

The other Rivet instruments illustrated comprise the *Famille de Clavicors* created between 1837 and 1844, ranging from an f tenor to a Bb baritone by way of models in eb, db and c. There are two types of baritone pitch, one of them the earlier version in which the first valve was some distance from the other two and operated by the left hand. They were all three-valve, trumpet-shaped instruments played in an upright position dictated by the mouthpipe's being at right-angles to the bell and valve-slides (Fig. 6.1(g)). The first part of the mouthpipe was adjustable and could be secured by means of a screw; the fixed section entered the first valve casing at the base—Stölzel valves, with the normal windways reversed.

As with the néo-cors, Rivet gives dates and customers' names to support his case but even so the clavicor was not his idea. It had been invented by the Parisian Danays and patented by its maker, Jean-Auguste Guichard: French Patent 6034 of 22 September 1838. Rivet claimed that his own clavicors were first made in 1837. The clavicor had a narrow bore and intonation problems, but in the specification Guichard states that it was invented to replace the even less satisfactory alto ophicleide. It was used to some extent in wind bands, as far south as Italy and as far north as England—Jullien's solos at Drury Lane in 1841 and the Brighton Proms in 1842 are documented—but it was soon replaced by the alto saxhorn.

Makers of instruments of these types were not restricted to France, or even to Europe. Joseph Anton Rohé, who moved from Philadelphia to New York in 1840 and was to remain in business there as an instrument-maker until 1863, advertised the wide range he had available for purchase in 1846. The *New York Business Directory* for that year shows him as making 'cornets, trombones, hibocornos, clavicor, neocor, bombardon, valve trumpet, & etc' (G[24], 133). Thomas Paine of Woonsocket, Rhode Island produced his Bassonet about the same time. Made in alto, tenor and baritone pitches, this tuba-shape intrument had marked German outlines and the model in c (French Tuba pitch) three rotary-valves for each hand: the right-hand giving drops of a semitone, tone, tone-and-a-half; left-hand, semitone, one-and-a-half tones and a fifth.

258 Saxhorns and Other Families

Sax's claims were also contested by foreign manufacturers. Giuseppe Pelitti of Milan was asked if he made Sax's instruments there and replied with some heat in the negative: it was Sax who made *his* instruments in Paris. His *Flicorno Baritono* or *Bombardino* of 1835 and *Pelittone* or *Controficleide* in contrabass pitches of 1845 were virtually indistinguishable from Sax instruments. In 1845 Wieprecht met Sax at Coblenz accompanied by Liszt after they had all been to a Jenny Lind recital. Wieprecht gave Sax a previously-existing German equivalent for each of the Frenchman's 'inventions'. Pontécoulant (P[20], 301-3) provides a detailed and apparently verbatim account, concluding somewhat surprisingly with Wieprecht's decision to drop the matter, although there was little he could have done anyway, apart from pistols at dawn.

However, Parisian lawyers were still being kept in cigars and boxes at the Opéra by litigation involving Sax, who produced testimonials from players stating that his instruments were preferable to others. Here is one from two members of the profession:

Paris, 1 March 1851

I have had my latest Sax valve instrument five years without a single accident. I the undersigned declare that to the best of my knowledge the four-valve Saxhorn-basse, invented by Monsieur A. Sax, is preferable to ophicleides and similar instruments in that if offers great advantages like a good tone, resonance, intonation and above all facility in the handling and fingering of the instrument, as one of the first to play it,

Holtzem
Extra-player at the Opéra
Dortu
Replacing the ophicleide by the Saxhorn at the Prado.

In the same year Sax was represented at the Great Exhibition in London not only by over fifty exhibits but also by his friend Berlioz, the anonymous juror responsible for comments on the brass instruments on display (G[20], 330). M. Sax's instruments 'possess additional power, sharpness and impressiveness, obtained in a great measure from their remodelled proportions (proving that it is not the quality of the metal brought into vibration by the air-blast which influences to any great extent the quality of the tone produced, and that successful results have ensued from an improved modification of form)'. The 'Sax-horns' introduced a 'quality of tone unheard until the introduction of these instruments by M. Sax'. He makes a note that the English and French instruments are generally better than the German, but cost half as much again. Sax's Sax-horns and Sax-trumpets (translation of *Saxotromba* plural) have produced a 'total revolution of military music . . . Sax-horns (double bass in E♭ and B♭) have left ophicleides very far in arrear; and his small treble Sax-horn, in B♭, is the only instrument known that can reach with certainty and just intonation the notes of the upper octave of the flute'. He has 'adapted to bugle-horns of infantry bands a set of portable tubes . . . which transform them into cylinder bugles of various keys . . . producing all the intervals of the musical scale'. And he has invented a 'contrivance' with 'mechanical cylinders' to enable sound to be 'continued (as in the violin, slide-trombone and voice) from one note to another through all the enharmonic intervals'. (This was presumably some sort of portamento device like Wieprecht's *Piangendo*, a spring-loaded tuning-slide, the subject of Prussian Patent 10803 of 27 October 1838.)

Sax came away from the exhibition with a Council Medal, leaving thousands of factory workers England and Wales seeking ways to buy his new instruments for their new brass bands.

In 1852 he introduced his system of ascending valves, six *indépendant* pistons each cutting off a length of tubing (Fig. 6.2). Since it was never necessary to use them in combination intonation was theoretically perfect. Mahillon, who had a number of these instruments in his care in the Brussels Musée Instrumental, goes into the reasons for the failure of the system:

Unfortunately the instrument is dull, precisely because of the independence of the pistons, each of which needs a special tube of determined length while the normal system allows additions to their length when used in combination. There is another thing: it is extremely difficult to construct a valve with two air passages absolutely air-tight, an essential condition for a good quality of tone. The normal system takes the air-column through only three pistons while the system with six independent valves submits the air-column to the disadvantages resulting from its passage through twelve pistons [twice through each of six] (M[7],II,450).

He might also have mentioned that these instruments are extremely heavy and that the system is so different from any of the other valve-systems in existence then (or now) that it was inevitable that players would not find it to their liking. The application of the system to saxhorns was a failure and later in the year Sax went bankrupt.

Springing up again like a well-regulated valve at the Paris Exposition of 1855 Sax was awarded a Gold Medal, and four years later had the good fortune to be in business when, owing to pitch reforms, the entire French army needed completely

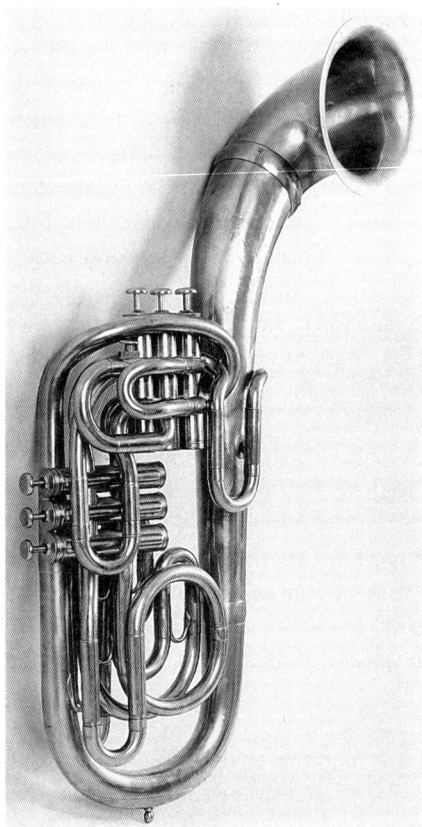

Fig. 6.2. *Saxhorn nouveau basse* in C/B♭ with six *indépendant* valves by Adolphe Sax, 1867.

new sets of instruments. It was during this period that he developed his instruments with six valves and seven bells, surpassed visually only by Distin's £400 alto horn which also included an echo bell. (This magnificent construction is illustrated by Bate (B[16], 175).) Sax took out another patent on 3 January 1859 for the addition of keys to valve instruments, showing a number of examples at the 1862 London International Exhibition (Fig. 6.1(f)). By this time all of his significant contributions to instrument design had been made and his business was in decline. Gautrot, with magnificent impudence, took out French Patent 56,450 on 22 November 1862 for

La nouvelle construction d'instruments de musique de cuivre a peur but de remédier principalement au grave inconvenience que présente le forme actuelle des instruments dits saxhorns et saxotromba. (The new form of brass instruments aimed principally at remedying the great inconvenience presented by the present design of instruments called saxhorns and saxtubas.)

Sax died in 1894, the year in which a number of distinguished French composers petitioned the Minister of Fine Arts to assist him in his extreme poverty, just as in 1846 Sax himself, though not particularly affluent, had helped the even poorer Berlioz with 1,200 francs.

The extent and speed at which the saxhorn group was established is graphically demonstrated in Jérome Thibouville-Lamy's 1878 catalogue. Saxhorns in the following pitches were offered in four qualities, the last being *nickelé* (nickel-plated). Prices are given in francs.

| | | | | |
|---|---|---|---|---|
| Soprano mib | 29 | 36 | 52 | 61 |
| Contralto sib | 35 | 44 | 60 | 70 |
| Ténor fa | 48 | 56 | 74 | 86 |
| Alto mib | 50 | 60 | 76 | 88 |
| Ténor sib | 52 | 60 | -- | -- |
| Baryton ut/sib | 54 | 64 | 87 | 103 |
| Basse ut/sib | 67 | 80 | 100 | 116 |
| Basse ut/sib *[4 pistons]* | 80 | 94 | 120 | 136 |
| Contre-basse fa/mib | 90 | 100 | 130 | 150 |
| Contre-basse fa *[4 pistons]* | 103 | 114★ | 150 | 170 |
| Contre-basse ut/sib | 107 | 125 | 170 | 194 |
| Contre-basse ut/sib *[4 pistons]* | 120 | 140 | 200 | 224 |
| Contre-Bombardon ut/sib | -- | 215 | 215 | 246 |

| | | | |
|---|---|---|---|
| ★also available: Contre-basse mib | 114 | -- | -- |

Also available was a *Saxhorn à clé rectificative* with four piston-valves and a key on the bell on the pattern of the 1859 French patent. This was offered as part of a range of *instruments circulaires* and had curved forward-facing bells. It is stated that the function of the key is to bring into tune the treble clef fourth space E (fifth harmonic) which is flat in comparison with other notes. The catalogue prints an air from Halévy's *La Juive* indicating where the key might be activated. Intonation is given serious attention elsewhere in the catalogue, which shows the third valve lowering the pitch by a minor third (like the first and second in combination), but first and third giving the normal perfect fourth (see pages 196-7 above).

Sax's name will live as long as saxhorns and saxophones. The latter he invented, the former systematized by regular pitch relationships within the family. Makers in other countries established similar families but never with such confidence.

In Italy, for example, the *flicorni* provide the mellow background in wind bands. They evolved over a period as a group and the name seems gradually to have been used by players and makers. There is an obvious similarity between the Italian word *flicorno*, the Spanish *fliscorn* or *fiscorn* and the Austrian *flügelhorn*.

Ex. 6.3.                    COMPASS OF THE FLICORNI

N.B. The Flicorno Basso, Basso-grave and Contrabbasso in this example are four-valved.

*Flicorno Sopracuto in Sib o La.* It is not clear whether this instrument was ever included in the band, but it was advocated for Bach and Handel high trumpet parts. The rare model in a' was to be utilized to avoid complicated fingering on the b'b instrument.

*Flicorno Sopranino in Mib o Re.* This instrument plays the florid high parts in the band, like the Eb soprano cornet.

*Flicorno Soprano in Do, Sb o La.* This is virtually the Bb cornet, the important brass melodic instrument in the band (sometimes called by the colloquialism *Sax*). An extremely ingenious version, of unknown make, for cavalry use is illustrated in *Brass Bulletin*, 59 (suppl., [7]). Both held and played by the left hand, the fingers operate touch-pieces arranged like a keyboard through which all valve combinations are available.

*Flicorno Contralto in Fa, Mi♭ o Re.* Normally called *Genis*, although the reason has yet to be discovered. Meucci suggests that the genis may have been introduced by Pelitti in 1847. (M[33], 312) This flicorno was also sometimes also known as *Clavicorno*. The pitch is the same as that of the most widely-used clavicor, which it usurped from its position in the band.

All the flicorni above are written in treble clef as transposing instruments. The lower models which follow are written in bass clef at sounding (concert) pitch:

*Flicorni Tenore e Baritono in Do o Si♭.* Here again are two baritone instruments of identical pitch but different bores. The *tenore* has the narrower bore and was considered advantageous in the higher part of the compass. Note that 'tenore' = English 'baritone'; 'baritono' (sometimes called *bombardino*) = English 'euphonium'. Like all the flicorni these are normally three-valved but may have four.

*Flicorno Basso in Do o si♭.* Identical in bore to the *baritono*, but the *basso* always has four valves. It is often called *eufonio* and sometimes *bombarda a 4 pistoni*. The version in c is at the same pitch, and orchestrally fulfilled the same functions, as the French *saxhorn-basse*, the Small French C Tuba. The B♭ model is to all intents and purposes a four-valve euphonium and is used as such in the band.

*Flicorno Basso-grave in fa o Mi♭.* This is usually called *bombardone* and is used also as an orchestral instrument, equivalent to the bass tuba in F or E♭.

*Flicorno Contrabbasso in Do o Si♭.* This is also found in the orchestra as well as the band, the equivalent of the CC or BB♭ tuba.

In the Italian version of Verdi's *Don Carlo*, prepared for La Scala in 1884, the stage band included 2 *Flicorni* (b'♭ soprano), 4 *Genis in Re* (d), *Flicorno Basso*, 2 *Bombardini* and 2 *Bassi*.

Spanish bands also have a range of saxhorn-type instruments, the *fliscornos*:

*Sopranino en mi♭.* Rarely used. Sometimes called *fliscornito* or *trombino*.

*Fliscorno en si♭.* The B♭ flügel horn, solo instrument in bands, where at least two are found and often many more. It is not considered to be a virtuoso instrument but valued for its powers of cantabile.

*Onnoven en mi♭.* 'Perhaps the least interesting instrument of the family . . . its timbre is very weak . . . its function in a band, for example, goes unnoticed . . . In bands that are not well organized it is used as a substitute for [french] horn.'(F[10], 57). Notwithstanding its alleged inferior status, it is interesting to find that in Spain, as in

Italy, there is a distinctive name for the instrument of this pitch. Kenyon de Pascual has researched its origins and finds that it may have initially been closely related to the *onnoves* shown by Stowasser of Vienna at the 1862 London International Exhibition (K[11], 133-4). This was possibly a type of *Schwanenhorn*, with a bell in swan's neck shape like the Lyraphone in Fig. 15.4. Her interesting article includes a reproduction of Romero's *Método elemental* with an illustration of the instrument as known in 1870. Significant from the etymological angle is that, as with 'Clavicorno' in Italian band parts, the name of a defunct instrument may have become a generic term for valved bugle horns of eb pitch.

*Barítono en sib*. Baritone. Normally written at concert pitch, and in some scores uses the bass clef. 'Complements the lower ranger of *fliscorno*, with a beautifully expressive warm tone. Less virtuosic than the other instruments; nor does it blend well. It is at its best in contributing the melody or playing a part in the harmony' (F[10], 58).

*Bombardino*. Four-valved euphonium. Pitched in c or Bb and written in bass clef. It is indispensible in bands where it has a bigger sound than the *barítono*. Its timbre is mellow and very sonorous. Frequently found as a soloist (F[10], 59).

*Bajo en mib; bajo en do o sib*. Basses in Eb, C' and B'b. Written in bass clef. 'French composers write the part an octave higher than it sounds, as in writing for string bass' (F[10], 60).

The *flügel horns* are another group which gradually evolved. There is a direct connexion between the three- or four-valve instrument and the *Flügelhorn* without valves used in Germany as a duty bugle. This descended in line from a small hunting-horn carried by the eighteenth-century *Flügelmeister*. The German *Flügel*—which can be traced back through Middle High German and Middle Low German to Middle Dutch *vlōgel* derived from the English *fly*—means 'wing' and the *Flügelmeister* signalled on his horn to each wing, or flank, of drivers beating the undergrowth to draw out the game during hunting. At one period *Flügelhorn* was the German name for a keyed bugle, but later was applied to what was quite possibly the earliest group of valved bugle-horns.

In Britain and America the only flügel horn (U.S.A *fluegel horn*) in use is the soprano or alto in bb, identical in overall shape and pitch to the cornet but of larger bore, the mouthpipe going directly into the first valve and the valves lying on the opposite side of the bell (Fig. 6.3). Originally a funnel-mouthpiece was used, but over the years cornets and flügel horns have tended to appropriate each other's characteristics to some extent. It is common in Germany and Austria for valved bugle-horns of all sizes to be included in the family. *Altflügelhorn*, *Tenorflügelhorn* and *Bassflügelhorn*, meaning Eb alto horn, Bb baritone and euphonium respectively, are terms in current use in those countries for valved bugle-horns, which are almost always trumpet-shaped. (Miraphone make a bb soprano in 'post horn' style.)

*Bugle* is the French equivalent of 'flügel horn' (the French for English 'bugle' is *clairon*). In addition to the bb bugle, Couesnon make a model in e'b—the *petit bugle*—normally found only in larger bands. The *bugle alto* is unison with the eb alto horn, or sometimes a tone higher (Fig. 6.3). Besson's French Patent 127953 of 16 December 1878 was for a *bugle contralto* in eb. He claimed that its particularly sweet tone made it 'superior to the "vulgar" *cornet-à-pistons*'. The mouthpipe went straight to the first valve (as in all flügel horns) and 'the water accumulates in the lower part'.

Fig. 6.3. *Saxhorn-alto* in flügel horn shape, c. 1895. The instrument is approximately 400 mm in length.

From 1882-5 Červený developed a range of 'Kaiser' instruments of large bore and conical profile right through the valves (Austrian Patent 13773 of 1884). From *Kaisertenorhorn* in c or Bb downwards through the *Kaiserbaryton* to *Kaiserbass* they were built in oval shape, eventually giving their name to similar instruments built elsewhere. ('Kaiser' translates conveniently as 'Imperial'.) Červený's were beautifully-constructed instruments, and the free response, enormous breadth of tone and mechanical perfection of the four-rotary-valve *Kaiserbaryton* enable it to hold its own alongside any twenty-first-century euphonium (Fig. 5.2).

In 1888 the *Herculesophones* appeared, made by Sediva of Odessa. Like the saxhorns they were a complete family from soprano to contrabass. They had a wider bore than existing instruments in order to give a greater volume and were intended for band use. To prove their point Sediva published the cubic capacity of each instrument. The two types of alto manufactured were respectively 5,520 and 6,640 cc. The baritone was 10,180 cc, the euphonium 14,190 cc, the EEb 33,400 cc, and the BBb 58,720 cc. These details lose much of their point, however, in view of the lack of comparable statistics from other makers.

In Italy the *Bersag Horns* (*Trombe per Fanfara per Bersaglieri*) form a group still in use by the *fanfare* of the 1st, 2rd and 8th *Reggimenti Bersaglieri*. These valved bugles were introduced into the Italian army on its establishment in 1861. The original maker may have been Pelitti of Milan, although Meucci's research has indicated that his *tromba alla bersagliera* was not invented until shortly before 1870 (M³², 319). The family consists of *Soprano in sib*, *Contralto in mib*, *Tenore in sib*, *Baritono in sib* and *Bass in fa*; once again the two instruments in Bb differ only in bore. The distinctive characteristic of the Bersag Horns is that with the exception of the three-valve soprano they each have only one valve. This lowers the pitch by a fourth, giving the notes shown in Ex. 6.4. H. H. Slingerland, in business in Chicago from 1916 to 1950, went one better, inventing a bugle with two valves, the main one piston and the secondary rotary.

Ex. 6.4.          NOTES PLAYABLE ON THE BERSAG HORN

Similar one-valve bugles are made  by Amati, who produce two *Trumpet Bugles*, one a soprano in g and d, the other a bariton [sic.] in G; and by D. Hüttl of Baiersdorf/Mittelfranken who make a valve bugle in bb/f and another in g/d. At one time the Premier Drum Co. of Wigston made a *Bb-f Piston Bugle*, but all of these are characterized by a profile approaching that of the trumpet (and the U.S. military bugle). Alexander correctly call their single-valve Bb/Eb instrument *Fanfare* The Bersag Horn is the only true one-valve bugle-horn. (The Portuguese army uses flügel horns with two piston-valves, a variety not observed elsewhere.)

Such are the families of valved bugle-horns, intended in the first place for use in bands and soon becoming confused, cross-bred and indistinguishable from other, similar instruments. This was inevitable with so many prolific inventors operating within such a limited field, and it is a matter of no concern that, for example, the euphonium is identical with the *saxhorn-basse* and the *flicorno basso*. But we should be wary of confusing the euphonium and baritone.

In Britain there is no question of which is which: they are the same pitch, but the baritone never has more than three valves and its bore is narrower than that of the euphonium (Fig. 6.4). This gives the  baritone a  lighter  tone. In the U.S.A. matters

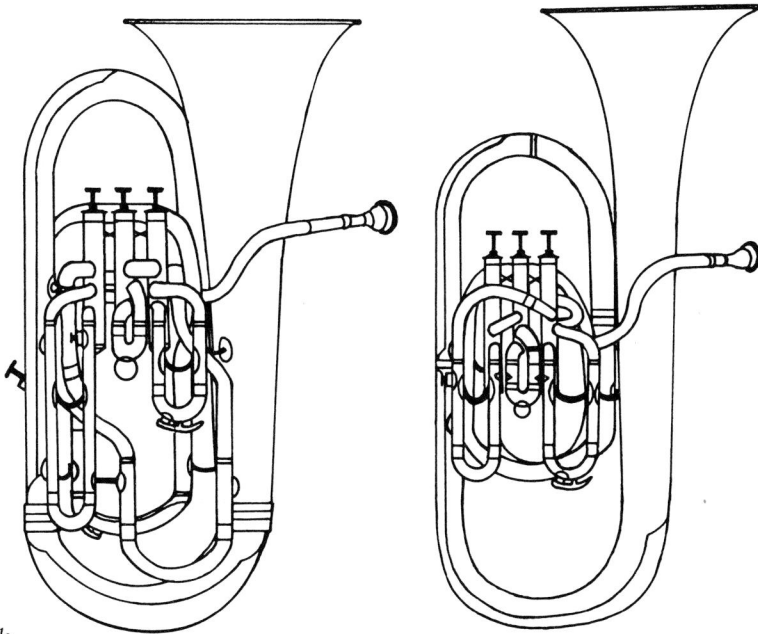

*To scale*

Fig. 6.4. Instruments by Hawkes of London, c. 1935. On the left a four-valve euphonium with compensating pistons, on the right a three-valve baritone with compensating pistons. Many of these superb instruments are still being played today.

have not been always been so straightforward. Despite assurances by many manufacturers that they are different instruments, some makers market one under the name of the other, or under the name of both. The Yamaha Marching YEP 210 Euphonium has a bore of 14.5 mm, identical to the YBH 310 Marching Baritone, though most American companies do now differentiate between the two instruments. (Holton, however, make no euphoniums, only a range of baritones.) For many years the *Encyclopaedia Britannica* claimed that in the United States the euphonium was called 'baritone', although more recent editions have reflected current practice. The reason for this confusion may lie in the nineteenth-century adoption by Americans of the German term 'baryton' for euphonium—perfectly correctly. The British type of instrument (increasingly favoured in the U.S.A.) is sometimes described as having 'English bore' to differentiate it from indigenous euphoniums which have inclined to a generally narrower profile. Since the early twentieth century the true baritone (i.e., *saxhorn baryton*) in Britain has occupied a relatively ignominious position in a five-part backing group with the three Eb horns in the brass band—and is found nowhere else. The baritone and euphonium are really two instruments with very different profiles and timbres, though similar pitch and configuration. The baritone is the lowest of the high saxhorns, the euphonium the highest of the deeper saxhorns. During the last fifteen years of the twentieth century Americans increasingly called the euphonium by its correct name, encouraged by Tubists' Universal Brotherhood Association which has lost no opportunity to become involved in euphonium-orientated activities. Their publishing house is now actually called Tuba-Euphonium Press.

A more confused situation applies in the many other cases of instruments which are really modified forms of existing types. By 1867 they were found in profusion and Fétis, who wrote the report on musical instruments shown at the Paris Exposition that year, was not very impressed.

> Bugle and saxhorn families. It is not without difficulty to report on this category as several manufacturers have tried to vary the shapes and names. Červený of Königgrätz, Distin of London and Schreiber of New York are particularly remarkable for their singular shapes, where fantasy has played a greater part than necessity . . . Sonority and intonation are lacking . . . several makers exaggerate the bore of the basses, attempting immense power; this is completely wrong. First, the instrument is too loud for the others; second, only human lungs provide the wind for the low notes of these sonorous monsters. . .
> Sax has made rotatable bells in curved shape, which can double the sound to the listener . . . Distin's Tenor Cor, with mute, has a bastard sound, neither true horn nor bugle. Another tenor cor in F by the same maker is in a bizarre shape with a bell which passes under the arm. The sound is not so good as the ordinary horn.

Some attempts to increase the bore of the deeper instruments have already been noted; rotatable bells and tenor cors are dealt with in Chapter XV. Apart from differences in overall shape and conformation few changes have been made to the saxhorns. There was a type of Eb alto called the *Baryton aigu*, designed by Fontaine-Besson in conjunction with Sellenick in the 1880s and given a bore like that of the Bb baritone in an attempt to improve the quality of the tone. Fontaine-Besson's most significant innovation was no doubt the 'Prototype' range of instruments built on 'conical steel mandrels of exact mathematical proportion'. Červený's *Althorn-obligat* (1859) was made in tuba, oval or helicon shape and apparently had an unusually sweet tone. Recommended as a solo instrument, it was adopted by a number of bands including those of the Russian army.

Červený also built a Bb baritone with rotary change to A in 1846 called the *Glycleide;* Lamperhoff of Berlin designed a type of alto horn called the *Contrahorn* in 1845; no more details of either seem to be available.

Today the deeper saxhorns and *flicorni*, indistinguishable from the bass and contrabass tubas, are found in both the orchestra and the band. The large-bore tenor instruments have merged with the Baroxytons, Sommerophones and Tenor Tubas to become the euphonium. The narrow-bore instrument of the same pitch—the baritone—occupies a place in school bands, some American wind bands and British brass bands. In 1890 A. Stein played baritone alongside J. H. Guilmartin, euphonium, in The London Military Band (B[55], 4.1.1890, 149) and Turner (T[15], 99) reproduces a photograph of the band of 1st Battalion the East Surrey Regiment during the North Russia Campaign of 1919 including both instruments. The last baritones in British military bands were pensioned off in the 1950s. However, the baritone appears in the symphony orchestra under the German name *Tenorhorn* in Mahler's seventh symphony where, during the first movement, it plays an extremely important and exposed solo part, notable for a striking entry in the second bar of the work (Ex. 6.5). The compass is concert B-b', written in transposed treble clef. Many players prefer to use a medium-bore euphonium for the part, which needs to carry across the entire orchestra, but the Continental oval *Tenorhorn* can often produce a considerable volume without losing its characteristically concentrated sound. Mahler was quite clear about his requirements here.

In Respighi's *Pini di Roma* the two *Flicorni tenori* parts are usually played on baritones. The baritone has also appeared on the jazz scene in the role of a doubling instrument: the names of players like Joe Comfort, Maynard Ferguson and Gus Mancuso come to mind (although they may, of course, actually have played euphoniums). Occasionally it joins the tuba in television comedy cartoon music. It has been a favourite solo instrument in the United States but not for many years in Britain. Gone are the days when Charles Godfrey conducted the Crystal Palace Military Band accompanying Mr. Farren playing the althorn solo *Let Me Like a Soldier Fall*. In his youth Sousa played the baritone and violin.

The next higher instrument, the Eb alto horn, is still in wide use despite a century of criticism. In Britain and the Commonwealth (where it is restricted to the brass band) it is called 'tenor horn', all the more confusing since as recently as 1953 the baritone was still being called the 'althorn' in British literature ('Althorn, another name for the Baritone'—Farmer (F[2], i, 127)). Farmer refers to the transfer of the name 'tenor horn' to the higher instrument, the Eb saxhorn, but fails to point out the Gilbertian situation that thus came into existence, with the higher instrument being called 'tenor horn' and the lower, 'althorn'. Jacquot wrote, from the opposite point of view, 'ALTO ... destined to replace the horn in military bands. It is in Bb.' Perhaps he was confusing it with the *cor alto*. Yet there are indications that 'tenor horn' came originally from the French as Kastner illustrates a *Saxhorn en mi bémol, ténor* side by side with a *Saxhorn en si bémol, contralto* (K[5], Pl. XX).

Ex. 6.5

Mahler: Symphony 7

Three E♭ tenor horns are found in the brass band score, designated solo, first and second. But solos are few as there is a tradition that these easy-blowing instruments are most suitable for old men and young boys. The tradition is now being followed less rigidly (in many cases the young boys have been replaced by young girls) and contemporary band composers give the tenor horns more to look forward to than the opening of *The Caliph of Bagdad* and the overture to *Coppélia*. So accustomed is the player of this instrument to the repetitive off-beats which are his staple fare in marches and older orchestration that the term 'Peck-horn' is used in the United States: the player pecks away at his part for bar after bar! The parts played by the tenor horn which is known to have existed in the Hellesveor Chapel Choir, Cornwall about 1900 may well have been more interesting (W²⁶, 100). Church bands in these isolated western communities probably benefited from the active industrial brass band movement in the county.

Awareness of the E♭ horn began to be raised initially through the efforts of one man, the virtuoso player Gordon Higginbottom who had played with top-class bands like Black Dyke Mills and CWS (Manchester) before joining James Shepherd's Versatile Brass. Several composers wrote solos for him, culminating in *September Fantasy*, composed by Eric Ball and played at the Royal Albert Hall after the 1978 National Championships.

In 1996 Sheona White, Solo Horn with the Yorkshire Building Society Band, won the BBC Radio 2 Young Musician Award, successfully persuading the judges that this rarely-heard saxhorn was worthy of serious consideration. In the following year the Tenor Horn Society was founded in the U.K., marking the final stage in drawing together the players of this hitherto under-rated instrument.

Since early French attempts to involve massive numbers of saxhorns the E♭ alto horn has never been found in the orchestra, and experiments with not only tenor cors but even french horns occasionally occur in Britain with the object of finding a substitute for it in the brass band which is, in this country, the only large ensemble where it finds a place. It has frequently formed part of small ensembles, including the standard brass band contesting quartet of two cornets, E♭ horn and euphonium, and the Russian equivalent: two cornets, alto horn in E♭ and tenor horn (i.e. baritone) in B♭ introduced by Červený in 1876. Later, Karl Brandt, trumpet at the Bolshoi from 1890, established a quartet of two cornets, alto horn and trombone for which several Russian composers have written (T², 2).

The British jazzman Django Bates has made E♭ horn an important part of his refreshingly different approach. It has also been used as a doubling instrument, on both sides of the Atlantic, often by trumpeters, including Humphrey Littleton and Mercer Ellington. Its jazz pedigree actually goes back to the earliest days with Papa Jack Laine (1873-1966) and New Orleans contemporaries.

Ex. 6.6

(a) Brass band notation

(b) Sounding pitch

Bevan: *Meditation on 'Austria'*

The bugle horn which proved itself the grooviest is the flügel horn (Ex. 14.6), although at one time the mellophone made a strong bid for the position. Though Joe Bishop played flügel with Woody Herman in 1936, it is since Miles Davis recorded *Miles Ahead* with Gil Evans in 1957 and *Porgy and Bess* the following year that the flügel's cotton-wool tone, straight and cool without vibrato, has become familiar not only to jazz addicts but also to the millions of non-hearers subliminally affected by television background music. Davis had adopted the instrument under the influence of Clark Terry, who was primarily responsible for introducing the flügel horn to jazz, though Terry's technique of quickly alternating flügel and trumpet (one held in each hand) remains unique. Also uniquely, the singer Maxine Sullivan, who had connexions with Claude Thornhill (see page 441 below) played both flügel and trombone. In the early 1960s trumpeter Art Farmer chose to use flügel for all his solos. Most trumpet players involved in jazz and sessions now carry cases containing both a trumpet and a flügel horn.

It also has a place in the rigidly standardized instrumentation of the British brass band—just one player whose part, until recently, was shared by the irrelevantly named Repiano Cornet. The flügel should really, of course, be treated as the highest instrument of the saxhorn group, as composers now realize (Ex. 6.6). This is reflected also in rationalized seating arrangements, with Flügel Horn next to Solo Horn rather than in the back-row cornets between Soprano and Repiano. Continental bands make much more use of the instrument than others. Gorgerat (G[17], III, 111) lists the recommended instrumentation of *la grand fanfare* (the full brass band), including, out of a total sixty to seventy players (excluding percussion) two E♭ piccolo bugles (*bugle*: flügel horn), two solo bugles in b'♭, six to ten first bugles and another six to ten second bugles. There are also between four and six E♭ altos, two or three baritones or euphoniums, six or eight B♭ basses (presumably four-valve euphoniums), three EE♭ basses and three BB♭ basses.

Occasionally the flügel horn is used in the orchestra. Vaughan Williams's ninth symphony has a solo part, sometimes muted and at one point marked *lontano senza vibrato*. So concerned about the timbre was the composer that he put on the first page of the score: 'The Flügel Horn part must *never* be played on a Cornet; also the conductor must make sure that the player uses a real Flügel Horn mouthpiece'. He obviously had nightmare visions of his cool lyricism being ruined in a cut-price performance on a cornet with vibrato!

A flügel horn may be used for the posthorn asked to play offstage in Mahler's third symphony. Respighi specifies 'Tre Buccine in Si♭ (Soprano) (opp. Trombe)' in his *Feste Romane*. The three *buccine*, often in unison, are normally played by flügel horns. Does one infer from the 'opp. [opposto = opposite] Trombe' a composer fearful not only that they will be in the wrong place but also that they will have the wrong sound? Two flügels normally play the *Flicorni soprani* parts in the same composer's *Pini di Roma*.

The cornet, so charmingly described by Lavignac as 'the *gamin de Paris* of the orchestra': by Prout as 'coarse and vulgar'; by Widor as 'thick and vulgar'; and by Mahillon as 'a true bastard', superseded the B♭ soprano saxhorn. The piccolo trumpet in bʹ♭ is now used for the *petit saxhorn suraigu* in Berlioz's *Te Deum* and the offstage band of his opera *Les Troyens*.

# CHAPTER VII

# *The Contemporary Tuba*

Before we leave the brasses let us dwell for a moment on the lowly and lonely tuba player. There is only one in the entire orchestra and he enjoys a certain amount of prestige—and loneliness. Tuba players never talk. They are silent, morose, uncommunicative, but they sing to themselves. They have no common interests with any of their colleagues and, as a matter of fact, most tuba players feel they don't even belong in the orchestra. They normally strike up a strong friendship with the stage manager.
—Harry Ellis Dickson *Gentlemen, More Dolce Please!*

The souped-up Pittsburgh Symphony has . . . a tuba that rests on a frame so that the player, in this case Sumner Erickson, simply stands up and blows into it. The freedom allows Mr Erickson to be more agile and less Tubby the Tuba-ish than players who have to hug the instrument awkwardly between their legs as if kissing someone fat . . .The Bolero is really the first piece of conscious minimalism. . . Everyone gets a look in except Mr Erickson who is the only player in the orchestra not to be asked to step into the limelight at some point during the piece. Tuba players so rarely get a mention. —review by Rick Jones of a Henry Wood Promenade Concert
*Evening Standard,* 9 September 1994

. . . slow learners, and those who are happily plodding away at the back, are content to play with the other engaging members of the tuba or bass section . . .   —A. Ben-Tovim & D. Boyd *The Right Instrument for Your Child*

SO FAR the development of the valved bugle-horns has been traced from the keyed bugles through the invention of the valve, up to its application to brass instruments having widely conical profiles. The history to the present day of the euphonium and higher instruments has been surveyed; their use in ensembles old and new by composers up to and including those writing now has been investigated. It is time to turn to the bass and contrabass tubas, the valved bugle-horns built in pitches lower than Bb.

National preferences emerged almost immediately the instruments were introduced into bands and orchestras. These affected not only players but composers to such an extent that until relatively recently an orchestral tubist in France, for example, normally played upon an instrument pitched a whole octave higher than his counterpart in the United States.

In the global village these differences are now giving way to a much more universal concept of tuba practice, but the bulk of the orchestral repertoire still shows the influence of national tuba preferences. The tubist is therefore expected to be able to play over a wide compass. Contemporary solo works demand up to five octaves, but while the lowest note in the symphonic repertoire is the A'' in Max Trapp's fifth symphony, the possible altitude depends upon the player and the pitch of his instrument. John Stevens's *Liberation of Sisyphus* exceptionally ends on a c' and A'' is probably the lowest note playable with any definition on the F tuba, but it does not follow that deeper instruments permit lower notes *pro rata*.

Stipulation of the desirable compass of tuba parts is a difficult task. Tubists, rather like their trumpet-playing colleagues, have accepted that in order to produce the notes requested by the composer they will need to have at hand instruments in at least two pitches. The easiest-playing, best-sounding range of the valved bugle-horns generally lies between the open instrument's first playing mode (second harmonic) and sixth harmonic but tubists generally aim at a well-developed lower register, in partnership with manufacturers who normally provide at least one extra valve to fill the gap between the open fundamental and second harmonic.

Grade VIII tuba examinations of the Associated Board of the Royal Schools of Music—the highest grade, leading to the recital certificate and performing diploma—ask for scales to be played within the brass band treble clef range F♯ below the stave to c above the stave (sounding A'-e'♭). The lowest note is the lowest second harmonic of a three-valve E♭ tuba and the highest should be possible on a CC without too much perspiration. As a rule-of-thumb this might be taken as a good practical range for bass tuba. (This register has been christened 'the cash register' by the American tubist Daniel Perantoni: highly advisable for composers who want their tuba music to sell!) If exceeded it should be downwards rather than upwards as tone quality becomes non-characteristic above the stave.

Treble clef brass band parts are normally written up to the top of the stave. It is wise to include *ossia* notes for anything beneath written F♯ three ledger lines below as in some bands E♭ bass parts are even now played on three-valve instruments, while still relatively few brass band players have four-valve BB♭ basses. (The increase in the number of these instruments following disbursements to bands from the National Lottery regularly incurred the wrath of record reviewers in the band press. They quite rightly objected to the practice of playing notes down the octave as an expression of the players' delight with the capabilities of their new four-valve BB♭ basses.)

Bass and contrabass tubas are currently built in F, E♭, C' and B'♭. Kappey's tutor (c. 1874) was for 'Bombardons in F, E♭, D♭, C and B♭', but he conceded that 'the F, D♭ and C [were] rarely employed'. The application of the term 'bass tuba' to the euphonium in the form *basse* or *saxhorn-basse* continues in France. Instruments pitched in B♭ and c were dealt with in Chapter V under the names 'tenor tuba' and 'euphonium'.

Tubas have been built in lower pitches than those common today—for example the instruments in E'♭ and B'♭ shown in Paris at the 1855 Exposition. Those built in the former pitch are generally termed 'subbass', in the latter 'subcontrabass'. The *Rottophone* was a four-valved tuba, apparently in F', built by Augustin Rott of Prague some time before 1885 (W[3], 336). A chronological list of giant tubas is given in Table 7.1, but none of them compares with the natural B♭ tuba made by Ernst Emil Köerner (1885-1945). This instrument has neither valves nor bends and is adjustable in length between 4650 mm and 5200 mm. The diameter of the bell, made as his masterpiece to celebrate the end of his apprenticeship in 1913, is 1020 mm. Köerner completed his tuba in 1928 and gave it to Markneukirchen sportsmen to display at a festival in Cologne that year. It seems that two athletes carried it and a third blew it. It is presently in the Musikinstrumentenmuseum at Markneukirchen. Arnold Myers, who provides the above details, also prints an amazing photograph of the tuba on a float in a Markneukirchen Hornmakers' Guild procession in 1933 (M[55], 30-1).

The system used to describe tubas by size and proportion is of limited use owing to the inconsistency with which it is applied by different makers. Under this, a 4/4 instrument is full size, while 1/2 and 3/4 represent instruments with smaller dimensions, 5/4 and 6/4 larger instruments. However, it is indisputable that even the smallest tuba is still a large brass instrument, and the question of weight cannot be ignored. G. C. Conn, manufacturers with a particular interest in bands, have found it worth their while to address this problem seriously, while in 1997 Jupiter Band Instruments of Austin, Texas, introduced a 3/4 size marching BB♭ tuba with a medium (17 mm) bore and a weight of only 6.5 kg. Amati and Boosey & Hawkes also make instruments of around this weight. Medical conditions resulting from the excessive weight of some sousaphone bells are discussed on page 457 below.

While different nationalities have varied considerably in their conception of what constitutes a bass or contrabass tuba, the instruments themselves have tended to follow similar forms with variations in bore and favoured valve-systems contributing the essential differences. Later the preferences of each group of

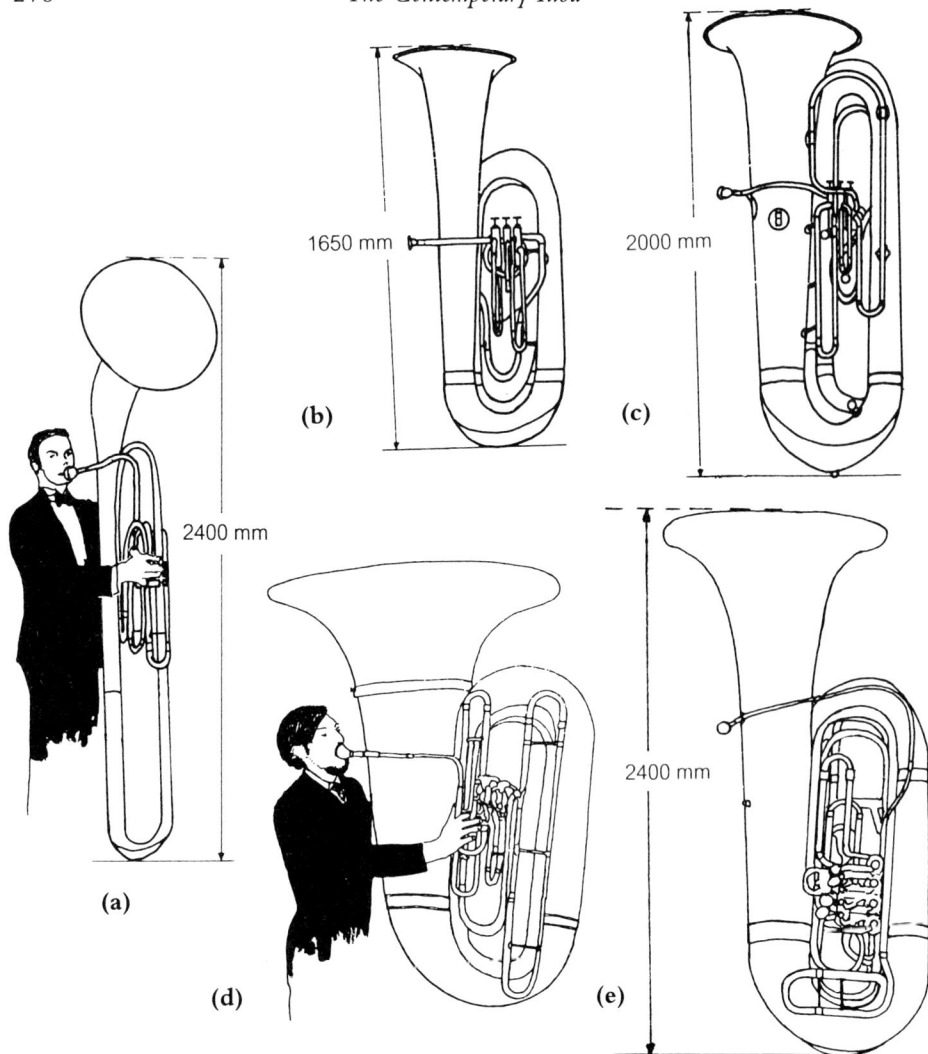

*Approximately to scale*

Fig. 7.1. Giant tubas: (a) tuba used in 1928 Broadway production of Yellen, Ager and Murphy's musical comedy *Rain or Shine* (valve-slides partly conjectural), played by a tubist standing in the orchestra pit; (b) *Sax-bourdon mib* by A. Sax, 1851; (c) subcontrabass tuba made for Sousa by Boosey, 1896-8, now at Harvard; (d) tuba which stood at the entrance to the Paxman workshop in Gerrard Street, London for many years, played by Gerard Hoffnung in the 1950s, taken by Ron Schneider (tubist with Johnny Dankworth) to South Africa and, having surfaced in the United States in 1978, seems to have disappeared; the player here is George Wall, c. 1967; (e) *Riesen-Kontrabass* by Bohland & Fuchs, 1910-11, built for New York World Exhibition 1913, now at Technical School for Music, Kraslice, Czech Republic.

Table 7.1 GIANT TUBAS

[All dimensions are in mm]

| Date | Maker | Tube length | Height (mm) | Width (mm) | Bell dia. (mm) | Valves | Notes |
|---|---|---|---|---|---|---|---|
| 1851 | A. Sax | — | 1650 | — | 800 | — | *Saxhorn bourdon mi bémol* |
| 1855 | A. Sax | — | 2750 | — | 1500 | — | *Saxhorn bourdon si bémol* |
| 1855 | G. Besson | — | 3000 | — | — | — | *Trombotonar.* Made in Eb, BBb for Rivière at Jardin d'hiver, Paris. Only Dortu could play it. Fétis thought it 'barbarous'. |
| 1862 | H. Distin | — | 'nearly 8 ft' | — | — | 3 | For 'Flügel Horn Union'. Only two windways through each valve. |
| 1873 | Červený | 15000 | 1550 | — | 1050 | — | In C. |
| 1893 | — | 11100 | 2080 | 780 | 800 | 3 | |
| 1896 | — | 5300 | — | — | 810 | — | For T. P. Brooke (Chicago Marine Band). |
| 1896 | — | 5300 | — | — | 830 | — | For Innes Concert Band. Weight 28.5 kg. |
| 1896 | ?Boosey | 12000 | 2000 | — | 1000 | — | For Sousa Band. |
| 1899 | Sander | — | 1550 | — | 1050 | — | For Sousa Band. |
| 1910 -11 | Bohland & Fuchs | 13680 | 2400 | 950 | — | — | *Riesen-Kontrabass* for 1913 NY Fair. Now in Kraslice. |

countries will be outlined, but all tubas are built in one of the shapes shown in Fig. 1.7, or a combination of two or more of them. With the exception of the giant tubas there is a valid reason for the general gradual adoption of instruments of lower pitch: the deeper the fundamental the smaller the number of valves it is necessary to use to play the lower notes which tend to form the tuba's staple diet. Not only is the quality of sound maintained but it is easier for the player to deal with fast passages (Ex. 4.1).

Often the overall form of the instrument is dictated by another feature—for example the necessity for a left-facing bell when rotary-valves are used. Until the introduction of the front-valve piston-valved instruments had to have right-facing bells. Although the prime purpose of front-valves was to bring the valve caps more conveniently under the player's fingers, a further advantage resulted from the valve casings being at right-angles to the valve tubing which consequently was able to dispense with the more abrupt curves previously necessary in piston-valved instruments. Some early saxhorns had valve tubing arranged in circular shape in an attempt to overcome this same problem. This solution was not acceptable, however, as the tubing has to be adjustable for tuning purposes. In practice, it is usually extended into as smooth a form as possible in order to diminish resistance. It is, though, easy to over-estimate the undesirable effects of bends in the tubing. In 1859 Mandel wrote of the bombardon that the only pedal note available was that of the open instrument. Notes involving all three valves 'have to force a passage through so many twistings and twinings, that it is impossible for their tone to be certain and definitive'. He suggested using two bombardons—one in F, one in E♭—to cover up each other's poor low notes (cf. Berlioz's ophicleides, page 157 above). As recently as 1929 Andersen warned student orchestrators that 'the pedal tones are weak and practically useless' (A[12], 154). (He also wrote '. . . where a boisterous climax is required, finds the tuba in its natural element'.)

The position of the valve-slide in relation to the valve chamber is a problem different makers tackle in various ways. French top-valve instruments often have at least two slides on the side away from the player. On compensated instruments the compensating-system slides are placed here (see Fig. 4.5). One of the important factors governing the position of the valve-slides on uncompensated instruments is the necessity for their being convenient for the player to adjust while playing. It is essential that the first valve-slide should be adjustable and desirable that the third should also; at least one manufacturer feels an adjustable fourth valve-slide gives the player more control over intonation.

Since the right hand operates the valves (or, at least, the most frequently-used valves), in a rotary-valve or front-valve instrument the left is used to manipulate the valve-slides. These must therefore be positioned so that they draw out in an upwards direction. Some makers find this in any case preferable as moisture condensing in the slide runs down through the valve and thence to the water-key, while the possibility of moisture from the valve chamber running into the slide is avoided. Other makers position the bulk of the fourth valve-tubing above the valve but the actual slide below, solving the drainage problem though preventing convenient manipulation. Yet other makers (and players) feel that the valve-slides should be below the valve chambers as the moisture tends to pick up some of the slide lubricant which may cause the valve to stick if the slide is positioned above the valve. (Lubricants for the valve itself are extremely lightweight and normally include a cleansing agent. The traditional lubricant for piston-valves was saliva, and it must be admitted that many old instruments seem to respond to its use with more enthusiasm than to sophisticated modern products. It is also cheaper and generally available.)

Slides adjustable during performance are shown in a photograph of the three tubist Hellebergs, August sr with sons August jnr and John, reproduced by Taylor (T[6], 39). Dating from 1904, each has a rotary-valve instrument with the first, third and fourth valve-slides accessible to the left hand. Some players, notably the American Don Butterfield, feel that the only way really fine control can be exercised is by the use of push-rods operated by the finger and moving through guides. Butterfield began his experiments in this direction as long ago as 1949 and six instruments incorporating his proposals were built by King. It has been suggested that the fine-tuning facilities available make a fourth valve necessary only for bridging the gap between the fundamental and lowest second harmonic. Roger Bobo, however, advocates tuning the fifth valve to give a drop of rather less than two tones. Three different positions of the slide—controlled by a lever system—then give perfect intonation between fundamental and second harmonics. Meinl-Weston give players the option of having triggers on first, second or fourth valves, with the possibility of a Viennese valve system for certain models (Ex. 4.1). In conjunction with the German tubist Walter Hilgers they have also developed the *quintventil*: a sixth valve giving a drop of three-and-a-half tones. Flügel horns are now increasingly benefiting from the trumpet-designer's practice of fitting a trigger to the first or third valve-slide (or both). This facility is also sometimes available on alto horns, baritones and euphoniums.

The individual player is often a strong advocate of either piston- or rotary-valves. The major disadvantage of the piston-valve is its unsuitability for use with bores exceeding 19 mm (hence the common use of a rotary when there is a fifth valve positioned at a point where the bore of the tubing is wider than at the main four-valve assembly fitted closer to the mouthpipe). It is generally agreed that the rotary is quicker (it has a shorter action), but its more intricate mechanism gives extra expense in construction and extra difficulty in cleaning and oiling. The piston-valve is in general slower but easier to maintain. Normally the piston is lighter to the touch, especially if a euphonium valve spring is substituted for the often unnecessarily strong spring fitted by the makers. Besson's French Patent 13668 of 18 January 1855 includes pistons made from *aluminum argenté* (silver-plated aluminium) to decrease their weight. (V. Scully and B. J. Heywood in Provisional British Patent 20844 of 15 September 1855, and F. W. Gerhard in British Patent 2980 of 16 December 1856, proposed the use of aluminium for all the parts liable to corrode.) Materials in current use for pistons, which tend to suffer from corrosion, include stainless steel, nickel-silver (German Silver) and monel (approximately 67 per cent nickel, 28 per cent copper and 5 per cent other elements). The pistons are then silver- or nickel-plated. Valve stems are sometimes anodized, and valve springs normally made of phosphor bronze. In general a piston-valved instrument can be left unplayed for far longer than a rotary-valved instrument and still function on being picked up, perhaps after many months of inactivity.

Červený seems to have been the first manufacturer to make it possible for the player to adjust a rotary-valve spring, customizing the pressure needed for its operation. Introduced more recently, Miraphone's presto system for tubas allows the player to make adjustments to each individual lever. This company also offers a choice of light-weight spiral spring or compact clock-type spring operation. Many years ago hollow rotors were made: a few are still in existence and apparently very light and fast. Rotary-valves seem to wear before piston-valves, and mechanical action before string action. Meinl has used for some years a straight rod action with ball-and-socket joints incorporating Unibals on both ends of the connecting arm. Miraphone's Direct Valve Stroke Assembly (DVS) utilizes a system of steel balls with nylon sockets, the steel CPU system forming a compact precision unit of ball-and-socket. The Miniball Linkage, introduced by Červený in 1997, consists of a self-lubricating compact ball-and-socket unit made of stainless steel, providing a smooth and quiet action. Boosey & Hawkes fit piston-valve guides made from a variety of nylon called Delrin. The same firm also fits silicone rubber spring dampers and 'super-resilient soft stops'. It might be possible to fit stops of the same material to rotary-valves, although neoprene (a synthetic rubber) is now in general use. Attempts to use natural rubber (first suggested in 1866) have been unsuccessful owing to its tendency to harden when subjected to moisture, thus losing resilience and causing noise—a characteristic shared in the long-term by neoprene. Cork, even the close-grained type from Champagne bottles, tends to break down over time.

One final point concerning valves is their position on the instrument. In Britain they have traditionally been top-valves (hence the inevitable right-facing bell). These are without any doubt the least comfortable for the player as the hand is never allowed to fall naturally on the valve caps. Conn addressed a similar problem in their sousaphones by using offset valve caps for the first and third valves to bring them closer to the second valve and within a normal hand's span, and this has increasingly become the general practice of other makers.

Another solution lies in the use of front-valves, but they are more liable to accidental damage when the instrument is carried in a non-playing position. The front-facing valve originated in the United States, quite possibly inspired by the early nineteenth-century American string action valve. The Allen valve could be positioned either as a top-valve or a front- (side-) valve, as Garofalo & Elrod illustrate in many of their photographs of Civil War instruments. Early in the century the London firm of Boosey made a number of front-valved tubas. It is thought that the reason was to give left-facing bells and hence symmetry to marching bands, although they are sometimes known as 'cavalry tubas' (Fig. 7.2). A photograph of the 11th Hussars, a mounted band, in Paris in 1931 shows a tuba of this type (T$^{14}$, 74), while a photograph on the facing page allows the visual effects of two left-facing and two right-facing tubas in the same band to be appreciated more fully. A photograph of the Coldstream Guards Band in 1911 shows similar instruments, and also a rotary-valve model of unknown provenance. By 1921 the regiment had five left-facing Boosey tubas (T$^{14}$, 24). Some others using them are listed in Table 7.2.

In 1997 Besson (Boosey & Hawkes) introduced EE♭ and BB♭ Sovereign tubas following the pattern of the Boosey 'cavalry tubas'. They share with the Hirsbrunner HBS 488 EE♭ Tuba the distinction of having front piston-valves as well as an automatic compensation system, but in practice players choose not to carry the extra weight of the compensation system (and pay the financial cost of the extra materials and labour involved) when fine-tuning is available through manipulating the slides.

Rotary-valves suffer from the same practical disadvantage as front-valves, sometimes standing out several centimetres from the rest of the instrument. Where robust construction is essential, as in school instruments, top piston-valves are thus desirable. Rotaries seem rarely to have appeared in British army bands, although a photograph of the Royal Horse Guards (The Blues) in London between 1880-90 shows a tuba with three valves of this type (T[14], 24) and the 1st Battalion The Hampshire Regiment had another c. 1913 (T[16], 129). For many years rotary-valves, although generally much more conveniently situated for the hand, often had spatulae which were much too short, but manufacturers do now ensure that these are of sufficient length to be manipulated by average fingers. The first four rotary-

Fig. 7.2
Freelance London tubist
Jim Anderson with
early twentieth-century
left-facing 'cavalry tuba'
by Boosey of London.

valves on any tuba are normally positioned alongside each other with any others situated some distance away; if there are more than one these extra valves may form a subsidiary cluster. Until relatively recently it was customary for the fifth and further valves to be operated by the left hand (as in the original Baß–Tuba and later clavicor), but it is now more normal for the right hand to be used, connexion with the valve being made by means of a lever mechanism. This allows the left hand to remain free to manipulate the valve–slides.

Allied to the position of the valves, which sometimes still seems to have been chosen by reference to a deformed giant, is the position of the mouthpipe. Attempting to play the only British BBb tuba in production in the 1960s, John Fletcher, six foot tall, found the mouthpiece level with his forehead (F[18], Winter 1974, 117). The Besson Sovereign BE994 model was designed to be 'shorter, putting the player completely in touch with this instrument's superb sound'.

Sousaphone mouthpipes are built in a number of adjustable sections which can be locked into position to suit the individual player but this tends to impair the acoustic functions of the mouthpipe. In 1896 Fontaine-Besson took out a French patent for a 'cup mouthpiece in bent form to enable the player to move it'. Named *Guerrière*, it was apparently not a success. Taylor refers to a pair of Holton tubas owned by Luca Del Negro, a sometime Sousa tubist who worked as a freelance player in New York. Both of these instruments had front-action piston–valves and mouthpipes that could be positioned on either side of the bell with the intention of giving consistency of bell direction when playing in any position in the pit (T[6], 40).

The mouthpipe, or leadpipe, is an element that has received much attention during recent years, particularly in relation to the trumpet and trombone. Players are often given the opportunity to choose a bore profile with which they feel particularly comfortable. This is a terrifying decision to have to make swiftly and live with for a long time. The B&S 4098 MC (marketed under the VMI name in the United States), designed in conjunction with Mel Culbertson, is supplied with two leadpipes to enable the player to continue to experiment. While there is at first glance much to be said for a compact design of tuba (like the Červený *Tornister-Bass* of 1908 or current 603 'Piggy' model), this approach can result in the loss of the instrument's distinctive tonal qualities.

Don Butterfield's interest in tuba design was initiated by the discovery that the vision of his left eye was deteriorating owing to its seeing no further than the bell when he was playing; the right eye was both reading the music and observing the

Table 7.2    SOME LEFT-FACING TUBAS IN BRITISH ARMY BANDS

| DATE | REGIMENT AND NOTES | REFERENCE |
|---|---|---|
| c. 1890 | 1st. Bttn. Leinster Regiment (1) | T16, 232 |
| 1910 | 1st Bttn. Leicestershire Regiment (1) | T15, 186 |
| 1911 | Coldstream Guards (2 + rotary-valve tuba) | T14, XX |
| 1912 | King's Rifle Corps (BB flat: possible rotary-valves) | T16, 204 |
| 1915 | 5th Bttn. Royal Irish Regiment (1) | T15, 190 |
| 1920 | 1st Bttn. Quen's Own Royal West Kent Regt. (1) | T15, 109 |
| 1921 | Coldstream Guards (5) | T14, 24 |
| 1921 | 2nd Bttn. Lancashire Fusiliers (1) | T15, 148 |
| 1922 | 2nd Bttn. Royal Yorkshire Regiment (1) | T16, 225 |
| 1924 | 1st Bttn. Black Watch (1) | T15, 72 |
| 1929 | 1st Bttn. Norfolk Regiment (1) | T15, 156 |
| 1930 | 2nd Bttn. Queen's Royal Regiment (1) | T15, 97 |
| 1931 | 11th Hussars (2 + 2 right-facing tubas) | T14, 74 |
| after 1945 | Scots Guards | T14, 31 |

conductor. One advantage of the right-facing tuba bell is that both eyes are allowed to function normally. A second advantage lies in the left hand's being free to *volti subito* when necessary as these instruments, even if not compensated, do not allow adjustment of the valve-slides while actually being played. Their inherent superior balance enables them to be steadied by the right hand if necessary as well as being manipulated by the right-hand fingers.

Reference has already been made to drainage problems in the tuba. Contrary to general opinion very little of the moisture is saliva. It is mainly the result of the condensation of warm breath inside cold tubing, and is thus particularly prevalent when giving alfresco performances on cold days—aggravated on wet days as rain collects in the bell. Even in the concert hall the extremes of the instrument can remain much cooler than the parts closest to the player. Although a relatively high temperature may often be felt by a hand inside the bell, the fifth valve-slide in uncompensated instruments and the third compensating slide in others can repay individual attention as they suffer the additional hazard of not being used so often as the other tubing in the instrument and thus cooling off quicker. Each individual model has its particular intentional or unintentional sumps. It is often found that rotary- and front-valve instruments drain down to the water-key very efficiently

Table 7.3              SOME BRITISH WATER-KEY PATENTS

| PATENT | DATE | NAME | DESCRIPTION |
|---|---|---|---|
| 342 | 22 Febrary 1858 | J. Davis | A reservoir with a sponge below one or more perforations in a bend of the instrument to collect condensed breath. |
| 2468 | 25 September 1866 | W. E. Newton, on behalf of Schreiber Cornet Mfc. Co. | A 'new type of self-acting water-valve'. (This was like the rotary-valve and sump type introduced by Schreiber in the United States the following year.) |
| 5432 | 14 November 1882 | W. Booth | A drainage device operated by a disc rotated by a handle attached to the mouthpipe. |
| 4542 | 7 March 1884 | D. J. Blaikley | A drainage device operated through the valve-cap. |
| 7173 | 15 March 1888 | G. T. Hyde, on behalf of A. Leforestier. | A very complicated drainage device operated through the valve-cap. |
| 21,807 | 2 October 1909 | J. H. Viol | 'Small reservoir traps' along a tube 'of sufficient total capacity to retain the accumulated water until the longest solo has been played'. |
| 297,185 | 23 July 1927 | J. Hutchison | '. . . an opening through which condensed moisture escapes continuously, the opening being plugged with wire gauze, sponge, a mass of fine wire or other porous material' along with a reservoir. |

owing to the tubing's lying simply in two vertical planes. Other types are now regularly fitted with as many as five water-keys, particularly when carrying the extra tubing required by compensation.

There was a water-key on Charles Sax's 1824 omnitonic horn, although most subsequent french horns were —and still are—without the benefit of this device. Cotter's Hibernicon carried a 'spring water-key on the bow at its lowest point' in 1823, possibly the first ever. The traditional water-key shown in Fig. 7.3(a) is highly efficient, the spring and cork easily replaceable when either is worn. Care has to be taken that it is situated as low as possible in order to allow the maximum amount of collected moisture to escape when opened; often there is only a second available during performance for it to be expelled. The arm should not be too exposed—

there is a model of euphonium in wide use on which it tends to catch in the player's clothing when the instrument is raised to the playing position. The Besson Sovereign 956GS baritone has no fewer than five water-keys (and finger tops inlaid with mother-of-pearl). Devices which clip to the nipples beneath some piston-valves may be obtained. They collect the moisture tending to accumulate in the casings and drip out of the base. Their use should be seriously considered on two counts: unless regularly drained they can (and do) overflow; and spillage can also occur when the instrument is not held vertically—when, for example it is rested across the knees. Vincent Bach's 'Grime Gutter' is made from a lightweight plastic and also fastens beneath the valves, in this case with the intention of absorbing excess oil.

A problem can be posed by the creation of undesirable harmonics as the air passes across the resonant cavity necessary to the water-key. Meinl-Weston have introduced the Amado Water Key (Fig. 7.3(b) and (c)) in which the cavity is reduced by eighty to ninety per cent. When the spring-loaded plunger is depressed the moisture may be evacuated through the resulting orifice.

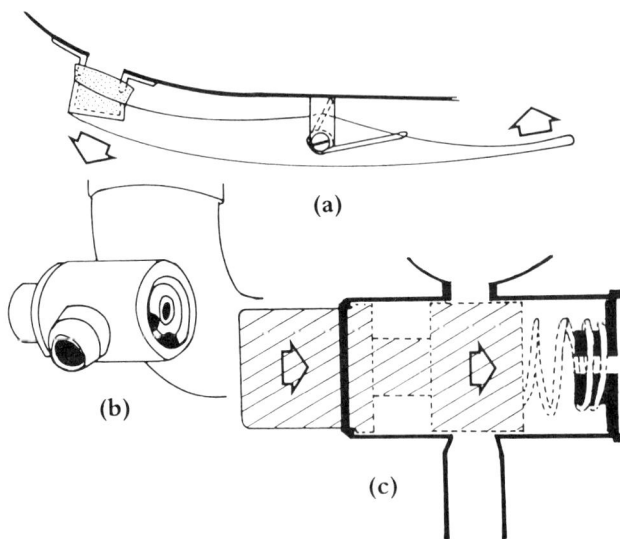

(a) and (c) to scale

Fig. 7.3. Water-keys. (a) Section *along* the tubing of the instrument, showing a traditional water-key. The arrows indicate direction of movement when the arm is depressed. (b) General view of Amado Water Key, showing position on the tubing. (This is not to scale.) (c) Section *across* the tubing, the arrows indicating direction of movement when the plunger is depressed.

A surprising amount of time and effort has been spent by inventors seeking the ideal drainage system for brass instruments. Table 7.3 lists merely a selection of British patents in this area.

Protection is normally given to the exposed sides of the main branches of the instrument by a guard wire which is either broadened on the bottom bow of the instrument or replaced by a comb or knob. It is more difficult to protect the bell, which by virtue of its size and shape is particularly vulnerable in the case of the tuba. In most models the rim is formed during spinning, a highly skilled process in which the craftsman places in position the bell bead consisting of a thin brass wire which he turns inside the outer edge of the bell. It contributes both to its strength and acoustic properties. Seamless bells are now customary and at one time Meinl-Weston tubas had the added protection of a clear plastic ring which prevented the scratches and other damage caused by standing the instrument upright on its bell.

Too large a bell can cause the sound to be too diffuse. A large bell, however, can make an instrument look impressive, and most makers have at some time offered a model with a range of bell sizes, a practice with little if any scientific basis. In fact the extremely directional large bell of the tuba can lead to problems for the player whether he sits on the right or left flank of the orchestra. Forward-facing or recording bells allow the sound to be directed forward, in common with the trumpets and trombones, but can give an unpleasant 'blurting' quality which tends to prevent the use of this pattern of bell in the orchestra. The euphonium or small bass built to this design shown in a photograph of a bandsman of the 16th (The Queen's) Lancers about 1890 is a rare example of this type of instrument in use by the British army. (T[15], pl. II). Most American and Continental makers produce instruments with bells at an angle of 45° which to some extent modifies the more unpleasant characteristics. This design was also proposed by G. Metzler and J. Waddell in their British Patent 1836 of 12 August 1858. They suggested that it might have either a circular or an elliptical shape.

It is possible to make the bell detachable, thus allowing the use of either an upright or recording bell at will. Stuart Roebuck's Barlow Tuba offered this facility, possibly one of only two made on this pattern (Fig. 12.5). DEG adopted this principle in the Caravelle Commuter Tuba (also made in a baritone version). The student tubist's brass bell stays at school while a fibreglass bell lives at home, with the eminently practical result that it is necessary to carry only a conveniently shaped case with the tuba body section inside. George McCracken of Barhamsville, Virginia, makes tuba bells of a special carbon fibre.

At the other extreme of the instrument is the mouthpiece, the part most intimately connected with the player himself. The acoustic functions are of extreme importance, followed by the comfort of the player (physical and psychological). Variations in mouthpiece dimensions have already been dealt with (see pages 51-6 above), but the finish is also important. Normally the mouthpiece is made from brass, usually plated in silver or even gold to protect both mouthpiece and player. Alternatively it may be made in German Silver. Walter Sear and Conn have made mouthpieces turned from transparent plexiglass for teaching purposes. DEG offer a nylon cup. Polycarbonate cups are available from Doug Elliott of Silver Spring, Maryland, while Discount Music (Chicago) and Josef Klier (Diespeck über Neustadt/Aisch, Germany) make analyzation rims. Vincent Bach offer an alternative Lucite rim (a plastic or acrylic resin made from polymerized methyl methcrylate) and the Perantucci range includes synthetic rims, all of which can add to the player's comfort in certain circumstances. Thomas Ghislin took out British Patent 1072 (28 April 1864) for mouthpieces made from seaweed. The plant was powdered or made into a paste prior to moulding, but there is no evidence that the process was actually tried out.

Occasionally the inventor's interest lay closer to the player's own contribution to sound generation. In J. Engelhard's British Patent 18,442 of 13 August 1913

> A device is inserted between the lips, gums, and teeth of a performer to facilitate the production of high and low notes. The device may be made of rubber and is so shaped that the sides of the lips are supported although the central parts are free to vibrate.

Several companies currently offer a range of mouthpiece components that can be assembled to suit the player's individual demands. Doug Elliott of Silver Spring, Maryland and Endsley Brass of Denver, Colorado, for example, allow a choice of rim, cup and shank, indications that in an electronic age there is still room for the ingenious mind and in 1997 Dillon Music, Woodbridge, New Jersey, designed an adjustable gap tuba receiver. This consists of a section soldered to the external end of the instrument's mouthpipe which includes a lock-ring and a separate section tapered like a conventional receiver but carrying an external screw thread. Inserting this into the lock-ring allows infinite adjustment of the gap between the mouthpiece and the end of the leadpipe. It is claimed that by this means the response of the tuba can be varied between a smooth, broad response with liquid slurs and a much sharper, focused response. Furthermore, the adjustable receiver is provided with inserts ('bits') for both large- and small-shank mouthpieces, giving rise to the claim that 'this is perhaps one of the most significant innovations in tuba technology since the invention of the valve'.

Numerous other inventors have applied their talents to modifications of the mouthpiece. Table 7.4 is restricted to British patents:

Table 7.4    SOME BRITISH MOUTHPIECE PATENTS

| PATENT | DATE | NAME | DESCRIPTION |
|---|---|---|---|
| 782 | 3 March 1875 | B. J. Mills (for C. G. Conn) | An elastic or soft india-rubber face welded on to the rim of the mouthpiece. |
| 4515 | 4 November 1881 | J. Dunbar & R. R. Harper | 'Positive and negative metals, conjoined with an insulator, are employed in connection with the mouthpieces, so as to obtain an electric current to the mouth.' |
| 24,366 | 14 December 1894 | W. P Thompson (for C. G. Schuster) | 'The mouthpiece is covered with cloth, leather, or other non-conductor. A mode of attaching the covering by rings is shown, but others may be adopted.' |
| 7677 | 16 April 1895 | J. Rüegg | 'An india-rubber or other soft ring is attached to the mouthpiece [rim].' |
| 8350 | 21 April 1899 | L. Antoine | 'The mouthpiece has its walls made hollow for lightness, and to prevent heating. It screws on the the stem, which is solid.' |
| 9470 | 23 April 1906 | M. M. Rubright | A shell of vulcanized rubber or other hard material for the mouthpiece. 'The form of the embrochure [sic.] may be changed by varying the thickness of the shell.' |
| 8849 | 10 April 1911 | W. Thomason & A. G. Brannan | An attachment for mouthpieces 'serving as a support for the upper lip of the performer'. |
| 261,419 | 14 November 1925 | P. Aka | 'The mouthpiece . . . has an integral elongated flange serving as a lip support.' |

During the 1990s there was a fashion for heavy mouthpieces, varieties in which the additional metal could add more than half as much weight again to that strictly required for the cup and rim. The reasons for this have been claimed as 'gives more resonance to the sound' (Jet-Tone); 'louder volume without distortion—softer playing with more control—better high register—better low register—cleaner articulation—faster tonguing' (Denis Wick); 'velvety, darkened sound quality and increased dynamics' (Dillon). While the internal dimensions of a mouthpiece are crucial in deciding its characteristics and thus directly influence those of the instrument, it is not easy to understand how the *outside* of a mouthpiece can affect the sound in any way (far less a player's ability to tongue faster!). Makers may here be exploiting players' natural inclinations to believe that it is always possible to achieve a higher standard given the right magical component. Jet-Tone actually state that their new, heavyweight models 'feature the exact same internal specifications as the standard models', while Dillon aim for improvement by using bronze, which is forty per cent heavier than brass. Brass itself is not cheap, and this conspicuous consumption of expensive materials may be seen as paralleling the contemporary fad for four-wheel drive vehicles to collect the children from suburban schools. Movement in the opposite direction may have been indicated in 1998 when euphoniumist Stephen Mead, in relation to his new range of mouthpieces, stated: 'I removed quite a bit of metal, since the more there is, the more prominent the central core of sound is, to the detriment of roundness. By removing some metal, you also improve response' (M[17], 35-36). It would have been interesting to overhear his next conversation with Denis Wick.

Tubas themselves are normally made of brass with ferrules, stays and other fittings often of German Silver (nickel-silver: fifty per cent copper; twenty per cent zinc; thirty per cent nickel) which is more resistant to corrosion. Yellow brass seems to be the favourite body material, especially for the bell section, but some makers also offer red brass. The Sander tuba made mainly from copper shown in Fig. 8.1 is exceptional. Brass may be nickel- or silver-plated, epoxy-resin lacquered or left as brass, although this soon dulls and frequent polishing is not recommended owing to the abrasive action of the polishes. Different makers have different approaches. Meinl-Weston's leadpipes and tuning-slides are made from nickel-silver, while UMI use rose brass (with a higher copper content) for flügel horn mouthpipes to overcome the corrosion caused by saliva. The L.A. flügel horn is available in either red or black.

In 1997 Glassl of Nauheim announced a range of BB♭ fibreglass tubas, roughly one-third lighter in weight than traditional brass tubas. The valves are conventionally made of nickel-silver and the leadpipe, of either nickel-silver or brass, can be conveniently removed. Similar materials have been used regularly for sousaphones since the early 1960s, but this was a revolutionary approach to the tuba. Further advantages include the use of a more robust material than brass in construction and the potential for colouring the body black, white, gold or silver. The advent of the first coloured tuba in a symphony orchestra is anticipated with sweet delight (Fig. 7.4).

The keen observer of tubas will have noticed accessories and gadgets not mentioned so far. Rings are prominent on the instrument: a thumb-ring for the

Fig. 7.4. Fibreglass BB♭ tubas by Glassl of Nauheim. From left to right, they are black, gold, silver and white. Glassl also make tubas with correctly-coloured national flag designs, etc.

right thumb is virtually obligatory on a left-facing tuba; pull-rings help to give purchase when valve-slides are to be moved; rings are often provided so that a strap may be clipped to the instrument to take the strain when marching. A bandsman on the move also needs a card-holder, or 'lyre' as it is invariably called, to hold his music. This is attached to the tuba when required by being fitted into a conveniently situated lyre-box where it is retained by the pressure of a screw (Fig.

7.5). Tubists may also fit a pencil-holder to the instrument if they often work in studios. Others may attach a small screwdriver, or even manage to wedge a plastic container of valve-lubricant amongst the tubing. The tuba, or euphonium, itself may be conveniently rested on a specially-designed support when playing. Models for use with sousaphones have been available for some years: it is quite awkward to play sousaphone seated since the instrument interposes a large-diameter tube between the player and the back of the chair. Stands for upright tubas are being used increasingly, and it is now possible to obtain miniature gig bags which fit into the tuba bell to hold the stand in transit.

It will surprise many Britons that such a wide choice is available to the tubist when he comes to buy an instrument. But technological improvements, new materials and scientific research notwithstanding, professional players constantly seek good, old models. These are not crocks of gold. They appear from time to time: a half-century-old York or Holton, a Heiser with hollow valve rotors; my own euphonium was made in 1914. Rightly or wrongly the sentiment is often expressed in bandrooms the world over that 'they aren't made like they used to be'. In general the larger manufacturers are not very interested in the professional tubist. In an entire career a player may buy only two or three new instruments and the firms' accountants are much happier to see 100 mass-produced instruments sold to an education authority.

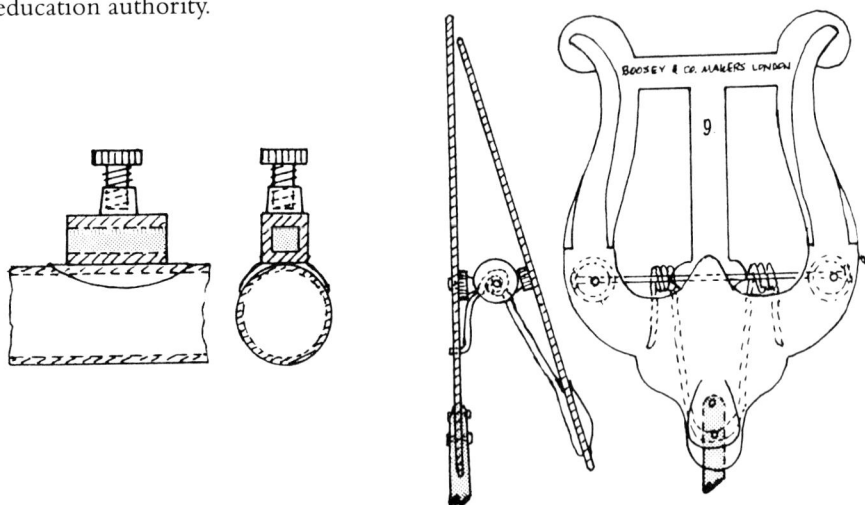

Fig. 7.5. Card-holder, or lyre, showing method of securing in the lyre-box soldered to the instrument.

It is difficult to avoid a degree of wry amusement when reading advice on brass instrument purchase given to parents. Here are Jill Phillips's comments:

> Metal instruments are subjected to a good deal of moisture, and with a great deal of playing they eventually suffer from metal-fatigue. Players must replace their instruments during the course of a playing career—sometimes quite often. It is common therefore to come across old instruments in a worn condition. It is not common to find a brass instrument in a second-hand shop which is going to prove to be just what you've been looking for (P[11], 101).

This statement is in striking contrast to the testimony of a number of distinguished American professional tubists in 1998:

> Fred Geib, my teacher, seemed to own and play Sanders tubas. All of his tubas were pre-World-War-Two vintage . . . The BB-flat, which he considered a band instrument . . . cost me $225 . . . In the late 1950's I began to use a Conn-Helleberg mouthpiece . . . as my main mouthpiece . . . that was the tuba/mouthpiece combination that I used for 35 years as a member of the Metropolitan Opera Orchestra. (Herbert Wekselblatt.)

> I found that the CC King that I used for 25 of the 26 years [in the Philadelphia Orchestra] did the job for me, and I never had any complaints from any conductor about my choice of instrument . . . I did use . . . a King E-flat that was made for Mr. Bell [1902-71] on some occasions . . . As for mouthpieces . . . I switched to a Bach 18, and used that for my entire playing career. (Abe Torchinsky, Philadelphia Orchestra.)

> The CC tuba that I use at the New York City Opera and for much of my other symphonic, ensemble and studio work is a four-quarter size Hirsbrunner with four rotary valves. It was built in 1976, and through the years I have become very comfortable with it . . . The more I play it, the better I like it. This horn responds well to many different kinds of mouthpieces. My personal preference is for an old mouthpiece that a former teacher spotted in a New York pawn shop in the 1960's. It belonged to Fred Geib, a well-known New York City tuba player from the 1930's and 40's. (Stephen M. Johns, Principal Tuba New York City Opera, American Symphony Orchestra.) (T[5], 34-6).

Some productive associations between manufacturers and players have reflected the concern for quality that characterises the dedicated maker and the professional tubist. In the late 1960s, for example, Meinl-Weston (selling under the name Melton in Europe) collaborated with Bill Bell and Arnold Jacobs in making a close copy of Bell's Model 1293 King CC which he used for many years in the New York Philharmonic Orchestra. This was marketed as the William Bell Model CC Tuba. In the 1990s Meinl-Weston introduced a virtually identical model, the Model 37 Tuba, a 17 mm bore, 4/4, five-valved instrument with a 420 mm detachable bell and first, third, fourth and fifth valve slides capable of adjustment by the left hand while playing. The same company has recently worked with Warren Deck of the New York Philharmonic in producing two types of CC tuba with different characteristics, and with jazz tubist Sam Pilafian in developing a versatile 4/4 CC instrument of relatively compact design. Daryl Smith, of the RAI Milan Orchestra, is another American who has collaborated with a European company, in this case Kalison of Milan. The essential requirements of the tubist have not changed in the past seventy years. It is reassuring to note that in both Europe and the United States tuba makers are increasingly looking to past best practice.

The tubist is, in fact, more likely to have to renew the case in which the instrument is carried around. The traditional case may be made from wood and can weigh as much 11 kg or more. In view of this, the majority of tuba cases made from this material now come with built-in wheels. There are two ways of reducing the weight of a tuba case. One is to make it out of a lightweight material like fibreglass or ABS plastic. Moulded to shape from hybrid-reinforced composites (in the case of Johnson Cases of Corona, California), these cases usually feature a soft interior utilizing a textile for maximum protection of the instrument's finish. The other approach to weight-reduction consists of the gig bag, a well-padded textile-lined bag with a leather or tough plastic outer.

Tubists, 'the lowly and lonely', have formed their own world-wide organization, Tubists' Universal Brotherhood Association—TUBA—to 'maintain a liaison between those who take a significant interest in the instruments of the tuba family'. In 2000 membership stands at over 2,000. Since 1979 International Tuba Day has been celebrated annually on the first Friday in May. A significant event occurred on 25 June 1995, declared by the city's mayor as 'Arnold Jacobs Day in Chicago' in celebration of the achievements of the distinguished American tubist, active from 1915-98. President Clinton himself sent his congratulations. Meanwhile, the twenty-first Annual William J. Bell Memorial Tuba Day took place on 6 November

1999 in Perry, Iowa. A steadily increasing number of regular tuba and euphonium-orientated events was typically indicated in *TUBA Journal* for Spring 1998 which, on page 11, listed no fewer than eight forthcoming major conferences in locations ranging from Austria to Finland, Sydney to Washington.

Apart from providing a very practical demonstration of methods of improving international understanding, these events also enable devotees of the tuba to benefit from a greater awareness of the ways in which manufacturers and composers in various countries have seen and heard their instrument, matters that have already been shown to cover an amazingly wide range of concepts. These will be considered in greater detail in the following chapters.

Table 7.5          SOME INSTRUMENT PRICES SINCE 1789

| SERPENTS | | | |
|---|---|---|---|
| *Date* | *Maker* | *Price* | *Notes* |
| 1789 | J. J. Régibo, Lille | 3 Louis | 'serpent nouveau qui est fait de même qu'un basson' |
| 1805 | Bernard, Lyons (retailer) | ½-litre Eau de Canel | Bought by the mayor of La Côte de S.-André, Berlioz's home town. |
| 1839 | D'Almaine, London | 5l. 15s.-7l. | 3 keys |
| | D'Almaine, London | 6l. 6s.- 7l. 10s. | 4 keys |
| | D'Almaine, London | 6l. 12s.- 7l. 17s. 6d | 5 keys |
| | D'Almaine, London | 3s. | Mouthpiece |
| | D'Almaine, London | 5s. | Crook |

| BASS HORNS | | | |
|---|---|---|---|
| 1839 | D'Almaine, London | 6l. 6s.. | 'Brass, with 4 Elastic Plug Keys' |
| 1839 | D'Almaine, London | 7l. 10s. | 'Copper, with 4 Elastic Plug Keys' |

| KEYED BUGLES | | | |
|---|---|---|---|
| 1817 | Imported into U.S.A. (?from Ireland) | $40 & $70 | Kent Bugles |
| 1839 | D'Almaine, London | 1l. 15s.- 5l. 10s. | 'Brass, with Tuning Slide and all the modern improvements' |
| | D'Almaine, London | 2l. 5s.- 6l. 10s. | 'Copper, with ditto' |
| | D'Almaine, London | 3s. | Crook |
| 1851 | Wright, Boston, Mass. | $350 & $480 | Silver presentation bugles |

| OPHICLEIDES | | | |
|------|------|------|------|
| 1839 | D'Almaine, London | 7l. 10s.–15l. 15s. | 9 keys |
| | D'Almaine, London | 9l. 9s.–16l. 16s. | 11 keys |
| | D'Almaine, London | 18l.–21l. | 'With Patent Valve Stops' |
| | D'Almaine, London | 5s–7s. 6d. | Mouthpieces |
| 1842 | U.S.A. [?] | $32 | Bought by G. Warren, Weston, Mass. |
| 1843 | Tredegar & Lewis, London (retail) | £4.16.0–£7.7.0 | 9- & 11-key ophicleides |
| 1851 | Jordan, Liverpool | 5–10 gns. | |
| 1851 | Jordan, Liverpool | £31.10.0 | Euphonic serpentcleide |
| 1851 | Köhler, London | 15 gns. | 11-key ophicleide |
| 1858 | Halary-Antoine, Paris | 140f. (£5.12.0) | keys on rod axles |
| 1916 | Couesnon, Paris | £3.2.5–£4.3.3. | |

| BARITONES | | | |
|------|------|------|------|
| 1828 | Stölzel, Berlin | 45 Rsf. | 'Tenorhorn oder Tenortrompete' |
| 1913 | Holton, Chicago | $57–$68 | Gold-plated: $170 |
| 1960 | King, Cleveland | $310–$350 | Fourth valve: $65 |
| 1974 | Selmer, London | £75 | |
| 1975 | Mirafone, Sun Valley | $650 | Fourth valve: $165 |
| 1999 | Besson, London | £3225 | Sovereign 4-valve compensating |

| EUPHONIUMS | | | |
|---|---|---|---|
| 1913 | Holton, Chicago | $60-$72 | Gold-plated: $185 |
| 1913 | Holton, Chicago | $77-$93 | with double bell |
| 1957 | Hüttl, Baiersdorf/ Mittelfranken | $133.35-$176.20 (£47.17.3-£63.5.0) | |
| 1973 | Boosey & Hawkes, London | £288 | Imperial |
| 1974 | Yamaha, U.K. | £301.25-£356.49) | |
| 1977 | Boosey & Hawkes, London | £730.85 | Sovereign |
| 1999 | Besson, London | £3595 | Sovereign 4-valve compensating |

| EE flat TUBAS (4 valves) | | | |
|---|---|---|---|
| c. 1874 | Boosey, London | £12-£25 | |
| 1906 | Holton, Chicago | $90-$120 | Monster E flat Bass |
| 1939 | Hilton, Chicago | $175-$220 | |
| 1960 | King, Cleveland | $645-$695 | |
| 1977 | Boosey & Hawkes, London | £867.25 | Imperial (+ case £72.10) |
| 1999 | Besson, London | £4700 | Sovereign 4-valve compensating |

| BB FLAT [CC] TUBAS | | | |
|---|---|---|---|
| c. 1874 | Boosey, London | £14-£24 | |
| 1908 | Holton, Chicago | $90-$120 | Mammoth B flat Bass |
| 1939 | Holton, Chicago | $290-$345 | |
| 1960 | King, Cleveland | $850-$905 | |
| 1974 | Yamaha, U.K. | £560.67 | |
| 1975 | Mirafone, Sun Valley | $2340 | |
| 1977 | Boosey & Hawkes, London | £893.60 | Imperial (+ case £93.00) |
| 1999 | Besson, London | £6060 | Sovereign 4-valve compensating |

# CHAPTER VIII

# *Instruments and Music: Germany and Austria*

Modern makers have elevated the Bombardon to a high
degree of importance in the orchestra. Wagner assured its
importance therein . . .
—*The Easy Way to Play Brass Instruments*
Liverpool, n.d.

He also said: 'I heard in your "Rienzi" an instrument that
you call "Bass-tuba"; I should not like to banish this
instrument from the orchestra: write a part for it into
Vestale' . . . When he heard the effect for the first time . . .
he threw me a truly tender glance of thanks . . .
—Richard Wagner *Prose Works*
'Mementoes of Spontini'

WITHIN a decade of its appearance the Baß-Tuba had adopted a more familiar shape. In the same showcase as the Wieprecht & Moritz tuba at the Musikinstrumenten-Museum Berlin is another, by an unknown maker, from about 1850 (No. 4368). The bell and bore are larger and there are three rotary-valves; it could almost be a current model. This rapid development was the result of fifteen years' activity by numerous instrument-makers in the German States.

Despite the economic problems brought about by unification, Germany still supports more professional orchestras than any other country. Craftsmen to build and repair instruments are a necessary adjunct, and there are many small workshops. Often certain towns became centres for brass instrument-making: Markneukirchen is one, with makers maintaining traditions established by the french horn maker Isaak Eschenbach in 1755. It is interesting—and reassuring—to see the emphasis placed on standards of craftsmanship by a company like Vogtländische Musikinstrumentenfabrik, makers of B&S tubas, who moved into their new factory in the town in 1994. Statements in their sales literature demonstrate their continuing faith in established practices:

B&S tubas are built by master craftsmen devoted to quality and perfection in the finest German tradition. An unprecedented amount of handwork goes into every B&S tuba before the name is engraved on the bell . . . All tapered bows are built up from sheet brass, carefully worked to their final form and hammered, filed and annealed for correct wall thickness and temper . . . The B&S staff consists entirely of people who have a strong traditional background in and orientation toward the handcrafting of wind instruments. Decades of experience are reflected and incorporated into all facets of the company's work. This begins with the training of apprentices and continues through all phases of manufacturing.

At the beginning of World War II there were 300 musical instrument-making companies in the Bohemian town of Graslitz, a staggering number, developing from the twelve violin-makers established there by 1669. Following his release as a prisoner of war, Anton Meinl, born in Graslitz and son of instrument-maker Wenzel Meinl, settled in Austria and worked for two years as an instrument-repairer before locating his father, who had in the meantime established a business in the German town of Geretsried. In 1991 Anton's own son Gerhard founded the TA-Musik group which took over Vogtländische Musikinstrumentenfabrik (B&S) and Courtois of France. TA-Musik is now part of TA Triumph-Adler AG. The company promotes its products through the musical media of the Melton Tuba Quartett and Gerhard Meinl's Tuba Sextett, both of which have made numerous recordings.

From Graslitz (now Hradec Králové, Czech Republic) thirty instrument-makers arrived as refugees at the Bavarian town of Waldkraiburg in 1946. Here they formed a co-operative, erecting their first workshop on a munitions dump. Now, in a factory purpose-built in 1983, they produce Miraphone instruments. They are proud of the combination of technology, tradition and craftsmanship which has earned a high reputation for their products. Computer analysis facilitates the assessment of intonation, along with the sound and tone qualities of each instrument, yet the company emphasises that 'the secret of our quality is the skill of our craftsmen'. Situated between Munich, with its operatic and symphonic activities, and the historic musical centre of Salzburg, the region is also a renowned centre of band activity.

The vitality of the German musical instrument industry is easily explained. The region in which Markneukirchen lies is known as the *Muikwinkel* (music corner), and the activities concentrated there help to explain why in the 1850s, after fewer than twenty years, the bass tuba became practically the instrument it is today, and why now the majority of professional orchestral tubists play on German instruments.

The liberation of the orchestral brass in nineteenth-century Germany was begun by Richard Wagner, yet when Wieprecht's Baß-Tuba appeared in 1835 Wagner was unaware of the event. Twenty-two years of age, he was attempting to compose, court his future wife, escape his creditors and earn a living from minor posts in undistinguished provincial theatres. He wrote his first significant opera, *Rienzi* (1840) with the Paris Opéra in mind, placing an ophicleide in the orchestra and four more in the stage band. There is also a serpent, an instrument for which he showed some affection. The different functions he ascribes to the two instruments are quite clear; the former is the bass of the brass, the latter the bass of the woodwind, an arrangement had had first adopted in the overture *Rule, Britannia!* of 1837. (In the score it is suggested that the serpent could be 'possibly third bassoon'.) When the two are used in octaves, the ophicleide takes the upper part.

*Photo: Tom Mason*

Fig. 8.1. Five-valved CC tuba by Rudolf Sander, Wolfstein (Pfalz) owned by Jack Allison of Lymm. It is made of copper and German Silver. The fourth valve lowers the pitch two tones, the fifth (a rotary operated by piston), two-and-a-half tones.

There are two passages deserving attention. The first is the trombone and ophicleide entry in the overture, where a substitute tuba gives completely the wrong sound (Ex. 8.1). The other is a passage where the low brass accompany Rienzi (Ex. 8.2). This would just about work with three trombones and ophicleide, despite Berlioz's warning (see page 157 above); there are similar passages by Verdi where the lowest part may have been intended for the same instrument. A more mature Wagnerian treatment of a comparable sequence is shown in Ex. 15.2. *Rienzi* was first performed in 1842 at the Dresden Court Opera in a production affected by certain economies. It is likely that the ophicleide part was played on a valved instrument since there was a Baß-Tuba or valved ophicleide there by 1844.

Ex. 8.1

Wagner: *Rienzi* Overture

Ex. 8.2

Wagner: Rienzi

At the time Wagner was second conductor at the Court Opera. He later wrote a touching account of a request by the sixty-eight-year-old Spontini:

> He also said: 'j'ai entendu dans votre 'Rienzi'' un instrument que vous appelez "Bass-tuba"; je ne veux pas bannir cet instrument de l'orchestre; faites m'en une partie pour la Vestale'. [I have heard in your *Rienzi* an instrument that you call 'Bass-tuba': I should not wish to ban this instrument from the orchestra: write me a part for it in *La Vestale*.] I was delighted to carry out his wish, with moderation and discretion. Whe he heard the effect for the first time, at rehearsal, he threw me a truly tender glance of thanks, and the impression made on him by this not very difficult enrichment of his score was so lasting that he sent me afterwards a most friendly letter from Paris, begging me to forward him a copy of this instrumental addition; ony his pride did not allow him to admit, in the expression used to signify his wish, that he was asking for anything from my own pen, but he wrote: "envoyez-moi une partition des trombonnes pour la march triomphale et de la Basse-tuba, telle qu'elle a té exécuté sous ma direction à Dresde' (E[8], III, 133). [Send me a score of the trombone parts for the 'Triumphal March' and the other that you made for the bass tuba under my direction in Dresden.]

There is evidence that Spontini was already aware of the existence of the tuba, as from 1840-42 he was Generalmusikdirector of the Berlin Opera and consequently involved in an episode in which the new instrument acted as a substitute horn. The French composer Adolphe Adam wrote an account of this in a letter dated 3 June 1840 to the horn-player Joseph Meifred reproduced in the preface to his 1840 *Méthode pour le cor chromatique ou a à pistons* (E[12], 75-76). Adam had included some low notes in the horn parts of his opera-ballet *Hamadriades*, already performed several times at the Paris Opéra where chromatic horns were in use. The Berlin horn-players told Adam that the notes were not playable on their instruments.

> I went to see Spontini who told me that these notes are found only on the three-valved horn which is not used in the orchestra; and I believe that they are not found in the wind band any more, where these notes are played only on the corno basso, an instrument that is completely unknown to us, and which has a powerful effect. In spite of my conviction of Spontoni's error and that of the Berlin hornists, I was obliged to have the part of the fourth horn performed on the tuba . . .

Wagner's first specific request for the tuba seems to have been in *Eine Faust-Ouvertüre*, completed in Paris in 1840. The first few bars of the work (Ex. 8.3) are often quoted for this reason, but the tuba part was probably added during revision of the orchestation prior to 1855. On the evidence of *Rienzi* it is likely that Wagner would have written for ophicleide as he hoped for a performance of the overture first of all in Paris. But this was not to be and we know from a letter written to Liszt that by 1855 he had revised the work, including the orchestration. The programme of the first English performance, at Crystal Palace, 10 October 1874, remarks: 'The orchestra . . . embraces Piccolo, three Bassoons, and Bass Tuba'.

Ex. 8.3

Wagner: *Eine Faust-Ouvertüre*

The Czech firm of Červený is generally credited with the invention of the contrabass tuba in CC in 1845 (Fig. 9.1). Wagner specified it from *Das Rheingold* (1853-54) onwards. The contrabass tuba gave an additional tone-colour, demonstrated in the opening bars of *Siegfried* (Ex. 8.4). It eventually became the practice in some German opera houes to employ two tubists, one specializing in the lower parts and the other in the higher F tuba parts, although by the end of the twentieth century economics dictated that one tubist should cope not only with both tubas but also with cimbasso (see page 421 below).

Wagner's tuba parts often extend to considerable heights, depending upon his specifying tuba or contrabass tuba. In 1867 he wrote the famous passage in the overture to *Die Meistersinger von Nürnberg* (Ex. 8.5). Despite the subsequent efforts of some conductors, it was the composer's intention simply to support the double-basses here, as was his habit, and not obliterate the orchestra by tuba tone. The trill was the sole example in the repertoire until Mahler's fifth symphony of 1902.

Fig. 8.2
George Wall (Royal Opera
House, Covent Garden)
with four-valved 163
Alexander BB♭ tuba.

*Photo: Jill Wall*

Wagner was concerned to clarify the tuba's position in the brass section and introduced the Wagner Tuben to provide a tonal link with the horns (see pages 461-5 below). The presence of a contrabass trombone throughout the entire *Ring* allowed the trombones four real parts and permitted the tuba to fulfil more individual functions, as discussed in Chapter XVI. Here his characteristic contrabass tuba writing is low, massive and majestic as in the passage already referred to with Wagner Tuben. These were the sounds that captivated Bruckner, who also delighted in the contrabass tuba and the Tuben, although as an organist he was normally content to allow the larger instrument to double the bass line at the octave.

Ex. 8.4

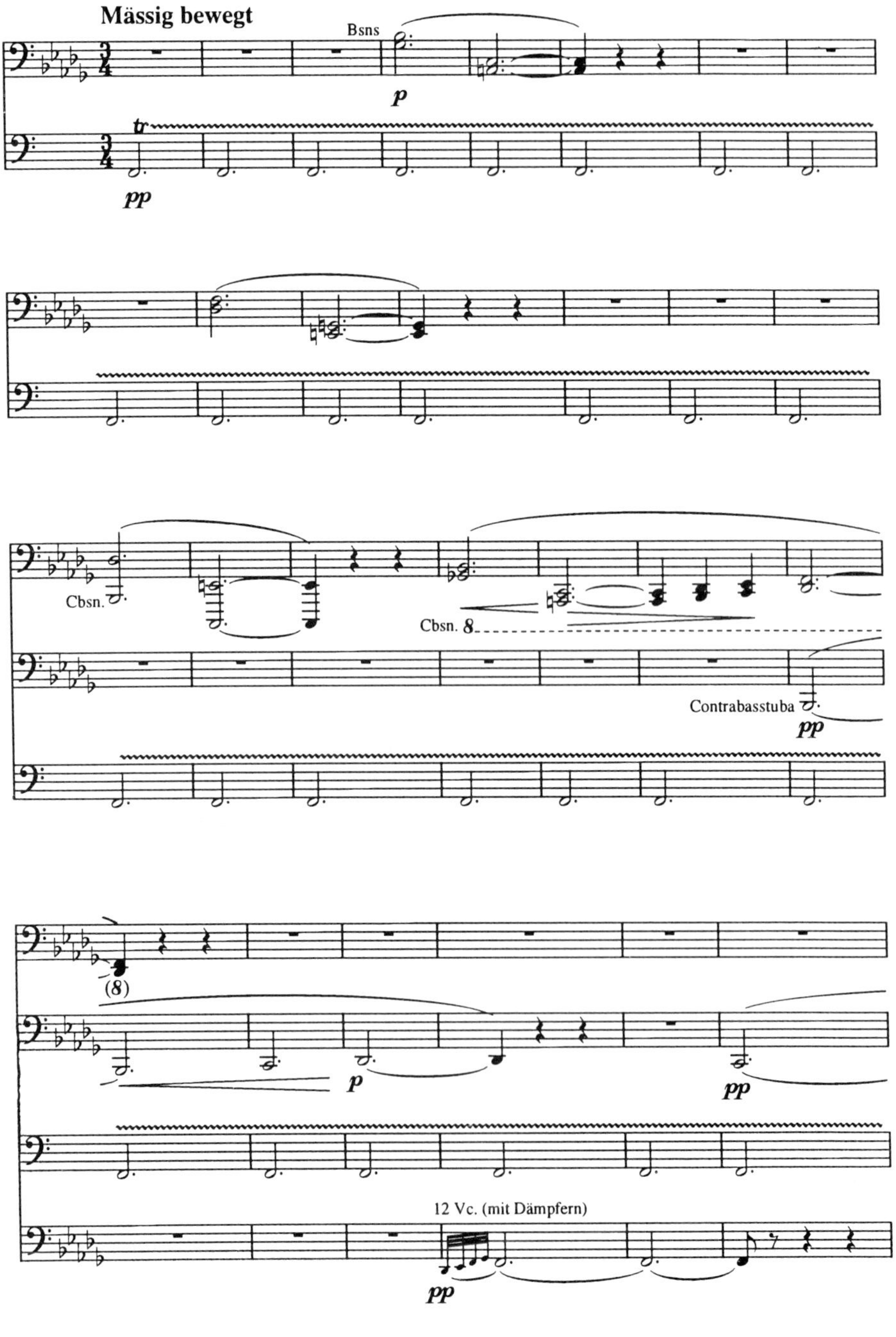
Mässig bewegt
Bsns
p
tr
pp
Cbsn.
Cbsn. 8
Contrabasstuba
pp
(8)
p
pp
12 Vc. (mit Dämpfern)
pp

Wagner: *Siegfried* Prelude

Ex. 8.5

**Sehr Mässig Bewegt**

*mf (aber sehr markirt)*

*(allmählich immer*

*stärker) f*

Wagner: *Die Meistersinger von Nürnberg* Overture

Johannes Brahms showed a consistent awareness of the tuba's partciular role. A full study of his treatment of the low brass has yet to be made, but he shows a masterly command of this section of the orchestra. The tuba is used in only a few works—one of the symphonies, two of the overtures, a work for choir and orchestra—and therein lies the secret: it is withheld (like the trombones) until the moment when it is essential for the desired effect.

Brahms was a master of chorale-style writing for the low brass. In the *Akademisch Festouvertüre* a modulatory phrase occurs, each time slightly varied, not only leading the listener to a new key but achieving this by way of something magic yet clear and simple (Ex. 8.6). Anyone can be a magician with coloured smoke and girl in tights, but Brahms enchants in his shirt-sleeves.

Ex. 8.6

Brahms: Akademisches Festouvertüre

During the first movement of the second symphony the four low brass instruments play a striking high chord (Ex. 8.7) finally clinching a long-built-up musical argument in the orchestra. The effect of this was probably even more powerful on Brahms's listeners in 1877 than Stravinsky's similarly-positioned and undeniably effective muted chords in 1910 (Ex. 9.6(b)). In the second movement of the same symphony Brahms uses the tuba for support during important passages for the lower strings, the other brass remaining silent. He sometimes writes the second trombone and tuba in octaves opposed to the first and bass trombones also in octaves, for example in the *Tragisch Ouvertüre*. Just as distinctive are his remarkable leaping tuba parts which appear at the end of the second symphony (Ex. 8.8(a)), the end of the *Akademisches Festouvertüre* (Ex. 8.8(b)) and in *Ein deutsches Requiem*. This latter work also contains a short passage of considerable range, fortunately with the support of the bass trombone (Ex. 8.9).

Ex. 8.7

Brahms: Symphony 2

Ex. 8 8

(a)

**(Allegro con spirito)**

Brahms: Symphony 2

(b)

**(Maestoso)**

Brahms: *Akademische Festouvertüre*

(Ex. 8.9

**(Allegro)**

Brahms: *Eine deutsches Requiem*

Robert Schumann's skill in writing for piano contrasts with the awkwardness of his orchestration, which so often looks, feels and sounds uncomfortable. His use of 'Ophycleide' in *Das Paradies und die Peri* is positively bizarre, and it is difficult to fathom what he understood by the designation. Daverio states: 'Echoes of the Offertorium from Berlioz's Requiem take the form of prominent passages for ophicleide in Nos. 6, 7 and 23 of the *Peri*' (D$^2$, 227). If so, they are only partial echoes, heavily distorted.

Ex. 8.10

Schumann: *Das Paradies und die Peri*

Davario correctly identifies the three numbers (out of twenty-six) in which the instrument (valved, unliked Berlioz's) appears. But what is its distinctive function, that it is restricted to such limited use? Certainly nothing as appropriate as Brahms's restricted use of tuba. In No. 6 the Ophycleide doubles the basses of the choir in nine *forte* bars and doubles the celli for twenty-four (at the same written pitch as the celli and double basses). In No. 7 it doubles the choir's second basses for twelve bars and the celli for six. Its appearances in No. 23 are simply weird:

4 bars octave below Clarinet 1 (in chord)
3 bars two octaves below Clarinet 2 (chord)
4 bars octave below Bassoon 1 (Bassoon 2 tacet)
4 bars chord with Trombones 1 and 2 (bass trombone tacet)
2 bars unison with bass trombone
3 bars octave below Violins I
13 bars doubling celli.

Schumann's compulsion to tangle with voices and orchestra next led him to his first opera, *Genoveva,* completed in 1848 and turned down by Dresden on the grounds that its four acts were 'highly boring' (D², 341), a reaction later shared by Bernard Shaw who described it as 'markedly silly' from the start and 'pure bosh' from the Act I finale (D², 344). It was first performed in 1850 at Leipzig. Schumann was to some extent under Wagner's influence in composing this opera, which may be why he required 'Tuba' in one number, 15, the finale to Act III. This is the moment when Drago's ghost appears to force the sorceress Margaretha to tell Genoveva's husband Siegfried the truth about his wife's supposed adultery with Drago (prior, of course, to his assuming a supernatural form). Harking back admirably to Mozart and Weber, Schumann brings on the trombones—but totally

Ex. 8.11

(a)

(b)

Schumann: *Genoveva*

ruins the effect by suddenly introducing a tuba. Having contributed its distinctive broad sound to eleven bars, it then disappears for good. His use of tuba in *Manfred* is restricted to sixteen bars (in a total of fifteen numbers). Placing the tuba note *two* octaves below the bassoons' unison G in the chords in No. 14 implies that he may have misunderstood the notation—which could help explain *Genoveva*.

It is reassuring to consider Richard Strauss, standing at the farther end of the spectrum of restraint from Brahms. There are examples of his use of tenor and bass tubas in Chapter V. The distinguished Hallé Orchestra tubist Harry Barlow contributed to a lively newspaper debate when in 1925 conductor Hamilton Harty programmed Strauss's *Symphonia Domestica* for performance by the orchestra. The long-serving Barlow reminded readers that Richter had called it 'a torture to the ears' (K[7], 225). Yet Strauss's tuba parts are, at least, interesting, conceived in terms of a contrabass instrument with the possible exception of *Der Rosenkavalier.* (In *Also sprach Zarathustra* there are two tubas.) Strauss wrote an extremely effective glissando for tuba (Ex. 5.4(a)) three years after Mahler had first introduced the effect in his third symphony (1895).

Fig. 8.3
The author photographed in the Philharmonic Hall, Liverpool in the 1960s with his GDR five-valved tuba in F and C. The third valve lowers two tones, the fourth two-and-a-half and the fifth gives a large semitone.

However, at this time the influence of Wagner was pervasive. From the tuba-player's point of view there is a strong argument for seeing the apotheosis of his style in a work by a relatively minor German composer, Engelbert Humperdinck (1854-1921). The one work of his which remains (firmly) in the repertoire is the opera *Hänsel und Gretel*, first performed at Weimar in 1893. The overture is a favourite concert item, much to the delight of tubists everywhere. While Ex. 8.12(a) manages to be more Wagnerian than Wagner himself, Ex. 8.12(b) bears remarkable similarities to some of the Brahms extracts printed above. Perhaps Humperdinck

Humperdinck: *Hänsel und Gretel* Overture

Fig. 8.4. Freelance London tubist Stephen Wick with Hirsbrunner HBS 392 CC tuba. Its five valves consist of four pistons and one rotary (cf. the Sander tuba in Fig. 8.1).

succeeded in forming a link between two composers each of whom was widely considered at the time to be the antithesis of the other.

With his awareness of the potential of individual voices Mahler probably allotted more soloistic parts to the tuba than any of his contemporaries. Sometimes they are low, quiet solos, audible because of their distance from the other instruments (Ex. 8.12); sometimes they take their place as a significant contribution to the working-out of melodic material (Ex. 8.13); sometimes they are tiny solos, the quick flash of some grotesque goblin (Ex. 8.14). It is impossible to deny Mahler's influence on twentieth-century writing for tuba.

Ex. 8.12

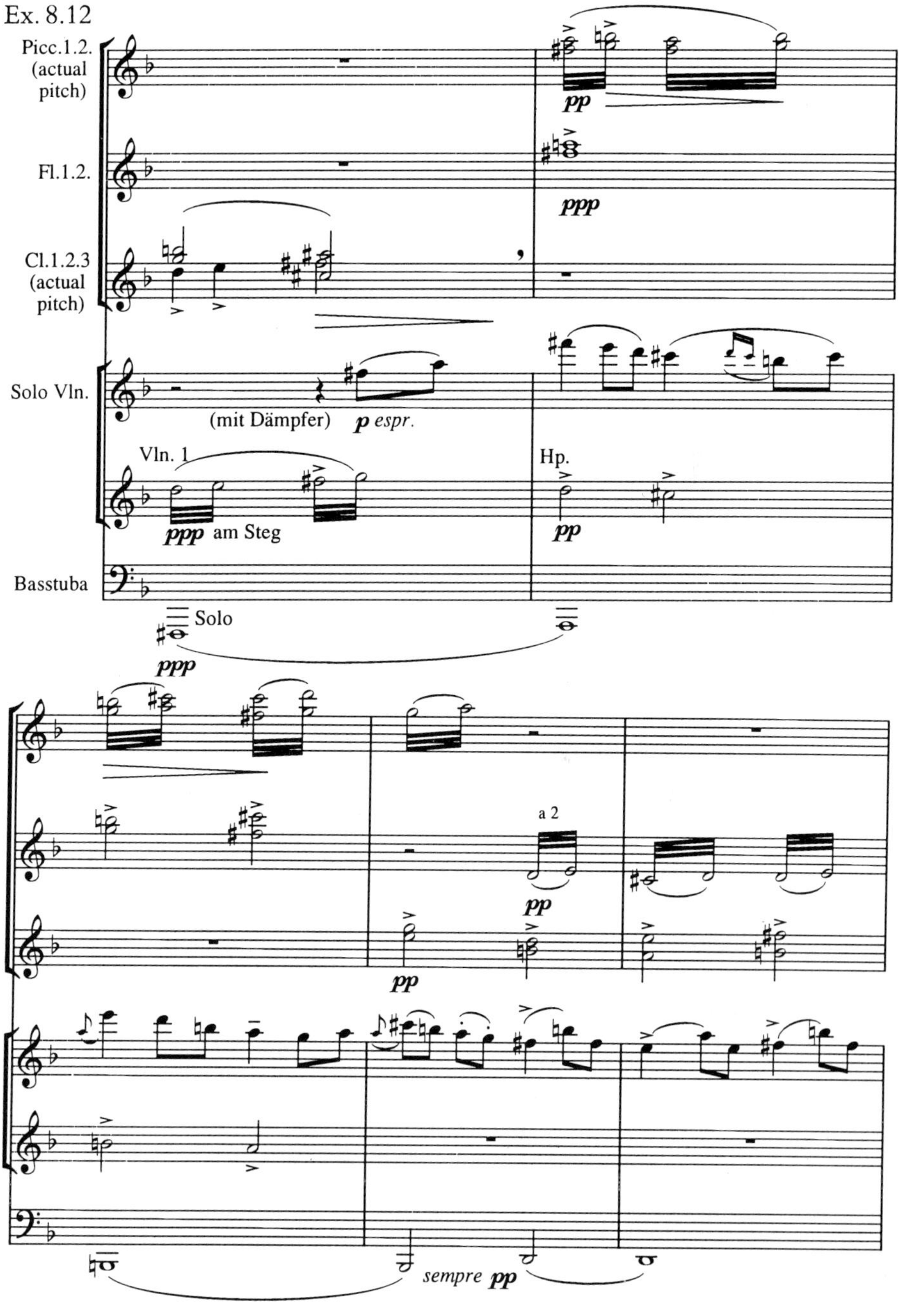


Mahler: Symphony 2

Ex. 8.13

*(Feierlich und gemessen, ohne zu schleppen)*

*pp* [In canon with solo muted double bass and solo cello]

Mahler: Symphony 1

Ex. 8.14

**(molto moderato)**

*poco rit.*    solo

*pp morendo*

Mahler: Symphony 5

In 1909, two years before the first performance of Mahler's *Das Lied von der Erde* with its thirty-four-note tuba part, Schoenberg's first atonal works appeared. There is in his compositions, and those of his disciples Berg and Webern, an overt interest in sounds, the qualities and textures possible with the delicate touch of the tip of the finest brush. Similar awareness and control can be traced back through Mahler, Wagner and Berlioz. Thus we find Berlioz's delight on being introduced to new instruments to give the timbres he had imagined, and Mahler's extreme care in handling the instrumental ingredients of his orchestral recipes.

Berg, in *Der Wein*, gives a perfect example of the continuation of timbre beyond the range of the initial instrument (Ex. 8.15). In his *Fünf Orchesterlieder* there is a part for 'Kontrabass tuba (auch Baßtuba)' covering a compass of almost three octaves, the lower instrument being asked for in the range E'-b, the other up to d'♭.

Ex. 8.15

Berg: *Der Wein*

But in *Lulu* the tubist is expected to cover an extensive range (Ex. 8.16). As the only member of the Second Viennese School to become seriously involved in opera, Berg was called upon to expand the dramatic content of his music, whilst operating within accepted operatic conventions. In *Wozzeck* (1925) the orchestral low brass consists of four trombones and *Kontrabaßtuba,* but there are in addition two stage bands, both involving tubas. In the military band that appears in Act I, Scene 3, there is another *Kontrabaßuba.* In the tavern music (Act II, Scene 4) the tubist is more directly involved in the action. Here the specified instrument is preferably a 'Bombardon in F'. Ex. 8.17(a) shows a section of the tuba part at this point (bars 504 to 517). At bar 625 the instrument is 'somewhat' muted (Ex. 8.17(b)). There then follows a truly dramatic moment as the Second Apprentice stuffs something down the tuba's bell. At bar 655 there is the instruction to play 'as though warming up with mute and out of tune', and at bar 662, 'hurries off to the main orchestra and takes the bass-tuba' (no doubt with a certain amount of relief). The lowest note in the orchestral part, incidentally, is C♯.

Ex. 8.16

(a)

(b)

Berg: *Lulu*

Berg and his contemporaries made frequent use of the tuba; it was a 'new sound', given new opportunities by their own new methods of composition. Their fastidiousness was not always observed by later serialists who seemed sometimes to be so much taken up with their permutations as to forget that a tuba mute needs more than a quaver rest for insertion or removal and that the lips are vibrating so slowly when producing the lowest notes that it is not feasible to articulate rapidly.

Hanns Eisler (1898-1962) studied with Schoenberg and often utilized complex serial techniques, though this approach did not always lie comfortably alongside his Marxist political philosophy. The latter took precedence in his First Orchestral Suite, opus 23, a reworking of material from his score for Walter Ruttman's 1927 film *Opus III*. Never has *Song of the Volga Boatman* been rendered in a more robust style!

Ex. 8.17

(a)

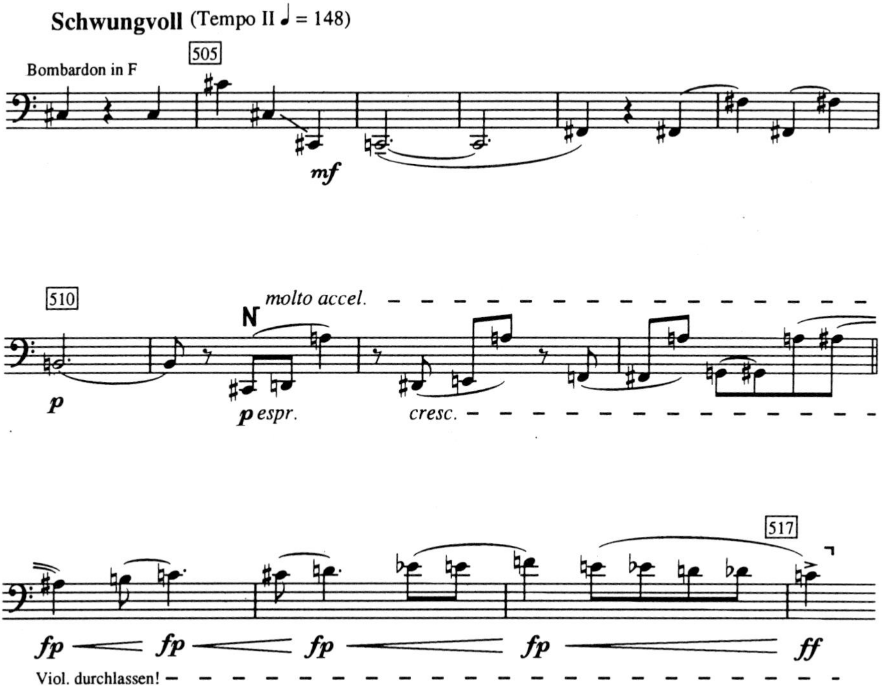


(b)

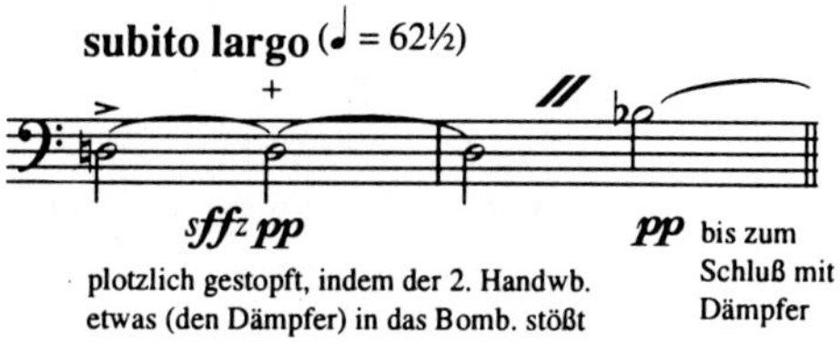


Berg: *Wozzeck*

# THE VIENNESE CONCERT TUBA

The Vienna Philharmonic Orchestra has always prided itself on a distinctive style of brass playing brought about to some extent through the use of distinctive instruments, notably the Vienna Horn and the *Wiener Konzerttuba*. In 1836, one year after the appearance of Wieprecht & Moritz's Baß-Tuba, the Austrian Leopold Uhlmann bult a type of F tuba with five rotary-valves rather than the Berliner-Pumpen favoured by Wieprecht.

The Vienna Opera, in the meantime, was following its own very distinctive low brass policy. In 1862 a contrabass CC helicon was introduced, initially, it appears, for performances of selections from Wagner's still incomplete *Ring* (Z⁴, 49-50). This remained in the orchestra until 1875 when Hans Richter, a horn-player who had become Wagner's assistant in 1866 and then a conductor, was appointed music

Fig. 8.5
Gerhard Zechmeister in 1983 with the prototype of the new Viennese Concert Tuba which he designed and which is now made by Musica.

*Photo: Walter Zechmeister*

director of both the Vienna Opera and the Philharmonic. He invited sixteen year-old *Wunderkind* Otto Waldemar Brucks from Berlin to become tubist at the Opera. At the same time he commissioned an F tuba from Paulus of Berlin which became the prototype Viennese Concert Tuba. Daniel Fuchs, a maker active in Vienna during the 1870s, added a sixth valve to improve intonation (the development of the instrument thus paralleling that of the French Small C Tuba), but few of these instruments were built. Gerhard Zechmeister ($Z^3$, 52) gives the complicated fingering as the reason, although it has to be said that complicated fingerings often imply tortuous routes for the passage of the air within an instrument, tending to create problems in tone production. Following World War I instruments of this type were no longer manufactured, but sufficient were in existence to enable the playing tradition to be continued.

In 1983 Musica of Steyr agreed to take up production of Gerhard Zechmeister's improved version of the Viennese Concert Tuba. The traditional comparatively narrow bore and limited bell-flare of this instrument have led to a clear, compact sound matching that of the Vienna Horn and contributing towards an orchestral sound considered to have been highly regarded by such composers as Bruckner and Brahms, a number of whose compositions were first performed by the Vienna Philharmonic. Perhaps even more important in determining its distinctive tone, however, is a conicity of some 1:20 throughout its length from mouthpipe to bell (compared with 1:6 or 1:8 for higher valved bugle-horns) ($Z^3$, 41).

The valve-system is also distinctive, the three upper valves played by the left hand giving respectively drops of around one tone, a semitone and just under one tone; the three lower, played by the right hand, giving one-and-a-third tones, two-thirds of a tone and two-and-a-half tones (see Ex. 4.1). The position of the hands will be seen to be similar to that adopted in playing the ophicleide and Wieprecht Baß-Tuba.

Just how distinctive the timbre of this type of instrument actually is may be arguable: the player could contribute the major role. Fritz Reiner, then conductor of the Chicago Symphony Orchestra, returned from fulfilling engagements with the Vienna Philharmonic in 1956 with the wish to confer some of the Austrian orchestra's characteristics on his American musicians. One of his suggestions was that Arnold Jacobs should use a Viennese Tuba, and he thus acquired a six-valve tuba made there by Dehmals. Jacobs had formidable problems in coping with this instrument. Not only did he find that he had to cross his hands to cope with the six valves, it was not even well made. 'Jim Palacek, a bass player in the orchestra, dubbed it *The brass accordion*', he later recollected. Nonetheless, Jacobs used it in a recording of Tchaikovsky's sixth symphony and then, realising that Reiner's eyesight was failing, returned to his venerable York CC tuba. Shortly afterwards Reiner congratulated him on his tone and Jacobs carefully hid the Dehmals instrument, which was not found until building work was being carried out on the basement of Orchestra Hall many years later (F21, 187-188).

The tuba style of the Vienna Philharmonic was preserved for many years through its tubists' being either German or Austrian. However a transatlantic influence was brought to bear when American Robert Tucci was appointed to the chair in the early 1960s. He moved to the Bavarian State Opera Orchestra in Munich, but Ronald Pisarkiewicz, the American who has occupied the position since 1979, favours a large Hirsbrunner tuba.

The Viennese Concert Tuba may have influenced the type of instrument adopted in British orchestras to succeed the ophicleide. From 1877 Hans Richter conducted regularly in London, initiating his own series of orchestral concerts two years later and arranging for Hillyard to make a tuba for the ophicleidist J. H. Guilmartin to play. Although this particular instrument seems not to have survived, it is said to have been pitched in F, with five valves, and been relatively compact, like the Vienna Tuba, thus establishing a British tradition that lasted into the early 1960s (see pages 376-80 below).

# CHAPTER IX

## Instruments and Music: Eastern Europe

The sun dissolves the whole of Moscow into a
single spot, which, like a wild tuba, sets all one's
soul vibrating.
— Wassily Kandinsky *Reminiscences*
Berlin, 1913

THE FIRM of Václav Frantisek Červený was founded in 1842 in the Bohemian town of Königgräz, now Hradec Králové in the Czech Republic, where it still operates. During the nineteenth century branches were established in New York and Kiev. Fig. 9.1 shows the type of tuba Červený was constructing before 1889; comparison with a model in current production (Fig. 9.2) shows that the basic concept remains.

Before setting up the Kiev factory in 1867 Červený exported instruments to Russia in considerable numbers. Even in 1890 Pierre stated that most Russian instruments were still imported, although Sediva was 'establishing a new industry in his country' (P[14], 224). Russian royalty was involved: in the Museum of Musical Instruments at St Petersburg is the tuba that was played by the future Tsar Alexander III (1845-1894) in the amateur ensemble at the Marine Museum of the Admiralty (K[20], 224-25). During the nineteenth century there was considerable French influence on intellectual and artistic matters in Russia. This seems never to have extended so far as the design of the tuba, which closely followed the Červený style. Massive construction, large bore and rotary-valves were general, typified by the renowned tubas made by Zimmermann of St Petersburg from 1875 onwards (L[11], I, 22, 24). The BBb 'St Petersburg Tuba' has for many years been used exclusively in Russian symphony orchestras. In the 1990s Vincent Simonetti of the Tuba Exchange, Durham, North Carolina arranged for improved valves to be fitted (with adjustable minibal linkage) and the instruments are now available in the U.S.A. with 420 mm bells and a second-valve bore of 2.15 mm. Current models have four rotary-valves, but a five-valve CC is being developed. Already the BBb is being played by Pat Sheridan, Marty Erickson, Ros Colvert, Bill Rose and other leading players. In 2000 the exchange rate allows it to be sold for under $3,000. The English virtuoso Steve Sykes is the first to own the new EEb version.

Meanwhile Miraphone, King, Hirsbrunner and B&S tubas, amongst others, have been imported into the various republics. Writing in 1997, Alexei Lévachkine stated that he knew of only one orchestra where the F tuba was used, and then only for specific purposes such as 'Bydlo'[!] (L[12], 40). At that time there were more than twenty symphony orchestras in Moscow, as well as sacred and military ensembles.

Following the devastating effects of occupation during World War II, in 1948 Červený became part of the state enterprise Amati Kraslice. In 1973 it relocated to a new factory close to its original site in Hradec Králové while Amati remained in Kraslice, a town with a 300-year history of musical instrument-making close to the German manufacturing centres of Markneukirchen and Klingenthal. In 1991 the company opened a new factory here, equipped with state-of-the-art machinery from Germany and Switzerland. Červený's present philosophy is demonstrated by its statement that 'today's production methods are a blend of modern technology and even more important, the world's finest craftsmen with generations of experience'. In practice, the associated companies of Červený and Amati (with between them over 800 employees) produce two quite different ranges of instruments. The former are of the highest quality, intended for professional use and featuring rotary-valves, while the latter are less expensive and often orientated towards the requirements of bands, including the specific requirements of marching bands such as convertible instruments and sousaphones, although intriguingly Červený seemed to be the only late twentieth-century maker of rotary-valve helicons. Amati remain resolute that 'full automation simply does not work in the making of brass and woodwind instruments. The finest quality will always be the result of hand-craftsmanship'. History shows that Červený has consistently led European manufacturers in the range of instruments invented, developed and marketed. Their current catalogue presents a choice of no fewer than thirty-three models of tuba—more, if alternative body finishes are included.

Amongst other companies nationalized in 1948 was Josef Lidl, founded in Brno in 1892 as the first musical instrument factory in Moravia. Since World War II the firm has specialized in brass instruments, and has become known particularly for its french horns. Recently it has added a tuba to its range of products, the LBB 701 BB♭ tuba. The instrument's design maintains links with traditional East European practices, including four rotary-valves with relatively short touch-pieces and enclosed clock-springs.

From the second half of the nineteenth century onwards the tuba in eastern Europe was expected to provide a uniquely solid tone-quality. At the same time the tubist was expected to be able to move around on his instrument. One contributory factor was Rimsky-Korsakov's work as inspector of Russian naval bands. As a composer he was surprised by the agile brass playing he found there; as composition and instrumentation professor at the St Petersburg Conservatory he was able to influence the next generation of musicians. Glazunov and Stravinsky were amongst his pupils, Borodin and Tchaikovsky amongst his friends.

Fig. 9.1. Červený Kaiserbass, c. 1880.

Rimsky-Korsakov thus had considerable influence on Russian orchestral music. His orchestration is vivid and colourful, exotic, to western ears markedly Russian. *Scheherezade* required the tubist to double-tongue for the first time and there is an unusual passage in the *Russian Easter Festival* overture for tuba and unison bassoons soli. But it is in the classic use of tuba in octaves with trombones that all the nineteenth-century Russian composers excelled. The sheer power of the

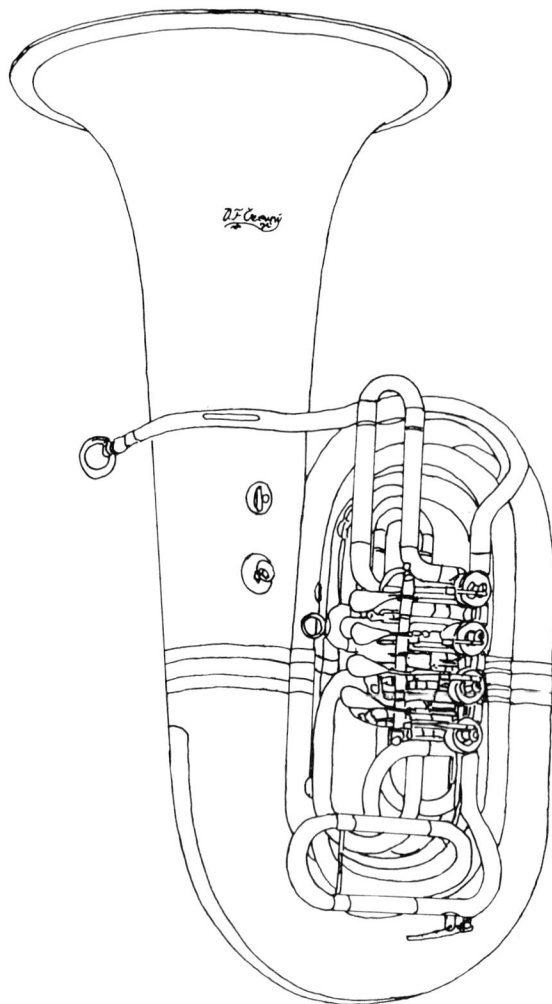

Fig. 9.2. Červený ABB 691-4 MR Kaiser-Tuba, 2000.

Ex. 9.1

Mussorgsky: *A Night on the Bare Mountain*

opening entry of Mussorgsky's *A Night on the Bare Mountain* (Ex. 9.1) and the wonderful octaves with bass trombone in the 'Wedding March' from Rimsky-Korsakov's *Golden Cockerel* (Ex. 9.2) are as unmistakably Russian as the balalaika. The immense sound capable of being generated by this particular combination has been regularly exploited by other east European composers, too, though never more dramatically, or extensively, than in Smetana's symphonic poem, *Wallenstein's Camp.*

Ex. 9.2

Rimsky-Korsakov: 'Wedding March' *(The Golden Cockerel)*

Rimsky-Korsakov and Glazunov together completed Borodin's *Prince Igor*, unfinished and unorchestrated at the time of his death in 1887. The tuba has an important entry in the overture, providing a cue for the rest of the brass. The two-note ascending motif which it introduces occurs elsewhere in the opera, most interestingly perhaps in Act III, No. 20, where it is treated in the stage-band rather as it is treated orchestrally in the overture. The band is a compact brass group with percussion, 2 B♭ cornets, 2 E♭ horns, 2 B♭ baritones, euphoniums and tubas (Ex. 9.3), possibly the work of the youthful Glazunov. Throughout *Prince Igor* the tuba part is carefully arranged to lie within the compass of a three-valve E♭, implying that in Russia, as in Britain, this instrument was found in orchestras of the time.

Ex. 9.3

Borodin: *Prince Igor*

Ex. 9.4

Tchaikovsky: *Romeo and Juliet*

ɔst, though not all, of Tchaikovsky's tuba parts may be played on an instrument ɔf this type. He asks it to fulfil numerous functions, but that of soloist only in a four-note figure in his sixth symphony and the long sustained B in *Romeo and Juliet* which provides a pedal an octave above pizzicato double-basses (Ex. 9.4). This note gives two peculiar problems: in all but the best orchestras there is a mysterious but definite discrepancy in pitch between the string and woodwind passages which can be embarrassing to the tubist; and the opportunities for taking quick, unnoticeable breaths are limited, probably to the places suggested. It is part of basic brass technique to be able to discern where to take breaths during long notes, but they are rarely so exposed as this.

There is an interesting dichotomy in the symphonies, dealt with in some detail by Roger Bobo in his monograph *Tuba: Word with a Dozen Meanings*. In the fourth symphony the instrument is given a bass role, consistently allocated foundation notes, often allied with the double-basses or an octave below the bass trombone—only twice at a dynamic quieter than *mezzo-forte*. In the sixth symphony, however, the tuba is clearly associated much more closely with the remainder of the brass and there are frequent examples of one of Tchaikovsky's trade-marks: a passage ascending from the tuba through the trombones into the

Ex. 9.5

Tchaikovsky: Symphony 6

trumpets or vice-versa. As Bobo puts it, 'The whole section sounds like one beautiful brass instrument with an extremely large range'. At the end of the symphony there is a sublime chorale passage in which the trombones and tuba, soli, grow quieter gradually until they reach the ultimate *ppppp* (Ex. 9.5). An enormous tuba, its character inevitably far different from the trombones, would obviously be quite wrong in this work; blend with the other brass is essential. Bobo suggests a small CC tuba in this symphony, a large CC for the fourth. Having regard to the relative bores of the instruments this could be yet more evidence that the E♭ was at that time found in Russian symphony orchestras.

The tuba part in Tchaikovsky's rarely-played opera *The Maid of Orleans*, first performed at the Maryinski Theatre, St Petersburg in 1881, is of particular interest. The player will feel that it is laid out very much like a cimbasso part, with characteristic independence from the three trombones and a closer working relationship with other bass woodwind and string instruments than is normal in tuba writing. Tchaikovsky's biographer, David Brown, makes a significant comment on this work, stating that his 'contempt for Verdi's *Giovanna d'Arco* did not leave him unwilling to take suggestions from the earlier opera' (B[60], 49).

The Bohemian composer Dvořák regularly included a tuba in his orchestral works but with remarkably little regard for its particular character. True, there is the solo sustained note near the beginning of his eighth symphony, but otherwise the impression is always that he included the instrument because there happened to be one available. In the 'New World' Symphony the tuba doubles the bass trombone at the unison in the slow movement, seven quiet notes at the beginning and seven quiet notes at the end . . . and that is its sole contribution to the work, including the exuberant last movement!

Undoubtedly this adds body to the brass chorale, but it might have added much more if it had been written an octave lower. Can anyone give a convincing reason for the tuba's not being used in the remainder of the work, especially in the last movement, where in the cause of recapitulation and manipulation of every motive from the symphony to the verge of disintegration the entire orchestra crashes away for page after page—leaving the tubist to doze in the middle of it all? Did Dvořák forget about the tuba line in the score? There is no evidence in this movement of a finesse necessitating the omission of the tuba to avoid spoiling the overall orchestral sound.

East European composers during the twentieth century—Rachmaninov, Stravinsky, Prokofiev and Shostakovich from Russia, Bartók and Kodály in

Hungary—retained an allegiance to their national folk-material and the tuba-style established by their predecessors. I use the phrase 'from Russia' rather than 'in Russia' as a number of composers worked mostly outside their native country. One palpable result is shown in Stravinsky's ballet scores *L'Oiseau de Feu* (1910), *Petrouchka* (1911) and *Le Sacre de Printemps* (1913) which were written for the *Ballets Russes* in Paris, using the Small French C Tuba. There are thus some passages in high tessitura in addition to a typically French demand for two tubas in *Sacre*. Tuba II descends only as low as D, but each needs to play as high as g'♭. Both this work and *L'Oiseau de Feu* require Wagner Tuben, incidentally. Russian composers for orchestra have shown great delight in discovering bright colours, none more than Stravinsky who can be credited with being the first to exploit the distinctively hard sound of loud notes in the tuba's high register (Ex. 9.6). As the century progressed and Stravinsky's style changed his writing for tuba became less characteristic, though always technically possible.

Prokofiev's use of the tuba is consistently decidedly Russian. The massive foundation notes in, for example, *Alexander Nevsky* seem to give the instrument at times almost a solo supporting role. The ballet *Romeo and Juliet* is typical: the tuba's enormous tone can be heard providing long sustained notes beneath the entire orchestra and the instrument is also required to display the agility demanded by earlier Russian composers. Shostakovich too has made considerable demands on the tuba. In his many symphonies the higher range has been exploited as well as the lower, and he has asked for effects like flutter-tonguing. (*Flutter-tonguing*, usually denoted by the German *Flatterzunge* in a score, involves rolling the tongue in the mouth to produced an R-R-R-R after articulating the note. Ex. 10.5(e) shows what must surely be the most extended passage in the tuba repertoire.)

Ex. 9.6

(a)

[Peasant leading a performing bear]
(♩ = 69) Solo

Ex. 9.6 (b)

Stravinsky: (a) 'Un paysan avec un ours' (*Petrouchka)*; (b) 'Danse infernale du roi Kastcheï' *(L'Oiseau de feu)*

Ex. 9.7

Shostakovich: Violin Concerto

One of Shostakovich's most striking tuba passages appears in the Violin Concerto, where there is a carefully scored section with solo violin, three clarinets, bassoon and tuba. The last two play in octaves, the composer choosing the tuba as the lower of the two despite the presence of a double-bassoon (Ex. 9.7). The work also includes a low passage where the composer needs to introduce a quiet E' sustained for thirty bars. He solves the problem by alternating the two instruments, four bars at a time; the timbres are indistinguishable at this dynamic and depth, whereas in the passacaglia the effect of putting the contrabassoon at the lower octave would have been a dryness incompatible with the three clarinets and bassoon in their middle registers. The tuba is often given a distinctive role in violin concertos from Britten to Chávez, but seldom is it so sublime. There are no trumpets or trombones in this score and the tuba sits in his rightful seat next to the four horns.

The Hungarian composers Kodály and Bartók evidence a keen appreciation of the tuba. Bartók, in fact, conceived one of the most tubaistic phrases in the repertoire. This is the remarkably urbane Concerto for Orchestra solo shown here in Ex. 9.8. It is like a very suave relative of *Tubby the Tuba*. The same work includes a beautiful chorale-like passage for two trumpets, two trombones, tuba and drum. Elsewhere a mute is required, a request made again in *The Miraculous Mandarin* in which the tuba has an entry beginning on g'.

In *Cantata Profana* Bartók provides yet another surprise: a passage where the tuba is very effectively written higher than the bass trombone.

One more point remains to be made in this survey of the tuba in eastern Europe. During much of the twentieth century political events and dogma caused long periods during which communication with the west was difficult if not impossible. It is a testimony to the power of art—and perhaps particularly music, a non-verbal form of communication—that the works of Russian composers were regularly heard elsewhere.

Even more remarkably, there is today not a serious tubist throughout the world who has not benefited from regular use of the two volumes of the *70 Studies for BBb Tuba* by the Russian trombone and tuba teacher, Vladislav Blazhevich (1881-1942). He taught at the National Conservatory in Moscow from 1920-42 (L[11], 2, 61), but posthumously also taught the bulk of the the world's advanced tubists when his studies became generally available through an edition published in 1965 by Robert King in the United States.

The studies are almost inevitably linked with the modest and supremely attractive concerto in one movement by Alexei Lebedev (1924-93). He taught the tuba class

Ex. 9.8

Bartók: Concerto for Orchestra

at the Conservatory from 1949 and was also principal tuba of the Bolshoi 1950-66 ($L^{11}$, 2, 64-5). Paradoxically, tubists never felt the influence of Russian style more strongly than when an Iron Curtain was in place as part of an attempt to divide the world. There is no doubt that this influence will continue, to the benefit of both east and west.

# CHAPTER X

## *Instruments and Music: France*

Its tone has great strength, great solemnity,
and is mysterious and gloomy in *pp* . . .
—A. Lavignac, *La Musique et les musiciens*
Paris, 1895

. . . powerful and terrible, it provides a full
and solid bass for the wind section.
— J. Rambosson, *Histoire des instruments*
Paris, 1897

ALTHOUGH the Baß-Tuba was a Prussian invention, and valved instruments had been familiar in Austria and Germany longer than anywhere else, the first major composer to succumb to the tuba's charms was the Frenchman Hector Berlioz. With his lively interest in musical instruments the 'new sound' of the tuba made a strong impression on him.

By 1843, when he first heard it during a tour of Germany, he was well into his composing career and accustomed to using several ophicleides in order to balance the large numbers of high woodwind and brass he often demanded. In his early *Messe solennelle*, rediscovered only in 1991, the bass of the brass consists of serpent, buccin and ophicleide (played respectively by Stephen Wick, Stephen Saunders and Marc Giradot on the first recording: by John Eliot Gardiner and the Orchestre Révolutionaire et Romantique, Philips 442 1372). The first work in which Berlioz specified tuba was *La Damnation de Faust* of 1846 (cf. Wagner's first, *Eine Faust-Ouvertüre*). Two ophicleides are also present in the score and it is quite possible that one of the players may have doubled on tuba in, for example, the 'Hungarian March' where one of each instrument was specified, sometimes in unison, sometimes in octaves.

Berlioz's scores have been marked by the pens of many editors, instrumentation has been changed and sometimes, as a result, passages have even been transposed into different octaves. Despite the carefully-researched complete edition now appearing it is often still the tubist who finds himself having to play parts originally written for 'ophicléide' (*Symphonie fantastique*), 'serpent d'harmonie et ophicléide'

('Resurrexit' of *Symphonie funèbre*) or 'ophicléide monstre à pistons' (*Grande Messe des morts*). In the Breitkopf edition of 'Marche Hongroise' a footnote to the tuba part instructs: 'In the fourteenth bar the tubist beats the triangle', but this is exceptional. The five tubas found in *Lélio* ('l'Impériale') were originally two tubas and three ophicleides. It would be impracticable to mix the different instruments now since the ophicleide is so different in tone from the tuba of today, although closer to that of the early tuba. There is a comparison of a Henri et Martin ophicleide (c. 1855) and a Johann Moritz Baß-Tuba from the 1830s below which shows that some of the dimensions of this late ophicleide are more generous than those of the tuba. That the the ophicleide's bell is twenty-five per cent larger than that of the tuba may well indicate a rearguard action on the part of its French makers.

Berlioz was attracted by the nobility of the Baß-Tuba, its tone unimpaired by emerging from side holes as in the ophicleide, and although when coupling the two instruments he would give the tuba the lower of two notes he admitted that he found the low register weak. The difference is summed up in a Spanish definition of *fiscorn*: it has 'sondos más suaves que los del figle'—smoother sounds than those of the ophicleide, not more powerful sounds. A practical approach to the problem often suggested but rarely acted upon is the employment of a euphonium in at least some of the Berlioz works. The overtures are a case in point. There would be much better blend in Ex. 10.1, while the satirical intent of Ex. 10.2 could perhaps be more effectively conveyed by the lighter-weight instrument. Generally speaking the euphonium is probably as close as it is possible to approach to the narrow-tuba/ ophicleide tone Berlioz knew without using the ophicleide itself, a procedure which may not always be appropriate to modern performances.

Table 10.1 COMPARATIVE DIMENSIONS OF BAß-TUBA c. 1840 AND OPHICLEIDE c. 1855

| | BAß-TUBA IN F & C (JOHANN MORITZ, c. 1840) | OPHICLEIDE IN Bb (HENRI ET MARTIN, c. 1855) |
|---|---|---|
| | mm | mm |
| Overall length of tubing | 3540 | 2598 |
| Length of main tube | ---- | 1628 |
| Length of crook | ---- | 970 |
| Bore where mouthpiece is inserted | 14.8 | 12 |
| Bore where crook is inserted | ---- | 34 |
| Diameter of bell | 193 | 236 |

The ophicleide was strongly established in France, more firmly even than in Britain, and it was many years before it finally disappeared from the orchestra. The popular transfer of the name ophicleide to the valve instrument, noted above (pages 213-20) also appears to have been relatively common in France. It seems that the new valved instrument was expected to act as a substitute rather than a completely new voice in the orchestral brass section.

In his admirable article on the tuba Joseph Brousse describes its progress in France:

> From 1845 until about 1875 the tuba in C with three and four valves was hardly ever used except in dance orchestras, where it carried out the functions of the ophicleide. In the small orchestra it was limited simply to playing the bass line while in the full orchestra it sometimes doubled the 'cello and excelled *con brio* in the ardent rhythms of the counter-melody [i.e., typical euphonium functions]. The tuba with four valves was introduced at the Opéra about 1874. In 1880 a five-valve instrument appeared which was considered the definitive tuba until the final instrument appeared from Courtois in 1892 with a supplementary

Ex. 10.1

Berlioz: *Benvenuto Cellini* Overture

Ex. 10.2

43 bars simile then—

*[le faux Balducci prend un couronne pour la donner à Pasquerello]*

Ah!ah!ah!
Ah!

*lourdement et un peu retenu*

Berlioz: 'Cavatine de Pasquarello' *(Benvenuto Cellini)*

transposing valve . . . For forty years the repertoire had not exceeded the ophicleide's low B♭ but with the four-, five- and six-valve instruments it was possible to reach C below, first employed by Wagner. Later composers followed the illustrious master's example and, in the orchestra, the tuba with six *dépendant* valves became indispensable (B[59], X, 1674-80).

As opposed to Sax's *indépendant* system, the six-valve *dépéndant* system was so successful that the tuba to which it was applied lasted in French orchestras until the 1960s. Interviewed in 1995, the virtuoso performer Michel Godard admitted to beginning his tuba studies on such an instrument at the Besançon Conservatoire in 1978. It is now known as the Small French Tuba in c *(Petite tuba français en ut)*, although there were some varieties made with proprietorial names, like Besson's *cornophone à pédale* of 1892 (W[3], 30). The tuba's basic pitch is a tone above the euphonium or *saxhorn-basse*, and for this reason, in addition to the historic influence of the ophicleide, French composers have inclined to write high passages for the tuba far more often than their colleagues in other countries. But the remarkable aspect of this instrument was not so much the possible high notes as its immense compass, which was thought of as covering at least four octaves, from C' to c". The open instrument stood in c; the first valve lowered it a tone, the second a semitone and the third two tones, the fourth two and a half tones, or a perfect fourth. The fifth valve, lowering a semitone, was used as a *transpositeur* to simplify fingerings in difficult passages, while the sixth dropped three and a half tones, or a perfect fifth. The fingering for the entire compass is shown in Ex. 10.3.

It is surprising that the Small French Tuba lasted as long as it did when much better instruments were available from makers elsewhere. The instrument was both heavy and difficult to hold as the amount of tubing that had to be crammed into its euphonium-sized area made the provision of spaces for supporting fingers extremely difficult. This problem could have been overcome by making it longer so that it rested on the thighs, like most bass tubas. Add to this the stuffiness found in blowing even the best models and the forebearance of the players becomes quite remarkable to contemplate.

The instrument's lightweight tone was no disadvantage. French composers up to the Impressionists and beyond were much more interested in the precisely calculated differences given by woodwind and brass which, while relatively narrow-bored by German standards, differed much more one from the other. On Debussy's palette the tones of horns and trombones, for example, could never be confused in

Ex. 10.3     FINGERING-CHART FOR SMALL FRENCH C TUBA

Row 1:
6 5 4   6 5 3   6 3   4 6 / 3 2 / 2 1   4 6 6 / 3 2 5   6 4 5 / 2 4 / 1 2   3 4 5 / 1 2 4   4 3 5 / 2 3

Row 2:
3 5 / 2 / 1   2 5 / 1 1   1 5 / 2   2 5   0 6 6 / 5 5 / 4 3 / 1   6 6 6 / 4 3 5 / 1 3   6 4 5 / 3 3 4 / 2 3 / 1 2   4 5 / 3 4 / 2 3

Row 3:
4 6 6 / 3 2 5   6 4 5 / 2 4 / 1 2   3 4 5 / 1 2 4   4 3 5 / 2 3   3 5 / 2 / 1   2 5 / 1 1   1 5 / 2   2 5

Row 4:
0 5 5 / 4 3 / 2 1   4 3 5 / 2 1 4   4 3 5 / 2 3   3 5 / 2 / 1   2 5 / 1 2   1 6 5 / 2   2 5 5 5 / 4 3 / 2   4 3 0 5 / 2 3

Row 5:
5 5 / 2 / 1   2 5 / 1 1   1 5 / 2   2 3 4 5 / 2   0 6 5 / 2 / 1   2 3 4 5 / 1 1 2 1   1 4 3 5 5 / 2 3 2   2 3 3 / 2 / 1

Row 6:
0 2 5 6 / 1 1 5   1 6 5 / 2   2 5   0 3 4 5 / 2 3   3 5 / 2 / 1   2 5 / 1 1   1 5 0 / 2   2 5   0

the way they might on Bruckner's. Each instrument had a completely individual voice, the tuba equally with the others, and it was quite adequate to support the trumpets and trombones with their narrow bores and brilliant timbres. So sufficient was it that Rambosson in 1897 could describe it as 'puissant et terrible, qui forme une basse ample et solide pour le groupe des cuivres' (R², 174).

Fig. 10.1
'Basse ut à 6 pistons' illustrated in an early twentieth-century Gustave Besson catalogue. This Small French C Tuba is about the same size as a modern euphonium.

The present-day tubist is aware of the French C Tuba through the 'Bydlo' (Polish: 'cattle') solo in Ravel's orchestration of *Pictures at an Exhibition* (Ex. 5.3), discussed on page 232 above. In the same work there are passages as low as Ex. 10.4, which led Walter Piston, in his book on orchestration, to suppose that French tubists used two different instruments for the piece (as is, indeed, universal practice today). The same phenomenon is found time and again in the French repertoire. The examples in Ex. 10.5 were all written with the same tuba in mind.

Ex. 10.4

**Moderato non tanto, pesante**

Mussorgsky-Ravel: 'Promenade' (*Pictures from an Exhibition*)

Ex. 10.5

(a)

**Movt. de marche**

[1 solo violin two octaves higher]

(b)

**Vif** (♩. = 66)

10.5

(c)

(d)

(e)

(a) Milhaud: *Les Mariés de la Tour Eiffel*; (b) Milhaud: *Suite Provençale*; (c) and (d) Poulenc: *L'Histoire de Babar*; (e) Honegger: Concerto for Cello and Orchestra

The French school's unique approach is perhaps best summed-up in the symphony composed by the Belgian César Franck in 1888. The lyrical approach to the brass shown in Ex. 10.6(a) is found elsewhere only in the British brass band,

Ex. 10.6

(a)

(b)

Franck: Symphony

while Ex. 10.6(b) shows a broad melody forging ahead over five octaves simultaneously like an incoming tide, with the tuba expected to play as fluently as the other instruments. No nods here in the direction of a lumbering giant.

French orchestral tubists developed their agility with little systematic instruction. At the Gymnase Musical Militaire (1836-1856) saxhorn was taught alongside valve trombone by Antoine Dieppo, solo trombone of the Opéra orchestra. He continued in his post when the school's activities were taken over by the Conservatoire, though all military classes were discontinued after the war of 1870-71 (S[28], 6). The first class for tuba and saxhorn at the Paris Conservatoire was not established until 1944, and only made official twelve years later. The teacher was Paul Bernard of the Opéra orchestra, who subsequently also assumed responsibility for teaching bass trombone. There were twelve students in his class, four each for bass trombone, bass saxhorn and tuba (S[28], 5). Sluchin remarks that at the beginning of the twentieth century most provincial music schools had only a single class for all brass instruments, and this situation still existed in many at the end of the century.

From the 1970s universal tuba practice began to be adopted in France, largely through the influence of emigré American tubist Mel Culbertson. The present generation of orchestral tubists tends to play mainly on German rotary-valve instruments. The Small C (often Courtois) is brought out only for 'Bydlo' and sometimes tenor tuba parts, although a *saxhorn-basse* (euphonium) is more often used for these, in parallel with the practice elsewhere.

Courtois, established in 1803, demonstrated their commitment to a wider European presence when in 1994 they became integrated into TA-Musik, president of which is Gerhard Meinl of the German brass instrument-making family. In that year they built a new factory in Amboise (where they had operated since 1956), and operations are now centred here. One result of their involvement with the German company was the introduction of the Worldline range of instruments, which gave brass players a wider choice but probably dismayed the Académie Française. During the nineteenth century a number of French makers, including Besson and Sax, had established a presence in London. Courtois was another, with Chappell & Co. as agents and a strong awareness of the importance of the brass band contest movement: their instruments were often given as prizes. The company's introduction in 1997 of a range of 'British Background Brass', with the involvement of British euphonium virtuoso Nick Childs, was therefore of historic as well as commercial interest. However, Courtois still manufacture three-, four- and five-valve B♭ saxhorns (euphonium pitch) for the French market.

# CHAPTER XI

## Instruments and Music: America

The collector of customs at New York has sent back an English tuba player whom Barnum had engaged, on the ground of his being a contract labourer. It was held by the authority in question that the mere playing of an E flat tuba does not make an artist. The collector got pretty near a truth capable of wide application.
—*The Musical Times,* 1 July 1890

Having selected the men, pick out the most intelligent and ambitious of the lot for Cornet players . . . the next most important place to be filled is that of the Tuba player. He should be a moderately stout fellow, capable of supporting the 'big horn' without getting tired, and besides having plenty of good common sense, his supply of patience should be practically inexhaustible, for in practising accompaniment parts with beginners a Tuba player, who has not the qualities of patience and good humour is likely to get disgusted, and if a man of profane habits is apt to swear in a disagreeable way at the stupid blunders made by his companions of the Althorns and Tenors, and this tends to make them angry in turn, and the disgust and swearing may become mutual, and so little private feuds spring up which will eventually undermine the band.
—'How to organize a brass band' in G. F. Patton, *A Practical Guide to the Arrangement of Band Music,* New York, 1875

IN CONTRAST to the well-established orchestras of the many states comprising Germany, the United States of America had, in 1835, not one single regularly constituted professional orchestra. The first opera season had been given in New York ten years earlier, but it was 1842 before the New York Philharmonic Society was inaugurated. Shanet reprints its consitution, showing three trombones but no lower brass instrument ($S^{23}$, 425, n. 46). There was a notable German influence on this orchestra's foundation as well as those at Boston (1881) and Philadelphia (1900), although the Chicago (1891) and Cleveland (1918) orchestras seemed from the outset to have been much more conscious of being American.

A great deal of the musical activity in the nineteenth-century U.S.A. was not orchestral. The rise of the wind band is dealt with in Chapter XIV; there is a parallel with the English brass band in that players tended to move from band to orchestra, and sometimes back again. The first to occupy the tuba chair in the

# MUSICIANS WANTED

## From a 1911 edition of Holton's Harmony Hints

**Musicians Wanted**—First class tuba or clarinet player who is a horse shoer and general blacksmith. Steady work. Good wages. All letters answered. Give service to band and orchestra. Musiciain, Fairmont, Ill.

**Musicians Wanted**—Clarinet and bass players wanted for the Grand Forks Military Band. Men with trades and clerks preferred. Boozers save your stamps. City of 15,000 population. E. L. Egermayer, Bandmaster, Grand Forks, N.S.

**Musicians Wanted**—A good barber who is a good tuba or baritone player. Permanent position in good shop. Must be of good reputation and sober. To play with a growing band of 25 pieces. S. A. Patterson, Macon, Mo.

**Musicians Wanted**—Cornet, baritone, tuba and clarinets, can furnish positions to painter and paper hanger and blacksmith. Some business openings. (College town.) J. B. Taylor, Lock Box 267, Tabor, Iowa.

**Musician Wanted**—Band man to locate in good town, that can purchase either pool hall with two tables, makes good money, or blacksmith shop, can be rented or bought. Good place for barber to start business. Can play either cornet, clarinet, trombone, alto, bass or snare drum. F. F. Osteloh, Martsburgh, Mo.

**Musicians Wanted**—For Odd Fellows band. A1 bass players, two B flat clarinets, one E flat clarinet, one alto. Other musicians write, all must be real musicians and work as carpenters, painters, cigarmakers, gun smiths, tailors, meat cutters, barbers, tool makers and horse shoers. City of 15,000. First class openings for good musicians. Geo. W. Wilson, No. 711 Broadway, Fulton, N.Y.

**Musician Wanted**—Blacksmith who is band man to open shop in good town of 400. Tuba player preferred. S. R. Burklew, Killbuck, Ohio.

**Musician Wanted**—Leader, playing cornet, 2 clarinets, 1 baritone, 1 slide trombone. Men with trades wanted who are willing to give services to band, but who would appreciate a good position in one of the best cities in the U.S. All enquiries answered. Phoenix Military Band, Suffolk, Va.

**Musicians Wanted**—With vaudeville show, must be gentlemen. Salary low but sure. Bob and Eve McGinley Co., 14 N. Fourth Str., Minneapolis, Minn.

**Musicians Wanted**—For the Cutler Hammer Co. Band. Bass, baritone, two slide trombones, mellophone, solo clarinet, first and second B flat clarinet, E flat clarinet, flute and piccolo. Must use low pitch instruments. First class jig and tool makers, good assemblers, bench, lathe and drill press hands. P. Johnstone, Cutler Hammer Co., 12th and St. Paul Ave., Milwaukee, Wis.

**Musicians Wanted**—For hospital work, cornets, clarinets, trombones, tuba, baritone, and double drums. Answer by letter. L. R. Davidson, A. F. of M., band director, State Hospital No. 2, St. Joseph, Mo.

**Musicians Wanted**—Lady musicians for Summer, Fall and Winter Season 1911. Good performers on reed, brass and string instruments. Members treated as ladies and expected to be ladies in every manner. Applicants state instruments played, age, experience, ability, salary commanded and send postal photo. Manager, Elmwood Ladies' Band and Orchestra, 722 Main St., Buffalo, N.Y.

Chicago Symphony Orchestra, for example, was August Helleberg. He stayed only for one season then went back to Sousa as principal tuba, later becoming a member of the Metropolitan Opera Orchestra. This sort of association led to the use of large instruments in the orchestra in contrast to the British practice where orchestral tuba-players had mainly been band euphonium-players, more at ease with the higher-pitched and smaller F tuba.

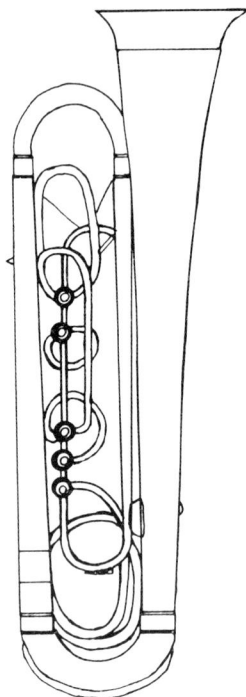

Fig. 11.1
Trombacello by
Graves, c. 1840.

Although the Trombacello made by Graves & Co. of Winchester, New Hampshire in the 1840s was clearly influenced by Wieprecht's Baß-Tuba, there are indications that subsequently the design of valved bugle-horn favoured in America tended to follow the French narrow upright conformation with top-valves. However, as the century progressed the instruments brought by German immigrants began to exercise increasing influence on native manufacturers, if only through sheer familiarity. Kouwenhoven reproduces an illustration of *The German Band*, painted by J. G. Brown in 1879 (K[22], 267). The five instruments include a rotary-valve tuba and E♭ alto horn. Originally published in *Harper's Weekly*, the caption remarked 'The German bands are becoming a feature here . . .' Despite the large numbers of instruments exported to the U.S.A. by the London firm of Besson and by several French companies, the British/French-shaped tuba thus found less favour with orchestral players, although it is still used in bands.

When Sousa formed his band in 1892 its three tubists used instruments made by Rudolf Sander of Wolfstein (Pfalz). During the 1904 season August Helleberg was joined by his two sons, August, jnr and John, each of whom remained members of the band for some years. A photograph taken in 1904 shows them playing almost identical tubas, all thought to have been made by the same maker (T⁶, 39). Father Helleberg had purchased a complete set, in BBb, CC and either Eb or F as the result of hearing a German band when in Chicago and being impressed by the sound of their Eb tuba. Sander also built a sub-contra C Monster Bass, 1550 mm in height with a 1050 mm-diameter bell for the Sousa Band. (A tuba by Sander is illustrated in Fig. 8.1.)

Probably the most important single development in native tuba design was the front-valve, giving rise to a distinctively American instrument—left-facing, like German rotary-valve models and, to this day, often made by German companies with American use in mind. All leading American manufacturers also currently produce instruments including this feature. Many of the improvements to the tuba detailed in Chapter VII were brought about by American designers or players, who still seem to be the most concerned with the instrument's potential. The recording bell, the sousaphone, valve-slides which are adjustable during performance and the use of non-metallic materials in brass instruments are all the result of American activity.

Reference has already been made to some early nineteenth-century American makers who often worked alongside or under the influence of European emigrants like Henry Distin and James Keat. It is claimed that the oldest continually-operating wind instrument company in the United States is that established by Frank Holton in Chicago in 1898. Holton had been first trombonist in Sousa's band and he began his typically American journey to fame and fortune with a new trombone slide lubricant called Electric Oil. His company moved to Wisconsin in 1917, where it remains despite having been acquired by the G. Leblanc Corporation in 1964. While many American tubists have collaborated with European companies, Holton's chosen performer is the distinguished Harvey Phillips. The tuba they jointly designed is the first to have been created entirely on computer. This instrument is an archetypal American tuba in CC, with four front-valves, a bore of 16.89-17.45 mm and a bell diameter of 457 mm.

The takeover of Holton was symptomatic of the upheavals in all western economies during the later twentieth century. In 1985 the renowned manufacturers Conn and King found themselves associated with companies less well-known to tubists as consituent parts of the new United Musical Instruments U.S.A. Inc. It has to be said that immediately prior to this the manufacturers were seen as not being in a particularly healthy state by either musicians or economists. With a lack of investment, research and forward planning, instruments were often being manufactured—sometimes abroad—to far lower standards than those previously associated with these particular brand-names.

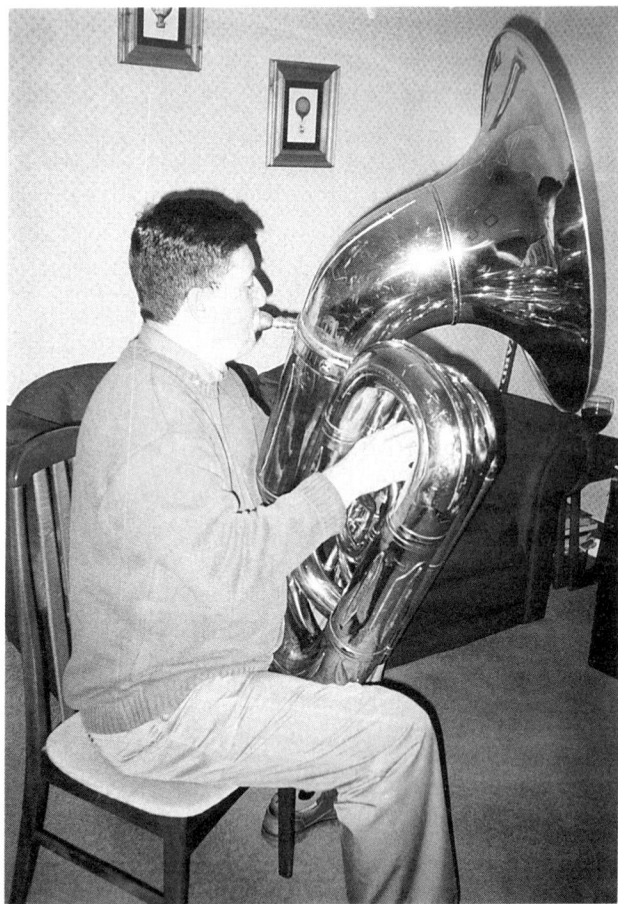

Fig. 11.2
Freelance London
tubist John Elliott
with four-valved
recording bell
Conn 24J
BB♭ tuba

*Photo: Barbara Elliott*

UMI dedicated itself to advanced technology, quoting Colonel C. G. Conn himself as saying: 'Only modern precision tools and machines can make a musical instrument with the fine accuracy required today. After all, workmen do not make the instruments with their bare hands—they use tools'. The company's arguments are persuasive. They quote the example of the difference between a bore of .460 inch and .464 inch when cutting piston ports. A three-valved instrument has nine ports, which could result in a total error of almost double the difference of the two bore sizes.

Fig. 11.3
Ron Davis (University of South Carolina, Columbia, S.C.) with Conn 20J BB♭ tuba

There is no doubt that after a period during which standards were variable, manufacture of quality instruments now seems to be under way once again. To the advantage of American players, the Japanese firm of Yamaha also has a strong presence in the United States along with German and other European companies opting for the continuation of traditional apprenticeships and production by individual craftsmen, so there is a unique breadth of choice for tubists.

Two things are quite certain: to the manufacturers' delight, there is an enormous demand for tubas in the United States; and the vast proportion of them are well played. This state of affairs was not foreseen by those who drew up the Constitution, nor did it find a place in the Declaration of Independence, but it became inevitable following the introduction of music into public education in 1835 (be it noted, thirty-five years before the first British Education Act which laid down compulsory schooling for all). In the years following the Civil War serious attempts were made to encourage music teaching at all levels of education and instrumental music was found in high schools later in the nineteenth century. Out of the problems associated with the isolation of many communities in such a vast country came the American educators' practice of analyzing aims and processes, breaking them down into their constituent parts and thus assisting those ultimately responsible for instruction in the schoolroom.

The English-speaking instrument-playing community worldwide has benefited from this approach. The greater number of instrumentalists has been initiated into the art through producing the first suggested note in one of the Boston Music Company's *A Tune a Day* books, where each new step is introduced carefully and gradually, preparing the pupil to pass on to more advanced material, like the Rubank *Supplementary Studies*. Over the years these methods have been much imitated, but the source of inspiration of subsequent publications is easily spotted. The disadvantages of Continental European philosophical and theoretical approaches to the process of learning to play are dealt with in some of the chapters dealing with the various countries. The disadvantage of the system outlined here is that it has produced a vast number of excellent instrumentalists with nowhere to perform (see John Fletcher's comments, page 438 below). The advantage to the entire musical world is that performing standards have been raised immensely.

The influence of American composers is another matter. There are those who consider John Philip Sousa as the greatest. Whether or not one would go along with this totally, it is generally acknowledged that the second greatest single influence on music in the U.S.A. has been the wind band.

Fig. 11.4. Meinl-Weston Convertible Tuba with an adjustable mouthpipe allowing it to be used either upright or as a marching instrument with forward bell.

A composer like Ives, who often reflected his musical surroundings, demanded band virtuosity of the tuba if only because he frequently expected the instrument to play a band part. On the other hand the prevalence of band activity has often led to a practical approach to brass writing following from the composer's enhanced awareness of the instruments. Thus in his second symphony Samuel Barber asks for 'Tuba (Tenor Tuba *ad lib*)' in order to cope with a moderately high solo passage in canon with first violins and cor anglais, showing a rare sympathy with the possible problems of a player with a large instrument accustomed to playing in the lower register. The American composer generally tends to write deep tuba parts, possibly because the standard pitch of tuba in school bands is BB♭: paradoxically, when tubists grow up and become orchestral players they often graduate to the CC. (It is interesting to note that some American retailers now promote the E♭ as a useful instrument for school band members transferring from treble clef instruments. The astonishing simplicity of changing clefs when taking up this pitch of tuba is explained on page 375 below.)

Ferde Grofé's *Grand Canyon Suite* of 1943 is typical: although the highest note in its tuba part is a, the bulk of the material is written in the register from E' to c. It requires virtuosity, too. Ex. 11.1 shows fingerings on four-valved EE♭ and CC tubas, showing the advantages of the deeper instrument in music of this kind.

A useful survey by Hope Stoddard of 'The tuba and its players in our bands and orchestras' was published in 1950 (S³⁸, 32-8). It includes a striking row of photographs showing twenty-two of the most distinguished orchestral players of the time. Their names and orchestras are as follows:

Vaughn Abbey, Seattle Symphony
Eugene Adam, St. Louis Symphony
Clyde Bachand, Kansas City Philharmonic
William Bell, New York Philharmonic
Gaetano Berardenelli, Portland Symphony
J. E. Booth, Minneapolis Symphony
Louis Chassagne, Dallas Symphony
Virgil Ester, Oklahoma Symphony
Fred Exner, New Orleans Symphony
Samuel Green, Cincinnati Symphony
Floyd Henderson, Toronto Philharmonic
Bruce Holcomb, Vancouver Symphony
Robert Ingram, Los Angeles Philharmonic
John Manuti, Metropolitan Opera
J. E. McAllister, Indianapolis Symphony
William Montieth, Buffalo Philharmonic
Adolf Moser, Cleveland Orchestra
Joseph J. Novotny, NBC Symphony
Louis Pirko, National Symphony
William Rose, Houston Symphony
Kilton Vinal Smith, Boston Symphony
Abe Torchinsky, Philadelphia Orchestra.

The instruments they are holding range from huge to absolutely enormous. Three of them are fitted with recording bells. Where the valves can be seen, four have front-facing piston-valves and the rest use rotary-valves. The smallest tuba seems, suprisingly, to be that held by William Bell, but even so all the instruments are large-bore, in CC or BBb. These were the tubas familiar to American composers in the mid-twentieth century. At the time orchestral trombonists were using instruments with a smaller bore than those in use towards the end of the century, giving an even greater discrepancy between the tone of the tuba and the trombone section alongside. This intentional lack of blend had already given rise to a very distinctive American low brass section sound, with the lowest notes of all providing tremendous harmonic and/or rhythmic support to the remainder of the brass without their being any attempt at homogeneity. The opposite situation had been heard in the Italian opera section with four trombones, while the French with three tenor trombones and a small-bore tuba and British with two tenor trombones, a G bass trombone and F tuba illustrated middle-of-the-road stances.

A list of the tubas reported to have been used in the Dallas Symphony Orchestra auditions in 1995 (T[13], 16) includes the following, presumably the players' favourite instruments for orchestral work:

B&S F, 4/4, rotary-valves (?) [4 players]
Besson EEb, 4 piston-valves [an English player]
Böhm & Meinl 5/4, piston-valves
Dillon/York CC, 6/4, piston-valves
F tuba, maker unknown
Hirsbrunner CC, 4/4, piston-valves
Hirsbrunner CC, five rotary-valves
Hirsbrunner CC, 5/4, rotary-valves
Meinl-Weston 2165 CC, 6/4, piston-valves [2 players]
Meinl-Weston 45s, 4/4, rotary-valves
Meinl-Weston 46, 4/4, rotary-valves
Meinl-Weston double tuba, 4/4, piston-valves
Meinl-Weston 1930 vintage
Mel Culbertson CC, 6/4, rotary-valves [2 players]
Rudolph Meinl CC, 5/4 rotary-valves
Yamaha F 4/4, piston-valves
Yorkbrunner CC 6/4, piston-valves

Fig. 11.5. An amazing variety of instruments in the class of 1976 at the University of North Texas. Donald C. Little (still Professor of Tuba) is standing to the left of the helicon-player in the centre of the back row. Third from the right in the same row is the renowned jazz euphoniumist Rich Matteson.

Ex. 11.1

[Allegro moderato $\mathJ = 66$ ]

| 4-v. EE♭ Tuba | 4 | 2 | 1 | | 2 | 4 | 2 | 2 | 4 | | 2 | 1 | 1 | | 4 | | 2 | 1 | | 2 | 4 | 2 | 2 | 4 | | 2 | 1 | 1 | 2 |
|---|---|---|---|---|---|---|---|---|---|---|---|---|---|---|---|---|---|---|---|---|---|---|---|---|---|---|---|---|---|
| | | | | | | | | 3 | | | 3 | | | 4 | | | 2 | | | | | 3 | | 3 | | | 4 | 4 | 2 | 3 |
| | | | | | | | | | | | | | | | | | | | | | | | | | | | | | 4 | 4 |

| 4-v. CC Tuba | 1 | | 1 | 2 | | 2 | 1 | 4 | 2 | 1 | | 1 | | 2 | 0 | | 1 | | 1 | 2 | | 2 | 1 | 4 | 2 | 1 | | 1 | 2 | 4 | 2 |
|---|---|---|---|---|---|---|---|---|---|---|---|---|---|---|---|---|---|---|---|---|---|---|---|---|---|---|---|---|---|---|---|
| | | 2 | 3 | | | | | | | | 2 | | 4 | | | | | 2 | 3 | | | | | | | | | 2 | 3 | | 4 |

Grofé: *Grand Canyon Suite*

Each player used two different instruments for the wide range of orchestral excerpts presented during the audition.

The CC tuba is made in a range of bores, from 16.89 mm to 22 mm. It follows that it would be possible to play orchestral music, ensemble music and solos using two or three instruments of the same pitch but different bore. Reading is simplified since notes of identical pitch need identical fingering.

The general orchestral preference for a CC with a proportionately wider bore (often a BB♭ built a tone higher) gives a distinctive American orchestral tuba tone. The archetypal American symphonic tuba is the York CC made in 1933 to satisfy the demands of Stokowski, at the time conductor of the Philadelphia Orchestra. Possibly because under the name of Stokes he had been organist of St. James's, Piccadilly before emigrating and taking up the baton, an important element in his concept of orchestral sound was that it should have a foundation of organ pedal-like tone. The Philadelphia tubist, Philip Donatelli, therefore arranged to have a large CC tuba made by the York Band instrument Company of Grand Rapids, Michigan. (The factory was closed in 1971 and proprietory rights were sold to Boosey & Hawkes.)

Two of these instruments were built, each with a number of distinctive characteristics. They had four front-facing piston-valves and a fifth rotary-valve dropping rather more than a whole tone. A short mouthpipe entered the valves directly (the main-slide was between the fourth and fifth valves), where the bore was 19.05 mm. The profile showed a rapid flare, terminating in a 508 mm. bell. There is a striking photograph of Donatelli with one of the instruments in

Photo: John Taylor

Fig. 11.6. Arnold Jacobs playing his renowned York tuba.

Frederiksen's book on Arnold Jacobs (F[21], 7). Jacobs had the opportunity of acquiring one instrument from Donatelli (his teacher) while still a student, and later exchanged two other tubas for the second instrument. On retiring, Jacobs sold one of these to the Chicago S.O. and the other to Gene Pokorny, his successor, who uses it regularly.

These legendary tubas have been copied by a number of manufacturers (but not by Boosey & Hawkes). A copy made in the 1950s by Holton reproduced many of their characteristics and in 1979 Hirsbrunner began to make copies with rather more success. This design remains in the catalogue as the HBS 500 York Model. In 1992-3 Floyd Cooley measured the other instrument when playing with the Chicago S.O. and as a result copies of this are now available from Walter Nirschl of Geretsried. The saga of the York is recounted in all of its fascinating detail by Brian Frederiksen (F[21], 182-86). The fact that so many of the world's leading orchestral tubists now play Swiss and German copies of an instrument originally made in the United States in the 1930s puts sales departments' gimmickry firmly in its place . . .

There is a certain vocal quality found in American brass playing. With the exception of countries like the Czech Republic, Russia and until the 1960s, France, where vibrato was part of the normal brass style, the U.S.A. is the only place where tubists are liable to adopt it when this is felt essential to musical expression. To the inhibited Anglo-Saxon it sometimes comes as a tremendous shock, but it must be admitted that he would sometimes like to do it if he dared!

Ex. 11.2

Bernstein: Symphonic Dances from *West Side Story*

Ex. 11.3

Gershwin: *An American in Paris*

Martin Williams wrote: 'Most of our musicians also know that American symphonic brass-men generally have an unorthodox vibrato because of the pervasiveness of the jazzman's vibrato' (W[22], 12). Since that was written a good deal has in fact happened to the jazzman's 'pervasive vibrato' (as Miles Davis, for one, has shown), but this does not affect Williams's premise and its implication that jazz has had a strong influence on the 'straight' American musician, whether player or composer. Jazz will be studied in some detail in Chapter XIV, but it is impossible to escape from it when discussing the United States since it is no doubt the most important single element contributed by that country to the development of twentieth-century music.

Jazz, like wind bands, affected many American composers at first hand. Stravinsky's *Ebony Concerto*, written when he was resident in the U.S.A., is one example of jazz influence; Bernstein's *West Side Story* is an example of jazz absorption. The tuba, liberated—albeit much later than most instruments—by jazz techniques, found itself playing a new part in the orchestra (Ex. 11.2).

Thirty years earlier, George Gershwin was raising the establishment's eyebrows during performances of his orchestral works. He was influenced not only by jazz but by *popular* music: an American phenomenon—the musician operating across the great divide. It may have been the familiarity of the dance band tuba that caused him so often to use the instrument in association with the double basses rather than with the trombones. Eric Blom wrote, one hopes ironically, '. . . *An American in Paris* shocked the audience of the 1931 I.S.C.M. Festival in London by its excessive commonness . . .' (B[45], III, 607). For the tubist, common or not, there was the satisfaction of recognition as an individual voice, not only a singing voice but an agile singing voice (Ex.11.3).

As a new generation of American composers was consciously following in the footsteps of Ives, with his open-eared absorption of vernacular music-making and subsequent processing into symphonic structures, and Gershwin, whose Russian-Jewish roots enabled him to empathize with many of the characteristics of jazz, a truly distinctive American orchestral idiom became evident before World War II. The tuba played a prominent role. Ex. 11.4, part of Roger Sessions's second symphony (1949), illustrates the further development of American tuba writing, here in what was rapidly becoming the normal American tessitura. The overall compass of the part is from D' to c, a tone short of three octaves, the highest note a mere third above the bass stave.

Types of music merge, styles become blurred, and it sometimes seems as though the distinctive CC foundation notes, long and sustained, met their final apotheosis on Mel Tormé albums while since the last twenty years of the twentieth century the orchestral tubist has been playing jazz rhythms, banging his bell or kissing his mouthpiece. The solo from Elliott Carter's Concerto for Orchestra (Ex. 11.5) shows that the later twentieth-century American composer was able to give the tubist plenty to think about without exceeding normal technical requirements or ignoring the instrument's particular individuality.

Ex. 11.4

Sessions: Symphony 2

Ex. 11.5

Carter: Concerto for Orchestra

The inclination of composers to exploit the tuba in violin concertos has already been pointed out, and the unlikely coupling of solo violin and solo tuba is likely to be enhanced when the composer concerned works within a distinctive musical climate. South of the border, the Mexican Carlos Chávez demonstrates an awareness of the tuba's personality within a very different but equally valid idiom from that adopted by Carter (Ex. 11.6).

Ex. 11.6

Chávez: Concerto for Violin and Orchestra

Silvestre Revueltas (also Mexican) judges the functions of the tuba perfectly throughout his *Janitzio*, a work that could be used as a model for aspiring orchestrators (Ex. 11.7).

Ex. 11.7

Revueltas: *Janitzio.*

# CHAPTER XII

## *Instruments and Music: Britain*

Trumpets, trombones and tuba represent, with a few exceptions, the
soldier returned to civilization—and not liking it overmuch . . . It is not
for nothing that they play instruments which are meant to he heard,
whose dominos resound throughout London, and whose mistakes cannot
be erased                                   —Thomas Russell *Philharmonic* (1942)

He [brass band trainer William Halliwell (1864-1946)] used to say that
Yorkshiremen always made the best bass players, because of the way they
speak, because of the Yorkshire accent—'Owt for nowt'.
—Euphoniumist Bert Sullivan, quoted by Arthur Taylor in *Labour &*
*Love: an oral history of the brass band movement* (1979)

There were some silver-plated instruments which came out a bit dull.
—Richard Holland, chief executive of Boosey & Hawkes, on the
company's £45.1m. loss, quoted in *The Daily Telegraph*, 24 April 1999

FROM the death of Henry Purcell at the end of seventeenth century until the
mature Elgar at the end of the nineteenth, English music, such as it was, lay very
much under the influence of Germany. In this there are parallels with the situation
in the United States and it would be reasonable to expect the British tuba, like the
American, to have followed German practice. But this it did not do, and if it had it
would have been an uncomfortable member of the British orchestra. Until well
into the twentieth century the normal horn and bassoon were the narrow-bore
French type. The trombone was of 'pea-shooter' bore, although in place of the third
tenor fround in France the British used an instrument pitched in G. The British
orchestral tuba was pitched in F and relatively small, but still totally adequate for
supporting the narrow-bore brass and woodwind, perfectly suited to the trombones
then in use. Until the end of the nineteenth century there were remarkable
similarities between French and British orchestral low brass sections. While both
had included ophicleide until the final two decades, the Small French Tuba in c and
British orchestral euphonium which normally replaced the keyed instrument were
only a tone apart in pitch and similar in bore and power.

In Britain the progression from euphonium to F tuba is graphically illustrated in
the programmes of the Norwich Festival. In 1890 Alfred Phasey played euphonium

(conveniently able to switch to fourth trombone for Schütz's 'Fili mi, Absolom'), but in 1896 J. H. Guilmartin was engaged on tuba, having played both euphonium and tuba in the Queen's Hall Orchestra the previous year. The change in tone was not dramatic, as demonstrated by the Higham F tuba shown in Fig. 12.3: the lower register of the tuba was fuller than that of the euphonium at the identical pitch.

Comparative practice in band and orchestra is shown in Farmer's *The History of the Royal Artillery Band*. To appreciate the significance of this account the reader should be aware that the Royal Artillery's headquarters are at Woolwich, within the boundaries of Greater London. In addition to the normal military band this regiment has a symphony orchestra, naturally with a full-time contract for its members. This was unique in nineteenth-century London, and owing to the resulting high standard of performance the orchestra played before Her Gracious Majesty and also gave a regular concert series in the Royal Albert Hall. It might be supposed that with the introduction of bombardons into the band—there were four by 1850—a tuba would have found its way across the barrack square into the orchestra. However, it was not until 1863 that the ophicleide finally disappeared from the orchestra list and in its place appeared an E♭ bombardon and a euphonium. (It should be noted, however, that this was more twenty years before most civilian symphony orchestras considered similar moves.) By 1884 only the euphonium was being used in the orchestra, and this apparently remained the practice until as late as 1926, when a tuba took its place.

It seems that outside the sphere of German influence there had been a tendency to view the ophicleide as an instrument to be played by orchestral artistes, while the tuba was a workhorse more suited to toiling away in bands. Thus in Italy the ophicleide remained firmly established in symphony orchestras until at least 1881, despite Verdi's strongly expressed feelings that it should give way to the contrabass trombone. In France, the ophicleide was not replaced at the Paris Opéra until the mid-1870s, although the deeper saxhorns had long been established in military bands there. In England the transition took place during the last fifteen years of the century, with a tuba supplanting ophicleide at the 1886 Leeds Festival, Richter's ordering an F tuba for his London orchestra in 1887 and a tuba replacing the ophicleide and euphonium in Manchester's Hallé Orchestra by 1897 at the latest.

Clearly there had been a need for tubas in orchestras earlier in the century. When, for example, Wagner conducted the Philharmonic Society in London in 1855 some of his works were included in the programmes. One of these was a selection from *Lohengrin,* and although the name of the tuba-player is unknown it is certain that

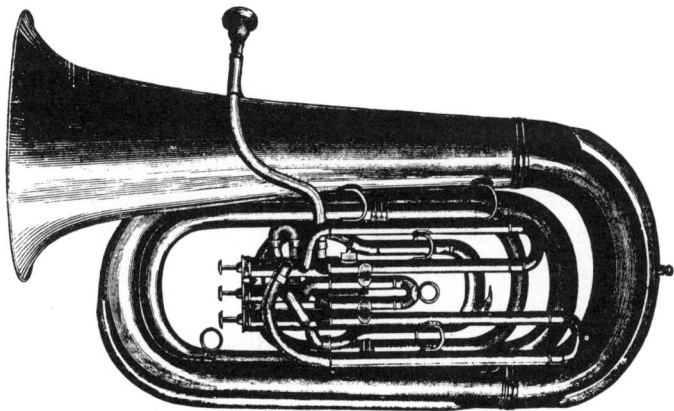

B♭ CONTRABASS Patent Compensating Pistons, £24.

B♭ CONTRABASSES from £14 to £24.

E♭ IMPERIAL BASS.   A 90b.

E♭ BOMBARDON, Imperial Model, £25.

E♭ BOMBARDONS, 4 Valves. from £12 to £25.
E♭ BOMBARDONS, 3 Valves, from £10 to £21.

Fig. 12.1. Tubas by Boosey & Co, shown in Kappey's *Complete Tutor*, c. 1874.

he will have been a military bandsman (like the other wind and brass) and equally certain that he will have played on his Eb bombardon (as, indeed, J. Wilson was named as doing for the Society in 1880). Since the orchestral tuba repertoire was severely limited until the last two decades of the century players from bands where brass basses were already in use were engaged for performances as required.

Although the Liverpool Philharmonic Society was formed in 1840 it did not have its own orchestra until 1943. Prior to that it shared players with Manchester's Hallé Orchestra, founded in 1858. The Bournemouth Symphony Orchestra was founded in 1893 as the Bournemouth Municipal Orchestra, while the first extant professional civilian London orchestra is the London Symphony Orchestra, founded in 1904. Written records show that tubists, like the earlier ophicleidists, serpentists or bass hornists, were for many years not shown in the accounts as full members of their orchestras. Thus, the Philharmonic Society's records up to World War I always show the tubist as an 'Extra Player'. In the Hallé Orchestra, until at least the beginning of the twentieth century, the player of the lowest brass instrument was put in a similar category. Richard Marsden, for instance, during the 1880s was not included in the 'Weekly Band' or 'Permanent Orchestra' along with the trombones but in the 'Additional Band' with the percussionists. These players were paid at a lower rate than the regular members. Marsden thus received a fee of 15s. 0d (75p.) for each performance of *Elijah* during the season, the lowest scale of payment.

The reason for this affiliated status is quite clear: there were still relatively few works that included a brass part below the trombones. In the Hallé's first season, 1858, the only calls upon orchestral ophicleide were in the opening concert on 30 January, when Signor Medina was required to play in Rossini's overture to *The Siege of Corinth;* and the *Midsummer Night's Dream* performances on 13 February, 6 March and 24 April (Sam Hughes playing in the last two, having already contributed *O, Ruddier than the Cherry* as a solo). Medina, too, was paid at the current lowest rate of £1.0.0d. His total earnings for the season seem to have totalled £10.16.8d plus an extra 10s.0d which was probably a subsistence payment. The most regular work available with the Hallé appears to have consisted of oratorio performances, particularly out of town.

While the Mendelssohn overture continued to be performed to excess, during the 1880s employment opportunities improved, with Richard Marsden playing works by Brahms, Wagner, Berlioz, Sullivan and others, sometimes in the Liverpool Philharmonic Society's concerts conducted by Julius Benedict or Max Bruch. (It must have been a great experience for his immediate predecessor, F. J. Batley to stay at the Pension Waldrand in St Beatenburg bei Interlaken while on a European tour with the Hallé Orchestra.) Marsden's professional activities were substantially the same as those of many present-day British brass players, covering both orchestras and brass bands. Solo euphonium in Bacup Band from 1863-71, he then occupied a similar position with the professional Belle Vue Gardens Brass Band and De Jong's Orchestra in Manchester, playing with the Hallé from 1876. He was also a contest adjudicator and in 1886 took over the Railway Hotel and Concert Hall in Ordsall Lane, Salford. Moving to Scotland, he conducted Alloa Burgh Band from 1889 and, from 1895, Kirkcaldy Band.

The lack of orchestral playing opportunities was not unique to British low brass players, of course. In the New York Philharmonic Orchestra's first season (1842-43) there was a performance of the overture to *A Midsummer Night's Dream* on 10 May 1843, but in general the mid-century concerts regularly included trombones though only rarely any lower brass instrument (S[23], App. II). It should also be borne in mind that initially the New York Philharmonic Society promoted only four concerts each year.

At the beginning of the twentieth century in London, where tubists were mainly serving or ex-military bandsmen, there was a certain amount of freelance work. The more restricted demands for freelance players elsewhere were often satisfied by local brass bandsmen or retired service personnel, leading to the regular use in British orchestras of the Eb tuba. Ebenezer Prout, in 1897, stated that the Eb bombardon was 'the tuba more frequently used', a statement supported by orchestral photographs (P[23], I, 235). One of the advantages was that brass band players accustomed to reading in treble clef could read bass clef instantly simply by reading the concert pitch part as treble clef and deleting three flats (or adding three sharps) to the key signature.

# THE ENGLISH F TUBA

Hans Richter was born into a family of professional musicians in Györ, Hungary in 1843. He studied at the Vienna Conservatory and for four years played horn in the orchestra of the Kärntnertortheater in Vienna. In 1866 he assisted Wagner as copyist of *Die Meistersinger*, acting as chorus master and repetiteur for the premiere. Later he was involved in other Wagner productions, from 1870 as conductor, directing the first complete performance of the *Ring* at Bayreuth in 1876.

Following the realization of his Bayreuth dream Wagner found himself suffering from a severe lack of funds and enthusiastically accepted an invitation to present a concert of his works in London with a view to bringing his bank account back into the black. He asked his young assistant Hans Richter to share the conducting, and thus Richter celebrated his first appearance in England, at the Royal Albert Hall in May 1877. He made a positive impression on both audiences and players, all of whom were quick to realise that his sheer craftsmanship and professionalism put him in a different league from the dilettante English conductors of the time. His popularity with orchestral players was unsurpassed until the arrival of Henry 'Timber' Wood and Thomas 'Tommy' Beecham in 1895 and 1906 respectively.

It has been claimed that 'first-class orchestral playing in England dates from 1877' (N[2], 220), and Richter was to continue inspiring players to outplay themselves in the great and popular German repertoire for thirty years. On the death of Sir Charles Hallé in 1893 the committee managing the orchestra, founded in Manchester in 1858 largely at the instigation of the city's German community, had no doubts about who should replace him. Richter took up his position in 1899, remaining until failing sight forced him to retire in 1911. His legacy remains, in the form of the Royal Northern College of Music which grew out of the Royal Manchester College of Music, founded to train players for the Hallé Orchestra.

It is impossible to over-estimate his importance in the establishment of the tuba in the symphonic orchestra. A professional brass-player who had worked intimately with Wagner, a composer with firm views on the functions and nature of the brass section, Richter swept from one extreme to the other of Europe, killing off the old and establishing the new like a nineteenth-century knight in shining brass armour. His replacement of the CC helicon(!) at the Vienna Opera by tuba on being appointed music director in 1875 is recounted on pages 323-4 above. This tuba was made by the Berlin maker Paulus, pitched in F and, as the prototype Viennese Concert Tuba, characterised by a distinctive clear sound. On initiating his series of concerts in London in 1879 he obviously decided that the low brass department in England was also not totally to his liking. Although at the time the ophicleide was the generally-accepted instrument in professional orchestras, tubists were available: obviously one had played in Wagner's Royal Albert Hall concert in 1877 and another had been involved in his Philharmonic Society concert as early as 1855.

In 1887 J. H. Guilmartin, a leading British orchestral player who had been a euphoniumist in the Scots Guards (and also, three years later, in The London Military Band, of which he was chairman), found himself having to play a tuba ordered by Richter from William Hillyard of London. Like the tuba commissioned for the Vienna Opera in 1875 it was pitched in F and had five valves, but they would certainly have differed in form. (If this had not been the case, rotary-valved, left-facing tubas would have become the norm in Britain.) Hillyard probably used an Eb saxhorn-shaped tuba with top piston-valves and right-facing bell (or even a euphonium) as the pattern for his F instrument, modifying the dimensions. Thus came into existence the prototype British F tuba, a relatively small instrument with the clear tone remarked upon a hundred years later by John Fletcher (F[18], Summer 1973, 61) and obviously to the liking of both Guilmartin and Richter himself as shown by the following letters, reprinted on the back cover of the *British Bandsman:*

118 Alderney Street, S.W.

Dear Mr HILLYARD—After playing upon the tuba you made for me, during the whole of the Richter concerts this season, I have had every opportunity of thoroughly testing it, and I am very pleased to say that it gives me entire satisfaction, moreover, I asked Dr. Richter's opinion of it, and the enclosed is the result, of which the maker, and I fancey [bis] also the player, may be justly proud. With kindest regards

Yours faithfully
J. H. GUILMARTIN
    July 5th, 1887

Richter's letter gives a hint of Teutonically-inflected English which no doubt helped to maintain the players' morale during rehearsals:

11 Bentinck Street, W.

Dear Mr. GUILMARTIN—The F Tuba made for you specially for my concerts by Mr. W. Hillyard is a magnificent Instrument. The intonation, considering the extraordinary compass, is so perfect that I with pleasure testify to the great excellence of the instrument.

Yours truly
HANS RICHTER
    July 4th, 1887 (B[55], 12.1887).

Guilmartin continued to use this instrument, playing it at the 1889 Leeds Festival, 1895 Gloucester Festival and 1896 Norwich Festival. (The dimensions of his mouthpiece, given in Table 3.1 above, should be compared with those in the Perantucci range, Table 1.3.) In 1894 Harry Barlow was appointed tubist of the Hallé Orchestra. Born in Besses o' th' Barn on 8 December 1870, he was to play euphonium in the famous local band and those of Rishton and Accrington. He also conducted Besses as well as Irwell Springs and Leicester Imperial, and his arrangement for band of a selection from Bellini's *I Capuletti* was published. Higham of Manchester made a five-valved F tuba for him to use in the Hallé (Fig. 12.1) which has been dated to 1896-7 by the organologist Frank Tomes on the basis of its serial number. The instrument in the 1895 photograph below is not identical: it is quite probably a euphonium. The tuba was no doubt specifically ordered by Barlow as Higham's 1889 price-list included 'bombardons' in various shapes and pitches but no F tuba (H[19], 185). Possibly Barlow himself had a hand in the design. The bell diameter is 300 mm and the bore at the second valve, 15.8 mm and the fifth valve gives a drop of a large semitone. Arnold Myers, curator of the Edinburgh University Collection of Historic Musical Instruments, points out that this system had previously been used by both Higham and Besson.

Fig. 12.2
Part of a photograph of the Hallé Orchestra taken in 1895. The tuba-player (top row, right) is assumed to be Harry Barlow, probably with a euphonium.

Fig. 12.3. Five-valved tuba in F by Higham, 1896-7, thought to have been used by Harry Barlow shortly after joining the Hallé Orchestra.

It was said of Richter that 'no other could unfold that splendid banner of tone with which *The Mastersingers* overture opens' (quoted in N², 226). Playing the famous part (Ex. 8.5) on the Higham instrument brought home just how far ideas of tuba tone have changed. The notes speak well, they have remarkable clarity, but little weight or power.

Barlow remained with the Hallé, living in Prestwich at 2 Elizabeth Street and then Douglas Villas, Clifton Road, both close to his birthplace, until enticed away by the newly-established BBC Symphony Orchestra in 1930. From the northern boundaries of Manchester he chose the southern outskirts of London, at 2 Highbarrow Road, Addiscombe, Surrey. Barlow seems to have been a suburban type of man, industrious and sober, staying at Llanrhos Cocoa Rooms in 1895, when presumably playing in one of Llandudno's two summer season orchestras, and marrying in the local church Deruchette from Bootle, daughter of a gasworks manager; later choosing the Bloomsbury (Young Men's) Club, 31-38 Cartwright Gardens (between Euston Station and Covent Garden) as his London base.

Richter was Elgar's favourite conductor, and Barlow is reputed to have advised the composer on his tuba parts. He will have played in the first performances of the *Pomp & Circumstance Marches 1 & 2* with the Liverpool Philharmonic on 19 October 1901 and the first symphony with the Hallé Orchestra on 3 December 1908. From 1905 he played for Richter at the Royal Italian Opera, Covent Garden; his *Radio Times* obituary (1 July 1932) states that he was invited to play at Bayreuth. He was also principal tuner for Besson, designing a series of tubas, pitched in F with five valves arranged to lower the pitch by a tone, a semitone, two tones, two-and-three-quarter tones and three-quarters of a tone in order to give true intonation. The majority of tubas in British hands incorporated the compensating system initiated by David Blaikley, Boosey's works manager, in 1874, as did Boosey's own F tubas. Besson's decision to provide an alternative system may therefore have been based on commercial considerations, but this is actually unlikely.

At the beginning of the twentieth century there was probably enough work to sustain two or three orchestral tubists (see App. C 3). Barlow was a member of the only permanently-established civilian orchestra, but owing to the seasonal nature of the work was still able to play in London and elsewhere. As a pianist he directed the Grosvenor Picture House orchestra, Oxford Street, Manchester, and as conductor took Besses o' th' Barn Band to participate in the first of the BBC's National Concerts at the Royal Albert Hall in 1926 when they joined the Hallé in Berlioz's *Grand messe des morts*. In London, series of symphony concerts like Richter's and

(b)

(c)

(a)

(d)

Fig. 12.4. Barlow F tubas: (a) a youthful George Wall with an early model; (b) Clem Lawton, Yorkshire Symphony Orchestra (Leeds 1947-55); (c) Wallace Jones, Hallé Orchestra, c. 1955; (d) Charles Brewer, BBC Symphony Orchestra, 1947.

Henry Wood's Queen's Hall Concerts, established in 1895, existed alongside the performances promoted by the Philharmonic Society and others. A select group of freelance London musicians developed amazing sight-reading skills to cope with under-funded and under-rehearsed performances. The first permanent symphony orchestra in the capital proper was the London Symphony Orchestra, founded in 1904. The pattern of provincial music festivals using London-based players has already been surveyed, leading to the conclusion that a maximum of two or three tubists was quite sufficient to cope with the available orchestral work, with others imported from service bands (usually Guards) as required.

The first tuba-player named in the list of musicians engaged for Philharmonic Society concerts (pages 502-4 below) is W. F. Young, in 1870. J. Wilson appears in 1880 and from 1890 R. Blake, R. W. Travis, J. W. Collins, F. Reynolds and W. Reynolds. Walter Reynolds (1866-1944) was, like Barlow, a man of many parts. Born in Hampshire and raised in a Barnado's Home, he became a euphoniumist and then orchestral tuba-player, his work including the Queen's Hall Orchestra and, as bass trombonist, Covent Garden Opera. He was also an eminent band trainer and adjudicator, judging the Championship Section of the National Contest at Crystal Palace. Subsequently he became musical director of the London County Council Parks Department. His son Frank (1887-1921) was both pianist and tubist, playing for the Royal Choral Society, Birmingham Promenade Concerts, Hammerstein's Opera Orchestra and, as second tuba, Queen's Hall Orchestra (M[16], 122). On his premature death, Walter returned to this orchestra, remaining for some thirty years in all (W[25], 11).

On 15 June 1932 Harry Barlow died at 496 Lower Addiscombe Road from 'Acute Septicæmia & Periodontitis & tonsilitis'. He left £2785.10.6 plus a life assurance of £250; 'furniture and instruments' were valued at £100. His *British Bandsman* obituary stated that about fourteen Barlow Tubas had been made (B[55], 26.1.74, 8). Table 12.2 lists those that it has been possible to trace. Interestingly, Barney Singleton, who came from the military to take over Barlow's Covent Garden work in 1932 on his going to the BBC, had a distinctive compensating F made by Besson (later played by 'Tug' Wilson, see page 436 below).

The Barlow F is still appreciated by connoisseurs. In 1998 Bart Cummings wrote a rave review of the CD *Killer Tuba Songs* recorded by Jay Rozen and Vern Nelson (C[26], 24-5). The music (by Nelson and the Englishman John White) was technically demanding. Cummings commented: 'The playing of Rozen is a real delight, and the entire album was played on a Besson F Tuba. His tone is rich and full, his

Fig. 12.5. Stuart Roebuck with the Barlow F Tuba he played in the Hallé Orchestra until his retirement in 1984. The instrument was provided with both upright and forward-facing (recording) bells.

Table 12.1                          EXTANT ENGLISH F TUBAS

**HIGHAM.** 5 valves, not compensated.
1. Edinburgh University Collection of Historic Musical Instruments. Dated to 1896-7; probably played in Hallé by Harry Barlow. Bell dia. 300 mm. 2nd valve-slide dia. 15.8 mm. 5th valve lowers by large semitone. (See Fig. 12.3.)

**BOOSEY.** 4 valves, compensated.
1. Mark Carter, Cwmbran<Nicholas Alford<Phil Parker Ltd<Jock Gordon.
2. Mark Carter, Cwmbran<James Gourlay<public school (scrapped c. 1975). Built in high pitch and fitted with long slide; slightly larger bore than above instrument.
4. Stephen Wick, London<Nigel Amherst<Denis Wick (principal trombone, LSO)<Arthur Doyle (CBSO).
5. ex-RMCM student (present whereabouts unknown)<Jim Anderson<John Sephton (cellist, RLPO)<John Williams (RLPO). Bought by JA for use in Bournemouth SO, mid-1960s.

**BESSON.** Barlow Tubas. Not compensated; dimensions of instruments vary considerably, tending to be larger in later models; distinguished by tubing running along back of large branch.
1. Marcus Cutts, Glossop<Stuart Roebuck<Terry Nagle (principal trombone, Hallé)<Wallace Jones (Hallé 1930-60). 5 valves. '124545' marked on back of 2nd valve. Bell dia. 390 mm. 2nd valve-slide 17.78 mm.
2. Steve Freeman, London<David Roberts, Denbighshire<player in Stockport S.O.<Stuart Roebuck. 5 valves. Marked 'Harry Barlow. No. 77176'. Bell dia. 370 mm. 2nd valve-slide 15 mm. 4th valve lowers 5 semitones, 5th lowers three semitones. Silver-plated apart from [replacement?] leadpipe.
3. Joyce Roebuck, Birch Vale<Stuart Roebuck (Hallé 1962-84). May have belonged to RMCM and been bought by Stuart who was initially a trombone student. If so it could have been the other of the Saywell pair (see 6 below) or, with recording bell, Barlow's own (see 5 below). 5 Valves. Marked 'Class A. Besson breveté' (valves made in Belgium). Upright bell 431.8 mm, flare less trumpet-like than other Barlow Tubas; recording bell c. 355.6 mm. 1 + 2 slides dia. 17 mm; 4 + 5 slides dia. 18 mm. 4th valve-slide at back, main-slide at front (unusual positioning). (See Fig. 12.5.)
4. ?Jay Rozen, Texas: see review in *TUBA Journal*. No response to enquiries. Could this be the tuba used by Arnold Jacobs in his 1978 recording of the Vaughan Williams Concerto?
5. Norman Shaw, Leeds<anon., London, c. 1972 (purchased through *British Bandsman* advertisement). 4 valves. Marked 'Class A New Standard. No. 237476'. Bell dia. 336.55 mm. 2nd valve-slide 19.05 mm. NS says his teacher, Clem Lawton (Yorkshire SO, 1947-55), believed some Barlow tubas were made in the early 1930s, one with a recording bell bought by Barlow himself. On HB's death CL bought both his tubas. CL also thought another batch was made c. 1950, players including Tom Atkinson (BBC Northern Orch) and Arthur Doyle (CBSO), the latter using it up to about a year before retiring c. 1970, having been persuaded to play Eb during his final year (ref. MC).
6. Sebastian Waller, Oberaudorf, Germany<Bob Tucci<Mike Johnson<Vic Saywell. Marked 'No. 14'. Present owner has had the tuba silver-plated. Possibly one of the last two Barlow tubas, dating from ?1950s.
7. Present whereabouts unknown<George Wall at West London College, c. 1960. Obtained on the advice of Tug Wilson. (See Fig. 12.4(a).)
8. Seen at RNCM by MC 1999. Besson 'New Standard'. Bell similar to 355 mm Eb bass. Thought to be possibly property of RNCM, bought in the 1960s. Might the college have actually bought two in the 1950s, the other being sold to SR (see 3 above)?
9. Present whereabouts unknown. Familiar to AM in Edinburgh orchestras in 1960s.

**BESSON.** Custom-made, compensated.
1. Paul Lawrence, Radlett<Tug Wilson<Barney Singleton (Covent Garden, 1932). Valves marked 'breveté'.

*Information from: Nicholas Alford (NA), Jack Allison (JA), Jim Anderson (JA), Mark Carter (MC), Marcus Cutts (MaC), Steve Freeman (SF), Mike Johnson (MJ), Paul Lawrence (PL), Arnold Myers (AM), Harold Nash (HN), Norman Shaw (NS), Bob Tucci (BT), George Wall (GW), Stephen Wick (SW).*

The author would be pleased to receive further details of existing English F Tubas.

technique is rock solid and his musicianship is impeccable.' Clearly no excuses need be made for this instrument. When, in 1978, Arnold Jacobs recorded the Vaughan Williams Tuba Concerto for the second time he used an instrument of this type, following the practice of Philip Catelinet who gave the work's premiere (F[21], 41). A Barlow F was used in the Hallé Orchestra throughout the century until the retirement of Stuart Roebuck in 1984 (Fig. 12.4).

The use of this pitch of instrument was not universally praised, however. George Millar, at the time bandmaster of the Portsmouth Division of the Royal Marines, gave as his considered opinion in 1912: 'An acquaintance with the orchestral tuba in F gives but a very poor idea of the present magnificent tubas, or basses, of the military band; even as the "parts" assigned to the orchestral tuba are but a mere index to what the solder-man plays in common' (M[36,] 57).

## POST-WAR PRACTICE

By the 1960s the English F tuba was no longer being produced. This was clearly a purely commercial decision on the part of the makers: the market for orchestral tubas was never large, but previously at least sufficient instruments to satisfy demand had been available. Jim Anderson recollects that when he was offered the Bournemouth Symphony Orchestra tuba position, as a nineteen year-old student in the mid-1960s, his main concern was to find one of the scarce F tubas to enable him to do the job properly. But a different tradition, along deviant lines from universal tuba practice, was already being established through force of circumstances. Unable to obtain one of the scarce foreign instruments, there was really no decision to be made. Just as some British orchestral players a century earlier had used their band Eb basses, those of the 1960s turned to the four-valved equivalent, the EEb. Ten years later probably only the two latest and largest Barlow F tubas were still being played professionally, by Victor Saywell (at the time freelance, previously with the London Philharmonic Orchestra) and Stuart Roebuck.

The standard British orchestral tuba is now the Besson compensated EEb, made by Boosey & Hawkes, which despite representations to the maker since the 1960s still often has to be modified by the excision of some 76 mm in order to bring it up to pitch when used with a reasonably large mouthpiece (Fig. 12.6). With a bore of 19 mm it is a versatile instrument, although until the introduction of the 'Sovereign' model in the early 1980s the g'b was often of poor quality or completely absent, causing difficulties in various repertoire works.

The use of the EE♭ in the orchestra would have horrified many of the older generation to whom accession to the F was proof of the successful move from band to profession. There is a famous (true) story of two tubists about to return from an engagement in the car belonging to one of them. 'You put your E♭ bombardon in the boot and my orchestral F can go on the back seat,' said the driver.

The first player to use the EE♭ professionally was John Fletcher, who raised eyebrows when he appeared with his 'band instrument' in the BBC Symphony Orchestra in 1964. (Curiously, even though born in Yorkshire, he had never played with a brass band.) Fletch moved to the London Symphony Orchestra in 1970 and within a few years had taken to using a Holton CC as his normal instrument. One reason for his decision was that he found that in the orchestral repertoire a large proportion of the notes lay in the fourth valve register of the EE♭ tuba, relatively lacking resonance compared with the range where fewer valves are used (F[18], Autumn 1973, 100). However, he discovered an unexpected bonus (also found by James Gourlay when he succeeded Fletch at the BBC and bought a CC tuba): the high register of these larger instruments is often remarkably clear, pure and very well in tune. Arnold Jacobs similarly found that when he was required to play 'Bydlo' at short notice, using a Penzel BB♭/F double tuba rather than the customary euphonium, he was more comfortable on the low, BB♭, side of the instrument than on the higher F side (F[21], 37, 187).

The general use of the EE♭ tuba—the 'man with van' of the tuba world, able to cope adequately with virtually all the demands made on it—has resulted in a distinctive tuba sound in British orchestras and a distinctive British concept of what an orchestral tuba is. However, it should not go unremarked that several trombonists have commented that they prefer the more concentrated tone of the F tuba since it is less removed from that of the trombones. If present practices and attitudes are to be understood fully it is necessary to bear two things in mind. The first is the large number of brass bands in the United Kingdom. Music for band demands at least one tuba pitched in E♭, and in practice there are normally two (see pages 430-1 below). As in all countries, the economics of brass instrument manufacture result in the makers' being more interested in the market for bands than the demands of a limited number of orchestral tubists. However, outside the influence of the British brass band and some European bands, tuba parts are written in concert pitch bass clef, leaving it to the player or the band director to make a decision about which pitch of instrument to use. This allows the developing player perhaps to begin on a

*Philip and Ursula Jones*

Fig. 12.6. John Fletcher playing his Boosey & Hawkes EEb tuba in the Philip Jones Brass Ensemble, BBC Pebble Mill Studios, 1984. The other players, from left to right, are Roger Harvey, Frank Lloyd, Philip Jones and Rod Franks.

single Eb or a small CC tuba at school, and experience other sizes and other pitches of instrument as time passes. (As any player or teacher will confirm, transposition is not really a problem: horn and trumpet players live with it all the time in various guises.)

Treble clef Eb tuba parts are, however, designed to be read and played only by Eb tubists, so there is a culture of Eb tuba thought in a country where not only are brass bands pervasive but it is normal for brass to be taught in schools using the treble clef methods which are widely available for all brass instruments. This notation is, in fact, a brilliantly simple idea, the effectiveness of which has been tried and tested ever since saxhorns first appeared halfway through the nineteenth century.

Alongside this tradition has existed the stranglehold imposed by the virtual monopoly exercised by the main British brass instrument manufacturer. During the nineteenth century there was a healthy brass instrument industry in the U.K., particularly England, with important makers in all the major cities. Such names as Higham and Mayers & Harrison of Manchester, Gisborne of Birmingham, Jordan of Liverpool, Besson, Boosey, Distin, Hawkes and Pace of London come to mind. When Boosey & Co. merged with Hawkes & Son in 1930 they had already taken-over Distin (1868) and the importers Lafleur (1917). During the 1940s Boosey & Hawkes bought out both Rudall, Carte and Besson. Provincial manufacturing virtually ceased when Mayers & Harrison, which had purchased Higham in 1923, ceased operations in the 1950s.

Steps were also taken to ensure that native manufacturers were protected, and until the 1960s the only way to obtain a foreign brass instrument was illegally, usually by exchanging an English one taken out for an American or German one bought while abroad and having the nerve to smuggle it into the UK. With the musical instrument industry represented on its advisory bodies, H.M. Customs were often effective in thwarting these efforts, ensuring that for tubists, in particular, there was no real choice. In effect, only the products of one company were available for purchase. During the 1980s and 90s, in comparison with the investment in advanced technology characteristic of the Japanese and Americans and the craft apprenticeships of Germany and other Continental Europeans, the British manufacturer turned to mass-production and assembly by semi-skilled workers.

Such practices are doomed to bring tragedy in their wake, and in 1999 nemesis appeared following a bizarre confluence of political decree and commercial greed. Five years earlier a National Lottery had been established, successfully raising vast sums of money. The first major grants were given to causes like the Churchill archives (£12,000,000), resulting in widespread expressions of disquiet. Casting around for ways to soothe the wrath of the electorate, the government lighted on the brass band movement as a politically-acceptable recipient of money for the many. Numerous bands ordered new sets of instruments and the bank accounts of the manufacturers began to look extremely healthy.

Not so their products. Faced with overwhelming demand, quality control was set aside and instruments were sold with poor silver-plating, rough valves, inadequately-brazed stays and other faults. In 1998 one retailer estimated that customers were returning sixty per cent of instruments; some bands sent back whole sets of basses. This contributed to the company's abrupt plunge into the red of the order of £45.1m, while in March 1999 shares fell to 352½p compared with a peak of £10.07½ two years earlier. While the National Lottery's television advertising featured its help for brass bands many players were already regretting that they had sold their Imperial tubas and euphoniums.

Tubas had been manufactured by Yamaha since the 1960s, with a four-valve EE♭ introduced in the 1970s. British players had shown little enthusiasm for these instruments as they were not compensated and there was an inbuilt expectation that the note a semitone above the first pedal would be available without too much fuss. The YEB 631 four-valve compensating EE♭ and YBB 631 compensating BB♭ tubas appeared in the early 1990s, providing viable alternatives to home-made products. In 1998 James Gourlay worked with the company on improving the EE♭ and the result was the superb YEB 632 which appeared the following year and seems set to become the professionals' EE♭ tuba. It needs more skilful handling than the Sovereign, but its amalgam of fulness and clarity (combining universal tuba sound and the traditional English ideal) more than justify its technical demands. Paul Smith now plays a Yamaha in the BBC Symphony Orchestra.

Meanwhile Mike Johnson of Manchester has successfully addressed many of the problems identified by John Fletcher through providing customised alternative mouthpipes, radically reconfiguring the fourth valve-tubing via a rotary-valve and introducing demountable sections, simplifying cleaning, maintenance and repair. These instruments have had a marked impact on professional players: London freelance Kevin Morgan has already invested in a pair of them.

The attitude of music colleges towards tuba students in the post-war years tended to be lacklustre. Traditionally brass players had entered the profession on retiring in early middle age from service bands. It is difficult to avoid the impression that

United Kingdom music colleges tolerated brass-players only because without them they would not have had in-house orchestras to accompany their student soloists. Immediately after World War II there was in any case a dearth of low brass students.

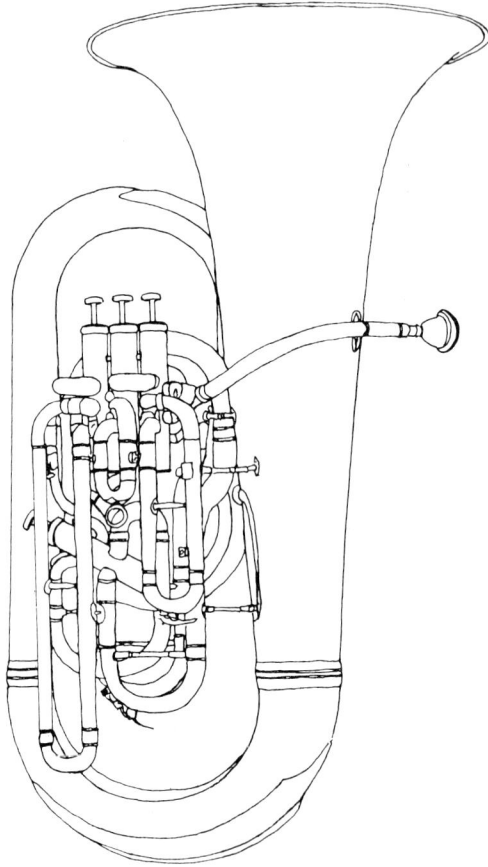

Fig. 12.7
Yamaha YEB 632
four-valve
compensating
EE♭ tuba.

I studied trombone at the Royal Academy of Music from 1956-60 and in my first year we had to borrow a tuba student from Trinity College of Music for concerts as we had no tubist of our own. Similarly, I played with the orchestra of the Guildhall School of Music & Drama as they had only two trombone students.

The quality of teaching was immensely variable at the time. It was freely acknowledged that some of the professors were reluctant to pass on their wisdom as they feared for their own jobs. (As trombonist Roger Brenner was to remark later: 'If you came out of college knowing as much you did when you went in, you were fit for the profession'.) At the R.A.M. there was no Professor of Tuba until John Fletcher was appointed in 1965, although Harry Barlow had taught there for a year until his death in 1932. Low brass was traditionally the province of the Professor of Trombone. My memories of tubists at the time I began my career in the late 1950s consist principally of a series of ex-military bandsmen who were very agreeable, who turned up at rehearsal dressed like bank clerks, who rarely talked, and whose playing was mainly inaudible. During a recent conversation concerning a professional tubist who had been forced to stop playing following continuing embouchure problems it was remarked: 'Yes, but remember he was taught by ——, the last of the non-playing tuba players'.

There were exceptions, notably John 'Tug' Wilson of the London Philharmonic and Philharmonia Orchestras and Philip Catelinet in the London Symphony Orchestra. The latter, who by virtue of his position, gave the first performance of Vaughan Williams's Tuba Concerto, was a remarkable musical polymath. As a renowned Salvation Army bandmaster he reached high office in the United States, while his entries in *Brass Band Cylinder and Non-microgroove Disc Recordings* (A[14]) show him as piano accompanist rather than as tuba soloist. (In fact there are no tuba soloists in the fifty-seven-year period covered by this comprehensive discography.) When, towards the end of his life, he was asked to provide details of his career for inclusion in *The Tuba Source Book* the requests were met by a steadfast silence as he was hard at work composing an immense oratorio.

Orchestral tubists often doubled in the capacity of orchestra manager, with an overall responsibility for ensuring that the right players were in the right place at the right time, paid correctly and behaving properly. In the Hallé, Wallace H. Jones fulfilled this function for many years, also playing double bass when no tuba was required and eventually retiring as tubist but remaining for some time as orchestra manager. Even Arnold Jacobs was for a short period personnel manager (the American equivalent) of the Pittsburgh Symphony Orchestra (F[21], 21) He also played double bass, though not in the orchestra. (In the Chicago Symphony Orchestra, though, Fredrick Otte doubled on the two instruments from 1895 to 1914; Heinrich Wiemann did likewise in the Philadelphia Orchestra, 1926-53.) I believe that I was the last tubist/orchestra manager with a permanent salaried orchestra in the U.K. when a member of the Royal Liverpool Philharmonic in the late 1960s, until it was realised that economies of this sort could not be allowed to continue if the ratio of administrative staff to players was to rise in the way that has since become international practice.

While the tuba crept into British orchestras from the 1880s onwards, the first real teachers did not appear until eighty years later, when during the 1960s John Fletcher and Stuart Roebuck began to nurture their students in the way that teachers of strings, woodwind, piano and voice had been doing for many years. In turn, their students have influenced others and a high level of tuition is now generally available, but a new threat exists in the lack of employment opportunities for their many gifted graduates. Both the United Kingdom and United States are net exporters of professional tubists, currently providing tubists for the prestigious Vienna Philharmonic and La Scala, Milan orchestras, amongst many others. The exponentially-increasing number of solo competitions in Continental Europe seems to produce relatively few outstanding orchestral players.

Within the last few years more professional British orchestral players have been following American practice. This is not because of an influx of American tubists, as elsewhere in Europe, but rather because international conductors expect the fuller sound that they find elsewhere, as John Fletcher sensed in the early 1970s. English trombonists have been using large-bore American instruments for many years, necessitating a consequent adjustment in the size of tuba, and tubists themselves more often hear players from the outside world, on record or live. Paul Lawrence, when with the London Philharmonic Orchestra, designed a successful CC based on the Boosey & Hawkes four-valve BB♭. This instrument was one of the few compensated right-facing CC tubas with top valves to be made, although another was played in the Concertgebouw Orchestra of Amsterdam in the 1950s.

However, British players still have to cope with the British composer's very distinctive attitude towards the instrument. Since early tubas in the U.K. were to some extent fulfilling the role of substitute ophicleides it might be reasonable to suppose that there would be a good deal of lively high writing in English tuba parts: there was, though not so much as in French. Equally, since English music was strongly affected by German music it could be expected that there would be a tendency to use the instrument's low register: there was—especially at the octave to the bass trombone. There are many examples of low French and high German writing, but English composers tend to include both in remarkably close proximity.

This inheritance may well be because of the virtuosity of the euphonium-players who took up tuba. From Elgar through Holst, Walton and Malcolm Arnold there is a tradition of tuba parts demanding the greatest dexterity and flexibility of embouchure. Edward Elgar (1857-1934) represented the first generation of British composers who expected to find a tuba in the orchestra and he spared no efforts in using this new instrument in a distinctive way. In doing so he laid down an approach followed by other (often lesser) composers. It is sometimes difficult when playing British music to put out of mind The Alberts, a comic musical duo who justified their chaotic performances by shouting: 'It might be rubbish, but at least it's British rubbish!' yet for the tubist many works of lesser inspiration, like Dyson's *The Canterbury Pilgrims* and Holst's uninspired *Fugal Overture* (Ex. 12.1), make interesting demands on technique. Holst also resorts to muted tuba in this extraordinary piece.

Ex. 12.1

Holst: *A Fugal Overture*

Ex. 12.2

Elgar: *Enigma Variations*, XI: G.R.S.

Ex. 12.3

Elgar: *Enigma Variations,* VII: Troyte

Ex. 12.4

Elgar: Overture *Cockaigne*

Elgar's first significant work, *Variations on an Original Theme ('Enigma')*, appeared in 1899, at a crucial time for the development of the tuba in Britain. Ex. 12.2 actually presents few difficulties despite its speed. It represents the manic organ-pedaling-cum-gyrating-bulldog effect of a cathedral organist and his pet. Elsewhere Elgar makes effective use of the heavy brass to illustrate a young architect's earnest but erratic attempts to play the piano (Ex. 12.3). He often allied tuba with the horns, as in Ex. 12.4, from *Cockaigne*, where the quiet chords support one of the overture's themes stated by the celli and a second developed by the upper strings. Another overture, *In the South,* makes virtuoso demands on the tubist (Ex. 12.5).

The tuba parts of Elgar's three oratorios, *The Dream of Gerontius, The Kingdom* and the more rarely-performed *The Apostles*, stand scrutiny. They still present technical problems, particularly *The Kingdom*, which has an overall range of virtually three octaves and two of the most exposed entries in the repertoire (Ex. 12.6). There is a wonderful, Mahlerian, phrase in the midst of the Demons' Chorus in *Gerontius* (Ex. 12.7). The symphonies, too, include many demanding passages. If Barlow really did advise Elgar, he clearly was not prepared to admit that there are things the tubist might find it difficult to play. In the first symphony Elgar sometimes follows Wagner in separating the tuba from the trombones and associating it with bass instruments

Ex. 12.5

Elgar: Overture *In the South*

Ex. 12.6

Elgar: *The Kingdom*

of other orchestral families (12.8). The second symphony is remarkable for the use of wide-ranging tuba phrases which at times are reminiscent of Brahms (Ex. 12.9, cf. Ex. 8.9). It is interesting to note that while Elgar specified mutes galore in his *Severn Suite* for brass band of 1930 (scored by another hand), the only demands for muted tuba in the orchestral works appear in the completion of his third symphony by Anthony Paine.

Ex. 12.7

Elgar: *The Dream of Gerontius*

Gustav Holst wrote for brass in a sympathetic way, having worked as a trombonist. In *The Planets* he demonstrates an acute awareness of the tuba's lowest notes (Ex. 12.10). Arnold Bax has also exploited the instrument's unusually wide range. In his fifth symphony the part extends downwards as far as E'♭ and there is a passage for muted tuba accompanied by one flute, harp and strings which reaches d'. 'Was solo tuba ever scored more poetically than in the central slow movement?' asked the critic Felix Aprahamian after attending a performance by the BBC

Ex. 12.8

Elgar: Symphony 1

Ex. 12.9

**Allegro vivace e nobilmente**

Elgar: Symphony 2

Philharmonic Orchestra at a 1984 Promenade Concert (A[17], 39). Bax is the only composer regularly to use the instruction 'Like pizzicato' on tuba parts.

His contemporary Havergal Brian was explicit in his awareness of the importance of the bass instruments in the orchestra, and freely acknowledged his distinctive method of composing from the bottom of the score upwards. Between 1927 and 1968 he composed thirty-two symphonies, many of them including one (or two) euphoniums (see page 238 above) and all except Symphony 21 demanding at least one tuba. The part in Symphony 29 is notably virtuosic. Symphonies 1, 2, 3 and 4 stipulate two tubas. Symphony 2 ('Gothic') additionally requires two euphoniums and, in the finale, 'four extra brass orchestras' with a tuba in each. Another instance of two orchestral tubas (if Australians may be included in the British category) is found in the revised 1924-25 version of Percy Grainger's *English Dance*, although as originally scored in 1899-1909 it included a tuba alongside the euphonium.

Constant Lambert composed little, unfortunately, spending most of his time as conductor and occasionally writing on music. In 1930 appeared *The Rio Grande*, in which the tuba contributes to a wistful yet lively score, written very much in the

Ex. 12.10

Holst:'Jupiter' *(The Planets)*

Ex. 12.11

(a)

(b)

Lambert: *The Rio Grande*

style of its time. Ex. 12.11(a) shows eight bars of the tuba part, covering a considerable range. Lambert places the tuba in its high register in the last four bars since it is the only instrument playing these two phrases which need to be heard through the tutti. Ex. 12.11(b) may be considered the 1930 equivalent of the Brahms passages quoted in Ex. 8.6. These bars follow immediately after the chorus has sung 'To where, in the square, they dance and the band is playing'.

Ralph Vaughan Williams, composer of the first concerto for tuba and orchestra, made considerable use of the instrument in his orchestral works. At first sight many of his tuba parts look remarkably similar to the concerto owing to his distinctive modal style of writing and the unique 'elf-music' found in the concerto's first movement. It is difficult to choose an extract from William Walton's compositions since so many of them involve the tuba and he has always felt free to write for it in a virtuoso manner. *Belshazzar's Feast* needs two additional tubas in bands situated to the left and right of the main orchestra. The extract from his overture *Portsmouth Point* shown in Ex. 12.12 is particularly distinctive.

Ex. 12.12

Walton: Overture *Portsmouth Point*

Benjamin Britten's *Young Person's Guide to the Orchestra* (1946) includes a passage for the low brass frequently misunderstood by conductors (Ex. 12.13). On seeing the canonic entries they expect the tuba line to balance the trombones. Three trombones playing forte in unison would need far more than a solitary tuba to fulfil this requirement. Britten intended a contrast, the three virile young men throwing out a challenge to the whole orchestra with a sort of Sancho Panza character following on some distance behind. There is a passage of a completely different type in his Violin Concerto, a solo with the accompaniment of two piccolos and divisi violins in harmonics (Ex. 12.14). The opera *Gloriana* covers a range of D' to e'. The

Ex. 12.13

Britten: *The Young Person's Guide to the Orchestra*

Ex. 12.14

Britten: Concerto for Violin and Orchestra

high note comes in a solo in Act II written throughout in a high tessitura. It is eminently possible on the F tuba, or sometimes a euphonium is used in this passage, though there is some very low writing elsewhere in the score.

Britten was uniquely sensitive to the tuba, which for him spoke of bestiality and excess. His biographer, Donald Mitchell, refers to the moment at the end of 'Rats Away', in his early work *Our Hunting Fathers*, when 'a baleful tuba solo is added to the texture, the most subversive and menacing sound of all'. Mitchell points out that almost forty years later, in his opera *Death in Venice*, 'it is the sonority of the tuba that acts, as it were, as the bearer of the plague, the symbolic and actual plague that kills Aschenbach. How extraordinary that already in 1936 it was the tuba that was associated in Britten's inner imagination with the idea of pestilence' (M[36], 37). Conrad also makes reference to *Death in Venice*, where the spreading Asiatic cholera 'is erotic, killing Aschenbach [the chief protagonist] by way of his love for Tadzio [the boy] . . . Tadzio is [Apollo's] deputy, playing Phoebus astride a pyramidal chariot

Ex. 12.15

Tippett: Concerto for Orchestra

of boys . . . In Aschenbach's dream, this fluting luminary is drowned by Dionysus, whose mysteries and reeling dance and sacrifice are a sexual debasement, announced by the beastly lowing of the tuba' (C[31], 23-231).

The only instance of tenor clef in an orchestral tuba part occurs on the last page of the finale of Britten's *Spring Symphony*. The eight bars concerned are not particularly high, and the reason for this aberration appears to be the literal

Ex. 12.16

Arnold: Harmonica Concerto

transcription by a copyist of the lower of two parts from a stave shared in the manuscript score with the third trombone.

Michael Tippett's 1964 Concerto for Orchestra gives the tuba a solo with piano, the latter part being marked 'accompagnando la tuba solo' to make sure that the melodic part remains prominent (Ex. 12.15). Tippett requires two tubas in his fourth symphony (1977). It has been stated elsewhere that these are tenor and bass, but the nature of the writing, in which they are consistently used as a pair of like instruments, does not support this assertion. Overall neither part is outstandingly high, and although Tuba 1 does reach g', Tuba 2 is written up to e'. Furthermore, in both the introductory notes and the score proper Tippett refers to them as 'two tubas'.

Malcolm Arnold, like Holst before him, was a professional brass player—a trumpeter. The brass find considerable use and pleasure in his compositions. He often puts the tuba with the trombones in chords, long or short, and there is a fair amount of oompah. The passage from the Harmonica Concerto shown in Ex. 12.16 illustrates another deft touch—a cantabile, wide-sweeping melodic line for the tuba. It is not every day that a tubist finds himself in duet with a mouth-organ.

# CHAPTER XIII

## *Instruments and Music: Italy*

In fact anything you like, but not that damned bombardon
which does not blend with the others.
—from a letter from Verdi to his publisher, Ricordi, prior to the
first performance of *Aida*, 1871

. . . the professors of the orchestra of La Scala have been the first
to put into effect the deliberations of the Congress of Musicians
of Milan. Thus they now have the four-string double bass, horns
with crooks for the various keys indicated in the score, and the
new bass trombone in place of the bombardon.
—'At Random' in *Gazetta musicale di Milano*,
18 December 1881

THE 1954 edition of *Grove's Dictionary of Music and Musicians* defined *cimbasso* as
'The Italian narrow-bore tuba in B♭', and later English-language music dictionaries
patently derived their inspiration from this definition, generally reprinting it more
or less intact. There was one exception, the *Cambridge Italian Dictionary* (Cambridge,
1962) which chose to define *cimbasso* as 'ophicleide'. Included in the Introduction
was a statement which read: 'The word *cimbasso*, for instance, meaning "ophicleide",
occurs in the score of Verdi's *Un Ballo in Maschera* (1859) but is not elsewhere
recorded'.

Although even comprehensive general dictionaries published in Italy tend not to
include the word it usually finds a place in Italian music reference books, where it is
defined as a bass or contrabass trombone introduced into the orchestra by Verdi and
sometimes known as the *Trombone Verdi*.

*The early cimbasso*

Vessella gives the following information on the cimbasso:

In the scores of the Italian masters the cimbasso is still found as the foundation of
the trombones, instead of the ophicleide. The cimbasso, no longer used, was made
of wood, sometimes copper, in bassoon shape with six finger-holes and two keys,
a metal bell and an S, to which was applied a mouthpiece somewhat larger than
that of the trombone; the compass was C-g, non-transposing (V[5], 348).

Renato Meucci suggests that the name is derived from an abbreviation of *corno basso* or *corno in basso*, written *c. basso* or *c. in basso*. This is confirmed by inconsistencies in written forms, which include *simbasso, gimbasso* and the abbreviation *gibas* (M[32] [GSJ], 145).

The cimbasso thus appears to be the distinctive type of Italian upright serpent or bass horn, differing from the Russian bassoon in always having a metal bell, and from the English bass horn in being partially made of wood. Other distinguishing features include the considerable proportion of the total tube-length made up by the crook (one-third), the position of its finger-holes, and the fact that it may have one, two or three keys, shown in the fingering-charts printed in M[32] [GSJ], 167-8 and M[54],135, in Vessella's description and by extant specimens This is doubtless the type of instrument seen at La Scala in 1816 and 1825 (see page 81 above) and used by composers including Bellini (the *serpentone* in, for example, *Il Pirata* of 1827) and Rossini (Ex. 2.2).

*Mid-nineteenth century performing practices*

The upright serpent identified as a Russian bassoon in the Shrine to Music Museum, No. 1275 (M[32] [GSJ], Fig. 4) is likely to be a prototype cimbasso. It has a maple body in three sections with brass bell and long brass mouthpipe, brass trim, six finger-holes and three keys. Stamped on the lower joint is 'P. Piana, a Milano', and the ivory mouthpiece is known to be the original. The instrument is thought to date from c. 1815. The earliest stipulation of cimbasso in a score so far found is that in Paganini's first violin concerto, composed in 1815-16 (M[32] [Studi Verdiani], 142). In the third concerto the part is actually for 'Serpentone, e Gimbaſſo', the implication being that it is suitable for either instrument rather than a requirement that both should play together. The part, which follows accepted cimbasso practice, sometimes providing the bass of the trombones and at other times more closely allied with other low woodwind or string instruments, was one of four that Paganini himself copied and is reproduced in facsimile by Canale (C[3], 122-3). There would not have been a cimbasso as such at the premiere of the work in Vienna on 24 July 1828, nor at its first English performance, in Liverpool Theatre Royal on 9, 10 or 11 January 1832 (B[32], 500). The orchestra list for performances in Manchester Theatre Royal on 12-14 and 19-21 June 1832 includes 'le chevalier Leisenring dit André' who, since no instrument is ascribed to him and no serpentist is named, may have been André, the leading English serpentist at the time. There were several other London players in the orchestra. Another instrumentalist is named Pretty, although whether this is the serpent-maker Francis Pretty who worked in London from 1829 to 1840 is not known. There seem to be no other references to his actually having played the instrument. The second and third movements only of the concerto were first played in London on 14 August 1832, but the names of the individual musicians are not known (C³⁴, I, 380).

The source of orchestral wind, brass and percussion players during much of the nineteenth century was the army band (with musicians often wearing their military uniforms in performances). In the earlier years of the century in Italy an army musician providing the lowest brass part would play it on his bass horn, his cimbasso. But when valved instruments began to appear in military bands (a process that had begun as early as the 1820s in Prussia) players would take their familiar valved bass to the opera house. Halfway through the century, therefore, a variety of keyed and valved low brass instruments will have been found in the Italian theatre, and it is reasonable to suppose that while the *oficleide* or *flicorno* was heard in the major cities the early cimbasso lingered in the more isolated towns, where it may actually have been more appropriate to its function than many valved basses. More appropriate still could have been a deep brass instrument which was a closer match to the three upper trombones in bore and consequently also in timbre.

Both keyed and valved ophicleides were known in Italy: Balbi's *Grammatica ragionata della musica* (1845) states that 'the oficleide or gimbasso is an instrument with a deep and penetrating tone' (B⁹, 143). The valved ophicleide *(oficleide a macchina)* was particularly popular in northern Italy, geographically and politically close to Austria. The Museo Civico at Modena contains two examples, one by Uhlmann of Vienna (Fig. 4.9) and the other by the local maker Antonio Apparuti dating from 1841. It comes as no surprise, therefore, to find ophicleides being referred to as *cimbassi* nor, with the appearance of the valved bombardon, to find this instrument sharing the name. Meucci provides numerous examples of this imprecise usage, leading to the conclusion that by the mid-nineteenth century in Italy any low brass instrument of any type could be called by any name.

This is confirmed by Francis Irving Travis, who observed that in some manuscript copies of early Verdi works 'the designation of the instrumental line in question seems to change from act to act, apparently depending on the copyist' (T¹⁰, 50). The implication is that 'cimbasso' was in familiar but not precise use, rather as 'bombardon' and 'ophicleide' were in Germany at various times or, in Italy itself, *Clavicorno* on band parts long after it had been superseded by the Eb alto horn, the mysterious *genis*.

Ex. 13.1

Since the earliest years of the nineteenth century, valved trombones have had a particularly strong attraction for southern Europeans, the Spanish and the Italians. In fact throughout the century playing the valve trombone was a surprisingly widespread practice. In England, D'Almaine included valved alto, tenor and bass trombones in their 1839 price-list (P[21, 25]). During the American Civil War valved trombones appear to have been more common than the slide variety (though both were relatively scarce). Contemporary comment makes it clear that (even in France) the main reason for this was that the slide trombone was considered too demanding. In 1895 Lavignac illustrated both slide and valved types, commenting: 'a few orchestras have alto and bass valve trombones; but in most the three parts are played by tenor trombones' (L⁴, 145-6). In order to establish the slide-trombone at the Vienna Opera in 1883 the older players had to be pensioned-off (Z², 53). In the late 1890s the Boston Symphony Orchestra included valved bass trombone.

But it was the Italians who showed most interest in applying valves to trombones. About 1880 G. Gabusi of Bologna built soprano, tenor and bass valve trombones in tuba shape. There is a four-valved *Gabusifono* in the Leipzig Musikinstrumenten-Museum, No. 1762 (H²², 62-63). Italians were especially enthusiastic about developing the lower pitches of valved trombone. The trombonist Giovacchino

Bimboni invented the *Bimbonifono* about 1850. Pitched in F with seven rotary-valves, five tone and one semitone descending, one semitone ascending, its keys are arranged as on a woodwind instrument *(Sistema Bimboni Brevettato)*, with a four-octave range. There is an example in the Horniman Museum, London (Fig. 13.3).

## The cimbasso from 1881

Continuing discussions about the ideal orchestra took place in Italy in the last thirty years of the nineteenth century. At the time the standard symphonic low brass section consisted of three tenor trombones and an ophicleide, as in France. In 1871 a committee for the reform of the conservatories (of which Verdi was president)

Verdi: *La Traviata*

recommended four trombones in the orchestras of large theatres, and did not mention any other low brass (G9, 4.6.1871, suppl.). This was in complete agreement with the sentiments expressed by Verdi in a letter to his publisher Ricordi prior to the first performance of *Aida* in December that year:

Again I insist on a fourth Trombone. That bombardon is not a possibility . . . I cherish a *Trombone Basso* because it is of the same family as the others; but if it should be too tiring and too difficult to play, try again one of the usual ophicleides that reach low B. In fact anything you like, but not that damned bombardon *[quel diavolo di Bombardone]* which does not blend with the others (A[1], III, 525-6).

As was to be expected, Verdi was well aware of the attributes of the *bombardone*, the bass tuba he regularly specified in opera stage bands. Meucci argues that the reference to ophicleides that reach low B shows that Verdi was referring to valved ophicleides, but this is the lowest note of the keyed ophicleide in C as well as of the valved ophicleide in F.

Ten years later the Congresso dei Musicisti Italiani recommended that orchestras should adopt the alto trombone, along with a bass trombone in F in place of the third tenor, while the *bombardone* or *serpentone* (terms often used synonymously at the time) should be replaced by a contrabass tuba (G$^9$, 13.11.81, 408). Verdi strongly disagreed with this decision having in August 1881 taken the practical step of listening to various instruments at Pelitti's workshop, including a contrabass trombone in B'♭, an octave lower than the tenor (P$^{10}$, 196). The new instrument 'gave splendid results for range, timbre, sonority, power, sweetness, and ease of playing, blending perfectly with the other trombones' (G$^9$,4.9.81, repr. in P$^{10}$, 312-13).

Although three-valved contrabass trombones in B'♭ existed (like the example in Fig. 13.3), it seems that the instrument that initially impressed Verdi may have been a valved version of a model similar to the familiar modern bass (slide) trombone in B♭/F/E♭ (which can in fact cope with Verdi's lowest brass parts) since he stated:

... the bass trombone in B♭ and E♭ ... achieved a perfect homogeneity of timbre with the tenor trombones, thus completing the harmony without distorting the bass notes, as occurs with the present ophicleides and similar instruments, all fine for a band, but absolutely out of place in an orchestra (P$^{10}$, 312-13).

Later Verdi returned to Pelliti's workshop along with his librettist, the composer Boito, a member of the committee of the recent Congresso Musicale, and publisher Ricordi to inspect a

... new bass trombone in B♭, an octave below the tenor trombone. This new instrument gave splendid results in range, sonority, power, sweetness and ease of playing, matching the other trombones perfectly. The final result would be the necessary adoption of two tenor trombones in B♭, one bass trombone in F, and the new bass trombone in B♭, thus creating a perfectly homogeneous, effective quartet of trombones, without bringing the distinctive sound of the band to the orchestra, which adulterates the blend of the various instruments (P$^{10}$, 312-13).

There were to be unexpected problems in implementing this plan, however. In a letter to Verdi dated 18 January 1882 Ricordi reported from Milan that

... everything is going very well — The professor in charge of the bass trombone wishes to reassure you again that shortly he will be able to manage, and is still taking time to overcome the inconvenience caused by the physical *weight* of the instrument ($C^{15}$, 8).

Writing from Geneva on 8 February 1882 Verdi replied:

They move very slowly *[Andante troppo adagio]* these reforms of the orchestra! once again, is the Bass trombone not ready? ($C^{15}$, 15).

But on that very same day Ricordi was able to reassure Verdi:

... meanwhile I must tell you that I visited Pelitti again, and he has now found a good way of stabilizing the support of the bass trombone, making it comfortable and sonorous: he has made a new one, and as soon as it has been tested we shall let you know ... ($C^{15}$, 14).

Although Pelitti named his instrument *trombone contrabbasso Verdi* the composer himself, who chose it for his later works, always called it *trombone basso* ($C^{15}$, 8). It is identified on orchestral parts and in scores as 'Trombone Basso' since existing Italian trombone sections consisted of three tenors. An example of the new instrument was displayed at the Esposizione Teatrale in Milan in 1894 (A. Soffredini in $G^9$, 24.6.94). Cella suggests that it is likely that the 'professor in charge of the bass trombone' mentioned in the letter above was the same performer who was eventually entrusted with the part for the cimbasso which the bass trombone was deemed to replace ($C^{15}$, 8, n.3).

That Verdi's preferred instrument was valved even towards the end of the century would not have surprised anyone. In 1897 Vessella wrote: 'In a word, with the trills and the passages entrusted to the trombone by modern composers the greatest virtuosi on the *slide* trombone would find the former an absolutely insurmountable obstacle' ($V^5$, I, 380). The tradition was already well-established. Almost fifty years earlier Tosorini's treatise on instrumentation had referred to '... trombones in use, that is: with pistons, or with a mechanism with cylinders' ($T^9$, 55). This was the *trombone a macchina*, and the bass trombone in F was quite capable of dealing with parts in the ophicleide or bass horn range, but in *Otello* the lowest note is E'. This is the lowest note of the three-valved Italian contrabass trombone in B'♭ and in that work, *Falstaff* and *Quattro Pezze Sacri* Verdi actually specifies four (valved) trombones.

There is evidence that this type of instrument became the normal bass of the brass in all Verdi opera performances, along with those of other composers. In his appendix to Berlioz's *Grande trattato di stromentazione e d'orchestrazione moderne con appendice di Ettora Panizza*, published in 1912, Ettora Panizza stated: 'Today this trombone has become extremely common in Italian orchestras, and almost all the parts for ophicleide or tuba are played on the Verdi trombone' (P[4], 277, fn). This despite the seating arrangement at La Scala, about 1890, in Henry Kling's *Der vollkommene Musik-Dirigent* which shows a tuba in the orchestra (K[15], 277). In 1881 the members of that very orchestra had stated their determination to use the 'new bass trombone as substitute for the bombardon' as recommended by the Congress (G[9], 18.12.81, 458).

Verdi's obsession with the matching sounds of a true quartet is explicit in the statement he made on his visit to Pelitti's factory, and his wish to contrast the sound of the orchestral low brass with that of the band makes it clear why he always chose a *bombardone* for the stage band. A general Italian preference for matching timbres in orchestral low brass is made clear by Ascalone in 1893: '. . . while on its own the bass tuba is an excellent orchestral instrument on account of its gentle voice, both agile and weighty, its dark sound is unpleasing to the ear when heard in conjunction with the clear tone of the trombones' (A[18], 43).

The widespread use of the contrabass valve trombone in Italy (the three-valved version providing at least a possible fourth lower than a four-valved Bb/Eb bass trombone, although these extra notes were not required by Verdi) is supported by the number of extant specimens. The model by Orsi of Milan shown in Fig 13.3(a) is typical, though variants were found. The John Webb collection contains two examples in tuba-shape, one of these by Cazzani, maker of the instrument traditionally used at the Rome Opera. An instrument of this type may well have inspired the false attribution in *Grove V*.

The manufacture of valved contrabass trombones in cimbasso form was not restricted to Italy. There is a contrabass trombone by P. Senecaust of Brussels in the Museum Vleeshuis, Antwerp (No. 322) in a similar shape. Made in the second half of the nineteenth century, it has three top piston-valves and a fourth valve horizontally below the bell, presumably for the left hand. There are four water-keys (M[47], 99). At least two Italian firms were still making valved contrabass trombones in the 1970s: Desidera (Bologna) and Orsi (Milan). The former included three models in their January 1974 catalogue, a three-valve (l. 350,000), four-valve (l. 1,420,000) and another, the 'Mahillon', with a fourth, top-facing, piston-valve. As Mahillon and Senecaust (see previous page) were both Belgian, this could indicate that the former may have had a hand in the Vleeshuis trombone. Instruments of this pitch were not restricted to the opera house, or indeed to the orchestra, but were widely used in wind bands. Present-day Italian publishers include a part for *Trombone contrabbasso in Si♭* in their arrangements for large bands like those supported by the municipalities of Venice and Rome. It is interesting to note that the instrument was neither made nor played in Spain, the other southern European country where wind bands with over 100 members are regularly found. Even so, the demand for valve trombones in general may still be more widespread than is generally supposed, with Miraphone, Blessing, Červený, Conn, Holton, Amati, Yamaha and Getzen all currently making them. Their products are sometimes aimed at the jazz market, but Červený and Miraphone's four rotary-valved models are clear exceptions. Červený also make a rotary-valve bass trombone in F.

*Present-day performing practices*

Anyone with a serious interest in the use of the low brass in Italy has cause to be grateful to Renato Meucci for the vast amount of painstaking, detailed research he has carried out into the cimbasso. However, in his conclusions he seems to overlook the need to listen to the music in performance. He refers to 'certain Italian orchestras [where] older conductors ask for the cimbasso part to be played on an instrument similar to . . . [one] made at the begining of the century by Cazzani of Milan . . . still occasionally in use at the Rome Opera under the name of "cimbasso", according to an unchanged tradition handed down through many generations of orchestral players . . .' (M[32] [GSJ], 158, n. 70). As a more appropriate alternative he recommends using a 1/2 or 3/4 tuba for parts written between the 1850s and 1920s. This instrument should be in F 'being that used in nineteenth-century orchestras . . . For works composed between 1835 and 1850, it is advisable not to exceed a tuba of 1/2; alternatively, both for this period and that just following (until the 1860s), a bass trombone (in F) might be used, an instrument certainly documented in some orchestras of the period'.

In giving this sincere advice, he seems to have forgotten that he himself stated, 'Almost twenty years were to elapse—almost forty since the Commission had expressed its opinion on the matter—before the bass tuba was to become finally accepted in Italy' (M[32] [GSJ], 160). In other words, the tuba was not regularly found in Italian orchestras until about 1920, a state of affairs confirmed by Panizza (see page 415 above). Furthermore, he admits to having no clear idea about the instrument to use in modern performances of works scored with the original bass horn type of cimbasso in mind. 'For the moment we should trust to the good sense of the performer, who as far as possible should control any "soloistic" instinct he might have . . .' (M[32] [GSJ], 162). Alas, those sitting in the pit providing the lowest part of the brass are, by definition, accustomed to inhibiting any vestigial soloistic instincts!

The first British opera company to invest in a *Trombone basso Verdi* was Welsh National Opera, and the player, Sean O'Neill, was kind enough to invite me to a performance of *Otello* in 1986 (Fig. 13.1). It was an experience I shall never forget, because for the first time I heard the low brass speak with a balanced clarity that totally complemented the higher brass, introducing an astonishing sense of space into the deeper notes of the orchestra.

The way in which Verdi treats the deepest of the low brass instruments in this work is not different in any significant way from the way in which he treats it in any of his other operas, from earliest to last. From a practical, performing point of view, therefore, since the instruments playing first, second and third trombones are going to remain constant in all but period orchestra performances, so should the lowest instrument. The imprecision of Italian terminology has already been noted, and Meucci's own statement that 'Verdi wrote for this instrument only in his last two works . . . and that its increasing use later was due to the practices adopted by orchestras and conductors' confirms the need for it to be used in works from the 1880s onwards. Since, therefore, earlier works by Verdi and others specifying cimbasso tend to utilize the instrument in a similar way to later works, so the same instrument should be used if in modern performances the same upper trombones (two tenors and a bass) play the other three parts.

One of the most striking instances of Italian slackness in terminology is found in Ponchielli's *La Gioconda,* premiered at La Scala in 1876. The score names the lowest of the brass 'Bombardone', the part prints 'Ophicleide', and the nature of the part puts it firmly into the category of cimbasso. (The two lower parts in the *banda* are termed 'Basso I' and 'Basso II' with 'Bombardino' above.)

*Photo: Brian Tarr*

Fig. 13.1. Sean O'Neil, Welsh National Opera, with Meinl-Weston cimbasso 41.

Another aspect which has been overlooked by musicologists, though seen as important by performers, is the direction in which the bell of the cimbasso faces. Whether used alongside valved or slide trombones the sound is projected in the same plane, thus making an additional contribution to the concept of four matching tone-qualities, and incidentally solving the problem of the tuba in the pit which can either be lost to the audience when facing through the proscenium arch into the stage area, or alternatively can distort sectional balance when facing outwards into the dress circle. My own reaction to playing in peformances of *Aida* on a Farnell cimbasso confirmed my impressions as a listener (B[34], 56-7). Verdi, of course, needed lessons from no-one in theatrical effect.

Until the 1980s performing practice outside Italy was totally the reverse of that deplored by Meucci, with the tuba being used for cimbasso parts, ophicleide parts and serpent parts indiscriminately. When in the 1970s I asked an Italian conductor about the type of instrument that played cimbasso parts (he was directing a production of *Il Pirata* in which I played the *serpentone* part on F tuba), he discussed the matter with his colleague, the word 'biscione' (serpent) ocurring several times in their conversation, before concluding: 'We use whatever we can get'. However there is some evidence that some twentieth-century Italian composers did occasionally (like Verdi) give serious consideration to the nature of the lowest of their brass. Otterino Respighi (1879-1936) stipulated 'B. Tuba' alongside 'Tromboni I e II, Trombone III' (a traditional Italian orchestral trombone section) in *Fontane de Roma* (1916). In *Pini di Roma* (1925) he included a Verdian section of '4 Tromboni'. Here, as in *Fontane*, the two lower parts are often in octaves, and the lowest descends as far as E', the deepest note of a three-valved B♭ contrabass trombone. The two different approaches were dictated by the inclusion in the fourth movement of *Pini* of a band of six 'buccine', representing Roman warriors marching beside 'I Pini della via Appia'. The 'buccini' are themselves represented by '2 Flicorni soprani in Si♭, 2 Flicorni tenori in Si♭, 2 Flicorni bassi in Si♭'. Like Verdi, in this instance Respighi wished to contrast the four trombones in the main orchestra with the flügel horns, baritones and euphoniums in the band.

However, the first stirrings of curiosity about the precise sounds composers had in mind when creating their works were becoming evident in the late 1950s. In 1959 Hans Kunitz designed a slide bass trombone in F for Otto Maenz, bass trombonist at the Berlin Komischen Oper. It had two valves for the left hand, conferring a potential range of up to four octaves from C' and facilitating fast passages. The *Cimbasso Bass Trombone* was manufactured by Alexander and described in detail by Gregory, who also prints a photograph (G[22], 96-97, pl. XIII). One of these instruments was bought by the Royal Liverpool Philharmonic Society and can be heard in its EMI recording of the overture to Verdi's *Nabucco*, contributing to the distinctive sound of four trombones in the chorale-like opening bars (Ex. 16.2). However, this was only an interim step, since in 1985 Josef Meinl of Neustadt an der Aich built a cimbasso for the Mannheim Oper. His instruments are now in use from Japan to the United States. Superbly made, the Meinl-Weston Cimbasso 41 is pitched in F (optionally Eb) with four rotary valves for the right hand and another for the left. Triggers are available for the first and second valves The bore is a generous 18.5 mm (comparable to many CC and BBb tubas) and the bell diameter 270 mm (Fig. 13.1).

Other makers have made cimbassi along similar lines. One of the most interesting is that by Derek Farnell of Manchester, built in Eb, the pitch with which most British tubists feel most comfortable, with four piston-valves and a thumb valve for the right hand. (Italian cimbassi are also sometimes made with piston-valves.) This instrument is described in detail in my article 'Final thoughts on the cimbasso', pt. 1 (B[34], 56-7). Other cimbassi have been made in more fanciful shapes, like the tuba-form model with forward-facing bell played by Stephano Ammannati (Fig. 13.3(b)). The appearance of the orchestra of the Academy of St Cecilia, Rome in the BBC Henry Wood Promenade Concert in the Royal Albert Hall on 12 August 1995 probably marked the first visit to the U.K. by an Italian orchestra including cimbasso.

In contrast to the finely-crafted output of makers like Sax, Červený and Mahillon, nineteenth-century Italian cimbassi seem to be deficient in airtightness and rich in intonation problems. Like the valved ophicleide, they beg the question of contemporary standards of performance and point to the impossibility of genuine authenticity in modern interpretations, short of a theatre where a largely tubercular audience listens to out-of-tune orchestral playing. Modern cimbassi are a delight to play and hear and it was not long before new uses were found for them. Typical of their utilization is the music composed by Patrick Doyle for the film *Mary Shelley's Frankenstein* in 1994. Here Doyle and his orchestrator Lawrence Ashmore contrast the broad, smooth sounds of four horns, two Wagner Tuben, euphonium and contrabass tuba with the more incisive timbres of four trumpets, three trombones and a cimbasso. All six tubists in the score of *Soldiers* (Joel Neely, 1998) were required to double on cimbasso. Heiko Triebener of the Bamberg Symphony Orchestra plays his cimbasso in the big band formed from its members.

The periodical *Das Orchester* now regularly includes Situations Vacant like: 'Eine Baßtuba mit Verpflichtung zur Kontrabaßtuba und Cimbasso' (O³). By the end of 1995 it was estimated that there were six *cimbassi* in the United Kingdom and there are now many more. 'Cimbasso' appeared for the first time as a heading in the *Musicians' Union London Branch Directory* in 1997-98. During the 1997 International Tuba-Euphonium Conference in Riva del Garda, Italy, cimbasso fanfares were played by an International Cimbasso Ensemble of ten players, from Italy, Germany, Hungary, Japan, U.S.A. and Australia.

Fig. 13.2
Manchester instrument-maker Derek Farnell testing his prototype five-valved
E♭ cimbasso.

Verdi's natural successor was Puccini. His *Messa da Gloria* of 1880, the graduation exercise at the end of his studies at the Istituto Musicale Pacini, Lucca, specified the three trombones and ophicleide normally found in Italian orchestras of the time. In his operas he stipulated four trombones. The last was *Turandot*, in 1926. Sometime during the following fifty years the general practice of substituting tuba for the lowest trombone crept in—except, it seems, for some Italian centres. Paradoxically, now that the rest of the world has rediscovered the correct instrument, there seem to be those in Italy who are recommending a return to the tuba.

(a)

(b)

*Photo: V. Andy Anders*

(c)

*Photo: Nicholas Perry*

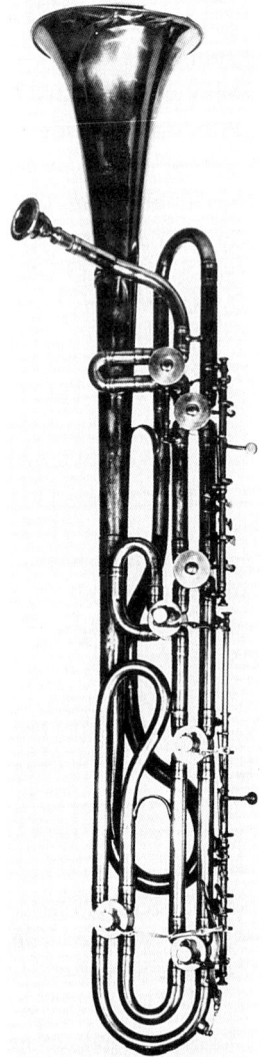

(d)

*Horniman Museum*
*& Gardens*

Fig. 13.3. Some types of cimbasso: (a) Alan Lumsden with three-valve BB♭ cimbasso by Maino & Orsi, Milan, late nineteenth-century; (b) Stephano Ammannnati with late twentieth-century Italian cimbasso; (c) early cimbasso with six finger-holes and three keys by Nicholas Perry, St Albans, 1988; (d) Bimbonifono in F by Bimboni, Florence, c. 1850.

*A blueprint for the future*

One problem relating to the designation 'cimbasso' remains: the correct realization of performances of early nineteenth-century works originally conceived with the upright bass horn in mind, an instrument which might now be called *early cimbasso* (cf. 'early clarinet') to avoid confusion. Until late 1998 it was known only through a small number of specimens in collections, but in the previous year Nicholas Perry, an instrument-maker from St Albans, fortuitously discovered several dismembered examples in store in a Continental museum. Having taken measurements he made a prototype which worked remarkably well. The majority of the notes were strong and clear in tone, not least because the thickness of the wood of the bassoon-like butt enabled him to experiment with the size and position of the tone-holes, boring them at angles more or less suiting the requirements of both the acoustic system and the player's fingers. Although its six finger-holes and three keys will be familiar to serpent-players, it is by no means simply another serpent, as the fingering-chart (Ex. 13.2) shows if compared with a

Ex. 13.2.   PRACTICAL FINGERING-CHART FOR EARLY CIMBASSO BY
NICHOLAS PERRY, ST ALBANS, 1998

serpent fingering-chart (Ex. 2.1). The practical early cimbasso fingering chart was developed from the three already known and published: two reprinted in M[31] [GSJ], 171-2 with, more bizarrely, another by Auguste Bertini published in London in 1830 with further editions in 1837 and 1849. This is described by Arnold Myers in an article in which he also reprints the chart (M[54], 135). There is evidence that the plates in this *New system for Learning, and Acquiring Extraordinary Facility on, All Musical Instruments* may well have been previously prepared for an Italian publication, but Bertini translates the names of the instruments into English—except for 'cimbasso'.

The instrument's clarity of tone is largely the result of the considerable proportion of narrow-bore tubing in the metal crook. With a total tuba-length of some 2510 mm, about 810 mm, or nearly one-third, is taken up by the crook which expands from a diameter of 12 mm at the point where the mouthpiece enters to 26 mm at the entry to the body of the instrument. The metal bell expands from 55 mm diameter where it leaves the wooden body to a flare diametere of 247 mm. The early cimbasso therefore possesses some trombone-like characteristics, marked by the relatively narrow internal profile of the wooden section and making it eminently suitable for its position alongside the trombones.

This instrument would certainly be suitable for use in performances by 'authentic' orchestras, but as a strong-toned bass instrument it could also be used in more mainstream musically-informed performances where the three trombone parts were perhaps all played on medium-bore tenors. An experiment along these lines at the 1999 Lacock Serpentarium, where Andrew van der Beek on cimbasso played extracts from the Italian repertoire (including that shown in Ex. 16.2) with Phil Humphries, Michèle Lomas and Clifford Bevan on trombones of this type, demonstrated the validity of this suggestion. While the serpent would be at a disadvantage in this context, the early cimbasso could have a great deal to offer, paralleling the modern valved cimbasso and contemporary (slide) trombone.

The sum total of evidence leads to the conclusion that, rather like a number of composers, the cimbasso went through three distinct periods in its career. In the first it was a bass horn; in the second, any brass instrument that could play the notes; in the third, a contrabass valve trombone in B♭. For modern performances with modern orchestral brass, the bulk of the repertoire might be played appropriately by the normal three trombones plus contrabass trombone.

The low brass requirements of Verdi, Puccini, Rossini and other Italian composers are further considered in Chapter XVI. Even today the variety found in Italian opera-house low brass sections tends to be greater than elsewhere. In the symphonic orchestra the tuba has been found since at least the beginning of the century, despite the Italian authorities' refusal to acknowledge the instrument's existence. Nonetheless, manufacturers like Kalison of Milan have actively worked at new designs and improved models to satisfy the requirements of players. Meanwhile an investigation of the Milan Conservatory by Mathez & Bonino (M[20], 54-71), from which the following information is taken, indicates shortcomings in the provision of tuition for low brass players.

The Conservatorio di Milano was established in 1808, under the influence of the Paris Conservatoire. The brass was taught solely by horn-players until 1881, although in 1864 the bombardon and ophicleide were amongst a number of brass instruments accorded the privilege of special classes. From 1882 the trumpet teacher also taught trombone, and although trombone was officially given its own class in 1965 the teachers were still mainly trumpet-players. Tuba is still not recognized by the administration, so teachers and students need to claim that they play bass trombone in order to carry out their activities legitimately. There is thus no reference to the tuba in the list of brass teachers at the Conservatory from 1808 to 1999.

The situation was aggravated by an Italian law of 1976 which banned state employees from holding more than one post. In consequence, players in the major subsidized orchestras are not allowed to teach in the conservatories. This apparently meets with the approval of Italian trades unions in their search for full employment. As a result, advanced students have either to take private lessons or, increasingly, study abroad. The present tubist in the prestigious La Scala, Milan orchestra is English: Brian Earl, who studied with Stuart Roebuck at the Royal Northern College of Music. At the Orchestra Sinfonica dell RAI di Milano (the Milan broadcasting orchestra), the tuba chair is occupied by the American Daryl Smith.

Verdi, a composer whose name has appeared with some frequency in the present chapter, was refused a place to study at the Milan Conservatory on the grounds that his piano technique was unconventional and that he was in any case too old: he was nineteen at the time. Perhaps the Conservatorio's decision not to recognize the tuba was a belated attempt to ingratiate itself with its most eminent student-that-never-was.

# CHAPTER XIV

## *The Tuba Outside the Orchestra*

Many slightly over-weight children who do not have a lot of spare
energy are very happy on the tuba . . .You do not need an agile
brain. The music is not difficult to read, it is repetitive and you rarely
have to play fast . . . Responsible, good-natured boys who are happy
belonging to a group can be content in band or orchestra playing
what seem like endless oompahs to an outsider.
— A. Ben-Tovim & D. Boyd *The Right Instrument for Your Child*

I remember playing a band transcription of the *New World
Symphony*, playing the bass parts. I never knew what I was
missing—it was marvelous. The orchestral tuba part consists of
fourteen notes but the band part is a different world.
—Arnold Jacobs, principal tubist Chicago Symphony Orchestra
1944-88, quoted in B. Frederikson *Arnold Jacobs: song and wind*

THE TUBA first came to the attention of a wider public during the 1950s: through
two events in 1954, Vaughan Williams's concerto and the signature tune to *Hancock's
Half Hour*; Bill Bell's recital LP of 1957; and the Hoffnung Music Festival of 1958.
In 1960 John Lanchbery gave it a wonderfully characteristic solo in his rescoring of
Hérold's *La Fille mal gardée* for the Royal Ballet.

## TUBA IN THE BAND

The tuba was conceived as a band instrument. The total number of models
currently available subdivides in the proportions EE♭ = 2; F = 4; CC = 5; BB♭ = 9,
with the 'deviant' British EE♭ available in the smallest range, orchestral F and CC
instruments in roughly twice the number, and U.S.A. school/wind band BB♭s in
the largest. The tuba first appeared in the Prussian Second Infantry Guard
Regiment in 1835, with a performance by Wieprecht's massed bands including
twelve Baß-Tubas in the presence of Berlioz shortly afterwards. Yet the Paris Opéra
retained the ophicleide for another forty years, and in 1887 Richter had to
commission a tuba for his London orchestra. Orchestral players, conductors and
composers seemed generally happy with what they had; few rushed to the nearest
tuba-builder when they heard of the instrument. Sometimes tuba parts would be
played on the ophicleide just as today ophicleide parts are played on the tuba.

In addition to Wieprecht's advocacy of his invention and its immediate adoption owing to his influential position, the tuba was taken-up in the German States for the simple reason that the ophicleide had not become widely known there. The double-bassoon, which was in quite common use as a band instrument, is not really suitable for use on the march. The tuba therefore fulfilled a long-felt want. In England, owing to an inclination to muddle through and the traditional lack of money available for music, army bands normally included serpents, bass horns—which were more suitable for carrying on the march—and ophicleides, which were tonally better but structurally impracticable for use in many of the conditions suffered by army bandsmen. Even in 1844 the Royal Artillery had no tubas, although the Grenadiers had at least one by 1848. Two years later the R.A. Band included four 'E flat Bombardons' and probably several Guards regiments, including the Grenadiers, had similar instruments. It is claimed that the tuba and baritone were introduced into the R.A. Band about 1846 from France by Collins, who was Master of the Band from 1845 to 1854.

French army bands had been reorganized in 1845, their new instrumentation consisting almost exclusively of Adolphe Sax's products, including saxhorns. It was easy to obtain these instruments in the U.K. as in 1846 Henry Distin became London agent for Sax. Not only were the military authorities anxious to re-equip their bands: under the influence of the touring Distin family and Jullien's provincial concerts members of the early brass bands were made aware of the saxhorns' possibilities.

In the United States the introduction of the tuba and development of the all-brass band occurred at roughly the same time as in England. Following bands of woodwind and brass, with generally an ophicleide or bass horn providing the lowest notes, the mid-1830s saw the establishment of several bands consisting entirely of brass instruments. The first was probably the Dodworth Band of New York which dispensed with woodwind in 1834, but similar developments occurred elsewhere in the United States. Manuscript music from the town band of Youngstown, Ohio, shows significant changes in instrumentation about 1850. An Eb keyed bugle superseded Eb clarinet as the lead instrument, with Eb tuba providing the bass. An Eb 'hibo corno' was also present, along with a Trombacello.

The *ebor corno* had been introduced in alto and tenor pitches by the Dodworths about the middle of the nineteenth century. L. J. Wagner (W[1], xi) points out that this was a definite Eb band, with thirty-nine of the fifty-five works in its repertoire pitched in that key. A high proportion of Eb instruments was characteristic of American bands from 1835 until the 1890s.

Allen Dodworth's 'bell-over-the-shoulder' instruments were patented in 1838, made to his design by Uhlmann of Vienna in considerable quantities and a wide range of sizes. Other European companies were also tempted to make them (presumably because of the potentially large American market), including J. Lecocq of Paris, but the enormous numbers required during the American Civil War (1861-65) encouraged their manufacture by native makers. Garofalo & Elrod illustrate instruments by Kummer & Schetelich, Baltimore; J. Lathrop Allen, Allen & Hall, G. Freemantle, Graves & Co. and E. G. Wright, all of Boston; John F. Stratton (who also manufactured for Harvey Dodworth and possibly William Hall of New York), Martin Pollmann & Co., Slater & Martin and Christian R. Stark in New York; Klemm & Brother and W. Seefeldt of Philadelphia; and Isaak Fiske of Worcester, Massachusetts. It has been estimated that there were in the order of 3,400 regimental bandsmen in the two armies, and although over-the-shoulder instruments were not used exclusively, OTS appears to have been the predominant conformation. A wide range of valves was fitted, and pitches ranged from Eb soprano to Eb bass. The former was the lead treble instrument, following on from the popularity of the Eb keyed bugle which had itself displaced the Eb clarinet. American bands thus had a generally higher tessitura than those in Europe, where Bb cornets generally carried the melody. BBb basses seem not to have been made in OTS shape, although there is an illustration of an Eb with a fourth valve lowering it to BBb (G[6,] 24). Considerations of size and weight must also have entered into this matter; resting on the ground, an Eb bass OTS instrument stood at shoulder height.

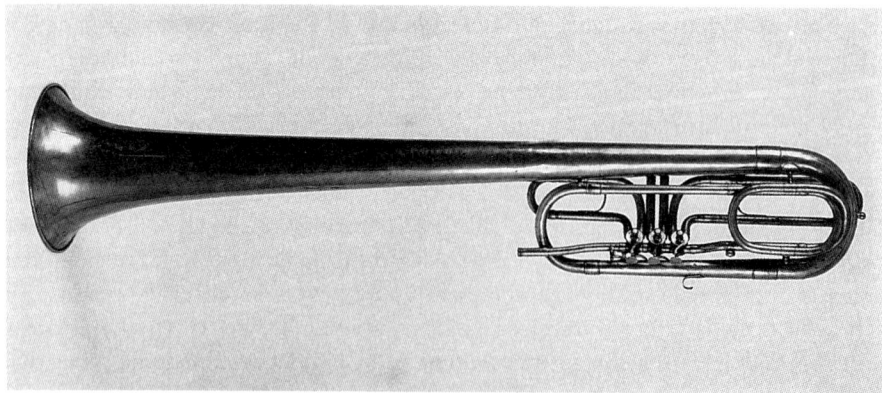

*Edinburgh University Collection of Historic Musical Instruments*         *Photo: Antonia Reeve Photography, Edinburgh*

Fig. 14.1. Contrabass saxhorn in Eb with three valves, over-the-shoulder model, by Klemm, Philadelphia, c. 1860.

Based on extant part-books, Garofalo & Elrod estimate the basic instrumentation of Civil War bands as follows:

1st & 2nd E♭ Cornet (saxhorn)
1st & 2nd B♭ Cornet (saxhorn)
1st & 2nd E♭ Alto Horn
1st & 2nd B♭ Tenor Horn (i.e., baritone)
B♭ Baritone (i.e., euphonium)
E♭ Bass
Snare drum, bass drum, cymbals

with possibly Solo Alto Horn, B♭ Bass, one or two flutes or clarinets. It is interesting to note the absence of trombones and also to compare the instrumentation above with that of the British brass band (see pages 430-1 below). Heritage Americana and the 4th U.S. Artillery Brass Band recreate the sights and sounds of that time at the present day.

The OTS design was intended exclusively for marching instruments and their inventor is on record as having stated their unsuitability for concert work. The appearance of Schreiber's graceful variant in 1867 may have been a reaction to the more utilitarian requirements of the Civil War which had ended two years earlier. In this design the bell was curved to allow it to face upwards, perhaps providing inspiration for the sousaphone thirty years later (see page 457 below). By 1875 OTS instruments were falling from favour, although in Britain Sir Michael Costa had backward-facing trombones made to counter his players' alleged 'over-blowing'.

In later years more American brass instrument manufacturers were established, including Henry Distin in 1877, though even 100 years afterwards Sear instruments were made in Belgium and Marzan in Switzerland. During the second half of the nineteenth century in America the all-brass ensemble gave way to mixed woodwind and brass bands, often of considerable size and variety of instrumentation.

If any one man was responsible for the establishment and development of the concert wind band it was Patrick Gilmore, but the most universally known name is that of John Philip Sousa. At the age of twenty-six he was appointed conductor of the U.S. Marine Band where he stayed for twelve years, leaving in 1892 to form his own band. He had very definite views on the capabilities of the tuba. 'The bass-tuba does all and more than a string bass can do, is richer, gives fuller and rounder harmonic basis for the volume of tone, and can be played on the march—which a string bass cannot' (S[30], 192). In 1917 he took charge of U.S. Navy bands at the

Great Lakes Naval Training Section. He was there for nearly two years, training bands for the navy and forming the Great Lakes Battalion Band of almost 300 players, including twenty-four tubas.

Over the years the instrumentation of military bands in each country has inevitably varied. It is not within the scope of this book to survey the development of these bands, but the part  played by the EE♭ bass is worthy of note. The contemporary British army 'concert-size' band of twenty-five players includes one EE♭ and one BB♭ bass, both playing from a concert pitch part written in the bass clef which exceptionally includes divisi passages. French bands also include instruments in these two pitches, written in the bass clef and transposed so that the key in which they are pitched is always thought of as C. Russian bands use BB♭ and EE♭ instruments, the EE♭ sometimes being called 'Middle Bass' since, as in the other bands, when not in unison with the deeper instruments it plays at the octave above. These, with the addition of Italy, seem to be the only countries where the BB♭ is not exclusively used in military bands although historically, of course, other pitches have been found. Kappey details those in British bands during the 1870s (see page 277 above) and in the United States the BB♭ was not available before its probable introduction by Harvey B. Dodworth, conductor of the Dodworth Band c. 1860-1890. The Austrians used basses in F at the beginning of the twentieth century and in the 1950s the Royal Artillery Band had a distinctive rank of eight BB♭s, plus just one EE♭.

In Britain the smaller three-valve E♭ instrument is more or less restricted to school bands and those where weight is a consideration (in marching), but the four-valve EE♭ is of some importance in the brass band. This unique organization has a rigidly-determined instrumentation laid down by the authorities responsible for promoting contests over a century ago. A handful of progressive bands has experimented with tenor cors, french horns, trumpets and additional trombones but for all practical purposes the standard contesting band is quite adequate. Part of a brass band score is reproduced in Ex. 6.6, but it may be of interest to list the officially stipulated numbers of players to each part:

One E♭ Soprano Cornet
Eight B♭ Cornets (three or four 'Solo'; one 'Repiano'; two 2nd; one or two 3rd)
One B♭ Flugel Horn
Three E♭ Tenor Horns ('Solo', 1st and 2nd)
Two B♭ Baritone (1st and 2nd)
Two B♭ Euphoniums (one part, almost exclusively in unison)
Two Tenor Trombones (1st and 2nd)
One Bass Trombone

Two EE♭ flat Basses (playing from the same part)
Two BB♭ flat Basses (playing from the same part)
Drums.

Although lacking in cylindrical brass tone this gives a versatile combination, rich and sonorous.

Fig. 14.2. Harpurhey & Moston Silver Prize Band leading a Sunday school procession in Rochdale Road, Harpurhey, Manchester at Whitsuntide 1947. From right to left, two Imperial BB♭ Basses and an Imperial E♭ Bass. Note the covers over the lower parts of the instruments (see page 187 above) and also the G bass trombone. The uniform jackets were scarlet . . . and my grandfather was eighty-four years old!

While rarely (though increasingly) exploiting the lower register, band tuba parts frequently make technical demands not found in the orchestra since much band music consists of transcriptions of orchestral works in which the tubas have to play notes originally given to bassoons, cellos and basses. On the other hand the band tubist is never expected to produce the volume of tone asked of his orchestral colleague who has, normally on his own, to support the weight of at least four horns, possibly four trumpets and three trombones. In consequence more of the band player's efforts can be spent on technique and fewer on tone production.

A tubist in a band of average attainment will normally use both a rather smaller mouthpiece and some vibrato, the former helping higher notes while inhibiting the production of a large tone which is not in any case required (pedal notes are seldom written in wind band parts, almost never in the brass band). Vibrato makes intonation less of a problem and, consciously or unconsciously, leads to a cantabile style of playing often described as a 'unique singing quality'.

Ex. 14.1

Greenwood: *Moments with Wagner*

Examples of band tuba parts have been intentionally restricted to the British brass band repertoire for a number of reasons. One is that at least as many demands are made on these mainly amateur players as on any other band tubists who may be full-time service bandsmen or have the advantage of high-quality tuition in, say, a college band. My second reason is that there have been too few opportunities for musicians outside the brass band world to discover the types of things that bandsmen customarily play. And the third reason, allied to this, is the unfamiliarity of most composers and arrangers with their system of notation. Ex. 6.6 was given in both the original notation and at concert pitch, but the examples in this chapter are shown only in their original form. With the exception of the bass trombone all brass band instruments are treated as transposing. Thus they all have identical fingering, a convention which began as an adaptation of saxhorn notation (see Sax's 1845 French Patent 1592) and was subsequently applied to the saxophones. It later proved its value in facilitating the rapid transfer of players from instrument to instrument when emergencies occurred in the normal brass band environment, frequently cut off from the remainder of civilization. This is still valid today, as the schools where so many brass bands are found in a similar way provide examples of isolated units.

Ex. 14.1 is taken from a classic nineteenth-century selection entitled *Moments with Wagner* by the renowned band arranger John A. Greenwood (1876-1953). In this arrangement of the 'Grand March' from *Tannhäuser* the basses have a nineteen-bar passage transcribed from the orchestral bassoon, cello and double-bass parts, showing how necessary it is to have more than one player to each band tuba part if continuous passages originally allocated to strings are not to be broken by the player's need to breathe.

Ex. 14.2

Ball: *Tournament for Brass*

Ex. 14.3

Leidzén: *Sinfonietta*

The more recent example by Eric Ball (1903-1986) demonstrates the possibilities available from using the two types of instrument, either in unison or octaves, and another characteristic of modern writing—a solo EE♭ bass which is quite sufficient to support the entire band in quieter passages and also provides a contrast to the more solid sound of four instruments in unison (Ex. 14.2).

The *Sinfonietta* by Eric Leidzén (1894-1962) indicates how far from the oompah tuba brass band writing has progressed without leaving a tonal idiom (that has been a later development still). Ex. 14.3 shows the euphoniums joining the basses in a magnificent wodge of sound.

## TUBA IN THE SMALL ENSEMBLE

Although it has been assumed that the tuba ensemble began in Britain, with some works by the brass band composers Kenneth Cook and Eric Ball written in the 1940s for a quartet of two Eb and two BBb basses, there is evidence that tuba quartets existed earlier in the century. Hubert Shergold, who played flügel horn with Foden Motor Works Band from 1912 to 1963, recollected that when he joined the band every member was in a quartet, nine in all. 'We even had the four basses in a quartet' (T[4], 27-28). These ensembles competed in the popular quartet contests (which are still held) and also helped out other bands from time to time.

All subsequent development has taken place in the United States, culminating in mammoth gatherings of perhaps 100 tubists and euphoniumists. The tuba ensemble is scarcely likely to rival television as an entertainment for the masses, but it undoubtedly fulfils an important didactic function. This is yet another example of the British genius for conceiving an idea and leaving it to someone else to carry it through. As long ago as 1923 the low-note fanatic Havergal Brian wrote the following after adjudicating the National Brass Band Contest at Crystal Palace and in anticipation of massed performances of arrangements of works by Wagner and Berlioz:

The low Bb basses in the brass band correspond with the low F tuba in the orchestra, and there are two or three of them in each band so that, massed, you would have some thirty-three to fifty double bass tubas. Counting the Eb basses, euphoniums, baritones, corresponding with tubas in higher registers, you would have a complete tuba band of one hundred and forty-six instruments, plus forty-eight trombones, forty-eight horns, and about two hundreed and fifty cornets, ranging from flugel to soprano in Eb. A combination like this has unlimited possibilities, muted or unmuted (B[53], 161).

The standard brass quintet of two trumpets, french horn, trombone and tuba has a considerable repertoire and can stand alongside the other generally-accepted ensembles of single-genus instruments. The first brass quintet of consequence was the Philip Jones Brass Ensemble, formed in 1951. It is difficult now to realise quite how revolutionary the idea of brass chamber music was at the time. Jones recounts how John (Tug) Wilson, the tubist from 1957 to 1966, found the absence of a conductor disconcerting when making the group's first recording to include tuba in 1965 (EMI 7EG 8960: *Brass*) (M$^{24}$, 22). Tug was one of the country's leading brass-players, a sometime member of the crack Royal Air Force Central Band and professor of euphonium at Kneller Hall before playing with the London Philharmonic Orchestra for many years. His playing, as heard on this recording, is extremely precise and very agile, the tone clear rather than solid.

Much of the brass quintet repertoire is of dubious quality, but the ensemble's potential has been displayed in a range of idioms. Although limited in tonal contrast it has a valid *raison d'être* both for the listener, to whom the capabilities of the orchestral brass can be conveniently demonstrated, and for the player, to whom it is the equivalent of the string-player's quartet. There are many similar brass combinations including tuba and sometimes euphonium. The brass band quartet, of long standing, consists of two cornets, Eb horn and euphonium. There have been opportunities for many years for quartets of these instruments to contest, and more recently they have formed the basis of effective group teaching methods.

A unique quintet was formed in 1989 by members of the Suhl Philharmonic, Germany. This consisted of the orchestra's four horn-players along with tubist Dorothee Kretschmann. Sadly no details of their repertoire are available. Probably more viable is the brass tentet: horn, four trumpets, three trombones, tuba and percussion. This is a miniature band which has the potential to cope with a range of styles and, at professional level, provide a full ensemble at an economical cost.

When the composer knows his idiom sufficiently well, the all-tuba ensemble is capable of a surprising degree of dramatic expression. *Liberation of Sisyphus* by the American tubist and composer John Stevens (1990) sets a virtuoso solo tuba against an octet of four euphoniums and four bass tubas in a work that is both remarkable and accessible.

## TUBA AS SOLOIST

The discographer Frank Andrews has compiled details of recordings by British brass bands from the first cylinder records in 1903 to the arrival of the long-playing record in 1960 (A$^{14}$). Amongst many hundreds of recordings there is not a single example of a tuba or bass solo. When, therefore, on his seminal album *Bill Bell and his Tuba* (Golden Crest LP CR 4027), this distinguished player included Herman Hupfeld's 'When Yuba Plays the Rumba on the Tuba Down in Cuba' the effect on unsuspecting listeners in 1957 must have been remarkable. Arnold Jacobs, when tubist with the Indianapolis Symphony Orchestra, gave the first performance of Arcady Dubensky's *Fantasy on a Popular Folk Song for Tuba and Symphony Orchestra* as early as 11 December 1938. Dubensky had been given the theme by Vincenzo Vanni, tubist with the New York Symphony Orchestra, for the low brass section of which he later composed his *Concerto Grosso for Three Trombones and Tuba* (F[21], 19). Neither work seems to have become firmly established in the repertoire—a characteristic fate of low brass features with orchestra.

The first 'serious' tuba solo was the Sonata for bass tuba and piano by the German composer Paul Hindemith, the last of a series of sixteen sonatas for solo instruments with piano accompaniment initiated in 1935. Hindemith's belief that music should be practical and useful was influenced by *Gebrauchsmusik*—the pre-Nazi philosophy of socially-relevant composition. There was certainly room for something to stimulate tubists to higher thoughts, but solo music did not begin to appear in any quantity until the late 1960s. Since then the flood-gates have remained jammed firmly open.

There was no concerto for tuba and orchestra until Ralph Vaughan Williams provided a new work for a concert in June 1954 marking the golden jubilee of the London Symphony Orchestra. John Fletcher points out that VW had intended for some time to write a tuba concerto, and it has to be said that very often sections of the tuba parts in his orchestral works approach a concerto level of difficulty.

Fletcher also states:

> . . . during the performance VW was visibly chuckling to himself for much of the time. Beneath the very English sense of humour lie some perfectly serious intentions. I think the VW concerto remains the best example of the tightrope act the tuba has to perform between the sad, melancholy, neglected monster on the one hand and the absurd non-musical results which are likely to occur if you give it its head (F[18], Spring 76, 13).

Fletcher's reference to the English sense of humour is pertinent: it seems to have been overlooked that the opening figure of the first movement of the concerto is virtually identical to that central to Vaughan Williams's 'romance on a poem by George Meredith' for solo violin and orchestra, *The Lark Ascending,* of 1914. What larks!

The tubist who first performed the concerto, Philip Catelinet (1910-96) became a celebrity, considerably to his surprise. He had played tuba with the BBC Theatre Orchestra and euphonium in the BBC Wireless Military Band, becoming a member of the Philharmonia and then the LSO after World War II. This versatility obviously contributed to his ability to respond so successfully to a challenge never previously presented to a tuba-player. There are indications in the manuscript score (in the British Library) of discussions between composer and soloist, resulting in the addition of a number of slurs in the faster passages and the excision of the higher notes in the cadenza, reinstated as an *ossia* in later editions of the work. But Catelinet's achievement in coping with the contrasting demands of speed and lightness in the outer movements, the high-register cantabile melody in the slow movement and the extended overall range deserves to be commemorated.

While a landmark in terms of tuba repertoire, this event may have been equally important in initiating a continuing expansion in concepts of the nature of the tuba. In two articles in *Sounding Brass* considering 'Is the tuba really a solo instrument?' (F[18], Spring 1976, 13,19; Summer 1976, 54, 63) John Fletcher discussed the phenomenon from his position as the performer whose own recording of the work has never been surpassed and whose own breadth of vision and objectivity continue to make tuba devotees pause and rethink.

Readers are strongly recommend to search out Fletch's articles: they are now widely available, reprinted in Philip Jones's compilation *A Celebration: John Fletcher, tuba extraordinary* (see bibliography). Sales of this book also benefit the John Fletcher Trust Fund. Here we find this remarkable man admitting, in 1976, that the sound of the tuba 'can be difficult to take seriously'; identifying 'the tuba explosion'; confessing to being bewildered by the American tuba scene, where he finds his own reservations about the tuba being ignored. 'This is a terrific example of positive thinking achieving results—the result being that all over the USA there are kids playing the tuba to a standard undreamed of in this country, and all reconciled to the prospect of never having a professional position'.

This state of affairs he identifies as the root of the numerous solo recitals and vast amount of solo compositions for tuba. '. . . I have said many times, at the risk of sounding snotty and ungrateful, that most of it sounds to me, to have been written by tuba players for tuba players to play to tuba players.'

Lest it be thought that these were the ramblings of a single, isolated, albeit peerless, tubist, it is also worth noting the comments of Arnold Jacobs, living in the midst of it:

However, I love to hear tubas, but I still say that when you put a tuba player in front of an audience, they will enjoy a great artist playing whether it is a tuba or any other instrument. Whether they would like to hear it constantly is another story. I leave that wide open for another generation (H[15], 167).

Dear John, how would you have reacted to the appearance of *The Tuba Source*

*Book* in 1996, with its lists of some 1,900 solos for tuba with piano, over 100 for tuba with orchestra, more than 1,100 for multiple tubas? And each quarter *TUBA Journal* carries reviews of additions to this ever-swelling list.

In the second part of his article Fletcher mentions that during the 1975-76 season he had played three concertos with the LSO. Of these, two have been lost in the mists of time and only one, by Edward Gregson, has established a place in the regular repertoire, not least because it is sensible, enjoyable for listeners and now exists in versions with brass band (the original), wind band, orchestra, brass ensemble and piano. Other concertos are longer, or phenomenally difficult, or make extraordinary technical demands, or are pleasant and forgettable. I must confess that I rather denigrated the VW in the first edition of this book, but now I accept that it is still as good as any subsequently composed ... and better than most.

Performers currently find themselves in something of a quandary so far as expectations of what might next be produced are concerned. While Hindemith's Sonata is difficult (particularly for the accompanist!) it is not impossible and, as in the Vaughan Williams and Gregson concertos, there are melodies that can be understood by the listener. Precedents were perhaps set in works for other solo instruments and orchestra by Mozart, Beethoven, Tchaikovsky and Alban Berg. A different trend appeared in Harrison Birtwistle's *The Cry of Anubis*, 'part concerto, part tone poem', for solo tuba and orchestra, premiered in 1995 by Owen Slade and the London Philharmonic. The solo part is not particularly difficult—it is said that Slade mastered it in a week—and it is not particularly satisfying, for either the player or the audience. The idiom is not especially tubaistic, and it is unlikely that a piano reduction could be made to enable more players to get to know it. This confusion of purpose is reflected in the piece of doggerel by Stephen Pruslin printed at the front of the score which utterly fails to differentiate between the two meanings of 'tuba', in the Roman trumpet and Wieprecht invention connotations. In contrast, it is significant that Rodney Newton's demanding but attractive *Capriccio* has quickly found itself in the Grade 8 examination syllabus.

As *The Tuba Source Book* demonstrated and *TUBA Journal* continues to confirm four times a year, there is no shortage of composers keen to write for tuba. The reason is simple: a composer promised a performance of his next composition will write for whatever medium is required. The composer may in fact be particularly anxious to write for the instrument, since unlike the piano or string quartet repertoires the standards of comparison are not particularly high: there is no Beethoven or Bartók to aim to match or surpass.

Ronald Davis, who teaches tuba and euphonium at the University of South Carolina, considered these and related matters in a ground-breaking article in *TUBA Journal*. In 'The Historian's Perspective', his first sub-heading read 'We are serious artists who have chosen this instrument', his second, 'Admit it, tubas are funny'. Not having been lynched, he continued to ponder the question of tuba players themselves:

> If we take a survey and have people describe tuba players in general, what would appear on that list? Hopefully 'artists' or 'musicians' would be suggested more often than in the past, showing that the organization [TUBA] has been successful in its mission. Other possible descriptions: easy going, laid back, supportive, share a genuine camaraderie' (D[3], 33).

His assessment is borne out from an unlikely source. One of the initial intake at the Royal Military School of Music, Kneller Hall, in 1859 described his lessons with Thomas Sullivan:

> He welcomed one with a smile and generally had a little joke to crack or tale to tell which made the lesson all the brighter . . . He also took the beginners on clarinet—in fact nothing came amiss to him, for he was as much at home teaching on the trombone or bombardon as the clarinet or violin (B[40], 60).

There is little evidence of consideration being given to these matters between John Fletcher in 1976 and Ronald Davis twenty years later. But I am certain that Wieprecht got it right: there is nothing more satisfying than providing a sympathetic foundation part on tuba. A tubist who gets more pleasure from playing a tune than contributing the two descending notes between the opening phrases of 'Nessun Dorma' should perhaps consider moving to a different instrument.

## TUBA IN JAZZ

In an account of a concert by the Gil Evans Band in *Melody Maker* Martha Sanders Gilmore wrote:

> Howard Johnson was phenomenal on bass trumpet, baritone sax and tuba. I've never heard so many fast notes spew forth from that instrument which has been known to bring up the rear of circus parades . . . sighing orchestral cushions deployed by French horns and bath-tub bound tuba sounds (M[28], 21).

That was in 1972. The part played by the tuba in earlier chapters of the short but fast-moving history of jazz was generally less impressive.

Following the end of the Civil War the pawnshops of the south were crammed with ex-Confederate army band instruments, many of which came to be used in the first New Orleans marching bands. This was the pre-jazz period, the bandsmen playing 'by ear', the germ of jazz being sown in the rhythmic and melodic styles they found natural. At the turn of the century the famous *New Orleans Blue Book* of ragtime 'standards' contained parts for tuba but they were in unison with, and probably alternative to, the string bass parts. The first jazz bands, in the early 1900s, seem to have included a string bass, the bull-fiddle, rather than the tuba. The literature has few references to this aspect of jazz history, but apart from the marching bands, which included brass bass, euphonium and on some occasions one or two alto horns, the tuba was rarely found in jazz until the 1920s. Then it was usually a sousaphone (sometimes a helicon) which helped the player provide the crisp attack necessary to the instrument's rhythmic function, for with the exception of an occasional solo break it played a purely oompah part. The playing of Cyrus St Clair, a member of bands directed by Wilbur de Paris, Charlie Johnson and Clarence Williams in the 1920s and 30s, stands out through his mastery of the instrument and his confidence in restricting its contribution to the notes necessary for a musicaly-conceived rhythmic bass part.

The Paul Whiteman Orchestra (1920-52) was much photographed with its two sousaphones spectacularly placed on each side of the band. One of the players doubled on string bass but Whiteman's tuba parts, mainly by his arranger Ferdé Grofé, could equally well have been played on anything low enough to cope. Page after page of undistinguished oompah, now and then a more interesting bar in a modulatory passage, but then back to two-in-a-bar.

In the big dance era of the 1920s and 1930s this remained the instrument's sole function. There was undoubtedly a visual attraction in the huge bell of the sousaphone which reared over the 'orchestra' like a mammoth wind-up gramophone horn, and this possibly accounted for its widespread use in night-club and hotel bands of the time. It disappeared from jazz proper during this period, to reappear in the Dixieland revival of the 1940s, some time after the advent of 'swing' which drove it from the dance bands. 'Traditional' jazz bands since then have often associated the tuba with banjo in their rhythm sections (alternatively double-bass and guitar, depending upon the period and sound of their choice). Many front-line players prefer the two-beat rhythm of the one or the four-beat rhythm of the other type of section (Ex. 14.4).

During the late 1940s the tuba began to appear in a very different role in jazz of a very different kind. Feather suggests that Bill Barber was probably the first tubist to play modern jazz. He worked with Claude Thornhill, who had introduced the french horn to jazz in 1941, and Miles Davis, who included the tuba in *Birth of the*

Ex. 14.4

Black: *When the Saints go Marchin' in*

*Cool* recorded in 1949. The others in the nine-piece group were french horn, trumpet, trombone, alto and baritone saxes with a rhythm section of piano, bass and drums. But to many the most striking early modern jazz tuba sounds resulted from the partnership of Miles Davis and Gil Evans, with the magic of *Miles Ahead* (five trumpets, flügel horn, two french horns, four trombones and tuba; flute, clarinet, bass clarinet, alto sax, bass and drums) and their wonderful version of *Porgy and Bess*. The tuba was treated as an instrument in its own right, related to the french horn, capable of playing quickly or slowly, a member of the brass section not the rhythm section . . . a partner in 'sighing orchestral cushions'.

Gil Evans has continued to use a tuba alongside the other mellow brass with, since 1966, the phenomenal Howard Johnson to play it. Through his lips the instrument has even achieved a solo role, passages like the lead in *Struttin' with some Barbecue* or improvised solos as in *Thoroughbred* confirming its status. Johnson himself has led several groups, the first, Substructure, initiated in 1968 with Jack Jeffers, Morris Edwards, Dave Bargeron and Bob Stewart. His 1990s group Gravity (with Bob Stewart, Joe Daly and Earl McIntyre) demonstrated his continuing enthusiasm. Pre-eminent in liberating the tuba from its antideluvian jazz functions, he is also a multi-instrumentalist, one of few to play both tuba and flügel horn.

Stylistically somewhat different, the Tubajazz Consort led by Harvey Phillips (tuba) and Rich Matteson (euphonium) made its initial appearance at the First International Brass Congress in Montreux in 1976 and subsequently did a great deal to encourage student tubists to venture into the world of jazz.

There were few discernible developments in the use of brass in jazz during the last quarter of the twentieth century and the 1970s were in many ways a high-water mark in writing for jazz tuba. Ex. 14.6 shows the last four bars of 'To Lady Mac: In Memory', a work by Michael Gibbs where the tuba is used with flügel horn, two soprano saxes and a new partner, the electric piano. The movement (from his *Lady Mac* suite) is slow and free, and it is notable that although the high tessitura is quite possible on a large instrument in the relaxed environment of Gibbs's music it would be far more difficult to play in a symphonic context.

Ex. 14.5

Runswick: *The Generals of Islamabad*

Jazz composers like the Canadian Kenny Wheeler and the British Alan Cohen and Darrell Runswick have all made effective use of the tuba. Ex. 14.5 shows the opening bars of Runswick's *The Generals of Islamabad*, a rhythmic part played absolutely solo by the tuba which is gradually joined by the other instruments

Ex. 14.6

Tpt. 1
Flg. 1
mf
Tpt. 2
Flg. 2
mf
1
Sopr.
Saxes
2
mf
mf
Tuba
mf
Vc.
p
(F Triad)
Gtr.
mp
Bass Gtr.
mf
(ad lib. etc.)
Bass
mp
Light bells - sparsely
Perc.
Elec.
Piano

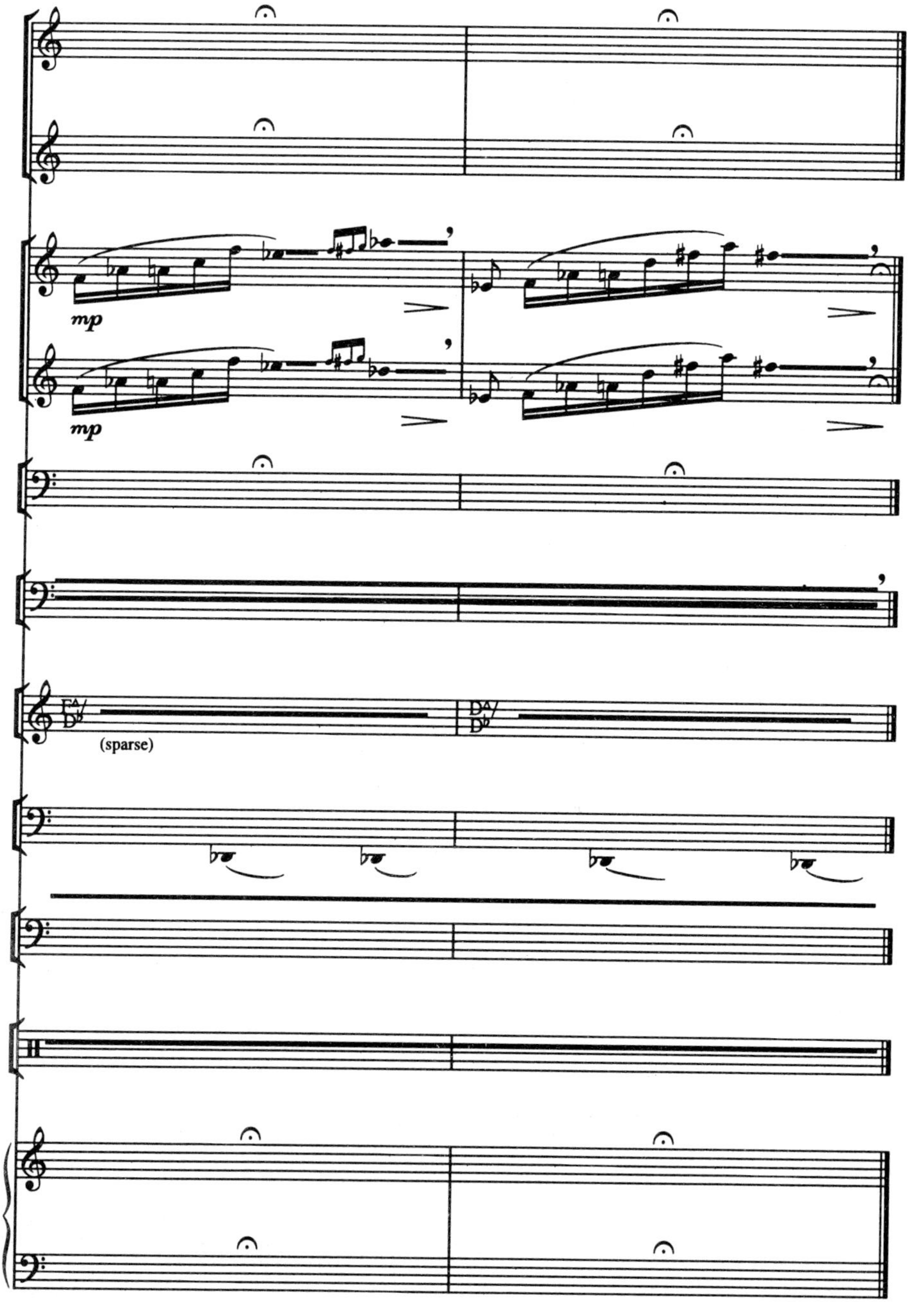


Gibbs: 'To Lady Mac : In Memory' (*Lady Mac* suite)

as the passage is repeated. The Swiss keyboard player, composer and bandleader George Gruntz, formed a big band with an exceptional emphasis on the more mellow brass in the late 1980s. The trombone section was replaced by french horn, two euphoniums and tuba (Howard Johnson, who also doubled on bass clarinet).

In jazz some individuals have shown an inclination to double, mainly on another bass instrument. Pops Foster (1892-1969) is known mainly as a New Orleans-style string bass player, but he also took up tuba in the 1920s. John Kirby (1908-1952) conversely changed from tuba to bass on joining the Fletcher Henderson Band in 1930. Currently the German free jazz exponent Peter Kowald plays both these instruments in addition to alphorn. The Canadian Ashley Slater has sought to extend parameters, playing both tenor and bass trombones and contributing tuba to bands led by Carla Bley, Andy Sheppard and, during the 1980s, London-based Loose Tubes. His funk band Microgroove was formed around a tuba bass. French tubist Michel Godard has ventured into world musics. One of three CDs on the Enja label, *Loose Wires,* includes a version of John Coltrane's 'Spiritual'; on the other two discs he is joined by oud-player Rabih Abou-Khalil.

There was an unexpected appearance of several members of the tuba family when the singer Tori Amos chose to use a brass group as backing in the mid-1990s. Tuba, euphonium, E♭ horn, flügel horn and trumpet doubling flügel provided a balanced and mellifluous ensemble to support the vocals and add instrumental passages. A CD issued in 1996, *Boys for Pele,* includes one track, 'Talula', where the group appears. On two others, 'Mr Zebra' and 'Putting the Damage on', the accompaniment is provided by nothing less than the entire Black Dyke Mills Band.

These are essentially legitimate ways of using the instrument. It was not through the demands of jazz composers but through those of the avant-garde that the tuba's extra-musical potential began to be exploited. The American alto sax-player Henry Threadgill has always shown an inclination towards avant-garde techniques and in the early 1990s his interest in unusual instrumentation led to the formation of the Very Very Circus. This group included two tubas (Marcus Rojas and Edwin Rodriguez) along with trombone, two guitars, drums and Threadgill on reeds.

## TUBA AND THE AVANT-GARDE

The tuba has been a favourite instrument with avant-garde composers ever since Berlioz. There have always existed things the tuba could do which had not been asked of it before. We have seen its potentially large range and its agility, both of which made the instrument an attractive proposition to composers seeking new sounds.

One of the technical difficulties presented by composers from Berg and Webern onwards results from the intervals between adjacent notes in atonal music. It is not so much their extent but their nature—augmented, diminished, inconceivable—which causes problems. Owing to its wide bore, notes on the tuba are easily bent, made to sound flat if approached from too low or sharp if from too high. It is therefore necessary to hear the note being approached before actually playing it (a problem found also on the french horn but not to anything like the same extent on trumpet and trombone where the cylindrical tubing tends to bring into line a note vibrated slightly slow or fast by the lips). It is difficult to auralize an extended and unusual interval.

Much avant-garde music requires the brass to be muted, but allowance should be made for the time taken to insert and remove the mute since the tuba often has to be lowered to the floor to allow the player to reach above the bell. This operation takes at least ten seconds. Gradual movement of the mute while playing is also precluded by this requirement. Since it is easy to bend notes it is not difficult to produce glissandi with the assistance of partially depressed valves. Kissing the mouthpiece and speaking or singing through the instrument are particularly effective owing to the capacious profile and gradually-opening wide bell. It should however be remembered that these factors give less distortion than in many other instruments and tubists not committed to the idiom may exploit this advantage. Working the valves without playing can also give interesting percussive effects, particularly piston-valves, but demands upon the player to strike his instrument will result in his using an instrument meriting that sort of treatment.

The English composer John White played tuba with the London Gabrieli Brass Ensemble for a time in the 1970s so there is an awareness of its practical potential and the problems to be avoided in his numerous compositions for the instrument. Cornelius Cardew (1936-81) composed a work for tuba and cello entitled *Machine*. Using a number square and chess moves it takes over four hours in performance. That a composition can utilize contemporary idioms and yet still grip an audience is demonstrated by Maurizio Kagel's *Mirum* of 1965, in which the tubist also needs to declaim. (Kagel refers here to the *Tuba Mirum*, or last trumpet, while cleverly managing to avoid the use of the contentious word 'tuba'!—cf. page 439 above.)

Daniel Perantoni has published a comprehensive list of special effects (P[9], 24-7). They include playing on the mouthpiece without the instrument and on the instrument without the mouthpiece; holding the mouthpiece, cup away from the player, at a slight distance from the mouthpipe entry and blowing into the shank; blowing into the instrument without producing tone, sometimes however giving the effect of rising or falling pitch; playing with the main-slide removed; playing with valve(s) partially depressed; and varying the rate of vibrato.

The most puzzling instruction found, for example in works by Siegmeister and Tansman, is 'Bells Up'.

## TUBA ON RADIO, STAGE AND IN FILM

In Britain the tuba regularly reached its widest audience from 1954 when radio listeners tuned in for their weekly episode of *Hancock's Half Hour*. The theme tune, by Wally Stott, opened with unaccompanied leaping tuba, a part played by Jim Powell (on, of course, F tuba). Since that highspot the instrument's radio appearances have been less frequent.

Appearances as part of the action in the theatre are also rare. A handful of plays in which sousaphones formed part of the visual delights comes to mind, all of them disastrous failures, although the same cannot be said of the musical *Barnum* (Cy Coleman, 1981) in which John Elliott not only played sousaphone but simultaneously rode a unicycle (Fig. 15.6(b). Alternatively the tuba tends to appear in surreal contexts like Tom Stoppard's *After Magritte* (1970), summarized as follows in a review of a 1999 production:

Here ballroom dancer Mr Harris, his wife and his tuba-playing mother are interrogated by Inspector Foot of the Yard about a non-existent crime while arguing over the identity of a one-legged footballer with a tortoise under his arm (C[39], 60).

However, in the early days of gramophone recording tubists were in great demand. It was much easier to record brass and woodwind than strings and this led to the use of bands rather than orchestras even where the original was an orchestral work or a soloist had to be accompanied. Tubas and euphoniums found themselves playing double-bass and cello parts, but the tuba had a distinct disadvantage at a time when all the instruments had to play directly into one or more gigantic horns aimed horizontally toward the players. Attempts to use actual string instruments led to their being equipped with miniature horns acting like gramophone transcription systems in reverse. The tuba was fitted with a recording bell, facing towards the recording horns (Fig. 11.2). These bells, still available, are normally removable as they increase the overall height of the instrument considerably, a factor to be borne in mind when portability is in question, and there are in any case occasions when the player will prefer to substitute a normal upwards-facing bell.

It was not until after World War II that with the interest in 'new sounds', shared by jazzmen, there came a general awareness that the voice of the tuba had a distinctive character. Film composers began to use it soloistically, as suitable accompaniment to the kitchen-sink films popular at that time. But it has also been featured with more awareness of its unique qualities—in films like *The French Mistress* (John Addison, 1960), *It's a Mad, Mad, Mad, Mad World* (Ernest Gold, 1963) and cartoons by Disney and others. Its voice was also heard when an atmosphere of fantasy or the grotesque needed to be evoked. In this context, Miklos Rozsa's score for *The Golden Voyage of Sinbad* (Columbia Pictures, 1973) is outstanding: the tuba plays an important part in the sequence of fencing skeletons regarded as seminal by many film historians.

Despite the new possibilities brought by advances in digital techniques for the manipulation of recorded sound, many composers still prefer to achieve their effects acoustically. While the score of *The Day the Earth Stood Still* (Bernard Herrmann, 1951) demanded no fewer than five tubas, *Soldiers* (Joel Neely, 1998) used three antiphonal brass choirs, a total of eighteen french horns (each player doubling Wagner Tuba), twelve trumpets, twelve trombones and six tuba-players doubling cimbassi. Tuba devotee John Williams made a breakthough in using the instrument as a type of *recitativo* solo voice in *Close Encounters of the Third Kind* (1977).

Less to be expected was the tuba's adoption by arrangers of pop music. It is, of course, an essential provider of oompahs, often doubled nowadays by bass guitar in unison, each contributing something of its own quality to the resulting timbre. But there are many examples of its use in numerous albums and television commercials. American west coast practice is often for the tuba player to double on contrabass trombone, a sensible idea from the point of view of embouchure, offering increased possibilities to orchestrators of studio music. For the fourth trombone (generally bass) to double on tuba has been accepted for many years in the sphere of theatre and film. Frederick Loewe's *My Fair Lady* (1956) is probably the best-known example, but more recently *Les Misérables* and *Miss Saigon* (Claude-Michel Schönberg, 1980 and 1989) have been scored in the same way. Less usual is the demand for tubist to double string bass, as in the musical *Chicago* (John Kander, 1975).

There have been occasions when the tuba has had a visual, as well as an aural, presence. Gary Cooper plays the title role in the film *Mr Deeds Goes to Town* (directed by Frank Capra in 1936). During the trial which forms the conclusion of the film, evidence of his alleged insanity includes playing the tuba, writing poetry and chasing fire-engines. In his defence he claims: 'Everybody does silly things to help them think. Well, I play the tuba.'

Inevitably, he is found not guilty.

# CHAPTER XV

## *Helicons, Sudrephones, the Duplex and other Exotica*

> Way back when I was with the Marines they used a helicon
> tuba wound around the body. I disliked it for concert work,
> because the tone would shoot ahead and be too violent. I
> suggested to the manufacturer that we should have an upright
> bell of large size so that the sound would diffuse over the
> entire band like the frostiness on a cake!
> —John Philip Sousa *Marching Along* (1928)

THERE are some interesting and important variants of the tuba family which need to be included in a comprehensive survey. Helicons and Antoniophones are tubas made in unusual shapes, Sudrephones valved bugle-horns with an attachment to change the quality of sound, Wagner Tuben, cornons, cornophones, tenor cors and mellophones resulted from the cross-breeding of valved bugle-horns with another brass family and duplex instruments were the twin-belled offspring of a similar union, while Saxotrombas and Kornett-instrumente were both cross-bred and in helicon shape.

## THE HELICON

The form of the helicon (Fig. 15.1) follows that of the Roman *buccina*, the bell resting on the player's left shoulder and the main tubing passing beneath the right arm. It is generally thought to have been invented in Russia about 1845 and was patented in western Europe by Ignaz Stowasser of Vienna in 1848 (Austrian Patent 5338), although in 1846 Giuseppe Pelitti of Milan had made his first rotary-valved helicon-shape *Pellitone*, also covered by an Austrian patent. Since both Vienna and Milan were part of the same empire it is interesting to speculate upon the significant difference between Stowasser's and Pelitti's instruments. Surprisingly, there was a CC helicon in the Vienna Opera orchestra from 1862-75 (Z[4, 49]).

Tubas built in helicon-form added to the comfort of marching bandsmen, particularly those of a tender age (Fig. 15.2) and those in service bands (Table 15.1). They were found in abundance in Britain: the 2nd Battalion, Royal Scots had two about 1890 and the 1st Battalion, Queen's Own Cameron Highlanders had one about the same time. There was a helicon in the band of the 2nd Battalion, Royal East Kent Regiment in 1899 , while the 2nd Battalion, Essex Regiment had no tubas but four helicons at the turn of the century. The 2nd Battalion, Gordon Highlanders took their helicons to India in 1907, in 1909 the 1st Battalion, Leicestershire Regiment had two helicons, and about 1910 the Royal Sussex Regiment also had two. The 5th Dragoon Guards had a pair of helicons and a pair of tubas about 1912, an arrangement also noted in the 1st Battalion, Norfolk Regiment at Aldershot that year. A photograph of 'the Life Guards' Band before the last war' (i.e., pre-1914) in M[41], x, 11, 222, shows two BB♭ helicons and two E♭ tubas. The 1st Battalion, Royal Fusiliers had a helicon alongside three tubas in 1920.

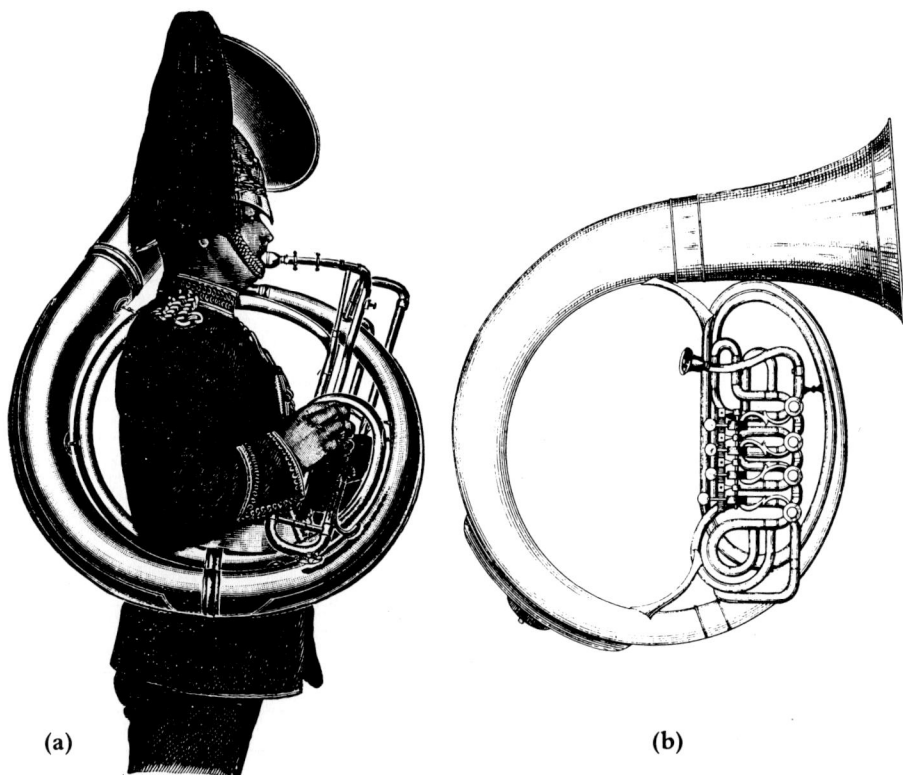

(a)  (b)

Fig. 15.1. (a) 'Monster Circular Contrabass' by Boosey & Co., c. 1894 (from K[2]); (b) *Helikon,* 1908 (from N[6]). This rotary-valved German model retains the profile of the original instrument with a gradually widening tube and limited bell-flare.

Table 15.1. SOME BRITISH ARMY HELICONS

| DATE | REGIMENT AND NOTES | REFERENCE |
|---|---|---|
| 1866 | 43rd Light Infantry (2) | T16, 196 |
| c. 1881 | 2nd Bttn. Duke of Wellington's Regiment (2) | T16, 79 |
| 1886 | 2nd Bttn. Green Howards (2) | T16, 42 |
| c. 1890 | 2nd Bttn. Royal Scots (2) | T15, 50 |
| c. 1890 | 1st Bttn. Queen's Own Cameron Highlanders (1) | T15, 81 |
| 1896 | 1st Bttn. East Yorkshire Regiment (2) | T16, 54 |
| c. 1896 | 1st Bttn. York & Lancaster Regiment (2) | T16, 85 |
| c. 1898 | 2nd Bttn. King's Shropshire Light Infantry (3) | T16,196 |
| 1899 | 2nd Bttn. Royal East Kent Regiment (1) | T15, 105 |
| 1901 | 4th Cavalry Band (1?) | R1, 49 |
| c. 1901 | 1st Bttn. Royal Welch Fusiliers (1) | T16, frontis. |
| 1906 | 2nd Bttn. King's Regiment (4 + 2 string bass) | T16, 20 |
| c. 1906 | 2nd Bttn. Sherwood Foresters (2) | T16, 137 |
| 1907 | 2nd Bttn. Gordon Highlanders (1) | T15, 88 |
| 1907 | 1st Bttn. Royal Berkshire Regiment (2 + rot-v. tba) | T16, pl. X |
| 1908 | 1st Bttn. Green Howards (1) | T16, 43 |
| 1909 | 1st Bttn. Leicestershire Regiment (2) | T15, 74 |
| c. 1909–10 | 2nd Bttn. King's Own Yorkshire Light Infantry (1) | T16, 175 |
| 1910 | 6th Bttn. Hampshire Regiment (1) | T16, 128 |
| c. 1910 | Royal Sussex Regiment (2) | T15, 115 |
| 1911 | Royal Dublin Fusiliers (2) | T16, 240 |
| 1911 | 1st Bttn. Worcestershire & Sherwood Foresters (1) | T16, 143 |
| c. 1912 | 5th Dragoon Guards (2 + 2 tubas) | T14, 49 |
| c. 1912 | 1st Bttn. Royal Norfolk Regiment (2 + 2 tubas) | T14, 137 |
| pre-1914 | Life Guards (2 B flat + 2 tubas) | M41, x, 11, 222 |
| 1915 | 1st Bttn. Border Regiment (2) | T15, 12 |
| 1920 | 2nd Bttn. Royal Munster Fusiliers (1) | T16, 236 |
| pre-1922 | 1st Bttn. Connaught Rangers (2) | T16, 227 |
| 1922 | 2nd Bttn. Royal Inniskilling Fusiliers (2) | T16, 48 |

*Hammersmith & Fulham Archives & Local History*
Fig. 15.2. West London District School Band playing at the opening of the Fulham Union Workhouse Chapel, 24 January 1890. Behind the helicons two valve trombones can be seen.

The instruments were particularly suited to use by the cavalry and Private Thomas, of the 4th Cavalry Band, was photographed with his helicon in 1901 (R[1], 49). Some fifty years later, jazz euphoniumist Rich Matteson played helicon in Bob Scobey's Frisco Jazz Band and elsewhere, and the shape was also adapted to the valve trombone, which thus found its way into the famous Dutch cycling bands.

Helicons have been made in many countries. Červený introduced a three- or four-valve *Kaiserhelikon* following the profile of his other Kaiser instruments and in 1851 Pelitti introduced a *Generale Pelittone* in B'♭. 'Pelittone' became synonymous with 'BB♭ Bass' in Italy, even to the extent of appearing on band parts, although the instruments were also constructed in CC and possibly other pitches. Pelitti's enthusiasm for the helicon design caused him to produce more varieties in 1863. These *al collo* ('in a sling') or *a tracolla* ('across the shoulder') models included an E♭ Clavicorno, B♭ Bombardino, Basso Flicorno in C and B'♭, and a B♭ valve trombone, all intended for cavalry use.

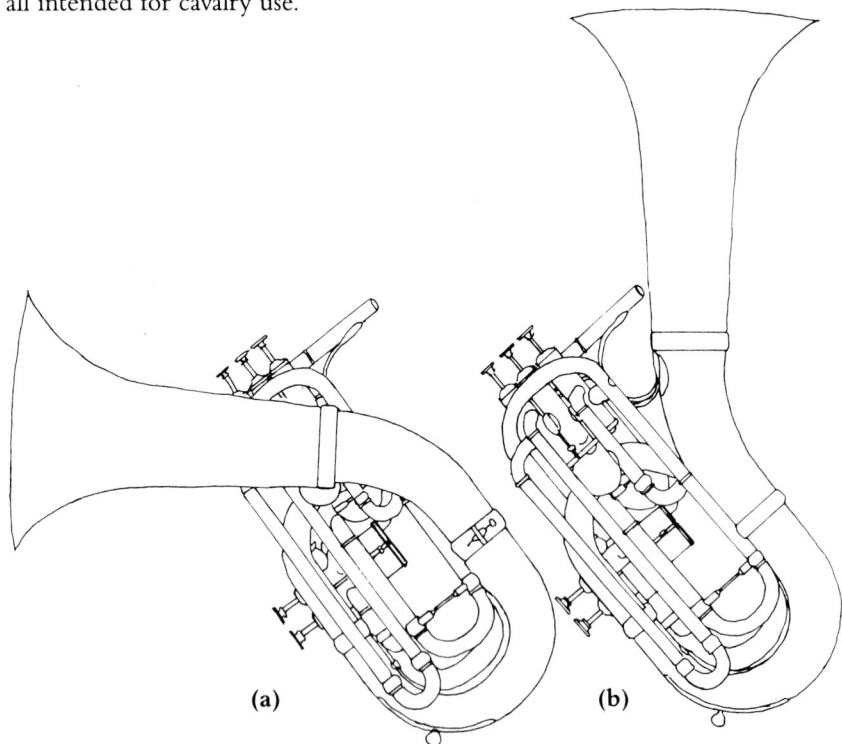

*(After the patent drawing.)*

Fig. 15.3. *Instrument de nouvelle forme* (Besson, 1855) showing the two positions of the bell: (a) when resting; (b) when playing.

Besson's *Trombotonar* (French Patent 12493, 18 January 1855 with *certificat d'addition* of 30 April 1856) was effectively a helicon, although it did not wind around the player. It was built in E'♭ and B'♭ as a military band instrument, anticipating to some extent Sousa's invention of forty years later. The Trombotonar was one of his *'instruments de nouvelle forme'* in pitches from *piccolo* to *contrebasse*, and the patent was claimed on the new principle that the bell was vertical during performance but at other times rested beside the left shoulder, facing in the same direction as the other instruments (see Fig 15.3). A slide-trombone on the same principle was also made. There is circular baritone marked Aggio of Colchester (a dealer), made in the second half of the nineteenth century, in the Horniman Museum (Fig. 15.4).

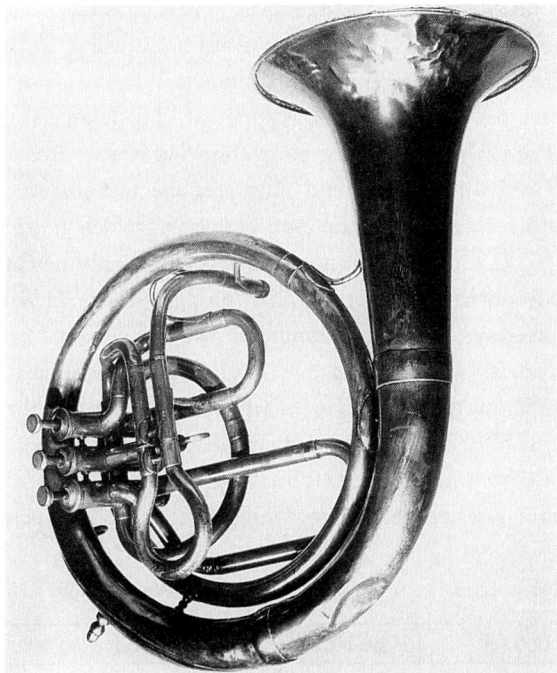

Fig. 15.4
Circular baritone, made in the second half of the nineteenth century, marked H. Aggio & Son, Colchester.

*Horniman Museum & Gardens, London*

In 1858 the London firm of Metzler patented their *Sonorophone* (British Patent 1836, 12 August 1858) in association with James Waddell, Bandmaster of the 1st Life Guards. This also bore similarities to the helicon but, somewhat like Besson's instruments, did not enclose the player, rather being supported in front of him.

There is an example pitched in C in the Edinburgh University Collection of Historic Musical Instruments (No. 1704) dating from 1865. It must have been pleasing for George Metzler and Bandmaster Waddell to learn that at the Crystal Palace contest ten years later the prize in the Solo Bass Players Competition was won by a bandsman playing a rotary-valve Eb Sonorophone.

Higham of Manchester made a large BBb helicon called 'Jumbo' with a bell 554 mm in diameter for the Chicago Exhibition of 1893. This was to be eclipsed by the most famous helicon of all: the sousaphone, the brainchild of John Philip Sousa, who had been dissatisfied with the helicons of the U.S. Marine Band because of the violent 'blurting' quality of tone given by their forward-facing bells. Sousa was all but obsessed by the need for smooth, round sounds—which probably contributed towards his success. He suggested that a BBb helicon be made with an extra-large bell facing not forward but upward 'so that the sound would diffuse over the entire band like the frostiness on a cake'. The prototype instrument seems to have been made by J. W. Pepper of Philadelphia in 1893, a year after the formation of Sousa's band. Taylor points out that it was 1923 before Sousa's entire tuba section played sousaphones and illustrates the five players in the section later during the 1920s, four playing the type with upright bell and one forward-facing (T[6], 38-9).

C. G. Conn began to manufacture sousaphones in 1898, although the year of the introduction of the familiar modern form in which the bell faces forward is uncertain. Sousa continued to use the original 'raincatcher' type, which Holton were still making as late as 1923. Bierley claims that the only occasion upon which he allowed a bell-front sousaphone to appear in the band was for part of the 1921 tour (T[12], 4-5). Other makers were quick to manufacture sousaphones. H. N. White of Cleveland, Ohio were making them by 1889, and two Russian sousaphones with 'rain-catcher' bells were photographed on 22 December 1906 (D[23], 1183).

Table 15.2.        SOME BRITISH ARMY SOUSAPHONES

| DATE | REGIMENT AND NOTES | REFERENCE |
|---|---|---|
| 1931 | Welch Regiment (1) | T16, 117 |
| 1933 | Oxfordshire & Buckinghamshire Light Infantry (1) | T16, 198 |
| 1937 | 1st Bttn. Loyal Regiment (1) | T16, 67 |
| 1939 | Wiltshire Regiment (2) | T16, 158 |
| c.1960 | Duke of Edinburgh's Royal Regiment (2) | T16, 159 |
| 1962 | 15th/19th King's Royal Hussars (1) | T14, 93 |

Fig. 15.5
Conformation of
the original model
of sousaphone, the
'raincatcher'.

The spectacular appearance of sousaphones led to their manufacture under proprietorial names like the Holton *Holtonphone* or Cuesnon *Soubassophone*. The ebullience indicated by their unashamedly extrovert shape and size inevitably link the instruments with United States music-making. Probably for this reason they have rarely appeared in the ranks of the more restrained British military, as Table 15.2 indicates. Turner's photograph of the band of the 15th/19th King's Royal Hussars in 1962 including a sousaphone is therefore of particular interest (T[14], 93).

As in all helicon-shape instruments the sousaphone requires the player only to stabilize and play the instrument. The concentration of weight on the left shoulder has, however, not been without problems. In a concert situation the instrument can be totally supported on a stand, an advantage not available to those who have to play while marching. A U.S. *Music Products Evaluation Index* pointed out that the concentration of weight on the left collar-bone tended ultimately to collapse the left lung. In order to reduce the weight a fibreglass bell was introduced (King made their first in 1963). Although diminishing the weight by something like 3.6 kg in the case of a BBb Sousaphone with a 660 mm bell, the quality of tone is adversely affected, so the potential player is put into something of a quandary. It is now normal for virtually the entire section between the valves and the bell in such an instrument to be made from fibreglass (in the case of Yamaha, fibreglass reinforced plastic, FRP). The lightest Sousaphone in current prodution appears to be the Conn 36K 'Artist', a three-valve BBb with 610 mm ABS Polymer bell designed for school use, weighing a mere 9 kg. The heaviest ever made, so far as can be discovered, was the Holton 130, available in 1939. This giant had a choice of

**(a)**

**(b)**

*Photo: Richard Wall*

Fig. 15.6. The ubiquitous sousaphone: (a) Martin Fry makes a telephone call in the 1960s; (b) John Elliott at the London Palladium in 1982 during the run of *Barnum*, for which he taught himself to ride a unicycle whilst playing.

bells from 560 mm to 660 mm, a bore of 19 mm, overall height of 1470 mm, and, pitched in BBb, a weight of 14.5 kg.

The 'Helikonposaune' by Richard Weller of Markneukirchen highlights an intriguing paradox, for by definition a slide-trombone must be mainly cylindrical in profile while a helicon must be mainly conical. Arnold Myers's investigations into a contrabass trombone invented in Yorkshire has shown this particular instrument to be in fact a slide-tuba. It was designed by John Midgley, bass trombonist in Marriner's Private Band, Keighley (where it is now in the Cliffe Castle Museum), and made by Besson of London. British Patent 3194 of 31 December 1860 for double slide trombone was in favour of Midgley, roller-coverer John Sugden and iron-founder William Clapham, a team which also took out several textile machinery patents. The prototype appears to have been built by George Wigglesworth of nearby Otley. The profile of the tubing is marked by an increase in diameter of each bow of the slide section and the whole terminates in a bell which is 321 mm in diameter, comparable to a reasonably large Eb tuba. Myers prints a photograph of this wonderful machine (M[56], 128).

## THE ANTONIOPHONE

The *Antoniophone* was described as a bombardon (therefore pitched in Eb) in the shape of a snail shell with three valves in the centre (cf. Fig. 15.4). The bell was detachable and could face upwards or under the arm, french horn fashion. A model by Sax was shown at the Royal Military Exhibition in 1890 but the instrument was actually invented by Antoine Courtois, after whom it was named. In 1889 Gilmore featured a quintet of Antoniophones, one played by his bass soloist, Elden Baker.

## THE SUDREPHONE

The French manufacturer François Sudre patented this unique family of instruments (French Patent 21958 of 18 February 1892; British Patent 22562 of 8 November 1901.) There was a complete range, the *Grand Bugle, Alto* and *Basse ut ou sib* having three valves, the *Baryton, ut ou sib* and *Contrebasse sib ou ut* having four. There were also a cornet and trombone, all built in ophicleide shape with the valves and branches to one side (Fig. 15.7). The distinguishing factor was their timbre. Covering a slit in the side of the bell was a cylinder containing a membrane which, when operated by appropriate 'flaps or slides', vibrated when the instrument was played just as the tissue paper in a kazoo or comb-and-paper. Although ostensibly merely a novelty, the intention was to make a real contribution to the timbres available in the wind band. The tone was claimed to approach that of string instruments, or the cylinder containing the membrane could be rendered inoperative and the original tone would then be available. Despite the inventor's laudable intentions there is, however, no indication that the Sudrephone achieved any success.

Fig. 15.7
*Sudrephone basse en ut,*
Sudre, 1892.

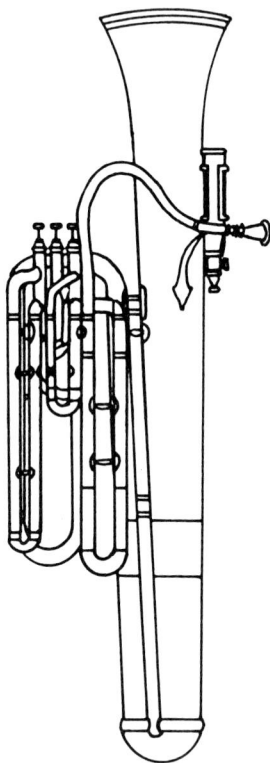

Sudre showed some persistance in seeking the best ways to exploit his idea. His British Patent 13605 of 13 June 1908 is a for a bell which includes a number of tubes each of which may have a diaphragm fitted to its side. This principle was appropriated for different purposes by T. J. Slechta in British Patent 277,153 of 31 July 1926. In tune with the times, Slechta claimed that the diaphragm on the wall of his instrument was 'to produce a tremolo ... or add a "jazz" quality'.

# THE WAGNER TUBEN

We have seen that the various valved bugle-horns interbred considerably and inevitably, but there were some cases in which other types of brass instrument were involved. It appears that Richard Wagner consulted the maker Alexander as early as 1862 about the provision of a new tone-colour in the orchestra, midway between horn and tuba, as a contrast to the trumpet/trombone sound. This may have been as the result of seeing some of Sax's instruments when he visited his Paris workshop in 1853, shortly before he began work on *The Ring*. In 1867 he ordered a set of narrow-bored tubas from Carl Moritz of Berlin who finally delivered them to Bayreuth in 1877. In an interesting article on the Tuben, John Webb points out that, as in the earlier instrument, these were played with the right hand, although they used a horn mouthpiece and leadpipe ($W^5$, 207-12). He supports his contention with an illustration from a Moritz catalogue. The instruments were clearly more tuba than horn, and they were replaced about 1890 by a set of Wagner Tuben built by Alexander for Bayreuth which were recognizably conceived along the lines of modern Tuben. The bore of these instruments was narrower than the tuba, wider than the french horn, and they were to be played with a funnel-mouthpiece. Modern tuben are invariably built in oval shape, the valves arranged to be played by the left hand. The Wagner Tuben were not, in fact, an original idea as Červený had made a similar set of instruments in 1846 which Wagner could well have seen since they were used by Dresden military bands at the time he was assistant conductor of the Court Theatre there, but the Wagner Tuben are the only instruments of their type to have remained in use to the present day.

They are built in two pitches, tenor in Bb and bass in F. Both sizes have four valves which in earlier models were arranged tenor: 1, ½, 1½, 2½ tones and bass: 1, ½, 1½, 3 tones but later rearranged to the familiar 1, ½, 1½, 2½ tones in both pitches. Until the introduction in the twentieth century of a variety in Bb/F the fourth valve served only to correct intonation in the low register. The instruments are played by horn-players using their normal mouthpieces, although the wider mouthpipes of early models imply the use of special mouthpieces. Wagner Tuben are always used in sets of four, two tenors and two basses. It is fortunate that the repertoire is limited as there is no standardized notation. Wagner, Bruckner, Draeseke, Nicodé, Schoenberg and Stravinsky used a variety of transpositions. Often the only way to decide which notation has been used is to look at the part in its context in the score, although horn-players are, of course, educated in these mysterious matters. There is some discussion of the problem in Gregory (G[21], App. A). Ex. 15.1 shows the note c' written in the various notations.

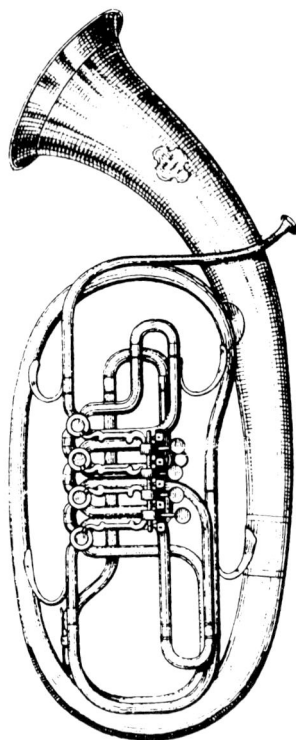

Fig. 15.8
Bass Wagner Tuba
in F (German,
c. 1908).

 Possibilities of using the tenor Wagner Tuba as a substitute french horn in marching bands are referred to on page 468 below. Further opportunites for using Tuben have been found in studio recordings where their distinctive characteristics of smooth sonority when blown moderately (as in Bruckner VII) or primeval wildness when blown hard (as in *Le Sacre du Printemps*) have attracted a number of composers. James Decker states that they were first used in Hollywood in 1964. Since then they have been used in situations as different as the MoTown Sound (Gene Page), *Ice Station Zebra* (Michel LeGrand, 1968) and the television series *Mission Impossible* (Lalo Schifrin, 1966-72).

Ex. 15.1                     WAGNER TUBA TRANSPOSITIONS

Despite Wagner's explicit demands, for many years performances of his works were given with Wagner Tuben substitutes. Cornophones were used in Paris (see page 467 below) and in London various instruments were tried. It was with expressions of delighted anticipation, therefore, that *The Stage* reported in its issue of 15 February 1894 that

> the Grand Wagner-Mottl concert at Queen's Hall in April will be remarkable for the introduction in this country of the bass-trumpet and four tenor-tubas, which are required for the Fauer [Trauer]-marsch. On former occasions at St. James's Hall the passages assigned to these instruments have been played by a trombone and four horns. The difference will be very marked, for the tenor-tubas are very noble instruments. Though the passages in question take only a few minutes to play, the instruments are being specially built, and some players will study them on purpose (S[33], 12).

Ex. 15.2

Wagner: *Die Walküre*

These instruments were thought to have been lost, perhaps in the air raid that demolished the Queen's Hall in 1941. However, in the 1990s Harold Nash, at the time principal trombone at the Royal Opera House, discovered three instruments with the characteristic tall, thin shape of saxhorns. Two were in F, one in B♭ and each had four top piston-valves. He realized that these were three-quarters of the set of Wagner Tuben bought by Henry Wood from Mahillon in Wardour Street for the Queen's Hall Orchestra. Later he discovered a fourth instrument. A similar set has now been identified in the Naples Museo Storico Musicale (W[5], 209).

The second half of the concert on the evening of 28 October 1908 at the Norwich Festival included the 'Trauermarsch' and 'Closing Scene' from Wagner's _Die Götterdämmerung_. The audience was informed: 'The four Wagner Tubas used in these numbers (specially constructed by Messrs. Mahillon) have been kindly lent by Mr. Henry J. Wood'. Wood recollected having for the previous two years left his train at Kettering to rehearse the players for two hours when on his way north (W[25], 214). The existence of Wagner Tuben exponents in this shoe-making town seventy-five miles from London may seem unlikely, but there were at least nine brass bands there at the time. The fame of Kettering Rifles Band was international as they had won first prize at the Dieppe contest in 1898. Possibly Wood chose players from amongst its ranks on the advice of his regular euphoniumist and tubist, Walter Reynolds, who lived close to Kettering at Burton Latimer. The bandsmen concerned were Thomas Seddon (bandmaster and solo cornet), G. York (solo trombone), D. Burditt (solo baritone) and J. Preston (solo euphonium). 'It was a notable event in music', enthused 'Cuivres', the London correspondent of _Wright & Round's Brass Band News_ (W32, 14.10.01, 9).

In the Royal Philharmonic Society's concert on 18 February 1913, including excepts from Wagner conducted by William Mengelberg, four tuba players are named: H. Tyler, A. Tyler, T. Cornish and R. Powis. There is a strong likelihood that their instruments were the Mahillon set as Wood occasionally conducted for the society. The players appear to have been drawn from the London tuba pool: Powis is shown as playing [bass] tuba in the Society's orchestra shortly before this event. It was not until 1935 that Alexander Tuben were heard in London, when Sir Thomas Beecham ordered a set for the London Philharmonic Orchestra which is now in the Edinburgh University Collection of Historic Musical Instruments.

The Mahillon instruments have recently been shown through practical demonstration (including a Bruckner performance by the New Queen's Hall Orchestra) to be extremely effective, conforming in all respects to the high standards of this company's workmanship (Fig. 15.9). Production of the sound seems more secure than on many 'conventional' Wagner Tuben, and their blend with each other and contrabass tuba is quite superb.

*Photo: Harold Nash*

Fig. 15.9. The Mahillon Wagner Tuben, two tenors on the left, two basses on the right. Each has four-in-line Périnet valves and a large-bore mouthpipe receiver indicating the requirement for mouthpieces of larger size than those now used by french horn players doubling on Tuben.

## CORNONS AND CORNOPHONES

The Červený instrument which Wagner quite possibly heard while in Dresden was the *Cornon*, probably invented for one of the very purposes which the Tuben later found themselves (with some surprise) being used: substitute french horns in infantry and cavalry bands. Cornon, the subject of Austrian Patent 4480 of 1844, were made in tuba, oval and helicon shapes, with three rotary- or piston-valves and

funnel-mouthpieces. Between the date of introduction and 1872 a range including
Eb alto, Bb tenor, Eb bass and BBb contrabass was built.

A similar family came from Fontaine-Besson of Paris in 1880. They were
originally patented as 'Cornon or Cornophone' (British Patent 16358, 14 October
1890) but were in fact known only by the latter name. There were five instruments,
notated like saxhorns in transposed treble clef. Their shape was unusual (Fig. 15.8)
but their true distinction was the completely conoidal profile through all the
tubing. The mouthpiece was funnel-shaped and to 'obtain homogeneous tone and
great accuracy' the mouthpipe was made in the form of a 'hollow, truncated cone',
7 mm at the entrance and 11 mm at the junction with the main tubing. The timbre
was claimed to be 'soft, round and velvety' and in addition to taking part in quartets
and quintets the alto and tenor were suggested for use as substitute french horns in
schools and amateur orchestras or to double the horns in large orchestras; the alto
itself could replace the Eb alto horn; and the tuba was particularly suited for church
use, 'its round yet soft penetrative voice being well adapted for sacred music and
leading choirs'. Here in the British patent specification is the basis for the often-
quoted passage in Sachs (S[3], 95) where he mentions the Cornophone's frequent use
in English churches! He may even have obtained this information from a secondary
source—Pierre (P[13], 18):

Il paraît que le clergé anglican adopte avec empressement le cornophone basse
pour accompagner le choer des fidèles; cet instrument prend ainsi le rôle de
l'antique serpent et de l'ophicléide au lutrin (P[13], 18).

Fig. 15.10
Cornophone in F
by Besson, London,
1890.

*Horniman Museum & Gardens, London*

[It seems that the Anglican clergy willingly adopted the bass cornophone to accompany the faithful; this instrument thus took over the role of the ancient serpent or ophicleide of the lectern.]

Ex. 15.3          COMPASS OF THE CORNOPHONES

They were used to play Wagner Tuben parts in the Lamoureux concerts in Paris during the 1888 season and were undoubtedly more satisfactory substitutes than many of the instruments used for this purpose elsewhere.

# TENOR CORS AND MELLOPHONES

In addition to the Tuben, Cornons and Cornophones there is another family of saxhorns crossed with the french horn, distinguished not only by its intermediate profile but by its french horn-like shape. The members came into being solely as horn substitutes. Of all brass instruments the french horn has been most prone to split notes owing to its use of the higher harmonics (the F horn's main tubing is roughly 3700 mm in length, the same as that of the F tuba). There would be an advantage in shortening the tubing so that the player could obtain the same notes as lower  harmonics with more certainty. A further disadvantage of  the french horn is

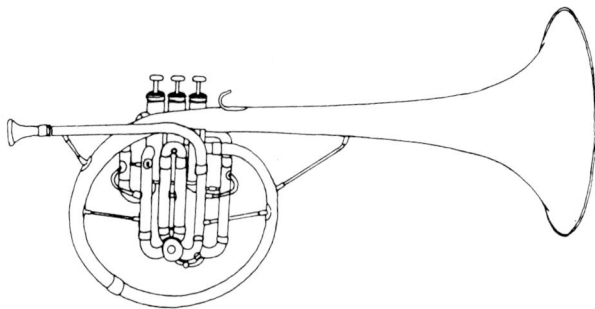

Fig. 15.11. Contempora ML-12 Straight Bell Mellophone by Reynolds, c. 1960. It is fitted with a rotary-change from f to e♭.

found when marching: the mouthpiece is kept on the lips with the utmost difficulty, the instrument is almost impossible to support and the bell faces into the players in the following ranks who absorb the sound.

A horn pitched an octave higher than normal would help. The distinctive horn tone would be lost, but using lower harmonics pitch would be more secure. The first instrument of this type was actually the Koenig Horn (Koenig, 1855) built by Antoine Courtois. Practically it was a saxhorn in bb put into French horn shape and played with the right hand. Koenig Horns were made up to the end of the century. Fig. 15.11 shows an example dating from 1890 in the Horniman Museum, London, built in c' with crooks for bb and a and compensating valves. The bell is 157 mm in diameter, larger than that of a saxhorn of equivalent pitch.

The *tenor cor* was introduced about 1860. It found ready acceptance, especially amongst amateurs and school bands. Since it is used for f horn parts as well as eb saxhorn parts, it is normally provided with an alternative main-slide; earlier models often had two crooks. Červený's *Primhorn* of 1873 was a similar instrument, as is the French *cor alto*, an eb alto horn invented about 1900 by Ligner, a bandsman in the Garde Républicaine; and the Dutch *Stellahoorn*, the German *Oktavwaldhorn* and *Corhorn* and American *Mellophone*. Conn make a Mellophonium in f which has the further advantage of a forward-facing bell, the valve tubing being contained within the main branches. In 1882 Henry Distin built a tenor cor in c—the *Ballad Horn, Amateur Voice Horn* or *Vocal Horn*—enabling music to be played direct from a piano copy without transposition. Judging by the numbers still in existence it was popular in Victorian drawing-rooms. (An American ballad horn was built in Bb.)

There were two ways to attack the problems of the french horn in marching bands. One was to build an eb/f saxhorn in trumpet shape. This made it into an alto flügel horn, known in France as *bugle alto en mib*, an octave below the *petit bugle*, often with four valves. An American example dating from c. 1856 is illustrated by Garofalo & Elrod (G[6], 28). It has three Vienna valves, is marked 'F. G. Kaiser, Cincinnati, Ohio' and comes complete with an alternative shorter mouthpipe to put the Eb instrument into F. The other method was to use a Bb Wagner Tuba. Since this was already familiar to many horn-players, who fingered it like the Bb side of the F/Bb horn, and since it was built in an oval shape, making it more suitable for marching, it is surprising that this practice was not more widespread. The Prussian Army adopted the Wagner Tuba as a substitute french horn in 1911.

French horn players in the bands of the Household Cavalry have traditionally solved their unique problem by playing Eb alto horns ('dog horns') when mounted, reverting to their normal instruments at other times. In the last few years of the twentieth century a different approach was taken by a number of makers who now offer marching instruments in trumpet shape. Thus Blessing, DEG–Dynasty, Getzen and Yamaha make marching mellophones in F; Blessing and Getzen make marching F french horns; DEG–Dynasty, Getzen, Holton and Yamaha make marching Bb french horns—the latter two varieties of instrument finally rendering redundant the tenor cor or mellophone as compromise solutions.

However, the requirements of jazz players should ensure that the mellophone continues to exist as a distinctive brass voice, with a long history in this area. The American Dudley Fosdick (1902-57) has been called 'the father of the mellophone' for his contribution to bands from Red Nichols to Guy Lombardo's Royal Canadians. Davey Jones (c. 1888-1953), who also played french horn, was another early jazzman whose mellophone playing has been acclaimed. Whole sections were found in the 1930s in London bandleader Lew Stone's dance orchestra and in 1960-63 in the somewhat different Stan Kenton 'progressive jazz' band.

## SAXOTROMBAS

In 1845 Sax patented a family of instruments distinguished by a profile lying midway between bugle and french horn and use of funnel-mouthpieces: the *Saxotrombas*. They ranged from sopranino in e'b to contrabass in B'b, including one in f to replace the french horn. Even the deeper instruments had only three valves since the relatively narrow profile inhibited the production of lower notes. The design originated in the cavalry's requirements for an instrument which would

Fig. 15.12. *Saxotromba en mi bémol basse* (a) compared with *saxhorn contre-basse en mi bémol* (b): both instruments are Eb tuba pitch.

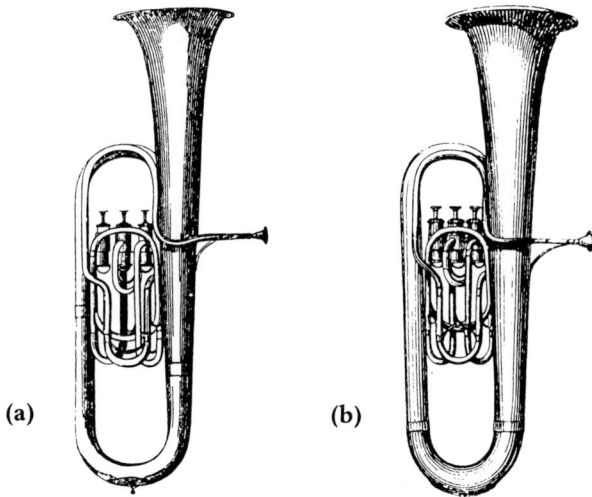

(a)          (b)

allow the player to use one hand for controlling his mount. Saxotrombas were tall, slim and well-balanced (Fig. 15.12). Kastner describes them as 'holding place, for quality of sound, between the Bugle, the Ophicleide and Cornet, the Trumpet and Trombone'. They were used as a family for twenty years at the most and probably manufactured for a much shorter period as all extant illustrations depict them with the Berliner-Pumpen abandoned by Sax relatively early during his career. The f or eb remained in use longer in both cavalry and infantry bands.

Much later in the century Sax made four Saxotrombas for performances of Wagner's *Ring* in Paris. Their distinctive feature was the *pavillon reversible*. The raised position added greatly to the effect of loud passages while the bell at floor level not surprisingly gave a subdued and mysterious sound. The two positions of the instrument are illustrated in Fig. 15.13.

Fig. 15.13
Saxotromba made for performances of Wagner's *Ring*: (a) with bell lowered; (b) with bell raised.

## SAXTUBAS AND KORNETTE-INSTRUMENTE

French Patent 4361 of 5 May 1849 (with *certificats d'addition* of 20 August 1849 and 23 April 1852) was granted to Adolphe Sax for 'Wind instruments'. They were built in the circular form of the Roman buccina in a range of pitches from piccolo in b'b to contrabass in Bb. Each had three valves and since the bell was positioned above the head of the player a very powerful sound could be produced. Sax claimed that they would benefit the sound given by military bands as all the bells faced in the same direction, while enhancing public ceremonies by being based on depictions found on Ancient Greek and Roman monuments. The painter and revolutionary Jacques-Louis David had been influential in the inclusion of two classically-inspired instruments, each capable only of playing the notes of a single harmonic series, in ceremonial performances between 1791 and 1807 in Paris. These were the *buccin*, based on the straight Roman trumpet, and the *tuba curva*, in which the tubing curved under the player's arm and terminated in a forward-facing bell above his head (C[17], 39-47). Sax ensured that to some extent the valves of his derivatives were hidden from the spectators' view, enhancing the archaic effect (Fig. 15.14). He also suggested the use of 'an appendix' to facilitate support and safeguard the valves, claiming the desirability for this on the grounds that

> . . . it is known that in order to obtain high notes in the scale the player increasingly presses the instrument against his lips; thus, the efforts that he makes in this direction are almost always accompanied by increased force of the hand on that section of the instrument which it grasps, and as very frequently this section is that which contains the valves, there result in that area deviations in the positions of the several parts, which, insignificant as they appear and they actually are, affect the working of the valves to the point of sometimes jamming them . . . this results in at least after a certain time the casings becoming oval . . .

Through the courtesy of Laurence Libin, Curator of Musical Instruments, it is possible to give the dimensions of a saxtuba in the Metropolitan Museum of Art, New York (No. 89.4.1109). These are compared below with those of a late twentieth-century tuba of similar pitch.

Table 15.3.     COMPARATIVE DIMENSIONS OF SAXTUBA AND EE♭ TUBA
[Dimensions in millimetres]

|  | SAXTUBA 13802 | EE♭ TUBA |
|---|---|---|
| Pitch | (?) E♭ | E♭ |
| Overall height | 1240 | 883 |
| Diameter of bell | 316 | 440 |
| Overall maximum width | c. 900 | 560 |
| Tube diameter at 2nd valve | 16.2 [external] | 16.8 |
| Mouthpipe diameter at entry | 14.2 | 16.0 |

This saxtuba has Berliner-Pumpe valves and both the standard of workmanship and design are of a high quality. Comettant felt that the position of the bell ensured

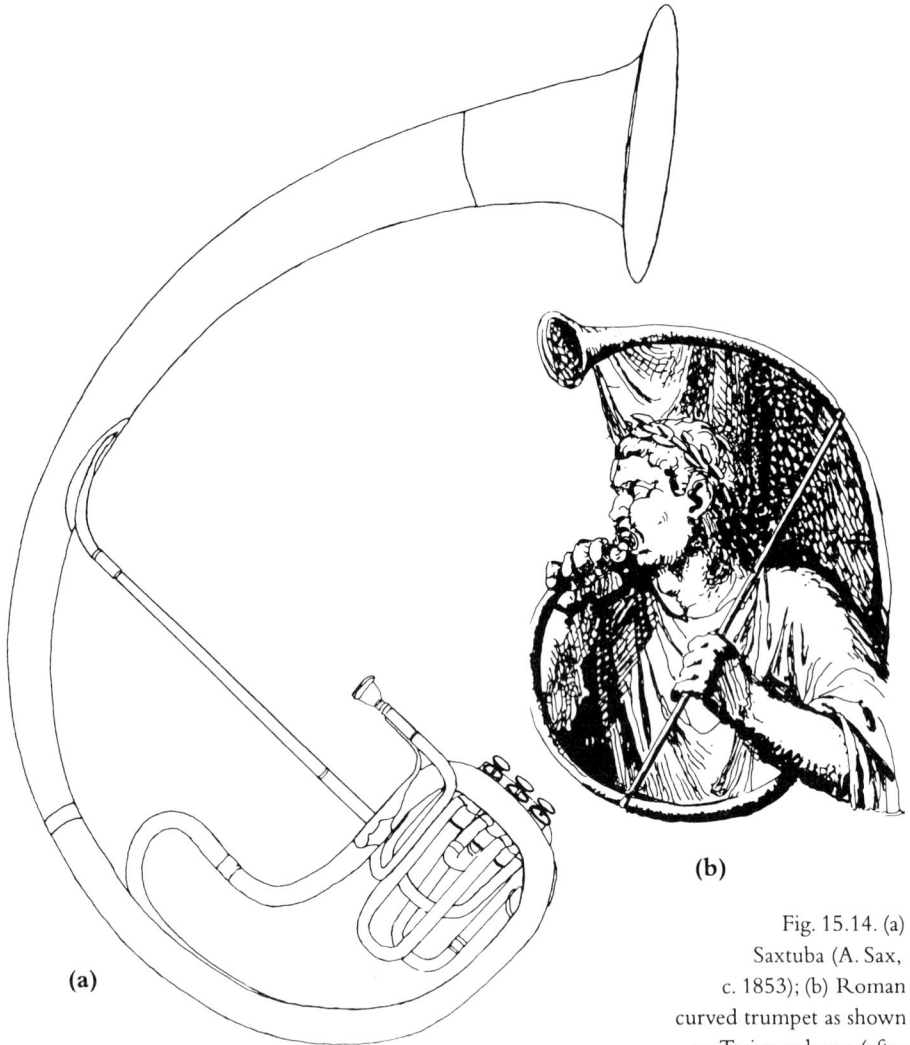

Fig. 15.14. (a)
Saxtuba (A. Sax,
c. 1853); (b) Roman
curved trumpet as shown
on Trajan column (after
engraving by Bartoli).

**(a)**

*Not to scale*

that 'the trombone, beside the saxtuba, is no more than a simple kazoo . . . the saxtuba surpasses in force all the instruments known today' (C[29], 369).

On 10 May 1852 twelve saxtubas were amongst the 1500 musicians who played on the Champ de Mars as the Emperor distributed the colours to his army. There were performances both with and without the new instruments, and Comettant was impressed by their strength of tone (C[29], 379). He aslo commented that they were played by civilians using the instruments they had previously played at the Opéra in a production of Halévy's *Le Juif errant*, premiered on 23 April 1852. As Sax was director of the stage band there were no particular problems in arranging for the saxtubas to appear in what turned out to be a spectacular failure. The score (in manuscript, in the library of the Opéra) shows that the instruments were made in the same pitches as saxhorns and, since the copyist named them 'saxhorns', may have been introduced at a late stage in the preparations for the first performance.

*Petite Sax=horn aigue en Si♭*
*Sax=horn soprano en Mi♭*
*Cornet à pistons en Si♭* [called *'Sax-horn au pistons en Si♭'* in Act IV, No. 17]
*Sax=horn Contre Alto en Si♭*
*1<sup>er</sup> Saxhorn alto en Mi♭*
*2<sup>e</sup> Saxhorn alto en Mi♭*
*Sax horn baryton en Si♭*
*Sax horn basse en Si♭*
*Sax horn C:basse en Mi♭*
*Sax horn C:basse en Si♭*

The *Collection de Mises en Scène* compiled and published by M. L. Palianti (Bibl. Op. C4247.107à13) shows that the instruments were used in the finale of Act III (No. 12, 'Triumphal March') and Act IV, No. 17. The music is reminiscent of Berlioz's orchestral marches: the rhythm of the first bar of the 'Apothéose' of his *Symphonie funèbre et triomphale* (1840) is identical to that of Ex. 15.4, although the melody is inverted. This was very much music in the style of its time.

The instruments achieved more fame (or notoriety) than they merited. Their existence was noted in London when, referring to an unreasonable delay in the appearance of Meyebeer's opera *L'Étoile du nord* the following year, *The Athenaeum* (A[20], 28.1.1854, 124) stated 'There are people in Paris who declare that the work is waiting . . . till its composer has, as usual, "tried conclusions" with harps, Sax-tubas, double-bass clarionets . . .' More amusingly, the severe criticism of the opera by Jule Janin of the *Journal des Débats* led to a protracted and lurid public correspondence with Roqueplan (Louis-Victor-Nestor Rocoplan), the Director of the Opéra, in which Sax's novel contribution played a prominent role amongst the factors deemed to have led to the opera's failure. This is reprinted in B[37], 135-46.

Ex. 15.4

Halévy: *Le juif errant.*

It is possible that the term 'Saxtuba' was previously used for other instruments made by Sax as in 1847, two years before they were patented, John Distin published in London a *Selection of the Most Fantastic Swedish Melodies for . . . Cornet . . . Sax-horn or Saxtuba. Distin's Journal for Sax Horn, Sax-Tuba, etc.* Pierre refers to the saxhorn-contrebasse as 'Sax-tubar' (P[14],136). It is easy to see how a colloquialism of this sort could come into being, and it may even be that John Distin's son Henry, who was Sax's London agent, used it himself in the course of trade since upright saxhorns of various pitches illustrated on the back cover of some of his published music are all called 'tuba'.

In 1876 Červený patented under the name *Kornett-instrumente* a similar family of instruments in the same range of sizes.

## DUPLEX INSTRUMENTS

A duplex instrument is played by one performer but has the characteristics of two different instruments; the performer is free to choose which of the two the duplex should be. Owing to difficulties in construction, the bass tuba itself has not suffered the indignity of this treatment, but many other valved bugle-horns have found themselves Siamese-twinned with other brass.

The first duplex seems to have burst upon an unsuspecting world in 1847 when Giuseppe Pelitti of Milan made his *Doppio Strumento*, a combined trombone and euphonium. In 1851 there followed a whole family of *duplex* or *gemelli* (twins) (*French* Patent 14737 of 18 December 1855—not 25863, as stated elsewhere). These were *Flicorno/Cornetta* (flügel horn and cornet), *Genis/Tromba* (alto horn and Eb trumpet), *Bombardino/Trombone Baritono* (euphonium and valve trombone) and *Bombardone/Trombone Basso* (four-valved euphonium and bass valve trombone), which won an award at the 1855 Paris Exposition. At the 1878 Exposition Giuseppe Clementi Pelitti showed a *Duplex Baritonali con Pistoni Traspositore* in which the secondary bell was placed *inside* the primary bell (M[33], 317).

In 1851 Gisborne of Birmingham combined an 'althorn and cornet'. Since an essential point of the duplex is a common valve system serving two instruments of identical pitch, the Gisborne duplex, referred to by Sachs (S[3], 123), presumably involved a flügel horn and cornet. In the same year, apparently going one better, John Mcneill of Dublin conceived a duplex combining 'un bugle contralto, un cornet à pistons et une trompet' (flügel or eb horn, cornet and trumpet) according to Pontécoulant. Another triplex was designed by Pelitti some time after 1855 although it is not certain that any of these instruments were actually manufactured (M[33], 317). His *bombardone tritonio*, designed after 1870, appears to have had a mechanism (of an unknown nature) enabling the player to switch quickly between its three pitches of F, Eb and Bb (M[33], 320). Rather than constituting a triplex, therefore, this instrument seems to have been more akin to the various types of bass tuba made in three nominal pitches—currently, for example, by Kalison of Milan (see page 200 above).

British patents of the period show a continuing interest in the gratuitous exercise of combining (natural) bugle and (valved) trumpet—gratuitous as the notes of the bugle can be obtained on the valved trumpet simply by not using the valves. M. J. Nyilassy's British Provisional Patent 140 of 18 January 1855 proposed effecting the change by means of a single valve. Henry Distin's British Patent 1465 of 26 June 1855 was simpler still, proposing the insertion of an assembly of three valves and associated tubing between the mouthpiece and the remainder of the instrument as required. (This idea was revived by W. Stasek (British Patent 6702, 28 March 1899) who suggested adding a section with three piston-valves to a bugle to convert it into a cornet.) Distin's Patent 2592 of 18 October 1861 was for a duplex bugle/trumpet in which the mouthpiece could be used for either instrument, while an alternative method introduced an additional tube for effecting the change.

Adolphe Sax's British Patent 1284 of 24 May 1859 included proposals for duplex instruments, while J. Lawson and H. Carter (British Provisional Patent 2596 of 18 October 1861) detailed a combined bugle and trumpet operated by a four-way rotary valve. At the 1873 Vienna Exhibition the *B-C-Clairon* by Hirschberg of Bratislava was shown. This was a somewhat more sophisticated pairing of B♭ soprano flügel horn and C cornet. Obviously it was much easier to combine two smaller instruments than two of deep pitch but during the 1870s Bohland & Fuchs of Graslitz paired a euphonium and trombone. In 1887 Sediva of Odessa made several instruments of different pitches under the name *Duetton* or *Lyraphon* also including a baritone/valve trombone. These utilized a common mouthpiece and valve system in the normal way but the bells of the two component instruments curved away from each other and upwards on each side of the player in the shape of a lyre, the bells facing either forward or upward (see Fig. 15.15). Higham of Manchester marketed a *Highamphone*, Besson of London a *Doublophone*, both combining the two contrasting tenor soloists, euphonium and trombone. Another *Doublophone*, pairing a baritone and trombone, was built by Bohland & Fuchs of Graslitz in 1890.

In the late 1880s Conn twinned euphonium and trombone to produce what was claimed as the earliest American duplex. Gilmore's soloist Harry Whittier was probably the first player to adopt the instrument (in 1888), followed a year later by Sousa's solo euphoniumist Michael Raffayalo. Edward Mallett, however, has shown

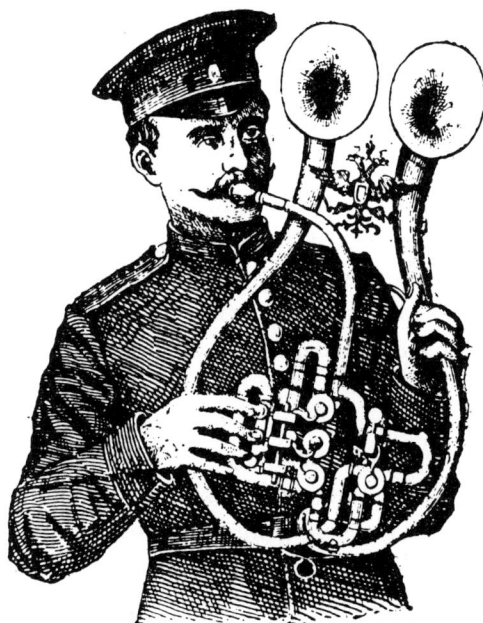

Fig. 15.15
Lyraphon by
Sediva, c. 1887.

that double-belled instruments were known in the USA at an earlier date, referring to a lithograph of the Gilmore band in 1885 which includes a player with a double-belled rotary-valved instrument similar to that built in 1892 by Missenharter of Stuttgart. In 1891 J. W. Pepper was importing double-bell euphoniums by C. A. Mouchel of Paris into the United States and Missenharter instruments were being imported by the Coleman Music Company of New York ($M^{10}$, 25).

While all of these duplex had a recognisably common form, the actual mechanics presented a wide range of variations, some with rotary-valves, others with top-action or front-action piston-valves. The position of the secondary bell also varied between models. Mallett makes the point that the other significant double-belled instrument, the echo cornet, in which the air-stream could be deviated to pass through a mute when required, retained its popularity in Europe while soon falling out of use in the U.S.A. while the reverse applied to the duplex euphonium/ trombone. (In this connexion it is interesting to note that whilst in America the English emigré Henry Distin designed an alto horn with echo bell, the *Melody Horn*, ($E^6$, I, 572).) In the United States double-belled euphoniums, with a fifth valve controlling the choice of tone, were popular not only with soloists but with tutti players, and there are wonderful newsreel shots of the Sousa Band showing a rank of upward-belled sousaphones and a front-line including two-belled euphoniums. To satisfy the demand several American companies produced the instrument. These included Conn (who introduced the Wonderphone and the Mantia Model), Buescher, Distin, King and York. The top-quality Holton instrument was the Pryorphone, named after Arthur Pryor, at one time Sousa's virtuosic trombone soloist, then composer, arranger, and later band director in his own right. By the 1930s the United States Marine band was using only Conn models and the United States Navy band only Kings (M[10], 25). Holton seem to have stopped production about that time, while Conn may have ceased around 1956 when the Marine band decided no longer to use double-belled instruments.

Mallett (who reproduces a number of fascinating double-belled euphonium photographs) suggests a reason why the instrument finally fell out of use. It appears that shortly after the outbreak of World War II in 1939 a British naval vessel docked at an American port for repairs. Noting the poor condition of the brass instruments used by the naval band, as a goodwill gesture a set of American instruments was presented to replace them. Harold Brasch, soloist with the United States Navy Band, thus came into possession of a Boosey & Hawkes four-valved compensating euphonium. Much taken by its full tone, he began to use it rather than his regulation King double-bell. As a result, by the mid-1950s the British instruments were in general use by American military bands. (The information was given to Mallett by Art Lehmann, soloist with the United States Marine band from 1947-71, and there are so many obviously true elements that there is no reason to doubt its accuracy.)

Apart from the weight of the instruments and their inconvenience (although the secondary bell was usually detachable) the common mouthpiece and valve sections were the main disadvantage of duplex instruments. These prevented the effective contrast given by the original individual instruments as only the final sections of tubing differed in bore, although the Besson Doublophone valve pistons had two sets of windways so that only the mouthpiece and the mouthpipe were shared by the euphonium and trombone sections. Arrangers had a little more colour at their disposal and soloists the opportunity to feature echo effects, but the last duplex instruments seem to have been those in the King catalogue during the 1960s.

As with the serpent, keyed bugle and ophicleide, the double-belled euphonium has had something of a revival in recent years. Turn-of-the-century solos are sometimes played on the stipulated instrument by players aiming for a more authentic performance. Ashley Alexander also used one with the Matteson-Phillips

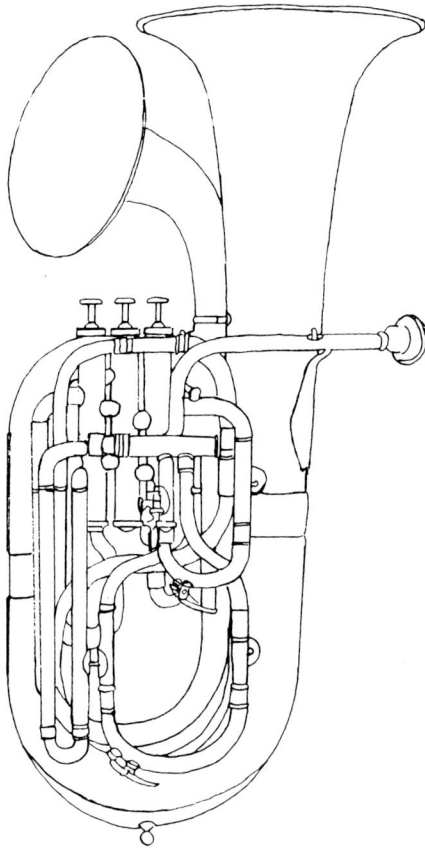

Fig. 15.16
Doublophone
(Fontaine-Besson)

Tubajazz Consort. Furthermore, in 1996 Edward Mallett developed a modern version, having investigated forty-nine different extant double-belled euphoniums. He allied a compensating Kurath euphonium to an Edwards Trombones bass trombone bell. Clearly, this is not an historic reconstruction but rather a new approach as the large-bore euphonium was not in common use in the United States until after World War II. However, Mallett found that he had a good contrast of timbres and any problems with intonation could be solved by the use of a conveniently-placed main-slide and another slide controlling only the extra bell (positioned vertically, like the main bell). The slides also allow microtones and glissandi to be performed. The new instrument is described in greater detail by Charles Guy (G[25], 64).

# CHAPTER XVI

# Low Brass in the Nineteenth-century Orchestra

It must be boring, it was suggested, spending your whole life
playing two notes on the tuba when you can't hear what
tune the rest of the orchestra is playing . . .
—from a student essay competition on big businesses versus
small in *The Observer,* 27 April 1980

Toscanini . . . laid down his baton and quietly asked Mr. Bell
[tubist] to 'Please play that passage again'. When Bell had
finished it, Toscanini said, 'Now please play it once again!' and
then, at the end, 'Still another time, please'. Mr Bell asked
him finally what there was to correct. 'Nothing,' said Mr
Toscanini, 'Only I never heard anything so beautiful'.
—quoted by Hope Stoddard, 'The tuba and its players in our
bands and orchestras' in *The International Musician,*
January 1950

THE HABIT of indiscriminately playing orchestral lowest brass parts on tuba
seems to have become generally established during the last fifteen years of the
nineteenth century. Although the ensuing period is short in historic terms, the
consolidation of the practice by several generations of players and teachers has
resulted in their now being as many difficulties in the way of reaching decisions
about an informed historic approach as those faced by singers of medieval
chansons. This chapter attempts to help clarify the situation, first by considering the
approaches to the low orchestral brass taken by some important nineteenth-century
composers and by two long-standing British concert-giving organizations; then by
tabulating the instruments stipulated in a number of scores; and finally by
presenting a graphic indication of low brass section instrument profiles in key
countries throughout the nineteenth and twentieth centuries. Readers may also find
the Composer Index of References to the Use of Low Brass (pages 597-602) a useful
tool when seeking information on the approaches taken by specific composers.

## MENDELSSOHN AND THE BASS PROBLEM

Felix Mendelssohn-Bartholdy was a phenomenally-gifted polymath. His talents
were nurtured by the considerable educational oportunities available to a member
of a rich family with intellectual and artistic interests in early nineteenth-century

Germany and he became a skilful visual artist, a prolific and colorful correspondent, a formidable linguist and a composer subsequently rated high in the second division. During his lifetime his musical works were universally praised in Continental Europe, in Britain (where the royal family led a fan club that united a class-ridden society more effectively than any Acts of Parliament), and in the United States.

He was a close personal friend of Berlioz, although incapable of understanding his French colleague's approach to music, for Felix suffered from good taste, from conformity, and, in consequence, lacked the vital spark that is essential in the true genius. His music is often described as Romantic in character, but Classical in presentation. It is unlikely that he would have found this description in the least offensive.

Given that his musical practices were so deeply rooted in tradition, the remarkable thing about Mendelssohn's scores is the number of times that he demands low brass instruments: serpent, bass horn, ophicleide and tuba. Many more flamboyant contemporaries asked at the most for a trombone section, and possibly the odd percussion instrument. What led this restrained and civilised, urbane and diplomatic composer to become so obsessed with the low brass?

To answer this question, it is necessary first to consider the works, their inspiration and development.

Mendelssohn was second only to Mozart in his precocity, so it is not surprising that when, in 1824 at the age of fifteen, he went on holiday with his father to Bad Doberan, near Rostock, and heard the court wind band, he should compose for it. The result was the *Ouvertüre für Vollstände Harmonie-Musik*, opus 24, published in 1852 and including parts for 'Contrafagotto und Basshorn'. (The band's serpent-player in 1812 is known to have been Seipoldsdorf and he could well have been playing bass horn twelve years later (S$^{40}$, 74).) These two parts are mainly, though not consistently, written in unison. This gives the effect of octaves as the contrabassoon sounds an octave lower than written. A strong bass line is thus provided.

Mendelssohn adopted the same approach elsewhere. In the *Ouvertüre: Meerestille und Glückliche Fahrt* (opus 27), composed in 1828, first performed in Berlin on 18 April 1828 and revised in 1833-34, he uses an octave combination of 'Serpente e Contra Fagotto', placing them in the score immediately below the woodwind. The *Trauer-Marsch*, opus 103, was composed for Harmonie-Musik (wind band) and completed about 8 May 1836. It was published in 1869, the year after an arrangement for orchestra had been issued. The Harmonie included 'Contrafagott und Basshorn', written in unison apart from the Trio, where only the contrabassoon plays. There is no bass horn in the orchestral version, implying that Mendelssohn correctly saw it as a band instrument.

He uses it again, in a non-orchestral situation, in three marches for the Düsseldorf town band, composed around 1833-34. The score and original parts are lost, but they are thought to survive in a set of manuscript parts, in an English copyist's hand of c. 1860, in the Bodleian Library, Oxford (MS. M. Deneke Mendelssohn c.50, fols. 67-75). The instrumentation is: Flauto, Eb Clarinetto, Bb Clarinetto 1°, Bb Clarinetto 2°, Fagotto, Eb Corni [2], Eb Trombe [2], Posaune [single part], Bass-Horn. One march also has a 'Contra Fagotto' part.

In the choral movement of his fifth symphony, 'Reformation' (completed in 1832), Mendelssohn established a method of using the serpent later adopted by Wagner in *Rienzi* and *Das Liebesmahl der Apostel*. It is placed below the bassoons, written in unison with the double-bassoon, fulfilling the function of bass to the woodwind section. Sometimes it contributes the bass part when the strings are tacet or playing different material from the winds, but it does not contribute to the activities of the brass section. However, in the oratorio *Paulus (St Paul)*, opus 36 (1836) the 'Serpente' is sometimes positioned in the score below the trombones and at others below the bassoons. In No. 45 the contrabassoon and serpent are again written in unison. The resulting octaves strengthen the bass line in a mainly contrapuntal movement where it is vital that the four parts should be as balanced as possible in order to emphasize the linear nature of the composer's approach. This work gives the clearest illustration of the influence of Carl Friedrich Zelter, Mendelssohn's teacher between September 1819 and January 1821. His methods were based on an admiration for J. S. Bach, with an emphasis on the traditional techniques of figured bass and counterpoint, along with a requirement for each of the parts in chorale harmonizations to form a satisfactory melodic line.

Mendelssohn was to work under the influence of Zelter for the whole of his composing career, often showing a strong inclination towards contrapuntal textures. In the choruses of works for choir and orchestra he was frequently faced with difficulties when doubling the vocal parts instrumentally owing to the lack of sufficient strength in available bass instruments. *Paulus* clearly shows his attempts to overcome these problems, with the serpent and contrabassoon adding security and sometimes prominence to the basses in the choir. It was first performed at Düsseldorf on 22 May 1836. The first English performance took place in

Liverpool on 7 October that same year, conducted by Sir George Smart 'who will preside at the ORGAN, To which a Long-Movement has been added by Mr. Gray, of London'. The programme book (in the Liverpool Record Office) lists Ponder as playing ophicleide, no serpent being present.

In June 1846 Mendelssohn's opus 68, *Festgesang an die Künstler*, was performed at the Deutsch-Vlaemischen Sängerfestes, Cologne. This work is scored for four-part male voice chorus and a brass ensemble consisting of 2 Trumpets in Eb, 1 Trumpet in Bb, 2 Horns in Eb, 2 Horns in Bb, 3 Trombones, Bass Trombone, Ophicleide and Tuba. The last two instruments play in unison throughout, and it appears that by using this technique Mendelssohn hoped to balance the large number of voices. Doubling them at the octave would, of course, have produced a greater strength of sound. Presumably the ophicleide part was for the valved *Ventil-Ophikleide* found in Germany at the time, along with a Baß-Tuba of the type invented only eleven years earlier in Berlin.

*Elias (Elijah)* was Mendelssohn's opus 70, commissioned by the Birmingham Music Festival and first played in the Town Hall there on 26 August 1847. (The first American performance was given by the New York Sacred Harmonic Society in the Broadway Tabernacle on 8 November 1847, the rival American Musical Institute peforming the same work in the same venue the following night.) Here keyed ophicleide is stipulated, an instrument in Bb being necessary to cover the part. There is not a great deal for it to play, and it is often written in unison with the bass trombone. The ophicleide has been used successfully in performances with modern orchestral brass so as not to detract from the trombone sound. Adding the very different' timbre of a tuba tends to cause the trombone section to sound unfocused.

While the effects of his choral techniques on Mendelssohn's low brass writing are evident, the most misunderstood and most frequently incorrectly performed of his works is purely orchestral.

A performance of the version for piano, four hands, of his overture to *Ein Sommernachtstraum (A Midsummer Night's Dream)* was given by Felix and his sister Fanny on 6 August 1826. The first performance of the orchestral version was given at Stettin, Prussia (now Szczecin, Poland), directed by Karl Loewe, on 20 February 1827. In the first draft of the score (MS. M. Deneke Mendelssohn b.5 fol 7-12, Bodleian Library) no low brass instrument is present. However, in the final version, dating from 1826 (MS. autogr. Mendelssohn vo. 32, Kraków) an English bass horn appears as 'Corno ingle. di basso', listed at the beginning of the score between

'Fagotti' and 'Corni in E'. It is highly likely that the orchestration was supervised by his friend, the composer Adolph Bernard Marx who made a number of suggestions for improving the work. This did not prevent Marx from reviewing the performance in *Berlin Allgemeine Musikalsiche Zeitung* (B[23], 95), where he observed that '. . . the clumsy English bass horn portrays perfectly the boorish Bottom.'

When Mendelssohn saw his first bass horn, in the court wind band at Bad Doberan three years earlier, he was so taken by its appearance that in a letter he wrote home to his sister on 21 July 1824 he included a sketch and a description, likening it to a syringe or watering-can. His musical characterization of Bottom the weaver through the medium of this bizarre, appropriately rustic ('watering can') and, as Marx says, 'clumsy' instrument provided a perfect contrast to the *leggiero* fairy music and sennets and tuckets of Theseus's court.

On 24 June 1829 the first British performance of the overture was conducted by Mendelssohn himself, at the Argyll Rooms, London, in a concert for the benefit of the victims of floods in Silesia. (Another was given on 13 July.) The orchestra had been assembled by Smart, who was immensely proud of his friendship with Mendelssohn whom he had previously met in Berlin. However, as Mendelssohn relates in a letter he wrote home to his sisters Fanny and Rebecka on 25 June, at the 10 o'clock rehearsal on the day before the concert the bass horn was missing, and an irate Mendelssohn took Smart to task. Smart promised that 'the man with the beer-bass' would be present, and the next morning 'along came the fellow with the bass horn.' (*Bierbaß* was a German dialect word for another instrument of the people, the Handbassel, a small string bass used for dance music.) Mendelssohn's account of the proceedings is graphic. 'I accompanied him at the keyboard . . . Neate [Charles Neate, a director of the Philharmonic Society] walking around me, while Smart encouraged the soldier [bass horn player], asking about his wife and children, giving him snuff . . .' Mendelssohn had to correct Smart's impression that the instrument should sound 'schön [noble]', and at the end the player went off home, taking his part with him. 'The scene was divine.'

It is clear from this account that Smart and others with Philharmonic Society connexions were involved in this charity performance (in which, incidentally, the overture was not particularly well performed, although an encore was more successful). It is unlikely that he was familiar with the bass horn, as it was a military rather than an orchestral instrument. There are no Philharmonic records extant for this period, but it would seem very likely that the unfortunate player of this very exposed part came from the Coldstream Guards. Annual performances of the work formed part of the Philharmonic Society's seasons from 1830 onwards. The accounts show that for the 1830 concert Willman, 1st Clarinet, engaged eight wind players. Thomas Willman was bandmaster of the Coldstreams until 1825 and Jepp, who became one of the country's leading serpentists and was regularly engaged to play with the Philharmonic Society's orchestra, was also a member of the Coldstream Guards. The other possibility is that the player was Ponder, who played 'Bafs Horn' in the society's 1832 performance of the overture (see page 502 below). Smart, incidentally, conducted the first Philharmonic Society performance at the King's Theatre on 1 March 1830, and all his later performances, from a copy of the score presented to him by Mendelssohn on 23 November 1829. This is now in the library of the Royal Academy of Music (MS. 2). The orchestral parts were copied by Charles, Smart's double bass-player brother, for a fee of £3.5.5.

When Friedrich Wilhelm IV later suggested to Mendelssohn that he write incidental music to *Ein Sommernachtstraum*, the composer included 'Corno Inglese di Basso' in Nos. 6, 9, 11 and 12. This, opus 61, was performed at Potsdam on 14 October 1843. The bass horn had generally been superseded in military bands by this time. The parts of the overture published by Breitkopf & Härtel in 1832 and the score (1835) label the part 'Ophicleïde', as do the parts and score of the incidental music published in 1848. The British Library copy of the first edition of the score of the overture is that given by Mendelssohn to the Society of British Musicians, so it would seem that the composer approved of the substitution of ophicleide for bass horn. It is likely, in any event, that the incidental music was first played on a *Ventil-Ophikleide*. When Berlioz conducted in Berlin in the year of the first performance he noted that at the Opera an additional bass trombone was present, but Gassner claims to have seen an ophicleide in another Berlin orchestra in that same year, presumably of the valved type. No evidence of valved ophicleides being used in Britain has so far been discovered, probably because the keyed ophicleide was well-established in orchestras while bands took up the saxhorns immediately they appeared.

In London the Philharmonic Society appears to have used a (keyed) ophicleide for the overture from at least 1843, when Ellison was engaged as player of the 'Ophycliede'. The printed orchestral parts specify this instrument and, in any case, by this time the last players of the bass horn would have been dying off. It is ironic that in the 1970s some conductors and orchestras, under the impression that they were giving historically-informed performances, began to use ophicleide rather than tuba. They were in fact ignoring Mendelssohn's express wish for a particular sound: though preferable to the tuba, the ophicleide is not a satisfactory substitute for bass horn.

# INTERNATIONAL DEMANDS ON ROSSINI

When the Italian composer Gioacchino Rossini (1792-1868) revised *Maometto II* for production at the Paris Opéra in 1826 he renamed it *Le Siège de Corinth*. Disappointingly, no manuscript score of either version survives: the earliest extant material consists of the score published by Troupenas in 1826. The overture to the opera became immensely popular and was played in the inaugural concert of the Hallé Orchestra in Manchester on 30 January 1858, providing an opportunity for Angelo Medina to contribute the ophicleide part. Inspection of the score of *Maometto II*, first performed in Naples on 3 December 1820, would allow a full assessment of Rossini's initial treatment of the low brass. In the Paris version this consists of three trombones and ophicleide. Since there was an ophicleide present in the Opéra orchestra a part had to be provided for it, but much of this is in unison with the third trombone and none of it contributes anything of significance. As Troupenas prints all four parts on one stave it is even difficult to decide in one passage (bars 29-56) whether the ophicleide is in unison with the third trombone or whether the trombone alone plays.

Rossini's failure to exploit his full low brass section is all the more surprising as he uses the trombones in a strikingly idiomatic and dramatic manner in the overture, particularly in the section headed 'Marche lugubre Grecque' in which the ophicleide is significantly silent until the last two bars. The only conclusion to be drawn is that Rossini had no idea what an ophicleide was—and nor should he, as it had made its first public appearance only six years earlier, in France. The instrument in general use for the lowest brass part in Italian opera houses at the time was, of course, the cimbasso, or bass horn. His awareness of the function of that instrument is shown in the *serpentone* part in the opening of the Sinfonia to *Armida* (Ex. 2.2).

Rossini retired at the age of forty-three and enjoyed himself eating regularly and composing from time to time. One of his few religious compositions is the *Petite messe solennelle*, a major work, initially accompanied by two pianos and harmonium but subsequently orchestrated and first performed in this version at the Théâtre-Italien on 28 February 1869. By this time he had lived permanently in Paris for some fourteen years and had had the opportunity to learn rather more about the ophicleide. During the work he sometimes uses individual brass instruments as solo voices. On several occasions the ophicleide takes over a melodic line from the first trombone to fulfil this function. There are even three bars marked 'solo' in the 'Agnus Dei' (Ex. 16.1). The Kalmus edition stipulates three trombones and a bass trombone as in Verdi, but even this later composer did not expect (or demand) four trombones in a Parisian orchestra and it has been found that three trombones and ophicleide provide a viable combination in performances of the *Petite messe* by modern orchestras.

Ex. 16.1

Rossini: *Petite messe solennelle*

# VERDI AND THE CIMBASSO

As with the other major composers considered this chapter, Verdi's ear for instrumental colour was finely attuned. Despite (or because of) having spent his formative years amongst performers with modest attainments, he was all but obsessed with minute differences in sound throughout the whole of his long working life. Julian Budden points out that he was filled with so much hatred for the valved horn, which had been in use at the Paris Opéra for thirty years before his *Don Carlos* was produced there, that he chose to use four natural horns, each crooked in a different key (B[63], III, 55). In the opening of *Jérusalem,* he clearly differentiates between trumpets and cornets (B[63], I, 353). Chapter XV gives details of how Verdi finally reached a decision about the lowest of the brass in his orchestra. His stipulated low brass requirements in some of the major operas are as follows (in chronological order):

*NABUCODONOSOR (NABUCCO)* (La Scala, Milan, 9 March 1842). 3 trombones, 1 cimbasso (lowest note B♭♭; Verdi goes out of his way to avoid the A♭ one tone below.) Trombones written on one stave in score.

   Meucci (M[33] [GSJ], 150, n. 37) mentions an *oficleide* in the orchestra at La Scala in 1846, and if this were in B♭ it could explain the inclusion of the B♭ but avoidance of the note a tone lower in this score. However, official documents show that there was a serpent at La Scala between 1854-60 (*Capitoli d'obbligo per l'Empresa degl'Imperiali Regj Teatri della Scala e della Canobbiana in Milano pel sejennio del 1° dicembre 1854 al 30 novembre 1860* (Milan, 1853), 37, quoted in H[14], 112), but it is unlikely that the early cimbasso (bass horn) noted in 1825 was still being used. Verdi, a careful orchestrator, gives the cimbasso a part that descends one tone lower than its official lowest note. A skilled player could, of course, obtain this through fingering low C and bending the note down at the embouchure. It is always possible that the 'serpentone' to which reference was made was in fact a different low brass instrument, though practical experiment shows that the low brass chorale which opens the overture does work well with three trombones and early cimbasso, so perhaps this was, after all, the low brass section at the premiere.

Ex. 16.2

Verdi: *Nabucco* Sinfonia

*ERNANI* (La Fenice, Venice, 9 March 1844). 3 trombones, 1 cimbasso (lowest note C). Trombones written on one stave in score.

In 1844 the orchestra list for La Fenice included three trombones and one *bombardone* ($V^4$, *Ernani*, xxvii). (A libretto dating from this period gives the name of the player as Ferdinando Rizzolini.) Claudio Gallico, who contributed the critical notes to this volume of the Verdi Complete Edition, points out that in that particular theatre the term 'Bombardone' seemed to refer generically to the lowest brass instrument. Both Verdi and the copyist wrote 'Cimbasso'. However, when Ricordi printed parts in the late nineteenth century these were for 'Trombone 1°', 'Trombone 2°', 'Trombone 3°' and 'Ophicleide', though on the covers of the various sets the latter part is always either 'Cimbasso' or 'Trombone Basso'.

*LUISA MILLER* (San Carlo, Naples, 8 December 1849). 3 trombones, 1 cimbasso (lowest note C). Trombones written on one stave in score.

In the score, the composer wrote 'Tromboni' and 'Cimbasso' respectively, but in his critical commentary Jeffrey Kallberg notes that on the manuscript part for 'Serpan' (presumably used at the Naples premiere) there is a pencilled annotation: 'First performance at Her Majesty's Theatre June 8th 1858'. It is unlikely that the part would have been played on serpent so late as this, the more so as there was an 'ophecleide' at this theatre in 1847 ($M^{53}$, 20.2.47, 113). If an ophicleide was used, it may have been played either by Alfred Phasey or Samuel Hughes.

*RIGOLETTO* (La Fenice, Venice, 11 March 1851). 3 trombones, 1 cimbasso (lowest note C).

The lowest brass part at La Fenice was always called 'Bombardone' ($V^4$, xxviii), and the player at this time was Ferdinando Rizzoli (see *Ernani*, above). In his critical commentary, Martin Chusid points out that Ricordi's printed parts were for 'Trombone 1$^{mo}$ e 2°', and 'Trombone 3° e Serpan'. References to this part in this particular opera use three different names: cimbasso (composer), bombardone (theatre management) and serpan (publisher) (compare with Ponchielli, *La Gioconda*, see page 510 below).

*IL TROVATORE* (Teatro Apollo, Rome, 19 January 1853). 3 trombones, 1 cimbasso (lowest note C).

In his critical comentary, David Lawton states that Verdi's manuscript shows 'Tromboni' and 'Cimbasso', although it is known that the orchestra at the Apollo for the 1852-53 season included three trombones and an ophicleide. Ricordi's printed parts were for 'Trombone 1$^{me}$ e 2$^{do}$', 'Trombone 3° e Cimbasso'.

LES VÊPRES SICILIENNES (Opéra, Paris, 13 June 1855). 3 trombones, 1 ophicleide (lowest note ?D).

The specified instruments are those which were available at the time at the Opéra. In Ricordi's score of *I Vespri siciliani* the lowest instrument is sometimes '[Tr.$^{ni}$] IV', sometimes 'Cimb'. It is interesting to note that by this time in Italy more 'modern' practices may have been in place as the *Archivio di Stato*, Rimini, 1855, show a bombardon at the Teatro Comunale, Rimini.

LA TRAVIATA (La Fenice, Venice, 6 March 1853). 3 trombones, 1 cimbasso (lowest note C).

The first Ricordi edition of the score, c. 1854, gave 'Trombone I e II/Trombone III e Serpentone', the libretto for the premiere: '*Bombardone* sig. Gaetano Bettini'.

SIMON BOCCANEGRA (La Fenice, Venice, 12 March 1857). 3 trombones, 1 cimbasso (lowest note C).

In the reconstruction of the Noseda Archivio Musical MS. by Alan Bousted the cimbasso part uniquely reaches g♯, but this may have resulted from transposition of the third trombone and cimbasso staves in the original score.

UN BALLO IN MASCHERA (Teatro Apollo, Rome, 17 February 1859). 3 trombones, 1 cimbasso (lowest note C).

LA FORZA DEL DESTINO (Imperial Theatre, St Petersburg, 19 October/10 November 1862; revised version, La Scala, Milan, 27 February 1869). 3 trombones, 1 cimbasso (lowest note B').

Verdi found the St Petersburg orchestra and chorus good though 'not educated in finesse' (A$^1$, II, 679, 681). It is possible that the cimbasso part may have been played on a [valved] ophicleide; one of these instruments was present in the orchestra of Moscow's Bolshoi Theatre at the time (see page 215 above).

DON CARLOS (Opéra, Paris, 11 March 1867; revised version as *Don Carlo*, La Scala, Milan, 10 January 1884). 3 trombones, 1 oficleide (lowest note B').

Verdi goes out of his way in this score to avoid writing a B'♭ for the lowest instrument, clearly having in mind an ophicleide pitched in C.

*AIDA* (Opera House, Cairo, 24 December 1871; La Scala, Milan, 8 February 1872). 3 trombones, 1 cimbasso (lowest note B'b).

In a letter to Verdi dated 23 May 1871, Giulio Ricordi reported that for the La Scala premiere of *Aida* a bombardon was to be used. The response was Verdi's strongly-voiced objection to that 'devilish bombardon'. Marchesi reports that the libretto for the Cairo performance on 24 December 1871 listed an ophicleide (M[12], n. 59).

By the time Verdi came to compose his two final operas the balanced low brass quartet for which he had been searching was at last available, with the *Trombone basso Verdi* as the lowest instrument. Since the three upper trombones were all tenors, on the covers of this lowest part 'Trombone Basso' was normally stamped, in accordance with the wishes of the composer, but the instrument itself, made by Pelitti, was a BBb contrabass.

*OTELLO* (La Scala, Milan, 5 February 1887). 3 trombones, 1 *trombone basso* (lowest note A').

*FALSTAFF* (La Scala, Milan, 9 February 1893). 3 trombones, 1 *trombone basso* (lowest note B'b).

*MESSA DA REQUIEM* (San Marco, 22 May 1874). 3 [tenor] trombones, 1 *oficleide* (lowest note B').

Verdi's two major sacred works for voices and orchestra were not intended for production in the opera house. Consequently, in the Requiem he uses the accepted Italian symphonic quartet of three trombones and ophicleide, although it should be noted that there are no significant differences between his approach to this ophicleide part and the cimbasso parts he wrote elsewhere (Ex. 16.3(a)). Verdi takes great care to avoid going below the compass of the ophicleide in C. In the 'Dies Irae', at bar 258 he gives the part a bar's rest. Up to this point it has been playing an octave below the third trombone: C♯ (two bars), C (two bars). In the next bar, while the third trombone goes down to B'b the ophicleide is tacet, playing again in the following bar where an ascending passage of B', C, etc. begins (Ex. 16.3(b)). At the end of No. 2, there is a B'b in the third trombone part (the [valve] trombone playing this as an open pedal note), while the ophicleide is in unison with the second trombone (Ex. 16.3(c)). Apart from this instance, the lowest note for Trombone 3 is the E below the bass clef, the lowest second harmonic of a Bb tenor trombone, played with all three valves. This treatment should be contrasted with that given to the *Trombone basso* in *Otello* (see above). The *Trombone basso Verdi in Sib* could, by definition, have played the Bb immediately below the bass stave.

A performance of the Requiem at the Teatro Regio di Parma in 1876 included cimbasso (i.e., *Trombone basso Verdi*) (M[12], 73-74). Rosen remarks that the hand-written names on the covers of the manuscript parts include 'Tromboni' [1 and 2], 'Trombone 3°' and 'Cimbasso'. A later hand has written 'Tuba' on both the cover and an inserted page of the 'Liber scriptus' used in the first English performance at the Royal Albert Hall on 15 May 1875. On the title-page and elsewhere is written 'Ophicleide', as in Verdi's manuscript. Modern performances using cimbasso contrabass valve trombone have been very effective as this instrument balances the contemporary symphonic trombone section perfectly.

Ex. 16.3

(a)

Ex. 16.3

(b)

**[Allegro molto sostenuto]**

(c)

**[morendo ed allargando]**

Verdi: Messa da Requiem

*QUATTRO PEZZI SACRI* (Opéra, Paris, 7 April 1898). 4 trombones (Trombone 4 lowest note B'♭).

The music was composed between 1888 and 1897. In the score, the three higher trombone parts (which descend as far as E) are written on one stave, the fourth on the stave below. That the B'♭ is not considered solely as a pedal note (i.e. for tenor trombone) is demonstrated by Verdi's also writing a B' in the fourth part.

Why did Verdi stipulate four trombones in the *Four Sacred Pieces*? The title gives the answer. The Requiem, though not intended for the opera house, was vividly dramatic (to the extent that initially Sunday performances were banned in England). The *Four Sacred Pieces* are, however, sublimely religious. Although apparently so spontaneous a composer, Verdi always carried out painstaking research before beginning work. In the case of the Requiem he made a thorough study of Palestrina's techniques. There is no doubt that he was also aware of the trombone textures in the church compositions of the Gabrielis in sixteenth- and early seventeenth-century Venice, so his reasons for specifying four trombones are not difficult to find.

Puccini, Verdi's generally-accepted successor, followed the master's operatic practice by stipulating three trombones and 'Trombone Basso', save for *Manon Lescaut* ('Basso Tuba') and *Turandot* ('Trombone Contrabbasso'). While Puccini's *Trombone Basso* parts tend to have a lower tessitura than Verdi's, *Turandot* is more consistently in tuba range, descending to A'♭. The Ricordi full score lists the performers in the first performance, at La Scala on 25 April 1926, including 'Basso Tuba: Saverio Scorza'.

# WAGNER AND THE CONTRABASS TROMBONE

On finding two bass trombones and no ophicleide at the Berlin Opera in 1843 Berlioz expressed his horror thus:

Berlin is the only German town where I found the deep bass trombone (in B♭). We have none in Paris . . . at the Berlin Opera there is no ophicleide, and instead of replacing it by a bass tuba in the French operas . . . they imagined that they could have this part played by a second bass trombone; but the result of combining these two terrible instruments—the ophicleide part being often written an octave below the third trombone—is most disastrous . . . I should be inclined to allow the presence of a bass trombone only if the music were in four parts, and there were three tenors capable of holding their own against it (B[27], 308).

However, it does need to be borne in mind that the German bass trombone of the time was normally no more than a large-bore tenor. This is a familiar situation: at the beginning of the twenty-first century the instrument used for playing bass trombone parts has reverted to being just that, with the addition of two valves, one to lower it into the traditional bass trombone pitch of F and the other primarily to fill the gap between the pedal B♭ and the note a tone above by controlling access to either a trombone in E♭ or a trombone in D. The earliest reference to a slide trombone with such a valve seems to have been in *Allgemeine Musikalische Zeitung*, 41, 1839, with Sattler of Leipzig named as the maker (G[22], 85). Carter cites Andrew Nemetz who states in his *Nueste Posaun-Schule* (Vienna, 1827) that at the time alto, tenor and bass trombones were all in B♭ but used different mouthpieces and had different ranges (C[11], 186). A quartet of alto, tenor, large-bore tenor and 'deep bass trombone' seems totally viable. The continuing presence of two bass trombones at the Berlin Opera was noted in 1848 (G[7], XVI, 6) and as late as 1865 (Z[1], 730).

In his apprentice years, Wagner had to accept what he found, which is why the lowest brass parts in the earliest works show a remarkable diversity. In 'Norma, il predisse' (an aria for solo bass, male voice choir and orchestra to be inserted in Bellini's *Norma*), composed in 1839 with hopes of a Parisian performance, he rather surprisingly chose serpent. Another work for choir and orchestra, *Nicolay*, composed in Riga in 1837, has 'Ophikleide'. There are two 'Baßtuba' parts in a work composed for male voice choir and military band, *Gruß seiner Treuen au Friedrich August den Geliebten bei seiner Zurückkunft aus England den 9. August 1844*.

In *Rule, Britannia!* of 1838 and *Das Liebesmahl der Apostel* (1843) there are indications of his beginning to associate particular bass wind instruments with different sections. Here a serpent is written below the bassoons while below the trombones in the earlier work an ophicleide, a tuba in the later piece. A similar, though more extended, treatment is applied throughout *Rienzi*, where below the bassoons is 'Serpent (Kontrafagott)' and below the trombones, 'Ophikleide (Baßtuba)'. The 'Militärmusik auf dem Theater' (stage band) includes '4 Ophikleiden': he hoped for a première at the Paris Opéra. For the same reason, the tuba part in *Der Fliegende Holländer* lies within the range of the ophicleide.

By the time he had concluded his deliberations on *Gesamtkunstwerk* and set out to demonstrate them in *Der Ring des Nibelungen*, produced in 1876, he had become convinced that the tuba was not a satisfactory bass to the trombone section which at that time in Germany consisted of two B♭/F tenor-bass trombones and one wider-bore B♭/F bass trombone. Wagner's development of the Wagner Tuben is described in Chapter XV above. The *Ring* section of '2 Tenortuben in B, 2 Baßtuben in F' (played by the fifth to eighth horn-players) seated beside '1 Kontrabaßtuba' contributed a rounder, smoother, fuller sound to the low to

Fig. 16.1

TYPICAL ORCHESTR

(Local variations in performi

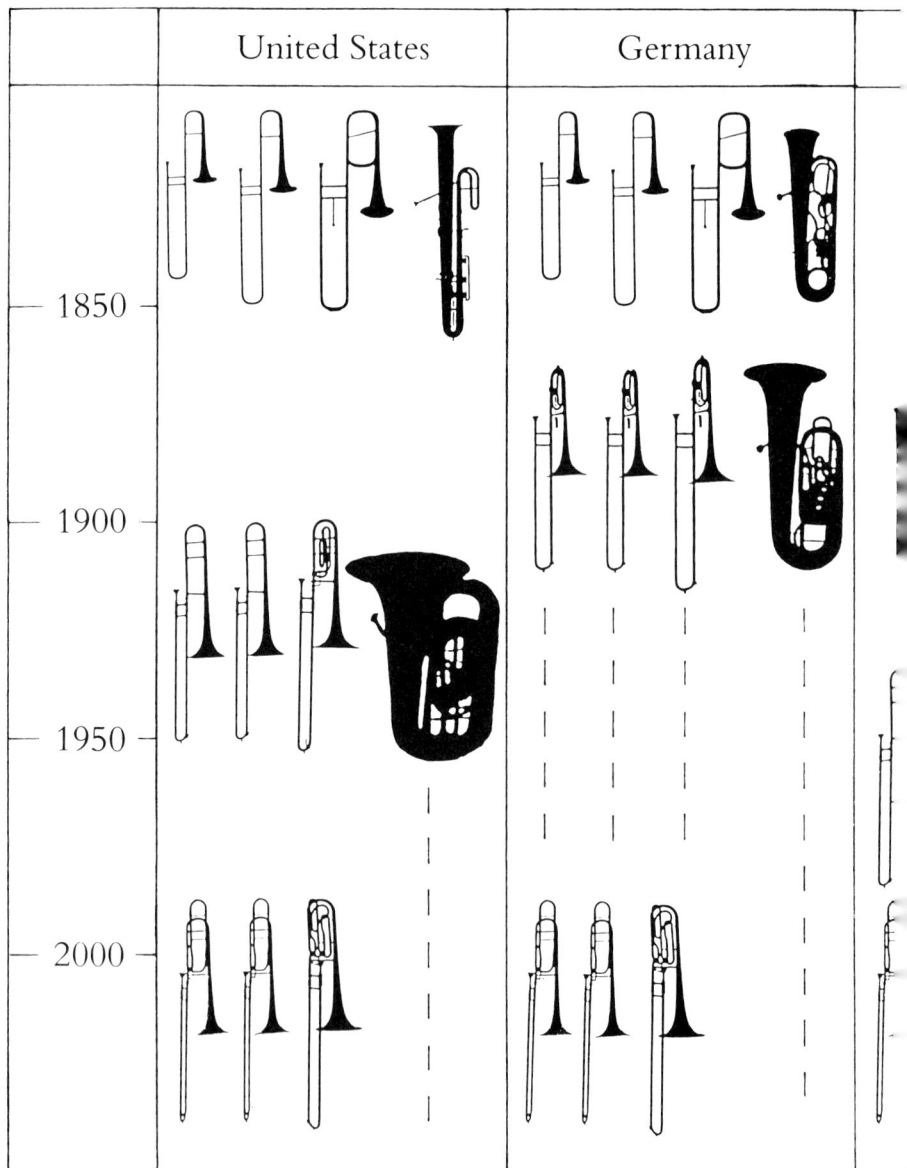

# LOW BRASS SECTIONS

ctice should be borne in mind)

| France | Britain | Italy |
| --- | --- | --- |

medium-high brass. He had explored this possibility over thirty years earlier when in 1841, in *Der Fliegende Hollander,* he had written a passage where the tuba (or ophicleide) is used not with the trombone section but in antithesis to it (Ex. 16.4). In the *Ring* Wagner specifies a low brass section of '3 Tenor-Baß-Posaunen, 1 Kontrabaßposaune, welche abwechselnd auch die gewöhnliche Baßposaune übernimmt' ('3 Bb/F trombones, 1 contrabass trombone which alternates with the ordinary bass trombone as appropriate'). In practice, this instrument is sometimes played by a tubist.

It would be totally wrong, therefore, to assume that only the Italians regularly used the contrabass trombone. Praetorius had actually illustrated such an instrument in his *Syntagma musicum* of 1619, but that prototype was unwieldy and little used. A specimen dating from 1639 by Oller of Stockholm is in the Musikmuseet, Stockholm (illustrated in S[5], III, 633 (b)). In Mannheim in 1841 there was no tuba but a specially-made valve trombone capable of playing down to C or B' (presumably therefore in Eb, or Bb/Eb). We have already noted Berlioz's pained surprise on finding two bass trombones in use at the Berlin Opera in 1843, at a time when the Baß-Tuba had already been adopted by army bands in Prussia. However, these instruments appear to have been in Bb, the same as the tenor, but with a larger bore. This was common practice at that time and in that place and explains the German enthusiasm for bass trombone solos of the type that brought fame to Carl Queisser (1800-1846) and Friedrich Belcke (1795-1874) (R[3], V, 1, 3-17). A quartet of trombones assembled to this recipe, all in Bb but with a wider-bore instrument playing the lowest part, is not all that far removed from Verdi's ideal.

While the literary and intellectual approach of Wagner would appear to have little in common with the apparent spontaneity of his contemporary Verdi, in his orchestration of *Der Ring des Nibelungen,* first produced in 1876, Wagner was equally concerned to differentiate between the mellow and the incisive brass instruments. Unlike Verdi, Wagner did not use tuba in his stage bands, but central to his approach to the brass in the orchestra pit was the separation of the tuba from the trombones, which he achieved through the introduction of a quartet of Wagner Tuben (see page 461 above) to sit on top of the contrabass tuba and form a new tonal group in the orchestra. In contrast to this, the more incisive sounds were provided by a trumpet section augmented by a bass trumpet of tenor trombone pitch, while the lower notes were played by a quartet of three Bb/F trombones supported by a contrabass trombone.

Ex. 16.4.

Wagner: *Der Fliegende Holländer*

From the middle of the nineteenth century there was a slow but regular flow of contrabass trombone patents, many utilising the double-slide principle which, according to Kastner, was conceived by Gottfried Weber and first manufactured by Schott of Mainz in 1816 (C[11], 189-190). Kastner illustrates a double-slide trombone (K[5], pl xvii, No. 7). Halary's model of 1855 is illustrated in L[5], x, 1652, Fig. 718. British Patent 3194 of 31 December 1860 for double slide trombone was taken out by John Midgley, John Sugden and William Clapham. Arnold Myers has shown this to be a slide-tuba (see page 459 above). In 1861 Boosey of London introduced the 'Basso Profundo', a double slide contrabass in CC. This fearsome instrument is illustrated by Gregory, where it is held by Godfrey Kneller (G[22], pl. XIV). Similar instruments appear to have been made and used by the Salvation Army early in the twentieth century (G[22], 97). It is difficult to imagine the role played by such an instrument in converting the fallen masses; perhaps it provided a form of penance for the bandsman. The double-slide instrument Wagner commissioned from Carl Moritz, pitched in BB♭, thus benefited from the work of previous makers. Later inventors included C. A. Goodwin, British Patent 3951 of 26 February 1884 for a double-slide trombone and Richard Weller (Markneukirchen 1898) German Patent 103298 for 'Helikonposaune' (contrabass slide trombone in helicon shape).

Mahillon showed in their 1896 catalogue what farther south might have been called a cimbasso as part of a set of extra brass instruments for *Ring* performances. This included four Wagner Tuben, a BB♭ contrabass bombardon, a bass trumpet and a BB♭ contrabass valved trombone (W[5], 210). Valved trombones were more widespread at the time: there was one in the band of the 24th Foot in 1879 (T[15], 113) and the late nineteenth-century English boys' band shown in Fig. 15.2 includes both tenor and bass instruments of this type.

In 1921 Ernst Dehmal of Berlin took out a patent for a contrabass trombone in F with two valves for Wagner performances. A model made by A. Sprinz was played by Dehmal at Bayreuth in 1924 (although he was succeeded by Friedrich Tritt of Vienna in 1927). The double-slide trombone enabled the positions to be located more conveniently, but the considerable weight of the slide contributed to its lack of popularity with players, and it is interesting to note that the 1921 double-valve approach was taken by a player rather than a manufacturer. During the early twentieth century it became normal for instruments of this type to be used for *Ring* performances.

A taste for contrabass trombone is evident amongst many German composers who indulged in the excesses of post-Romantic or serial idioms: Richard Strauss

(*Salome*, 1905, *Elektra*, 1909, *Die Liebe der Danae*, 1944); Schoenberg (*Gurrelieder*, 1913); Berg (*Wozzeck*, 1925); and Webern (*Six Pieces*, op. 6, 1910). Zechmeister has explored in some depth the role of the contrabass trombone in Vienna, showing that valved trombones were introduced at the Vienna Opera during the 1830s while it was under Italian management ($Z^4$, 20). A contrabass slide trombone was used for the first time 1927, replaced by a six-valve contrabass in F made in Vienna by Anton Dehmal's successor. (This was the instrument used in Solti's recording of the *Ring* in 1965, illustrated in $Z^4$, Fig. 6.) In 1998 Zechmeister successfully developed a new model (Fig. 16.1). This utilized the fingering of the Viennese Concert Tuba (see Ex. 4.1) and was thus convenient for players of that instrument.

Fig. 16.1
Gerhard Zechmeister with the new six-valve Viennese Contrabass Trombone, 1997.

Photo: *Karl Breslmair*

Elsewhere the contrabass was usually played by a bass trombonist, but this was not always the case: in the Royal Philharmonic Society's concert of Wagner excerpts conducted by William Mengelberg on 18 February 1913 it was played by Frank Reynolds, who normally played tuba.

# [ROYAL] PHILHARMONIC SOCIETY, LONDON

The following information has been compiled from the manuscript account books, correspondence and diaries of Sir George Smart, one of the founders of the society in 1813 (BL Add. MS. 41771, 41772, 41777, 41778, 41779); details of the society's programmes printed in the *Musical Courier*, 25 June 1896 (BL Loan MS. 48.15/2); accounts of the Royal Philharmonic Society (BL Loan 48. RPS); and C. Ehrlich: *First Philharmonic*, Oxford, 1995, Appendix 3. The Philharmonic Society was formed in London in 1813 for the encouragement of orchestral and instrumental music. On reaching its centenary in 1912 it became the Royal Philharmonic Society. The London Philharmonic Orchestra was formed in 1932 by Sir Thomas Beecham; the Royal Philharmonic Orchestra was founded in 1946, also by Beecham, but there are no formal connexions between these three organizations.

| | | |
|---|---|---|
| 1814–1815 | Wilmshurst. Serpent. | £1.1.0 |
| | Wilmshurst was serpentist in the band of the Guards First Regiment. He presumably played in Haydn's *Grand March* on 28 March 1814. | |
| 1830 | Accounts for one concert include 'Willman [1st Clarinet] for 8 Extra Wind instruments £4.4.0.' This probably was the performance of *A Midsummer Night's Dream Overture* on 1 March 1830. | |
| 1832 | Ponder. Baſs Horn. | £1.1.0 |
| | This was in *A Midsummer Night's Dream Overture* on 18 June 1832. | |
| 1836 | Ponder [no instrument stated] | £3.13.6 for 4 rehs, 2 concerts. |
| | The work was *Meerestille und Gluckliche Fahrt* (which includes a serpent part) on 22 February 1836. | |
| 1837 | Ponder          „ | £3.13.6 for 4 rehs, 3 concerts. |
| | These included *A Midsummer Night's Dream Overture* (27 February | |

|  |  |  |  |
|---|---|---|---|
|  | 1837). | | |
| 1838–41 | Ponder | ,, | £1.1.0 |

On 11 May 1840 he performed in *A Midsummer Night's Dream Overture.*

| 1842 | Jepp | ,, | £1.1.0 |
|---|---|---|---|

This was *A Midsummer Night's Dream Overture* on 18 April 1842.

| | Ellison | ,, | £1.1.0 |
|---|---|---|---|

This was *A Calm Sea and Prosperous Voyage* on 16 May 1842.

| 1843–46 | Ellison. Ophycliede. | | £1.11.6 for 3 rehs, 3 concerts. |
|---|---|---|---|

From 1844 works by Verdi regularly appeared in the society's concerts.

| 1847–50 | Prospére. | ,, | £1.1.0 |
|---|---|---|---|

This included the complete music to *A Midsummer Night's Dream* on 26 April 1847.

| 1850 | Jepp | ,, | £1.1.0 |
|---|---|---|---|
| 1851–58 | Prospére | ,, | £1.1.0 |

This included the complete music to *A Midsummer Night's Dream* on 26 April 1851.

On 28 May 1855 Wagner conducted a concert including the overture to *Tannhäuser* and a selection from *Lohengrin*, both requiring tuba.

| 1859 | Phasey | ,, | £1.1.0 |
|---|---|---|---|

This was the complete music to *A Midsummer Night's Dream* on 21 May 1859.

| 1863–65 | Phasey | ,, | £1.1.0 |
|---|---|---|---|
| 1866 | Standen. Serpent. | | |

The concert on 5 March 1866 included Schumann's *Paradise and the Peri* which has a part for Ophycleide. Perhaps Standen was engaged to play this.

Phasey.

The concert on 11 June 1866 included the 'Wedding March' from *A Midsummer Night's Dream.*

| 1870 | W. F. Young. Bass Tuba. | | |
|---|---|---|---|
| 1873 | A. J. Phasey | | |

The season included Brahms: *A German Requiem* (2 April 1873), and Wagner: *The Flying Dutchman Overture* (28 April 1873) and

*Tannhäuser Overture* (23 June 1873). Phasey probably played bass trombone rather than ophicleide.

| | |
|---|---|
| 1880 | J. Wilson. Bombardon. [A. J. Phasey. Bass trombone] |
| 1890 | F. Blake. Tuba. |
| 1900, 1905 | R. W. Travis. Tuba. |
| 1908-09 | W. Reynolds. Tuba. |
| | J. W. Collins. Tuba. |
| 1910-11 | R. Powis. Tuba. |
| 1912-20 | F. Reynolds. Tuba. [Also contrabass trombone in Wagner concert, 18 February 1913] |
| 1920 | W. Reynolds. Tuba. |

In the concert on 18 February 1913, which included excepts from Wagner conducted by William Mengelberg, the trombonist Arthur Falkner played bass trumpet while the contrabass trombone was played by Walter Reynolds, who had appeared with the orchestra on tuba in 1908-9 and was to reappear in 1920. Four tuba players are also noted in the printed programme, presumably playing the Mahillon Wagner Tuben: H. Tyler, A. Tyler, T. Cornish and R. Powis (though Powis played orchestral bass tuba in 1910-11).

# HALLÉ ORCHESTRA, MANCHESTER

The Hallé Orchestra is the longest-established permanent symphony orchestra in the U.K. Information up to 1895 has been obtained from Thomas Batley *Sir Charles Hallé's Concerts in Manchester. A List of Vocal and Instrumental Soloists . . . Members of the Orchestra . . . Programmes of Concerts . . . 1858 . . .1895,* Manchester, 1896 with expansion and correction from various other sources. Information on subsequent players has been provided by Stuart Robinson, whose long connexion with the orchestra (primarily as concerts manager) began during Wallace Jones's time as tubist.

| | |
|---|---|
| 1858-9 to 1867-68 | Angelo Medina (ophicleide and tuba) |
| 1858 | Samuel Hughes (ophicleide) [guest soloist] |
| 1868-69 | [      ] Dodsworth (ophicleide) |
| 1868-69 | Richard Hopkinson (ophicleide) |

| | |
|---|---|
| 1869-70 to 1875-76, | |
| 1877-78 | F[    ] J. Batley (?) |
| 1873-74, 1876-77, | |
| 1878-79 to 1885-86 | Richard Marsden (tuba, [?ophicleide], serpent) |
| 1885-86 to 1893-94 | [T    ] Moss (tuba) |
| 1894-95 to 1929-30 | Harry Barlow (ophicleide, tuba) |
| 1930-31 to 1959-60 | Wallace H. Jones (tuba) |
| 1959-60 to 1962-63 | Allan Jenkins (tuba) |
| 1962-63 to 1983-84 | Stuart Roebuck (tuba) |
| 1984-85 to 1999-00 | Andrew Duncan (tuba) |
| 2000- | |

Barlow is shown as playing ophicleide only on 7 March 1895, in the 'Air de ballet' and 'Angelus' from Massenet's *Scènes pittoresques*. His first season was Charles Halle's last and during the interregnum, before Richter became musical director (his inaugural concert was on 19 October 1899 and included Wagner's *Meistersinger* and *Parsifal* overtures), Frederick Cowen, another Wagner devotee, held the post. Significantly, during the season following Halle's death Sullivan also conducted the orchestra: his views on the ophicleide are printed on page 166 above.

# APPROPRIATE INSTRUMENTS AND TECHNIQUE

That most practical of historically-informed brass players, Crispian Steel-Perkins, has observed in relation to performances of period orchestra trumpet parts:

One must accept, even if reluctantly, that the degree of accuracy expected in modern performances and the volume required in large, acoustically dry modern halls make demands upon both players and instruments beyond the capabilities available 250 years ago (S[34], 11).

He concluded that a totally 'authentic' performance is an impossibility, if only because the act of performing requires an audience, and the socio-economic make-up of a modern audience, along with its accumulated experience of hearing music, is never going to be the same as that of an audience in earlier times. Here is Beethoven writing to his publishers after the first performance of his fifth symphony in December 1808:

To begin with, the musicians had lost their place and made a mistake in the simplest passage imaginable. So I stopped them sharply and cried out loud, 'Begin it again!' (B[12], 301)

In 1828 the Musikverein of Vienna found Schubert's ninth symphony too difficult to play in public. When Mendelssohn tried to rehearse it with the orchestra of the London Philharmonic Society in 1844 the string players laughed at the last movement and it was withdrawn. In 1837 some sections of Queen Victoria's coronation had to be repeated owing to omissions with serious implications for the legitimacy of her power. (In those days there were no rehearsals for mere coronations.) How much control a conductor actually had over a rehearsal or a performance in the mid-nineteenth century might also seem open to question when Louis Dietsch, conductor at the Paris Opéra from 1860 to 1863 was known to conduct from a Violin I part (B[63], III, 22). (It is perhaps worth mentioning that he was the conductor involved in the scandalous first production of *Tannhäuser* there (see page 255 above).) Hubert Parry made a rather despairing entry in his diary on 8 May 1880 about the deficiences in the accompaniment to his piano concerto provided by the Crystal Palace Orchestra under Richter (the best conductor of the time) on 3 April owing to problems with 'the 6 sharps business' (D[8], 8.5.80). The performance of Busoni's *Fantasia contrappuntistica* announced for the Royal Philharmonic Society's concert on 1 March 1913 had to be cancelled owing to 'difficulties at rehearsals'.

In terms of appropriate technique, is it advisable to follow to the letter the advice of the late eighteenth-century trumpet-player Altenburg and form the embouchure by 'a tight closing together of the teeth and lips' (A[9], II, 2, 60), or when playing high notes, adopt a 'tight drawing together of the lips'? (A[9], II, 1, 21). Articulation according to Mersenne, in which 'the end of the tongue must enter into the cup, so as to lead the wind into it' (M[29], 317) was still being taught well within living memory.

In terms of appropriate instruments it may be productive to consider a performance of a mid-nineteenth-century Italian opera. In this case the composer is likely to have written with the sounds of three tenor valved trombones and a cimbasso (of one sort or another) in his mind. Practical experience shows that even the best available modern tenor valve trombones are disappointing to play: stuffy to blow and poor in intonation. They cannot be seriously recommended for any type of music with longer notes than those found in bebop. Thus a decision has to be made between using cimbasso with three tenor valve trombones (unacceptable to modern audiences) or three slide trombones (inauthentic). The type of cimbasso to complete this section is another question to be pondered, but it should not lead our friendly music director to contemplate suicide. He needs to remember that unlike Mendelssohn, Wagner and Verdi, the majority of nineteenth-century Italian opera composers were not too concerned about the precise nature of the lowest instrument in the brass section.

In terms of audience reaction, it is salutory to remember the increase in acceptable levels of volume during the twentieth century. In the mid-nineteenth, complaints were made in both France and England about the unacceptably loud tone of the ophicleide, an instrument which to us is markedly weaker in sound than the modern tuba. Somewhat earlier, military bands consisted of a mere eight players and the image of a lone fiddler playing for public dances is familiar from many illustrations. The battery of megawattage expected in any disco, the deafening passage of open-topped cars through summer streets and our shared ability to turn up the sound by the twist of a knob or the flick of a slider has changed for ever our ideas of loudness in music. The broader soundscape against which the game of life is played is not appropriate for consideration here, but it is worth reflecting on the contrast between the sounds of two common methods of transport: the stage-coach of the nineteenth century and the jet airliner of the twenty-first.

Perhaps a more productive approach to the question could result from addressing the problems of nineteenth-century national performing styles. It must be borne in mind that there was no abrupt change in tone or volume during the period under consideration. The transition from ophicleide to Small C Tuba in French orchestras or ophicleide to euphonium to compact F tuba in England was probably the result of the pursuit of secure intonation: changes in timbre or power were imperceptible except to those most closely involved. The sudden introduction of the 'big sound' in these countries occurred after World War II.

Some of the most dramatic illustrations of performing practice in relation to the lowest brass instrument are found in the orchestrations of operas. We have already seen that composers hoping for a premiere abroad conformed to the conventions of the foreign opera house. The following list is not restricted to opera, but includes mainly works by composers who have varied their stipulated lowest brass instrument for whatever reason. As far as possible it is based on modern collected editions and is thus as correct as can be from the scholarly viewpoint. Composers are listed in alphabetical order with their works printed chronologically.

Table 16.1.     LOWEST BRASS INSTRUMENT STIPULATIONS

| Composer | Title | Date & place of premiere | Instrument |
|---|---|---|---|
| Auber, Daniel Fr. 1782-1871 | La muette de Portici | 29.2.1828 Paris Opéra | Ophicleïde |
| | Gustave | 27.2.1833 Paris Opéra | Ophycléide |
| Bellini, Vincenzo It. 1801-1835 | Il Pirata | 27.10.1827 Milan La Scala | Serpentone |
| | La Straniera | 14.2.1829 Milan La Scala | Cimbasso |
| | Norma | 26.12.1831 Milan La Scala | Cimbasso |
| Berlioz, Hector Fr. 1803-69 | Messe solennelle | 22.11.1827 Paris [?] | Serpent |
| | Les francs-juges (ouverture) | 26.5.1828 Paris Cons. | Ophicléide I (Ut) Ophicléide II (Si♭) |
| | Resurrexit | 26.5.28. Paris Cons. | Serpent et Ophicléide |
| | Scène héroïque (orch.) | 26.5.1828 Paris Cons. | Ophicléide |
| | (band) | [pre-1833; unperf.] | Ophicléides |
| | Waverley | 26.5.1828 Paris Cons. | Ophicléide |
| | Huit scènes de Faust | 29.11.1829 Paris Cons. | Ophicléide |
| | Symphonie fantastique | 5.12.1830 Paris Cons. | Serpent et ophicléide |
| | | [rev.] | 2 Ophicléides |
| | Le roi Lear (grande ouverture) | 12.12.1833 Paris Cons. | Ophicléide |
| | Harold en Italie | 23.11.34 Paris Cons. | Ophiclëide ou Tuba |
| | Grande messe des morts | 5.12.1837 Paris Invalides | |
| | Tuba mirum | | 4e Orchestre: Ophicléides (4) I/II 1er Orchestre: Tubas (2) |
| | 4. Rex Tremendae | | Orchestre 4: Ophicléides (2) |
| | 6. Lacrimosa | | Orchestre 4: Ophicléides (4) I, II Orchestre 1: Tubas (2) |
| | 7. Offertoire | | Orchestre 4: Ophicléides (2) |
| | 9. Sanctus | | Orchestre 4: Ophicléides (4) |

| | | | |
|---|---|---|---|
| | 10. Agnus Dei | | Orchestre 4: Ophicléides (4) |
| | Benvenuto Cellini | 10.9.1838 Paris Opéra | Ophicléide |
| | Roméo et Juliette | 24.11.1839 Paris Cons. | Ophycléide ou Tuba |
| | Grande symphonie funèbre et triomphale | 7.8.40 Paris | 1rs Ophicléides en Ut (3) [parade]  2mes ophicléides en Sib (3) |
| | Tristia 3. Marche funèbre pour la dernière scène d'Hamlet | [ ].11.1844; unperf. | Basse tuba ou Ophicléide |
| | Le Corsaire (ouverture) | 19.1.45 Paris Cirque Olympique | Ophicléide ou Tuba |
| | La damnation de Faust | 6.8.46 Paris Opéra Comique | Ophicléide et Tuba |
| | Vox Populi 1. La menace des Francs | 25.3.51. Paris Salle Ste.-Cécile | Ophicléïde ou Tuba |
| | Lélio | 21.2.55 Weimar | Ophicléide |
| | Te Deum | 30.4.1855 Paris S.-Eustache | Ophicléide et Tuba |
| | L'Impériale | 15.11.1855 Paris Palais de l'industrie | Tubas (2) et Ophicléides (3) |
| | Les Troyens | 4.11.1863 Paris Th. Lyrique [in part] | Ophicléide ou Tuba |
| Donizetti, Gaetano It. 1797–1848 | Parisina | 17.3.33 Florence Pergola | Cimbasso |
| | Les martyrs | 10.4.1840 Paris Opéra | Ophicléide |
| | La favorite | 2.12.1840 Paris Opéra | Ophicléide |
| | Dom Sebastién | 29.2.1828 Paris Opéra | Ophycleide |
| Halévy, Fromental Fr. 1799–1862 | La juive | 23.1.1835 Paris Opéra | Ophicléide |
| Mendelssohn-Bartholdy, Felix Ger. 1809–1847 | Ouvertüre für Vollstände Harmonie-Musik | [ ].[ ].1824 Bad Doberan | Basshorn |
| | Ein Sommernachtstraum Ouverture | 20.2.1827 Stettin [Szcecin] | Basshorn |
| | Ouvertüre: Meerestille und Glückliche Farht | 18.1.1828 Berlin | Serpente |

|  |  |  |  |
|---|---|---|---|
|  | Paulus | 22.4.1836 Düsseldorf | Serpente |
|  | Ein Sommernachtstraum |  |  |
|  |   VI, IX, XI, XII | 14.10.1843 Potsdam | Basshorn |
|  | Festegesang an die |  |  |
|  |   Künstler | [ ].6.1846 Cologne | Ophicleide und Tuba |
|  | Elias | 26.8.1846 Birmingham | Ophicleide |
|  | Trauer-Marsch | [publ. 1869] | Basshorn |
| Meyerbeer, Giacomo Ger. 1791-1864 | Robert le diable | 21.11.1831 Paris Opéra | Ophyclëide |
|  | Les Huguenots | 29.2.1836 Paris Opéra | Ophyclëide |
|  | Le prophète | 16.4.1849 Paris Opéra | Ophiclèide |
|  | L'africaine | 28.4.1865 Paris Opéra | Ophicleide |
| Ponchielli, Amilcare It. 1834-1886 | La Gioconda | 8.4.1876 Milan La Scala | Bombardone [score] Ophicleide [part] |
| Puccini, Giacomo It. 1858-1924 | Manon Lescaut | 1.2.1893 Turin Reggio | Basso tuba |
|  | La Bohème | 1.2.1896 Turin Reggio | Trombone basso |
|  | Tosca | 14.1.1900 Roma Costanzi | Trombone basso |
|  | Madama Butterfly | 17.2.1904 Milan La Scala | Trombone basso |
|  | La fanciulla del West | 10.12.1910 New York Metropolitan | Trombone basso |
|  | Il trittico | 14.12.1918 New York Metropolitan | Trombone basso |
|  | Turandot | 25.4.1926 Milan La Scala | Trombone contrabbasso |
| Rossini, Gioacchino It. 1792-1868 | Armida | 9.11.1817 Naples San Carlo | Serpentone |
|  | Mosè in Egitto | 5.3.1818 Naples San Carlo | Serpentone + serp. in banda |

|  | | | |
|---|---|---|---|
| | Ricciardo e Zoraide | 3.12.1818 Naples San Carlo | Serpentone + serp. in banda |
| | Maometto II | 3.12.1820 Naples San Carlo | Serpentone |
| | La siège de Corinth [reworking of Maometto II] | 9.10.1826 Paris Opéra | Ophiclëide |
| | Moïse et Pharaon | 26.3.1827 Paris Opéra | Ophiclëide |
| | Cantata in onore del Sommo Pontefice Pio Nono | 1.1.1847 Rome Palazzo Senatorio | Serpentone + serp. in banda |
| | Petite messe solennelle | 28.2.1869 Paris Italien | Ophiclëide |
| Sullivan, Arthur Brit. 1842-1900 | Overture di Ballo | 31.8.1870 Birmingham Town Hall | Ophicleide (Bass tuba ad lib.) |
| | The Golden Legend | 16.10.1886 Leeds Town Hall | Bass Tuba |
| Verdi, Giuseppe It. 1813-1901 | Oberto | 17.11.1839 Milan La Scala | Cimbasso |
| | Nabucodonosor | 9.3.1842 Milan La Scala | Cimbasso |
| | I Lombardi alla prima crociata | 11.2.1843 Milan La Scala | Cimbasso |
| | I due foscari | 3.11.1844 Rome Argentina | Cimbasso |
| | Ernani | 9.3.1844 Venice La Fenice | Cimbasso |
| | Jérusalem | 26.11.1847 Paris Opéra | Oficleide |
| | Gerusalemme | Ital. version [not perf?] | Serpente |
| | Luisa Miller | 8.12.1849 Naples San Carlo | Cimbasso |
| | Rigoletto | 11.3.1851 Venice La Fenice | Cimbasso |
| | Il Trovatore | 19.1.1853 Rome Apollo | Cimbasso |
| | La Traviata | 6.3.1853 Venice La Fenice [Serpentone in 1st pub. score, c. 1854] | Cimbasso |
| | Simon Boccanegra [revised version] | 12.3.1857 Venice La Fenice 24.3.1881 Milan La Scala | Cimbasso ? |
| | Les vêpres siciliennes [rev. as I vespri siciliani] | 13.6.1855 Paris Opéra Ricordi score: [Tr.[ni]] IV or Cimb.[asso] | Oficleide |

|  |  |  |  |
|---|---|---|---|
|  | Un ballo in maschera | 17.2.1859 Rome Apollo | Cimbasso |
|  | Don Carlo(s) | 11.3.1867 Paris Opéra | Oficleide |
|  | Aida | 24.12.1871 |  |
|  |  | Cairo Opera | Ophicleide |
|  |  | [8.2.1872 Milan La Scala | Cimbasso] |
|  | Messa da requiem | 22.5.1874 Venice San Marco | Oficleide |
|  | Otello | 5.2.1887 Milan La Scala | Trombone basso |
|  | Falstaff | 9.2.1893 Milan La Scala | Trombone basso |
|  | Quattro pezzi sacri | 7.4.1898 Paris Opéra | Trombone 4 |
| Wagner, Richard Ger. 1813-1883 | Rule, Britannia | ?19.3.38 Riga | Serpent (with ww.) Ophicleide (with br.) |
|  | Norma, il predisse [intended for performance in Paris] | comp. 1839 | Serpent |
|  | Nikolay | 21.11.37 Riga | Ofikleide |
|  | Gruß seiner Treuen au Friedrich August den Geliebten bei seiner Zurückunft aus England den 9 August 1844 | | 2 Baßtuba |
|  | Das Liebesmahl der Apostel | | Tuba |
|  | Rienzi [A production in Paris was anticipated] | 1840 | Ophikleide (Baßtuba) |
|  | Der Fliegende Holländer [A production in Paris was anticipated] | 2.1.843 Dresden Opera | Ophikleide (Baßtuba) |
|  | Tannhäuser | 19.10.1845 Dresden Opera | Baßtuba |
|  | Lohengrin | 28.8.1850 Weimar Court Th. | Baßtuba |
|  | Die Meistersinger von Nürnberg | 21.6.1868 Munich Opera | Baßtuba |
|  | Der Ring der Nibelungen | 13-17.8.1876 Bayreuth | Kontrabaß-tuba |
|  | Parsifal | 26.7.1882 Bayreuth | Baßtuba |

# APPENDIX A

# *The Baß-Tuba Patent (Die Chromatische Baß-Tuba)*

## Translated by Veronica Lawson

*Prussian Patent 9121*
*Wieprecht 12. Sept. 1835*

The Chromatic Baß-Tuba:—

1) Possesses the property that it surpasses in compass every wind instrument yet existing, seeing that all woodwind and brass instruments have a compass of only 2, 3 or at most 3 and one half octaves, whereas the Baß-Tuba covers 4 full octaves through the chromatic scale, namely, from second octave C down to pedal C.

2) Supersedes by virtue of its compass, in wind band and military band music, the double-bass found in the string band, and does so to perfection, since the Baß-Tuba can descend three notes lower yet than the double-bass, and so now stands as the deepest of all musical instruments, excepting only the organ.

3) Is, owing to the special design of its tubing and bell, distinguished from all other brass instruments by the strength, fullness and beauty of its timbre, while on the other hand the ultimate pianissimo can be brought forth from it.

For 10 years now I have been working with military bands, and have felt, I suppose, most sorely the need of a true contrabass wind instrument.

None of the bass wind instruments, such as: 1) the English bass horn, 2) the serpent (both with an effective compass of at the most 2½ octaves, viz. from treble G down to contrabass C) and 3) the bass trombones (with a compass of 3 octaves from second octave C to contrabass C), could fill the place of the wanting contrabass which wind band music demanded.

Proof that this need was felt in all countries is offered by the invention of the ophicleide. Although the latter can go only one and one half tones deeper than the

English bass horn and the serpent, this instrument was still looked upon as a major advance in all countries; this would surely indicate how important and advantageous for music is the invention of the chromatic Baß-Tuba, which can descend one octave lower than the serpent and English bass horn, and six notes lower than the ophicleide, while yet retaining the high notes of these three said instruments. The wish, indeed, the burning desire for such a contrabass instrument spurred me on to all kinds of researches, and my reflections at last led me to compare the natural notes which may be found in every brass instrument without resort to artificial means to the segments of a stretched catgut string on any stringed instrument.

This brought me close to my goal, and I owe the invention of the Baß-Tuba to this idea, and this idea alone, for the entire contrivance is built hereupon as to both its compass and its harmonic arrangement, and I refer in my exposition to the accompanying chart.

**Figure 1**. If one tunes a catgut string on any stringed instrument to a particular note, and divides this string into two equal parts (with a flageolet-touch, not by firm pressure with the finger, since the string would otherwise lose its vibrations), and then bows the second part, the string will sound a pure octave higher. If this second part is now again divided into two equal parts, it will rise a further pure octave, and there will appear in the centre of the second segment a new note which is termed the fifth, which is to say the 5th note up from the fundamental. It now remains to divide the fourth part of the string; if this also is divided into two equal parts, two more new notes are created in the third segment, with the fifth in the centre again but joined on one side by the third and on the other by the seventh. This would leave an eighth part of the string; if this, too, is divided, we have in the fourth segment a diatonic scale, with the augmented fourth. Should one proceed with all these investigations, the division of the sixteenth string part would give the chromatic scale, and, finally, the division of the thirty-second string part would produce pure quarter-tones. In the event of still further division the notes would come so close together that the ear would be unable to distinguish them. These researches led me to the conviction that all bass wind instruments hitherto existing were pitched a whole octave too high, and hence the idea came to me of a bass instrument which was precisely as long again as the English bass horn and the serpent.

**Figure IV** formulates the vibration-segments for these two said instruments, but nonetheless it should be noted that they can reach only as high as second octave C (the note marked★), because the notes above the same are met in theory only. Were it vital to blow these notes this would require a smaller mouthpiece, and the lower notes of the two instruments would be lost in their stead. It would be impossible to use all the natural notes inherent in the tube except by perpetually changing mouthpieces—if the technique of the instrument were to allow of such expedients.

If, therefore, **Figure II** is now compared with Figure IV, it becomes clear that, to achieve the real pedal notes, the length of the English bass horn and that of the serpent would need to be doubled; the notes which

1) lay in the first segment in Figure IV appear in the second segment in Figure II, and between them we also find the fifth, G, missing from the first segment in Fig. 4;
2) the notes which lay in the second segment in Fig. 4 now appear in the third in Figure 2, but with the difference that the third segment in the second Figure also includes the third, E, and the seventh, Bb;
3) the notes which lay only in the third segment in Fig. 4 appear in the fourth in Fig.2 with the addition of the second, augmented fourth, major sixth and minor seventh. The plain tube of an English bass horn or serpent will therefore sound only eight, the plain tube of the Tuba, on the other hand, 15 natural and usable notes.

In order now to obtain the missing fourth, F, in the first segment in Figure II, I computed a second tube and pitched this in F, that is, four notes higher than pedal C; (Figure II) both tubes combined now produced the notes remarked in **Figure III** naturally and without using artificial means, and the foundations for one of the widest-ranged and deepest wind instruments had been laid at last.

These discoveries made, I took myself to J. G. Moritz, Wind Instrument Maker to the Royal Court, whom I now commissioned first to build a tube in F. After numerous experiments very difficult to devise, the aforementioned Moritz succeeded in making me a tube in the prescribed key, which despite its extraordinary length and the bulk of its tubing and bell not only was very pure in intonation and very responsive, but also established the exceedingly beautiful timbre of this instrument.

After I had confirmed by testing this tube that all notes hypothesized from the segmenting of a catgut string were truly present in this tube, I had an attachment made for it which pitched the F tube (Figure I) down to pedal C, and at this pitch, also, the notes computed in Figure II were exhibited. A contrabass instrument with two differently pitched *Mutter-Töne*† had now been created.

To render the instrument usable at last in all keys, I sought to compute the various harmonics of the *Mutter-Töne* so that all major keys found in music, of which there are 12, could be produced on this instrument.

Consequently I superimposed on each *Mutter-Ton* one semitone and one whole tone harmonic, both harmonics in combination thus created a 1½ tone harmonic. Hence each *Mutter-Ton* acquired three different harmonics, and so with this arrangement, as **Figure V** manifests, could be got: from *Mutter-Ton* F, to E, E♭, and D major, from *Mutter-Ton* C, to B, B♭, and A major. The keys still wanting, which were D♭, A♭ G and G♭ major, were formed by combining both *Mutter-Töne* with their harmonics, as indicated in **Figure VI**.

So in consequence of this computation of harmonics we arrive at the 12 major keys to be found in music, namely;

F: (first *Mutter-Ton*)

E: 1st. valve

E♭: 2nd. valve

D: 1st. and 2nd. valves

D♭: 1st. and 4th. valves

C: 3rd. valve (as 2nd. *Mutter-Ton*)

B: 5th. and 4th. valves

B♭: 5th. and 3rd. valves

A: 5th., 4th., 3rd. valves

A♭: 5th., 4th., 3rd. and 2nd. valves

G: 5th., 4th., 3rd. and 2nd. valves

G♭: 5th., 4th., 3rd., 2nd. and 1st. valves

and so also at the perfection of this instrument, in all keys.

Since, moreover, each of these keys also produces its own notes in accordance with the vibration-segments computed above, this instrument has thereby attained such a degree of perfection in its technique as is not to be found in any other wind instrument, inasmuch as, as is precisely illustrated in **Figure VII**, one and the same note can frequently be fingered in two, three, four, five, even six different ways. This Figure also indicates in which chord each note has its root, and at what interval this appears as a harmonic. Comparison of the notes in Figure VII with those in Figures V and VI is facilitated by numerals, and it may be seen how the numerals in the 7th. Figure are often to be found two, three, four, five or six times in Figures 5 and 6.

†[By Mutter-Ton Wieprecht meant the fundamental of the open instrument. The Baß–Tuba was built in F and C which were consequently the pitches of the two Mutter-Töne.]

Having completed all my calculations, and having myself tuned all the harmonics in the workshop of the aforementioned Moritz, I entrusted this specimen to the skill and, as regards the external design of this instrument, to the further consideration of Court Instrument Maker J. G. Moritz, who gave the instrument a pleasing form, and rendered it most easily playable, and built the same at last most tastefully and serviceably to the satisfaction of not only myself, but also the most worthy Musical Division of the Academy of Arts and Sciences, and all other experts.

The Baß-Tuba has a height of 3 foot when upright, and a weight of 7 to 8 pounds; the manner of playing it is as the English bass horn or bassoon, that is, the top two valves with the left hand, the bottom three with the right.

Berlin, August 9th, 1835

Friedrich Wilhelm Wieprecht
Musician to the Royal Court
of Prussia and Member of the
Academy of Arts

*The Drawings of Letters Patent N$^0$. 9121*
*granted to Court Musician W.Wieprecht*
*and to Court Instrument Maker J. G. Moritz,*
*in Berlin, on September 12th., 1835,*
*for a wind instrument, the Baß-Tuba.*

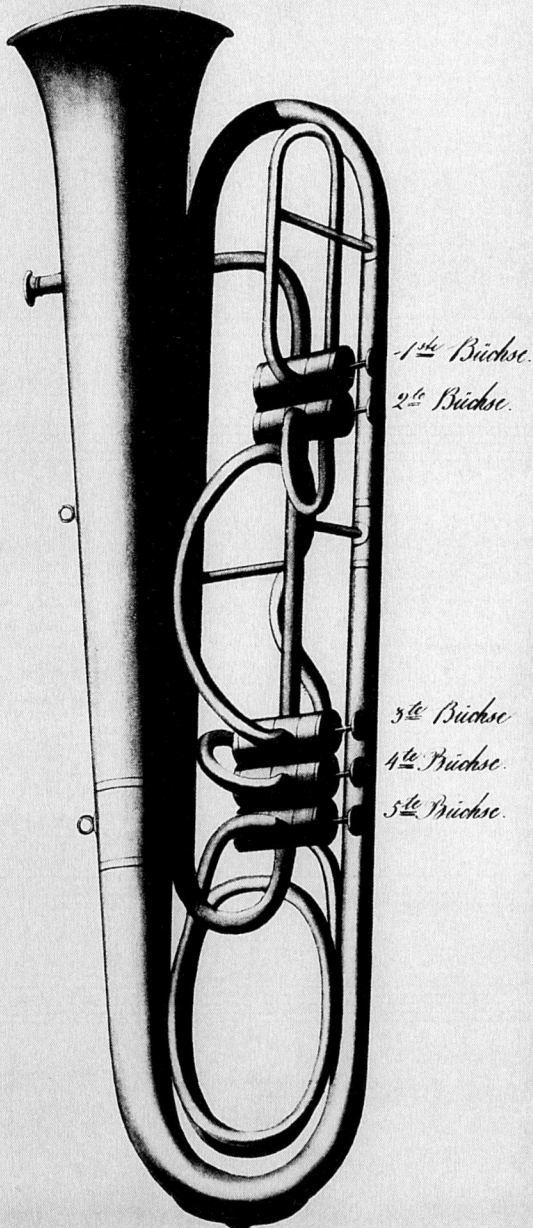

*Chromatische Baß-Tuba*

1ste Büchse.
2te Büchse.

3te Büchse
4te Büchse.
5te Büchse.

CHART
for reference, concerning the invention of the chromatic

BAß-TUBA
with accompanying specification and complete drawing,
drafted by
F. W. Wieprecht

Fig. I

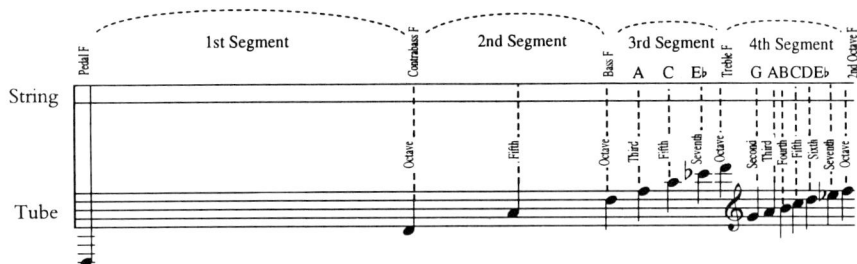

Fig. II

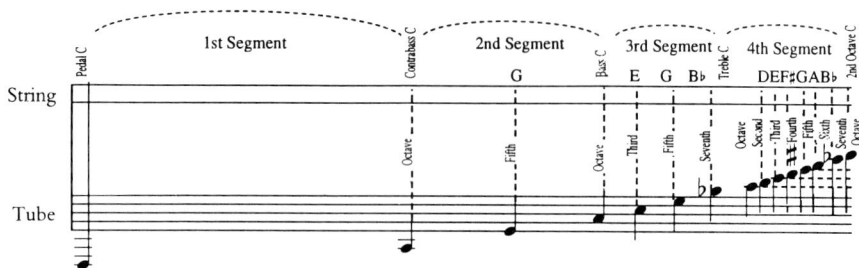

Fig. III

Fig. IV

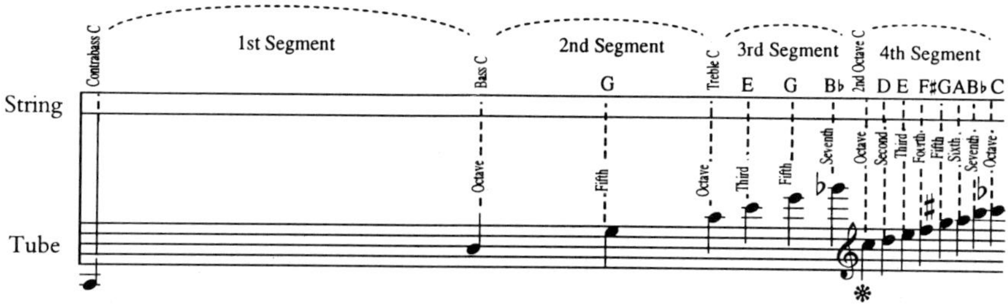

Fig. V

String

1/2 Segment    1/4 Segment    1/8 Segment

Pedal 8ve   Contrabass 8ve   Fifth   Bass 8ve   Third   Fifth   Seventh   Treble 8ve   Second   Third   Fourth   Fifth

1st Mutter-Ton
F major

½-tone harmonic
E major

1-tone harmonic
E♭ major

1½-tone harmonic
D major

2nd Mutter-Ton
C major

½-tone harmonic
B major

1-tone harmonic
B♭ major

1½-tone harmonic
A major

[*Wieprecht numbers this 42 in error]

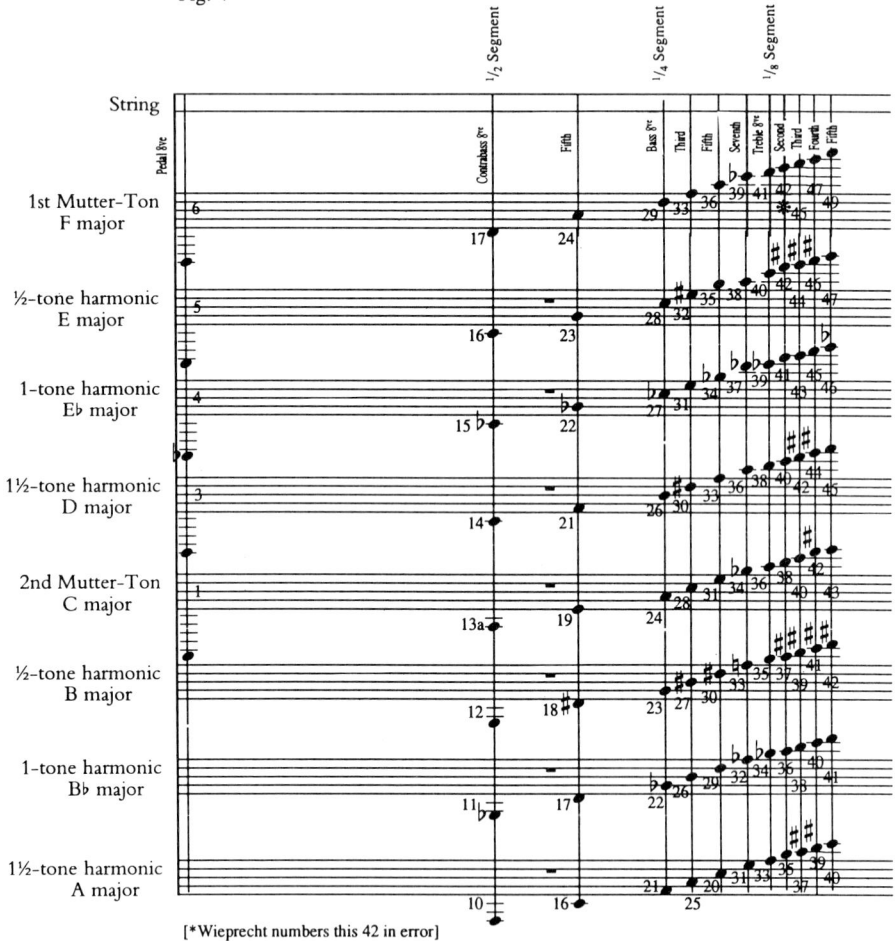

NB. The lower pedals of the second *Mutter-Ton* are not perceived because the ear cannot adequately distinguish them, although, like the high notes above second octave C, they can be hypothesized. Hence only the specified compass of four octaves, that is to say, from pedal to second octave C, applies in practice.

Fig. VI

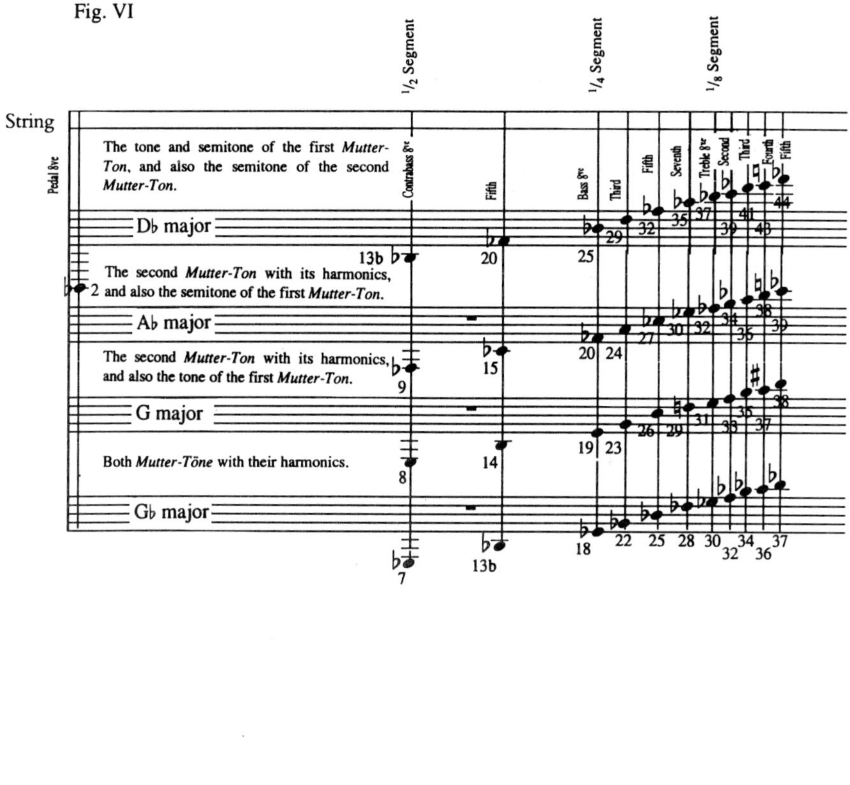


Relationship of both *Mutter-Töne* to their harmonics

Fig. VII

All the octaves of pedal-notes appear as harmonics.

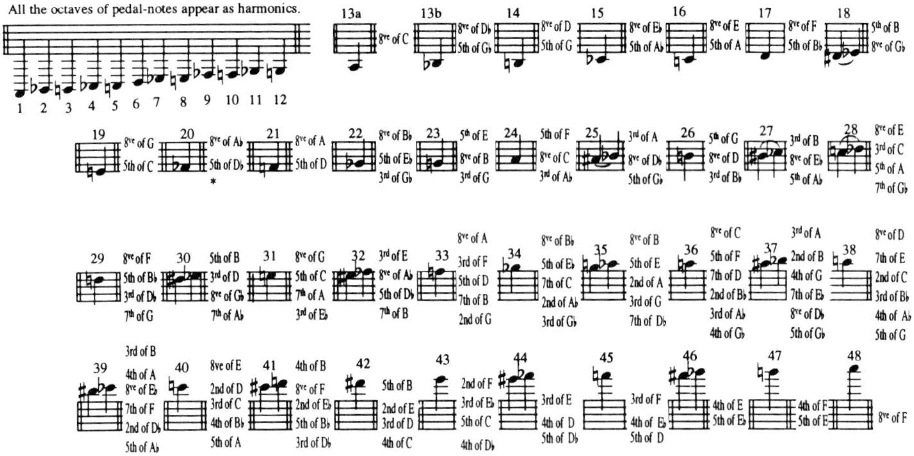

[*Wieprecht states 'in Es als 5te' in error.]

# APPENDIX B

# *Glossaries*

WHEN Wieprecht named his deep valved bugle-horn *Baß-Tuba* he unwittingly created a major problem for organologists. The new instrument's conical profile put it into a completely different class from the first tuba—the long, straight Roman trumpet with cylindrical profile from which today's trumpet and trombone are descended. Bernard Sarrette (see 'Tuba Curva' below) had in 1791 paid much more attention to correct terminology (as was to have been expected of the Director of the Paris Conservatoire).

The terms defined in Glossary I have all been derived from the Roman *tuba*. Here they are dealt with in some detail, but they are also included in the general Glossary II where they are only briefly defined.

In the glossaries names in parentheses give maker and, where known, date of invention—e.g. (A. Sax, 1855). Names in square brackets indicate the source of the definition if only one reference has been found—e.g. [Sachs (S³)]. Details of the reference will be found in the Bibliography (pages 577-600 below).

## GLOSSARY I

### Terms derived from the Roman *Tuba*

TAUREA—*Lat.* A type of Roman tuba that sounded like the bellowing of a bull. [Marcuse (M¹³)]

TOB—*Old Irish.* Trumpet. [Downey (D¹⁷)]

TROMPETTE-TUBA—A long straight trunmpet manufactured by A. Sax for use at the funeral of Napoleon I, 15 December 1840. [Chouquet (C²²)]

TUB—*Old Irish.* Trumpet. [Downey (D¹⁷)]

TUBA (1)—*Lat.* Trumpet, specifically the straight Roman infantry trumpet, about 1250 mm in length, ancestor of the trumpet and trombone of today.

TUBA (2)—*Fr.* Contrabass valve trombone 'producing raucous disagreeable sounds . . . so found only in mounted brass bands'. [Lavignac (L⁵)]

TUBA (3)—An organ-stop with trumpet-like tone of 4 ft, 8 ft, or 16 ft pitch, often found in large organs as the instruments' most powerful solo stop.

TUBA (4)—One of the eight Gregorian Psalm tones, one for each church mode. The main note of the recitation, always the dominant of the mode, is called the *tenor,* *repercussion* or reciting note. [Apel (A[16])]

TUBA (5)—A high-powered radar transmitter used to jam enemy radar. [Webster W[7])]

TUBA (6)—*Fr.* Snorkel.

TUBA CLARION—A 4 ft pipe-organ stop of Tuba (2) type.

TUBA CORNEA—*Lat.* Bronze horn or trumpet in animal horn shape.

TUBA CURVA—Natural horn designed by Bernard Sarrette, Director of the Paris Conservatoire, in imitation of the Roman instrument shown on Trajan's column (a *buccina*). Able to sound only a few notes, the tone was loud and resonant. It was first used in Paris on 12 July 1791 in Voltaire's funeral procession and later appeared in the second act finale of Méhul's opera *Joseph* (1807). The example by Jean Cormeri in the Paris Musée de la Musique is presumably one of the original instruments as Cormeri is known to have given up his business in 1791.

TUBA DIRECTA—The straight Roman trumpet.

TUBA DUCTILIS—A trumpet made from metal drawn out or thinned by the hammer. For many years the term was taken to mean that the Romans had a trumpet which was played by being drawn out—in other words, a trombone. The fallacy was exposed by Galpin in his famous 1906 treatise on *The Sackbut, its Evolution and History* to which he applied the approaches of both classical scholar and organologist.

TUBA EBURNEA—*Lat.* Oliphant (of Roland).

TUBA HERCOTECTONICA—A species of trumpet made by the mathematician Christian Otter (1598-1668) for the King of Denmark. It presumably pleased the king who gave Otter 200 of his recently-introduced thalers.

TUBA MAGNA—High-pressure organ reed stop.

TUBA MAJOR (1)—The *Quartposaune* or bass trombone. [Praetorius (P[22])]

TUBA MAJOR (2)—Name given to two different organ-stops: a 16 ft pipe-organ tuba and an 8 ft pipe-organ mirabilis.

TUBA MAXIMA—The *Oktavposaune* or contrabass trombone. [Praetorius (P[22])]

TUBA MINOR (1)—The 'ordinary, correct trombone' in A. [Praetorius (P[22])]

TUBA MINOR (2)—Small, smooth-toned organ-stop. [Scholes (S[16])]

TUBA MIRABILIS—A loud organ-stop invented by Hope-Jones

TUBA OBLONGA—*Lat.* Trombone. [Scholes (S[16])]

TUBA ORIEL—*Lat.* Positive organ. [Scholes (S[16])]

TUBA PASTORALIS—*Lat.* Pastoral trumpet: a type of alphorn. [Stoneham (S[40])]

TUBA SONORA—A variety of organ-stop introduced by Hope-Jones.

TUBA STENTOROPHONICA—A speaking-trumpet invented in 1760 by Sir Samuel Morland and manufactured by Simon Beale, Suffolk Street, London. [Langwill (L[1])]

TUBA TYMPANODIS—Small medieval flûte-a-bec played simultaneously and by the same player as a drum—i.e. the pipe of a pipe and tabor. [Kunitz (K[24])]

# GLOSSARY II

Comprehensive list of valved bugle-horns and related
(or apparently related) instruments

ALTFLÜGELHORN—Ger. Alto flügel horn in e♭.

ALTHORN (1)—*U.K. (arch.), Fr., Ger.* Alto saxhorn in e♭.

    (2)—Austrian narrow-bore valved bugle-horn in d, e♭ or f; tuba-, helicon- or trumpet-shaped (1820s).

    (3)—*U.K. (arch.)* Baritone in B♭.

    (4)—Wagner Tuba in B♭.

ALTHORN-OBLIGAT—Ger. Obbligato alto horn.

ALTKORNETT—Ger. Alto saxhorn, flügel horn or cornet in e♭ (f).

ALTO (1)—*Fr.* Alto saxhorn in e♭.

    (2)—*Fr.* Alto saxhorn in B♭.

    (3)—*Fr.* Alto clarinet.

    (4)—*Fr.* Viola.

    (5)—*(coll.)* Alto saxophone.

ALTO-CLAVE—Quinti-clave.

ALTO-COR—*Fr.* Tenor cor.

ALTO CORNOPHONE—Cornophone in f (e♭).

ALTO FLUGELHORN (1)—Flügel horn in b'♭.

           (2)—Ger. Flügel horn in e♭.

ALTO HORN B♭—Baritone or euphonium (1) in B♭.

ALTO HORN E♭—*U.S.A.* Saxhorn in e♭.

ALTO OBLIGÉ—Fr. Obbligato alto horn.

ALTO OPHICLEIDE—Ophicleide in e♭ (f) (Halary, 1822).

ALTOPHIKLEÏDE—*Ger.* Alto ophicleide.

ALTO SAXHORN—(1) Saxhorn in e♭ (f).

        (2)—Soprano saxhorn in b♭.

ALTO SAXOTROMBA—Saxotromba in e♭.

ALTO TUBA (1)—Wagner Tuba in B♭.

      (2)—*Ger.* Alto saxhorn in e♭.

ALTSAXHORN—*Ger.* Alto saxhorn, flügel horn or cornet in e♭ (f).

ALT-TROMPETE—*Ger. (arch.)* Probably valved bugle-horn in e♭, trumpet-shape (adopted by Wieprecht, 1829).

ALT-TUBA—*Ger.* Alto saxhorn in e♭.

ALWEDDGON—*Wel.* Keyed bugle. [Sachs (S³)]

AMATEUR VOICE HORN—Ballad Horn (1).

AMORSCHALL—Hunting horn with perforated bulbous bell anticipating keyed bugle (Kölbel, 1760).

ANTONIOPHONE—Bombardon designed by Courtois in shape of a snail shell with three valves positioned centrally.

APOLLO-LYRA—Psalmelodicon with new name 'on account of its shape' (Schmidt, n.d.). [Pontécoulant (P²⁰)]

BAJO EN MIb—*Sp.* Tuba in Eb with three or four valves.

BAJO EN DO—*Sp.* Tuba in C with three or four valves.

BAJO EN SIb—*Sp.* Tuba in B'b with three or four valves.

BALLAD HORN (1)—Valved bugle-horn in french horn-shape, pitched in c (Distin, 1870).

        (2) U.S.A. Similar to (1) pitched in Bb.

BAMBARDINO BAJO—Sp. Euphonium (1).

BARITON—Ger. euphonium (1).

BARÍTON HORITZONTAL—*Cat.* Baritone saxhorn in trumpet shape.

BARITONE—Medium-bore saxhorn in Bb.

BARITONE SAXOTROMBA—Medium-bore Saxotromba in Bb.

BARITONE TUBA—Euphonium (1) [Roy Harris].

BARITONO—*It.* Euphonium (1) with three valves [Shostakovich scores, from *Flicorno Baritono*].

BARÍTONO EN SIb—*Sp.* Euphonium (1).

BARITON-SAXHORN—*Ger.* Baritone in Bb.

BARLOW TUBA—Tuba in F with five valves (*des.* H. Barlow, *mfc.* Besson, London, first half 20th century).

BAROXYTON—(1) Tuba in Bb, F or Eb in tuba-, helicon- or ophicleide-shape (Červený, 1848).

        (2) 'Four-valved bombardon' (Stegmaier, c. 1848). [Waterhouse W³)]

BARYTON(E) (1)—*Fr.* Baritone saxhorn in c or Bb.

        (2)—*Ger.* Euphonium (1).

        (3)—*(arch.)* Baritone saxhorn in Bb.

        (4)—*Fr.* Oboe pitched an octave lower than normal (1539).

        (5)—16ft. Vox Humana organ stop.

        (6)—*Fr.* Large violin or small viol. [Jacquot (J²)]

        (7)—*Ger.* Type of bass viola d'amore for which Haydn composed many works.

BARYTON AIGU—Large-bore eb alto saxhorn (F.-Besson, 1880s).

BARYTON-À-BOCAL—*Fr.* Sommerophone.

BARYTONHORN—*Ger.* Euphonium (1).

BARYTON IMPÉRIALE—*Fr.* Imperial euphonium.

BARYTONKORNETT—Narrow-bore valved bugle-horn in Bb, helicon-shape (Červený, 1876).

BARYTON-SAXHORN (1)—*Ger.* Baritone in Bb.

                    (2)—*Ger.* Euphonium (1).

BARYTONTUBA—*Ger.* Euphonium (1).

BASS—Contrabass tuba in Eb or B'b.

BASS CORNETT—Tenor cornett.

BASS CORNOPHONE—Four-valved Cornophone in c (Bb).

BASSE (1)—*Fr.* Tuba in Bb or c. (In the current Couesnon catalogue it is translated as 'Euphonium-Baritone'.)

        (2)—*Fr.* Ophicleide (1).

BASSE-À-CYLINDRES—*Fr.* Euphonium (1).

BASSE À PISTONS—*Fr.* Euphonium (1).

BASSE-CHROMATIQUE—*Fr. (arch.)* Bass tuba in F.

BASSE-COR—Upright serpent by Frichot (1806) subsequently improved and called *Basse-trompette.*

BASSE DE CORNET—*Fr.* Early bass wind instrument (e.g. serpent).

BASSE DE SERPENT—'Instrument made from wrought iron with a bell like a huge candle-snuffer' ('d'un énorme éteignoir'). [Chouquet (C[22])].

BASSE D'HARMONIE (1)—*Fr.* Ophicleide.

                (2)—10-key ophicleide (Labbaye, 1821).

                (3)—11-key ophicleide (Sautermeister, 1827).

                (4)—*Fr.* Hibernicon.

                (5)—*Fr.* Double bassoon. [Kastner (K[5])].

BASSE-TROMPETTE—Bass horn with immense potential range depending upon type of mouthpiece (Frichot, 1810).

BASSE-TUBE—Bass clarinet by Lot (1772). [Pierre (P[14])]

BASS-EUPHONIUM—Upright serpent by Haseneier (c. 1850).

BASS FLUGEL HORN—Bb Euphonium (1).

BASSFLÜGELHORN (1)—*Aus.* Baritone in Bb.

              (2)—*Ger.* Euphonium (1).

BASS-FLÜGELHORN—*Ger.* Baritone in Bb.

BASSHORN (1)—Valved instrument in f (eb) by Stölzel (1828) probably in ophicleide-shape.

            (2)—Baritone by Červený (1840).

(3)—*Fin*. Bass. [Karjalaien (K[4])]

BASS HORN (1)—Upright serpent (Frichot, 1790s).

    (2)—*U.K. (arch)* & *U.S.A*. Bass brass instrument.

BASSE IMPÉRIALE—*Fr.* Imperial bass (B♭, E♭ or B'♭).

BASS-KLAPPENHORN—*Ger.* Ophicleide (1).

BASSKORNETT—Narrow-bore valved bugle-horn in f (e♭) in helicon-shape (Čerkený, 1876).

BASSKORNOPHON—*Ger.* Tenor cornophone in c (B♭).

BASSO FLICORNO—*It.* Flicorno tenore or baritono.

BASSON RUSSE—*Fr.* Russian bassoon.

BASSONET—Alto, tenor or baritone valve bugle-horn in tuba-shape (Paine, c.1845).

BASS OPHICLEIDE—Ophicleide in c or B♭.

BASSOPHIKLEÏDE—*Ger.* Bass ophicleide.

BASS-OPHYKLËIDE—Upright serpent (Siering, n.d.). [Leipzig]

BASSO TUBA (1)—Basse-tube.

    (2)—*It.* Bass tuba.

BASS SAXHORN—Wide-bore saxhorn in B♭ (euphonium (1)).

BASS SAXOTROMBA—Saxotromba in B♭.

BASSTROMPETE—Valved instrument in f or e♭ by Stölzel (1828) probably in trumpet-shape.

BASSTUBA (1)—Bass tuba.

    (2)—*Ger.* Bass saxhorn in B♭ (euphonium (1)).

BASS-TUBA—Valved bugle-horn in F (Wieprecht and Moritz, 1835).

BASS TUBA—Tuba in B♭, F, E♭, C or B'♭.

BASSTUBE—*Ger.* Bass tuba.

B♭ BASS—Medium/small-bore tuba in B'♭ with three valves.

BB♭ BASS—Tuba in B'♭.

B♭ TUBA—Euphonium (1).

BB♭ TUBA—Tuba in B'♭.

B-C CLAIRON—Soprano flügel horn in B♭/cornet in C duplex 1873 (F. Hirschberg, Bratislava, pre-1873). [Gorgerat (G[17])]

BEN BUABHALL—*Mid. Irish.* Bugle horn (2). [Downey (D[17])]

BERSAG HORN—Member of family of Italian valve bugles, all having one valve apart from the soprano which has three.

BIERBASS—*Ger. coll.* Bass horn (1). Term used by Mendelssohn in letter to his sister, originally applied colloquially to *Handbassel:* small German cello or double bass used in dance music. [Mendelssohn]

BILLENTYÜS KÜRT—*Hun.* Keyed bugle.

BIMBONIFONO—Brass instrument in F with seven rotary-valves operated by keys (G. Bimboni, c. 1850).

BIUCOLO—*It.* Term for flicorno (2) in Neapolitan bands (lit. 'of the bugle').

BOMBARDA A 4 PISTONI—*It.* Four-valved euphonium (1).

BOMBARDÍ—*Cat.* Euphonium (1).

BOMBARDIN (1)—Bombardon (1). [Kappey (K[2])]

      (2)—Euphonium (1). [Rose (R[9])]

BOMBARDINO (1)—*It. & Sp.* Wide-bore flicorno in B♭ or c (euphonium (1)) with three or four valves.

      (2)—*It.* Tenor shawm.

BOMBARDINO TRITONIO—Bombardon pitched in F, E♭ and B♭ (Pelitti, after 1871). [M[31], 320]

BOMBARDON (1)—Tuba, especially in F or E♭, particularly in a band.

      (2)—Tuba (B. W. Riedl, 1835). [Kunitz (K[24])]

      (3)—12-key bass ophicleide (Joh. Riedl, *c.* 1820).

      (4)—*Ger.* Valve ophicleide (2).

      (5)—Bass instrument of *Néo-alto* family (Rivet, before 1845).

      (6)—Tuba by Červený, 1845. [Pontécoulant (P[20])]

      (7)—16 ft. or 32 ft. organ pedal reed stop.

BOMBARDON-À-CYLINDRES—*Fr.* Bombardon (1).

BOMBARDÓN CONTRABAJO—*Sp.* Tuba in E♭ or B'♭.

BOMBARDON CONTREBASSE—*Fr.* Bass tuba in E♭ or B'♭.

BOMBARDONE (1)—*It.* Flicorno in F or E♭.

      (2)—*It.* Bass shawm.

BOMBARDON IN TIEF B—*Ger.* Tuba in B'♭.

BOMBARDON IN TIEF C—*Ger.* Tuba in C.

BOMBARDON OPHOCLEIDE—Four-valved ophicleide (2) exhibited at 1851 Great Exhibition (Pfaff, n.d.).

BORDUNSAXHORN—*Ger.* Contrabass saxhorn.

BUABHALL—*Old Irish.* Bugle horn (2). [Downey (D[17])]

BUABHALL EBOIRE—*Mid. Irish.* Oliphant (of Roland). [Downey (D[17])]

BUAL—*Wel.* Bugle horn (2). [Downey (D[17])]

BUALGORN—*Wel.* Bugle horn (2). [Downey (D[17])]

BUELIN—*Wel.* Bugle horn (2). [Downey (D[17])]

BÜGELHORN—*Ger.* Valved bugle-horn.

BUGLE (1)—Bugle-horn (1).

      (2)—A (military) signalling instrument belonging to the bugle-horn family, sometimes slightly modified.

(3)—*U.S.A.* As (2) but with more cylindrical profile and sometimes one valve.

(4)—*Fr.* Flügel horn.

(5)—Keyed bugle.

BUGLE À CLEFS—*Fr.* Keyed bugle.

BUGLE-À-CLÉS—*Fr.* Keyed bugle.

BUGLE-À-CYLINDRES—*Fr.* Flügel horn.

BUGLE A LLAVES—*Sp.* Keyed bugle.

BUGLE ALTO (1)—*Fr.* Alto saxhorn in e♭.

(2)—*Fr.* Flügel horn in e♭.

BUGLE À PISTONS—*Fr.* Flügel horn.

BUGLE BARYTON (1)—*Fr.* Baritone in B♭.

(2)—*Fr.* Euphonium (1).

BUGLE-BASSE—*Fr.* Euphonium (1). [Sachs (S³)]

BUGLE CONTRALTO—Contralto Flügel horn in e♭ (*pat.* Roblin, 1878; *mfc.* Besson, Paris, 1879).

BUGLE EN MI BÉMOL—*Fr.* Sopranino saxhorn in e'♭.

BUGLE-HORN (1)—Brass instrument of widely conical profile.

(2)—(*arch.*) Horn of bugle (wild ox) used as a drinking vessel or musical instrument.

(3)—Keyed bugle.

BUGLE OMNITONIQUE—Bugle-horn with omnitonic valve system (Chaussied, 1889).

BUGLE TÉNOR (1)—*Bel.* Soprano saxhorn in b♭.

(2)—*Fr.* Alto horn in e♭.

(3)—*Fr.* Baritone in B♭.

(4)—*Fr.* Flügel horn in c. [Kastner (K⁵)]

CATUBA—*It.* Bass drum. [Sachs (S³)]

CC TUBA—Tuba in C.

CHROMATIC BASS—Three-valve bugle-horn in trumpet shape with range F'-a'. [*Harmonicon* (H¹⁰), 1830]

CHROMATIC BASS-HORN—Type of Russian bassoon (Streitwolf, 1820).

CHROMATISCHE BASSHORN—*Ger.* Chromatic bass-horn.

CIMBASSO—*It.* Designation used in nineteenth century for contrabass instrument to trombone section, initially bass horn, subsequently sometimes valve ophicleide (2), and particularly contrabass valve trombone used by Verdi. Parts should normally be played on contrabass (valve) trombone.

CIRCULAR BASS—(*coll.*) Helicon or Sousaphone.

CLAIRON—*Fr.* Duty bugle.

CLAIRON-À-CLEFS—*Fr.* Keyed bugle.

CLAIRON-BASSE (1)—*Fr.* Tenor duty bugle.

(2)—*Fr.* Bass ophicleide, especially of valved variety. [Sachs (S³)]

CLAIRON-CHAUSSER—Bugle-horn in French-horn-shape (Millereau, 1883).

CLAIRON-CHROMATIQUE—*Fr.* Keyed bugle.

CLAIRON-CONTREBASSE—*Fr.* Bass tuba.

CLAIRON SCOLAIRE—Duty bugle in b♭ used by *bataillons scolaires.* [Jacquot (J²)]

CLAIRON-SOPRANO—*Fr.* Keyed bugle in e'♭.

CLAIRON-TÉNOR—*Fr.* Keyed bugle in e♭.

CLARÍN DE LLAVES—*Sp.* Keyed bugle.

CLARÍN DE SEÑALES—*Sp.* Duty bugle.

CLAVICOR—Three-valve, tuba-shaped instrument in several pitches, familiarly e♭, introduced as substitute for alto ophicleide but superseded by saxhorn (*inv.* Danays, 1838; *mfc.* Guichard).

CLAVICOR ALTO—*Fr.* Clavicor in e♭.

CLAVICORNO (1)—*It.* Clavicor, especially pitched in e♭.

(2)—*It.* (*coll.*) Flicorno, especially soprano in b♭.

CLAVICORNO FAGOTTO—Euphonium (1) (Rossano, 1887).

CLAVITUBE—Keyed bugle in f', e♭', c' or b♭ in trumpet-shape (Halary, 1817).

CONTRABAJO—*Sp.* Contrabass tuba.

CONTRABASS CORNOPHONE—Cornophone in F (E♭).

CONTRABASS OPHICLEIDE—Ophicleide in F' (E'♭).

CONTRABASS SAXHORN—Saxhorn in E♭ or B'♭.

CONTRABASS SAXOTROMBA—Saxotromba in B'♭.

CONTRABASS SERPENT—Serpent in E'♭ (Jordan, exhibited at 1851 Gt. Exhibition).

CONTRABASS TUBA (1)—Tuba in C or B'♭.

(2)—Subcontrabass tuba.

CONTRAHORN—Alto saxhorn in e♭ (Lamperhoff, 1845).

CONTRALTO—*Fr.* Saxhorn in b♭.

CONTRALTO HORN—Four-valve Wagner Tuba in f or e♭ intended as substitute for French horn or alto horn in marching bands (Miraphone).

CONTRALTO SAXHORN—Saxhorn in b♭ (tuba-shape).

CONTRA-OPHICLEIDE—Contrabass ophicleide in E'♭ (Wright, c. 1841-71).

CONTRA-SERPENT (1)—Double-sized serpent (Wood Brothers, 1840).

(2)—Bass instrument by Jordan (possibly his *Euphonic serpentcleide*).

CONTREBASSE (1)—*Fr.* Tuba in E♭ or B'♭.

(2)—*Fr.* Contrabass ophicleide in F (Halary, 1817).

(3)—*Fr.* String bass.

CONTREBASSE D'HARMONIE (1)—*Fr.* Ophicleide.

(2)—*Fr.* Contrabass ophicleide in F (Halary, 1819).

(3)—*Fr.* Bass tuba. [Berlioz (B[24])]

CONTREBASSE RONDE—*Fr.* Helicon.

CONTRE-CLAIRON—Experimental French reconstruction of ancient deep bugle by 'the performer Hostié', 1791. [*Journal de Paris* (J[8])], 1793]

CONTRE-HORN—*Fr.* Contrahorn

CONTROFICLEIDE—Contrabass Pelittone (Pelitti, 1845).

COR (1)—Four-valve 'bass valve horn' (? maker, 1841). [Lavoix (L[6])]

(2)—*Fr.* Horn.

COR À CLEFS—*Fr.* Keyed bugle.

COR ALTO—*Fr. & Ger.* Tenor cor.

COR-BASSE TÉNOR—*Fr.* Euphonium (1). [Sachs (S[3])]

COR DE BASSE ANGLAIS—*Fr.* English bass horn. [Kastner (K[5])]

COR DE KENT—*Fr.* Keyed bugle.

CORHORN—*Ger.* Tenor cor.

CORN BUABHALL—*Old Irish.* Bugle horn (2). [Downey (D[17])]

CORN BUELIN—*Wel.* Bugle horn (2). [Downey (D[17])]

CORNET À BOCAL—Small serpent with six holes and one key (? maker, n.d.).

CORNET À BOUQUIN—*Fr.* Treble cornett.

CORNETA DE CLAUS—*Cat.* Keyed bugle.

CORNETA DE LLAVES—*Sp.* Keyed bugle.

CORNETT (1)—Instrument with finger-holes and cup mouthpiece.

(2)—Organ stop: 4 ft. or 2 ft. pedal solo reed.

CORNETTA A CHIAVI—*It.* Keyed bugle.

CORNETTA SEGNALE—*It.* Duty bugle.

CORNETTINO—Cornett pitched a fourth or fifth higher than the treble.

CORNETTO TORTO—Bass cornett.

CORNET-TROMPE—Copper wide-bore hunting-horn, the first part of the tubing spiralling round the exterior (Adolphe Sax, n.d.).

CORNO—Bass cornett.

CORNO Á CIGNO—*Sp. (arch.)* Onnoven (1).

CORNO BASSO—*It.* Bass horn (1).

CORNO BASSO CROMATICO—Bass horn (1).

CORNO KENTH—*Ger.* Keyed bugle.

CORNON (1)—Bass cornett.

(2)—Member of helicon-, oval- or tuba-shaped family, bore between bugle and French horn, played with funnel-mouthpiece (Červený, c. 1846).

(3)—Cornophone.

CORNOPHONE—Member of cornon-type family, bell tilted forward (Besson, Paris, 1890).

CORNOPHONE ALTO—Alto Cornophone in eb (f).

CORNOPHONE CONTRABASS—Contrabass Cornophone in Eb (F).

CORNOPHONE CORNETTITO—Soprano Cornophone in bb.

CORNOPHONE PÉDALE—Small French Tuba in c (Besson, Paris, 1892).

CORNOPHONE TENOR—Tenor Cornophone in Bb (C).

CORNOPHONE TUBA—Bass Cornophone in B'b (C).

CORNU—Medium-bore horn in helicon-shape, c. 3.5 m long, used by Romans.

COR PERFECTIONNÉ—*Fr.* Cornon in French-horn-shape (Červený, n.d.). [Pierre (P[13])]

COR TÉNOR—*Fr.* Tenor cor. [Chevalier (C[20])]

COR-TUBA—Instrument by G. Besson—no further details. [B[46], 'Besson']

COUNTER BOMBARDON—Tuba shown at 1851 Gt. Exhibition (Gautrot, n.d.).

CYWEIRGORN—*Wel.* Keyed bugle. [Sachs (S[3])]

DEEP BASSSAXHORN—Bass tuba in Eb.

DISKANTTUBA—*Ger.* Flügel horn in e'b.

DOG HORN—(*coll.*) Alto saxhorn in eb.

DOUBLE B—(*coll.*).Tuba in B'b (i.e. BBb).

DOUBLE BASS—(*coll.*). BBb Tuba.

DOUBLE-BASS OPHICLEIDE—Contrabass ophicleide.

DOUBLE-BASS SAXHORN—Contrabass tuba in B'b.

DOUBLE-BASS SAXOTROMBA—Saxotromba in B'b.

DOUBLE C—(*coll.*)—Tuba in C (i.e. CC).

DOUBLE E—(*coll.*).Tuba in Eb (i.e. EEb).

DOUBLOPHONE—Combined euphonium and valve trombone (Besson, Paris, 1890).

DUDACH—*Wel.* duty bugle. [Sachs (S[3])]

DUETTON—Duplex instrument in the shape of a lyre (Sediva, 1887).

DUPLEX INSTRUMENT—Two different instruments leading from a single mouthpipe usually through common valves.

DUTY BUGLE—Bugle (2).

Eb BASS—Medium/small-bore tuba in Eb with three valves.

EBOR CORNO—Valved alto and tenor bugles in bb and eb. (Dodworth, mid-19th century).

EEb BASS—Tuba in Eb.

EEb TUBA—Tuba in Eb.

ELICON—*It.* Helicon.

EMBOLICLAVE—Type of euphonium (1) (Coëffet, 1844).

ENGLISCHES BASSHORN—*Ger.* Bass horn (1).

ENGLISCHES HORN—*Ger.* Bass horn (1).

ENGLISH BASS HORN—Bass horn (1).

Eb TUBA—Medium/small-bore tuba in Eb with three valves.

EUFONIO—*It. & Sp.* Euphonium (1).

EUPHONIC HORN—Sommerophone or euphonium (1).

EUPHONIC SERPENTCLEIDE—Serpentcleide one octave lower than normal, shown by Jordan at 1851 Gt. Exhibition (possibly identical with *Contra-serpent*).

EUPHONIKON (1)—*Ger. (arch.).* Euphonium (1).

(2)—Combined harp and pianoforte (Beale, 1842).

EUPHONION—*Engl. & Ger. (arch.).* Euphonium (1).

EUPHONIUM (1)—Tuba in Bb Sommer, c. 1843).

(2)—Chromatic bass horn.

FAGOTTSERPENT (1)—*Ger.* Russian bassoon.

(2)—*Ger.* Bass horn (1).

FIGLE—*Sp.* Ophicleide.

FISCORN—*Sp.* Valved bugle-horn.

FISCORNIO—*Sp.* Fiscorn.

FLICORNO (1)—*It.* Valved bugle-horn.

(2)—*It.* Flügel horn or cornet in bb.

FLICORNO BARITONO—*It.* Three-valve euphonium (1) in Bb (c).

FLICORNO BASSO—*It.* Euphonium (1).

FLICORNO BASSO-GRAVE—*It.* Bass tuba in F or Eb; also *bombardone*; *Pelittone* or *elicon* when in helicon-shape.

FLICORNO CONTRABASSO—*It.* Contrabass tuba in C or B'b; also *Pelittone* or *elicon* when in helicon-shape.

FLICORNO CONTRALTO—*It.* Alto saxhorn in eb (f), normally called *Genis*.

FLICORNO SOPRACUTO—*It.* Saxhorn, cornet or flügel horn in b'b.

FLICORNO SOPRANINO—*It.* Saxhorn, cornet or flügel horn in e'b (f', d' or c').

FLICORNO SOPRANO—*It.* Soprano saxhorn, cornet or flügel horn in bb (a).

FLICORNO TENORE—*It.* Baritone in Bb.

FLISCORNITO—*Sp.* Sopranino saxhorn in e'b.

FLISCORNO—*Sp.* Fiscorn.

FLISCORNO ALTO—*Sp.* Onnoven (1).

FLISCORNO EN SIb—*Sp.* Flügel horn in bb.

FLISCORNO EN SOPRANO MIb—*Sp.* Flügel horn in eb.

FLUGELHORN—*U.S.A.* Flügel horn.

FLÜGEL HORN—Valved bugle-horn, particularly soprano in bb.

FLÜGELHORN (1)—*Ger.* Flügel horn.

        (2)—*Ger.* Valved bugle-horn.

        (3)—*Ger. (arch.)* Horn used by Flügelmeister.

        (4)—*Ger. (arch.)* Keyed bugle.

        (5)—*Sp. (arch.)* Onnoven (1).

        (6)—Organ 8 ft reed stop.

FLUGELHORN IN B—*Ger.* Flügel horn in bb.

FLUGELHORN CONTREBASS—Three-valve tuba in Eb or B'b (Rivet, pre-1845).

FLÜGELHORN PIKKOLO IN ES—*Ger.* Sopranino flügel horn in e'b.

FLÜGEL-HORN À PISTONS—*Fr. (arch.)* Valved bugle-horn.

F TUBA—Tuba in F.

FUGEL HORN—*Ger. (arch.)* Keyed bugle. [Kappey (K$^2$)]

GABUSIFONO—*It.* Four-valve soprano, tenor or bass trombone in tuba-shape (Gabusi, c. 1880). [Heyde (H$^{22}$)]

GEMELLI—Varieties of duplex instruments (Pelliti, 1855).

GENIS—*It.* Alto saxhorn in eb (f) (derived from Italian maker's name?).

GLAGOL—Euphonium (1) with adjustable bell (Rott, 1861).

GLAS-EUPHONION—*Ger.* Type of glass harmonica (c. 1790).

GLYCLEIDE—Baritone in tuba-shape, Bb with rotary-change to A (Červený, 1846).

GRAND BUGLE—*Fr.* Flügel horn in Bb.

GROSSER BASS—*Ger.* Tuba in Eb.

HARMONIEBASS (1)—*Ger.* Ophicleide.

        (2)—Nine-key bass horn (?, 1829). [Kalkbrenner (K$^1$)]

HARMONIE KONTRABASS—*Ger.* Bass ophicleide by Griessling & Schlott, 1833. [Geiringer (G$^{11}$)]

HELICON—Tuba in circular-shape (?Russia, c. 1845).

HELICÓN—*Sp.* Helicon.

HELIKON—*Ger.* Helicon.

HELLHORN—Type of euphonium (1) (Hell, 1843).

HELL'S-HORN—Hellhorn.

HERCULESOPHONE—Member of large-bore valve bugle family (Sediva, 1888).

HERKULESOFON—*Fr. & Ger.* Herculesophone.

HIBERNICON—Type of bass horn (1) in two sizes, tenor and bass (*inv.* Cotter, 1823).

HIBOCORNO—Ebor corno (Roché, c. 1846).

HIGHAMPHONE—Duplex instrument in eb with euphonium and trombone bells

(Higham, n.d.).

HIPPOCORNO—*U.S.A.*Ebor corno

HOCHFLÜGELHORN—(1) *Ger.* Sopranino flugel horn or cornet in e'♭.

(2) *Ger.* Soprano flugel horn in bb· [Geiringer (G[11])]

HOLTONPHONE—Sousaphone in E♭ or B'♭ with forward bell (Holton, early 20th century).

HONNOBE—*Sp. (arch.)* Onnoven (1). [Kenyon de Pascual (K[11])]

HONOBEN—*Sp. (arch.)* Onnoven (1). [Kenyon de Pascual (K[11])]

IMPERIAL BARITONE—Large-bore four-valve baritone in c or B♭, oval-shape, completely conical profile (Červený, 1885).

IMPERIAL BASS—Large-bore tuba or helicon in F, E♭, C or B'♭, with completely conical profile. (Červený, 1883).

IMPERIAL EUPHONIUM—Large-bore euphonium in B♭ or c with completely conical profile (Červený, 1882).

IMPERIAL HELICON—Large-bore helicon in C (B'♭) with completely conical profile (Červený, 1883).

IPOCORNO—*U.S.A.* Ebor corno.

JUBELHORN—Type of tenor cor (1) (Conn, c.1900). [Geiringer (G[11])]

KAISERBARITON—*Ger.* Imperial euphonium.

KAISERBASS—*Ger.* Imperial bass.

KAISERHELIKON—*Ger.* Imperial helicon.

KAISERTENOR—*Ger.* Imperial baritone.

KAISERTUBA—*Ger.* Imperial bass.

KENT BUGLE—Keyed bugle.

KENTHORN—*Ger.* Keyed bugle.

KEY BUGLE—Keyed bugle.

KEYED BUGLE—Bugle (1) with six or more keys (*inv.* Haliday, 1810).

KLAPPENBASS—*Ger.* Ophicleide.

KLAPPENFLÜGEL—*Ger.* Keyed bugle.

KLAPPENFLÜGELHORN—*Ger.* Keyed bugle.

KLAPPENHORN—*Ger.* Keyed bugle.

KLAPPENHORNBASS—*Ger.* Bass ophicleide.

KLAPPHORN—*Ger.* Keyed bugle.

KLEINER BASS—*Ger.* Euphonium (1).

KLEINE SAXOTROMBA—*Ger.* Sopranino saxotromba in e'♭.

KLEINES KORNETT—*Ger.* Sopranino saxhorn in e'♭.

KLEINES SAXHORN—*Ger.* Sopranino saxhorn in e'♭.

KLEPHOORN—*Dutch.* Keyed bugle.

KOENIG HORN—Flügel horn in French-horn-shape (*inv.* Koenig, 1885; *mfc.* Courtois).

KÖNIGHORN—*Ger.* Koenig Horn.

KONTRABASOWA—*Pol.* Tuba.

KONTRABASSKORNETT—Narrow-bore valved bugle-horn in helicon-shape in B'♭ (Červený, 1876).

KONTRABASS-KORNOPHON—*Ger.* Contrabass Cornophone.

KONTRABASSSAXHORN—*Ger.* Contrabass saxhorn.

KONTRABASSSAXOTROMBA—*Ger.* Contrabass saxotromba.

KONTRABASSTUBA—*Ger.* Contrabass tuba.

KONTRABASSZUS SZAXKÜRT—*Hun.* Contrabass tuba.

KONTRAHORN—*Ger.* Contrahorn.

KONTRASTBOMBARDON—Deep tuba; no more details available (Barth, 1840). [Sachs (S³)]

KORNETT (1)—*Ger.* Flügel horn, soprano saxhorn or bugle in b♭.

       (2)—*Ger.* (*arch.*) Valved bugle-horn.

KORNETTINSTRUMENTE—Family of narrow-bore valved bugle-horns in helicon-shape (Červený, 1876).

KORNON—*Ger.* Cornon (2).

KORNOPHON—*Ger.* Cornophone.

KUHLOHORN—Flügel horn in b♭ for *Posaunenchöre* use. [Heyde (H²²)]

LYRAPHONE—Duplex instrument with forward- or upward-facing bells in shape of lyre (Sediva, 1887).

LYSARDEN—English name for deepest cornett.

MELODY HORN—*U.S.A.* Alto horn with echo bell (Henry Distin, c. 1880). [Eliason (E⁶)]

MELLOPHONE—*U.S.A.* Tenor cor (1) (Conn, n.d.).

MELONICOR—*It.* Tenor cor (1) (*des.* Italian pianist Meloni, 1853; *pat.* France, n.d.). [Geiringer (G¹¹)]

MELOPHON—*Sp.* Tenor cor.

MINIBASS—Three- or four-valve tuba for use in small ensembles (Finke, n.d.).

MOIENEL—*Fr.* (arch). Medieval name for helicon(!). [Geiringer (G¹¹)]

MOIIEMAU—*Fr.* (arch.) Medieval name for helicon(!). [Geiringer (G¹¹)]

MONSTER OPHICLEIDE (1)—Contrabass ophicleide.

       (2)—Ophicléide monstre (2).

MONSTREOPHIKLEÏDE—*Ger.* Contrabass ophicleide.

NÉO-ALTO—French valved bugle-horn (Rivet, 1844-5).

NÉOFORM—Instrument in tuba shape with bell turnable in any direction (G. Besson,

1851-5).

OBBLIGATO ALTO HORN—Sweet-toned alto horn in f, e♭, C or B♭ (Červený, 1859).

OBLIGAT-ALTHORN—*Ger.* Obbligato alto horn.

OFICLEID—*Rom.* Ophicleide.

OFICLEÍD—*Russ.* Ophicleide.

OFICLEIDE—*It.* Ophicleide.

OFICLEIDE A MACCHINA—*It.* Valved ophicleide.

OFICLEIDE SOPRANO—*It.* Alto ophicleide in A♭. [Geiringer (G[11])]

OFIGLE—*Sp. (arch.)* Ophicleide.

OFIKLEID—*Hun.* Ophicleide.

OFIXLIER—*Sp. (arch.)* Ophicleide.

OKTAVWALDHORN—*Ger.* Tenor cor.

OLIFANT—Oliphant.

OLIPHANT—Wide-bore signal instrument derived from elephant's tusk.

OMNITON—Improved ophicleide (Halary, 1849).

OMNOBE—*Sp. (arch.)* Onnoven (1). [Kenyon de Pascual (K[11])]

ONNOVEN (1)—*Sp.* Alto saxhorn in e♭.

      (2)—*Sp.* (rarely) Tenor cor. [Kenyon de Pascual (K[11])]

      (3)—*Sp.* (arch.) Alto saxhorn in oval or circular shape (possibly Romero, c. 1870). [Kenyon de Pascual (K[11])]

OPHECLEIDE—Ophicleide.

OPHIBARITON—Type of Russian bassoon (Bachmann, 1840). [Pontécoulant (P[20])]

OPHIBATERION—Type of French upright serpent (? maker, n.d.).

OPHICLEIDE (1)—Bass keyed bugle in bassoon-shape (Halary, 1817). Alto and contrabass versions were also made.

      (2)—Bass tuba in ophicleide shape.

      (3)—Powerful high-pressure organ-stop, usually 16 ft pedal.

OPHICLÉIDE—*Fr.* Ophicleide.

OPHICLÉIDE À CYLINDRES—*Fr.* (arch.) Bass tuba.

OPHICLÉIDE-ALTO À PISTONS—*Fr.* (arch.) Alto saxhorn in e♭.

OPHICLEIDE-À-PISTON(S)—*Fr.* (arch.) Narrow-bore bass tuba in ophicleide-shape.

OPHICLÉIDE-À-ROTATION—Rotary-valve ophicleide (2). (Kraus, 1878).

OPHICLÉIDE BASSE—*Fr.* Bass ophicleide.

OPHICLÉIDE MONSTRE (1)—*Fr.* Contrabass ophicleide.

      (2)—*Fr.* (arch.) Narrow-bore bass tuba in F or E♭ in ophicleide-shape.

OPHICLÉIDE QUINTE—*Fr.* Alto ophicleide.

OPHIKLEÏDE—*Ger.* Ophicleide (1) or (2).

OPHIMONOCLEIDE—Type of upright serpent (Coeffet, 1828).

OPHY-BARYTON—Type of Russian bassoon (*des.* Forveille; *mfc.* Turlot, 1823). [Sachs (S³)]

OPHYCLÉÏDE—*Fr.* Ophicleide.

PECK HORN—*U.S.A.* (*coll.*) Alto saxhorn in eb.

PELITTIFERO—Wooden instrument covered in thin skin with three cylinders (Pelitti, 1843).

PELITTONI (*sing.* PELITTONE)—Helicons in Bb, Eb and B'b, especially the latter (Pelitti, 1846).

PETIT BUGLE—*Fr.* Sopranino saxhorn or flügel horn in e'b.

PETIT SAXHORN—*Fr.* Saxhorn in b'b.

PHONEION—*Fr.* Phonikon.

PHONIKON—Euphonium (1) with cor-anglais-type bell (Červený, 1848).

PIKKOLO IN ES—*Ger.* Sopranino saxhorn in e'b.

PISTON-BASSE—Bass tuba (Périnet, 1841).

PRIMBASS—*Ger.* (*arch.*) Euphonium (1).

PRIMHORN (1)—Valved bugle-horn in French-horn-shape in f (eb) (Červený, 1873).

        (2)—*Aus.* Tenor cor.

PRIMWALDHORN—*Ger.* Tenor cor.

PRYORPHONE—Duplex euphonium/valve trombone (Holton, pre-1930).

PSALMELODICON—Type of serpent with 25 keys (Weinrich, 1828).

QUINTE—*Fr.* Alto ophicleide.

QUINTE À CLEF—Quinticlave.

QUINTE-TUBA—Name engraved on ophicleide by Turton, 1829.

QUINTICLAVE—Keyed bugle in f or eb in bassoon-shape, (Halary, 1817). Also called *alto ophicleide.*

QUINTI-TUBE—Quinticlave.

QUINTON—*Sp.* (*arch.*) Onnoven (1)

RIESENOPHIKLEÏDE—*Ger.* Contrabass ophicleide.

RINGTUBA—*Ger.* Wagner Tuba.

ROYAL KENT BUGLE—Keyed Bugle.

RUSSIAN BASSOON—Serpent in bassoon-shape. The prototype was Régibo's upright bassoon, c. 1780.

RUSSISCHES FAGOTT—*Ger.* Russian bassoon.

SARFFUDGORN—Wel. Ophicleide or serpent. [Sachs (S³)]

SAX (1)—*It.* (*coll.*) Flicorno, particularly soprano in bb.

(2)—*(coll.)* Saxophone.

SAX-BOURDON EN MI BÉMOL—*Fr.* Subbasss tuba.

SAXHORN (1)—One of a family of valved bugle-horns in tuba-, helicon- or
            trumpet-shape (A. Sax, from 1845).

        (2)—Valved bugle-horn by any maker.

        (3)—Alto saxhorn in e♭.

SAXHORN ALTO—*Fr.* Saxhorn in e♭.

SAXHORN BARYTON—*Fr.* Euphonium (1) or baritone in B♭.

SAXHORN BASSE (1)—*Fr.* Euphonium (1).

        (2)—*Fr.* Bass tuba in F (E♭).

SAXHORN BOURDON (1)—Tuba in E'♭ (A. Sax, 1855).

              (2)—*Fr.* Contrabass tuba in C or B'♭.

SAXHORN CONTRALTO—*Fr.* Saxhorn in b♭.

SAXHORN CONTREBASSE—*Fr.* Contrabass tuba in B'♭ or C.

SAX-HORN IN B ALTO—*Ger.* Saxhorn suraigu.

SAXHORN SOPRANO—*Fr.* Saxhorn in b♭.

SAXHORN SURAIGU—*Fr.* Saxhorn in B'♭.

SAXHORN TENOR—*Sp.* Onnoven (1).

SAXHORN TÉNOR (1)—*Fr.* Baritone in B♭.

        (2)—*Fr.* Alto saxhorn in e♭. [Kastner (K[5])]

SAXOR—*Sp.* Alto saxhorn in e♭.

SAXOTROMBA—Member of family of valve instruments with bore between bugle
  and French horn using funnel-mouthpiece (A. Sax, 1845).

SAXOTROMBA ALTO-TÉNOR—*Fr.* Saxotromba in e♭· [Kastner (K[5])]

SAXOTROMBA BARYTON—*Fr.* Saxotromba in B♭.

SAXOTROMBA BASSE—*Fr.* Saxotromba in E♭.

SAXOTROMBA CONTRALTO—*Fr.* Saxotromba in b♭.

SAXOTROMBA CONTREBASSE—*Fr.* Saxotromba in B'♭.

SAXOTROMBA SOPRANO—*Fr.* Saxotromba in e'♭.

SAXOTROMPA—*Port.* Alto saxhorn in e♭.

SAXTROMPETE—*Ger.* Saxotromba.

SAX-TRUMPET—Term for Saxotromba at 1851 Gt. Exhibition.

SAXTUBA—Member of buccina-like family of valve instruments (A. Sax, 1852).

SAX-TUBAR—Contrabass tuba. [Pierre (P[13])]

SCHLANGE—*Ger.* Serpent.

SCHLANGENHORN—*Ger.* Serpent.

SCHLANGENROHR—*Ger.* Serpent.

SCHWANENHORN (1)—Saxhorn with swan's-neck bell, Stowasser, pre-1842
  [Kenyon de Pascual (K[11])]

(2)—Bugle horn with bell bent at an angle (Červený, 1846). [Sachs (S³)]

SERPÀN—*N. It.* Serpent.

SERPANO—Serpent.

SERPENT—Development of *bass cornett* in convoluted shape with cup-mouthpiece and six finger-holes, but no thumb-hole (Guillaume, late sixteenth century). Subsequently it was made in other shapes, more keys being added.

SERPENT À CLEF—*Fr.* Ophicleide (1).

SERPENT ANGLAISE—*Fr.* English bass horn.

SERPENT À PAVILLON—Serpent with clear tone and notes of consistent quality (Coëffet, 1839). [Wright (W³⁰)]

SERPENT-BASSON—*Fr.* (*arch.*) Russian bassoon.

SERPENT BASSON—*Fr.* (*arch.*) Russian bassoon.

SERPENTBOMBARDON—Contrabass (?valved) ophicleide in F (Červený, c. 1840).

SERPENTCLEIDE—Wooden ophicleide (*inv.* Beacham, Glen or Huggett, n.d.).

SERPENT CONTRE-BASSE—Unsuccessful 1835 attempt at making contrabass serpent. [Wright (W³⁰)]

SERPENT DE CAVALRIE—Fr. Bass horn (1) for cavalry use. [Morley-Pegge (M⁴³)]

SERPENT D'HARMONIE—*Fr.* Keyed serpent (literally 'band serpent').

SERPENT DROITE (1)—*Fr.* Ophybaryton.

               (2)—*Fr.* Russian bassoon.

SERPENTE—*N. It.* Serpent.

SERPENTEAU—Fr. 'Small serpent used in churches.' [Wright (W³⁰), quoting Stendahl, *Vie de Rossini,* 1824, p. 254: 'Mais l'ottavino, le gros tambour, le serpenteau des églises, ont même ambition, et y arrivent, à peu près avec le même succès']

SERPENT FORVEILLE—Type of upright serpent (Forveille, 1822).

SERPENT MILITAIRE—Type of upright serpent (Piffault, 1806).

SERPENTONE—*It.* Serpent.

SERPENT ORDINAIRE—*Fr.* Serpent without keys.

SERPENT PIFFAULT—Type of upright serpent (Piffault, 1806).

SERPENT RUSSE—*Fr.* Russian bassoon.

SERPENT TORDU—*Fr.* 'Bent' (i.e., traditional ) serpent (cf. upright 'serpent droite').

SIGNALHORN—*Ger.* Duty bugle.

SODDUDGORN—*Wel.* Bass horn or ophicleide. [Sachs (S³)]

SOMMEROPHONE—Euphonium (1).

SONOROPHONE—Type of helicon (Metzler & Waddell, 1858).

SOPRANINO EN MI♭—*Sp.* Sopranino saxhorn in e'♭.

SOPRANINO SAXHORN—Saxhorn in e'♭ (f').

SOPRANINO SAXOTROMBA—Saxotromba in e'♭.

SOPRANO CORNOPHONE—Cornophone in b♭.

SOPRANO FLUGELHORN—Flügel horn or saxhorn in e'♭.

SOPRANO SAXHORN—Saxhorn in b♭ (c').

SOPRANO SAXOTROMBA—Saxotromba in b♭.

SOPRANO-SAXHORN—*Ger.* Soprano saxhorn.

SOUBASSOPHONE—Sousaphone in E♭ or B'♭ (Couesnon, n.d.).

SOUSAPHONE—Helicon in E♭ or B'♭ with large bell originally upward but later forward, conceived by Sousa (Pepper, late 1890s).

STELLAHOORN—*Ned.* Alto horn in e♭ in french horn-shape.

SUBBASS TUBA—Tuba in E'♭ (A. Sax, 1855).

SUBCONTRABASS TUBA (1)—Subbass tuba.

                              (2)—Tuba in C' and F' (Červený, 1846).

                              (3)—Tuba in B"♭ (A. Sax, 1855).

SUDREPHONE—Family of valved bugle-horns with vibrating membranes (Sudre, 1892).

SUPER-ACUTE SOPRANO SAXOTROMBA—Saxotromba in b'♭.

SUSAFÓN—*Sp.* Sousaphone.

SUSAPHONE—*Ger.* Sousaphone.

TAUREA—Tuba (4) with sound like bellowing of a bull. [Marcuse (M[13])]

TENOR (1)—Alto saxhorn in e♭.

           (2)—*Sp.* Baritone in B♭.

           (3)—*(coll.)* Tenor saxophone.

TENORBASS—*Ger.* Euphonium (1).

TENORBASSHORN—*Ger.* Euphonium (1).

TENOR BOMBARDON—Instrument (tenor tuba?) by Pelitti, 1835. [Pontécoulant (P[20])]

TENOR COR (1)—Valved bugle-horn, profile between French horn and bugle with the shape of the former, in f (e♭) (?maker, c. 1860).

                  (2)—Ballad Horn (2).

TENOR CORNETT—Cornett fifth lower than treble.

TENOR CORNOPHONE—Cornophone in c (B♭).

TENORE IN SI♭—*It.* Baritone in B♭.

TENOR EUPHONIUM—Baritone in B♭.

TENOR FLUGEL HORN—Alto flügel horn in e♭.

TENORFLÜGELHORN—*Ger.* Baritone in B♭.

TENORHORN (1)—*Ger.* Baritone in B♭.

             (2)—Valved bugle-horn in B♭ probably in ophicleide shape (Stölzel,

1828).

TENOR HORN (1)—*U.K.* Alto saxhorn in eb.

(2)—*U.K.* (*arch.*) Baritone in Bb.

TÉNOR IMPÉRIALE—*Fr.* Imperial baritone.

TENORKORNETT—Narrow-bore valved bugle-horn in Bb, helicon-shape (Červený, 1876).

TENORKORNON—Cornon (2) in Bb.

TENORKORNOPHON—*Ger.* Tenor Cornophone in c (Bb).

TENOR SAXHORN—*U.K.* Alto saxhorn in eb.

TENORTROMPETE—Valved instrument in Bb, probably in trumpet-shape (Stölzel, 1828).

TENOR TUBA (1)—Tuba in Bb (c) (C.W. Moritz, 1838).

(2)—Euphonium (1).

(3)—Wagner Tuba (tenor in Bb).

TENOR-VALVE OPHICLEIDE—Alto or tenor horn by Jordan, Liverpool, exhibited at 1851 Great Exhibition.

TENOR WAGNER TUBA—Wagner Tuba in Bb.

THURNERHORN—Wide-bore curved cornett used by medieval *Türmer* (watchmen stationed on a tower) to sound the fire-alarm.

TIEFES BASS-SAXHORN—*Ger.* Contrabass saxhorn.

TIEFES BASS SAXHORN—*Ger.* Tuba in Eb.

TIWBA—*Wel.* Tuba.

TOB—*Old Irish.* Trumpet.

TORNISTER-BASS—Type of compact tuba (Červený, 1908).

TREBLE CORNETT—Cornett with a compass of g-d"'.

TROMBA (1)—Basse-trompette.

(2)—*It.* Trumpet.

TROMBA A CHIAVI—*It.* Keyed bugle.

TROMBA PER FANFARA PER BERSAGLIERI—*It.* Bersag Horn.

TROMBACELLO—Bass tuba (Graves, mid-19th century).

TROMBE—Basse-trompette.

TROMBINO—*Sp.* Sopranino saxhorn in e'b.

TROMBOTONAR—Tuba 3000 mm in height shown at 1855 Paris *Exposition* (Besson, Paris, 1855).

TROMPA ALTO—*Sp.* Tenor cor.

TROMPE DE LORRAINE—Type of oliphant containing a spiral tube joining the mouthpiece to the bell (Grégoire, 1855).

TROMPETTE À CLEF(S) (1)—*Fr.* Keyed bugle.

(2)—Keyed bugle in f′, e′♭, c′ or b♭ (Halary, 1817).

TROMPETTE À CLÉS—*Fr. (arch.)* Keyed bugle.

TROMPETTE-CHROMATIQUE—*Fr. (arch.)* Keyed bugle (subsequently *clairon chromatique*).

TROMPETTE-QUINTE—Keyed bugle in f or e♭ in bassoon shape (Halary, 1817).

TROMPETTE-TUBA—Type of trumpet designed for funeral of Napoleon I (A. Sax, 1840).

TUB—*Old Irish.* Trumpet.

TUBA (1)—Valved bugle-horn in tuba-, ophicleide- or helicon-shape generally pitched in B♭ or below.

    (2)—Wagner Tuba.

    (3)—Bass saxhorn in B♭ (euphonium (1)).

    (4)—Roman military trumpet, about 1250 mm in length.

    (5)—*Fr.* Contrabass valve trombone. [Lavignac (L[5])]

    (6)—High-pressure organ reed stop.

    (7)—Tenor, or main-note or recitation in Gregorian chant. [Apel (A[16])]

    (8)—Powerful transmitter used to jam enemy radar. [Webster (W[7])]

    (9)—*Fr.* Snorkel

TUBA ALTO in Es—*Ger.* Alto horn in E♭. [Geiringer (G[11])]

TUBA BAIXA—*Cat./Port.* Bass tuba.

TUBA BARYTON—*Ger.* Euphonium (1). [Vessella (V[5])]

TUBA BASSA—*It.* Bass tuba.

TUBA BASSE—*Fr.* Euphonium (1) or bass tuba.

TUBA CLARION—4 ft tuba organ-stop.

TUBA CONTREBASSE—*Fr.* Bass tuba in F or E♭.

TUBA CORNEA—*Lat.* Bronze trumpet.

TUBA CURVA (1)—Medium-bore helicon-shape horn in D, based on *cornu* (*dev.* Sarrette; *mfc.* Cormeri, 1791).

    (2)—Cornu. [Jacquot (J[2])]

TUBA DIRECTA—Tuba (4).

TUBA DUCTILIS—*Lat.* Trumpet made from metal drawn out by hammering.

TUBA-DUPRÉ—Wooden ophicleide (Dupré, 1824).

TUBA EBORNEA—*Lat.* Oliphant (of Roland).

TUBA HERCOTECTONICA—Type of trumpet, details unknown (Otter, 1598-1668).

TUBA MAGNA—High-pressure organ reed stop.

TUBA MAJOR (1)—Quartposaune (bass trombone). [Praetorius (P[22])]

(2)—Variety of tuba organ-stop.

TUBA MAXIMA—Octavposaune (contrabass trombone). [Praetorius (P[22])]

TUBA MINOR (1)—'Ordinary trombone' (tenor in A!). [Praetorius (P[22])]

(2)—Variety of tuba organ-stop.

TUBA MIRABILIS—Powerful reed organ-stop (Hill, n.d.).

TUBA OBLONGA—*Lat.* Trombone. [Scholes (S[17])]

TUBA ORIEL—*Lat.* Positive organ. [Scholes (S[17])]

TUBA PASTORALIS—*Lat.* pastoral trumpet. [See Stoneham (S[40]) for works by Havel, and Volkert involving this type of alphorn]

TUBA SONORA—Type of loud organ-stop (Hope-Jones, n.d.).

TUBA SOPRANO in B—*Ger.* Soprano flügel horn in Bb. [Geiringer (G[11])]

TUBA STENTOROPHONICA—Type of speaking-trumpet (*inv.* Morland; *mfc.* Beale, 1760).

TUBA TENORE—*It.* Tenor tuba.

TUBA TYMPANODIS—Pipe used by pipe-and-tabor player.

TUBE (1)—*Fr.* Tuba.

(2)—*Ger.* Wagner Tuba.

TUBE DE CONTREBASSE—*Fr.* Contrabass tuba.

TUBE DE KIRCHER—Elliptical tube like monster Roman tuba (4) (Kircher, n.d.). [Jacquot (J[2])]

TUBEN—Wagner Tuben.

TUBETTE—*Fr.* Tenor Wagner Tuba in Bb with four valves (Evette & Schaeffer, Paris, n.d.). [Geiringer (G[11])]

TUBULA—*Lat.* Little tuba. [Sachs (S[3])]

TURNERHORN—Fire-brigade horn in four pitches (Červený, 1867).

VALVE BUGLE—Flügel horn [translation of French *bugle* in B[25]]

VALVE-OPHICLEIDE (1)—Valved bugle in eb (Guichot, 1832).

(2)—(*arch.*) Narrow-bore bass tuba in ophicleide-shape.

VENTIL-FAGOTTHORN—Valved horn in bassoon-shape (Zetsche, 1841). [Schubert, 1883]

VIOLONCEL-SERPENT—Type of serpent by Embach, Amsterdam, c.1830-35. [Nagy (N[1])]

VOCAL HORN—Ballad horn.

WAGNER TUBA/TUBEN—Instrument(s) developed by Wagner from cornons (2) and used in pairs pitched in Bb and F in the *Ring*; also used by some later composers and occasionally in bands.

WALDHORNTUBA—*Ger.* Wagner Tuba.

WONDERPHONE—Combined euphonium and valve trombone (Conn, 1920s).

ZUNKOROH—Phonikon.

# APPENDIX C

# 1

# *Serpent presence indicated in extant sets of parts, scores and in band instrumentation from 1698 to the end of the nineteenth century*

There are no significant indications of serpent presence between the later nineteenth century and the mid–twentieth century.

The following list is not intended to be comprehensive. Its purpose is to show the various contexts in which the serpent and bass horn were used during different periods and in different places.

Eccles, J.: *(A* serpent plays in *Rinaldo & Armida* (1698) though the music for this number is lost.) *Music to Macbeth* (c. 1700): four parts (incl. basso continuo) and serpent in 'Symphony' (i.e., overture). (BL Add MSS. 12219/293781).

French Revolutionary music for choir and band (1770s) (P[15]): pic (fl), 2 cl, 2 bsn, 2 hn, tpt, trb, serp, tp.

Establishment of Conservatoire (Paris, 1795): fl, 6 cl, 3 bsn, 2 hn, tpt, serp, tp, bd. (K[5], 165); for grander occasions: 10 fl, 30 cl, 18 bsn, 12 hn, 4 tpt, 2 tba cva, 3 trb, 2 buc, 8 serp, 2 tp, 2 sd, 2 bd, 2 cym, 2 tri. (K[5],165-66)

Abington, W.: *Royal East India Slow March* (London, 1777): 2 ob, 2 bsn, hn, 2 tpt, serp. (W[16], 264)

Wesley, S. *March in D* (London, 1777): 2 ob, 2 bsn, 2 tpt, serp.

Mozart *Don Giovanni* arr Richter (1780?): 2 cl, 2 bsn, 2 hn, 2 tpt, b-trb, serp/cbsn. (S[40], 275)

attrib. Haydn *St Antoni Chorale,* etc (FJH-1d, -4d, 6d) (Breitkopf, pre-1782): 2 ob, 3
  bsn, 2 hn, serp. [S[40], 191-2 discusses likely composers in detail]

Coldstream Guards Band (London, mid-1780s): 2 ob, 4 cl, 2 bsn, 2 hn, tpt, serp. [A
  band imported from Hanover.] (S[40], 267)

Godfrey, W. *The Thrush* (London, c.1785): solo picc, 2 cl, 2 bsn, 2 tpt, serp. (W[16],
  270)

Anon. *The Band of a Regiment of Guards Entering the Colour Court, St. James's Palace* ):
  2 ob, 1 (?3) cl, bsn, hn, tpt, serp, tp, longh d, cym, tri, tamb, fifes and ds. (Line-
  engraving, BM.)

*Wiener Zeitung,* 25.2.1789: 'Newly-invented bass serpent, never before made in this
  area' by Frederick Lempp (M[21], 464)

Anon. *Marsch Julius Caesar* ('pour tout la Musique turque Du Regiment d'alsace'
  c.1790): 2 fl, 2 cl, bsn, 2 hn, 2 tpt, serp. (W[16], 316)

Sarti, G., C. Canobbio & V. Pashkevich *Nafshalnoie oupravlanie Olega* (St Petersburg,
  1790): 4 hn, 2 trb, 2 serp, tri. [stage band in the first opera publ. in F.S. in
  Russia]. (M[25], iv, 184)

Spencer, J. *Favourite Troop for the Oxfordshire Militia* (London, 1793): 2 fl, F cl, 2 Bb cl,
  2 bsn, hn, 2 tpt, serp.

Catel, C.-S. *Overture in F* (perf. Paris, 1794): 8 fl, 14 cl, 8 bsn, 6 hn, 2 tpt, 3 trb, 4
  serp, 2 tp, 4 db. (W[16], 181)
     *The Battle of Fleuris* (perf. Paris 1794): 6 fl, 8 cl, 8 bsn, 6 hn, 4 tpt, 3 trb, 10
  serp, 6 tp, 6 bd & cym, 6 db. (W[16], 219)

Cherubini, L. *Hymn to the Panthèon* (perf. Paris, 1794): 6 fl, 16 cl, 8 bsn, 8 hn, 4 tpt, 3
  trb, bucc, tba cva, 4 serp, tp, bd, cym, 12 db, (W[16,] 226)

Gossec, F. *Hymn of Liberty* (perf. Paris, 1794): 4 fl, 13 cl, 4 bsn, 4 hn, 2 tpt, 2 serp, tp.
  (W[16,] 226)

Lesueur, J. *Scène patriotique* (perf. Paris 1794): 4 fl, 4 ob, 20 cl, 6 bsn, 12 hn, 4 tpt, 3
  trb, 3 serp, tba cva, tp, 4 db.(W[16,] 181)

Mèhul, E. *Hymn of the Victories* (perf, Paris 1794): 6 fl, 14 cl, 8 bsn, 6 hn, 4 tpt, 3 trb,
  1 buccin, 6 serp, 1 bd, 1 cym, 6 db. (W[16], 223)

Eley, C. *Hercules and Omphale March* (London, 1794): 2 ob, 2 cl, 2 bsn, hn, 2 tpt, serp.
  (W[16], 268)

Haydn, J. *Two Marches for Sir Henry Harpe[u]r, Bart . . . presented . . . to the Volunteer
  Cavalry of Derbyshire* (London, 1795): 2 cl, 2 bsn, 2 hn, tpt, serp.

Lefèvre, [ ]. *Hymn* (perf. Paris, 1795): 4 fl, 4 ob, 8 cl, 8 bsn, 8 hn, 2 tpt, 3 trb, 4 serp,
  tp. (W[16,] 223)

McClean, [ ]. *Brighton Camp Quick March* (London, 1795): 2 cl, bsn, hn, 2 tpt, serp. (W[16], 274)

Royal Artillery Band (Woolwich, 1795): fl, 2 ob, 4-5 cl, 2 bsn, 2 hn, tpt, 2 serp, ds, cym. (F[4,] 25)

Schroeder, H. *Duke of York Quick March* (London, 1795): 2 cl, 2 bsn, hn, 2 tpt, serp, tp. (W[16,] 277)

　*West London Slow March* (London, 1795): 2 cl, 2 bsn, hn, 2 tpt, serp, tp. (W[16], 278)

Attwood, T. *Royal Exchange [Slow] March* and *Quick March* (c.1795): 2 fl, 2 cl, 2 bsn, 2 hn, tpt, serp ['serpano'].

Griesbach, C. *Twelve Military Divertimento's* . . . *composed chiefly for the use of their Majesties band . . . Dedicated . . . to the Prince of Wales* (London, c.1795): 2 fl, E♭ cl, [ ] B♭ cl, bsn, 2 hn, tpt, serp.

Essex. T. *Hampstead Loyal Assoc. March* (London, 1797): fl, 2 cl, 2 bsn, hn, 2 tpt, serp, tp. (W[16], 269.)

Busby, Thomas *British Valour March* (London, 1798): 2 fl, 2 cl, 2 bsn, 2 hn, 2 tpt, serp. (W[16], 267)

　*The Field of Honor March* (London, 1798): 2 fl, 2 cl, 2 bsn, 2 hn, 2 tpt, serp. (W[16], 266)

King, M. *The British March* (London, 1798): fl, 2 fife, 2 ob, 2 cl, 2 bsn, hb, 2 tpt, serp, tp, sd, long d. (W[16], 266)

Busby, Thomas *The Triumph March* (London, 1799): 2 fl, 2 cl, bsn, 2 hn, 2 tpt, serp. (W[16], 266)

Dayes, E. *King George III reviewing Eight Thousand Volunteers in Hyde Park* (BM, pen and ink with water-colour, 1799): 12 players, incl. 2 hn, tpt, serp, pc.

Hoberecht, J. *A Grand Military Piece* (London, c. 1799): 4 cl, 2 bsn, 2 tpt, serp. (W[16], 272)

Percival, J. *Bristol Volunteer Troop* (London, 1799): 2 cl, bsn, hn, 2 tpt, serp. (W[16], 275)

Cherubini, L. *Les deux journées* arr. Gopfert (?Paris, before 1800): fl, ob, 2 cl, 2 bsn, hn, 2 tpt, serp. (P[3], 126)

Pick, H. Scores of several compositions (BL RM 21.b.16; c.1800): 2 E♭ cl, 2 B♭ cl, 2 bsn, 2 hn, 2 tpt, b-trb, serp, sd ['tamburo']

　Scores of several arrangements (BL RM 21.c.32 and 21.d.2; n.d.): 2 fl/ob, 2 bthn, 2 bsn, 2 hn, serp ['serpano']

　Scores of several arrangements (BL, RM 21.d.4; n.d.): 2 fl, 2 ob, 3 cl, 2 bsn, 2 hn, 2 tpt, 2 trb, serp.

French Imperial infantry bands 1802: picc, F cl, 16 C cl, 4 bsn, 4 hn, 2 tpt, 1 bs tpt, 3 trb, 2 serp, pc. (K[5], 171)

*Journal de Musique Militaire* (Prussia, c.1804): 'Musique Turque': 2 pic, 2 quart-fl, 2 bsn, 2 hn, 2 tpt, 2 serp, bd, sd, cym. (S[40], 25)

Prussian military bands until 1805: 2 fl, 2 ob, 2 cl, 2 bsn, cbsn, 2 hn, 2 tpt, 2 b-trb; from 1806: 2 fl, 2 ob, E♭ cl, 2 B♭ cl, 2 bsn, 2 hn, 2 tpt, 2 trb, 2 b-trb, serp, pc. (K[1], 34)

Royal Artillery Band, c.1805: picc, 3 ob, small cl, 6 cl, 2 bsn, 2 hn, 2 tpt, 3 trb, bass hn, serp, small d, long d, cym, tamb. (F[3], 4)

*Journal de Musique Militaire* (France, c.1806): 2 fl, 2 F cl, 2 C cl, 2 bsn, 2 hn, tpt, serp, bd. (S[40], 22)

Hummel, J.: *Parthia in E♭ a 8 parti per 2 clarinetti 2 oboe 2 corni e 2 fagotti con serpente ad libitum* (Vienna, 1808): 2 cl, 2 ob, 2 bsn, 2 hn (serp ad lib). (S[40], 200-1)

*Journal de Harmonie* (Prussia, c. 1808): terz-fl, 2 B♭ cl, 2 hn, tpt, b-trb, (2 bsn, serp, timp, bd, sd, cym ad lib). (S[40], 27)

*Nouveau Journal d'Harmonie* (France, 1808-09): fl, F cl, 2 cl, 2 bn, 2 hn, tpt, serp/trb, bd, cym, tri (playable by fl, 2 cl, 2 hn, 2 bsn, serp). (S[40], 21)

French line infantry band 1809: picc, small cl, 6-8 C cl, 2 bsn, 2 hn, tpt, 2 trb, serp, pc. (K[5], 171)

Walch, J.: *Three Marches* (Gotha, 1809): fl, 2 ob, 2 cl, 2 bsn, tpt, serp. (S[40], 323)

Deschalumeaux, [ ] Overture *(Monsieur des Chalumeaux)* arr Schmitt (c. 1810): fl, 2 ob, 2 cl, 2 bsn, 2 hn, trb, serp, pc. (W[17], 392)

Musique Turque (Hesse-Darmstadt, 1812-18): pic, 2 E♭ cl, 2 B♭ cl, 2 bsn, 2 hn, 2 tpt, b-trb, serp, bd, sd; later, fl, 2 cl, 2 bsn, 2 hn, or 2 E♭ cl, 3 B♭ cl, 2 bsn, 4 hn, 5 tpt, 2 trb, serp, bd, sd. (S[40], 27)

Meyerbeer, G. *Der Bayerische Schützenmarsch* ([ ] , 1814): 4 bsn, cbsn, 4 hn, 5 tpt, 4 trb, serp, pc. (W[17], 346)

*Musique Militaire* (France, 1814-15): pic, 2 F cl, 2 B♭ cl, 2 hn, tpt, serp, bd. (S[40], 24)

Bochsa, K. *Messe de Requiem de Louis XVI* (?Paris, 1815): 2 fl, 2 ob, 2 cl, 2 bsn, 4 hn, 4 tpt, trb, serp, tp, pc. (P[3], 121)

Jouve, J. *The Austrian Retreat* (London, 1815): 2 fl, 2 cl, 2 bsn, hn, 2 tpt, serp, pc. (W[17], 534)

Mašek, Paul [see accent p. 17]: Harmonie mit Türkischen Musick, c.1815; 'Turkish group' pic, 2fl, cl, b-trb, serp, perc. (S[40], 230)

Guest, G. *A Third Grand Bugle Horn Troop* (London, 1815): 2 fl, 2 cl, 2 bsn, 2 tpt, bugle, serp, pc. [also *Fourth, Fifth* and *Sixth Troops*] (W[17], 531)

*Wisbech Volunteer Troop* (London, 1815): 2 fl, 2 cl, 2 bsn, 2 tpt, bugle, serp, pc. (W[17], 531)

Blasius M.: *Harmonie Militaire* (Versailles, 1815-16): fl, F cl, 2 C cl, 2 bsn, 2 hn, tpt, b-trb, serp, bd. (S[40], 139)

*Harmonie Militaire contenant Marches, Pas Redoublés, Rondeaux et Walze* (France, 1815-16): fl, F cl, 2 C cl, 2 bsn, 2 hn, tpt, b-trb, serp, bd. (S[40], 24)

Beethoven, L. van *Marsch in D* ([ ], 1816): 2 picc, 2 ob, 5 cl, 2 bsn, cbsn, 8 hn, 6 tpt, 2 trb, serp, perc. (W[17], 411)

Prince Regent's Band (Brighton, 1818): 3 fl, 2 ob, 8 cl, 4 bsn, 4 hn, 4 tpt, 4 trb, 4 serp, tp; later, 3 fl, 3 ob, 12 cl, 2 bsn, 4 hn, 4 tpt, 6 trb, serp, 2 tp. (Carse: 'The Prince Regent's Band' in *Music & Letters*, XXVII, July 1946, 149-50)

*Pièces d'harmonie pour Musique Militaire* (Paris, c.1818-40s): fl, Eb cl, 3 Bb cl, 4 hn, 2 bsn, 3 trb, serp, bd, sd. (S[40], 22)

Berlin line infantry band (Allerhöcheste Kabinett-Order, 16 October 1820): 2 fl, 2 ob, 2 F cl, 6 C cl, 4 bsn, cbsn, 2 hn, 3 trb, basshorn, 5 pc. (W[17], 26)

Royal Artillery Band, 1820: 2 fl, 3 ob, 11 cl, 3 bsn, 2 hn, 2 tpt, 3 k-b, 3 trb, oh, 2 serp, 2 bs-hn, 5 pc (F[5], 98)

Anon. *Echo & 6 Ländler* (c. [ ], c.1820): 2 fl, 3 cl, 2 bsn, 2 hn, 2 tpts, 1 trb, serp. (P[3], 115)

Beethoven, L. van *Eggmunt Simphonie* arr. Schneider ([ ], c.1820): 2 ob, 2 cl, 2 bsn, 2 hn, 2 tpt, trb, serp, pc. (W[17], 390)

*Fidelio* arr Schneider ([], c. 1820): 2 ob, 2 cl, 2 bsn, 2 hn, 2 tpt, trb, serp, pc. (W[17], 390)

Bochsa, K. *Overture militaire*, op. 29 (Paris, c. 1820): 2 fl, 2 ob, 2 cl, 2 bsn, 2 hn, 2 tpt, trb, serp, pc. (W[17], 38)

Göpfert, C. *Allegrino alla Turca* ([ ] , c.1820): 2 fl, 2 ob, 2 cl, 2 bsn, 2 hn, 2 tpt, trb, serp, pc. (W[17], 337)

*Journal d'Harmonie et de Musique Militaire* (France, c. 1820): fl, Eb cl, 2-4 Bb cl, 2 bsn, 2 hn, tpt, trb, serp, bd.; later, pic, 2 Eb cl, 2-3 Bb cl, 2 bsn, 2 hn, 2 trb, 2 serp, bd or fl, 2 ob/cl, 2 cl, 2 bsn, 2 hn, tpt, trb, db ad lib. (B[40], 24)

Lindner, [ ] *Musique Militar* ([ ], c. 1820): 2 fl, 2 ob, 2 cl, 2 bsn, 2 hn, 2 tpt, trb, serp, pc. (W[17], 337)

Schneider, A. arr. and comps, publ. 1820-23 in 6 vols for following ensembles: 2 fl, 2 ob, 2 cl, 2 bsn, hn, 2 tpt, trb, serp, db; 2 fl, 2 ob, 2 cl, 2 bsn, 2 hn, 2 tpt, trb, serp, pc; fl, 2 ob, 2 cl, 2 bsn, 2 hn, 2 tpt, trb, serp, db; fl, 2 ob, 4 cl, 2 bsn, hn, 2 tpt, trb, serp; fl, 2 ob, 4 cl, 2 bsn, hn, 2 tpt, trb, serp.

Mejo, G. *Sextet* (Silesia, c.1821): 2 bsn, 2 hn, 2 serp/cbsn. (S[40], 234)

La Musique de la Garde Nationale du Mans (Le Mans, 1823): 1-2 picc, 2 ob, 1-2 Eb cl, 6-12 Bb cl, 2 bsn, 2 hn, 1-2 tpt, 1-3 trb, 2 serp, td, bd, cym, tamb, tri, 2 jj (D[24], 39)

Regiments Bande (Vienna, 1823): picc, Ab cl, 4 Eb cl, bsn, 4 hn, Eb, low Eb, F, C tpts, 3 trb, serp, tambour. (Lithograph in Heeresgeschichtliches Museum) (W[15], 51)

Mejo, G. *Variation on 'Gaudeamus Igitur'* (Silesia, c.1824): fl, Eb cl, 2 Bb cl, 2 bsn, 3 hn, b-trb, (cl, 2 trb, serp ad lib). (S[40], 234)

Scharf, G. I, *The Band of the Royal Marines, 1825* (Woolwich, 1825): fife, bsn, hn, kb, trb, serp, 2 sd, 2 ld. (Water colour over black lead, BM)

Beethoven, L. van: *Septet,* op. 20 arr B. Crusell (Leipzig, c. 1825): terz-fl, Eb cl, 2 Bb cl, 2 bsn, 2 hn, tpt, b-trb, serp. (S[40], 134)

Scharf, G. I. *Band of the Royal Marines in the Officers' Mess, Woolwich, 1826* (Woolwich, 1826): fl, 3 cl, bsn, 2 hn, tpt, kb, trb, serp [reading off bsn part] (Water colour over black lead, BM)

*Journal de Musique Militaire Authorisé par S.E. le Ministre de la Guerre* (Lyon, 1826): fl, Eb cl, 3 Bb cl, 2 bsn, 2 hn, tpt (cnt), b-trb, serp, bd & cym, tnr-d. (S[40], 25)

Austrian infantry band (1827): picc, 2 Ab cl, Eb cl, 9 Bb cl, bsn, 2 Eb hn, 2 Ab hn, 4 Eb tpt, 2 Ab tpt, F tpt, C tpt, 3 trb, serp, sd. (F[5], 99, after Swoboda)

Bishop, H. *Grand March composed Expressly for . . . The Royal Society of Musicians . . .* [in Eb] May 26th 1827 (London, 1827): fl, 2 ob, 2 bsn, 2 tpt, trb, serp. (BL Add M.S. 34725, ff. 1-7)

Haydn: various symphonies arr C. Bochsa (Paris, c. second decade 19th century): 2 fl, 2 cl, 2 bsn, 2 hn, tpt, trb, serp. (S[40], 139-40)

Prussian infantry band 1830s: piccs, fls, F, Eb, C, Bb, A cl, basset hns, obs, bsns, cbsn, 4 hn, 4 tpt, altohn, trbs, English-basshorn, Harmoniebass (bass horn with nine keys, inv. 1829), serp, large d, small d, cym, tri. (K[1], 34-35)

Ostreich, C. *Symphony fur Bläsinstrumente* ([ ], c. 1830-35): fl, 2 ob, Eb cl, 4 cl, bsn, 2 hn, 4 tpt, kb, 3 trb, serp, pc. (P[3], 153)

Neithardt, A. *Festgesang* (?Berlin, 1832): 2 fl, 2 ob, 3 cl, bst-horn, 2 bsn, hn, 4 tpt, 3 trb, serp, pc. (W[17], 349)

*American Musical Journal* (1835) article defining 'a full band': pic, 8 cl, 1 Eb cl, 2 bsn, 2 hn, 2 tpts, 2 trb, serp, bs hn, bd, cym, muffled d, tri. (A[10])

Prussian Jäger bands 1837-50 (W[15], 30 quoting T. Rode: 'Zur Geschicte der Kgl. Preuss. Inf.- und Jäger-Musik' in *Neue Zeitschrift für Militärmusik*, XLIXI,149,

161, 173 ff.): 9-10 hn, 3 kb (after 1847, cnts), 3 tpt, alto hn (after 1847 alto cnt), tnr hn, b-trb, Harmoniebass (later, tba), bomb (later tba).

Royal Artillery Band, 1839: picc, 2 fl, 2 ob, 3 E♭ cl, 4 B♭ cl, 4 bsn, 2 hn, 4 tpt, 3 cnt, 4 trb, oph, 2 serp, 2 bs-hn, 4 pc (F[5], 114)

Prussian infantry band, by 1848: 2 fl or picc, 4 ob, 16-20 cl, 2 bt-hn, 4 bsn, 1-2 cbsn, 4 hn, 4 tpt, 4 trb, serp, tba (bomb or bshn), 1-2 sd, cym, tri. (K[5], 196-7)

Chelard, H. (arr.) *Die Hermannschlacht* ([ ], c. 1850): fl, 5 cl, 2 bsn, 2 hn, 4 tpt, 3 trb, serp, pc. (W[17], 390)

Albert, Prince Consort (orch. Costa). *Invocazione all'Armonia* (London, before 1859): pic, fl, 2 ob, 2 cl, 4 hn, 2 tpt, 2 cnts, 3 trb, oph, serp [unis], tp, b.d., stgs.

# APPENDIX C

# 2

## Some historic players of the serpent, bass horn and ophicleide

*[For biographies of English tubists c. 1870-1930 see Appendix C 3; biographies of other tubists are in THE TUBA SOURCE BOOK (M[44], 457-522)]*

### SERPENT AND BASS HORN

AINSWORTH. Huddersfield, Yorkshire. Serpent Yorkshire Musical Festival, York, 1838 (see p. 112).

ANDRÉ. London. Principal serpent in a section of three, Prince of Wales's Private Band, Brighton 1811-20; obbligato City of London Amateur Concert 16.12.1819; George IV's Private Band, Windsor, 1820-30; Montpellier Band, Cheltenham 1830–; Birmingham Musical Festival 19-22.9.1837; Queen Victoria's Private Band, Windsor 1837; Yorkshire Musical Festival, York 1838; Subscription Evening Concerts 1842. Licensee of Cheltenham public house pre-1840 (see pp. 112, 116-17, 407).

ANDRÉ, Étienne. Paris. Priest from Sedan, Ardennes and a novice playing serpent, ordinary chaplain, St-Chapelle 23.1.1726 (see p. 115).

ANDRÉ, Jacques. Versailles. Serpent Chapelle-Musique du Roi c. 1670. d. 1676 (see p. 556).

AUBERT, ABBÉ. Paris. Serpent Notre-Dame c. 1752-72 (M[41], 6.3.1940).

BALLARD. Dampierre, Seine-et-Oise, France. Professor of serpent 1836 (see p. 100).

BARBIER, Carpentras, Vaucluse, France. Serpent cathedral 1639 (see p. 113).

BARNABÉ. Paris. Serpent St-Chapelle; awarded f.15 23.6.1700 (B[20]).

BARRARD. Paris. Serpent Garde Nationale VIIIe. légion 1836 (see p. 100).

BASTOW, Thomas. Ashburton, Devon. Serpent parish church 1836 (see p. 120).

BATTY, ?Worcester. Serpent Worcester Festival ?1842 (M[52], 1.1.1842).

BEAUGEOIS, ABBÉ. Amiens, Somme, France. Serpent 1827. Compiled method 1827 (see pp. 65, 91).

BELARD [BILART] DE BEAULIEU, Jacques. Versailles. Serpent Chapelle-Musique du Roi 4.9.1676-d. 9.9.1680 (B[20]).

BÉLÉ. François. Paris. Serpent St-Chapelle; interviewed 11.5.1686 (see p. 115).

BELLARD, Jacques. Paris. Succeeded J. ANDRÉ as serpent Chapelle-Musique du Roi 4.9.1676 (B[20]).

BENTINCK, Richard. ?London. 23rd Regiment of Foot (later Royal Welch Fusiliers). Played at Battle of Waterloo 1815 (S[22], 1.4.1995).

BIEDAU. Basoche, Landes, France. Professor of serpent 1836 (see p. 100).

BONVOUST. Paris. Serpent Garde Nationale V[e]. légion 1836 (see p. 100).

BOULIN. Paris. Novice (serpent) St.-Chapelle 21.7.1728 (B[20]).

BRALLE, Jacques. Paris. From Châlons-sur-Marne, Marne. Novice (serpent) St-Chapelle 29.10.1727 (B[20]).

BRINDEL. Paris. Serpent Garde Nationale IXe légion 1836 (see p. 100).

CALLINGHAM. Tunbridge Wells, Kent. Serpent (after six months' practice) in *St Paul* performed by Tunbridge Wells Vocal Association 29.3.1897, playing instrument owned by Frank Pickett (see p. 120).

CAPELLE, François Pierre. Paris. Novice (serpent and bassoon) St-Chapelle 18.12.1727; later bassoon at Opéra and Concerts Spirituel (see p. 115).

CARTY, GUNNER Patrick. ?Dublin, Ireland. Bass horn Royal Irish Artillery pre-1802 (see p. 87).

CHABOUD. Bologna, Italy. Serpent and bassoon San Petronio 1679-85 (see pp. 112-13).

CHEIN, François Louis. Paris. Serpent St.-Chapelle 30.5.1674; allocated own room; appointed churchwarden 11.4.1682, continuing to play serpent (see p. 115).

CHERON. Paris. Serpent Garde Nationale VIIIe légion 1836 (see p. 100).

COLLINS. Cheltenham, Gloucestershire. Serpent and ophicleide Montpellier Band 1840 (see p. 117).

CORNU, Jacques. Paris. Serpent and bassoon Notre-Dame 1789; taught serpent Institut Nationale de Musique 1793; bassoon Théâtre Feydeau 1794; trombone Opéra 1805-26; 'sous-maître de musique de la cathédrale' (see p. 99).

COSTELLO. York. Serpent Yorkshire Musical Festival, York 1838 (see p. 112).

DECOMBE [DECOMBES]. Paris. Novice (serpent) St-Chapelle; appointed cleric 5.6.1779; became alto chorister 22.10.1785 (see p. 115).

DOURDE, Jacques Philippe. Paris. Cleric of diocese of Paris, appointed serpent and bassoon St-Chapelle 29.11.1767 (B[20]).

DU QUESNE, Jean. Paris. Serpent St-Chapelle from 8.10.1701; d. of smallpox 5.12.1723 (see p. 115).

DUBOIS [DU BOIS], Pierre. Versailles. Succeeded P. FERRIER Chapelle-Musique du Roi 8.2.1729; serpent, bassoon, *symphonist* 1717-31. d. ?1731 (see p. 114).

DUNAND. Paris. Amateur player of serpent and ophicleide 1836 (see pp. 100, 155, 170, 562).

FAIVRE. Paris. Serpent Garde Nationale V[e] légion 1836 (see p. 100).

FERRIER, Antoine François. Versailles. Son of PIERRE, brother of LOUIS. Serpent Hautbois et Musettes de Poitou (see p. 114).

FERRIER, Claude. Versailles. Father of PIERRE. 3.8.1662-d. ?1703. On death of P. LAURENT appointed serpent Chapelle-Musique du Roi 4.9.1676-77, also 1680, 1683, 1685, 1688-91, 1698, 1703 (see p. 114).

FERRIER, Pierre. Versailles. Baptised 18.1.1663, d. 27.7.1701 (B[57]) or 2.12.1728 (B[21]). Son of CLAUDE. Serpent, cornett and bassoon Chapelle-Musique du Roi c. 1668-1729 and also Hautbois et Musettes de Poitou (see p. 114).

FERRIER, Louis. Versailles. Brother of ANTOINE FRANÇOIS. Serpent Chapelle-Musique du Roi c. 1714-27 ; d. 18.3.1724 (sic.) aged 20 (B[20]).

FOURNIOLS. Le Mans, Sarthe, France. Serpent Musique Municipale du Mans c. 1808-40, also band treasurer 1815-40 (see pp. 97-8).

FRICHOT, Alexandre. London. French immigrant. Played in Antient Concerts Orchestra 1793; invented bass horn (published scale 1800); returned to France 1804 and developed other types of upright serpent (see pp. 86, 91, 116, 141).

GIRARD, Jean. b. 1696 Saint-Privé-les-Bourges, Cher, France. Novice (serpent) St-Chapelle, Bourges 1712; appointed cleric and in 1724 emigrated to Montreal, Canada as organist and choirmaster at Notre-Dame (see pp. 115-16).

GOUBERT. Paris. received as novice, a cleric, 'to play the serpent' St-Chapelle 24.12.1723 (see p. 115).

GRÉGOIRE DE LA FERTÉ, Charles François. Versailles. Serpent (and possibly cornett) Vingt-Quatre Violons de la Chambre 1731, 1733 (see p. 114).

GUILLAUME, CANON Edmé. Auxerre, France. Credited with invention of serpent late 16th century (see p. 65).

HARDY, Alexandre. Paris. Bassoon. Taught at Paris Conservatoire, probably also serpent. Compiled serpent method c. 1815 (see page 91).

HINTON, Thomas. ?Warwickshire. Bass horn, 24th (2nd Warwickshire) Foot, 1812 (see p. 89).

HOLTZEM. Paris. Amateur. Serpent Garde Nationale X[e] légion 1836 (see p. 100). Later played *saxhorn basse* (see p. 258).

HULL. Brighton, Sussex. Hibernicon Yorkshire Musical Festival, York, 1835 (see p. 112).

HURST, London. Serpent First Guards Regiment 1794 (see p. 116).

HURWORTH. London. From Richmond, Yorkshire. Serpent George III's Private Band (see p. 112).

JEPP, London. Serpent Coldstream Guards, c. 1829. Concert Richmond [Surrey] Harmonic Society 10.1837; Guildhall 9.11.1837; Philharmonic Society 1842, 1850 (serpent or bass horn) (see pp. 101, 117, 485, 503).

JOLY, Melon. Paris. Novice (serpent) 24.12.1723 St-Chapelle; received as novice, a cleric 'to play the serpent' ; 23.1.1726 received as a cleric (see p. 115).

JONGHMANS. Paris. Serpent Garde Nationale VIII$^e$ légion 1836 (see p. 100).

LABEAU. Carpentras, Vaucluse, France. Serpent cathedral 1611 (see p. 113).

LAURENT, Paul. Versailles. Serpent Chapelle-Musique du Roi. d. 1676 (B[20]).

LE RICHE. London. Possibly of French origin. fl. 1685-1701. Considered the leading London player of the time (see p. 68).

LEFÈVRE. Dampierre and Rochefort, Seine-et-Oise, France. Professor of serpent 1836 (see p. 100).

LEWIS. London. fl. 1685-1701. Player of serpent (see p. 68).

LUNEL, Abbé. Paris. Serpent Notre-Dame 1772-80, succeeding Abbé Aubert. Credited with adopting diagonal playing position (see pp. 70-1).

MACCHEOW. London. Bass horn Guildhall concert 9.11.1830 (see p. 89).

MARCHAND, Jean. Paris. b. 14.8.1666. Player of serpent (B[57]).

MARCHAND, Jean-Baptise. Paris. Admitted as novice (serpent) St.-Chapelle 2.5.1697; repairs to instrument reimbursed 29.1.1698 (see p.115).

MARCHAND, Joseph. Versailles. 25.11.1700-28.1.1746. Appointed serpent Chapelle-Musique du Roi on death of R. Masselin 14.7.1717, also 1721-24, 1726-33 (B[57]).

MARSDEN, Richard. Manchester. Played serpent in *St Paul* 1882; ophicleide Hallé Orchestra 1873-74, 1876-77, 1878-86. Licensee Railway Hotel and Concert Hall, Ordsall Lane, Salford, 1886 (120, 374, 505, 559; *see also* Ophicleide).

MARTIN. Rochefort, Seine-et-Oise, France. Professor of serpent 1836 (see p. 100)

MASSELIN, Robert. Versailles. Serpent Chapelle-Musique du Roi 9.9.1680, 1683, 1685, 1688-91, 1698, 1700, 1704-15, 1717-20, succeeding de Beaulieu. d. 1717 (sic.) (B[57]).

MATHIEU, Jean. Paris. Professor of serpent École de Musique de la Garde Nationale Parisienne from 1790 (see p. 99).

MAYNARD, Thomas. Minstead, Hampshire. 1780-1807. Serpent 8th Hants

Yeomanry and probably also All Saints, Minstead (see p. 105).

MONNET, Pierre. Paris. Choirboy St-Chapelle. Bought serpent for 32 l. on 3.6.1679 (see p. 115).

MONTENOT, Joseph Sebastian. Paris. Admitted as novice (serpent) St-Chapelle 2.1700; left 1.10.1701 (B[20]).

PELISSIER. Carpentras, Vaucluse, France. Serpent. Deputy for Barbier at cathedral 1639 (see p. 113).

PETERS. Paris. Serpent Garde Nationale V[e] légion 1836 (see pp. 100, 169; possibly also ophicleide).

PONDER, William. London. Serpent Drury Lane, Covent Garden and Oratorio Concerts 1830; Yorkshire Musical Festival, York 1835; Philharmonic Society concert 22.2.1836; bass horn Philharmonic Society concert 18.6.1832; also 1836-41 bass horn or serpent (see pp. 101, 117, 120, 149-50, 155, 168, 170, 485, 502; *see also* Ophicleide).

POUSSON [PUSSON], J. J. Paris. Serpent, tenor and cleric St-Chapelle. Reimbursed for purchase of serpent 24.6.1651 (see p. 115).

REED, Thomas. Mabe, Cornwall. Serpent Trenoweth Chapel; emigrated to U.S.A. 1851 (see p. 94).

RÉGIBO. Lille, Nord, France. Musician college of St-Pierre. Invented *basson-serpent* 1788 (possibly first upright serpent) (see p. 79).

ROGAT, Joseph. Paris. 1789 bassoon and c. 1793 also serpent Notre-Dame; professor of *solfège* and bassoon Institut National de Musique 1836 (see p. 91).

ROZE, ABBÉ Nicholas. Paris. 1745-1819. Serpent, composer, cleric, first librarian Paris Conservatoire. Compiled method 1814 (see pp. 90-1, 116).

ROUX. Carpentras, Vaucluse, France. Serpent cathedral 1641 (see p. 113).

SHARP, James. London. Amateur. Shown with serpent in painting by Zoffany 1779-81 (see p. 69).

SICKEL, London. Serpent Second Guards Regiment 1794; also Drury Lane Oratorio Concerts (see p. 116).

SIEPOLDSDORF. Mecklenburg-Schwerin (Ludwigslust), Germany. Serpent Harmonie of Duke Friedrich Franz 1812. May have been the bass horn player heard by Mendelssohn in 1824 (see p. 481).

STANDEN. London. Serpent Coldstream Guards; deputy for André in Evening Subscription Concerts 1842; Philharmonic Society concert, 5 March 1866 (see p. 503).

STEAD. Halifax, Yorkshire. Serpent Yorkshire Musical Festival, York 1838 (see p.

112).

TIDDY, David. Modbury, Devon. Serpent Modbury Band; new instrument delivered 18.7.1836 (see p. 105).

TINGY. London. Serpent Third Guards Regiment 1794 (see p. 116).

TORNATORIS, Michel. Avignon, Rhône, France. Serpent, bassoon, organ, *maître de chapelle* Notre-Dame des Doms 1602-3 (see p. 113).

TOUSEZ. Dampierre, Seine-et-Oise, France. Professor of serpent 1836 (see p. 100).

VEILLARD, Gaspard. Paris. Serpent École de Musique de la Garde Nationale Parisienne 1.10.1793-1801; teacher of *solfège* 1804; Musique des Guards Françaises 21.2.1771; Opéra until 1813 (see p. 99).

VINCHON. Le Mans, Sarthe, France. Serpent Musique Municipal du Mans c. 1808 (see p. 97).

WATEL, Nicholas Paul. Paris. Novice (serpent) 18.12.1727 (B[20]).

WILMSHURST, Joseph. London. Serpent First Guards Regiment 1794, Philharmonic Society 1814-15 (see pp. 116, 502).

YOUNG. New York. Serpent. Played concerto Park Theatre 24.2.1835 (see p. 117).

# OPHICLEIDE

ARNAULT. Paris. Ophicleide Garde Nationale IXe légion 1836 (see p. 155).

AUSSANDON. Paris. Alto ophicleide *(quinte)* Garde Nationale IIIe légion 1836 (see p. 155).

BARLOW, Harry. Manchester. Tuba Hallé Orchestra 1894-1930 and also ophicleide 1894-95 (see p. 505; also pp. 168, 316, 372, 378-82, 391, 395).

BATLEY, F. J. Manchester. Ophicleide Hallé Orchestra 1869-70, 1875-76, 1877-78 (see pp. 374-5, 505).

BECHERIAS. Paris. Ophicleide Garde Nationale IIe légion 1836 (see p. 155).

BERNARD. Paris. Amateur. Ophicleide Garde Nationale X[e] légion 1836 (see p. 156).

BOSSUS. Paris. Amateur. Ophicleide Garde Nationale XIIe légion 1836 (see p. 156).

BROCA, Domingo. Madrid. Player of ophicleide and trombone, first trombone teacher at Real Conservatorio de Música, founded 1830 (see p. 153).

BRUYAS. Paris. Ophicleide Garde Nationale XIIe légion 1836 (see p. 156).

BUTRY. Paris. Ophicleide Garde Nationale X[e] légion 1836 (see p. 156). Possibly identical to BUTTRY below.

BUTTRY. Paris. Ophicleide Garde Nationale 1er légion 1836 (see p. 155). Possibly identical to BUTRY above.

CACHELEUX. Paris. Ophicleide Garde Nationale X$^e$ légion 1836 (see p. 156).

CAUSSINUS, Joseph. Paris. b. 1806. Ophicleide Théâtre-Italien, Garde Nationale IV$^e$ légion and XI$^e$ légion 1836; Musard's concerts 1837. Professor of ophicleide, cornet, piano, etc.; director of ophicleide class Gymnasium Musicale Militaire. Compiled method 1843. Highly regarded by Berlioz (see pp. 100, 142-3, 145-6, 155-6, 159-60, 169-70, 215).

CHARRAMOND. Paris. Ophicleide Garde Nationale VII$^e$ légion 1836. (see p. 155).

COGNET. Paris. Amateur. Ophicleide Garde Nationale VI$^e$ légion 1836 (see p. 155).

COLEMAN. Merthyr Tydfil, South Glamorgan. Solo ophicleide Cyfarthfa Band early 1850s; made ophicleide out of paper; later emigrated to U.S.A. (see pp. 148, 171).

COLLINS. Cheltenham, Gloucestershire. Ophicleide and serpent (succeeding ANDRÉ) Montpellier Band 1840 (see p. 117).

COLOSANTI. Naples, Campania. Ophicleide soloist in Jullien concerts; also Florence 1853, Bordeaux 1855, Leipzig 1858. Composed for ophicleide. d. Aix-la-Chapelle 1858 (see p. 177).

CORNETTE, Victor. Paris. 1795-1868. Military musician and member of orchestra Théâtre de l'Odéon 1836; played several instruments, including ophicleide and trombone. Compiled method 1835 (see pp. 159-60).

CROZIER(S). Paris. Ophicleide Garde Nationale XI$^e$ légion 1836; also played double bass (see p. 156).

DANNBY, C. London. Ophicleide Hallé Orchestra in *Symphonie fantastique*, St James's Hall 1.6.1880 (see p. 156).

DAYAT. Paris. Ophicleide orchestra of Gymnase Musicale and bands of Garde Nationale VIII$^e$ and X$^e$ légions 1836 (see pp. 155-6, 161).

DEMAUSE. Le Mans, Sarthe, France. 'Ophycléïde' Musique Municipale du Mans c. 1827 (see p. 97).

DETHEUX. Liège. Ophicleide Théâtre de Liège 1839, paid 2 francs a day (Martiny, *Histoire*).

DEVISE. Paris. Professor of ophicleide and trombone 1836 (see p. 170).

DIVOIRE. Paris. Ophicleide Garde Nationale II$^e$ légion 1836 (see p. 155).

DODSWORTH. Manchester. Ophicleide Hallé Orchestra 1868-69 (see p. 534).

DORTU. London. Ophicleide Drury Lane Jullien *Concerts d'hiver* 1850. In 1851 at Prado (Paris) playing *saxhorn-basse* (see p. 258).

DROBERT. Paris. Player of ophicleide, violin and double bass 1836 (see p. 170).

DUNAND. Paris. Amateur. Ophicleide Garde Nationale 1$^{er}$, VII$^e$ and IX$^e$ légions 1836 (see pp. 100, 155, 170).

DUPORT. Paris. Player of ophicleide 1836 (P[19]).

DUZART. Paris. Ophicleide Garde Nationale XIe légion 1836 (see p. 156).

EL(L)ISON. London. Ophicleide Philharmonic Society 1842-46 (see pp. 485, 503).

FRANCE. Paris. Amateur. Ophicleide Garde Nationale XIe légion (see p. 156).

FREISING. New York. Ophicleide on Jullien's U.S.A. tour (with S. Hughes) 1853 (see p. 170).

GAILLY. Paris. Player of ophicleide 1836 (P[19]).

GALÊME. Paris. Ophicleide Garde Nationale Ier légion 1836 (see p. 155).

GARRÉ. Paris. Alto ophicleide *(quinte)* Garde Nationale IIIe légion; ophicleide VIIe légion 1836 (see p. 155).

GUILLON. Paris. Amateur. Ophicleide Garde Nationale IIe légion 1836 (see p. 155).

GUILMARTIN, J. H. London. Ophicleide soloist Royal Aquarium Concerts 1876; 1893 Promenade Concerts. Professor of ophicleide 1901. Also played bass tuba from 1884 (see pp. 143, 171, 173, 325, 372, 377-8).

HANDLEY. London. Ophicleide soloist in Jullien's London concerts (year unknown).

HENRICET. Paris. Ophicleide Garde Nationale X[e] légion 1836 (see p. 156).

HOPKINSON, Richard. Manchester. Ophicleide Hallé Orchestra 1868-69 (see pp. 171, 504)

HORROCKS. London. Ophicleide Hallé Orchestra *Symphonie fantastique* St James's Hall 1.6.1880 (see p. 171).

HUBBARD. London. Ophicleide Westminster Abbey 6.1834 (with PONDER) (see p. 168).

HUGHES, Samuel. 19.12.1823-1.4.1898. Solo ophicleide Cyfarthfa Band c. 1850-53; soloist on Jullien's U.S.A. tour 1853; Covent Garden Promenade Concerts 1855; Jullien north of England tour 1856; Royal Italian Opera, Covent Garden, c. 1860-70s; Royal Albert Hall Concerts 1874-75; Hallé Orchestra 30.1.1858; Leeds Festival 1874, 1877, 1880, 1883; Crowe's Covent Garden Concerts 1881. Professor Guildhall School of Music 1881-94, Royal Military School of Music, Kneller Hall c. 1859. Contest adjudicator; made improvements to ophicleide mechanism. Arguably best English ophicleidist, commanding high fees (see pp. 120, 143, 146-7, 156, 166, 170-3, 175, 374, 540).

HUSSON. Paris. Amateur. Ophicleide Garde Nationale XIe légion 1836 (see p. 156).

LABALTE. Paris. Ophicleide, bassoon, double bass, trumpet 1836 (see p. 170).

LAHOU. Paris. Opéra, mid-19th century; soloist at Conservatoire concerts 1859 (C$^{10}$).

LANCE. Paris. Amateur. Ophicleide Garde Nationale I$^{er}$ légion 1836 (see p. 155).

LARSILLIÈRE. Paris. Ophicleide Garde Nationale à Cheval 1836 (see p. 156).

LEBEAU. Paris. Ophicleide Garde Nationale I$^{er}$ légion 1836 (see p. 155).

LEBRUN. Paris. Ophicleide Garde Nationale VI$^e$ légion 1836 (see p. 155).

LECLUS. Paris. Amateur. Ophicleide Garde Nationale X$^e$ légion 1836 (see p. 156).

LENDET [LEUDET]. Paris. Ophicleide Garde Nationale IV$^e$ légion 1836 (see p. 155).

LEREY. London. French musician? Ophicleide and monster ophicleide Jullien's Concerts d'hiver *Drury Lane* 1850 (see page 152).

LIMBERGER. Paris. Ophicleide Garde Nationale à Cheval 1836 (see p. 156).

LYDYARD. Ophicleide 1st Battalion Connaught Rangers India 1914 (B$^3$).

MARCHAL. Paris. Player of ophicleide and trombone 1836; also professor of trombone (see p. 170).

MARCHAND. Paris. Ophicleide Garde Nationale IV$^e$ légion; also played violin 1836 (see pp. 155, 170).

MARCHE. Paris. Ophicleide Garde Nationale IX$^e$ légion 1836 (see p. 155).

MARSAUX. Paris. Ophicleide Garde Nationale VII$^e$ légion 1836 (see p. 155).

MARSDEN, Richard. Manchester. Ophicleide Hallé Orchestra 1873-74, 1876-77, 1878-86 (also played tuba and serpent) (see pp. 120, 374, 505; *see also* Serpent).

MAURAGE. Paris. Ophicleide Garde nationale I$^{er}$ and XII$^e$ légions 1836 (see p. 156).

MEDINA, Angelo. Manchester. 1822-13.1.1869. Ophicleide Hallé Orchestra 30.1.1858-69 (see pp. 172, 174-5, 374, 486, 504).

MERRICK, Robert. London. Played monster ophicleide; translated Schiltz's method 1853 (see p. 149).

MONGIN. Paris. Ophicleide Garde Nationale V$^e$ légion 1836; first to perform publicly on ophicleide (Opéra, 22.12.1819); took out French Patent 4636 in 1849 (see pp. 155, 161).

MOREAU. Dijon, Côte-d'Or, France. Professor of ophicleide and stringed instruments, also piano tuner 1836 (see p. 170).

MOREAUX. Paris. Amateur. Ophicleide Garde Nationale XI$^e$ légion 1836 (see p. 156).

MUTEL. Paris. Ophicleide Opéra, Opéra-Comique, Garde Nationale VI$^e$ légion and (as amateur) VI$^e$ légion 1836 (see pp. 155, 161).

OBEZ. Paris. Ophicleide Garde Nationale IVᵉ légion 1836 (see p.155).

PAVART. Paris. Ophicleide Société des Concerts 9.3.1828; Conservatoire Concerts 1828; Garde Nationale IIIᵉ légion; '1er trombone à l'Opéra', and professor 1836 (see p. 170).

PAYNE, James. Penshurst, Kent. Ophicleide Penshurst church early 19th century (see p. 163).

PETERS. Paris. Professor of ophicleide 1836; Musard's concerts 1837 (see pp. 100, 169; possibly also Serpent).

PHASEY, Alfred James. London. 19.2.1834-17.8.1888. Ophicleide, euphonium, Coldstream Guards; Philharmonic Society and Her Majesty's Theatre, Orchestral Union, Musical Amateurs' Society, 1859, 1863-66, 1873; Costa's Crystal Palace Concerts 1862-1884. Also played bass trombone, composed and arranged. d. Chester, possibly while there for festival (see pp. 165, 171, 173, 227, 229, 372, 489, 503-4).

POISSON. Colombe[s], ?Seine, France. Professor of ophicleide 1836 (p. 170).

PONDER, William. London. Monster ophicleide Birmingham ·Musical Festival 1834); Yorkshire Musical Festival 1835; ophicleide Covent Garden, Drury Lane, Oratorio Concerts 1830; Westminster Abbey 6.1834; Norwich Festival 1836; Liverpool Music Festival 7.10.1836 (serpent part in *St Paul*); Guildhall 9.11.1837; Manchester Grand Music Festival 1836, 1837; Sacred Harmonic Society 1838; Three Choirs Festival, Gloucester 1841, where he died 5.9.1841 (see pp. 120, 149-50, 169; *see also* Serpent, Bass horn).

PROSPÈRE, Jean. b. 30.2.1814 [old-style Russian]-18.11.1862. Studied horn Paris Conservatoire; took up ophicleide 1830s. Ophicleide Jullien Concerts Jardin Turc, Paris, 1836, 1838; moved to London 1840; Musard's Drury Lane Concerts 1846; Jullien *Concerts d'hiver* Drury Lane 10.1840, 1841, 1843, 1851, 1852; English Opera House 1841-42; Philharmonic Society 1847-58; tours 1849; Grand National Concerts, Her Majesty's Theatre 1850; soloist Moirato's Promenade Concerts 1853, 1854; Leeds Music Festival 1858; soloist with Jullien until 1859; monster ophicleide Birmingham Musical Festival and Hanover Square Rooms 1843; serpentcleide Jullien's *Concerts d'hiver* Covent Garden 1846; also Antient Concerts. Biography and portrait *Illustrated London News* 24.6.1843 (see pp. 148-51, 158, 164, 169-70, 173, 503). Identical to PROSPERT below?

PROSPERT. Paris. Player of ophicleide 1836 (P[19]). Identical to PROSPÈRE above?

REINHART. Paris. Professor of *ophicleide-quinte* and *cor-à-pistons* 1836 (see p. 170).

RENIARD. Paris. Alto ophicleide *(quinte)* Garde Nationale à Cheval 1836 (see p.

156).

RIVIÈRE, Jules. 1819-1900. Paris-London-Llandudno. Conductor, publisher. As bandboy played alto ophicleide in French 12th Regiment of Light Infantry (see pp. 141, 279).

SAULT. Paris. Amateur. Ophicleide Garde Nationale IIIe légion 1836 (see p. 155).

SCHÖNEKERL, Wilhelm. Moscow, Russia. Appointed ophicleide Bolshoi Theatre 1861; tuba 1865. Ophicleide was probably valved (see p. 215).

SEYDER. Paris. Ophicleide Garde Nationale XIIe légion; professor of ophicleide and trombone 1836 (see pp. 156, 170).

TAFALL, Mariano. Burgos, Spain. Army musician appointed ophicleide Burgos cathedral 1836 (see p. 153).

TERRIEN. Paris. Professor of ophicleide 1836 (P[19]).

THURMSTON. London. Ophicleide Yorkshire Musical Festival, York 1835 (see p. 149).

THURSTON. Birmingham. Ophicleide Birmingham Festival 1834 (see p. 149).

TUCKWELL. Blackburn, Lancashire. Ophicleide Yorkshire Musical Festival, York 1838 (see p. 565).

VALLOD. Paris. Ophicleide Garde Nationale XIIe légion 1836 (see p. 156).

VIMEAUX. Orléans, Loiret. Professor of ophicleide 1836 (see p. 170).

WALKER, John. Merthyr Tydfil, South Glamorgan. 1822-90. Solo ophicleide Cyfarthfa Band pre-1863; best ophicleide solo prize Crystal Palace Contest 1860 (see p. 171).

WARREN, George. Weston, Massachusetts. Ophicleide Weston Town Band and Unitarian Church 1842-c. 50 (see p. 171).

WESTWELL, Adam. 1824-4.10.1859. Accrington, Lancashire. Ophicleide Wombwell's Circus Band; Accrington Band 1850-c. 59; awarded spectacular funeral as 'best ophicleidist in the country' (see pp. 169, 175-7).

WOLFER, George J. Aurora Colony, Oregon. Ophicleide 1917, possibly then oldest surviving player in United States (see p. 168 ).

WOODWARD. Rockhampton, Gloucestershire. Ophicleide parish church 1850 (see p. 163).

# APPENDIX C

# 3

# *English Orchestral Tubists c. 1870-1930*

THE FOLLOWING list offers some information on the pattern of work for English tuba-players in the period 1870-1930, but the topic will stand research in much more depth. In order to understand their working environment it needs to be borne in mind that the bulk of players in London were freelance. An interesting article on the professional civilian London Military Band, formed in 1890 (of which Guilmartin was chairman), indicates that virtually all of its members had been, or were still, in army bands, and that the majority of them subsequently earned their living in theatre orchestras (B[55], April 1890, 149). More details of those who played for the Philharmonic Society are given on pages 502-4 above. Other orchestras came into existence as follows: Crystal Palace Orchestra (wind players doubling in Military Band), 1855; Queen's Hall Orchestra, 1895; Richter Concerts, 1896; London Symphony Orchestra, 1904; BBC Symphony Orchestra, 1930. The next great outburst of new orchestras did not take place until the formation of the London Philharmonic, Philharmonia and Royal Philharmonic between 1932 and 1946. Outside the capital, the Hallé (which also provided the orchestra for the Liverpool Philharmonic Society until 1943) was founded in 1858; Bournemouth Orchestra (>Municipal Orchestra>Symphony Orchestra), 1893; Birmingham City Orchestra (>City of Birmingham Symphony Orchestra), 1920.

The London orchestras were freelance, while those elsewhere were seasonal. Traditionally members of the latter spent the summer playing in seaside resorts. Although these venues gave no scope for the employment of bass tuba-players, there was work for euphonium-players, sometimes doubling bass trombone. Then, as now, flexibility was essential. Harry Barlow successfully divided his time between Manchester and the Richter and Royal Italian Opera seasons in London as well as fitting in many of the major festivals (sometimes with the assistance of deputies). As outlined on page 380 above, he was also involved in various other musical activities.

| Name & Instrument(s) | Background | Work | Notes |
| --- | --- | --- | --- |
| Alfred Phasey<br>oph, euph, b.trb. | Coldstream Guards (oph) from 1849 | Crystal Palace Orch. (oph/b.trb.) 1862–80; H.M. Theatre 1865 (euph); Norwich Fest (euph/b.trb.) 1890. Renowned as euph player | Marked the transition from oph to euph but also was often b.trb beside a tubist |
| W. F. Young<br>tba | | Philharmonic Soc. 1870 | Probably a serving bandsman |
| F. J. Batley<br>tba, ?oph | | Hallé, 1869–76, 77–78 | |
| J. Wilson<br>bombardon | | Philharmonic Soc. 1880 | Probably a serving bandsman |
| T. Moss<br>tba, ?oph | | Hallé 1885–94 | |
| J. H. Guilmartin<br>oph, euph, tba | Scots Guards (euph) | From oph to tba for Richter 1887; Leeds Fest. 1889 (tba); Ldn. Mil. Band 1890 (euph); Queen's Hall Orch. 1895–?1898 (euph/tba); Norwich Fest. 1896, Crystal Palace, Henschel and Glasgow Choral Union (tba) | Almost certainly the first player of orchestral F tuba in England, 1887 |

| | | | |
|---|---|---|---|
| Richard Marsden<br>oph, euph, tba, serp. | Bacup Band, Belle<br>Vue Gardens B.B. | De Jong's Orch (?euph);<br>Hallé 1873-4, 76-7, 78-<br>9, 85-6 (oph, tba) | Played serp<br>in perfs of<br>*St Paul* |
| Felix A. Lee<br>tba | | Leeds Fest. 1886 | No other<br>refs. found.<br>May have<br>been local<br>Eb bass player |
| F. Blake<br>tba | | Philharmonic Soc.<br>1890 | Probably a<br>serving<br>bandsman |
| Handel Phasey<br>euph, b.trb. | | Bournemouth<br>1893 (euph/b.trb.) | |
| Harry Barlow<br>ophi, euph, tba | Rishton, Accrington,<br>Besses o' th' Barn Bands | ?Llandudno, 1895 (?euph);<br>Hallé 1894-1930<br>(?tba/euph/oph); also<br>1899/1902 Norwich<br>Fest. (tba); from 1905<br>Royal Italian Opera<br>(Covent Garden) (tba);<br>to BBC 1930.<br>Taught at R.A.M.<br>1931-2 | The first<br>British tubist<br>to make an<br>impact |
| R. W. Travis<br>tba | | Philharmonic Soc.<br>1900, 1905; Norwich<br>Fest. 1902 | |
| A Tyler<br>tba, Wagner Tuba | | Norwich 'Interim Concert',<br>Philharmonic Soc. 1901;<br>1913 Philharmonic Soc.<br>(Wagner Tuba) | |

| | | |
|---|---|---|
| J. W. Collins<br>tba | | Philharmonic Soc.<br>1908-9 |
| Walter Reynolds<br>tba, b.trb., cb.-trb. | ex–Barnado's<br>Home (euph);<br>brass band<br>conductor,<br>euphonium<br>soloist, contest<br>adjudicator | Philharmonic Soc<br>1908-9, Queen's Hall<br>Orch. (tba). Also<br>Royal Italian Opera<br>(b.-trb.); cb.-trb.<br>Philharmonic Soc. 1913;<br>succeeded Guilmartin<br>in Queen's Hall Orch (euph/tba)<br>(?1898) and then his own<br>son Frank (see below)<br>on his early death,<br>remaining until c. ?1928 –<br>some 30 years in all |
| R. Powis<br>tba, Wagner Tuba | | London Symphony<br>Orchestra, Norwich,<br>1905; Philharmonic<br>Society 1910-11 (Wagner<br>Tuba 1913) |
| Frank Reynolds<br>tba | | Philharmonic Soc.<br>1912-20; Royal Choral<br>Soc., Birmingham Proms,<br>Hammerstein's Opera<br>Orch.; succeeded father<br>Walter in Queen's Hall<br>Orch. and was succeeded<br>in turn by him on his early<br>death |

# APPENDIX C

# 4

# *Contemporary makers of musical instruments and accessories mentioned in this book*

*[Details of defunct instrument-makers will be found in*
THE NEW LANGWILL INDEX (W³) *and* THE NEW GROVE
DICTIONARY OF MUSICAL INSTRUMENTS (S⁵)*]*

ALEXANDER. Gebr. Alexander Mainz, Postfach 1166, 55116 Mainz, Germany.

AMATI. Amati-Denak, sro, Dukelska 44, Kraslice 358 25, Czech Republic.

APPERSON, RON. Ron Apperson Tuba Mutes, 3008 Riva Ridge Way, Boise, Idaho 83709, U.S.A.

B&S. Vogtländische Musikinstrumentenfabrik GmbH, 08258 Markneukirchen, Germany.

BACH, VINCENT. The Selmer Company, Inc., PO Box 310, Elkhart, Indiana 46515-0310, U.S.A.

BENGE *see* UMI.

BESSON *see* BOOSEY & HAWKES.

BLESSING. E. K. Blessing, 1301 Beardsley Avenue, Elkhart, Indiana 46514.

BOOSEY & HAWKES. Boosey & Hawkes Musical Instruments Limited, Deansbrook Road, Edgware, Middlesex, HA8 9BB, U.K.

ČERVENÝ. Amati-Denak, sro, Pouchovská ul., Hradek Králové, Czech Republic.

CONN *see* UMI.

COURTOIS. Antoine Courtois S.A., Z.I. de Boitardière, B.P. 341-61, rue de Colombier, 37401 Amboise, Cedex, France.

DEG. DEG Music Products, P.O. Box 968, Lake Geneva, Wisconsin 53147, U.S.A.

DILLON MUSIC, Inc., 325 Fulton Street, Woodbridge, New Jersey 07095, U.S.A.

DISCOUNT MUSIC, Inc., P.O. Box 148027, Chicago, Illinois 60614, U.S.A.

EDWARDS INSTRUMENT Co., *see* Getzen Co.

ELLIOTT, DOUG. Doug Elliott Mouthpieces, 13619 Layhill Road, Silver Spring, Maryland 20906, U.S.A.

ENDSLEY. Endlsey Brass Instrument Mouthpieces, 2253 Bellaire Street, Denver, Colorado 80207, U.S.A.

FARNELL, DEREK. Derek Farnell, 82 Crumpsall Lane, Crumpsall, Manchester, M8 5SG, U.K.

GETZEN. Getzen Co. Inc., P.O. Box 440, Elkhorn, Wisconsin 53121, U.S.A.

GLASSL. Musik Glassl, Adam-Open-Straße 12, 64569 Nauheim, Germany.

GRIFFITH. N. P. Griffith Co., 1436 11th Street, Omaha, Nebraska 68108, U.S.A.

GRONITZ. Gronitz-Matallblasinstrumente OHG, Haydnstraße 10, 22761 Hamburg, Germany.

HARDING, DAVID. David Harding, 56 Netherton Road, Appleton, Abingdon, Oxfordshire, OX13 5JZ, U.K.

HIRSBRUNNER. Hirsbrunner & Co. A.G., Musikinstrumenten-Fabrik, Dorfgaße 6, 3454 Sumiswald, Switzerland.

HOLTON. G. Leblanc Corporation, 7001 Leblanc Boulevard, P.O. Box 1415, Kenosha, Wisonsin 53141-1415, U.S.A.

HUMES & BERG. Humes & Berg Manufacturing Co., Inc., 4801 Railroad Avenue, East Chicago, Indiana 46312, U.S.A.

JET-TONE. Jet-Tone, P.O. Box 1462, Elkhart, Indiana 46515, U.S.A.

JOHNSON, MIKE. Mike Johnson, 62 Higher Croft, Barton, Eccles, Manchester, M30 7ET, U.K.

JOHNSON CASES. Walt Johnson Cases, 951 Primrose Lane, Corona, California 91720, U.S.A.

JUPITER. Jupiter Tubas, P.O. Box 90249, Austin, Texas 78709-0249, U.S.A.

KALISON S.N.C., Via P. Rossi 96, 20161 Milano, Italy.

KING see UMI.

LIDL. Lidl, Brno, Czech Republic.

McCRACKEN, GEORGE. George McCracken, 19230 Tabernacle Road, Barhamsville, Virginia 23011, U.S.A.

MEAD, STEPHEN see BOOSEY & HAWKES.

MEINL, RUDOLF. Rudolf Meinl, Blumenstraße 21-23, 91456 Diespeckt/Aisch, Germany.

MEINL, WENZEL. Wenzel Meinl GmbH, Postfach 710, 82532 Geretsried, Germany.

MEINL-WESTON see MEINL, WENZEL.

MELTON see MEINL, WENZEL.

MIRAPHONE. Miraphone eG, Postfach 1129, 84464 Waldkraiburg, Germany.

MONK, CHRISTOPHER. Christopher Monk Workshops, Workshop 4, 30-32 Devonshire Road, Forest Hill, London, SE23 3SR, U.K.

MUSICA STEYR [UMI Austria] *see* UMI.

NIRSCHL, WALTER. Meister Walter Nirschl, Geretsried, Bavaria, Germany (tel +11 4981 719 935999; fax +11 4981 719 935590).

PAXMAN. Paxman Musical Instruments Limited, Unit B4, Linton House, 164-180 Union Street, London, SE1 0LH, U.K.

PERANTUCCI. Horn & Tuba Center, Haupstraße 17-19, 82223 Eichenau bei München, Germany.

PERRY, NICHOLAS. Nicholas Perry, 20 Queen Street, St Albans, Hertfordshire, AL3 4PJ, U.K.

SCHILKE. Schilke Music Products, Inc.,4520 James Place, Melrose Park, Illinois 60160-1007, U.S.A.

STEWART, ROB. Rob Stewart Brass instruments, 140 E. Santa Clara Street #18, Arcadia, California 91006, U.S.A.

UMI. United Music Instruments U.S.A., Inc., 1000 Industrial Parkway, Elkhart, Indiana 46516, U.S.A.

VMI see B&S.

WICK, DENIS see BOOSEY & HAWKES.

WILLSON. Willson Band Instruments, 8890 Flums, Switzerland.

WOODWIND & THE BRASSWIND, THE. The Woodwind & the Brasswind, 4004 Technology Nr., South Bend, Indiana 46628, U.S.A.

YAMAHA. Nippon Gakki Co., Ltd, Hamamatsu, Japan.

# APPENDIX C

# 5

# *Collections of musical instruments mentioned in this book*

**Austria**
SALZBURG. Carolino Augusteum, Salzburger Museum für Kunst und Kulturgeschichte, Museumsplatz 6, 5020 Salzburg.

**Belgium**
ANTWERP. Museum Vleeshuis, Vleeshouwersstraat 38-40, 2000 Antwerpen.
BRUSSELS. Musée Instrumental, 16-17 Place du Petit-Sablon, 1000 Bruxelles.

**Denmark**
COPENHAGEN. Musikhistorisk Museum og Carl Claudius' Sammlung, Aabenraa 30, 1124 København K.

**France**
PARIS. Musée de la Musique, 221 Avenue Jean Jaures, 75019 Paris.

**Germany**
BERLIN. Staatliches Institut für Musikforschung, Preußischer Kulturbesitz, Tiergartenstrasse 1, 10785 Berlin.
FRANKFURT. Historisches Museum, Saalgasse 19, 60311 Frankfurt am Main.
LEIPZIG. Musikinstrumenten-Museum der Universität Leipzig, Täubchenweg 2c-e, 04103 Leipzig.

MARKNEUKIRCHEN. Musikinstrumentenmuseum, Bienengarten 2, 08258 Markneukirchen.

NUREMBERG. Germanisches Nationalmuseum, Kartäusergasse 1, 90402 Nürnberg.

## Italy

MODENA. Museo Civico di Storia ed Arte Medioevale e Moderna, Palazzo dei Musei, Piazza S Agostino, 41100 Modena.

NAPLES. Museo Storico Musicale, Conservatorio di Musica, S Pietro a Maiella 35, 80138 Napoli.

## Netherlands

HAGUE, THE. Haags Gementemuseum, Stadhouderslaan 41, 2517 HV Den Haag.

## Russia

ST PETERSBURG. Gosudarstvenny teatrainy muzei (State Museum of Theatrical & Musical Art), ul Inzhenernaya 4, 191011 Sankt-Peterburg.

## Spain

BARCELONA. Museu de la Música, Avenida Diagonal 373, 08008 Barcelona.

## Sweden

STOCKHOLM. Musikmuseet, Sibyllegatan 2, Box 16326, 103 26 Stockholm.

## Switzerland

BASLE. Musikinstrumenten-Sammlung, Historisches Museum Basle, Leonhardsstrasse 8, 4051 Basel.

## United Kingdom

EDINBURGH. Edinburgh University Collection of Historic Musical Instruments, Reid Concert Hall, Bristo Square, Edinburgh, Lothian, EH8 9AG.

LONDON. Horniman Museum & Gardens, London Road, Forest Hill, London SE23 3PQ.

Royal College of Music Museum of Instruments, Prince Consort Road, South Kensington, London SW7 2BS.

Royal Military School of Music, Kneller Hall, Kneller Road, Twickenham, Middlesex TW2 7DY.

KEIGHLEY. Cliffe Castle Museum, Spring Gardens Lane, Keighley, West Yorkshire BD20 6LH.

NUNEATON. Nuneaton Museum & Art Gallery, Riversely Park, Nuneaton, Warwickshire CV11 5TV.

OXFORD. The Bate Collection of Historical Instruments, University of Oxford, Faculty of Music, St Aldates, Oxford, Oxfordshire OX1 1DB.

SAFFRON WALDEN. Saffron Walden Museum, Museum Street, Saffron Walden, Essex CB10 1JL.

## United States

ANN ARBOR. Stearns Collection, University of Michigan, Ann Arbor, Michigan 48109.

NEW HAVEN. Yale University Collection of Musical Instruments, 15 Hillhouse Avenue, New Haven, Connecticut 06520.

NEW YORK. Metropolitan Museum of Art, 1000 5th Avenue at 82nd Street, New York, NY 10028-0198.

VERMILLION. The Shrine to Music Museum, Clark–Yale Streets, Vermillion, South Dakota 57069-2390.

WASHINGTON. National Museum of American History, Smithsonian Institution, 14th Street & Constitution Avenue NW, Washington DC 20560.

# BIBLIOGRAPHY

A[1]     Abbiati, F., *Giuseppe Verdi,* 4 vols, Milan, 1959.

A[2]     A.D., 'Brass Bands' in *The Message Bird,* New York, 15 June 1850, 361.

A[3]     *Accrington Free Press, The,* Accrington, 15 October 1859, 4.

A[4]     Adam, A., *Souvenirs d'un musicien,* Paris, 1857.

A[5]     Adams, W. E., *Memoirs of a Social Atom,* 2 vols, London, 1903.

A[6]     Adkins, H. E., *Treatise on the Military Band,* London, 1931/1958.

A[7]     *Allgemeine Musikalische Zeitung,* Leipzig, 3 May 1815, 26 November 1817, cols 814-16.

A[8]     *Allgemeine Preussische Staats-Zeitung,* Berlin, 16 September 1835.

A[9]     Altenburg, J. E., *Versuch einer Anleitung zur heroisch-musikalischen Trompeter- und Pauker-Kunst,* Halle, 1795, Eng. tr. of Part 2 by M. Rasmussen as 'An essay on the instruction of the noble and musical art of trumpet and kettledrum playing' in *Brass Quarterly,* Durham, N.H., i, 3, 133-141; i, 4, 201-13; ii, 1, 20-30; ii, 2, 53-62, 1958.

A[10]    *American Musical Journal,* New York, March, 1835.

A[11]    Andersen, A. O., *Practical Orchestration,* Boston, Mass., 1929.

A[12]    Anderson, G., 'Fourteen ways to improve intonation on tuba and euphonium' in *TUBA Newsletter,* Cookville, Tenn., Winter 1975.

A[13]    Andral, M., 'Serpent' in Michel, F. (ed.), *Encyclopédie de la Musique,* 3 vols., iii, Paris, 1961, 1013.

A[14]    Andrews, F., *Brass Band Cylinder and Non-microgroove Disc Recordings 1903-1960,* Winchester, 1997.

A[15]    Anon., '"Giant" Ophicleide, with a notice of Mons. Prospere, The' in *Illustrated London News,* London, 24 June 1843, 442.

A[16]    Apel, W., *Harvard Dictionary of Music, The,* Harvard, 1945; article 'Tuba'.

A[17]    Aprahamian, F., 'Fit for the gold of Elgar' in *The Sunday Times,* London, 29 July 1984, 39.

A[18]    Ascaloni, G., *Manualetto per l'allievo di strumenti d'ottone a bocchino,* Milan, 1893.

A[19]    Aspin, C., *Surprising Lancashire,* Helmshore, 1988.

A[20]    *Athenaeum, The,* London, 28 January 1854, 124.

A[21]    Ayars, C. M., *Contributions to the Art of Music in American by the Music Industries of Boston 1640-1936,* New York, 1937.

B[1]     Bach, V., *Embouchure and Mouthpiece Manual,* Mount Vernon, N.Y., 1954.

B[2]     Backus, J., *Acoustical Foundation of Music, The,* London, 1970.

B[3]   Baines, A., *Brass Instruments, their history and development,* London, 1976/1980/ 1993.

B[4]   ——,'Bugle' in S. Sadie (ed.), *The New Grove Dictionary of Musical Instruments,* 3 vols., i, London, 1984, 280.

B[5]   ——, *European and American Musical Instruments,* London, 1966.

B[6]   ——, 'James Talbot's manuscript' in *Galpin Society Journal,* i, London, 1948, 9-26.

B[7]   ——, (ed.), *Musical Instruments through the Ages,* Harmondsworth, 1961.

B[8]   ——, 'Tenor cor', 'Tenor horn', 'Tuba' in E. Blom (ed.), *Grove's Dictionary of Music & Musicians,* 9 vols., viii, London, 1954, 394, 578-80.

B[9]   Balbi, M., *Grammatica ragionata della musica,* Milan, 1845.

B[10]  Banister, H. C., *Music,* London, 1897.

B[11]  Barzun, J., *Berlioz and the Romantic Century,* 2 vols, New York, 1950/3rd edn. 1969.

B[12]  ——, *Pleasures of Music,* London, 1954.

B[13]  Bate, P., 'Cornophone', 'Saxhorn', 'Saxotromba', 'Sudrephone', in E. Blom (ed.),*Grove's Dictionary of Music & Musicians,* 5th edn., 9 vols., ii, vii, viii, London, 1954, 451, 426-30, 434-5, 162-3.

B[14]  ——'*Serpent d'église, A:* notes on some structural details' in *Galpin Society Journal,* xxix, London, 1976, 47-50.

B[15]  ——'Some further notes on serpent technology' in *Galpin Society Journal,* xxxii, London, 1979, 124-9.

B[16]  ——*Trumpet and Trombone, The,* London, 1966/1972.

B[17]  Batley, T., *Sir Charles Hallé's Concerts in Manchester. A list of vocal and intrumental soloists . . . members of the orchestra . . . programmes of concerts . . . 1858 . . . 1895,* Manchester, 1896.

B[18]  Beaugeois, l'Abbé, *N^{elle} méthode de plain-chant, de musique et de serpent,* Amiens, 1827.

B[19]  Benade, A. H., *On the Tone and Response of Wind Instruments from an Acoustical Standpoint,* Cleveland, Ohio, 1972.

B[20]  Benoit, M., *Musiques de Cour, 1661-1733,* Paris, 1971.

B[21]  ——*Versailles et les Musiciens du Roi,* Paris, 1971.

B[22]  Ben-Tovim, A. & D. Boyd, *Right Instrument for your Child, The,* London, 1985.

B[23]  *Berlin Allgemeine Musikalische Zeitung,* iv, Berlin, 1827, 95.

B[24]  Berlioz, H., *Grand traité d'instrumentation et d'orchestration modernes,* Paris,

1844, ed. of 1904 with appendix by C. M. Widor.

B²⁵ ——, *Grand traité d'instrumentation et d'orchestration modernes*, Paris, 1844; rev. ed. R. Strauss, Leipzig, 1905; Eng. tr. Theodore Frost, New York, 1948.

B²⁶ ——, 'Instrumens de musique: M. Ad. Sax' in *Journal des Débats*, Paris, 12 June 1842, [3].

B²⁷ ——, *Memoirs*, 2 vols, Paris, 1870, tr. R. & E. Holmes, rev. E. Newman as *Memoirs of Hector Berlioz*, New York, 1935.

B²⁸ ——, *Memoirs*, 2 vols, Paris, 1870, tr. D. Cairns as *The Memoirs of Hector Berlioz*, London, 1969.

B²⁹ ——, [New edition of the complete works], Kassel, 1969-

B³⁰ ——, *Requiem*, 1837, ed. Roger Fiske, London, 1969.

B³¹ ——, *Symphonie fantastiqe*, ed. C. Malherbe & F. Weingartner, Leipzig, 1900.

B³² Berri, P., *Paganini,* Milan, 1982.

B³³ Besarrabott, N., *Ancient Egyptian Instruments*, Boston, Mass., 1941.

B³⁴ Bevan, C. J., 'Final thoughts on the cimbasso', pt. 1, in *TUBA Journal*, xxvi, 3, Austin, TX, Spring 1999, 56-7.

B³⁵ ——, *Musical Instrument Collections in the British Isles,* Winchester, 1990.

B³⁶ ——, '(P)russian trumpet, The' in *Galpin Society Journal,* xli, London, 1988, 112-14.

B³⁷ ——, 'Saxtuba and organological vituperation, The' in *Galpin Society Journal,* xliii, London, 1990, 135-46.

B³⁸ ——, 'Stephen Wick and the informed approach' in *TUBA Journal,* xxv, 4, Austin, TX, Summer 1998.

B³⁹ Bierey, G. B., 'Neue Erfindung' in *Allgemeine Musikalische Zeitung*, Leipzig, iii, May 1815.

B⁴⁰ Binns, P. L., *Hundred Years of Military Music, A,* Gillingham, 1959.

B⁴¹ *Blackburn Weekly Times, The,* Blackburn, 8 October 1859, 2.

B⁴² Blaikley, D. J., *On Quality of Tone in Wind Instruments*, London, 1880.

B⁴³ ——, *Acoustics in Relation to Wind Instruments*, London, 1890.

B⁴⁴ ——, 'Bersag Horn' in E. Blom (ed.), *Grove's Dictionary of Music & Musicians,* 5th edn., 9 vols., i, London, 1954, 684-5.

B⁴⁵ Blom, E., 'Gershwin' in E. Blom (ed.), *Grove's Dictionary of Music & Musicians*, 5th edn., 9 vols., iii, London, 1954, 607.

B⁴⁶ ——, (ed.), *Grove's Dictionary of Music & Musicians,* 5th edn., 9 vols., London, 1954.

B⁴⁷ Bobo, R., *Tuba, Word with a Dozen Meanings*—obtainable from Miraphone

Corporation, n.d.

B[48]   Borland, J. E., *The Brass Wind Instruments*, London, 1903.

B[49]   Bowsher, J. M. & P. S. Watkinson, 'Manufacturers' opinions about brass instruments' in *Brass Bulletin*, xxxviii, Bulle, 1982, 25-32.

B[50]   Bragard & Hen, *Instruments de Musique, Les,* Vissoner, 1967.

B[51]   Brenet, M. [M. Bobillier], *Musiciens de la Saint-Chapelle de Paris, Les,* Paris, 1910.

B[52]   ——, *Musique militaire, La,* Paris, 1917.

B[53]   Brian, H., 'Brass Band, The' in *Musical Opinion*, London, November, 1923, 160-1.

B[54]   Briggs, G. A., *Musical Instruments and Audio*, Bradford, 1965.

B[55]   *British Bandsman, The,* London, December 1887, back cover; November 1888, 33-4; April 1890, 149; 12.4.1901, 114; 21.3.1908, 423; 26.1.1974, 8.

B[56]   Brooks, J. A., *Railway Ghosts*, Norwich, 1985.

B[57]   Brossard, Y. de., *Musiciens de Paris, 1535-1792,* Paris, 1965.

B[58]   *Brother Jonathan,* New York, 16 April 1842, 75.

B[59]   Brousse, J., 'Tuba' in Lavignac & Laurencie (ed.), *Encyclopédie de la Musique,* 11 vols, x, Paris, 1927, 1674-80.

B[60]   Brown, D., *Tchaikovsky: a biographical and critical study*, 4 vols., iii: 'The years of wandering (1878-1885)', London, 1986.

B[61]   Bryant, A., *Years of Victory, 1802-1812,* London, 1944/1945.

B[62]   Bryant, C., 'Sousaphone' in S. Sadie (ed.), *The New Grove Dictionary of Musical Instruments,* 3 vols, iii, London, 1984, 433-4.

B[63]   Budden, J., *Operas of Verdi, The,* 3 vols., Oxford, 1992.

B[64]   Burney, C., *Present State of Music in France and Italy, The,* 2 vols, London, 1771.

B[65]   ——, *Present State of Music in Germany, the Netherlands, and United Provinces, The,* 2 vols., London, 1773.

B[66]   Burstow, H., ed. W. Albery, *Reminiscences of Horsham*, repr. ?London, 1975.

B[67]   Butterfield, D., *It is Time to Modify the Bass Tuba*—obtainable from King Musical Instruments, n.d., repr. in part in *The Instrumentalist*, Evanston, Ill., February 1973.

C[1]    *Caeciliá*, Mainz, 3, 3 July 1824, 58; 34, 1827, 129; 34, 1828, 130; 39, 1829, 12.

C[2]    *Cambridge Italian Dictionary,* Cambridge, 1962.

C[3]    Canale, M., *Paganini Edizione Nazionale* [Introductory notes to *Terzo concerto per violino e orchestra*], v, Rome, 1990, 11-29.

C[4]     Carr, I., D. Fairweather & B. Priestley, *Jazz, the rough guide,* London, 1995.

C[5]     Carse, A., 'Adolphe Sax and the Distin Family' in *Music Review*, London, November 1945, 193-201.

C[6]     ——, *History of Orchestration, The,* Cambridge, 1951.

C[7]     ——, *Life of Jullien, The,* Cambridge, 1951.

C[8]     ——, *Musical Wind Instruments*, London, 1939, repr. New York, 1965.

C[9]     ——, *Orchestra, The,* London, 1948.

C[10]    ——, *Orchestra from Beethoven to Berlioz, The,* Cambridge, 1948.

C[11]    Carter, S., 'Georges Kastner on brass instruments: the influence of technology on the theory of orchestration' in Carter, S. (ed.), *Perspectives in Brass Scholarship* (Bucina: The Historic Brass Society Series, 2), Stuyvesant, N.Y., 1997, 171-92.

C[12]    —— (ed.), *Perspectives in Brass Scholarship* (Bucina: The Historic Brass Society Series, 2), Stuyvesant, N.Y., 1997.

C[13]    Castil-Blaze, F., *Académie Impériale de Musique, L'*, 2 vols, Paris, 1855.

C[14]    Caussinus, J. L. V., *Solfège-méthode pour l'ophicléïde basse, en 2 parties,* Paris, 1843.

C[15]    Cella, F., M., Ricordi & M. Di Gregorio Casati (ed.), *Carteggio Verdi-Ricordi 1882-1885,* Parma, 1994.

C[16]    Cellini, B., tr. J. A. Symonds, *Life of Benvenuto Cellini, The,* ?London, n.d.

C[17]    Charlton, D., 'New sounds for old: Tam-tam, Tuba Curva, Buccin' in *Soundings,* iii, Cardiff, 1973, 39-47.

C[18]    Chase, G., *America's Music*, New York, 1955/1966.

C[19]    Chaucer, G., ed. N. F. Blake, *Canterbury Tales, The,* London, 1980.

C[20]    Chevalier, M., *Rapports du Jury International, Paris Exposition Universelle de 1867,* Paris, 1868.

C[21]    Chickering & Sons (pub.), *Historical Musical Exhibition: Catalogue of the Exhibition*, Boston, 1902.

C[22]    Chouquet, G., *Musée du Conservatoire National de Musique, Le: Catalogue Raisonné des Instruments,* Paris, 1875.

C[23]    ——, 'Sax'—the family, in E. Blom (ed.), *Grove's Dictionary of Music & Musicians,* 5th edn., 9 vols., vii, London, 1954, 425-6.

C[24]    Christout, M.-F., 'Plain-chant' in F. Michel (ed.), *Encyclopédie de la musique, 3 vols.,* iii, Paris, 1961, 453-4.

C[25]    Clagget, C., *Musical Phenomena*, i, London, 1793.

C[26]    Clappé, A. A., *Wind-band and its Instruments, The,* London, 1912.

C[27]   Collier, G., *Inside Jazz*, London, 1973.

C[28]   Coltman, J. W., 'Effect of material on flute tone quality' in *Woodwind World,* 9, Oneonta, NY, 1972.

C[29]   Comettant, O., *Histoire d'un inventeur au dix-neuvieme siècle*, Paris, 1860.

C[30]   Conner, R., *How to Care for a Rotary Valve Tuba*—obtainable from the Getzen Co. Inc., n.d.

C[31]   Conrad, P., *Song of Love and Death, A: the meaning of opera,* London, 1987/1989.

C[32]   Conservatoire Impériale de Musique, *Méthode pour l'étude du Serpent*, Paris, 1812, repr. Geneva, 1974.

C[33]   *Correspondance des amateurs musiciens, La*, 23 May 1804.

C[34]   Courcy, de., G. I. C., *Paganini: the Genoese,* 2 vols., Norman, Okla., 1957.

C[35]   Croft-Murray, E., 'Wind-band in England, 1540-1840, The' in T. C. Mitchell (ed.), *Music and Civilisation* (British Museum Yearbook 4), London, 1980, 135-80.

C[36]   Cummings, B., 'Killer Tuba Songs' [CD review] in *TUBA Journal,* xxv, 3, Austin, TX, Spring 1998, 24-5.

C[37]   Crystal Palace (pub.), *Programmes of Concerts, 1853-91*, London, 1853-1891.

C[38]   Crystal Palace (pub.), *Programmes of the Saturday Concerts,* 1867-1904, London, 1867-1904.

C[39]   Curtis, N., 'Singer hits the surreal notes' in *Evening Standard*, London, 7 May 1999, 60.

D[1]   Daubeny, U., *Orchestral Wind Instruments*, London, 1920.

D[2]   Daverio, J., *Robert Schumann,* New York/Oxford, 1997.

D[3]   Davis, R., 'The historian's perspective' in *TUBA Journal,* xxv, 1, Austin, TX, Fall 1997, 32-4.

D[4]   Day, C. R., *Descriptive Catalogue of the Musical Instruments Recently Exhibited at the Royal Military Exhibition, London, 1890, A,* London, 1891.

D[5]   Decker, J., *Double or Nothing*—obtainable from Miraphone Corporation, n.d.

D[6]   Del Mar, N., *Richard Strauss*, London, 1962.

D[7]   Densmore, F., *Handbook of the Collection of Musical Instruments in the U.S. National Museum,* Washington, D.C., 1927, repr. New York, 1971.

D[8]   Dibble, J., *C. Hubert Parry: his life and music,* Oxford, 1992.

D[9]   Dickens, C., *Martin Chuzzlewit*, New York, ed. of 1844.

D[10]  ——, *Posthumous Papers of the Pickwick Club, The,* London, ed. of 1847.

D[11]  ——, 'Flight, A' in *Reprinted Pieces*, London, n.d., 127-35.

D¹²    Dickey, B. 'Cornett, The' in Herbert, T. & J. Wallace (eds.), *The Cambridge Companion to Brass Instruments*, Cambridge, 1997, 51-67.

D¹³    Dickson, H. E., *Gentlemen, More Dolce Please!*, Boston, Mass.,1969.

D¹⁴    Doane, J., *Musical Directory*, London, 1794.

D¹⁵    Dollfus, C. & E. de Geoffroy, *Histoire de la locomotion terrestre: les chemins de fer*, Paris, 1935.

D¹⁶    Donington, R., *Instruments of Music, The*, London, 1949, 3rd rev. ed. [=4th], London, 1970.

D¹⁷    Downey, P., " 'If music comes from many horns, then the sound is sweeter": trumpets and horns in early medieval Ireland' in *Historic Brass Society Journal*, 9, New York, 1997, 130-74.

D¹⁸    Draper, F. C., *Notes on the Boosey & Hawkes System of Automatic Compensation of Valved Brass instruments*, London, 1953.

D¹⁹    Drinker, P. A. & J. M. Bowsher, 'Application of noninvasive acoustic measurements to the design, manufacture and reproduction of brass wind instruments, The ' in *Historic Brass Society Journal*, 5, New York, 1993, 107-31.

D²⁰    Dudgeon, R., *Keyed Bugle, The*, Metuchen, N.J., 1993.

D²¹    Duffin, R. W., 'Backward bells and barrel bells: some notes on the early history of loud instruments' in *Historic Brass Society Journal*, 9, New York, 1997, 113-29.

D²²    Duffy, M., *Erotic World of Faery, The*, London, 1972.

D²³    Dullat, G., *Metallblasinstrumentenbau-Entwicklungsstufen und Technologie*, Mainz, 1991.

D²⁴    Durand, G., *Notice historique sur la Musique Municipal du Mans*, Le Mans, 1899.

E¹    Ehrlich, C., *First Philharmonic*, Oxford, 1995.

E²    ——, *Music Profession in Britain since the Eighteenth Century, The*, Oxford, 1985.

E³    Eliason, R. E., 'Early American valves for brass instruments' in *Galpin Society Journal*, XXIII, London, 1970, 86-96.

E⁴    ——, 'Graves, Samuel' in S. Sadie (ed.), *The New Grove Dictionary of Musical Instruments*, 3 vols., ii, London, 1984, 74.

E⁵    ——, *Keyed Bugles in the United States*, Washington, D.C., 1972.

E⁶    —— & L. P. Farrar, 'Distin' in S. Sadie (ed.), *The New Grove Dictionary of Musical Instruments*, 3 vols, i, London, 1984, 572.

E⁷    Eliot, G. [M. A. Evans], 'Sad misfortunes of the Reverend Amos Barton,

The', in *Scenes of Clerical Life*, 2 vols, Leipzig, 1859.

E[8]  Ellis, W. A. (tr.), *Richard Wagner's Prose Works,* 8 vols, London, 1894, repr. New York, 1966.

E[9]  Emerson, J. A., 'Plainchant—2: Western Plainchant', in S. Sadie (ed.), *The New Grove Dictionary of Music & Musicians*, 20 vols. xiv, London, 1980, 805-44.

E[10]  Engel, C., *Musical Instruments of all Countries*, London, 1869.

E[11]  Enrico, E., *Orchestra at San Petronio in the Baroque Era, The* (Smithsonian Studies in History and Technology, 35), Washington, D.C., 1976.

E[12]  Ericson, J. Q., 'Heinrich Stoelzel and early valved horn technique' in *Historic Brass Society Journal*, 9, New York, 1997, 63-82.

E[13]  Evans, E., *Method of Instrumentation*, 2 vols, London, n.d.

E[14]  *Evening Standard,* London, 9 September 1994, 49; 7 May 1999, 60.

E[15]  *Exposition Internationale, Genève, 1927, L'*, Geneva, 1927.

F[1]  Farkas, P., *Art of Brass Playing, The*, Bloomington, Ind., 1962.

F[2]  Farmer, H., 'Althorn', 'Bugle' in E. Blom (ed.), *Grove's Dictionary of Music & Musicians,* 5th edn., 9 vols., i, London, 1954, 127, 1005-6.

F[3]  ——, *Handel's Kettledrums, and other papers on military music,* London, *c.* 1950.

F[4]  ——, *History of the Royal Artillery Band, 1762-1953, The,* London, 1954.

F[5]  ——, *Rise and Development of Military Music, The,* London, 1912.

F[6]  Farrington, F., 'Note on the dissection of a serpent, A', in *Galpin Society Journal* xxii, London, 1969, 81-96.

F[7]  Feather, L., *Encyclopedia of Jazz, The,* London, 1956/1961.

F[8]  Feder, G., 'Haydn, Joseph' [lists and bibliography] in S. Sadie (ed.), *The New Grove Dictionary of Music and Musicians*, 20 vols., viii, London, 1980, 360-401.

F[9]  Fender, G., 'UK higher education: successes and challenges' [address to Convocation of the University of London, 20 October 1998], repr. in London University *Meeting of Convocation,* London, 11 May 1999, 22-8.

F[10]  Ferrero, B. A., *Bandas de música en el mundo, Las,* Madrid, 1986.

F[11]  Fétis, F. J. *Biographie Universelle des Musiciens*, Paris, 11 vols, 1834-44; articles 'Clagget' (i, 309-10), 'Sommer' (viii, 62).

F[12]  ——, 'Considérations sur quelques instruments et sur leur emploi' [troisième article], in *Revue musicale*, viii, 44, Paris, 2 November 1834, 345-6.

F[13]  ——, *Curiosités historiques de la musique,* Paris, 1830.

F[14]  *Field, The: the country gentleman's newspaper*, London, 17 May 1873, 464; 24 May 1873, 487; 7 June 1873, 542; 21 June 1873, 597; 12 July 1873, 43.

F[15]    Fisher, P. H., *Notes and Recollections of Stroud, Gloucestershire*, London/Stroud, 1871.

F[16]    Fiske, R., *English Theatre Music in the Eighteenth Century,* Oxford, 1973.

F[17]    Fletcher, G., London's Pavement Pounders, London, 1967.

F[18]    Fletcher, J., 'Tuba Talk', etc., in *Sounding Brass,* London, Summer 1973, 59-61; Autumn 1973, 78-9; Winter 1973/4, 110-12; Winter 1974/5, 116-17; Spring 1976, 13, 19; Summer 1976, 54, 63.

F[19]    Forsyth, C., *Orchestration,* London, 1914/1935.

F[20]    Foster, M. B., *History of the Philharmonic Society of London, 1813-1912, The,* London, 1912.

F[21]    Frederiksen, B., *Arnold Jacobs: song and wind,* Gurnee, Ill., 1996.

F[22]    Froelich, C., *Serpent-Schule,* Bonn, c. 1811.

F[23]    Fromrich, Y., *Musique et Caricature en France au XIX^e Siècle,* Geneva, 1973.

G[1]    Gallat-Morin, E., *Livre d'orgue de Montréal, Le* [notes accompanying CD Sacem 300 002.2].

G[2]    Galpin, F. W., *Old English Instruments of Music,* London, 1910/1965.

G[3]    ——, *Textbook of European Musical Instruments, A,* London, 1937.

G[4]    Galpin Society (pub.) 'Provisional index of present-day makers of historical musical instruments (non-keyboard)', *Galpin Society Journal,* xiii, London, 1960, 70-87.

G[5]    ——, ed. Melville-Mason, *European Musical Instruments at the Edinburgh International Festival, 1968,* London, 1968.

G[6]    Garofalo, R. & M. Elrod, *Pictorial History of Civil War Era Musical Instruments and Military Bands, A,* Charleston, W.Va, 1985.

G[7]    Gassner, F. S., *Dirigent und Ripienist,* Karlsruhe, 1844.

G[8]    Gatti, G. M., *Musica: Dizionario I, La,* Milan, 1968.

G[9]    *Gazzetta musicale di Milano,* Milan, 4 June 1871, (Suppl.); 4 September 1881, 319; 13 November 1881, 408; 18 December 1881, 458; 24 June 1894, [ ].

G[10]    *Gazette musicale,* Paris, 15 February 1834.

G[11]    Geiringer, E., tr. B. Miall, *Musical Instruments,* London, 1943.

G[12]    Gevaert, F.-A., *Nouveau traité d'instrumentation,* Paris/Brussels, 1885.

G[13]    Giampiero, T., *Gli Strumente Musicale,* 2 vols, Turin, 1971.

G[14]    Gibson, W. J., 'Life Guards Band, The' in *The Leading Note,* i, 6, Twickenham, February 1931, 16-23.

G[15]    Gillaspie, J. A., M. Stoneham & D. L. Clark, *Wind Ensemble Catalog, The*

(Music Reference Collection, 63), Westport, Conn., 1998.

G[16]   *Gloucester Journal,* Gloucester, 11 September 1841, [3].

G[17]   Gorgerat, G., *Encyclopédie de la musique pour instruments à vent,* 3 vols, Lausanne, 1955.

G[18]   Grace, H., 'Note on the serpent, A', in *The Musical Times,* London, 1 November 1916, 549-50.

G[19]   Great Exhibition (pub.), *Offical Catalogue,* corrected ed., London, 1851.

G[20]   ——, *Reports by the Juries,* London, 1852.

G[21]   Gregory, R., *Horn, The,* London, 1961/1969.

G[22]   ——, *Trombone, The,* London, 1973.

G[23]   Gray, B., *George Eliot and Music,* London, 1989.

G[24]   Groce, N., *Musical Instrument Makers of New York,* Stuyvesant, N.Y., 1991.

G[25]   Guy, C., 'Exploring the *new* double-bell euphonium: a review/commentary of Edward Mallett's lecture/recital' in *TUBA Journal,* Austin, TX, xxiii, 4, Summer 1996, 64.

H[1]    Haags Gemeentemuseum (pub.), *Catalogus van der Muziekinstrumenten,* Amsterdam, 1970.

H[2]    Hague, B., *Tonal Spectra of Wind Instruments, The,* London, 1947.

H[3]    Hall, J. C., *Proper Selection of Cup Mouthpieces, The,* Elkhart, Ind., 1963.

H[4]    —— & E. L. Kent, *Language of Musical Acoustics, The,* Elkhart, Ind., 1957.

H[5]    *Hallische Händel-Ausgabe,* iv, Halle, ?1978

H[6]    Handford, M., *Sounds Unlikely: 600 years of music in Birmingham,* Birmingham, 1992.

H[7]    Hardy, T., *Short Stories of Thomas Hardy, The,* London, 1928.

H[8]    ——, *Under the Greenwood Tree,* London, 1872.

H[9]    Harper, C. G., *Stage-coach and Mail,* 2 vols, London, 1903.

H[10]   *Harmonicon, The,* London, August 1825, 140; July 1830, [ ].

H[11]   Harper, T., *Instructions for the Trumpet,* London, 1835/37.

H[12]   Harris, R. G., [footnote to repr. of U[1]] in *Journal of the Society for Army Historical Research,* lvi, London 1978, 1-3.

H[13]   Harrison, F. & J. Rimmer, *European Musical Instruments,* London, 1964.

H[14]   Harwood, G. W., 'Verdi's reform of the Italian opera orchestra' in *Nineteenth Century Music,* x, Berkeley, Ca., Fall, 1986, 108-34.

H[15]   Haugan, P. 'TUBA profile—Arnold M. Jacobs tubist of the Chicago Symphony Orchestra' in *TUBA Journal,* New York, iv, 2, Winter 1977, 2-10.

H[16]    Hayburn, R. F., *Papal Legislation on Sacred Music 95 A.D. to 1977 A.D.*, Collegeville, Minn., 1979.

H[17]    Hellier, S., 'Catalogue of musicall instruments, A' in *Galpin Society Journal*, xviii, London, 1965, 5-6.

H[18]    Hen, F. J. de, 'Folk instruments of Belgium', pt. 2, in *Galpin Society Journal*, xxvi, London, 1973, 86-129.

H[19]    Herbert, T., & A. Myers, 'Instruments of the Cyfarthfa Band' in *Galpin Society Journal*, xli, London, 1988, 2-10.

H[20]    —— & J. Wallace (eds.), *Cambridge Companion to Brass Instruments, The*, Cambridge, 1997.

H[21]    Hermenge, C., *Méthode elémentaire de serpent ordinaire et à clé*, Paris, c. 1817.

H[22]    Heyde, H., *Musikinstrumenten-Museum der Karl-Marx-Universität, Leipzig. Katalog.* Band 3: *Trumpeten, Posaunen, Tuben*, Leipzig, 1980.

H[23]    ——'On the early history of the valve and valved instruments in Germany (1814-1833)' in *Brass Bulletin*, xxiv, Bulle (1978), 9;, xxv (1979), 41; xxvi (1979), 69; and xxvii (1979), 51.

H[24]    ——, *Das Ventilblasinstrument*, Leipzig, 1987.

H[25]    ——, 'Early Berlin Valve and an unsigned tuba at the Shrine to Music Museum, The' in *Journal of the American Musical Instrument Society*, Lyme, N.H., xx, 1994, 54-64.

H[26]    Hiley, D., *Western Plainchant*, Oxford, 1993.

H[27]    Hillsman, W., 'Instrumental accompaniment of plain-chant in France from the late 18th century' in *Galpin Society Journal*, xxxiii, London, 1980, 8-16.

H[28]    Hind, H. C., 'Brass Band', 'Military Band' in E. Blom (ed.), *Grove's Dictionary of Music & Musicians*, 5th edn., 9 vols., i, v, London, 1954, 913-17, 766-73.

H[29]    ——, *Brass Band, The*, London, 1934.

H[30]    Horniman Museum (pub.), comp. Ridley, *Wind Instruments of European Art Music*, London, 1974.

H[31]    Howard, J. T., *Our American Music*, New York, 1946.

H[32]    Howes, F., *Full Orchestra*, London, 1942.

H[33]    Howey, H., 'Revival of Ponchielli's *Concerto per flicorno basso* opus 155, Cremona, 1872, The' in *Tuba Journal*, xxiii, 4, Austin, TX, Summer 1996, 42-9.

H[34]    Hughes, H. P., *Mr T. J. Down and his Bands*, Warrington, 1905.

H[35]    Huneker, J. G., *Philharmonic Society of New York, The*, New York, 1912.

I¹    *Illustrated London News*, London, 10 December 1842, 491; 24 June 1843, 442; 25 May 1844, 336; 7 December 1844, 365; 14 December 1844, 384; 31 May 1845, 349; 6 December 1845, 366; 9 May 1846, 306; 1 August 1846, 78; 12 December 1846, 378;, 19 December 1846, 397.

I²    *Instrumentalist, The*, [Special Tuba Issue], Evanston, Ill., February 1973.

I³    *Italia musicale, L',* Milan, v, 30, 13 April 1853, 88; vii, 34, 28 April 1855, 121; x, 22, 17 March 1858, 136.

J¹    Jackson, E., 'Origin and promotion of brass band contests' in *Musical Opinion*, London, March, October 1896, 101-2.

J²    Jacquot, A. (ed.), *Dictionnaire des instruments de musique*, Paris, 1886.

J³    Jacobs, A., *Arthur Sullivan*, Oxford, 1984/Aldershot, 1992.

J⁴    Jeans, J., *Science and Music*, Cambridge, 1937.

J⁵    Jones, P. (ed.), *John Fletcher: tuba extraordinary*, London, 1997.

J⁶    Jones, P. W. (comp.), *Mendelssohn: an exhibition to celebrate the life of Felix Mendelssohn Bartholdy (1809-1847)* [catalogue of the exhibition at the Bodleian Library, Oxford, June-August 1997], Oxford, 1997.

J⁷    Jones, R., 'Going with the flow' in *Evening Standard*, London, 9 September 1994, 49.

J⁸    *Journal de Paris*, 21 November 1793.

J⁹    *Journal des Débats*, Paris, 12 June 1842, [3].

J¹⁰   *Journal of the Society for Army Historical Research*, lvi, Twickenham, 1978, 1-3.

K¹    Kalkbrenner, A., *Wilhelm Wieprecht, sein Leben und Wirken*, Berlin, 1882.

K²    Kappey, J., *Bombardon and Contrabass Tutor*, London, c. 1874.

K³    ——, *Military Music*, London, n.d.

K⁴    Karjalainen, K., 'Brass band tradition in Finland, The' in *Historic Brass Society Journal*, 9, New York, 1997, 83-96.

K⁵    Kastner, J. G. *Manuel général de musique militaire*, Paris, 1848, repr. Geneva, 1973.

K⁶    Keepnews, O. & B. Grauer, jnr, *Pictorial History of Jazz, A*, London, 1956.

K⁷    Kennedy, M. *Hallé Tradition, The*, Manchester, 1960.

K⁸    Kent, E., *Inside Story of Brass Instruments, The*, Elkhart, Ind., 1956.

K⁹    Kenyon, N., *BBC Symphony Orchestra, The*, London, 1981.

K¹⁰   Kenyon de Pascual, B., 'Brief survey of the late Spanish bajón, A' in *Galpin Society Journal*, xxxvii, London, 1984, 72-9.

K¹¹   ——, 'Onnoven, The ' in *Galpin Society Journal*, xlv, London, 1992, 142-8.

K¹²   ——, 'Ophicleide in Spain, with an appendix on some nineteenth-century brass tutors in Spain, The' in *Historic Brass Society Journal,* 7, New York, 1995.

K[13]   Keyte, H., 'English "gallery" and American "primitive" traditions, The'; Appendix 3 to H. Keyte & A. Parrott, *The New Oxford Book of Carols,* Oxford, 1992, 669-75.

K[14]   Kirk, E., K., *Music at the White House,* Urbana/Chicago, 1986.

K[15]   Kling, H., *Vollkommene Musik-Dirigent, Der,* Hannover [1890].

K[16]   ——, tr. Saenger, *Modern Orchestration,* New York, 1902.

K[17]   Knaack, M. 'Origins a mystery, but its inspiration clear' in *TUBA Journal,* xxvi, 3, Austin, TX, Spring 1999, 51-3.

K[18]   Knight, E., 'Music in Winchester, Massachusetts: a community portrait' in *American Music,* ii, 3, Champaigne, Ill., Fall 1993, 263-82.

K[19]   Knouse, N. R., 'American Moravian brass players: what did they play?' in S. Carter (ed.), *Perspectives in Brass Scholarship* (Bucina: The Historic Brass Society Series, 2), Stuyvesant, N.Y., 1997, 135-50.

K[20]   Koshelev, V., 'Trumpets, cornets, trombones and horns in the St Petersburg Museum of Musical Instruments: a checklist' in S. Carter (ed.)., *Perspectives in Brass Scholarship* (Bucina: The Historic Brass Society Series, 2), Stuyvesant, N.Y., 1997, 223-37.

K[21]   Koechlin, C., *Traité de l'orchestration,* Paris, 1954.

K[22]   Kouwenhoven, J. A., *Columbia Historical Portrait of New York, The,* New York, edn. of 1972.

K[23]   Kuehn, D. L., *Toward Better Tuba Players*—obtainable from the Getzen Co. Inc, n.d.

K[24]   Kunitz, H., *Instrumenten-Brevier,* Leipzig, 1961.

K[25]   ——, *Instrumentation, Die, Teil 9: Tuba,* Wiesbaden, 1968.

K[26]   Kurath, W., snr & jnr, 'ROTAX—the rotary valve with the ideal tube geometry' in *Brass Bulletin,* ii, 2, Bulle, 1997, 26-33.

L[1]   Langwill, L. G., *Index of Musical Wind Instrument Makers, An,* Edinburgh, 1960 /62.

L[2]   ——, 'Two rare eighteenth-century London directories' in *Music & Letters,* xxx, London, January 1949, 37-43.

L[3]   Larkin, C., 'Félicien David's Nonetto en ut mineur: a new discovery and new light on the early use of valved instruments in France' in *Historic Brass Society Journal,* 5, New York, 1993, 192-202.

L[4]   Lavignac, A., *Musique et les musiciens, La,* 8th edn., Paris, 1895.

L⁵ —— & L. de la Laurencie (eds), *Encyclopédie de la musique*, 11 vol, Paris, 1927.

L⁶ Lavoix, H., *Histoire de l'instrumentation*, Paris, 1878.

L⁷ Lawrence, V. B., *Strong on Music,* 4 vols, ii: 'Reverberations 1850-1856', Chicago, 1995.

L⁸ L.C.C. (pub.), *Catalogue of the Adam Carse Collection of Old Musical Wind Instruments*, London, 1951.

L⁹ *Leading Note, The,* i, 6, Twickenham, February 1931, 16-23.

L¹⁰ Lebœuf, J., *Mémoire Concernant l'Histoire Ecclésiastique et Civile d'Auxerre*, 2 vols, Paris, 1743.

L¹¹ Lévachkine, A., 'Short history of the tuba in Russia, A', pt. 1 in *Brass Bulletin,* cvii, 3, Bulle, 1999, 18-25; pt. 2 in cvii, 4, Bulle, 1999, 58-66.

L¹² —— & P. Umiarov, 'Something of the life of the tuba in Russia' in *TUBA Journal*, xxiv, 4, Austin, TX, Summer 1997, 40-1.

L¹³ Lichtenthal, P. (ed.), *Dizionario e Biografia della Musica*, Milan, 1826.

L¹⁴ Lindsay, J. & M., *Music Quotation Book, The,* London, 1992.

L¹⁵ Lindsay, K. C. & P. Vergo (eds.), *Kandinsky: complete writings on art,* New York/London, 1982.

L¹⁶ Lomas, M., *Amateur brass and wind bands in southern England between the late eighteenth century and circa 1900* (Thesis PhD, Open University, 1990) (unpub.).

L¹⁷ ——, 'Secular civilian amateur wind bands in southern England in the late eighteenth and early nineteenth centuries' in *Galpin Society Journal*, xlv, London, 1992, 78-98.

M¹ MacDermott, K. H., *Old Church Gallery Minstrels, The,* London, 1948.

M² ——, *Sussex Church Music in the Past*, Chichester, 2nd edn., 1923.

M³ MacDonald, H., *Berlioz Orchestral Music*, London, 1969.

M⁴ ——, *Troyens, Les* [introductory note to Berlioz New Edition], Kassel, 1969.

M⁵ Mackenzie-Rogan, J., *50 Years of Army Music*, London 1926.

M⁶ Mackim, T., 'Tubafours: take one lights . . . camera . . . action!' in *TUBA Journal*, xxv, 3, Austin, TX, Spring, 1998, 34-6.

M⁷ Mahillon, V.-C., *Catalogue descriptif et analytique du Musée instrumental du Conservatoire Royal de Musique de Bruxelles*, 4 vols, Brussels, 1893.

M⁸ Malet, H. E., *Annals of the Road*, 2 vols, London, 1876.

M⁹ Malherbe, C. & F. Weingartner, *Symphonie fantastique* [introductory note to edn. of Berlioz's work], Leipzig, 1900.

M¹⁰ Mallett, E. K., 'Double-bell euphonium, The: the history of a forgotten instrument ' in *TUBA Journal*, xxi, 3, Austin, TX, Spring 1994, 24-8.

M[11]   Mandel, C., *Treatise on the Instrumentation of the Military Band, A*, London, 1859.

M[12]   Marchesi, G., *Giuseppe Verdi e il Conservatorio di Parma (1836-1901)*, Parma, 1976.

M[13]   Marcuse, S., *Musical Instruments*, New York, 1964.

M[14]   Marek, G. R., *Richard Strauss*, London, 1967.

M[15]   Marr, R., *Music & Musicians at the Edinburgh International Exhibition 1886*, Edinburgh, 1887.

M[16]   Matthews, B., *The Royal Society of Musicians of Great Britain: List of Members 1738-1984*, London, 1985.

M[17]   Mathez, Jean-Pierre, 'Artistic rise of the euphonium, The' in *Brass Bulletin*, ciii, 3, Bulle, 1998, 32-6.

M[18]   ——, 'Forty years of brasses' in *Brass Bulletin*, cviii, 4, Bulle, 1999, 98-121.

M[19]   ——, 'Tuba in Germany, The: meeting with Dietrich Unkrodt' in *Brass Bulletin*, lxxi, 3, Bulle, 1990, 34-7.

M[20]   —— & G. Bonino, 'Milan Conservatory, The' in *Brass Bulletin*, cvi, Bulle, 2, 1999, 54-71.

M[21]   Maunder, R., 'Biographical index of Viennese wind-instrument makers, 1700-1800, A' in *Galpin Society Journal*, li, London, 1998, 170-91.

M[22]   Maupassant, G. de., *Vie, Une*, Paris, 1883.

M[23]   Mayhew, H. (ed. P. Quennell), *Mayhew's London*, London, 1951/1984. [Abridged edn. of *London Labour and the London Poor*, London, edn. of 1861.]

M[24]   McDonald, D., *Odyssey of the Philip Jones Brass Ensemble, The*, Bulle, 1986.

M[25]   McLymonds, M. P., 'Sarti, Giuseppe' [Works] in S. Sadie (ed.), *The New Grove Dictionary of Opera*, 4 vols, iv, London, 1997. 182-5.

M[26]   Medici, M. & M. Conati (ed.), *Carteggio Verdi-Boito*, 2 vols., Parma, 1978.

M[27]   Meer, J. H. van der, 'Curt Sachs and Nürnberg' in *Galpin Society Journal*, xxiii, London, 1970, 120-5.

M[28]   *Melody Maker*, London, 8 April 1972, 12.

M[29]   Mersenne, M., *Harmonie universelle*, 2 pts, Paris, 1636-37; facs. edn., 3 vols, Paris, 1963.

M[30]   *Message Bird, The*, New York, 15 June 1850, 361; 1 October 1851, 56-7.

M[31]   Métoyen, *Méthode de serpent*, ?Paris, c.1792-1812.

M[32]   Meucci, R., 'Cimbasso e gli strumenti affini nell' ottocento italiano, Il' in

Studi Verdiani, v, Parma, 1988-9, 109-62; Eng. tr. W. Waterhouse as 'The cimbasso and related instruments in 19th-century Italy' [without list of works] in *Galpin Society Journal*, xlix, London, 1996, 143-79.

M[33]   ——, tr. E. Pelitti, 'Pelitti firm, The: makers of brass instruments in nineteenth-century Milan' in *Historic Brass Society Journal*, 6, New York, 1994, 304-33.

M[34]   Miller, D. C., *Sound Waves*, New York, n.d.

M[35]   Miller, G[eoffrey], *Bournemouth Symphony Orchestra, The*, Milborne Port, 1970.

M[36]   Miller, G[eorge], *Military Band, The*, London, 1912.

M[37]   Mitchell, D., *Britten and Auden in the Thirties: the year 1936*, London, 1981.

M[38]   Morgans, D., *Music and Musicians of Merthyr and District*, Merthyr Tydfil, 1922.

M[39]   Morelot, S., 'Du Vandalism musical dans les églises' in *Revue de la musique religieuse, populaire et classique*, i, Paris, 1845, 129-45.

M[40]   Morley-Pegge, R., '"Anaconda" The,' in *Galpin Society Journal*, xii, London, 1959, 53-6.

M[41]   ——, 'Evolution of the large bore bass mouthpiece instrument, The' in *Musical Progress & Mail*, London, x, 6, March 1940, 136-7; 7, April 1940, 160-1; 8, May 1940, 172; 9, June 1940, 199; 10, July 1940, 207.

M[42]   ——, 'Hibernicon' in S. Sadie (ed.), *The New Grove Dictionary of Musical Instruments*, 3 vols., ii, London, 1984, 216.

M[43]   ——, 'Ophicleide', 'Russian Bassoon', 'Serpent', 'Valve' in E. Blom (ed.), *Grove's Dictionary of Music & Musicians*, 9 vols., i, iv, vi, vii, viii, London, 1954, 241-6, 333, 712-17, 658-67, 565-75.

M[44]   Morris, R. W. & E. R. Goldstein (ed.), *Tuba Source Book, The*, Bloomington, Ind., 1996.

M[45]   Murray, D., 'Strauss, Richard' in S. Sadie (ed.), *The New Grove Dictionary of Opera*, 4 vols, iv, London, 1992, 565-75.

M[46]   Museu de la Música (pub.), *Catàleg d'instruments*, Barcelona, 1991.

M[47]   Museum Vleeshuis (pub.), *Catalogus van de Muziekinstrumenten uit de verzameling van het Museum Vleeshuis*, Antwerp, 1981.

M[48]   *Music Review*, London, November 1945, 193-201.

M[49]   *Musical Courier, The*, London, 25 June 1896.

M[50]   *Musical Opinion*, London, March 1896, 392-3; October 1896, 101-2; November 1923, 160-1.

M[51]   *Musical Standard, The*, London, 15 December 1862, 132.

M⁵² *Musical Times, The,* London, 1 September 1846, 26; 1 February 1860, 216; 1 March 1860, 237; 1 September 1888, 552; 1 February 1891, 83-4; 1 November 1891, 500-1; 1 December, 1916, 549-50; 1 June 1917, 264; 1 July 1927, 635-7.

M⁵³ *Musical World, The,* London, 22 August 1835; 12 September 1835; 16 September 1836, 12; 24 February 1837, 10; 3 November 1837, 22, 137; 22 December 1837, 552; 29 December 1837, 254; 19 August 1838, 264; 3 June 1841; 1 December 1842, 384; 1 August 1846; 1 September 1846, 26; 20 February 1847, 113.

M⁵⁴ Myers, A., 'Fingering charts for the cimbasso and other instruments' in *Galpin Society Journal,* xxxix, London, 1986, 134-6.

M⁵⁵ ——, 'Museums' in *TUBA Journal,* xxiv, 3, Austin, TX, Spring 1997, 30-1.

M⁵⁶ ——, 'Slide tuba?, A' in *Galpin Society Journal,* xlii, London, 1989, 127-8.

M⁵⁷ —— & F. Tomes, 'PCB cornets and Webster trumpets: Rudall Carte's Patent Conical Bore brasswind' in *Historic Brass Society Journal,* 7, New York, 1995, 107-22.

N¹ Nagy, M., 'Serpent und seine Verwendung in der Musik der deutschen Romantik, Der' in *Bläserklang und Blasinstrumente im Schaffen Richard Wagners. Kongreßbericht Seggau/Österreich, 1983* (Alta Musica, Band 8), Tutzing, 1985, 49-71.

N² Nettel, R., *Orchestra in England, The,* London, 1946.

N³ Newman, E., *Life of Richard Wagner, The,* 4 vols, London, 1933-47.

N⁴ Newsome, J., 'American brass band movement, The' in *The Quarterly Journal of the Library of Congress,* 36, Washington, D.C., Spring 1979, 119.

N⁵ *New York Business Directory,* New York, 1846.

N⁶ Niloff, A., *Instrumentations-Tabelle,* Vienna, 2nd ed., 1908.

N⁷ *Nineteenth Century Music,* x, Berkeley, Ca., 1986-7.

N⁸ Nuitter, C., tr. E. Forbes, '146 répétitions et les 3 représentations du Tannhäuser à Paris, Les', in *About the House,* London, Summer 1975, 34-7.

O¹ Offenbach, J., *Offenbach en Amerique,* Paris, 1877, tr. L. MacClintock as *Orpheus in America,* London, 1958.

O² O'Loughlin, N., 'Sattler, Christian Friedrich' in S. Sadie (ed.), *The New Grove Dictionary of Musical Instruments,* 3 vols, iii, London, 1984, 303.

O³ *Orchester, Das,* Mainz, February 1998.

O⁴ Otis, P. A., *Chicago Symphony Orchestra, The,* Chicago, 1924.

P¹ Pacey, R., 'Unusual serpent, An' in *Galpin Society Journal,* xxx, London, 1980,

        132-3.

P[2]     Pallansch, R., D. Butterfield & R. Bobo, 'Tuba design—improvements are
        needed' in *The Instrumentalist*, Evanston, Ill., February 1973, 31-2.

P[3]     Palmer, P., *The Serpent: an historical survey of the instrument and its literature,
        performance practice and problems, and past and present uses*, Diss. PhD,
        Columbia Pacific Univ., 1987 (unpub.).

P[4]     Panizza, E., appendix to H. Berlioz., *Grande trattato di stromentazione e
        d'orchestrazione moderne con appendice di Ettora Panizza,* 3 vols., Milan,
        1912.

P[5]     Pass (pub.), *Instruments of the Orchestra*, Birmingham, n.d.

P[6]     Patent Office (pub.), *Abridgements of Specifications Relating to Music and Musical
        Instruments*, London, 1871.

P[7]     Patton, G. F., *Practical Guide to the Arrangement of Band Music, A,* New York,
        1875.

P[8]     Pedrell, F., *Catàlech de la Biblioteca Musical de la Diputació de Barcelona*, 2 vols.,
        Barcelona, 1908.

P[9]     Perantoni, D., 'Contemporary systems and trends for the tuba' in *The
        Instrumentalist*, Evanston, Ill., February 1973, 24-7.

P[10]    Petrobelli, P., M. Di Gregorio Casati & C. M. Mossa (ed.), *Carteggio Verdi-
        Ricordi 1880-1881,* Parma, 1988

P[11]    Phillips, J., *Give Your Child Music*, London, 1979.

P[12]    Pierre, C., *B. Sarrette et les origines du Conservatoire National de Musique et
        Déclamation*, Paris, 1895.

P[13]    ——, *Facteurs d'instruments de musique, Les,* Paris, 1893.

P[14]    ——, *Facture instrumentale à l'Exposition Universelle de 1889, La,* Paris, 1890.

P[15]    ——, *Hymnes et chants de la Revolution, Les,* Paris, 1904.

P[16]    *Pigot & Slater's General and Classified Directory*, Manchester, 1841.

P[17]    Piston, W., *Orchestration,* London, 1955.

P[18]    Pistone, D., *La musique en France de la Révolution à 1900*, Paris, 1979.

P[19]    Planque, [ ], *Agenda musical pour l'année 1836,* 3 vols, Paris, 1836, repr. in 1
        vol, Geneva, 1981.

P[20]    Pontécoulant, A. De., *Organographie*, 2 vols, Paris, 1861.

P[21]    Poole, H. E., 'Catalogue of musical instruments offered for sale in 1839 by
        D'Almaine & Co., 20 Soho Square, A' in *Galpin Society Journal,* xxxv,
        London, 1982, 2-36.

P[22]    Praetorius, M., *Syntagma Musicum*, 3 vols, Wittenberg and Wolfenbüttel,

1614-20, ii, Wolfenbüttel, 1618 (*Theatrum Instrumentorum*, 1620), facs. of ii, Kassel, 1929/1964.

P[23]   Prout, E., *Orchestra, The,* 2 vols, London, 1897.

P[24]   *Punch*, xxiii, London, December 1852.

Q[1]   Q [Quiller-Couch, A.], 'Looe Die-Hards, The' in *Wandering Heath*, London, 1895.

Q[2]   *Quarterly Journal of the Library of Congress, The*, 36, Washington, D.C., Spring 1979, 119.

R[1]   Railsback, T. C. & J. P. Langellier, *Drums Would Roll, The*, Poole, 1987.

R[2]   Rambosson, J., *Histoire des instruments*, Paris, 1897.

R[3]   Rasmussen, M., 'Two early nineteenth-century trombone virtuosi: Carl Traugott Queisser and Friedrich August Belcke' in *Brass Quarterley*, v, 1, Durham, N.H., Fall 1961, 3-17.

R[4]   Read, G., *Thesaurus of Orchestral Devices*, London, 1953.

R[5]   *Revue de la musique religieuse, populaire et classique,* i, Paris, 1845.

R[6]   *Revue musicale*, Paris, vii, 46, 14 December 1833, 372; viii, 44, 2 November 1834, 345-6.

R[7]   Richardson, E. G., *Acoustics of Orchestral Instruments and of the Organ, The*, London, 1929.

R[8]   Ridley, E. A. K., *Wind Instruments of European Art Music*, London, 1974.

R[9]   Rose, A. S., *Talks with Bandsmen*, London, 1895, repr. 1995.

R[10]   Russell, J. F. & J. H. Elliott, *Brass Band Movement, The*, London, 1936.

R[11]   Russell, T., *Philharmonic*, London, 1942.

R[12]   ——, *Philharmonic Decade*, London, 1945.

R[13]   Russo, W., 'Interview with Arnold Jacobs, An' in *The Instrumentalist*, Evanston, Ill., February 1973, 28-30.

S[1]   Sachs, C., *Handbuch der Musikinstrumentenkunde*, Leipzig, 1920.

S[2]   ——, *History of Musical Instruments, The*, New York, 1940.

S[3]   ——, *Real-Lexicon der Musikinstrumente*, Berlin, 1913.

S[4]   Sadie, S. (ed.), *New Grove Dictionary of Music and Musicians, The*, 20 vols, London, 1980.

S[5]   ——, *New Grove Dictionary of Musical Instruments, The*, 3 vols, London, 1984.

S[6]   ——, *New Grove Dictionary of Opera, The*, 4 vols, London, 1992.

S[7]   Sala, G. A., *Life and Adventures of George Augustus Sala, The*, 2nd edn., London, 1895.

S[8]   Salman, W., *Kontrabaß und Baßfunktion* (Innsbrucker Beiträge zur Musikwissenschaft, Band 12), Innsbruck, 1986.

S⁹ Sayers, D. L. (tr.), *Song of Roland, The,* Harmondsworth, 1957.

S¹⁰ Schlesinger, K., *Instruments of the Modern Orchestra, The,* 2 vols, London, 1910; edn. of 1969.

S¹³ Schmid, E. F., *Neue-Mozart Ausgabe, iv,* Kassel, 1955- [Introductory notes to *Ascania in Alba*].

S¹⁴ Schneider, F., 'Wichtige Verbesserung des Waldhorns' in *Allgemeine Musikalische Zeitung,* 48, Leipzig, 26 November 1817, cols. 814-16.

S¹⁵ Schnoebelen, A., 'Performance practices at San Petronio in the Baroque' in *Acta Musicologica,* xli, Basel, 1969, 37-55.

S¹⁶ Scholes, P., *Listener's Guide to Music, The,* London, 1910; 10th edn., 1942.

S¹⁷ ——, *Oxford Companion to Music,* London, 1938; edn. of 1970.

S¹⁸ Schubert, F. L., *Blechinstrumente der Musik, Die,* Lipsia, 1883.

S¹⁹ ——, *Traité d'harmonie et de composition,* ?, 1864

S²⁰ Schwab, H. W., *Musikgeschichte in Bildern,—Konzert,* Leipzig, 1972.

S²¹ Schwartz, H. W., *Bands of America,* New York, 1957.

S²² *Serpent Newsletter,* Mundelein, Ill., 1 April 1995, 6; 1 April 1999, 6.

S²³ Shanet, H., *Philharmonic: a history of New York's orchestra,* Garden City, N.Y., 1975.

S²⁴ Shaw, G. B., *London Music in 1888-9,* London, 1937.

S²⁵ Shive, C. S. jnr, 'First music for brass published in America, The' in *Historic Brass Society Journal,* 5, New York, N.Y., 1993, 203-12.

S²⁶ Sitwell, S., *Spain,* London, 1950.

S²⁷ *Slater's General and Classified Directory,* Manchester, 1851.

S²⁸ Sluchin, S. & R. Lapie, tr. Bonn, Ecklund & Snedeker, 'Slide trombone teaching and method books in France (1794-1960)' in *Historic Brass Society Journal* 9, New York, 1997, 4-29.

S²⁹ *Sounding Brass,* London, Summer, Autumn, 1973, Winter 1973/4, Winter 1974/5, Autumn 1976.

S³⁰ Sousa, J. P., *Marching Along,* Boston, Mass., 1928.

S³¹ Spark, F. R. & J. Bennett, *History of the Leeds Musical Festivals 1858-1889,* Leeds/London, 2nd edn., 1892.

S³² Spohr, L. (tr. Anon.), *Autobiography,* 2 vols, London, 1878.

S³³ *Stage, The,* London, 15 February 1894, 12.

S³⁴ Steele-Perkins, C., 'Trumpet, The' in *Early Music Today,* vi, 1, London, February/March 1998, 11-15.

S³⁵    Stevens, J., rev. G. Ferrari, 'Besson, G. A.' in E. Blom (ed.), *Grove's Dictionary of Music & Musicians,* 5th edn., 9 vols., i, London, 1954.

S³⁶    Stewart, G., *Restoration and Cataloging of Four Serpents in the Arne B. Larson Collection of Musical Instruments, The,* Diss. MMus, Univ. S. Dakota, 1975 (unpub.).

S³⁷    Stoddard, H., *From These Comes Music,* New York, 1952.

S³⁸    ——, 'Tuba and its players in our bands and orchestras, The' in *The International Musician,* January 1950, (repr. in *TUBA Journal,* xxiv, 3, Austin, TX, Spring 1997, 32-8).

S³⁹    Stone, W. H., 'Sommerophone' in E. Blom (ed.), *Grove's Dictionary of Music & Musicians,* 5th edn., 9 vols., vii, London, 1954, 886.

S⁴⁰    Stoneham, M., J. A. Gillaspie & D. L. Clark, *Wind Ensemble Sourcebook and Biographical Guide* (Music Reference Collection, 55), Westport, Conn., 1997.

T¹    Tarr, E., 'Besson' in S. Sadie (ed.), *The New Grove Dictionary of Musical Instruments,* 4 vols., i, London, 1984, 224.

T²    ——, Introductory notes to Ewald, *Brass Quintet No. 1,* Coburg, 1990.

T³    ——, 'Romantic trumpet, The', pt. 1 in *Historic Brass Society Journal,* 5, New York, 1993, 213-61.

T⁴    Taylor, A. R., *Labour & Love: an oral history of the brass band movement,* London, 1983.

T⁵    Taylor, J. (ed.), 'Great tubists talk' in *TUBA Journal,* xxv, 2, Austin, TX, Winter 1998, 34-36.

T⁶    ——, 'Sousaphone men of Sousa, The' in *TUBA Journal,* xxi, 1, Austin, TX, Fall, 1993, 38-41.

T⁷    Tennyson, A., *Lady of Shalott, The,* Nottingham, 1852.

T⁸    Thibouville-Lamy, J., *Manufacture d'instruments de musique,* Paris, 1878. [Catalogue of company's products.]

T⁹    Tosorini, A., *Trattato pratico di strumentazione,* Florence, 1850.

T¹⁰    Travis, F. L., *Verdi's Orchestration,* Zurich, 1956.

T¹¹    *TUBA Newsletter,* Cookesville, Tenn., Fall 1974, Winter 1975.

T¹²    *TUBA Journal,* xxi, 2, Austin, TX, Winter 1994, 4-5. ['Letters' column includes several dealing with the Sousa Band's tubas and sousaphones.]

T¹³    *TUBA Journal,* xxiii, 2, Austin, TX, Winter 1996, 16. [Report on Dallas S.O. auditions, 5 December 1995.]

T¹⁴    Turner, G. & A. W., *Cavalry & Corps, including the Parachute Regiment, the*

*Brigade of Ghurkas* (The History of British Military Bands, 1), Staplehurst, 1994.

T[15]   Turner, G. & A. W., *Guards & Infantry, including the Guards Division, the Scottish Division, the Queen's Division* (The History of British Military Bands, 2), Staplehurst, 1996.

T[16]   Turner, G. & A. W., *Infantry & Irish, including the King's Division, the Prince of Wales's Division, the Light Division, the disbanded Irish regiments* (The History of British Military Bands, 3), Staplehurst, 1997.

U[1]    *United Service Journal & Naval & Military Magazine*, ii, London, 1831, 263 ['Presentation of silver kettle drums to the 2nd Life Guards'].

V[1]    Valdrighi, L.-F., *Alcune ristrette biografie di musicisti modenesi e dell' antico dominio estense specie degli ultimi tempi* (Musurgianan. 14, ser. 1ª), Modena, 1886.

V[2]    ——, *Nomocheliurgografia,* Moderna, 1884/1888.

V[3]    Venables, A. C., *Choral and Orchestral Societies*, London, 1901.

V[4]    Verdi, G., [scholarly edition of works], Chicago/Milan, ?1983-

V[5]    Vessella, A., *Studi d'Istrumentazione per Banda*, 2 vols., Milan, 1897.

V[6]    Vincent, C., *Brass Band and How to Write for it, The*, London, 1908.

V[7]    Viret, J., *Chant grègorien, Le*, Lausanne, 1986.

W[1]    Wagner, L. J. (ed.)., *Band Music from the Benjamin H. Grierson Collection* (Recent Researches in American Music, 29), Madison, Wisc., 1998.

W[2]    Wagner, R., *Sämtliche Werke* [scholarly edition of works], Mainz, ?1974-

W[3]    Waterhouse, W., *New Langwill Index: a dictionary of musical wind-instrument makers and inventors, The*, London, 1993.

W[4]    Webb, J. 'Designs for brass in the Public Record Office' in *Galpin Society Journal*, xxxviii, London, 1985, 48-54.

W[5]    ——, 'Mahillon's Wagner tubas' in *Galpin Society Journal*, xlix, London, 1996, 207-12.

W[6]    Webster, M., *Johann Zoffany, 1733-1810*, London, 1976.

W[7]    *Webster's Third New International Dictionary*, Encyclopaedia Britannica, Chicago, edn. of 1966, article: 'Tuba', iii, 2459.

W[8]    Weldon C., 'Tuba Ensemble, The' in *The Instrumentalist*, Evanston, Ill., February 1973.

W[9]    Wells, H. W., *Handbook of Music and Musicians, A*, London, n.d.

W[10]   Weston, S., 'Choir-band instrumentation: two county surveys' in *Galpin Society Journal*, lii, London, 1999, 305-13.

W[11]   ——, 'Improvements to the nine-keyed ophicleide' in *Galpin Society Journal*, xxxvi, London, 1983, 109-14.

W[12]  ——, *Samuel Hughes, Ophicleidist*, Edinburgh, 1986.

W[13]  Westrup, J., 'Sidelights on the serpent' in *The Musical Times*, London, 1 July 1927, 635-7.

W[14]  Wheeler, J., 'New light on the "Regent's Bugle": with some notes on the keyed bugle' in *Galpin Society Journal*, xix, London, 1966, 65-70.

W[15]  Whitwell, D., *Nineteenth Century Wind Band and Wind Ensemble in Western Europe, The* (The History & Literature of the Wind Band & Wind Ensemble, 5), Northridge, Ca., 1984.

W[16]  ——, *Wind Band and Wind Ensemble Literature of the Classic Period* (The History & Literature of the Wind Band & Wind Ensemble, 8), Northridge, Ca., 1983.

W[17]  ——, *Wind Band and Wind Ensemble Literature of the Nineteenth Century* (The History & Literature of the Wind Band & Wind Ensemble, 9), Northridge, Ca., 1984.

W[18]  ——, *Wind Band and Wind Ensemble of the Classic Period (1750-1800), The* (The History & Literature of the Wind Band & Wind Ensemble, 4), Northridge, Ca., 1984.

W[19]  Wick, D., *Trombone Technique*, London, 1971.

W[20]  Widor, C. M., *Technique de l'orchestre moderne* [sup. to Berlioz 'Traité'], Paris, 1904, tr. Suddard, London, 1906.

W[21]  *Wiener Zeitung,* Vienna, 25 February 1789, 170-9.

W[22]  Williams, M., *Jazz Tradition, The,* New York, c. 1970.

W[23]  Wills, S., 'Brass in the modern orchestra' in Herbert, T. & J. Wallace, *The Cambridge Companion to Brass Instruments*, Cambridge, 1997, 157-74.

W[24]  Wit, P. de., *Katalog des Musikhistorischen Museums von Paul de Wit, Leipzig,* Leipzig, 1903.

W[25]  Wood, H. R., *My Life of Music,* London, 1938/1946.

W[26]  Woodhouse, H., *Face the Music,* St. Austell, 1997.

W[27]  Wotton, T., *Hector Berlioz*, Oxford, 1935.

W[28]  Wright, C., *Music & Ceremony at Notre Dame of Paris 500-1550,* Cambridge, 1989.

W[29]  Wright, F. (ed.), *Brass Today*, London, 1957.

W[30]  Wright, R., *Dictionnaire des instruments de musique,* London, 1941.

W[31]  Wright & Round (pub.), *Easy Way to Play Brass Instruments, The,* Liverpool, n.d.

W³²  ——, *Wright & Round's Brass Band News,* Liverpool, 1 January 1898, 3; 1 November 1901, 9.

Y¹  *York Courant,* York, 24 January 1817, [ ].

Y²  *Yorkshireman, The,* York, 22 August 1835, 1; 12 September 1835, 2.

Y³  Young, K., *Music's Great Days,* London, 1968.

Y⁴  Young, T. C., *Making of Musical Instruments, The,* London, 1919.

Z¹  Zaslaw, N. & J. Spitzer, 'Orchestra' in S. Sadie (ed.), *The New Grove Dictionary of Opera,* 3 vols, iii, London, 1997, 719-35.

Z²  Zechmeister, G., 'From the bombardon to the Vienna Concert Tuba,' in *Brass Bulletin,* lxxv, 3, Bulle, 1991, 46-55.

Z³  ——, *Entwicklung der Wiener Konzerttuba, Die,* Vienna, 1985.

Z⁴  ——, 'Role of the contrabass trombone in the Vienna sound, The' pt. 1 in *Brass Bulletin* iiic, 2, Bulle, 1998, 19-28; pt. 2 in ciii, 3, Bulle, 1998, 93-99.

Z⁵  ——, *Systematic Embouchure Development, Training and Review Programme for the Viennese Six-Valve Tuba in F (Viennese Concert Tuba),* Vienna, n.d.

# Composer Index of References to the use of Tuba Family etc. Instruments

# Index

The following major categories appear in capital letters: BRASS INSTRUMENTS, LONDON, MILITARY, NEW YORK, PARIS, PATENTS, TUBA, VALVE. Geographical locations are normally followed by county (in U.K.), state (U.S.A.) region (EU) or country as at 2000; companies, institutions etc. are listed under location with instrument-makers also appearing under name. Individuals are identified by trade or profession. Titles of works are normally given under author, composer, etc.

# Index

# 629
168, 265, 457; Courtois, *see* Amboise; Cousin, J., 195;
Darche, 82; Forveille, 83, 91, *123*; Gambaro, J., , 145;
Gautrôt aîné, 141, 255, 261; Guichard, J.-A., 215-16, 219,
256-7; Halary, 140, 145, 152-3, 159, 190, 255, 500; Henri
et Martin, 143, 341; Labbaye, J., C. *père*, 183; Labbay, J., *fils*,
145; Lecocq, J., 428; Mouchel, C., 477; Piffault, 79;
Raoux, 145, 217; Sax, A(dolphe), 32, 57, 158, 189, 209,
213, 227, 244-62, 259, 278-9, 344, 352, 420, 427, 461;
Sax, A(lphonse), 190, 195-6, 259, 459, 469; Sudre, F., 196,
199, 220, 459-60; Thibouville-Lamy, 166, 190, 195-6, 261,
Turlot, 82.

Isle de la Cité, 114
Jardin Turc, 169
Keyed bugle-teacher, 130
Mazarine, rue, 145
Musée de la Musique, 148, 152 (*see also* Conservatoire,
instrument collection).
Numerous ophicleideists in, 170
Open-air concerts, 101
Publishers: Framéry, 79; Imbault, 92; Palianti, M. 473; Schott,
B.,159; Troupenas, 486.
Salle Herz, 249
Serpente, rue, 145, 217
Société libre des Beaux Arts, 250
—— Lyricale, 164
Theatres: Opéra, 99, 111, 113, 115, 161, 166, 170, 213, 248,
253, 303, 305-6, 342, 351, 410, 426, 473, 486-7, 490, 493,
495, 506; Opéra Comique, 159, 161, 249; Prado, 258;
Théâtre des Variétés, 93; Théâtre Feydeau, 99; Théâtre
Italien, 159, 170, 486; Théâtre Lyrique, 253.
Vieux-Augustins, rue des, 145.
Paris, Wilbur de (bandleader & trombonist), 441.
'Pariser Modell' (ophicleide), 154.
Parker, Phil, Ltd (dlr, London), 384.
Pashkevich, Vassily (composer), 99.
Pask, John (mkr, London), 146.
PATENTS:
circumventing, 208; International Patents Convention,
183; Sax, 229.
American:
4132, 4.8.1845 [keyed bugle], G. W. Shaw, 128.
Austrian:
1558, 1833 [*Bass-Pumpathon*], W. Riedl, 217; 2053, 1830
[valve], J. Uhlmann, 183; [   ], 4.9.1833 [valved
instruments], W. Riedl, 207.[   ], 1835 [valve], J. Kail & J.
Riedl, 183; [   ], 1.4.1844 [Euphonion], F. Bock, 226;
[   ], 5.4.1844 [Hellhorn], F. Hell, 226; 4480, 1844
[Cornon], V. Cervený, 465; 5338, 1848 [helicon], I.
Stowasser, 450; 13773, 1884 [Kaiser instruments], V.
Cervený, 265.
Belgian:
[   ], 1840 [Ophibariton], Bachman, 82; 4363, 3.5.1848
[compensation], Sax, A(lphonse), 190.
British:
112, 13.1.1865 [inner jacket], A[dolphe]. Sax, 62; 140,
18.1.1855 [duplex], M. Nyilassy, 476; 342, 22.2.1858
[water reservoir], J. Davis, 287; 782, 3.3.1875
[mouthpiece], B. Mills, 291; 1072, 28.4.1864
[mouthpieces], T. Ghislin, 290; 1284, 24.5.1859 [duplex],
A. Sax, 476; 1465, 26.6.1855 [duplex], H. Distin, 476;
1664, 15.8.1788 [two horns of different pitches], Clagget,
181; 1836, 12.8.1858 [compensation/Sonorophone], G.
Metzler & J. Waddell, 195, 289, 455; 2468, 25.9.1866

[water-valve], W. E. Newton, 287; 2592, 18.10.1861
[duplex], H. Distin, 476; 2596, 18.10.1861 [duplex], J.
Lawson & H. Carter, 476; 2661, 31.10.1860
[ornamentation], T. G. Ghislin, 61; 2967, 3.12.1860 [brass
instruments], Macfarlane, Newton & Carte, 157; 2980,
16.12.1856 [aluminium parts], F. Gerhard, 282; 3194,
31.12.1860 [double slide], J. Midgley, J. Sugden, W.
Clapham, 459, 500; 3334, 5.5.1810 [keyed bugle], J.
Haliday, 127; 3662, 20.2.1902 [mouthpiece], H. Herring
& G. E. Case, 51; 3941, 26.2.1884 [double-slide], C. A.
Goodwin, 500; 4515, 4.11.1881 [mouthpiece], J. Dunbar
& R. Harper, 291; 4542, 7.3.1884 [drainage], D. Blaikley,
287; 4618, 14.11.1878 [compensation], D. Blaikley, 198-9;
4849, 9.10.1823 [Hibernicon], J. Cotter, 90; 5013,
7.10.8124 [valve], J. Shaw, 183; 5432, 14.11.1882
[drainage], W. Booth, 287; 6166, 9.3.1897 [mouthpiece],
H. H. Lake, 56; 6649, 30.1.1890 [compensating system],
O. Hawkes & P. Maurice, 199; 6702, 28.3.1899 [duplex],
W. Stasek, 476; 7173, 15.3.1888 [drainage], G. Hyde, 287;
7677, 16.4.1895 [mouthpiece], J. Rüegg, 291; 8350,
21.4.1899 [mouthpiece], L. Antoine, 291; 8849, 10.4.1911
[mouthpiece], W. Thomason & A. Brannan, 291; 9470,
23.4.1906 [mouthpiece], M. Rubright, 291; 13601,
24.4.1851 [wooden ophicleide], Robertson, J. C., 148;
13605, 13.6.1909 [modified bell], F. Sudre, 460; 13865,
13.10.1887 [valve], Bossi, J., 189; 16358, 14.10.1890
[Cornophone]. F.-Besson, 465-7; 18442, 13.8.1913 [gum
support], J. Engelhard, 290; 20844, 15.9.1855 [aluminium
parts], V. Scully & B. Heywood, 282; 21026, 6.10.1908
[compensating system], C. Moore & J. Clay, 200; 21295,
31.12.1903 [conical bore], Klussman, H., George, M.,
Zambra, J., 190; 21807, 2.10.1909 [drainage], J. Viol, 287;
22562, 8.11.1901 [Sudrephone], F. Sudre, 459; 24366,
14.12.1894 [mouthpiece], W. Thompson, 291; 24526,
5.11.1907 [mouthpiece], A. J. Burr, 52, 55; 27746,
16.12.1907 [bugle], M. B. Martin, 33; 261419, 14.11.1925
[mouthpiece], P. Aka, 291; 277153, 31.7.1926
[diaphragm], T. Slechta, 460; 297185, 23.7.1927
[drainage], J. Hutchison, 287; 679158, 19.3.1951 [mute], J.
W. T. Roope, 61.

French:
404, 31.12.1810, A. Frichot [Basse-trompette], 86; 1327,
9.2.1827 [ophicleide], Labbaye *fils*, 145; 1592, 13.10.1845
[saxotromba], A. Sax, 245; 1849, 24.3.1821 [ophicleide],
Halary, 140-1, 159; 2338, 2.5.1828 [Ophimonocléide], J.-
B. Coëffet, 82; 3226, 21.3.1846 [saxophone], A. Sax, 158;
4361, 5.5.1849 [saxtuba], A. Sax, 245-6, 470-1; 4636,
19.10.1849 [chromatic brass], Mongin, 161; 4936
14.6.1836 [valved ophicleide], J.-A. Guichard, 215, 217;
6034, 22.9.1838 [clavicor], J.-A. Guichard, 257; 9434,
17.8.1843 [compensation], A. Sax, 245; 12493, 18.1.1855
[Trombotonar, etc.], G. Besson, 454-5; 12823,14.9.1855,
[aluminium instruments], Martin, 61; 13668, 18.1.1855
[valves], Besson, 282; 14737, 18.12.55 [duplex]. G. Pelitti,
475; 16752, 9.10.1856 [valves], A. Sax, 246; 21958,
18.2.1892 [Sudrephone], F. Sudre, 459; 22148, 3.1.1859
[keys on bell], A. Sax, 196, 246, 261-2; 54212, 19.5.1862
[valves], A. Sax, 246; 56450, 22.11.1862 [internal glazing],
A. Sax, 62; 76072, 7.7.1867 [Trompe de Lorraine],
Grégoire, 32; 127953, 16.12.1878 [bugle contralto],
Besson, 265; 2141575, 8.3.1881 [valves, etc.], A. Sax, 247.

German: